PERSONALITY
Strategies and Issues

1982
fourth edition

Personality

STRATEGIES AND ISSUES

Robert M. Liebert
State University of New York
Stony Brook

Michael D. Spiegler
Providence College

THE DORSEY PRESS
Homewood, Illinois   60430

ISBN 0-256-02670-X
Library of Congress Catalog Card No. 81–70954

Printed in the United States of America

1 2 3 4 5 6 7 8 9 0 H 9 8 7 6 5 4 3 2

for Suzanne Arink
RML
and Charles F. Behling
MDS

Robert M. Liebert received his B.S. degree from Tulane University in 1963 after studying psychology both at Tulane and at University College, London. He received a Ph.D. in clinical psychology from Stanford in 1966, after which he joined the faculty at Vanderbilt. He subsequently served as Senior Investigator at Fels Research Institute and as a member of the faculty at Antioch College. He is now Professor of Psychology and Psychiatry at the State University of New York at Stony Brook. He has published widely in the fields of personality, social development, and methodological issues, and is coauthor of several other books, including *Developmental Psychology* and *Science and Behavior: An Introduction to Methods of Research*. He also has strong avocational interests in poetry and philosophy.

Photo by Joy Sherman

Michael D. Spiegler received his A.B. degree from the University of Rochester in 1964 and his Ph.D. in clinical psychology from Vanderbilt University in 1969. He has taught at Vanderbilt University and the University of Texas at Austin and was Director of the Community Training Center at Veterans Administration Hospital in Palo Alto, California. He is currently Associate Professor of Psychology at Providence College. His research has been in the areas of anxiety, modeling, treatment of chronic psychiatric patients, assertion training, and most recently in obesity and exercise addiction. He is author of *Contemporary Behavioral Therapy* and coauthor of *The Community Training Center*. He has a practice in psychotherapy and directs a program for the treatment of obesity and related risk factors. He is frequently observed running, sometimes in training for ultramarathons, eating ice cream, and listening to early music.

Our fundamental aim in this fourth edition of *Personality* is fourfold: *(a)* to introduce the undergraduate student to the major theoretical and practical issues involved in the scientific study of personality, *(b)* to present our readers with interesting and accurate information about the application of psychology to important and universal human concerns, *(c)* to provide an understanding of the methods used by personality psychologists both in conducting basic research and in applying their knowledge to personality assessment and personality change, and *(d)* to prepare and interest the reader in more advanced study.

To meet these goals we have organized the book around four conceptional *strategies* that have been used by psychologists in their study of personality, the *psychoanalytic, dispositional, phenomenological,* and *behavioral* approaches. Presentation of these four strategies preceded by a general overview of the field at the outset constitutes the five sections of the book. To help orient our readers to the major concepts and frameworks of the strategies, each strategy section begins with a short introductory chapter that outlines and summarizes the major assumptions of the approach. Then, after a more detailed presentation of the theories that fall within the strategy and the manner in which they have been researched and applied, the section concludes with a concise "liabilities" chapter in which the strategy's weaknesses as voiced by its critics are presented.

This edition, like its predecessors, aims at an evenhanded presentation of the various current ideas about the nature of human personality. Therefore, each of the strategies is presented in an affirmative light and in the tone and format which might be selected by its adherents.

A major thesis of this book is that any comprehensive strategy for the study of personality must come to grips with the same four major issues: a clear *theoretical statement,* a set of procedures for *personality assessment,* a systematic body of *research,* and an explicit basis for understanding and implementing *personality change.* The scientific investigation of personality is thus presented in such a way as to bring the critical interplay of the four basic strategies (psychoanalytic, dispositional, phenomenological, and behavioral) and the four fundamental issues (theory, assessment, research, and personality change), into clear focus. We believe that the presence of this superordinate organizational structure is critical in surveying the field for the first time, so that differences and similarities among the various viewpoints do not seem to be an incomprehensible hodgepodge of arbitrary opinions.

As in the preceding editions of *Personality,* complete coverage of every individual theory and viewpoint is *not* a goal of the book; even if such a goal could be attained (which is highly doubtful), we do not believe that an encyclopedic presentation is a sound way to introduce students to the field of personality. Instead, our emphasis continues to be on presenting enduring principles and contemporary issues and illustrating them with selected examples rather than exhaustive listings.

The field of personality is alive and vital, and much new research as well as several important theoretical advances have appeared in the past four years. Thus we have added a new section on sociobiology and its implications, described recent trends in psychoanalytic thinking, and expanded our discussion of the cognitive behavioral approach. Research coverage in each section has also been thoroughly up-dated, and there have been a number of organizational changes within each section so as to thoroughly integrate (rather than append) the new material. Not all of the material appearing for the first time in this edition is "new," however. In several instances our own re-reading of the older literature has led us to introduce a classic and still significant idea or piece of research omitted from earlier editions, to provide a more fully rounded picture of the major theorists whose ideas we discuss. In the case of the phenomenological strategy, for example, we have given greater emphasis to the work of Abraham Maslow and to the most recent writings of Carl Rogers in this edition.

Personality courses are among the most popular offerings of a psychology department, but they are often disappointing to students who want information which bears on their own lives. To serve this need (which we feel is a legitimate one), we have tried to illustrate concepts and principles through examples that are relevant to the contemporary college student. We have also expanded further on a feature of the previous editions which we believe capitalizes on, and perhaps helps to stimulate, the college student's intellectual skepticism. Periodically, the reader is invited to perform small, easily implemented *Demonstrations,* so that he or she can personally examine the validity of various propositions discussed in the text. These "personalized studies" have been tested repeatedly in our own personality classes and revised on the basis of student feedback. A Demonstration is included in each of the strategies' introductory chapters to provide an additional way for the student to experience the "way of thinking" that is characteristic of each strategy.

We believe that visual illustrations that are related in meaningful ways to the substance of a text can increase its instructional value.

We have also become increasingly aware that a book's appealing format serves more than a cosmetic function; an attractive, well-designed book makes reading easier and more enjoyable and thus can serve as a real aid to learning. Accordingly, we have worked to enhance the illustrations, design, and format of this edition.

As in the previous edition, we have written without sex bias by neuterizing the language and using feminine and masculine examples (the only exception being direct quotations from other sources).

We wish to thank the following reviewers: Professor Bertram J. Cohler, University of Chicago; Professor William L. Simmons, University of New York-Albany; Professor Robert C. Bennion, Brigham Young University; Professor Bonnie Spring, Harvard University; Professor Damaris J. Rohsenow, University of Wisconsin-Madison; Professor Robert Hogan, Johns Hopkins University; and Professor Auke Tellegen, University of Minnesota.

Once more we must acknowledge our debt to the many undergraduates in our personality courses over the past 14 years whose comments, questions, and challenges have provided the single most important source of continuing input we have available in our efforts to make this a better book. We wish to thank Sandi Cohen and Gretchen Daly for typing various parts of the manuscript, Catherine A. Jahn for her careful reading of proofs and indexing, and Madelyn Roesch for her expert copy editing. We are especially grateful to Suzanne Arink for her help with design issues and to Jean Steinberg for outstanding research and editorial assistance. Lulac Spiegler's presence provided perspective when things became harried. Special thanks are extended to David C. Guevrement for his competent research assistance, thoughtful criticisms and suggestions, and tireless efforts and dedication during all phases of the writing and production of this fourth edition of *Personality: Strategies and Issues*.

Robert M. Liebert
Michael D. Spiegler

contents

x

PERSONALITY
Strategies and Issues

section **1**

Introduction

Arthur Tress

1 *Introduction*

Strategies for the study of personality

In the theater of ancient Rome the actors used no makeup. Instead they wore one of a small number of masks, or *persona,* that told the audience to expect a consistent pattern of attitudes and behavior from the player who wore it. Soon persona came to refer not only to the masks but also to the roles they implied, and, finally, they referred to the actors themselves (cf. Burnham, 1968).

"Persona" is the source of the English word *personality,* and the link is more than historical. The term as we use it today also implies that we expect from other people a consistent pattern of attitudes and behavior or at least an "orderly arrangement" in the behavior of those whom we know. All people exhibit recognizable individual actions that serve to identify them.

Where, though, do these individual characteristics and regularities come from? Are they ever truly unique, or just particular combinations of characteristics all people possess? Are they learned, inherited, or both? Can personality be altered, and if so, how? Discerning the character of human nature has been called one of the "limited number of common human problems to which all people at all times must find some solution" (Kluckhohn & Strodtbeck, 1961, p. 10), and so it should come as no surprise that the questions just raised have puzzled thoughtful people for thousands of years. Originally the quest for answers to them was the domain of philosophy and religion, and these fields continue to be involved in such problems. But scientific psychology, born about 100 years ago, has also turned its attention to personality.

This book offers a general introduction to the psychological study of personality and deals with the issues involved in developing an approach to the systematic study of human behavior and experience. So many approaches to personality have been advanced by psychologists, philosophers, and theologians, and by social commentators in other disciplines, that it would be impossible to discuss all of these positions in detail. Even if complete coverage were possible, a mere catalog of viewpoints would probably not be the best way to introduce the scientific study of personality. Therefore, instead of detailing an exhaustive list of approaches, we have stressed the major *strategies* which psychologists have followed in developing conceptualizations of human behavior. This format is designed to give a general picture of the diversity of existing positions, the points they emphasize, the nature of the evidence they consider, and the assumptions they make. In this way, we have tried to explain both the logical and the empirical bases which underlie major theoretical positions and, at the same time, to summarize existing knowledge in the field.

To proceed systematically, the study of personality, like other scientific endeavors, requires a strategy. All of the approaches to personality that we shall discuss can be examined in terms of their explicit or implicit strategies, and to understand and evaluate those approaches we must be familiar with their strategic components. Thus, we shall first consider the elements involved in a strategy for studying personality.

Strategy, as we shall use the term here, refers to a four-phase plan for understanding human personality. It includes a *theory* of personality, an approach to the *assessment* (or measurement) of personality, *research* procedures for testing hypotheses or propositions derived from the theory, and methods of *changing personality* (i.e., therapeutic interventions). There is considerable overlap in the role played by each of the four phases of the study of personality. Thus, theories suggest ideas or *hypotheses* which are tested in research while, at the same time, the nature of the research is determined by what the particular theory leads us to expect. In order to do research, assessment techniques must be employed. The model of personality measurement used is dictated by the assumptions about personality the theory involves. The success of the personality-change techniques serves to partially validate the therapeutic principles which are derived from the theory. The interdependence of theory, assessment, research, and personality change is indeed complex, and it becomes difficult to talk about one phase without referring to one or more of the other three phases.

THE SCOPE OF THE STUDY OF PERSONALITY

Interest in understanding ourselves and other human beings has compelling justification. To begin with, it is natural for us to be curious about our own behavior and feelings, and "how we got that way." Furthermore, our daily lives are filled with concerns that relate to the assessment and prediction of personality. Virtually all social interaction requires that we evaluate and try to understand the behavior of other persons with whom we must deal. For example, on the basis of relatively short interactions, college students must attempt to determine whether a new acquaintance will make a suitable roommate or whether a given professor will be sympathetic to a student handing in a term paper two weeks after it is due. Psychology is the branch of science most concerned with such questions.

Modern psychology is a very broad field, comprised of specialty areas. Interest in interpersonal relations, attitude change, and the influence of major social forces has typically fallen in the domain of *social psychology. Developmental psychology* places emphasis on the historical antecedents of a person's behavior and is concerned with maturational and social influences as human beings advance from infancy through childhood and adolescence to adulthood and old age. When someone's behavior is markedly different from the usual norms of society, and especially when these differences may jeopardize the person or others, then the phenomena are of particular interest to workers in the field of *abnormal psychology,* which includes the theoretical and experimental work of *psychopathology* and the applied work of *clinical psychology.*

Fields such as *human engineering, industrial psychology, personnel psychology, educational psychology,* and *school psychology,* are concerned with specific human enterprises. *Experimental psychology* may involve the study of single aspects of the organism, such as physiology, sensation and perception, learning, motivation, or emotion. Recently, *cognitive psychology* has emerged as a unified branch within psychology, focusing on the operation of thought processes. A burgeoning interest in cognitive processes has influenced all of the major strategies we will discuss.

In many ways, *personality psychology* lies at the crossroads of all these other branches of psychology. Personality psychology generally refers to the study of the functioning of the individual person in all its aspects. The person[1] is influenced by all of the basic processes studied by experimental psychologists (e.g., perception, learning, memory, problem solving), by all of the interpersonal and group forces studied by social psychologists (e.g., group norms, peer pressure), and by all of the individual processes studied by experimental psychologists (e.g., brain functions, glandular secretions, sensory processes). At the same time, personality psychology provides the theoretical and research base from which our understanding of psychopathology and psychotherapy is derived and, often, justified.

THE CONCEPT OF PERSONALITY

Thus far we have spoken of *personality* without specifically defining the term. There are, in fact, many definitions used today by personality psychologists. Which definition a particular personality psychologist selects or constructs depends upon the psychologist's theoretical orien-

---

[1] Speaking of "the person" in this way is probably unique to personality psychology and a few subareas of psychology. The Roman philosopher Boeces defined the person as "an individual substance of a rational nature" (Müller, 1888). The reference, then as now, is to the thinking, feeling, living part of the human being. A person may be young or old, male or female, black or white, kind or cruel. A person only needs to *be.*

tation. Psychologists with a deterministic, genetic orientation often choose a definition that emphasizes the operation of psychological processes within the person. For example, Hans Eysenck, one of the many personality psychologists whose work we shall consider later, defines personality as "the more or less stable and enduring organization of a person's character, temperament, intellect and physique, which determines his unique adjustment to his environment." On the other hand, psychologists who view human beings as adaptive creatures whose behavior is determined largely by experience tend to stress past learning and current situational factors in their definitions. Thus, Walter Mischel defines personality as "the distinctive patterns of behavior (including thoughts and emotions) that characterize each individual's adaptation to the situations of his or her life" (1976, p. 2). Still other psychologists emphasize the measurement of personality in their theories, and not surprisingly, come up with definitions that stress the predictive utility of their measurements. Raymond Cattell, a prominent psychologist with this orientation, defines personality as "that which permits a prediction of what a person will do in a given situation."

Because of the diversity of the definitions which have been used, there is little point in searching for *a* definition of personality. As we shall see repeatedly in this book, a complete definition of personality always implies at least a partial theory of personality as well. Therefore, to fully understand what a particular psychologist means by the term *personality,* it is necessary to examine his or her theoretical approach. For example, conspicuously missing from the small sample of definitions presented above is the name of Sigmund Freud. Since for Freud personality is synonymous with the *psyche* (mind), his theory of personality (see Chapters 4 and 5) is a theory of psychology in general. Freud posited that personality is made up of the *id,* the *ego,* and the *superego,* three agencies of the psyche, and that it is their interaction which determines behavior. Much of Freud's personality theory deals with these three agencies and their interrelationship, and, therefore, Freud's definition of personality is his theory of personality.

Even from our brief remarks so far, it has probably become apparent that a number of specific issues regarding the definition of personality will be raised in almost any psychological discussion. Some of the more important ones are introduced below.

Objective versus subjective aspects

Philosophers have long understood that our direct knowledge of others is limited to what we can see of their behavior. We can never know directly what is "inside" a person; that is, we cannot observe another's subjective experiences ourselves. We may say that Tom is happy in order to provide a summary label for his smiles, his jovial conversation, or his invitation to take us all out for a beer, but we are speaking of his overt behavior and not necessarily of any private, internal state that he is experiencing. Psychologists who subscribe to the *behavioral* view (which holds that our primary concern should be with observable responses rather than with presumed internal states [see Section 5]) argue that the scientific study of personality can be no more than an examination of objective information and observable responses. Others, though, have argued that personality must refer to some private, subjective experiences as well. Tom, who *appears* happy, may in fact be miserable inside; Mary, who seems to be self-assured and "put together," may actually have numerous doubts and fears about her adequacy and competence as a person; and, in general, one's behavior may not reflect one's "real" personality. This orientation has a good deal of intuitive appeal, but we will see that the problem of measuring private experiences is a thorny one.

The person versus the situation

To what extent are people consistent in the way they think, act, and respond to various situations? In our daily language we often hear such things as "John is quiet" or "Sharon is irresponsible." People talk as if these were properties of individuals rather like the color of their eyes, which is always apparent and virtually unchangeable. But such statements are not likely to be true without exception. John may be very outspoken about his hobby, stamp collecting, and Sharon may be very careful in keeping her club's records despite the fact that she has not gotten a single class assignment in on time in the past three years. Both a definition and a theory of personality must therefore account for the inconsistencies as well as the similarities in a given person's behavior across situations and time. Some theorists have minimized the importance of situational differences, while others have argued that such differences are not sources of spurious "error," but rather are the primary data for understanding why people act as they do.

In fact, both personal consistency and striking situational variability can be found in studying human behavior. The real issue faced in all theories of personality is to specify precisely how personal characteristics and life circumstances influence (or interact with) one another to determine what we think, feel, and do. Here, viewpoints differ markedly, as we shall see.

The nature of individuality (the idiographic-nomothetic distinction)

There can be little doubt that, in some ways at least, each of us has a unique and distinctive personality. Each person is a product of all the forces that produce an individual and, like the uniqueness of the fingerprint, represents a combination that will not occur again. However, although personality psychologists generally agree that each of us is in some way unique, there is great controversy over the implications of this fact for the study of personality.

One view is that each of us is so distinctive that we can only be understood in terms of our own particular life and experiences. Comparison with others, according to this approach, is really not meaningful. This view, called the *idiographic* approach (from the Greek *idios*, meaning personal), has inspired exhaustive studies of the lives of individuals in all their aspects, with the aim of achieving a unique understanding of each person.

The alternative view, the so-called *nomothetic* approach, assumes that our uniqueness is a product of general physical, biological, and psychological laws. (*Nomos* is the Greek word for law.) The nomothetic approach assumes that each of us is a unique combination of ingredients. Each ingredient or aspect, though, is assumed to be contributed by general processes that can be understood by investigating specific aspects of personality in a wide variety of persons with the aim of formulating laws of behavior which hold for people in general. In this book, we consider both the idiographic and the nomothetic viewpoints.

Prediction, control, and understanding

In developing a perspective on personality, we must decide whether it is proper to describe our goal as solely *prediction* and *control* of behavior, or whether an additional goal, usually called *understanding*, is necessary for an adequate theory of personality. Whereas prediction and control are easily defined and specified, the meaning of "understanding" is elusive and ambiguous. By understanding we usually mean comprehension of the process involved in a phenomenon, but the level of comprehension sufficient for a person to say "I understand" varies from individual to individual. Understanding is thus a highly subjective matter.

Personality and adjustment

One thread that runs through many definitions of personality might be called the *adjustment emphasis* (Lazarus, 1961). Simply, this is the idea that each human enters the world with certain bodily needs and requirements. The person adjusts to the environment in order to satisfy these needs as smoothly and safely as possible. The individual's personality is his or her habitual forms of adjustment, which are shaped in part by the individual's particular mental and physical capacities and limitations. Although no theorist subscribes to this definition as complete, most agree that personality is in part understandable in terms of the struggle to adjust. "Personality," according to one theorist, is roughly summarized as "the formula an individual has evolved to assure his survival and mastery within the framework of his existence" (Allport, 1961, p. 82).

Philosophers of science have written a great deal about the nature of theory in general and about the nature of personality theories in particular. Our aim here is not to outline the subtleties of theoretical analysis; rather, we have tried to provide a simple overview of theory in personality psychology.

In science, theory serves three general goals: (1) to organize and clarify observations; (2) to explain the causes of past events in such a way that future events can be predicted from the same causes; and (3) to provide a sense of understanding of their subject matter.

Most theories are built on a relatively small number of terms or theoretical constructs (CON′-structs). *Theoretical constructs* identify phenomena considered important to the theory. Energy is a construct from physics, oxidization is a construct from chemistry, and natural selection is a construct from biology. Personality theorists have used many constructs; among the more familiar ones are ego, anxiety, conditioning, and self-awareness. Theoretical constructs do not actually exist, nor can they be seen or touched. They are merely useful inventions which help to give order to observed phenomena. Theoretical constructs are often shorthand summaries of relationships among many different variables, and they therefore serve to facilitate communication about these relationships. Many of the concepts to be discussed in this book are theoretical constructs.

Why is it necessary or even desirable to use such convenient fictions? A major reason is that they economically tie together meaningful relationships among observations that would otherwise soon become a hopeless quagmire of raw facts. As seen in Figure 1–1, the advantage of using the theoretical construct "anxiety" is striking even in the case of only three situations and three outcomes.

As building blocks, constructs are used to make theoretical statements, that is, general claims about the phenomena with which the theory deals. From these statements a scientist derives specific expectations, or *hypotheses,* which can be tested through research. Thus, although theories are themselves never tested directly, the hypotheses which can be derived from a theory must be testable and capable of being verified. Sociologist Jonathan Turner (1974) has put it aptly:

> Hypotheses must be vulnerable. It is this concern with *disproving* . . . that distinguishes science from other kinds of idea systems; for if statements cannot be disproven, "theory" is simply a self-maintaining body of statements which bears little relationship, except in their framers' minds, to real phenomena. (p. 7)

PERSONALITY THEORIES

Purpose of theories

Theoretical constructs in personality

FIGURE 1–1
An illustration of the advantages of using anxiety as a theoretical construct, defined differently in a number of circumstances (B), over a mere listing of observed, separate relationships (A)

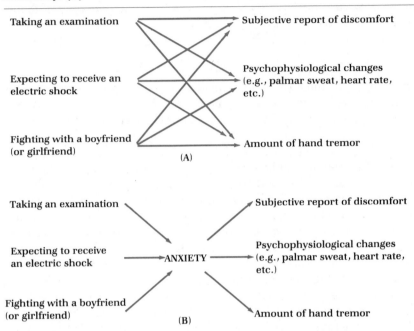

Source: Modified from Miller, N. E. Liberalization of basic S-R concepts: Extensions to conflict behavior, motivation, and social learning. In S. Koch (Ed.), *Psychology: A study of a science.* Vol. 2. New York: McGraw-Hill, 1959.

Criteria for evaluating personality theories

Epstein (1973) has identified six criteria by which a theory can be evaluated: empirical validity, parsimony, extensiveness, internal consistency, testability, and usefulness.

The *empirical validity* of a theory is the degree to which the theory is supported by observation and evidence. A theory, like a hypothesis, is never proved or disproved by empirical evidence. The most that research can do is to find support for a theory, whereas the absence of such findings does not usually refute the theory.[2] With each new substantiating piece of evidence, the psychologist gains more confidence in the theory. If, after a number of experimental tests, a theory has failed to receive support, the psychologist would be forced to turn to a new theory or to revise the existing one. In this case, for all practical purposes the theory would have been rendered useless. Strictly speaking, though, it would not have been proved false.

---

[2] A theory can be decisively refuted if some empirical consequence that is *absolutely* necessary for the theory turns out not to occur. However, psychological theories are rarely this determinate and "tight."

Any phenomenon can be described and explained in different ways. When everything else is equal, the simpler an explanation is and the fewer assumptions it requires, the better. The underlying principle here is referred to as the *law of parsimony*.

Extensiveness refers to the breadth of the phenomena with which the theory can deal. All other things being equal, the more extensive the theory, the better the theory. The more extensive the theory, the larger will be the scope of the research efforts which it inspires. On the other hand, restricted theories tend to be *restrictive* theories, in the sense that they belittle phenomena and problems with which they are unable to deal.

Some theories grow into such a loose confederation of ideas and concepts that the parts do not fit together. When this happens, the theory as a whole loses some of its explanatory power and "meaning." A theory has *internal consistency* to the degree that its various propositions and assumptions are logically consistent with one another, fitting together into a coherent, larger explanation.

Certain types of explanations are easily stated, simple, and all encompassing, but are not subject to verification or refutation. Explaining all natural phenomena as the will of a deity whose ways are mysterious is one example. Untestable claims greatly weaken a theory's scientific credibility. Thus, *testability* is a major criterion by which theories of personality can be judged.

"Theory," wrote the Irish poet James Stephens, "is but the preparation for practice." Though scientists often object to public demands for the practical applications of their ideas, the history of science shows that the theories which have survived have often had great practical *usefulness,* at least in the long run. Both personality assessment and efforts at personality change (e.g., psychotherapy) provide opportunities for testing the usefulness of personality theories.

We all have implicit theories of personality. If this does not seem immediately obvious, you will almost certainly be convinced by the time you have finished this book. For example, many people find that Freud's emphasis on the importance of early sexual impulses for personality development "seems wrong" to them, at least at first. Others immediately describe as "absurd" the behaviorist's idea of leaving subjective, personal feelings out of the scientific study of personality altogether. The list could be expanded. The point is that you will soon find that many theorists say things with which you do not agree, because you already have a set of ideas about how your own personality and the personalities of others work—that is, an "implicit theory of personality."

Individual implicit personality theories differ from the theories we

Implicit theories of personality

shall discuss in this book in several important respects. First, the theories we shall examine in later chapters are formalized and set down in terms that can be communicated to others. It is not that we cannot formalize or communicate our own personal theories of human behavior to others; it is just that we generally do not do so. Second, formalized theories are based on observations of many different people. Although we may meet different individuals in our daily lives, we usually do not make an explicit effort to observe and analyze their behavior. Third, most personal theories are based more on the observation of ourselves than on observation of other persons. Finally, formalized personality theories are tested repeatedly in studies having relatively rigorous standards, often by critics of the theories. Implicit personality theories are not subjected to such testing.

PERSONALITY ASSESSMENT

Traditionally, modern psychology is said to have begun in 1879, when Wilhelm Wundt established a psychological laboratory at the University of Leipzig. Only five years later, formal personality measurement was proposed by Francis Galton (1884) who wrote: "The character which shapes our conduct is a definite and durable 'something,' and therefore . . . it is reasonable to attempt to measure it" (p. 179). Toward this end, Galton made a number of specific proposals, including ratings by teachers and peers and direct observation of the person in social situations. Modern personality psychologists recognize that they have several distinct sources of information from which inferences about personality can be drawn.

Interviews, questionnaires, and personality tests

One way to find out something about a person is to ask the person directly through an interview, by questionnaire, or using a combination of the two. Data based on direct questions to the person have been used heavily in studies of personality, the form used ranging from structured and semistructured interviews to a myriad of psychological tests. Such procedures have the advantage of providing information quickly, and are also our only access to the person's subjective experiences (e.g., "How are you feeling today?").

Despite their appeal, direct questions alone present an incomplete picture. What people say about themselves is subject to memory lapses, misunderstanding, and a variety of distortions, especially when "sensitive" content is involved. As we will see, there are ways to limit these problems or take them into account, but they are imperfect.

When there is reason to believe that direct self-reports will be invalid or inaccurate indicators of personality phenomena, indirect personality assessment techniques are used. In most cases, these techniques "disguise" their purpose so that the person being assessed cannot easily distort the measurement. Projective techniques, which are discussed in Chapter 6, are a prime example of indirect personality assessment. The difficulty with projective techniques and other disguised test methods is that responses must be interpreted, and psychologists have often disagreed as to what constitutes a valid interpretation of, say, what a person reports seeing in an inkblot. Again, ways to deal with the problem of validating indirect tests have been suggested, but none is entirely satisfactory.

A second way to learn about people is to observe them in situations of interest. Such situations may be simulated or contrived, or they may occur naturally. For example, there have been studies of aggression in which the test situation involved leading subjects to believe they were "teachers" in an experiment on punishment and learning. In this context, they were asked to administer electric shocks to a learner (in fact, a confederate of the experimenter who was never really shocked) with the severity of shock subjects were willing to administer serving as the response measured. In contrast, a psychologist interested in aggression might simply observe children on a playground, noting and recording the nature, severity, and circumstances of various acts of aggression that occur spontaneously. Such personal observation by the psychologist (whether as a clinician or as a researcher) has a credibility not to be found in interviews or questionnaires. But personal observation is often expensive or otherwise impractical, so that observation of even a single individual in more than a small number of situations is usually out of the question for personality assessment. Then, too, even a psychologist's observations provide only part of the information needed for a complete understanding of personality.

Direct observation of behavior

Personality, as sociologist Erving Goffman (1959) has suggested, includes both the way we *express* ourselves and the way others are *impressed* by us. The way we are seen by other people, including friends, family, supervisors, and peers, is an important part of who we are. Moreover, these people have an opportunity to observe us in many situations and often over a considerable period of time. As we shall see, personality psychologists have increasingly turned to these sources of information as useful for personality assessment.

Using the impressions of others to judge someone's personality has a subtle implication, though. It blurs the line between objective judg-

Perceptions and impressions of others

ment and mere opinion. Thomas Szasz (1960), for example, believes that the term *mental illness* and related terms such as *abnormal personality* are really value judgments expressed about persons whose values, thoughts, and actions simply differ from those of the majority of people. Szasz, a psychiatrist, has been warning for years that "mental illness is a myth, whose function is to disguise and thus render more palatable the bitter pill of moral conflicts in human relations" (p. 117).

Personal history and life record

Finally, a great deal of information is to be found in a person's history and life record, including educational, employment and marital history, and personal accomplishments. Such data have the advantage that they can be obtained or confirmed objectively (e.g., by consulting school records or contacting past employers).

Bogus personality assessment

So far, our discussion has focused on personality assessment from the point of view of the assessor. An equally interesting question concerns personality assessment procedures from the point of view of the person being assessed.

A variety of popular techniques for assessing people are available on the commercial market, including everything from horoscopes to handwriting analyses. These techniques have never been shown to have real merit, yet they enjoy many enthusiastic endorsements. Why should this be so if the techniques tend to be invalid?

Snyder (1974a, 1974b) has shown that most people are quite credulous when they are given interpretations of their own personality based on sources that they trust. As a result, "generalized" or "bogus" personality descriptions that could actually apply to anyone are often accepted by otherwise thoughtful people as unique and remarkably accurate descriptions of their inner selves. What this means, of course, is that a general faith in some procedure, regardless of whether it is an astrological reading or a personality test administered by a Ph.D. psychologist in a prestigious clinic, does not necessarily prove much about whether or not the procedure can accomplish what it purports to accomplish.

Demonstration 1–1[3] serves to illustrate how personality assessments may seem to be "true" to the person who is offered them when, in fact, like cotton candy, they have very little real substance. The Demonstration will also allow you to try your hand at some research, the next issue we will consider in this chapter.

---

[3] This book contains a number of Demonstrations that will allow you to test for yourself both the principles and the problems associated with the study of personality.

THE CREDIBILITY OF BOGUS PERSONALITY ASSESSMENTS

Most of us have read horoscopes in the newspapers and may well have commented that it is difficult to imagine anyone being "taken in" by these overly general descriptions and predictions. It is possible, however, that a more sophisticated version of the same kind of generalized descriptions can be extremely effective and can even lead persons to believe that they have an entirely unique description of themselves. Testing this hypothesis, Ulrich, Stachnik, and Stainton (1963) asked students in educational psychology classes to take two personality tests. A week later, the students were given a written interpretation of their test scores which appeared to represent the careful efforts of the professor. As a second part of the study, other students were given instructions in administering the same two personality tests to a friend. For both phases of the study, the people whose personalities were being "interpreted" were asked to rate the accuracy of the "interpretation" (on a scale ranging from excellent to very poor) and to make any additional comments about the "interpretation" which they felt were important.

Despite the individualized appearance of the personality description, ***all persons were given exactly the same "interpretation"*** (though the order of the statements varied), and, in fact, ***no actual interpretations of the tests were made.*** The description read:

> You have a strong need for other people to like you and for them to admire you. You have a tendency to be critical of yourself. You have a great deal of unused capacity which you have not turned to your advantage. While you have some personality weaknesses, you are generally able to compensate for them. Your sexual adjustment has presented some problems for you. Disciplined and controlled on the outside, you tend to be worrisome and insecure inside. At times you have serious doubts as to whether you have made the right decision or done the right thing. You prefer a certain amount of change and variety and become dissatisfied when hemmed in by restrictions and limitations. You pride yourself as being an independent thinker and do not accept others' opinions without satisfactory proof. You have found it unwise to be too frank in revealing yourself to others. At times you are extroverted, affable, sociable, while at other times you are introverted, weary, and reserved. Some of your aspirations tend to be pretty unrealistic. (Ulrich et al., 1963, p. 832)

When the students who had been administered the personality tests by the professor rated the "interpretations," virtually all rated them as good or excellent. In the second phase of the study, approximately 75 percent of the subjects who had been tested by admittedly inexperienced students also rated the assessments of themselves as good or excellent. Furthermore, the comments that subjects made clearly indicated an acceptance of these interpretations as accurate and individualized descriptions of their own personalities. One student who had been given the tests and interpretation by the professor said: "On the nose! Very good. I wish you had said more, but what you did mention was all true without a doubt. I wish you could go further into this personality sometime." A subject who had been given the tests and interpretation by a student commented: "I believe this interpretation fits me individually, as there are too many facets which fit me too well to be a generalization" (Ulrich et al., 1963, p. 833).

More recently, Snyder and Larson (1972) replicated this study, extending it to show that college students accept these global evaluations as relevant, regardless of whether they are presented by a psychologist in an office or a graduate student in the laboratory. Indeed, in the Snyder and Larson study, even among students who had been led to believe that their tests had been computer scored (rather than evaluated by a human scorer), most rated these statements as between good and excellent. From their own and earlier experiments of this sort, Snyder and Larson (1972) conclude that the evidence provides:

> an object lesson for the users of psychological tests. People place great faith in the results of psychological tests, and their acceptance of the results as being true for them is fairly independent of test setting, administrator, and scorer. Furthermore, it must be realized that presentation of the results of psychological tests, typically presented to the individual as being for him personally, maximizes the acceptance of the psychological interpretation. Thus, the individual's acceptance of the interpretation cannot be taken as a meaningful "validation" of either the psychologist or his tests. (p. 388)

To replicate this experiment for yourself, tell a friend that you are learning how to use personality tests in class and have the person make two different drawings for you. First, ask your friend to draw a picture of her- or himself and another picture as he or she would like to look. (The Draw-a-Person Test is a projective technique which uses this procedure to assess personality; we shall have more to say about projective techniques in Chapter 6.) Then, in your own handwriting, copy the interpretation used by Ulrich et al. quoted on page 17 and, about a week later, offer this assessment to your friend. After he or she has had an opportunity to read it, ask your friend to rate the interpretation (excellent, good, average, poor, or very poor) and give you some feedback as to how well you are doing as a "psychological examiner." After this part of your experiment is completed, it is important that you reveal to your friend the real nature of the experiment. Complete explanation of the experimental deception, often called *debriefing*, may evoke further comments of interest and also remove the possibility that permanent misconceptions about psychological testing will result.

THE IMPORTANCE OF RESEARCH

Earlier we mentioned that a strategy for the study of personality includes theory, assessment, research, and personality change. The importance of the theory and assessment aspects of the study of personality, introduced briefly above, is obvious to most beginning students of personality because we all implicitly theorize about and assess other personalities (and our own) long before studying the field of psychology. Often, the importance of research seems less obvious.

Until about 100 years ago, the formal study of personality was rooted in philosophy and proceeded almost entirely on *rational* grounds. Discussion, argument, the opinions of various authorities, and a general appeal to "reason" formed the basis for settling disputes among adherents of differing viewpoints. But people often cannot agree on what is reasonable, and so the rational approach to the study of personality, by itself, offers no solid way of resolving differences of opinion. What one person may regard as a great insight may seem to be no more than a preposterous fantasy to another person.

An alternative to the rational approach, which can be traced at least to the 17th century and John Locke, is the *empirical* approach. Empiricism dictates that disputes can be settled by only admitting as "facts" those assertions which are verifiable by direct observation. Thus empiricism brought with it a demand for "hard," rather than circumstantial evidence. Rational considerations might give rise to theories, but they were not strong enough to validate theories.

Empirical research refers to any activity that systematically attempts to gather evidence through observations and procedures which can be repeated and verified by others. All four of the strategies that we shall consider are committed to supporting the validity of their theories, assessment procedures, and personality-change techniques through empirical research. It is this commitment to research that distinguishes the scientific approach to knowledge from other approaches (Neale & Liebert, 1973). As Frank (1977) has noted, approaching personality through scientific psychology and research entails accepting the "humanist-scientific" belief system. This belief system

> assumes a single reality existing independently of the observer and consisting of objects and events anchored in a space-time continuum which relate to each other according to laws of cause and effect. It can be perceived correctly only by the waking, unintoxicated brain and is to be comprehended by the intellectual analysis of sensory data. According to this view, the ultimate test of the validity of any phenomenon is the ability to meet the criteria of scientific evidence, including replicability and the use of controls. (pp. 555–56)

Scientific personality research is not a stereotyped or rigid enterprise, however. There are a host of scientifically legitimate ways of investigating personality, issuing from the three basic methods we shall consider in Chapter 2. We will also see, throughout this book, how often research has helped to dispel an "obvious" but incorrect idea or to establish a less obvious principle or process that seemed implausible until the evidence came in. Scientific demonstration is never superfluous.

Every complete strategy must speak to the possibility of intervening in the lives of other people in order to produce personality change.

PERSONALITY CHANGE

Strategies differ, though, in what exactly they mean by personality change. They also differ in how they go about producing such change. This should really not be surprising, given the very different definitions of personality with which the various strategies begin.

**PLAN OF
THE BOOK**

The book is divided into five sections. Section 1 includes this introductory chapter and the next chapter, which deals with methods of personality research that will be illustrated throughout the book. Each of the four succeeding sections is devoted to a description of the theory, assessment techniques, research methods, and change procedures which characterize one of the four strategies for the study of personality—*psychoanalytic, dispositional, phenomenological,* and *behavioral.* The strategies are the navigational tools of personality theorists and researchers; they can be likened to the constellations by which navigators steer while trying to cross a still-unfamiliar sea.

Our aim is to convey a responsible sense of the nature of these strategies. The strategy sections begin with brief introductory chapters which also serve as summaries; the introductory chapters should be read before the other chapters in the section have been read, and then again after these chapters have been read in order to help integrate what has been learned.

Another kind of summary can be found in the outline overviews with which each chapter begins. These overviews show all the topical headings that appear in the chapter, and the headings themselves have been worded so as to suggest to the reader the material the chapters contain. The overviews permit the reader to see the logic and progression of each chapter in advance and are quite helpful in reviewing the highlights of the chapter once it has been read. They are also useful for identifying gaps in one's memory when studying.

The format, emphasis, and writing style of Sections 2 through 5 vary somewhat so as to be consistent with the "flavor" and "customs" of each of the four strategies. Each strategy is presented in a positive light, emphasizing its assets. The last chapter in each strategy section, however, deals with the "liabilities" of the strategy as judged by its critics. In these liabilities chapters, we have adopted the stance of presenting arguments that a harsh critic would make in order to highlight the weaknesses of each strategy and, thus, to complement the positive light in which it was originally presented. The liabilities chapters are not intended to be complete critiques or even-handed evaluations of the strategies; rather, they are presented to illustrate the range of limitations and problems each strategy entails when it is applied to the full scope of the study of human personality. We believe that this approach will afford readers an opportunity to evaluate the merits and limitations of the strategy, thereby providing an optimal introduction to the scientific study of personality.

Beginning students of personality often ask why no single strategy is used by all personality psychologists. In fact, as the philosopher of science Thomas Kuhn (1962, 1970) has shown, mature sciences do tend to proceed under a single strategy or "paradigm" and to go about the business of refining and extending their understanding according to established traditions. But personality psychology has not yet achieved the status of a mature science; rather, modern personality psychology is characterized by "paradigm clashes" (cf. Katahn & Koplin, 1968) in which the proponents of various approaches to the study of personality insist that others have defined the problems incorrectly. Essentially, we feel that the four strategies considered in this book are alternative paradigms for the study of personality which are currently vying to establish themselves.

2 | *Introduction*

Asking and answering questions about personality: Research

The importance of empirical research in the scientific study of personality was pointed out in the previous chapter. In this chapter, we shall describe the basic methods of personality research so that the reader will be able to understand the research described in the book. The fundamental aim or purpose of personality research is quite simple, although the methods occasionally are complex and technical. Personality research involves asking and answering questions about human behavior, an endeavor that has intrinsic interest for curious individuals and in which many people engage on an informal and unsystematic basis. For instance, if we are curious as to why the same people sometimes seem very warm and loving and at other times appear very cold and aloof, we might, for a few days, take special note of the circumstances under which the people are at one extreme or the other. We might even attempt to elicit the two types of response in different people. However, like our personal, implicit theories of personality (which were discussed in Chapter 1), the results of our informal personality research efforts are likely to be limited in their generality, scope, and depth. The reason is that our casual investigations typically lack the systematization, rigor, and objectivity which characterize formal personality research. The nature of these characteristics will become clear as we describe the fundamentals of personality research in this chapter.

Three major research methods have been used to gather information about personality—the *case-study, correlational,* and *experimental* methods. The three methods have one essential element in common—they all involve *observation* of behavior. The major differences lie in the types of observations made, the circumstances in which the observations are made, and how the data from the observations are examined. Briefly, the case study involves a detailed *qualitative*[1] *description* of the behavior of a *single* individual and achieves a depth of informa-

AN OVERVIEW OF THE THREE BASIC APPROACHES TO PERSONALITY RESEARCH

---

[1] Qualitative measurement involves assigning observations to categories rather than assigning them numerical values.

tion not usually available in either the correlational or the experimental method. The correlational method examines the *quantitative*[2] *relationship* between two or more events for a group (sample) of people who are observed under the *same* conditions. The experimental method looks at the *quantitative relationship* between one or more conditions which are *systematically varied* and are expected to *cause* specific changes in people's behavior. (Note that the terms *experiment* and *experimental* will be reserved for investigations using the experimental method, in contrast to the correlational and case-study methods.)

In most cases, a problem can be studied by any of the three basic methods of personality research. How the research questions are stated and the type of answers desired determine which method will be employed. Before examining each of the methods in depth, we shall look at how a single, broad question—What are the effects of violence depicted on television on the aggressive behavior of children?—has been investigated using each of the methods. The purpose of this comparison is to point out with a concrete example how the same issue can be studied in different ways.

The earliest investigations of TV violence and children's aggressive behavior were case studies of individual youngsters who had apparently become more aggressive by learning from or copying antisocial behavior which they had seen on television. The following are two excerpts from case studies involving television violence and aggression (Schramm, Lyle, & Parker, 1961).

> In Los Angeles, a housemaid caught a seven-year-old boy in the act of sprinkling ground glass into the family's lamb stew. There was no malice behind the act. It was purely experimental, having been inspired by curiosity to learn whether it would really work as well as it did on television. (p. 161)
>
> A 13-year-old . . . boy, who said he received his inspiration from a television program, admitted to police . . . that he sent threatening notes to a . . . school teacher. His inspiration for the first letter came while he was helping the pastor of his church write some letters. When the minister left the office for an hour, the boy wrote his first poison pen letter. "I got the idea when I saw it happen on TV," he told Juvenile Sgt. George Rathouser. "I saw it on the 'Lineup' program." (p. 164)

Although such reports represent isolated incidents, they certainly raise the possibility that viewing television violence is related to aggressive acts. However, to actually determine whether such a relationship exists for the general population (i.e., for more than the few particular children who were the subjects of the case studies), it is necessary to examine more children in a somewhat more standardized manner

---

[2] Quantitative measurement involves assigning numerical values or scores to observations.

than is possible with single case studies. Furthermore, if we are interested in knowing the degree or magnitude of the relationship between television violence and aggression among children, it is necessary to collect quantitative data (i.e., numbers) to supplement the qualitative descriptions that case studies yield. These additional requirements are met by the correlational method.

In fact, numerous correlational studies have provided quantitative evidence for the relationship (Liebert, Neale, & Davidson, 1973). For example, McIntyre and Teevan (1972) examined the relationship between viewing habits and deviant behavior in 2,300 junior and senior high school boys and girls in Maryland. First, to obtain viewing information, the youngsters were asked to list their four favorite television programs, "the ones you watch every time they are on the air." A numerical violence rating was assigned to each program, and then an average violence score was computed for every subject. Second, a measure of deviance was obtained by having each youngster complete a self-report checklist of various antisocial behaviors such as engaging in serious fights at school, petty delinquency (e.g., trespassing) and involvement with legal officials. The subjects indicated the frequency with which they engaged in each behavior on the checklist using a simple numerical scale (0—never, 1—once, 2—twice or more). McIntyre and Teevan thus had two numerical scores for each of the 2,300 youngsters, one of the degree of violence in their preferred TV fare and the other of the extent of their deviant behavior. It was then possible to examine (mathematically) the relationship (correlation) between these two sets of scores to see whether or not they were systematically associated and, if they were, the nature of their association. The results indicated that there was a direct relationship between the various types of deviance and the violence ratings of the four favorite programs— the more violent the programs were, the greater the deviance.

Although this evidence is impressive, it does not indicate that television violence *caused* the aggressive behavior. It is possible that being aggressive makes a youngster more likely to be interested in watching violent entertainment, rather than vice versa. Cause-and-effect relationships can be most clearly demonstrated by means of the experimental method. For example, in one experiment, Liebert and Baron (1972) hypothesized that children who viewed a violent film would be significantly more willing to hurt other children than would children who viewed a nonviolent film. Boys and girls between the ages of five and nine were taken to a room containing a television monitor and told that they could watch television for a few minutes, until the experimenter was ready. The sequences they saw came from actual television shows, but had been videotaped earlier. For all the children, the first two minutes of film consisted of humorous and attention-getting commercials. The following 3½ minutes constituted the experimental treatment. Half of the children viewed a sequence from "The Untouchables" which contained a chase, two fist-fighting scenes, two shootings, and a knifing. The other children saw an exciting sports sequence. For everyone, the final minute seen was another commercial.

Each child was then escorted to another room and seated in front of a large box which had wires leading into the next room. On the box were a green button, labeled HELP, and a red button, labeled HURT. Over the two buttons was a white light. The experimenter explained that the wires were connected to a game that another child in the adjoining room was going to play. The game involved turning a handle, and each time the child started to turn the handle, the white light would come on. The experimenter explained that, by pushing the buttons, the subject could either help the other child by making the handle easier to turn or hurt the other child by making the handle hot. The subjects were told that the longer they pushed the buttons, the more they helped or hurt the other child and that they had to push one of the buttons every time the light came on. The experimenter then left the room and the light came on 20 times.

Using the total duration of pushing the HURT button as the measure of aggression, the investigators found that children who viewed the aggressive program were significantly more willing to hurt another child than were those who watched the sports sequence. As seen in Figure 2–1, the pattern appears for boys and girls in both age groups. Because the only difference between the two groups of children was the nature of the critical 3½-minute TV sequence they observed—violence or sports—it is possible to conclude that the differences obtained can be confidently attributed to an instigating effect of viewing violence.[3]

We now turn to a detailed examination of each of the three major research methods. It should be kept in mind that the same basic question can be approached using different methods of research, as we have just illustrated. Although each of the strategies for the study of personality to be discussed in subsequent sections of the book tends to favor particular types of research, we shall see numerous examples of the use of converging lines of evidence from varied research methods in support of hypotheses developed within each strategy.

THE EXPERIMENTAL METHOD

The major distinguishing characteristic of the experimental method is that the variables which are hypothesized to be causing the behavior in question are systematically varied while all other possible causative

---

[3] It was possible that children who viewed the violent television scene pushed the HURT button longer because they were more excited or aroused. If this line of reasoning were correct, *any* response of this group of subjects would have been of higher intensity; these subjects also should have pushed the HELP button longer. In fact, they did not. The programs used made no difference in the duration or number of HELP responses.

FIGURE 2–1
Mean total duration of aggressive responses in Liebert and Baron's (1972) experiment

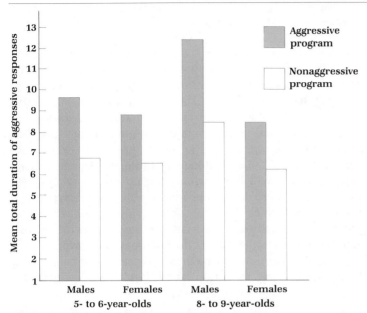

Source: Liebert, R. M., & Baron, R. A. Some immediate effects of televised violence on children's behavior. *Developmental Psychology*, 1972, *6*, 469–75.

factors are held constant. For example, in Liebert and Baron's (1972) experiment, discussed in the previous section, the only difference between the two groups of subjects was the nature of the critical 3½ minutes of film they saw. In all other respects, the subjects were treated identically. Assuming that the subjects in the two groups did not differ in any relevant way before the experiment began (e.g., more "aggressive types" in one group than in the other), it was possible to conclude that the difference observed in aggressive behavior (i.e., pressing the HURT button) was caused by the one essential difference in the way the two groups were treated (i.e., whether they saw violence or sports).

The essential elements of experimental research will be presented in the context of an investigation of the responsibility which people feel during an emergency (Darley & Latané, 1968). The experiment was instigated by a provocative incident which Darley and Latané described in the following way:

> Several years ago, a young woman was stabbed to death in the middle of a street in a residential section of New York City. Although such murders are not entirely routine, the incident received little public attention until several weeks later when the *New York Times* disclosed another side of the case; at least 38 witnesses had observed the attack—and

none had even attempted to intervene. Although the attacker took more than half an hour to kill Kitty Genovese, not one of the 38 people who watched from the safety of their own apartments came out to assist her. Not one even lifted the telephone to call the police. (p. 377)

Why did none of the more than three dozen observers come to Kitty Genovese's aid? The fact that no one intervened in her behalf appears to be inconsistent with all of the humanitarian and cooperative norms which our society attempts to foster. There are a number of possible explanations which would account for the fact that no assistance was rendered to the victim. It is possible that, contrary to our common belief, people are simply not willing to assist strangers, even in an obvious emergency. More likely, however, there are some circumstances in which people will be unwilling to aid others whom they do not know. Perhaps there are some identifiable characteristics of an emergency situation which diminish an individual's feelings of responsibility toward and willingness to aid another person in distress. Darley and Latané suggested that one of the circumstances which weakens norms favoring intervention may be the presence of other onlookers. With other witnesses present, there may be a *diffusion of responsibility*.

> For example . . . each observer, by seeing lights and figures in other apartment house windows, knew that others were also watching. However, there was no way to tell how the other observers were reacting. These two facts provide several reasons why any individual may have delayed or failed to help. The responsibility for helping was diffused among the observers; there was also a diffusion of any potential blame for not taking action; and finally, it was possible that somebody, unperceived, had already initiated helping action. (Darley & Latané, 1968, p. 377)

These possibilities may now be seen to converge upon a single, testable hypothesis, namely, that "the more bystanders to an emergency, the less likely, or the more slowly, any one bystander will intervene to provide aid" (p. 378). At this point, the hypothesis is still untested. It is no more than one possible explanation, but the idea is now formulated as a specific proposition that can be tested.

Information regarding the hypothesis could be gathered by any of the three methods of research used to study personality. For example, using the case-study method, people who witnessed various emergency situations could be interviewed to ascertain whether the number of other people present influenced their willingness to help the victim. Data from actual emergency situations could also be subjected to a correlational analysis to see whether an inverse relationship existed between the number of people who witnessed an emergency and the amount of assistance offered (i.e., the more witnesses, the less help offered). However, a major problem in using such naturalistic data is that factors other than the number of witnesses might influence people's feelings of responsibility to help. The type of emergency (e.g., store being robbed versus a person falling in the street) might very well affect people's willingness to intervene, as would such factors as the severity of the emergency, the danger of helping, the time of day, the location, and so on. Thus, to test Darley and Latané's hypothesis, people would have to be faced with the *same* emergency situation. Furthermore, it would be unethical to create a real emergency situation. Both these constraints can be dealt with by setting up a *controlled* situation which simulates an emergency.

Control in psychological research refers to systematically varying, randomizing, or holding constant the conditions in which observations are made. The purpose of instituting such controls is to reduce the number of alternative explanations of the variables influencing the behavior observed. The controlled situation must meet all of the logical demands of the hypothesis being tested and, at the same time, exclude other factors which have not been hypothesized to be relevant but could be. What are the demands in the present example? First, a situation must be created in which subjects believe that a true emergency is occurring. Second, each subject must be aware of the number of other "bystanders" present. Third, subjects must be unaware of the reactions or behavior of the other bystanders. Finally, precise measurement of the speed and frequency of reaction to the seeming emergency must be possible.

To meet these requirements, Darley and Latané designed an experiment in which college students were told that they were going to participate in a discussion of the personal problems college life involves. When subjects arrived for the experiment, they were taken to a small room, instructed to put on headphones with an attached microphone, and told to listen for instructions. By means of the headphones, the experimenter explained how the "discussion" was to be run. Subjects were told that the purpose of their being placed in individual rooms was to preserve anonymity—actually other persons were simulated by tape-recorded statements—and that, in order to foster more open discussion, the experimenter would not listen to the discussion while it was in progress. Finally, each subject was to speak for two minutes, in turn, during which time only the subject's microphone would be turned on. Thus, only one person at a time could be heard.

The first person to speak, the "victim" to be, mentioned in the course of his comments that he was subject to seizures similar to epilepsy. After the subject spoke (always last), it was the victim's turn again. Following several calm and coherent comments, the victim began to stutter and his words became increasingly incoherent as he verbally feigned a seizure.

Each subject was placed in the situation just described, but the number of other people the subject believed were participating in the discussion varied. In one instance, subjects heard only the victim's voice (two-person group); in a second, subjects listened to one other voice besides the victim's (three-person group); subjects in a third instance heard four other voices besides the victim's (six-person group). Thus, all subjects were exposed to a constant "emergency" situation except that the number of other people present varied. Since the only difference among the groups of subjects was the number of other "witnesses," any differences among the groups in their reactions to the feigned emergency could be attributable to the number of persons present.

"The number of persons present" was directly varied by the investigators. In an experiment, the condition which is directly varied is called the *independent variable*. The object of an experiment is to observe the influence of the independent variable on subjects' behavior. The specific behavior under investigation is called the *dependent variable*. The term "dependent variable" comes from the fact that this variable is hypothesized to depend upon or be influenced by the conditions varied by the experimenter—that is, the independent variable. In our example, there were two dependent variables: the *speed* and *frequency* of the subjects' reaction to the "emergency." The speed of reaction was defined as the time that elapsed from the beginning of the victim's seizure until the subject left his or her room to summon aid. The frequency of reaction was simply the proportion of subjects in each group who summoned aid within six minutes after the emergency began.

An *experimental hypothesis* involves a statement about the effect of the independent variable upon the dependent variable. It was hypothesized in the experiment that the more witnesses there are to an emergency (the independent variable), the less likely it is that any one witness will intercede and the more slowly will any one witness intercede (the dependent variables). If the three groups of subjects differed (on the dependent variables) from one another in the predicted direction (i.e., the most aid coming from subjects in the two-person group and the least from those in the six-person group), the experimenters would then want to be in a position to say that the differences were due to the independent variable and only to the independent variable. Suppose, for example, that the two-person group had a higher percentage of "civic-minded" subjects than did either of the other groups. In that case, the greater aid given by these persons might be due to a difference in the characteristics of the sample of subjects rather than to the number of people in the discussion group. To eliminate or minimize the possibility that such alternative explanations were as viable as the experimental hypothesis, every effort was made to equate the groups with respect to characteristics of the subjects that are *relevant* to the experimental hypothesis. Usually, this is accomplished by assigning subjects *randomly* to each of the variations of the experiment so that every subject has an equal chance of being assigned to each condition. Since subjects are not placed in the experiment in any systematic way, their characteristics, such as civic-mindedness, tend to equalize across groups of subjects so that no group has a disproportionate number of subjects with a particular characteristic.

Once the groups have been made as similar as possible, it is necessary to give all subjects exactly the same treatment except for the independent variable. (The only difference among the three groups in our example was the number of people perceived to be part of the discussion.) Otherwise, changes in the dependent measure could be attributable to extraneous differences in the treatment the groups received. For instance, if the six-person group heard a less convincing seizure by the victim, this could account for the reluctance of its members to render assistance. To ensure the same treatment for all groups, standard procedures were employed. For example, by using tape-recorded simulation of other discussants, all subjects heard identical voices.

The major results of Darley and Latané's experiment are shown in Figure 2–2, from which it can be seen that the experimental hypothesis was supported for both dependent variables. The two-person group had the highest percentage of subjects responding to the emergency and the fastest average reaction time, whereas the six-person group

FIGURE 2–2
Effects of group size on likelihood and speed of response to an "emergency" in Darley and Latané's experiment

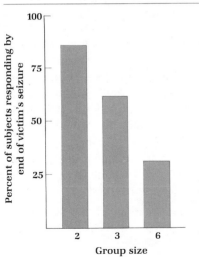
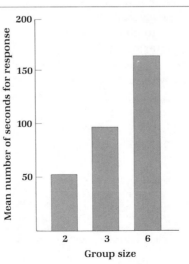

had the lowest percentage of subjects responding and the slowest average reaction time.

In considering these data, it is important to keep in mind that, *on the average,* people who were supposedly alone with the victim were more helpful than people who thought four other people were also aware of the victim's plight. When experiments are done with groups of subjects, the average performances of the groups are compared. There may have been subjects in the two-person condition who took longer to respond to the emergency than did some of the subjects in the six-person condition. But, overall, the performance of the subjects in the two-person group was considerably more helpful than was that of the subjects in the six-person group.

The single-subject experiment

The crucial element of the experimental method is the systematic variation of a specified event (the independent variable) to determine its influence on a specific aspect of behavior (the dependent variable). Usually this is done by comparing the behavior of two or more groups of people with each group being treated differently with respect to the independent variable. It is also possible to employ the basic strategy of the experimental method (i.e., systematic variation of an event) with just one person. In such *single-subject experiments,* the independent variable is changed successively over time (rather than among groups). For example, hypothetically the intervention behavior of a single individual could be studied under the same conditions as in the Darley and Latané experiment.[4] The person would have to be observed more than once under each condition. Then, if the person's behavior were *consistent* within each condition, it might be possible to conclude that the independent variable (i.e., the number of other people in the "discussion") was influencing the person's intervention behavior. For example, in order to conclude that being in a two-person discussion would result in a faster response to the emergency than would being part of a six-person discussion, the subject would have to average faster reaction times when in the two-person situation. (When groups of subjects are used in an experiment, consistency is required among people in each group or situation.) Single-subject experiments are employed extensively by behavioral psychologists, particularly those who subscribe to an operant approach (see Chapter 21).

---

[4] This example is useful for comparison of group and single-subject experiments. However, it is unlikely that a single-subject experiment would be used to investigate this particular research question because repeated exposure to the emergency situation presents numerous logical and methodological problems (e.g., practice effects as well as credibility regarding the "emergency").

The major advantage of the experimental method is that it can be used to determine definitive cause-and-effect relationships. Changes in the dependent variable can be directly attributable to changes in the independent variable when all other relevant variables (influences) except the independent variable are held constant. This is accomplished through experimental controls, and often involves setting up the experiment in the psychological laboratory, where rigid controls over conditions can be maintained. The price paid for such controls is frequently some artificiality. For example, to what degree is it possible and reasonable to translate an interest in the behavior of witnesses to crimes or sudden emergencies into an experimental investigation of the reactions of college students to the verbal anguish of another person heard over headphones? Can we generalize from this laboratory setting to the streets of our large urban centers?[5] Would it not be better to observe bystander behavior during an actual incident like the one which prompted the experiment? These are important questions, and they have no pat answers. *In laboratory experiments, we gain less information about the total problem of interest, but we gain more reliable and precise information about specific aspects of the problem.* As we shall see shortly, both the correlational and case-study methods involve less control over relevant variables but, at the same time, more naturalness is preserved. The decision as to which method to use in studying a particular problem is complex because each method has both advantages and disadvantages.

An assumption made about all of the personality research discussed in this book is that the results are generalizable beyond the narrow confines of the particular research investigation. Generalization may be to the total population of persons of whom the subjects in the study were a representative sample, or to the conditions under investigation of which the particular conditions in the study were representative. To make such generalizations, it is necessary to have confidence in the reliability of the findings. *Reliability* refers to consistency or repeatability, and in the context of psychological research, we are interested in results that are obtainable more than once. Any event which occurs only once might be attributable to chance. ("Anything can happen once," as the saying goes.)

A standard of the reliability of quantitative research findings is called *statistical significance*. Statistical significance is computed by mathe-

Evaluation of the experimental method

STATISTICAL SIGNIFICANCE AND PRACTICAL IMPORTANCE

---

[5] With this particular research question, the reader may be interested to know that experiments in real-life settings (e.g., a New York City subway) have confirmed the findings of laboratory experiments (Piliavin, Rodin, & Piliavin, 1969).

matical formulas called *statistical tests* (the details of which are not necessary to know in the present context.)[6] The statistical test gives the researcher the likelihood or probability that the results, such as a difference between two groups in an experiment or a correlation between two variables in a correlational study, are due to chance alone.[7] Obviously, a researcher is interested in having that probability as low as possible. If it is low enough, the researcher will be in a position to conclude that the results of the investigation were reliable rather than just a fluke (i.e., an accidental or chance finding). Traditionally, in psychological research, a result is considered *statistically significant* if the odds are less than 5 in 100 that the finding is due to chance factors alone. This is written "$p < .05$" and is read "probability less than 5 percent (or 5 in 100)."

It should be noted that, in discussing statistically significant results, the word "statistically" is often omitted (as: "A significant difference was found . . ."); however, it is assumed that the designation of a "significant" result refers only to its reliability and in no way implies that the finding is important, socially relevant, or practically meaningful. A highly reliable finding (one with a very low probability that the results are due to chance) may, in fact, have little or no practical import. For example, one could consistently obtain highly (statistically) significant differences in the observed ages of samples of elementary and high school students, but this is hardly surprising or earthshaking. Furthermore, there are conditions in which very small differences or relationships can be statistically significant, such as with very large samples of subjects (e.g., several hundred). The question still remains whether such a finding is important practically. With reference to Darley and Latané's experiment dealing with intervention in emergencies, one would not consider a group of people who, on the average, summonded aid one second faster than another group to be more concerned with helping in an emergency (although potentially such a finding could have been statistically significant). To be useful, research findings must be both statistically significant and practically meaningful. For instance, the difference between 52 and 166 seconds (the reaction times of the two-person and six-person groups in Darley and Latané's experiment) certainly could mean the difference between life and death for a victim in an actual emergency.

Although we are discussing the topic of statistical significance immediately following the section on the experimental method, it is important

---

[6] For a more detailed discussion of statistical significance as well as other statistical and methodological concepts touched upon in this chapter, the interested reader should see Neale and Liebert's *Science and Behavior* (1980).

[7] It is assumed that chance factors or factors that have been unaccounted for usually play *some* role in determining behavior, but the issue is whether the behavior is primarily a function of systematic factors rather than of random variation.

to keep in mind that the topic is equally relevant to the correlational method to be discussed in the next section. Correlations obtained between variables need to be reliable for them to be of any use, just as differences between experimental groups must be. Statistical significance is thus always computed for a correlation.

Correlation, as the name implies, deals with the co, or joint, relationship between two or more variables. The method answers research questions put in the form of: "Do variable X and variable Y go together or vary together?" Questions of relationship are frequently asked in psychology (e.g., Is there a relationship between late toilet training and compulsiveness in adulthood? Is the frequency of dating in college related to marital success and happiness?). Using the correlational method, *observations of all subjects are made under the same conditions.* The variation that occurs in the observations is due to each subject and to the common "natural" situation in which all subjects are exposed. (This approach should be contrasted with the experimental method, in which the conditions under which subjects are observed are systematically varied rather than naturally occurring.)

THE CORRELATIONAL METHOD

The basic data for a correlational analysis are pairs of observations collected for each member of a group of subjects.[8] To take an example, suppose a college professor were interested in finding out whether a relationship existed between how close students sat to the front of the classroom and how much they learned in the course. To find this out, the professor could record the row in which each student sat (let us assume that students sat in the same row each class period) and the student's final grade in the course. The data from such a study might look like those in Table 2–1, and these data could be used to correlate seating and final grade.

Notice that all of the subjects (students) in this correlational study were observed under the same conditions. In contrast, the same basic question—the relationship between seating and learning—could have been investigated by using the other two basic methods for studying personality. An experimental approach addressing the question might *randomly* assign students to seats at the beginning of the semester, and the final grades of the students sitting in the front half of the room might then be compared with those of the students sitting in the back half. Using a case-study approach, the professor might have interviewed several students and questioned them about where they sat and how well they did in their classes.

There are two specific questions which psychologists ask about the

---

[8] It should be noted that any number of variables can be correlated with one another. However, for the sake of illustration, the examples in this section refer to the simplest case—that is, only two variables.

TABLE 2–1

Data from a hypothetical study of the relationship between how close a student sits to the front of the classroom and final course grade

Subject	Row	Final grade	Subject	Row	Final grade
Andy	2	76	Linda	5	71
Ann	5	60	Mary	1	95
Bill	4	79	Pam	1	87
Bob	3	67	Pat	3	80
Eric	1	82	Polly	3	75
Howie	2	91	Robert	4	81
Jerry	2	86	Sam	2	82
Joan	5	64	Sheila	5	55
John	4	62	Shelley	3	90
Ken	4	66	Steve	1	99

relationship between two variables. First, if there is a correlation between the two variables, how strong is it? The *magnitude* or strength of a correlation refers to the ability to predict one variable from the other. The stronger the correlation, the more accurate the prediction will be. The second question involves the *direction* of the correlation or the way in which the variables relate to each other—either directly or inversely. A direct or *positive correlation* between variable X and variable Y means that high scores on X tend to be associated with high scores on Y and that low scores on X tend to go along with low scores on Y. For example, a positive correlation is regularly found between a person's height and weight. Conversely, an inverse or *negative correlation* is one in which high scores on X tend to be associated with low scores on Y and low scores on X tend to go with high scores on Y. Age and quickness of reflexes are negatively correlated; as people grow older, their reflexes become slower.

If the number of pairs of observations is small, an estimate of the correlation between two variables can be made by plotting the scores on a *scatter diagram*. Figure 2–3 presents several such scatter diagrams. The horizontal axis represents the values of one variable, and the vertical axis represents the values of the other. Each point corresponds to the scores of one subject on the two variables. The magnitude of the correlation is estimated by examining how closely the points in the scatter diagram deviate from a straight line.[9]

---

[9] The discussion in this chapter concerns *linear* correlations, so that a perfect correlation is a straight line. Variables can also be related curvilinearly, in which case a perfect correlation would be represented graphically as a curve. Anxiety-level and performance tend to be curvilinearly related—performance is poor at extremely low and extremely high levels of anxiety (with too little anxiety there is no motivation to perform, and with intense anxiety a person becomes immobilized), and performance is optimal at a moderate level of anxiety. If this relationship were plotted on a scatter diagram, with anxiety-level on the horizontal axis and performance on the vertical axis, the resulting curve would look approximately like an inverted "U" (∩).

FIGURE 2–3
Scatter diagrams showing various degrees of relationship between two variables

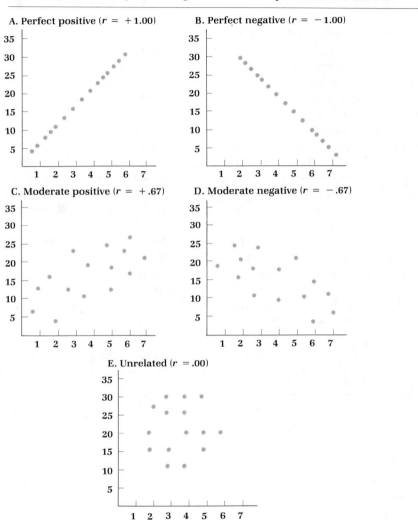

In the case of *perfect* positive or *perfect* negative correlation, all the points fall in a straight line. Thus, by knowing a person's score on one of the variables (it makes no difference which one), we can perfectly predict his or her score on the other variable. Where there is perfect correlation, either positive or negative, the plot shows no "scatter" or deviation from the perfect line of correlation.

Virtually no correlations are perfect, and so prediction of the value of one variable from knowledge of another can be reasonably accurate but will not be consistently exact. In the case of a high (but not perfect) correlation, there is some scatter about the line of perfect correlation, but the scores tend to fall within a narrow ellipse. Finally, where there is virtually no correlation, there is much scatter of the scores, and the plotted points tend to lie approximately within a circle.

The direction of the correlation is determined by the angle in which the points are oriented. If they go from bottom left to top right, the correlation is positive or direct (Figures 2–3A and 2–3C). If they are oriented from bottom right to top left, the correlation is negative or inverse (Figures 2–3B and 2–3D).

The data from our hypothetical study of the correlation between where students sit in class and their grades (Table 2–1) are plotted in Figure 2–4. Most of the data points fall in a narrow ellipse, which indicates a high correlation or strong relationship. The points are oriented from lower right to upper left, indicating that the correlation is negative. This means that there is a general tendency for students who sit closer to the front of the room to earn higher grades.

A scatter diagram is an efficient way to estimate the magnitude and direction of a correlation when there are a small number of pairs of observations. The procedure becomes cumbersome as the number of data points to be plotted becomes large. Furthermore, communicating a relationship between two variables becomes difficult and sometimes very inaccurate when such descriptions as "high negative correlation"

FIGURE 2–4
Scatter diagram of data (presented in Table 2–1) from a hypothetical study of the relationship between how close a student sits to the front of the classroom and final course grade ($r = -.79$)

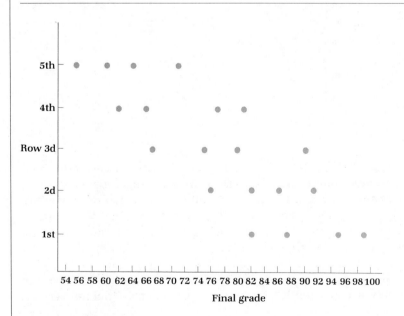

Final grade

or "moderately high positive correlation" are used. The modifying phrases "high" and "moderately high" are inexact and may very well connote different meanings to different people.

A more precise index of the correlation between two variables is provided by a *correlation coefficient,* often abbreviated *r,* which is calculated by means of a mathematical formula.[10] The direction of the correlation is indicated by the sign of the coefficient, while its magnitude is indicated by the absolute value (i.e., disregarding algebraic sign) of the coefficient. A correlation coefficient may range from +1.00, which indicates a perfect positive relationship, to a value of −1.00, which indicates a perfect negative relationship. Thus, when the coefficient is equal to 1.00 (+ or −), either variable can be exactly predicted from the other. As the coefficient decreases in absolute value from 1.00, the ability to predict one variable from the other decreases. In the extreme, a correlation of 0.00 indicates that the variables are unrelated, meaning that knowledge of one variable would not assist at all in predicting the other. It must be emphasized that how closely two variables are related depends only on the absolute size of the correlation coefficient. Thus, correlation coefficients of +.60 and −.60 are equivalent with respect to the extent to which one variable can be anticipated from the other. (Of course, the direction of the correlation must be known to make the prediction.) Examples of the correspondence between correlation coefficients and scatter plots can be seen in Figures 2–3 and 2–4 where the correlation coefficient is given in parentheses.

To conceptualize how well one variable can be predicted from the other, the correlation coefficient must be *squared.* The squared correlation coefficient (r^2) is a rough estimate of how much overlap there is between the two variables, or how much they *share in common.*[11] The greater the overlap, the stronger is the relationship and the more accurately one variable can be predicted from the other. A correlation coefficient of .80 indicates that the two variables have an overlap of roughly 64 percent ($.80^2 = .64 = 64\%$), and a correlation coefficient of .40 indicates that the two variables have an overlap of only 16 percent. A correlation coefficient of .80 cannot be considered twice as strong as one of .40. The relative strengths of correlation coefficients can be estimated only by comparing the squared correlation coefficients. Thus, a correlation of .71 is approximately twice as strong as a correlation of .50 ($.71^2 = .50$, and $.50^2 = .25$).

---

[10] There are a number of different correlation coefficients. The reader will have an opportunity to compute one type, a rank-order correlation coefficient, in Demonstration 15–1.

[11] The squared correlation estimates what is technically called the "percentage of variance the two variables have in common," and the discussion in the text of this statistical concept is simplified, albeit sufficient for our purposes.

The statistical significance (reliability) of a correlation coefficient is based only on its magnitude (not its direction—positive or negative) and the number of subjects in the study (i.e., the number of pairs of observations made). It should be noted that a finding can be statistically significant, but have little predictive value. The worth of a correlation relates to how well it predicts, and that is determined by squaring the correlation coefficient to estimate the percentage that the two variables share. For example, with a very large number of subjects, a very small correlation coefficient, such as .20, could be statistically significant meaning that the finding is likely to be obtained in subsequent studies. However, squaring the correlation coefficient, we find that the two variables have only 4 percent in common, which would not be very useful for predicting one variable from the other.

Correlational research does not always employ the correlation coefficient. Correlation should be viewed as a general approach to gathering information concerning the relationship between variables and not as a statistical procedure. The key elements of correlational research are that *all subjects are studied under the same existing conditions* (i.e., no events are systematically varied by the researcher, although the observations may be made under circumstances which are set up by the researcher) and *quantitative measurements are made of two (or more) variables for each subject.*

Evaluation of the correlational method

In considering the strengths of correlational research, it is useful to contrast it with experimental research, the other method of personality research that deals with quantitative data. Since the correlational method involves making observations without controlling the subjects' behavior or varying the circumstances under which the subjects are observed, the naturalness of the situation is maintained. As we shall see shortly, lack of control can make it difficult to draw conclusions about causation. However, this same absence of control may bring the investigation closer to "real life" than is possible with the experimental method.

Behavior is almost always *multiply determined*—that is, it is caused by a number of variables operating at the same time and in conjunction with one another. The correlational design can easily take this "fact of nature" into account by studying the relationship among many variables. Although experimentation can also deal with multideterminants by examining the effect of more than one independent variable, it is rare in practice for a single experiment to employ more than three independent variables, and many experiments involve only one.

Generally, there are three reasons for using the correlational method instead of the experimental method. First, a number of variables of interest to personality researchers are difficult or impossible to vary systematically. So-called *organismic variables* such as sex, age, birth order, and body size cannot be changed by a researcher. In the study of child-rearing practices, it would be virtually impossible to successfully place controls over the lengthy and complex procedures that parents use to train their children. And such phenomena as death, suicide, and mourning cannot ethically be controlled.

Second, direct variation of a relevant variable may be possible only at relatively "weak" levels, whereas collecting data on the variable as it naturally occurs may allow study of the variable in its extreme. For example, inflicting very mild pain or discomfort might (or might not) be an experimentally legitimate procedure, but inflicting extreme pain would clearly not be. However, it would not be difficult to find individuals who have suffered extreme pain. The correlation between such experiences and subsequent behavior might provide fruitful information that could not be legitimately obtained by the experimental method.

Third, correlational research is often more economical in terms of time, effort, and expense than is experimental research because correlational data are frequently collected under conditions that already exist so that there is no need to "set up" situations. For example, it has been shown in laboratory experiments that firstborn persons tend to exhibit more anxiety (e.g., Schacter, 1959) and a greater preference to be with other people (e.g., Darley & Aronson, 1966) when confronted with stress-inducing conditions than do others. Contriving a stressful situation in the laboratory is likely to be complex and hence costly in terms of time, at least, and most probably money, as well. Furthermore, producing highly stressful conditions in the laboratory is likely to prove impractical and unethical, as was discussed above. On the other hand, observing persons in an actual stress-inducing circumstance could be a relatively economical way to collect data bearing on this issue.

The massive power failure which encompassed much of the Eastern Seaboard of the United States on November 9–10, 1965 offered a rare opportunity to test laboratory findings concerning individual differences in anxiety and affiliation in relation to birth order in an actual crisis. The blackout occurred in New York City at about 5:30 p.m., at the height of the rush hour. The result was that thousands of people on their way home from work were forced to spend the night in public places. In the early morning hours, three psychologists from Rutgers University (Zucker, Manosevitz, & Lanyon, 1968) went to New York City to collect data from people in a large bus terminal and a hotel lobby, which were illuminated by emergency power. They asked people to complete a questionnaire concerning such information as age, education, and birth order, and their feelings about being stranded for the night. The subjects were asked to rate their preference for being alone or with other people, on a five-point scale, and to assess their anxiety by responding to the following question, also on a five-point scale: "How nervous or uneasy did you feel during this experience (i.e., the blackout experience) over the course of the evening?" The investigators also noted, before approaching a subject, whether he or she was talking to or standing with someone else, and this information became a dichotomous index of actual gregariousness (i.e., affiliative or nonaffiliative behavior). The data that Zucker and his associates collected confirmed the laboratory findings that, in anxiety-evoking situations, firstborn persons tend to exhibit more anxiety than do those born later, and that firstborn women prefer to be with other people during periods of stress.

Correlation and causation

The major limitation of correlational research is that conclusions about *cause-and-effect* relationships usually cannot be drawn. When two variables are correlated, we do not know which is the cause of the other—the *directionality* problem—or whether both are caused by some other factor—the *third-variable* problem.

A correlation between two variables tells us only that they are related or tend to covary, but does not tell us whether one is caused by the other. For example, a positive correlation can be found between grades and attendance in class. One possible interpretation of this relationship is that greater attendance in class increases the amount learned and thus results in higher grades. A second and equally plausible hypothesis is that good grades lead students who obtain them to attend class more frequently. In many correlational studies, the problem of directionality cannot be resolved. Hence the oft-cited dictum "Correlation does not imply causation."

But the directionality of the relationship is not always impossible to determine. Some relationships can be conceptualized in only one direction. For example, a manufacturer of certain exotic foods might calculate the relationship between the frequency with which products are purchased and the income of the purchasers. Suppose that the manufacturer finds a positive relationship between these two variables—the wealthier a person is, the more likely he or she is to buy the product. It is extremely unlikely that buying or eating a particular food would make an individual rich, but the possession of wealth might cause the person to buy something.

Although correlational research often does not allow statements about causation, it may contribute to disconfirming certain causal hypotheses. Causation always implies correlation, though the reverse is not necessarily true. Let us suppose that an investigator has asserted that cigarette smoking causes lung cancer. This causal relationship implies that lung cancer and cigarette smoking will be positively related. If a correlation between cigarette smoking and lung cancer were *not* obtained, our confidence in the hypothesis should be reduced. The *presence* of a correlation between cigarette smoking and lung cancer still does not allow the causal inference to be drawn, because the directionality of the relationship has not been specified. Furthermore, the relationship must be examined in terms of the other major problem in interpreting the results of correlational research, the third-variable problem.

The *third-variable problem* concerns the possibility that neither of the two variables involved in a correlation produces the other. Rather, some unspecified variable or process has produced the relationship. There is, for example, a high positive correlation between the number of churches in a city and the number of crimes committed in that city; the more churches a city has, the more crimes are committed in it. Does this mean that religion fosters crime? Probably not. That crime fosters religion? Unlikely. The relationship is due to a third variable—population—the growth of which leads to an increase in both churches and crime. Or consider the high positive correlation between the number of drownings on any given day and the consumption of ice cream on that day. Here, too, a third variable—temperature—is responsible for the relationship. When the weather is warm, more people are likely to be swimming (which is directly related to the frequency of drowning) and coincidently, more ice cream is likely to be eaten.

The fact that we cannot infer causation directly from correlational evidence does not mean that a cause-and-effect relationship does not exist; it merely means that, in contrast to experimental findings, a correlation does not enable us to identify the nature and the direction of causal relationships *without further information.*

There are instances in which it is not necessary to know whether one of the measured variables is causing the other or whether a third variable is responsible. One such case is in applied areas of psychology in which prediction of a criterion is all that is required. For example, a college admissions committee needs information to predict success in college. Typically there is a high positive correlation between grades in high school and academic achievement in college. Using this information, the committee can do its job effectively without reference to the causes of college academic achievement.

THE CASE-STUDY METHOD

A familiar method of studying personality is the biography. When a detailed account of a single individual is used in psychological, sociological, or anthropological research, it is typically called a *case study* or a *case history.* Oscar Lewis' (1961) classic study of family life in a Mexico City slum area *(The Children of Sanchez)* was based on extensive interviews in which the then-grown children were asked to relate their life histories. The following summary of one of the children, as it appeared in White (1976), illustrates the detailed, individualistic nature of the case study method:

> Manuel, the eldest son, came closest to the pattern of traits held to be typical in a disorganized slum environment. He recalled little about his home life, though his brother and sisters remembered all too well his crude assertions of authority when father was not at home. Having an "aversion to routine," as he put it, he remembered only "the exciting things," and these occurred mainly with his gang of friends who soon became the most important part of his life. Stocky and strong, he was from the first a good fighter and earned the other boys' respect. One of his fiercest fights, started to defend his brother, led oddly to a firm friendship; he and his new companion became inseparable, exchanged many confidences, and for years supported each other during emotional hard times. Manuel did poorly in school, which after the sixth grade he gladly gave up in favor of jobs, pocket money, and girls. At 13 he was inducted into sexual intercourse, after which "the fever, this sex business," got hold of him "in such a way that all I did was to go around thinking about it. At night my dreams were full of girls and sex. I wanted every woman I saw." Presently he fell into the grip of another fever, gambling at cards. "If a day passed without a game," he said, "I was desperate." This fever soon mounted to a point where he would bet a whole week's pay, but when he won he would go out with his friends and "throw it all away." Regretfully he recalled that he "never did anything practical" with his winnings.

> There is a certain charm about Manuel. His narrative is full of vitality and drama, and he sometimes reveals generous impulses, especially toward male friends. On one occasion he took over a sick friend's job to hold it for him, thereby sacrificing a much better job of his own. On another occasion, set up in a small business making shoes, he paid his three helpers so well that he went bankrupt. This mishap extinguished an already feeble spark: "I lost the little confidence I had in myself and lived just from day to day, like an animal. I didn't have the will power to carry out plans." At 15 he started a family and presently had four children. He never provided a home for his family, which finally became part of his father's household, and he increasingly neglected his wife, staying away and having a torrid affair with another woman. When his wife died he was grief-stricken. With his boyhood companion he departed for some months to work and gamble elsewhere, leaving the children to his father's support. No doubt this behavior contained some element of revenge for the humiliations and belittlements received from his father, but there was a strong undertone of shame and sadness in Manuel at having led a life "so sterile, so useless, so unhappy." (pp. 132–33)

The case study is mainly descriptive in nature, and its data are qualitative. It is the least systematic and least controlled research method, which, as we shall discuss shortly, has both advantages and disadvantages (cf. Ross, 1963). The case study is the major research method used in idiographic approaches to personality. (The experimental and correlational methods are typically used in nomothetic research.) Many case studies deal with *abnormal,* rather than normal, personality phenomena.

Case studies are used to present data concerning unusual cases. One of the most famous of these is "A Case of Multiple Personality" (Thigpen & Cleckley, 1954), an account of a 25-year-old married woman, "Eve White," who displayed three very distinct personalities. Eve White had been seen in psychotherapy for several months because of severe headaches and blackouts. Her therapist described her as a "retiring and gently conventional figure." One day during an interview,

> as if seized by a sudden pain she put both hands to her head. After a tense moment of silence, her hands dropped. There was a quick, reckless smile and, in a bright voice that sparkled, she said. "Hi there, Doc!" The demure and constrained posture of Eve White had melted into buoyant repose. . . . This new and apparently carefree girl spoke casually of Eve White and her problems, always, using *she* or *her* in every reference, always respecting the strict bounds of a separate identity. When asked her own name she immediately replied, "Oh, I'm Eve Black." (p. 137)

Following this startling discovery, Eve was observed over a period of 14 months in a series of interviews amounting to approximately 100 hours. (During this time, still a third personality emerged.) This case study is especially valuable because it is one of only a few detailed accounts of a rare phenomenon, a true multiple personality.

Case studies can be extremely useful in *illustrating procedures,* such as methods of personality change, when it is often insufficient to merely learn the principles involved. One must also be able to see how the principles are applied. Ayllon (1965) illustrates the management of "some behavioral problems associated with eating in chronic schizophrenic patients" in the following case study.

> Anne was a near mute catatonic who for the last 16 years would not eat unless a nurse led her to the dining room, gave her a tray, silverware, and food, and seated her at the table, then urged her to eat and occasionally spoonfed her.
>
> A 14-day baseline of Anne's behavior associated with meals was obtained. Not once during this period did she go to the dining room on her own, nor did she help herself to food. This information suggested that her difficulty in both these behaviors was being maintained by the attention she received from the nurses as a function of this difficulty. The nurses were instructed not to take the patient to the dining room but to help her as much as before once she entered the dining room.
>
> During the 21st week of this program, it was decided to shape her behavior in the dining room so that the patient would go through the

cafeteria line completely on her own, without the nurse's assistance (for four weeks previous to shaping, no records were taken once she had entered the dining room). The nurses were instructed not to help the patient in the dining room, but to reinforce her by dropping some candy on her tray, only after she had picked up a tray, silverware, and one edible item. (p. 74)

Case studies are sometimes used to test hypotheses and support theories, but the justification of such use is questionable. Freud used case studies extensively to support psychoanalytic theory, and, in fact, they were the major source of the evidence he presented for his hypotheses. Freud's case studies all suffer from the critical flaw of being open to many interpretations. Although Freud used these studies as evidence for his hypotheses, others can (and have) explained the same observations from entirely different theoretical viewpoints. For this reason, and others which will be mentioned shortly, case studies are poor substitutes for controlled experimentation when one's purpose is to muster support for a theory.

On the other hand, case studies can sometimes be helpful in *disconfirming* the implications of a theory. When a theory purports to be universally true (i.e., to hold in all cases), case studies can provide *negative instances* of the theory. A single negative instance—an example that is covered by the domain of the theory yet does not conform to the theory—is sufficient to disprove the claim of universality. For instance, Freud theorized that *all* male children experience an Oedipus complex (see Chapter 4). Accordingly, the anthropological studies which demonstrated that there are cultures in which young boys do not exhibit the Oedipus complex (Malinowski, 1927) cast serious doubt on Freud's original hypothesis. Of course, a somewhat modified position may still be tenable (e.g., limiting the phenomenon to Western society).

Evaluation of the case-study method

As a method of personality research, the case study has several advantages. It is an excellent method for examining the personality of a single individual in great detail. A closely related advantage is that the case study allows an individual's idiosyncrasies, complexities, and contradictions to be examined. However general the laws of human behavior are, each person is unique. Occasionally, a psychologist primarily interested in making statements about human behavior in general will use a large number of case studies, and in this situation the inconsistencies which appear may be of special significance.

Data from case studies can reflect the richness and complexity of personality. Although such data may not be specific enough to be used in *support* of a theory, they are often the source of hypotheses about human behavior. These hypotheses, once formulated on the basis of the case-study material, can then be tested by a more controlled and rigorous research method.

Another advantage of the case-study method is that it typically deals with people in their natural environments as opposed to an artificial laboratory setting. Since, ultimately, theories of personality are intended to explain the behavior of persons in "real-life" situations, it is apparent that case studies have compelling *external validity*. That is, they directly examine the phenomena of ultimate interest.

It is ironic that the most glaring deficiency of the case-study method can be its most redeeming quality. Here we are speaking of the *lack of control* which usually characterizes case studies. By allowing circumstances to vary as they will, the case study has a greater potential for revealing new and sometimes serendipitous findings. This is especially true with regard to control over the observations made. If the variables measured are specified in advance and only those measures are collected, the investigator may miss some vital observations which had not been planned for. Usually the case-study method does not specify the observations to be made but rather attempts to record as much of the entire situation as possible. [Sometimes unexpected data become even more significant than the anticipated data and subsequently become the subject of further investigation.] However, the advantage of placing no restrictions on the measures to be taken is sometimes outweighed by the problem of sorting through the data and making sense out of them. (Anyone who has sat down for an evening of editing reels of home movies has some idea of what a problem this could turn out to be.)

There are several distinct limitations of the case-study method. First, to circumvent the major practical problem of being in the right place at the right time, the psychologist typically waits for the critical event to occur and, at some later time, collects the data. These data come from detailed *retrospective* reports by the subject and any other people who happened to have observed the subject. The problem with such post hoc data collection is that the observers (the subject and others) tend to forget what has happened and to lose the feelings that accompanied the original critical situation. Moreover, observers not only forget details, but their "stories" also tend to change with the passage of time. Things are now seen in a different perspective, especially when the incident under study has been somewhat stressful. Memories are mixed with present thoughts and feelings in a process similar to that which occurs when someone tries to reconstruct a dream upon awakening. Thus, unless the data for the case study are gathered at the time the crucial incident occurs, the accuracy of the case material is open to question. Lewis' (1961) case study of Manuel Sanchez is clearly subject to the problems of retrospective data collection. The case of

Eve White is an example of a *non*retrospective case study. Once it was decided that she was to be the subject of an extensive investigation, the data were systematically collected at each interview.

A second limitation of the case-study method is that the data it yields are unique in that they generally come from a single individual, and therefore it is difficult to generalize from them to other people. A third limitation is that case studies are open to a variety of interpretations, since there are no definite guidelines for deciding among seemingly tenable hypotheses which account for the same data. Finally, the data from case studies are qualitative rather than quantitative, and quantification is an important element of scientific research because it leads to finer, more precise descriptions of behavior.

Whether the disadvantages of the case study method outweigh its advantages for studying personality depends upon the purpose of the investigation. At the very least, it is reasonable to think of the case study as a preliminary and adjunct research method.

The psychoanalytic strategy

Arthur Tress

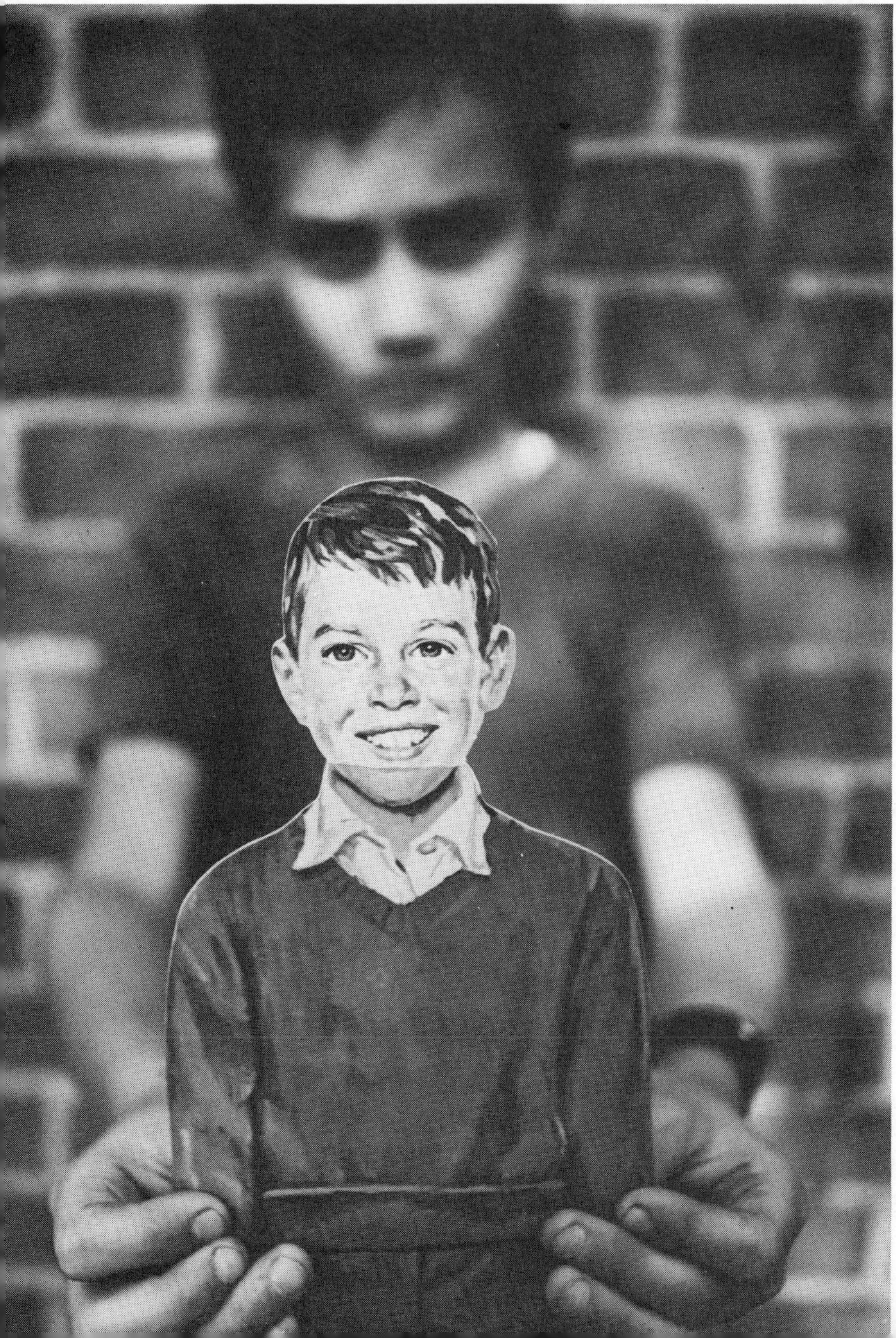

3 | *The psychoanalytic strategy*

Introduction

Psychoanalysis is, first of all, a strategy which emphasizes the importance of *intrapsychic events* (i.e., events within the mind) as central to personality. Beyond this general characteristic (shared with the phenomenological strategy discussed in Section 4), the term *psychoanalysis* has three common referents: a theory, an approach to research, and procedures for changing personality. First, it refers to a theory of personality (particularly personality development from its earliest stages in childhood) which was originally advanced by Sigmund Freud (1856–1939) and has subsequently been extended and modified by other psychoanalysts. The second meaning of psychoanalysis is a method of scientific investigation, a way of studying intrapsychic phenomena. This includes *psychoanalyzing* a person's random thoughts, dreams, mistakes, and other behavior so as to determine their intrapsychic significance, or their meaning for the person. This process is the same as that used to bring about personality change, and psychoanalysis as therapy is the third meaning of the term. As might be expected given these closely related meanings, theory, research, assessment, and personality change are quite intertwined in the psychoanalytic strategy.

More than any of the other three strategies, the psychoanalytic strategy has been dominated by the work and writings of a single individual. But, as we shall see, Freud's pursuit of a total theory of the mind involved a number of separable but interrelated mini-theories which he subjected to frequent revision. Thus, each of Freud's major ideas underwent many important changes during the course of his lifetime. Also, many of Freud's associates and disciples "defected" to establish theoretical camps of their own, taking some but not all of Freud's ideas with them. As time passed and psychoanalytic concepts came to be widely known to psychiatrists, psychologists, and educated lay people, drastic modifications of some of Freud's theories were also proposed.

In the brief discussion below we have introduced some of the major

WHAT IS PSYCHOANALYSIS?

Sigmund Freud

National Library of Medicine

PSYCHOANALYTIC THEORY

themes that run through Freudian and post-Freudian[1] psychoanalytic theory. Our aim is to provide an initial overview of theoretical perspectives and issues in psychoanalysis. Each of the themes introduced below will be developed more fully in Chapters 4, 5, and 6.

Ideas emerging in the late 19th century

We have already said that Sigmund Freud played an extremely important role in launching the psychoanalytic strategy. It is therefore useful to begin our journey into psychoanalysis by looking at the times in which Freud's theories developed. The second half of the 19th century was a period of great intellectual excitement. During its course, two extremely daring ideas about the human condition were published.

The human species is in all its aspects a natural result of evolution, not different in this way from animals. In 1871, Charles Robert Darwin (1809–1882) reached this conclusion in a compelling naturalistic theory of evolution that accounted for "the descent of man." In brief, Darwin showed that the human life form had gradually evolved from other life forms through the processes of random variation and environmental selection.

Darwin's accomplishment was based on brilliant insights that allowed him to see the underlying processes that lay behind and explained a wide range of natural observations. By treating a host of facts and details like pieces in a puzzle, Darwin was able to create a systematic biological theory that accounted for the appearance, disappearance (extinction), and evolution of species. Darwin's claim was that all life forms are motivated by two forces: (1) the will to survive, and (2) the urge to reproduce. Darwin was also impressed with the elaborate and sometimes remarkable mechanisms which could evolve to serve these ends. Darwin stopped short of providing a scientific analysis of the mind, and this was the task Freud set for psychoanalysis. (Ernest Jones, Freud's official biographer, called Freud "the Darwin of the mind.")

Unconscious, irrational, and primitive forces play a central role in human motivation. Philosophers Arthur Schopenhauer (1788–1860) and Friedrich Nietzsche (1844–1900) observed that human behavior is often impelled by forces that are unconscious and irrational, and both emphasized how easily the intellect could be self-deluding. Schopenhauer considered sex to be the most important human instinct. Nietzsche suggested that we repress certain memories, turn aggression inward to become a basis for ethics and conscience, and derive our ultimate

---

[1] We have used the general term *post-Freudian* to refer to psychoanalytic thinkers other than Freud and his original group of followers. Post-Freudians can be divided into several discrete theoretical camps (e.g., neo-Freudians, ego analysts, and so on), with many subtle differences among them.

strength from the most primitive part of ourselves. By the late 19th century, these ideas had come to hold sway among intellectual Europeans (Ellenberger, 1970; Kern, 1973; Sulloway, 1979; Whyte, 1960). They find clear expression in psychoanalytic theory, as we shall see.

A fundamental assumption for Freud and virtually all of his followers is that a person's inner world, rather than objectively observable external events themselves, is responsible for what the person feels and does. Psychoanalysts thus search for the intentions and meanings that lie behind every bit of behavior, even offering interpretations for what, at first, seem to be chance happenings.

The search for underlying motives is not unique to psychoanalysis, of course. For example, a hitchhiker who has just gotten a ride might ask, *"Why* did the motorist stop for me?" The hitchhiker is curious about the motorist's *intention.* "Did the motorist want company?" "Did the driver feel sorry for me?" "Is the driver going to ask me to do something in return?" Or consider our criminal justice system, which puts great emphasis on the degree to which harmful acts are premeditated. For example, the law prescribes incarceration for as little as one year for killing another person if intent cannot be shown. But if intent to murder is clearly established, the penalty can be upward of 20 years' imprisonment or even death. In everyday life we often base judgments about other people and their behavior by evaluating the "worthiness" of their intentions. Consider such common questions as: "Why did Jenny offer to help me with my work—because she likes me or because she felt she owed me something?"

In Western society, the importance of intent is learned early. Jean Piaget, a famous Swiss developmental psychologist, has found that children as young as seven may acknowledge that a small amount of purposeful damage is "naughtier" than substantial damage that occurs through ignorance, oversight, or accident. Our culture is filled with customs and attitudes which reflect the high status given to noble intentions, even when their outcome is undesirable. When a gift is given, it is the *thought* (the giver's intent) that counts, and parents feel justified in severely punishing their children *because* they love them.

From the preceding examples, it is evident that knowing other people's intentions is important in daily interpersonal relations. We are also concerned with the extent to which others understand our own intentions. When Wylie walks hurriedly past a close friend without stopping to say hello, he is likely to explain his "behavior" the next time he sees his friend. If Wylie had been late for an important appointment, for example, he would tell his friend that he did not *mean* to be rude but was concerned about being late for his appointment. Actually, he is explaining his intention rather than his behavior.

Interpretation and the search for meaning

Just as we sometimes explicitly make our intentions for a given act clear to another person, so, too, there are times when we try to conceal our intentions. A student who volunteers to do some additional research for a class in the hope of getting on the teacher's good side might tell the teacher that he or she is very interested in the topic.

Informing another person about the purpose of our behavior does not guarantee that the person will accept our statement of intent as valid. In our previous example of Wylie on his way to an appointment, if Wylie had had an argument with his close friend the night before, the friend might not be so sure that Wylie was merely concerned with his important engagement. Similarly, if the "diligent" student had shown little interest in the course throughout the semester, the teacher might question the student's motivation in volunteering to do extra work. In each case, there is a question raised as to the validity of people's reports of their intentions. The issue becomes one of finding the "true" intent of the act, the "real" reason it was performed. People frequently use the word *really* to emphasize the validity of a statement of intent. "Do you really like how I'm dressed?" "Phil really meant well." "I really love Lil."

The psychoanalytic strategy is characterized by the fact that it emphasizes the importance of questions of motivation and intention for understanding personality. In turn, this interest leads to the other emphases of the strategy. For example, as implied by terms like *really*, people may not always be aware of their own intentions and motivations; some of the most important aspects of an individual's personality may be *unconscious* and therefore the products of motivations of which the person is entirely unaware.

Intention is always inferred from behavior. But people vary in the degree to which they use behavior to evaluate interpersonal interactions or go beyond the behavior to infer intentions. Demonstration 3–1 will give you an opportunity to explore your relative use of behavior and intentions to evaluate personal interactions.

Demonstration 3–1

INTENTION VERSUS BEHAVIOR

In our daily lives we have many interactions with people: roommate, salesperson, friend, teacher, bus driver. In each interaction we have certain expectations, either explicit or implicit, about what should take place. For example, the bus driver is supposed to get us to work on time, a teacher is supposed to assign grades, a friend should listen sympathetically to problems, and so on. Some of our expectations are doubtless satisfied (e.g., teachers almost never forget to give grades), whereas others are not (e.g., friends are not always eager to hear about our frustrations). When our expectations about how another person is supposed to act are not met, our reactions and feelings about that person are based on two sources of information: the person's **behavior** (what he or she has done or failed to do) and the person's **intent** (what he or she meant to do).

Suppose that a bus driver failed to stop at your corner. You might have been very annoyed if you were consequently late for an appointment. It would have made little difference to you in that situation that the driver "had good intentions" of stopping. The driver's intent and behavior were at odds, and your reaction of annoyance was based on the bus driver's **behavior** of driving past your corner and not on the driver's intent.

It is important to note that, in this instance, the driver did not explicitly state an intention to stop, but the intention was a reasonable inference. **Intent frequently has to be inferred.** In the next example, the person's intention is explicitly stated.

Suppose you met your friend Dave at lunch, hoping to share with him the events of your frustrating morning. Dave said he wanted to listen (intent) but that he had to rush off (behavior) to study for a physics test scheduled that afternoon. You appreciated Dave's desire to listen to you and wished him well on his exam. Here again, a person's intent and behavior were inconsistent, but in this situation you evaluated the interaction in terms of Dave's **intention** to listen rather than his behavior of rushing off.

A third way of reacting to an inconsistency between intention and behavior would take both factors into account. In the preceding example, if Dave had left to play tennis, it is likely that you would have felt less good about your interaction with him than if he had "had" to leave for an exam. You would have understood that Dave had an appointment to play tennis but, at the same time, would have thought that he might have given your feelings and needs higher priority. By considering both behavior (Dave's playing tennis) and intention (he would have liked to listen to you), you would have viewed the situation differently than if you had taken only his intention or only his behavior into account.

The purpose of this Demonstration is to sensitize you to the role which other people's intentions and behavior and the relation between the two play in some of your daily interpersonal transactions. To achieve this, you will first compile a list of people with whom you have dealt recently and whom you either know very well or with whom you merely have a passing acquaintance. Then you will consider interactions you have had with these people in which their intentions and behavior were inconsistent.

PROCEDURE

1. First, make a list of the people with whom you have interacted over the past few weeks. Try to include as many persons as you can, but there is no need for the list to be exhaustive.

2. Next, divide the people on your list into three categories:

"Close"—people you know well, interact with frequently and regularly, think about, and so on (e.g., roommate, good friend, parent);

"Distant"—people you do not know well, interact with infrequently and irregularly, may have met only once or twice, have only brief business-type dealings with (e.g., salesperson, teacher with whom you have minimal personal contact);

"Other"—people who do not fit into either the "close" or the "distant" category (as defined above), whom you would not consider intimate acquaintances but with whom you have had more than just a brief encounter (e.g., many classmates, people who live in your dorm, your mail carrier). The people in this category will **not** be used in the Demonstration.

Keep in mind that the object of this preliminary step in the Demonstration is to provide you with a list of a number of people with whom you have recently interacted and whom you would consider either "close" or "distant." Thus, if you are having difficulty coming up with six to eight people in **each** of the two categories, your criteria for either "close" or "distant" relationship may be too stringent. If this seems to be the case, adjust your criteria accordingly.

3. Having compiled a sizable list of persons whom you might construe as "close" and "distant," you are ready to proceed with the major part of the Demonstration. This involves identifying as many interactions as you can with the persons on your "close" and "distant" lists *in which the persons' intentions and behavior were somehow inconsistent with each other.* Certainly all of your interpersonal interactions will not meet this requirement. Your goal should be to come up with at least four instances of intention-behavior discrepancies for each of the two categories of people (i.e., four for "close" and four for "distant"), and more, if possible.

4. For recording each of the intention-behavior discrepancies, make a large copy of the chart in Table 3–1 (omitting the examples, of course). Then, for each interaction in which intention and behavior were inconsistent, record the information outlined below. Note that the top half of the chart is designated for interactions with "close" acquaintances and the bottom half for interactions with "distant" acquaintances.

In Column I: give the **name** of the person with whom you had the interaction.
In Column II: give a brief description of the **interaction.**

TABLE 3–1
Sample chart for Demonstration 3–1

	I Other person	II Nature of interaction	III Other's behavior	IV Other's intent	V Your evaluation	VI Basis for evaluation
"Close" relationships	Dick	Met Dick after having rough morning	Went to study	Wanted to talk with me	Understood why he couldn't talk and felt okay about it	I
"Close" relationships	Dick	Met Dick after having rough morning	Went to tennis game	Wanted to talk with me	Appreciated that he had a tennis date but was a bit angry with him	B and I
"Distant" relationships	Bus driver	On bus going to appointment	Drove past my stop	To stop	Annoyed at the driver for making me late to my appointment	B

In Column III: give a brief description of the other person's **behavior.**

In Column IV: give a brief description of the other person's **intention.**

In Column V: give a brief description of how you *evaluated* the incident—that is, how you felt about and reacted to the other person and to the outcome of the incident.

In Column VI: state whether the **basis for your evaluation** in Column V was primarily the other person's behavior (B), primarily the other person's intention (I), or definitely a combination of behavior and intention (B and I).

The examples in Table 3–1 are taken from those discussed in the introduction of the Demonstration.

DISCUSSION

By the time you complete the Demonstration, you should have gained a greater understanding of the difference between intention and behavior which is an essential distinction made by the psychoanalytic strategy. We usually do not differentiate between intention and behavior when they are consistent with each other. However, when they are discrepant, as was the case in each of the interactions you considered in the Demonstration, a need arises not only to distinguish between them but also to decide whether to evaluate the situation and its consequences for ourselves in terms of the person's intent, the person's behavior, or some combination of the two.

The Demonstration should have given you an indication of how you tend to use intention and behavior in dealing with situations in which they are inconsistent. Is there any pattern in your reliance on intention versus behavior? There are any number of variables which might affect this, and one has been built into the Demonstration. By comparing your Column VI entries for "close" relationships with those for "distant" relationships, you may find that you tend to use intention as a basis for your evaluation of situations involving one of these groups of people, and behavior for the other group. Clearly this is an individual matter. The more interactions you have considered, the greater is the likelihood that consistent patterns or trends will emerge. You might wish to examine your relative use of intention and behavior in relation to other factors, such as the importance of the interaction to you, the sex of the other person, whether or not your evaluation of the other person's intention-behavior discrepancy had direct consequences for the person (e.g., if you mentioned how you felt), and so on.

In addition to what you have already done in Demonstration 3–1, you might also wish to examine those instances in which your own intentions and behavior were inconsistent. How did you evaluate such situations? How did others who were aware of your inconsistencies react with regard to the relative emphasis they placed on your intention versus your behavior?

Freud believed that the natural biological instincts of the individual (e.g., to satisfy its needs for defecation and urination, food, and sexual gratification as conveniently and immediately as possible) are inevitably in conflict with the requirements of adult society. His clinical observations convinced him that, in human beings, impulses of a sexual

Conflict and resolution

and/or aggressive nature are driven or kept from conscious awareness by a dynamic process called *repression.*

Freud said that his concept of repression was at the heart of psychoanalytic theory. Repressed intentions, that is, impulses of which we are unconscious, are the critical determinants of what we think, feel, and do. According to Freud, repressed impulses draw their strength from powerful, dammed-up biological instincts and are thus highly energized; though repressed, they are likely to manifest themselves in disguised form in dreams, fantasies, and behavior that is seemingly "accidental" (Freudian slips).

Repressed impulses fighting for expression may also produce psychopathology. Intense anxiety, specific phobias, and various illnesses with no physical basis were all treated by Freud through psychoanalysis. The theoretical goal of such analysis was to penetrate the barrier between the unconscious and conscious, thereby bringing unconscious wishes and conflicts into conscious awareness.

Psychoanalysts of all schools of thought place considerable importance on conflict, but they differ significantly in their explanations of the nature of this conflict. There is also disagreement concerning how readily conflict can be resolved and through what therapeutic means.

The course of personality development

Psychoanalytic thinking places a great premium on the importance of early experience and suggests that many of the earliest social and personal experiences of the child become the models for the formation of the individual's unique personality.

Freud cast personality development into a sequence of discrete *psychosexual stages,* triggered in a fixed order by the shift in sexual excitability (from the mouth to the anus to the genitals) that accompanies the natural course of biological development that has evolved for our species. The notion of unfolding sequences programmed by evolution—called the *ontogenetic principle*—was taken from the writings of Darwin, whom Freud and his intellectual contemporaries greatly admired.

Freud suggested that each stage in the ontogenetic sequence involved a specific conflict which required resolution, such as the conflict over toilet training at the anal stage. The psychological residue left by experiencing the full set of conflicts and struggling toward their resolution is the individual's basic personality, which is virtually complete by age five. Freud was extremely explicit concerning the overriding importance of early experience. At one point he said: "The little creature is often completed by the fourth or fifth year of life, and after that merely brings gradually to light what is already within him" (quoted by Roazen, 1975, p. 106).

Post-Freudians have generally accepted the necessity of considering personality from a developmental perspective, looking to the individual's prior history of conflicts and resolutions. There is also agreement that behavior may regress to earlier or more primitive forms under stress. (Think of how some people have childish temper tantrums when they get angry.) Beyond that, many viewpoints and several important disputes have emerged. For one thing, a number of theorists agree with pioneering ego psychologist Erik Erikson that it is more useful to think of stages and their associated conflicts as social than as sexual; Erikson speaks of psycho*social* stages. Also suggested by Erikson is the *epigenetic principle,* which differs from Freud's ontogenetic principle (see above) by asserting that each of life's conflicts is always potentially present with some degree of intensity and normally continues to be present, to some degree, throughout life. The epigenetic sequence, for Erikson, involves conflicts which come into ascendancy at various times because of social pressures. This process does not end at age five, but rather continues throughout life.

Analysts generally agree with Freud that each individual has a psychological distinctiveness—a personality—which is the active psychological residue of dealing with conflicts in the past. Analysts are also in general agreement that most people are not likely to come to understand the true nature of their own personalities by themselves. But Freud's belief that *character structure* (a phrase he would have preferred to personality) is fixed by the end of early childhood has been challenged from many sides, as we shall see.

Freud's theory of intrapsychic conflict identified three "agencies of the mind," representing the conflicting interests of primitive impulses *(id),* the rational self *(ego),* and internalized societal values *(superego).* Freud emphasized id impulses and the unconscious in his writings, but many post-Freudians have redressed the imbalance by emphasizing rational, conscious ego processes. A line of psychoanalysts beginning with Heinz Hartmann have also pointed to conflict-free ego functions, about which we shall have a good deal to say later. Nonetheless, Freud's three agencies of the mind have been adopted or absorbed into most psychoanalytic theories.

Agencies of the mind

If we are to deal with an individual's private motivations, we must ascertain the degree to which the person is aware of them. To get a feel for the problem of people's degree of awareness about their motives and attitudes, you might ask yourself such questions as: Why am I attending college? Why do I like (dislike) my roommate (friend, relative)? (If the answers to these questions are readily apparent, try inserting the word *really* before the words *attending* and *like.)* Can people be ignorant of their own motives and unaware or mistaken about their

PSYCHOANALYTIC ASSESSMENT

feelings regarding other persons, places, or events? It is now common-place, for example, to speculate that individuals who express an excessive degree of certainty about their own abilities, like the roaring lion, are expressing not self-confidence, but self-doubt. Are there grounds for such assumptions? How often do they hold? What is the value and what are the limitations of looking at people in this light? The answers to these crucial questions about *unconscious* processes are the burden of the psychoanalytic strategy.

The psychoanalytic strategy relies almost exclusively on *indirect* personality assessment (e.g., interpretation of free associations, dream analysis, projective techniques) because psychoanalytic theory makes the basic assumption that most of one's personality is unconscious and therefore cannot be assessed directly.

The psychoanalytic strategy is sometimes referred to as *depth psychology,* because psychoanalytic personality assessment involves probing into the hidden and the veiled. In psychoanalysis, one's understanding grows and things continue to reveal themselves more fully as one explores. Freud was committed to the concept of depth, repeatedly observing that, in psychoanalysis, one achieves understanding at various depths of meaning. The implication is that there are also many levels to each personality. Freud was passionate in his conviction that the deepest levels, arising from the earliest experiences and most primitive impulses, are the ones which most need to be sought and understood.

Another characteristic of psychoanalytic personality assessment is that it assumes observations are *nonadditive* (Mischel, 1971). This means that the strength of a personality attribute, such as generosity, cannot necessarily be measured by summing various observations (overt behavior) which are taken to indicate the presence of the attribute. Suppose that Eric frequently helped his friends, gave expensive Christmas gifts to his relatives, and donated money to half-a-dozen charities each year, whereas Harry rarely offered aid to friends, sent Christmas cards but no presents, and was an ardent adherent of the saying "Charity begins at home." If a nonadditive measurement model were used, Eric would not necessarily be considered more generous than Harry. In fact, it might be inferred that Eric's behavior is indicative of an underlying stinginess and that his generous behavior serves to cover up this more reprehensible personality characteristic.

To summarize, personality assessment in the psychoanalytic strategy involves making observations of behavior from which the processes that cause behavior are inferred in an indirect and nonadditive manner.

PSYCHOANALYTIC RESEARCH

Freud relied almost entirely on case studies he obtained from individual psychoanalyses to substantiate his theoretical propositions. Following in Freud's footsteps, many analysts have presumed that the "scientific" base of psychoanalysis can rest exclusively on data gathered in the clinical practice of psychoanalysis. As a consequence, a huge amount of data about single individuals has been collected; no other personality strategy has accounted for such a wealth of observations.

After hearing a patient repeat a given theme a number of times, the psychoanalyst will present the patient with an interpretation of its meaning. The validity of the interpretation is partially assessed by the degree to which the patient accepts it as true, and partially by whether it leads to any changes in the patient's behavior. In turn, interpretations that are frequently made by a number of psychoanalysts and have been validated in the manner just described become principles of the theory, developed from published psychoanalytic case studies.

Modern research methodologists flatly reject Freud's argument that the goings on during the treatment hour represented convincing evidence in their own right. So, research-minded psychologists, psychiatrists, anthropologists, and others have used the more conventionally acceptable correlational and experimental methods to investigate a variety of ideas suggested by Freud's theories. Various hypotheses and propositions derived from psychoanalytic theory have thus been subject, over the past two decades, to increasingly vigorous research conducted within the traditional framework of the psychological laboratory rather than through the understandings of a clinician. These studies have produced some fascinating and quite interesting information about the workings of the mind, as we shall see in Chapters 4, 5, and 6.

Some of Freud's hypotheses present unique problems for research. For example, much of psychoanalytic theorizing concerns the importance of early childhood events for later personality development, but it is extremely difficult to systematically vary the conditions under which children are raised, as would be done in an experimental investigation. It is possible to collect information about the way in which children were raised and to correlate this with measures of adult personality. Unfortunately, though, such studies are often weakened by the use of retrospective data.

PSYCHOANALYTIC PERSONALITY CHANGE

If personality were made up of motivations and intentions, many of which are unconscious, then in order to change personality, the intrapsychic events accounting for those motivations and intentions must be modified. Personality change in the psychoanalytic strategy involves dealing with thoughts, feelings, wishes, biological drives, and intentions, particularly those which are unconscious.

How can events about which a person is unaware be dealt with? The answer is that they cannot, at least not directly, and therefore a major aim of psychoanalytic personality change procedures is to make the patient aware of his or her unconscious processes and motives— to make conscious what is unconscious. Personality change comes about primarily through the lengthy process of having patients discover and come to understand (gain insight into) their inner motivations. This is often accompanied by intense emotional release. Frequently it is discovered, in the course of psychoanalysis, that the patients' motives are based on early childhood adjustment problems and conflicts, and they must learn to accept the fact that such motives are no longer relevant to their lives and are therefore unrealistic guides for their present behavior. As we will see, though, the goals and efficacy of psychoanalytic therapy have been hotly debated for years.

THE OVERLAP OF PSYCHOANALYTIC PERSONALITY THEORY, ASSESSMENT, RESEARCH, AND CHANGE

Personality theory, assessment, research, and change are interrelated in each of the strategies we shall be studying. Two of many possible examples will serve to illustrate this interdependence. The validity of a personality theory is tested in research which involves devising assessment procedures to measure the theoretical concepts under investigation. The theory of the development of personality disorders often suggests therapy procedures for changing personality, and the observations of clients in psychotherapy can be a rich source of data for expanding or revising the personality theory.

This interdependence among the four aspects of the study of personality certainly holds for the psychoanalytic strategy. Furthermore, there is considerable overlap and blending among them, more so than in any of the other three strategies. The best example of this phenomenon is Freud's use of his treatment of neurotic patients as a means of assessing personality, as a procedure for gathering evidence for his existing theory, and as a source of data for further developing his theory.

4 | *The psychoanalytic strategy*

Origins and development of personality

Psychoanalysis can be usefully conceptualized as involving four perspectives. First, psychoanalytic theory is *deterministic*. Freud held that all behavior is determined, or caused, by some force within us and that all behavior therefore has meaning. One of Freud's earliest and most widely cited clinical observations was the finding that even the simplest examples of human behavior can be traced to complicated psychological factors of which the individual may be totally unaware. Perhaps the best known occurrences are the so-called Freudian slips made in speech, writing, and reading. The errors presumably reveal something about the person's "inner" thought, or "real" intent. Examples in which the unconscious ideas are obvious include substituting "playbody" for "playboy" and "Fraud" for "Freud."

Among the clearest examples of the thoroughgoing determinism which Freud (1963)[1] used are those related to "accidental" forgetting and losing of objects:

> If anyone forgets a proper name which is familiar to him normally or if, in spite of all his efforts, he finds it difficult to keep it in mind, it is plausible to suppose that he has something against the person who bears the name so that he prefers not to think of him. (p. 52)

> We lose an object if we have quarreled with the person who gave it to us and do not want to be reminded of him; or if we no longer like the object itself and want to have an excuse for getting another and better one instead. The same intention directed against an object can also play a part, of course, in cases of dropping, breaking, or destroying things. (p. 54)

> Here is the best example, perhaps, of such an occasion. A youngish man told me the following story: "Some years ago there were misunderstandings between me and my wife. I found her too cold, and although I willingly recognized her excellent qualities we lived together without any tender feelings. One day, returning from a walk, she gave me a book she had bought because she thought it would interest me. I thanked her for this mark of 'attention,' promised to read the book and put it

[1] The dates used in this book refer to the actual references used (sometimes translated or reprinted editions) and thus do not always correspond to the original publication date of the work.

on one side. After that I could never find it again. Months passed by, in which I occasionally remembered the lost book and made vain attempts to find it. About six months later my dear mother, who was not living with us, fell ill. My wife left home to nurse her mother-in-law. The patient's condition became serious and gave my wife an opportunity of showing the best side of herself. One evening I returned home full of enthusiasm and gratitude for what my wife had accomplished. I walked up to my desk, and without any definite intention but with a kind of somnambulistic certainty opened one of the drawers. On the very top I found the long-lost book I had mislaid." (p. 55)

Freud noted that he could "multiply this collection of examples indefinitely," and he used incidents like these as an indirect assessment technique to understand facets of an individual's personality that would otherwise be inaccessible.

A second major characteristic of psychoanalytic theory is that it is a *dynamic* point of view. "Dynamic" in the present context refers to the exchange and transformation of energy within the personality. Like most other personality theorists, Freud thought that it was essential for a comprehensive understanding of personality to have a statement of the source of motivation for human actions. Freud postulated that this source of motivation was a unitary energy source called *psychic energy,* which can be found within the individual.

Third, psychoanalysis is *organizational.* Freud organized personality into three basic functions—the *id,* the *ego,* and the *superego*—and believed that it is the dynamic interaction or conflict among them which determines behavior. Also, these personality functions operate at three levels of awareness—*unconscious, preconscious,* and *conscious.*

Fourth, psychoanalytic theory is *developmental.* Freud held that human development follows a more or less set course from birth, and he divided development into a series of stages which all persons must pass through. Freud's theory is also developmental in the sense that it stresses the importance, indeed the dominance, of early childhood development as a determinant of adult personalities.

DRIVES AND LIBIDO

The psychoanalytic term *drive*[2] refers to an inborn, intrapsychic force which, when operative, produces a state of excitation or tension.

---

[2] "Drives" are frequently referred to as *instincts* in the psychoanalytic literature, but the latter translation of the German *Triebe* can be misleading. Unlike the common usage of "instinct" as an inherited predisposition to behave in a characteristic way, a "drive" refers only to a source of internal excitation and not to the motor response which follows. More in keeping with psychoanalytic usage, "drive," connotes a force whose energy can be modified and can be expressed in a variety of responses. The sex-drive, for example, can be satisfied rather directly through sexual intercourse or masturbation and indirectly through such artistic endeavors as painting and sculpting (see discussion of sublimation in Chapter 5).

Like much of his theory, Freud's conceptions of drives underwent considerable revision in the more than 40 years he was engaged in developing them. Freud's early formulation divided drives into two classes. The first class are *self-preservative,* dealing with the basic physical needs of existence, including breathing, hunger and thirst, and the excretory functions. When these drives are not satisfied, the organism experiences tension, as when we hold our breath or have not eaten in some time and feel hunger pangs. Usually, objects or circumstances satisfying these drives are available in direct form; their satisfaction is typically simple and straightforward, allowing relatively little tension to build up. However, under unusual circumstances, a drive such as hunger can become strong and exert a powerful influence on behavior. When a plane carrying a Uruguayan rugby team and their supporters to a series of matches in Chile crashed in the Andes Mountains in October 1972, the passengers and crew were given up for lost. Miraculously, 16 men survived for 73 days in subfreezing temperatures with no fuel and only enough food to be rationed for 20 days. When they were finally rescued, it was discovered that the survivors had remained alive by eating parts of the bodies of those who had died.[3]

The second group of drives are those related to *sexual urges;* the psychic energy of sexual drives is called *libido.* In this context, "sexual" refers to all pleasurable actions and thoughts, including, but not confined to, eroticism. (In his introductory lectures, Freud occasionally spoke of love and affection as possible goals of libidinal impulses.) Libido is also the energy for all mental activity (e.g., thinking, perceiving, imagining, remembering, problem solving) and is somewhat analogous to, though not the same as, physical energy.

Freud initially believed that most of human motivation is sexual in nature. Societies place obstacles in the way of living completely or even predominantly in terms of satisfying one's pleasure-seeking drives. In capsule form, Freud's theory of personality deals with the manner in which we handle our sexual needs in relation to society, which usually prevents direct expression of these needs. Each individual's personality is a function of his or her particular compromise between sexual drives and society's restraints on them.

For many years, Freud's theorizing was concentrated exclusively on the sexual drive. Later, around 1920, he revised his theory of motivation to include the aggressive drive along with the sexual drive.[4] The aggressive drive was hypothesized to account for the destructive aspects of human behavior. It possesses its own kind of psychic energy,

---

[3] A popular book titled *Alive: The Story of the Andes Survivors* (Read, 1974) was written about the incident and a movie, *Survive,* based on the book has been made.

[4] Freud also called the aggressive drive the death drive (death instinct), or *Thanatos,* which is in opposition to the life drive (sexual drive), or *Eros.*

although Freud gave this energy no special name. Freud's dual theory of drives assumes that both the sexual and the aggressive drive are involved in the motivation of all behavior, although their contributions are not necessarily equal. (Had Freud lived in contemporary America, he might well have cited as one piece of evidence for the close interrelationship of the sexual and the aggressive drive the common use of the word *fuck* to express anger.) Like the sexual drive, the aggressive drive is said to accumulate tension which must be released, and the aggressive drive develops in a manner parallel to that of the sexual drive. However, Freud's formulation of that development was never as clear-cut or complete as his formulation of the development of the sexual drive, and our discussion will focus on the latter.

Psychic energy is conceptualized as potentially building up in pressure or thrust in very much the same way as water might develop tremendous pressure in a series of pipes when no external valve is open. If there is an increase in pressure and there is no outlet for this pressure, the pipe will burst. Further, it will burst at its weakest point. Psychoanalytic theory argues that an increase in the pressure, or tension, of psychic energy is a natural consequence of an intrapsychic conflict. Reduction of this tension is necessary for an individual's functioning, and it also produces a highly pleasurable experience, since tension is experienced as unpleasant or painful. Tension reduction, which assumes a prominent place in psychoanalytic theorizing, is formally called the *pleasure principle*. If the individual's psychic energy does not have an opportunity to discharge in normal or socially acceptable ways, then the pressure will increase and finally, as with the water-pipe analogy, will burst out violently at the weakest point in the personality.

Freud's psychic energy system is a *closed* system. That is, each person may be thought of as possessing a fixed quantity of psychic energy which is invested in given objects, persons, and ideas. Psychic energy cannot literally be *cathected*,[5] or attached, to people and objects in the external world, but within the mind it can be cathected to their mental representations in the form of thoughts, images, and fantasies. The strength of a cathexis (i.e., the amount of energy invested) is a measure of the importance of the object. Since there is only a limited amount of psychic energy, the greater a given cathexis, the less psychic energy there is available for other cathexes and mental activities. Hence, the young man who is constantly thinking of a woman friend has difficulty in doing other things, such as reading an assignment in his personality textbook. Cathexes are not permanent, so that if psychic

---

[5] *Cathect* is the verb form of cathexis and refers to investing psychic energy in an object; *cathexes* is the plural of cathexis. Also, it should be noted that, in psychoanalytic terminology, all interactions with others are called "object relations."

energy is no longer cathected to one object, it is free to be reinvested in another.

Mention the name "Freud," and many people's initial association is "sex." Although Freud modified his view of the basic source of human motivation to include aggression, most of his theorizing deals with the influence of the sex drive on all behavior. It was Freud's insistence on this issue which made his views unpalatable to many psychologists, including two of his ardent followers at the beginning of the century, Carl Jung (1875–1961) and Alfred Adler (1870–1937). Early in their relationship, Jung (pronounced "Yoong") wrote Freud to ask:

> Is it not conceivable, in view of the limited conception of sexuality that prevails nowadays, that the sexual terminology should be reserved only for the most extreme forms of your "libido," and that a less offensive collective term should be established for *all* the libidinal manifestations? (Freud & Jung, 1974, p. 25)

Adler's dissension with Freud regarding the importance of the sexual drive was even more marked than Jung's. Essentially, Adler believed that the fundamental human motive was the *striving for superiority* as a compensation for feelings of inferiority. The origin of this conceptualization can be clearly traced to Adler's own life experiences. As a child, Adler was continually sick and weak. He suffered from rickets, a disease which softens the bones, and this made it extremely difficult for him to engage in physical activities with his peers. In later years, Adler would recollect his feelings of inferiority: "I remember sitting on a bench bandaged up on account of rickets, with my healthy elder brother sitting opposite me. He could run, jump, and move about quite effortlessly, while for me, movement of any sort was a strain and an effort" (quoted in Bottome, 1957, pp. 30–31). Adler had twice been run over in the street, and he almost died from pneumonia (Orgler, 1963). As a consequence, he decided early in life to become a physician in an effort to overcome death and his fear of death (Ansbacher & Ansbacher, 1956).

Adler did go on to become a physician, and before his interests turned to psychiatry, he practiced general medicine. During this time he developed and published, in 1907, a novel theory of disease titled *The Study of Organ Inferiority and Its Physical Compensation*. The theory stated that people develop a disease or malfunction in that organ or part of the body which is weakest. The general reaction to such weakness takes the form of compensating and over-compensating for it. For example, a person born with weak legs might spend many hours developing the leg muscles (compensation), with the result that the individual might eventually become a long-distance runner (over-compensation).

ALTERNATIVE VIEWS OF THE BASIC HUMAN MOTIVE: JUNG AND ADLER

Carl Jung

National Library of Medicine

Alfred Adler

National Library of Medicine

Several years later, when Adler began to practice psychiatry, he broadened his theory of organ inferiority to include all feelings of inferiority, including those arising from psychological or interpersonal weaknesses as well as those stemming from physiological impairment. The individual's perceived inferiority, be it from biological, psychological, or social weaknesses, leads to striving for superiority as a form of compensation. Adler believed that the existence of these two forces—the need to overcome inferiority and the desire to do so by becoming superior—is normal in all people. The two forces are the basic motivating tendencies in human beings and consequently account for individual growth and social improvement. In Adler's (1964) words, "to be a human being means to feel oneself inferior" (p. 96). In the normal process of development, striving for superiority compensates for the feelings of inferiority. In the resulting compensatory life-style which the individual adopts, feelings of inferiority, which are most prominent in childhood, may be forgotten. Adler (1964) was aware that "not every one . . . can remember that he has ever felt inferior. Possibly, too, many may feel repelled by this expression and would rather choose another word" (p. 96). It is interesting to note the similarity between Adler's view that adults are unaware of their childhood feelings of inferiority and Freud's view that adults are unaware of their infantile sexuality.

Abnormal behavior (neurosis) can occur if feelings of inferiority and/or strivings for superiority become exaggerated. Adler used the term *inferiority complex* to refer to such an exaggerated, neurotic reaction. Thus, the common usage of "inferiority complex," which equates the term with normal feelings of inferiority, is contrary to the narrower meaning which Adler intended.

PERSONALITY DEVELOPMENT

The exact manner in which personality develops is of great importance in psychoanalytic theory. There are more explicit divisions of opinion about personality development than about the definition of libido and the nature of human motivation, discussed in the previous section. This is because Freud's drive theory is metapsychological[6] and thus cannot be proved or disproved on the basis of objective evidence. In contrast, most of Freud's theories regarding personality devel-

---

[6] Psychoanalysts discriminate between Freud's clinical propositions and his metapsychological propositions (Silverman, 1976). Clinical propositions, such as the notion that conflicts may motivate psychological problems, are subject to empirical test; metapsychological propositions, such as the notion that hostile wishes result from an aggressive instinctual drive, are not even subject to verification *in principle* and would, at any rate, have little or nothing to do with the clinical application of psychoanalysis. Many psychoanalysts have rejected or ignored Freudian metapsychological propositions, focusing instead on clinical propositions which may be tested empirically. Accordingly, Freud's metapsychology will receive relatively less attention in our account.

opment were clinical propositions. Thus, each practicing psychoanalyst might obtain case evidence supporting or casting doubt on any of Freud's conclusions about personality development.

Freud believed each adult has a unique personality which is relatively fixed in the individual by about the age of five. One's personality is a result of the subtle interplay of inborn individual differences in constitution and temperament and the effects of passing through a set of universally experienced conflicts with parents. These conflicts occur because the free expression of the individual's biological impulses is unacceptable to others.

How, though, does character form? The answer is quite complex, and involves most of the remainder of this chapter. But it is useful to begin here by introducing and explaining a few of Freud's most important ideas and concepts, after which we shall consider the actual stages of development about which Freud and others have written.

Origins of character

Constitutional and genetic factors

Freud himself was strongly committed to the view that genetic and constitutional factors play an important role in determining one's personality. This conviction was consistent with what he saw to be the implications of Darwin's theories. In addition, the prevailing medical belief was that personality was highly dependent on such biological factors. (Interestingly, modern psychoanalysts have paid relatively little attention to constitutional factors.)

Early experience

Every psychoanalyst believes early experience to be important. Analysts differ about whether later experiences can also have profound effects and have pursued the fascinating questions of when and how underlying character changes might occur after childhood's end.

Character types

If given conflicts are not resolved, the individual will be likely to have an adult character reflecting these poorly resolved or unresolved conflicts, which remain active and potent in the psyche for the rest of one's life. Freud believed that there were identifiable character types associated with each stage of psychosexual development. Freud himself described only one character type in any detail, the anal character, but he encouraged his students to develop the others more fully.

Repetition

The concept of repetition played a central role in Freud's thinking. He was often struck by the variety of ways in which individuals managed to repeat the basic patterns and themes of their lives again and again. Such patterns have always seemed to have their roots in early childhood, more specifically, in the conflicts of psychosexual development. An essential part of the theory of repetition is that these early anxieties are irritated by current stimuli, giving rise to our reactions and behavior in the present.

Fixation

There are two basic conditions that result in an individual experiencing difficulty in leaving one stage and going on to the next: *frustration* or *overindulgence*. Either the person's needs relevant to the psychosexual stage have not been met (frustration), or the needs have been so well satisfied that the person is reluctant to leave the stage (overindulgence). Both problems result in *fixation* at a psychosexual stage. Fixation involves leaving a portion of libido permanently invested in a stage of development which has passed. The amount of libido fixated is dependent on the severity of the conflict.

Inevitably, some libido is fixated at each psychosexual stage. When the proportion of libido fixated at an earlier stage of development is small, only vestiges of earlier modes of obtaining satisfaction are seen in later behavior. However, when a substantial proportion of libido is fixated at an earlier stage, the individual's personality may become dominated by modes of obtaining satisfaction which were used in the earlier stage.

STAGES OF PSYCHOSEXUAL DEVELOPMENT

Freud divided human development into a series of universal stages which all persons pass through from infancy to adulthood. The stages are delimited by the *erogenous zone* (an area of the body which is particularly sensitive to erotic stimulation) which is dominant at the time. That is to say, at any particular time in the developmental sequence, one body area—specifically, the mouth, the anus, or the genital region—seems to outweigh other areas as a source of pleasure. The stages of development are called *psychosexual* to indicate that the development is actually that of the sexual drive as it moves through the erogenous zones.

At each psychosexual stage, a particular *conflict* must be resolved before the person can pass on to the next stage. The individual's libido is invested in behavior involving the erogenous zone which is predominant at the time; however, since each individual has a fixed amount of libido, the libido must be freed from the primary erogenous zone of the stage it is in (a consequence of resolving the conflict) so that it can be reinvested in the primary erogenous zone of the next stage. Freud used the analogy of military troops on the march to explain this process. As the troops march, they are met by opposition (conflict). If they are highly successful in winning the battle (resolving the conflict), virtually all of the troops (libido) will move on to the next battle (stage). If they experience greater difficulty in winning the battle, more troops will be left behind on the battlefield and fewer troops will be able to move on to the next confrontation.

The trauma of birth

Otto Rank (1929), whose name is most often associated with the concept of the *birth trauma,* argued that the initial biological separation of child and mother which is experienced at birth becomes the prototype for all subsequent anxiety. Biological separation becomes a prototype for loss and separation in later life. Rank suggested that every enjoyable act is oriented toward regaining the pleasure of the intrauterine environment. For example, for the male, sexual intercourse symbolically represents a return to the mother's womb.

Freud himself suggested that before birth the fetus is in fact leading a relatively calm, peaceful, and undisturbed existence. In a warm, safe environment, the fetus sleeps, exercises, and evacuates at will. After birth this "ideal" existence changes radically. Needs and desires are to a large degree now under the control of others, particularly parents, and immediate satisfaction and tension reduction are rarely, if ever, possible as they were during the previous nine months. Further, at the time of birth, the infant has not yet developed ways to cope with the immediate pressures (sources of anxiety) which are constantly present.

Oral stage and character

During the first year of life, the child's mouth is the most prominent source of both tension reduction (e.g., eating) and pleasurable sensations (e.g., sucking). The child is said to be in the *oral stage* of development because libido is centered in the oral cavity. Weaning is the crucial conflict of the oral stage. The more difficult it is for the child to leave the mother's breast or the bottle and its accompanying sucking pleasure, the greater will be the proportion of the child's libido which is fixated at the oral stage.

Freud suggested that there would be a distinctive "oral character" associated with fixation at the oral stage, and the idea was picked up and expanded upon by his early followers and by many post-Freudians. The generally held belief among psychoanalysts is that individuals who are fixated at the oral stage are likely to hold an optimistic view of the world, to develop dependent relationships in adulthood, to be unusually friendly and generous, and to expect the world, in turn, to "mother them." As Strupp (1967) points out, "the focal point of the child's personality organization at this period is not necessarily the mouth per se but *the total constellation of immaturity, dependency, the wish to be mothered, the pleasure of being held, the enjoyment of human closeness and warmth*" (p. 23).

What, then, would the prototypic oral character be like? Such an individual would be "centrally preoccupied with the issue of sustenance and all its ramifications" (Fisher & Greenberg, 1977, p. 85). This implies an unusual concern with social support; oral characters are expected to act in ways which will foster affiliation rather than separation from others. Moreover, their primary means of dealing with the world is expected to be oral. When frustrated they may resort to eating, drinking, taking drugs (orally), or sucking their thumbs. Oral characters would be expected to express their hostility through words.

Research on the oral character

Research suggests that the psychoanalytic concept of the oral character has some validity. For example, it would be predicted that people fixated at the oral stage would tend to eat and drink excessively. Masling and his associates have found a positive relationship between subjects' reporting oral imagery in Rorschach inkblots (see Chapter 6) and obesity (Masling, Rabie, & Blondheim, 1967) and alcoholism (Bertrand & Masling, 1969). It has also been found that college students who depend upon others for making decisions in ambiguous situations rather than trusting their own judgments report more oral imagery on the Rorschach than do students who hold to their own perceptions of the situation (Masling, Weiss, & Rothschild, 1968). Finally people who seem focused on the mouth and themes of incorporation on various projective tests appear to display a special motivation to gain closeness and support from others (Fisher & Greenberg, 1977, p. 400).

Oral eroticism and sadism

Some psychoanalysts, such as Abraham (1927), have divided the oral stage into two phases. Thus far in the discussion, only the first phase, *oral eroticism,* has been described. It is characterized by the pleasure of sucking and oral incorporation, and people fixated at this phase are called *oral-erotic characters.* The second phase, *oral sadism,* commences with the eruption of teeth and may be viewed as representing the development of the aggressive drive. The child is now capable of biting and chewing as well as behaving aggressively and destructively. A person fixated at this second phase of the oral stage is likely to be pessimistic, cynical, and aggressive in later life and would be called an *oral-sadistic character.*

Post-Freudian extensions of the oral stage

Erich Fromm (1900–1980), a well-known post-Freudian, also distinguished between these basic character types, though in keeping with his emphasis on social determinants of behavior, he conceived of their origins differently. Fromm (1947) believed that character types develop from the social interactions of children with their parents. He theorized that people who are receptive characters (Abraham's oral-erotic characters) were raised in home environments which fostered an attitude of expecting to receive because the demands of the home situation were best dealt with by being receptive, friendly, and pleasing. In contrast, when the home circumstances are more frustrating, children develop the attitude that they must *take* in order to receive and that the best source of security comes from exploiting others (Thompson, 1957). Fromm describes such persons as exploitative characters (Abraham's oral-sadistic characters).

Another extension of the basic Freudian notion of the oral character was made by Harry Stack Sullivan (1892–1949), who also emphasized interpersonal aspects of development. For Sullivan, the critical aspect of the first year of development (i.e., Freud's oral stage) was social interaction between the child and the mother which involves the child's learning to evaluate and discriminate the mother's emotions. This ability to "read" the mother's feelings can be viewed as a prototype of accurately perceiving and predicting other people's behavior. Masling, Johnson, and Saturansky (1974) obtained partial support for this proposition. Male college students who reported many oral images on the Rorschach were better than low-oral males at predicting the responses of other male students on a personality test. This finding was replicated with a second group of college students who knew each other well and were all enrolled in a pre–Peace Corps program. This made it possible to relate measures of oral dependence and interpersonal perception to a measure of progress in training for the Peace Corps which previous research had found to be the best single predictor of successful work in a foreign country. Certainly accurate perception of others would be essential to doing well in the Peace Corps program. Both oral dependence and accurate interpersonal perception were found to be positively related to the Peace Corps rating.

In an interesting extension of psychoanalytic thinking on the oral stage, Bettelheim (1976) conceptualizes the story of Hansel and Gretel as a tale of oral sadism. Hansel and Gretel are sent into the woods because they have been careless with milk. In the woods they greedily devour part of the gingerbread house of the witch, who (like their

Erich Fromm

René Burri/Magnum Photos, Inc.

Harry Stack Sullivan

Courtesy of William Alanson White Psychiatric Foundation, Inc.

mother) is at first gratifying (according to Bettelheim, "The original, all-giving mother, whom every child hopes to find again later somewhere in the world" [p. 161]). But the witch soon reveals her intention to eat the children. The children resolve their dilemma by abandoning their strictly oral impulses for reason. By outwitting the witch, they are able to kill her and return home as more mature children. The story is popular, according to Bettelheim, precisely because it facilitates dealing with oral conflicts.

Anal stage and character

With the weaning of the child, the libido shifts from the oral region to the area of the anus. Pleasure is obtained at first from expelling feces and later from retaining them. This is not to say that the child did not derive similar pleasure during the oral stage. However, during the second and third years of life, anal pleasure predominates, just as oral pleasure predominated during the first year of life. Up until the anal stage, relatively few demands are made on the child. During the second year of life, however, parents in most Western cultures begin to make demands on their offspring, particularly with respect to bowel and bladder control. The conflict in the anal stage pits the sexual drive for pleasure, derived from the tension reduced by defecation, against the constraints of society, which require that the child develop self-control with respect to excretion.

If children are able to easily accede to their parents' toilet-training demands, they will develop the basis for successful self-control. However, the child may have difficulty in developing sphincter control and thus meeting the increasing parental demands. Two fundamental strategies for coping with the frustrations of toilet training are open to the child.

One strategy leads to the development of an *anal compulsive character*. Consider, for example, the child who adopts the strategy of meeting parental demands by complete retention of feces. This in itself is pleasurable (i.e., gentle pressure against the intestinal walls), and in addition it may prove to be a powerful indirect way of striking back at one's parents (e.g., through provoking concern over the child's failure to have a bowel movement). If the tactic is successful, it may set the stage for unusually compulsive behavior patterns in later life. Anal compulsives are neat, careful, systematic, and orderly. They may be upset or even revolted by "mess."

An alternative strategy is to take a more directly oppositional, "you can't make me do that" attitude. This would include attempts to "counterattack" by defecating at moments which are particularly inconvenient, such as immediately *after* being taken off the "potty." If the child discovers that this is a successful means of social control, the child may come to employ the same type of strategy for handling frustration in general, becoming an *anal expulsive character.* It is interesting to note, for example, that in our culture verbal statements of extreme anger and hostility are often expressed in colloquial terms which refer to excretion (e.g., "Piss on it." "Oh, shit.") Anal expulsives would also be expected to be stingy, hoarding, and stubborn, and to rebel or express anger (originally against toilet training) by becoming wasteful, disorderly, or messy. Note, then, that anal expulsiveness and anal compulsiveness become the two sides of the same fixation; both are responses to being controlled and forced.

Research on the anal character

A few correlational studies have found some evidence for the configuration referred to as the anal character (Fisher & Greenberg, 1977; Kline, 1972). For example, people who are relatively stingy also tend to be relatively neat. There are also some interesting experimental demonstrations. In one (Rosenwald, 1972), male college subjects were asked to identify various geometric forms while they were immersed in a smelly fecal-like substance and while they were immersed in water. Comparison of the men's performance in the two conditions was taken as a measure of anal anxiety; the greater the difference in performance the greater the anal anxiety. The men who had the most difficulty managing in the fecal-like material tended to be the most obstinate and also were those who were most careful in arranging a set of magazines that had been left in disarray.

During the fourth and fifth years of life, the libido is centered in the genital region. Children at this age are frequently observed examining their genitalia, masturbating, and asking questions about birth and sex. The conflict in the phallic stage is the last and the most crucial one with which the young child must cope. The conflict involves the child's unconscious wish to possess the opposite-sexed parent and at the same time to eliminate the same-sexed parent. Freud called this situation the *Oedipus complex* (pronounced ED'ipus). The name is derived from the Greek myth in which Oedipus unknowingly kills his father and marries his mother.

Phallic stage

The Oedipus complex

The Oedipus complex operates somewhat differently for males and females. The little boy's first love object is his mother. As the libido centers in the genital zone, his love for his mother becomes erotically tinged and therefore incestuous. However, the boy's father stands in the way of his sexual desire for his mother, and thus becomes the child's rival or enemy. Accompanying his antagonism for and wish to eliminate his father are the boy's fears that his father will retaliate. The little boy's casual observations that women lack penises suggest to him that his father's revenge will be extracted in the form of castration. This threat of castration, experienced as *castration anxiety,* forces the boy to give up his wish to possess his mother. The resolution of the Oedipus complex is said to occur when the boy *represses* (puts out of consciousness) his incestuous desires for his mother and identifies with his father. The latter process is called *defensive identification* and follows from the boy's unconscious "reasoning": "I cannot directly possess my mother, for fear of being castrated by my father. I can, however, possess her vicariously. I can get some of the joy of possessing my mother *by becoming like my father.*" The boy thus resolves his conflict by incorporating his father's behavior, attitudes, and values, thereby simultaneously eliminating his castration anxiety, possessing his mother vicariously, and assimilating those qualities necessary for appropriate sex-role behavior.

The Oedipus complex for the little girl, sometimes called the *Electra complex,*[7] is considerably more complicated and less clear than that for the young boy.[8] The little girl's first object of love is also her mother. However, during the phallic stage, when her libido is centered in the genital zone, the little girl is likely to discover that while her father and other males (such as a brother) have penises, she and her mother (and other women) do not. She reasons that she must have had a penis at one time, and she blames her mother for her apparent castration. This, along with other disappointments in her mother, such as those revolving around conflicts in earlier psychosexual stages, leads to some loss of love for her mother and subsequent increased love for her father. Her love for her father, which is erotically tinged, is coupled with envy because he has a penis. *Penis envy* is the counterpart of castration anxiety. However, unlike castration anxiety, which motivates the little boy to renounce his incestuous desires, penis envy carries with it no threat of retaliation by the mother, since the ultimate punishment, castration, has no meaning for the girl. According to Freud, the female fantasizes sexual intercourse with her father, and imagines that she will therefore bear him a child. This child is unconsciously equated with a penis.

It is not clear exactly how the Electra complex is resolved, although the resolution occurs later in life and it is never complete. It is obvious

---

[7] In Greek mythology, Electra persuaded her brother to murder their mother and their mother's lover, who together had killed their father.

[8] In general, Freud had more difficulty theorizing about women than about men. Thompson (1950), among others, has argued that Freud's notions about women represent his own unexamined and distinctly Victorian attitudes.

that even though the mother does not hold the threat of castration over her daughter, she would express considerable displeasure over incestuous relations between her husband and her daughter. Presumably, the impracticality of fulfillng her Oedipal wish causes the girl to repress her desires for her father and to identify with her mother (i.e., defensive identification). This also protects the girl from loss of her mother's love.

We have presented the general "formula" for the Oedipus complex, but it should be kept in mind that the exact pattern it takes for each individual is a function of his or her history during the prephallic stages and of the specific familial circumstances during the phallic stage. Freud considered the resolution of the Oedipus complex to be crucial, since he postulated that all neuroses were due to an incomplete solution.

Of the views advanced by Freud, his ideas concerning infantile sexuality and especially the Oedipus complex are no doubt among the most difficult to comprehend or accept. This was true at the beginning of the century, when Freud introduced his revolutionary theory, as it probably is today for students being introduced to these notions for the first time. It is easy for us to accept the conflicts of the oral and anal stages; though we may not recollect being weaned and toilet trained, there is good evidence in our present behavior that we were. In contrast, not only is it unclear to us that we once had incestuous desires toward our opposite-sexed parent, but the very idea is completely contrary to our present morality. Freud's answer to an allegation such as "*I* never went through the Oedipus complex" was simply that people cannot remember or accept their Oedipus complex because they have long since repressed memories of it, which was part of their resolution of the conflict.

Evidence for the Oedipus complex

Most of the evidence for the concepts of the Oedipus complex, castration anxiety, and penis envy comes from case studies of patients in psychoanalytic treatment. However, there have been some attempts to study these important psychoanalytic notions nomothetically. In these investigations, a major problem has been to develop adequate research definitions of the concepts. A good definition should meet two requirements: it must be amenable to objective measurement, and it must be closely related to the theoretical concept so that research findings will have a bearing on the theory. In practice, it is often difficult to meet both requirements with psychoanalytic concepts, as can be seen in a study by Johnson (1966). He defined penis envy as not returning a borrowed pencil (a phallic symbol) and found that significantly more college men than college women returned pencils which they had been loaned during an examination. Although not returning the pencil is an objective measure, it could be argued that pencil hoarding is too far removed from the theoretical concept of penis envy to have much value. An example of a correlational and an experimental study will be presented to illustrate the nature of more definitive investigations of castration anxiety and penis envy.

Based on the differences between the Oedipal situation for males and females, Hall and Van de Castle (1963) hypothesized that men would have more dreams of castration anxiety than would women and that women would have more dreams of the wish to be castrated and penis envy. The content of 120 college students' dreams was examined. Examples of dream material taken to indicate castration anxiety included the dreamer's inability to use either his penis or a symbol of his penis (such as a pen or a gun). When another person in the dream had this difficulty, a castration wish was assumed to be indicated. Acquiring a penis or a phallic symbol or changing into a man in the dream was regarded as evidence for penis envy. The content analyses of the dreams supported the hypothesis being tested.

In a very different type of investigation, Sarnoff and Corwin (1959) studied the relationship between castration anxiety and the fear of death. If fear of death is assumed to be a derivative of repressed fear of castration, then the more castration anxiety people have, the greater should be their fear of death when castration anxiety is aroused. To test this proposition, Sarnoff and Corwin measured male undergraduates' fear of death before and after their castration anxiety was aroused. In the first part of the experiment, subjects indicated their agreement with statements about death (e.g., "I am disturbed when I think of the shortness of life") on a brief Fear of Death scale. Castration anxiety was assessed by means of a projective technique in which subjects were asked to choose one of three descriptions of a cartoon that was presumed to depict castration. On the basis of this test, subjects were divided into high and low castration anxiety groups.

In the second part of the experiment, subjects returned four weeks later, ostensibly to rate the esthetic value of some pictures. Half of the subjects in each of the castration anxiety groups rated pictures of nude women (high-sexual-arousal condition), and half rated pictures of fully clothed fashion models (low-sexual-arousal condition). Following this task, the subjects were again administered the Fear of Death scale. As predicted, under conditions of high sexual arousal, which were presumed to arouse castration anxiety, subjects with high castration anxiety showed significantly greater increases in the fear of death than did subjects with low castration anxiety. No differences were found when sexual arousal was low. If one assumes that fear of death is an indication of castration anxiety, this study lends support to an important psychoanalytic concept.

Horney's reinterpretation of the Oedipus complex

Few psychoanalysts (or other psychologists who study child development) question Freud's *observations* that children around the age of four or five experience jealousy, rivalry, and ambivalent feelings of love and hate for their parents. However, a number of post-Freudians (and other psychologists) have been skeptical about the origin and content of these occurrences. Specifically, they have disagreed with Freud's sexual interpretation. Analyst Karen Horney (1885–1952), for example, has reinterpreted the nature of the Oedipus complex in terms of interpersonal dynamics.

> The typical conflict leading to anxiety in a child is that between dependency on the parents . . . and hostile impulses against the parents. Hostility may be aroused in a child in many ways: by the parents' lack of respect for him; by unreasonable demands and prohibitions; by injustice; by unreliability; by suppression of criticism; by the parents dominating him and ascribing these tendencies to love. . . . If a child, in addition to being dependent on his parents, is grossly or subtly intimidated by them and hence feels that any expression of hostile impulses against them endangers his security, then the existence of such hostile impulses is bound to create anxiety. . . . The resulting picture may look exactly like what Freud describes as the Oedipus complex: passionate clinging to one parent and jealousy toward the other or toward anyone interfering with the claim of exclusive possession. . . . *But the dynamic structure of these attachments is entirely different from what Freud conceives as the Oedipus complex. They are an early manifestation of neurotic conflicts rather than a primarily sexual phenomenon.* (Horney, 1939, pp. 83–81; italics added)

Karen Horney

National Library of Medicine

In a similar vein, Horney, who, unlike Freud, theorized considerably about women, objected to Freud's use of the concept of penis envy to explain feminine inferiority and to Freud's view of motherhood as a means of compensating for that inferiority. Horney believed that Freud's image of women was distorted because he based it exclusively on observations of neurotic women.

Following the resolution of the Oedipus complex, at about the age of five, children of both sexes pass into a period known as *latency.* Latency is *not* a stage of psychosexual development because, during this period, which lasts from the end of the phallic stage to the onset of puberty, there is no further psychosexual development. According to Freud, the latency period involves massive repression not only of sexual impulses, but also of oral and anal ones. (Jung took serious exception to Freud's concept of a latency period, calling it a biological impossibility. He likened the idea to a plant whose buds would start

Latency period

to blossom, then fold into buds again, and then reappear once more.) During latency, the libido is channeled into such activities as school, interpersonal relations with children of the same age and sex, and hobbies. Freud said little about this period of life, although other psychoanalytic theorists (e.g., Erikson, Sullivan) have placed considerable emphasis on it.

Sullivan (1953) divided the period of development which Freud called latency into the *juvenile era* and *preadolescence*. For Sullivan (1953), "the importance of the juvenile era can scarcely be exaggerated, since it is the actual time for becoming social" (p. 227). This is the period in our society when children are in elementary school. Up until this time, children tend to play with peers in an egocentric manner. Each child is primarily interested in his or her own welfare, ideas, and needs. The juvenile era begins as the child develops a need for true cooperative play and a sharing of experiences with peers. During the juvenile era, the child learns to cope with the demands of authority figures other than parents, such as teachers, recreational leaders (e.g., in the Brownies or the Cub Scouts), and peers who assert authority in the form of bullying. An even more important contribution of the juvenile era to social development is that children come to recognize and effectively deal with people who are different from themselves.

Preadolescence begins when the child develops an intimate friendship with a "chum," a particular peer of the same sex, and it ends with the emergence of interest in and the need for a relationship with a peer of the opposite sex. The chum, or best friend, becomes the child's confidant. Most important, the child develops a true, nonselfish sensitivity to the needs of the other person, "not in the sense of 'what should I do to get what I want,' but instead 'what should I do to contribute to the happiness or to support the prestige and feeling of worthwhileness of my chum'" (Sullivan, 1953, p. 245). Sullivan held that this is the first time that a human being genuinely loves another. So critical is this relationship that Sullivan (1953) believed experiencing such genuine intimacy and love of a chum could be "fantastically valuable in salvaging one from the effects of unfortunate accidents up to then" (p. 227).

There are two essential differences between Freud's and Sullivan's theorizing about human development from about the age of five to puberty. First, in direct contrast to Freud, Sullivan considered this period of life to be rich in critical experiences. For Sullivan, the individual is anything but latent during this period. Second, although not denying the importance of earlier development, Sullivan viewed the juvenile era and preadolescence as very important stages in a person's life. In those two periods, the basis for all future social relationships is established. The contrasting views of Sullivan and Freud can be traced to their emphasis on different basic motivational factors—social for Sullivan and sexual for Freud.

The final stage of psychosexual development begins at puberty, when the young adolescent starts to mature sexually, and lasts through adulthood until the onset of senility, at which time the individual tends to regress to pregenital behavior (i.e., behavior of the oral, anal, or phallic stage). In the genital stage, the libido is again focused in the genital area, but now it is directed toward heterosexual, rather than autoerotic, pleasure. The greater an individual's success in reaching the genital stage without having large amounts of libido fixated in pregenital stages, the greater will be the capacity to lead a "normal" life, free of neurosis, and to enjoy genuine heterosexual relationships.

Anna Freud (1895–   )[9] brought psychoanalytic theory to bear more specifically on adolescence. She observed that the adolescent is suddenly faced with an onslaught of sexual and aggressive impulses that appear in stark contrast to the latency period. In defense against these new feelings, the adolescent tries to regain some sense of control. One strategy is ascetism, in which the individual tries to abandon physical pleasure (e.g., by strict diets or vigorous exercise). Alternatively, the adolescent may turn to intellectualization, developing personal theories about the nature of love or of life. Usually, the turmoil of adolescence is worked out without the need for therapy, but Anna Freud observed: "There are few situations in life which are more difficult to cope with than an adolescent son or daughter during the attempt to liberate themselves" (1958, p. 323).

The genital stage, we have said, begins at puberty and lasts until the onset of senility. Obviously, much goes on during those 50 or more years of a person's life. However, consistent with Freud's belief that the first five years of life are paramount and determine adult patterns of behavior, he did little theorizing about adulthood.

Jung (1933) did not delineate specific stages of development, but he was well ahead of his time in emphasizing that middle age (late 30s, early 40s) is a critical period in a person's life. Jung described this time as one in which people undergo a major transition from youthful impulsiveness and extroversion to thoughtfulness and introversion, from interests and goals which have their roots in biological urges to interests and goals which are based on cultural norms. The person's values become more social, civic minded, and philosophical or religious. In short, the individual develops into a spiritual being. These changes precipitate what Jung referred to as a midlife crisis. The crisis occurs even among quite successful people as they come to realize that many of their goals have been set from without, by others. Jung stated: "The

Genital stage

Anna Freud

National Library of Medicine

Jung's concept of the midlife crisis

[9] Anna was the last of Freud's children. Interestingly, she had no medical or scientific training and began her working career as an elementary school teacher. She was psychoanalyzed by her father.

achievements which society rewards are won at the cost of diminution of personality. Many—far too many—aspects of life which should have been experienced lie in the lumber-room among dusty memories" (1933, p. 104).

Jung believed that, if this transformation of energy within the personality did not occur smoothly, the personality might be seriously and permanently crippled. He was very successful in treating individuals who were having difficulties with this transition in their middle years. His principle of therapy was that the midlife crisis can only be resolved through *individuation*. Individuation refers, simply, to finding one's own individual way. Crain (1980) has nicely summarized the Jungian view:

> We are prompted to begin turning our energy away from the mastery of the external world, and to begin focusing on our inner selves. We feel inner urgings to listen to the unconscious to learn about the potentials we have so far left unrealized. We begin to raise questions about the meaning of our lives. . . . (p. 194)

Jung is equally notable for his recognition of the special problems of old age and his reflections on their intrapsychic meaning. He noted that the old person begins to try to understand death and suggested that universal images of eternity and the afterlife tend to appear in old age.

Erikson's eight stages of psychosocial development

Although all psychoanalytic theories of personality place a heavy emphasis on the importance of early periods of development for later life, post-Freudians have tended to de-emphasize the biological and sexual determinants of behavior and to focus upon social development. We have seen in the previous section an example of Sullivan's interpersonal view of development. To illustrate how the entire development sequence can be conceived of with greater stress on social factors within a psychoanalytic framework, the developmental stages proposed by the prominent ego analyst Erik Erikson (1902–   )[10] will be outlined. Although Erikson does not discount biological and psychosexual influences on the developing individual, he emphasizes the influence of society and culture. Thus, like Sullivan, Erikson considers Freud's latency period to be a time of growth rather than stagnation, and like Jung, Erikson views adult development as important, dividing it into three stages.

With the purpose of integrating Freud's theory of psychosexual development with the existing knowledge of human physical and social growth, Erikson (1963, 1968) outlined eight stages of psycho*social* devel-

---

[10] Erikson was a student of Anna Freud, and she was also his psychoanalyst.

opment, each of which represents an encounter with the environment. Each stage is designated by a conflict between two alternative ways of handling the encounter (e.g., basic trust versus mistrust), one adaptive and the other maladaptive. Unlike the conflicts in each of Freud's psychosexual stages, the eight critical conflicts or encounters with the environment which Erikson outlined are all present at birth in some form. For example, although in the first year of life the child's major problems center on developing basic trust (Erikson's first stage), the child is also struggling to develop autonomy (Erikson's second stage), as when it wriggles to be set free if held too tightly.

> However, under normal conditions, it is not until the second year that he begins to experience the whole *critical opposition of being an autonomous creature and being a dependent one;* and it is not until then that he is ready for a decisive encounter with his environment, an environment which, in turn, feels called upon to convey to him its particular ideas and concepts of autonomy and coercion in ways decisively contributing to the character and the health of his personality in his culture. It is this encounter, together with the resulting crisis, that we have tentatively described for each stage. (Erikson, 1963, p. 271)

Thus, each critical encounter with the environment predominates at a particular period of life, at which time it must be successfully resolved before a person is fully prepared for the conflict which predominates next. Successful resolution is relative and involves developing a "favorable ratio" between the adaptive and maladaptive alternatives (e.g., more basic trust than mistrust).

Not only are all eight conflicts represented in the individual at birth, but each of the conflicts continues to play a role, albeit a minor one, throughout life. This concept is illustrated in Figure 4–1, which is a diagram of Erikson's psychosocial stages, plotted against periods of physical and/or psychosexual development. Each row of the diagram represents one of the eight conflicts which are named in the shaded boxes. The location of the name of the conflict indicates the period in life when the conflict predominates in one's personality. For example, "identity versus role confusion" describes the central encounter for teenagers. However, the problem of feeling secure with oneself is also present at earlier and later stages. The particular forms that a person's search for identity assumes at each of the other seven periods of life (i.e., before and after adolescence) are described in the boxes to the left and the right of the box representing the time of ascendance of "identity versus role confusion." These descriptions indicate the nature of each of the first four conflicts as they are manifest in adolescence, when "identity versus role confusion" is the predominant, though not the only, conflict with which the individual must deal.

Erik Erikson

Harvard University News Office

FIGURE 4–1

Erikson's epigenetic diagram of the eight stages of psychosocial development

	1	2	3	4	5	6	7	8
VIII Maturity								Ego integrity vs. despair
VII Adulthood							Generativity vs. stagnation	
VI Young adulthood						Intimacy vs. isolation		
V Puberty and adolescence	Temporal perspective vs. time confusion	Self-certainty vs. self-consciousness	Role experimentation vs. role fixation	Apprenticeship vs. work paralysis	Identity vs. role confusion	Sexual polarization vs. bisexual confusion	Leader- and followership vs. authority confusion	Ideological commitment vs. confusion of values
IV Latency				Industry vs. inferiority	Task identification vs. sense of futility			
III Locomotor-genital			Initiative vs. guilt		Anticipation of roles vs. role inhibition			
II Muscular-anal		Autonomy vs. shame, doubt			Will to be oneself vs. self-doubt			
I Oral-sensory	Basic trust vs. mistrust				Mutual recognition vs. autistic isolation			

Source: Adapted from Erikson, E. H. *Childhood and society.* New York: W. W. Norton, 1963; *Identity, youth, and crisis.* New York: W. W. Norton, 1968.

Basic trust versus mistrust

Initially, according to Erikson, an infant must develop sufficient trust to let its mother, the provider of food and comfort, out of sight without anxiety, apprehension, or rage. Such trust involves not only confidence in the predictability of the mother's behavior but also trust in oneself. This conflict occurs during the period of life which Freud referred to as the oral stage of psychosexual development.

Autonomy versus shame and doubt

Next, the child must develop a sense of autonomy. This sense is originally developed through bladder and bowel control and parallels the anal stage of traditional psychoanalytic theory. If the child fails to meet parental expectations in this regard, shame and doubt may result. The shame of being unable to demonstrate the self-control demanded by parents may become the basis for later difficulties, just as the experience of attaining adequate self-control in childhood may lead to feelings of autonomy in later life. Erikson (1963) suggests:

> This stage, therefore, becomes decisive for the ratio of love and hate, cooperation and willfulness, freedom from self-expression and its suppression. From a sense of self-control without loss of self-esteem comes a lasting sense of good will and pride; from a sense of loss of self-control and of foreign overcontrol comes a lasting propensity for doubt and shame. (p. 254)

Initiative versus guilt

Initiative versus guilt is the last conflict experienced by the preschool child and thus occurs during the period Freud designated as the phallic stage. During this time, the child must learn to appropriately control feelings of rivalry for the mother's attention and develop a sense of moral responsibility. At this stage, children initially indulge in fantasies of grandeur, but in actuality they may feel meek and dominated. To overcome the latter feelings, the child must learn to take role-appropriate initiative by finding pleasurable accomplishment in socially and culturally approved activities, such as creative play or caring for younger siblings.

Industry versus inferiority

The conflict between industry and inferiority begins with school life or, in primitive societies, with the onset of formal socialization. At this time, children must apply themselves to their lessons, begin to feel some sense of competence relative to peers, and face their own limitations if they are to emerge as healthy individuals. Note that these important developments occur during the time when, from Freud's point of view, the child is in a period of psychosexual nondevelopment (i.e., latency).

Identity versus role confusion

With the advent of puberty the adolescent must begin to develop some sense of identity. *Identity,* as the term is used by Erikson, refers to the confidence that others see us as we see ourselves. Of particular importance for identity formation is the selection of an occupation or career, although other factors may be involved. If an identity is not formed, role confusion, which is often characterized by an inability to select a career or to further educational goals and by overidentification with popular heroes or cliques, may occur. Role confusion can be overcome through interaction with peers or elders who are informed about various occupational opportunities (if this is the locus of the conflict) or who accept the adolescent's self-perception.

Intimacy versus isolation

By young adulthood, people are expected to be ready for true intimacy. They must develop cooperative social and occupational relationships with others and select a mate. If they cannot develop such relationships, they will be, and feel, isolated. The conflict between intimacy and isolation occurs during the period which Freud referred to as the genital stage. Erikson (1963, p. 265) notes that when Freud was asked what a healthy person should be able to do well, he curtly answered: " *'Lieben und Arbeiten'* (to love and to work)." Erikson believes that "we cannot improve on 'the professor's' formula."

Generativity versus stagnation

According to Erikson, a mature person must do more than establish intimacy with others. The individual "needs to be needed" and to assist the younger members of society. *Generativity* is concerned with guiding the next generation, and if it is not accomplished, the individual may feel stagnant and personally impoverished.

Ego integrity versus despair

If all of the preceding conflicts are not suitably handled, despair may result in later life. Disgusted with themselves and correctly realizing that it is too late to start another life, such individuals live their last years in a state of incurable remorse. In contrast, to become psychosocially adjusted and have a lasting sense of integrity, the person must develop each of the adaptive qualities of the other seven stages. Erikson (1963) emphasizes that all human beings, regardless of their culture, can achieve such adjustment: ". . . a wise Indian, a true gentleman, and a mature peasant share and recognize in one another the final stage of integrity" (p. 269).

5 *The psychoanalytic strategy*

The organization
of personality

Psychoanalysis divides the mind into three levels of consciousness, or awareness. The *conscious* part of the mind includes all that we are immediately aware of at a given point in time. Freud's concept of the conscious is close to our everyday use of the term, except that only a very small proportion of our thoughts, images, and memories are conscious. The Freudian mind, like an iceberg, is nine tenths below the surface.

The *preconscious* includes cognitions which are not conscious but can be brought into consciousness with little or no difficulty. For example, as you read these words you are trying to think about the material being presented. However, unless a test on this information is imminent (and perhaps even then), you could easily begin to think of an upcoming vacation or next week's date. These thoughts were in your preconscious.

Finally, there is the part of the mind which plays the most important role in personality, the *unconscious*.[1] Freud contended that most of our behavior is directed by forces of which we are totally unaware—that is, they are out of consciousness. In contrast to preconscious thoughts, unconscious thoughts enter consciousness only in disguised or symbolic form.

Freud was certainly not the first to postulate the existence of an unconscious, but his emphasis on those aspects of personality of which we are unaware has had a profound influence on the scientific study of personality as well as on everyday conceptions about personality. Freud himself noted that we have suffered three blows to our narcissism and self-image. The first blow was dealt by Copernicus, who discovered that the earth was not the center of the universe. Next, Darwin made the human being an animal among animals. Finally, Freud made us conscious of our unconscious, aware of the degree to which we are controlled by unknown forces within us which are frequently beyond our control. Brown (1959) has commented: "It is a shattering experience

---

[1] The term *subconscious* is not part of formal psychoanalytic nomenclature, though presumably in its common usage it refers to everything that is below consciousness (i.e., the preconscious and the unconscious).

for anyone seriously committed to the Western tradition of morality and rationality to take a steadfast, unflinching look at what Freud has to say. It is humiliating to be compelled to admit the grossly seamy side of so many grand ideals. . . . To experience Freud is to partake a second time of the forbidden fruit" (p. xi).

In Freud's early theorizing, the concept of the unconscious played a major role. Later, around 1920, Freud revised his theory somewhat to posit three basic aspects of personality—the id, the ego, and the superego. The functions which were formerly relegated to the unconscious were now primarily taken over by the id. Basically, the relationship of the earlier and later constructs is that "all of the id is unconscious, but not all of the unconscious is id" (see Figure 5–1).

Before discussing the id, ego, and superego, we shall examine an alternative view of the division of personality conceptualized by Jung. This order of presentation is appropriate because Jung's division of personality is closer to Freud's earlier division into levels of consciousness.

JUNG'S ALTERNATIVE DIVISION

Like Freud, Jung divided the personality into three aspects, two of which are similar to Freudian concepts. There is the *conscious ego*, which includes the perceptions, thoughts, feelings, and memories of which we are aware. The *personal unconscious* is similar to Freud's preconscious in that it contains mental images of which we are not immediately aware, but which can readily come into our consciousness (i.e., be part of the conscious ego). Some of the content of the personal unconscious is out of awareness because we are attending to other matters or because of disuse. In other cases, images in the personal unconscious have been actively repressed because they are threatening or unacceptable to the conscious ego.

FIGURE 5–1
The relationship of the personality functions to the levels of awareness

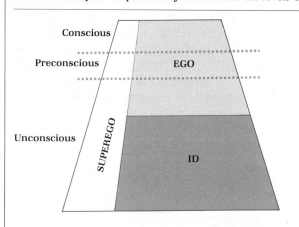

Jung differed with Freud in that he had less respect for the ultimate power of the intellect and considered the nonrational to be an important aspect of human capability. He overtly attacked the "totally erroneous supposition that the unconscious is a monster" (cited by Roazen, 1975, p. 267). For example, in contrast to Freud, Jung believed that the personal unconscious has both *retrospective* and *prospective* functions. Not only is the personal unconscious a repository for past experiences, but it also serves to anticipate the future. In addition, the personal unconscious has a *compensatory* function in that it is capable of adjusting imbalance in the personality if a person's conscious attitudes lean too heavily in one direction. This is accomplished by allowing the personality to experience the appropriate opposite tendency in dreams or fantasy (Jung, 1969a).

Jung's third aspect of the personality—the *collective,* or *transpersonal unconscious*—has no parallel in Freud's theory and is probably Jung's most original and controversial contribution to the study of personality.

Archetypes and the collective unconscious

Jung strongly believed that we are not only a product of our individual histories, but that we are also predisposed to act in various ways by experiences which have been common to all humans throughout the evolution of the species. In the collective unconscious—the dominant aspect of the personality for Jung—there are primordial images, called *archetypes,* which serve as models for our actions and reactions. "Archetypes are inherited modes of psychic functioning which can be recognized in the recurring motifs to be found in man's myths and dreams, in every time and every place" (Kopp, 1977, p. 186). (Much of Jung's evidence for the collective unconscious and its archetypes came from his extensive study of myths and symbols.) Thus, the collective unconscious is the same in all people. This does not mean, of course, that all people behave identically. The way an individual reacts in a particular situation is determined both by the relevant archetype and by the individual's experiences with the situation. For example, a child is born with a mother archetype which predisposes the child to react toward his or her mother (and other mother figures, such as a grandmother or an older sister) in a characteristic manner, such as perceiving her as nurturant and responding by being dependent on her. Throughout the history of the human race, mothers have behaved toward their children in essentially the same way. Thus, in most cases, children's perceptions of and reactions to their actual mothers are consistent with the mother archetype. If a mother were to deviate from the universal image, for example, by neglecting the child's needs and remaining emotionally detached from the child, the child's reaction would also be different from the usual pattern of child-mother interaction.

Bisexuality

The view that each of us has both a masculine and a feminine side, i.e., that humans are *bisexual,* was prevalent in the late 19th century, and was accepted as fact by Freud and most of his followers. Whereas Freud paid little attention to human bisexuality in his theories, Jung accorded it considerable importance in his writings. Bisexuality involves two complementary archetypes, the *anima,* which represents the feminine aspects of men, and the *animus,* which represents the masculine aspects of women.

Jung believed that satisfactory adult sexual relationships depended upon an adequate understanding of the sexual opposite within ourselves. Without a fully cultivated understanding of our own bisexuality, according to Jung, we will be left with a superficial understanding of the opposite sex.

Jung also believed that underdeveloped bisexuality could lead to a variety of psychological problems. For example, he suggested that a man with a weak anima will be subject to undifferentiated feelings of oversentimentality, moodiness, or touchiness which arise from his unconscious.

Other archetypes

Several other archetypes play a central role in personality. The *persona* is a person's public "mask," the personality one exhibits to others. The *shadow* serves as the model for the animal instincts in humans and for evil and socially unacceptable ideas. It has a function parallel to that of Freud's id. Other examples of archetypes include the *hero,* the *wise old man,* the *child,* the *demon, birth, death, magic,* and *god.*

Although the concept of a collective unconscious is intriguing, it is extremely difficult to provide a clear-cut demonstration that the collective unconscious exists. Interestingly, there may be some indirect support for the concept from an argument concerning the development of phobias via classical conditioning (see Chapter 20). Seligman (1971) argues that certain phobias or irrational fears not only appear to be learned very quickly (e.g., one or two instances of exposure to the phobic object or situation) but are also extremely difficult to eliminate. There seems to be a limited set of objects or situations of which many people are phobic (cf. Spiegler & Liebert, 1970). Examples include fear of the dark, snakes, insects, high places, and open spaces.

> All of these are relatively common phobias. And only rarely, if ever, do we have pajama phobias, grass phobias, electric-outlet phobias, hammer phobias, even though these things are likely to be associated with trauma in our world. The set of potentially phobic events may be nonarbitrary: events related to the survival of the human species through the long course of evolution. (Seligman, 1971, p. 312)

Seligman goes on to argue that humans may be *prepared* to fear such "nonarbitrary" and species-survival-based events. He raises the question: "Is it possible that there really is something to horses and wolves, etc., that makes them highly associable with certain kinds of traumas, perhaps even sexual ones?" (p. 317). He suggests that this may be a new way of construing symbolism.

Seligman's conclusions have a direct bearing on Jung's notion of a collective unconscious. ". . . does preparedness range beyond simple symbolic associations [which would be consistent with Freud's views]? Are there ways of thinking in which humans are particularly prepared to engage? . . . are there stories that man is prepared to formulate and accept? If so, a *meaningful version of the racial* [*collective*] *unconscious lurks close behind*" (pp. 317–18; italics added).

THE AGENCIES OF THE MIND

We have already mentioned the id, ego, and superego on several occasions. It is now time to examine these important psychoanalytic concepts in greater detail. First, however, a general point should be noted. The agencies of the mind, like the levels of consciousness, are theoretical constructs; they do not physically exist within the brain as do such structures as the frontal lobe and the hypothalamus. Although the id, ego, and superego are often referred to as "structures," it is more correct to think of them as *aspects* or *functions* of the personality. The three aspects of personality are frequently discussed in psychoanalytic writing anthropomorphically—that is, as if they possessed human capabilities, such as wishing, controlling, tolerating, and *being.* Nevertheless, the id, ego, and superego are not viewed by psychoanalysts as little people inside us but rather as convenient ways of conceptualizing complex psychological functions.[2]

Id

The *id*[3] is said to be the original system of personality because it contains everything psychological that is present at birth. The id is a reservoir for all drives and derives its power directly from bodily needs and processes. As bodily needs, such as hunger and thirst, build up, they must be satisfied, and the resulting increase in tension must be discharged. When the id alone governs this discharge, no delay of gratification is possible. The id is regulated by the *pleasure principle:* unable to tolerate increases in psychic energy, it presses for immediate satisfaction.

---

[2] Freud did believe that all mental functions would be ultimately tied to specific neural structures, but his theory of the divisions of the mind did not depend on the discovery of corresponding anatomical structures.

[3] Literally, the "it," since Freud used the German word *es* in his original description.

The id employs two basic techniques to reduce tension—*reflex action* and *primary process.* The primitive id is a reflex apparatus which reacts automatically and immediately to various internal and external irritants to the body, thereby promptly removing the tension or distress which the irritants create. Reflex action may be observed in such inborn mechanisms as sneezing, blinking, and coughing.

Since the id cannot tolerate any delay of gratification or any tension, it would be expected that very young children would "cry" for care as soon as an appetite or need appears which they cannot satisfy immediately. This seems to be exactly what happens. (Infants are, of course, quite capable of satisfying some of their needs, such as urination.) In addition, when the child's drive requires some object from the outside world, such as food or water, unless the object is immediately available, the id's *primary process* will form a memory image of the required object. For example, when the infant is hungry, the primary process will produce an image of food. This hallucinatory experience is called *wish fulfillment,* and remnants of it can be seen in adulthood, as when thirsty travelers imagine that they see water.

The primary process is a crude mechanism in that it is not able to differentiate between the actual object required to satisfy a need and a memory image of the object (e.g., between food and an image of food). Although the id may be temporarily satisfied with a memory image, the primary process does nothing to *actually* reduce tension. Obviously, one cannot eat or long survive on mental pictures of food. If the infant's needs were met immediately (as they were prior to birth), no problem would arise with the primary process. But inevitably there must be delay of gratification (a mother, for example, cannot be available constantly to nurse or feed her baby), and the infant must learn to tolerate the delay. The capacity to tolerate delay of gratification begins with the infant's growing "realization" that there is an external world—something which is "not me"—which has to be taken into account and considered apart from, but interrelated with, the infant. This comes about with the development of the second aspect of the personality, the ego.

Ego

The *ego* develops out of the id, which is to say that it "borrows" some of the id's psychic energy for its own functions. Recall that, at birth, all of the child's psychic energy is contained in the id and is used for primary processes. Therefore, the energy for ego functions must come from the id. An important consequence of the closed nature of the energy system is that, as psychic energy is transferred to the ego, there is less psychic energy for id functions. This shift of energy is an intrapsychic phenomenon which cannot, of course, be observed directly. However, it is manifest in such behavior as the child's becoming less demanding of immediate satisfaction of needs and more willing to delay gratification.

In contrast to the pleasure principle of the id, the ego is governed by the *reality principle* and has as its aim postponing the discharge of energy until an appropriate situation or object in the real world is discovered or produced. The ego does not attempt to thwart the pleasure seeking of the id, but rather it temporarily suspends pleasure for the sake of reality. According to Freud, the ego is representative of the external world to the id. Whereas the purpose of the primary process is to indicate what object or situation is necessary to satisfy a particular need (e.g., an image of food), the role of the *secondary process* is to create a strategy for actually obtaining the satisfaction (e.g., going to the cookie jar). The ego, then, is characterized by realistic thinking or problem solving and is the seat of intellectual processes. Daydreaming is an example of a secondary process which illustrates the reality-bound nature of the ego. Although we enjoy the pleasurable fantasy of a daydream, we do not mistake the fantasy for reality as we do in a nocturnal dream, which is a primary process.

For people to function both as individuals and as members of society, they must learn not only to deal with the direct constraints of physical reality but also to adhere to social norms and prohibitions. Further, they must conform to society's "laws" in the absence of external monitors (i.e., when there is no realistic fear of apprehension, punishment, or failure). Beginning around the third or fourth year of life, children start to judge and evaluate their own behavior independently of immediate threat or reward. Such self-control is the province of the third aspect of personality, the superego.

Superego

The *superego* serves as the internal representative of the values of one's parents and society. It strives for the *ideal* rather than the real. Independently of the utility of an act, the superego will judge it as right or wrong, as being or not being in accord with the moral values of the society.

The superego has two major functions. First, as the representative of society's demands regarding idealized behavior patterns, the superego, like one's parents, rewards the individual for acceptable behavior in the moral sphere. Second, by creating feelings of guilt, it punishes the person for engaging in actions and thoughts which society does not sanction.

The role of the superego in the life of an adult is threefold: (1) it inhibits rather than just postpones, as does the ego, the impulses of the id, particularly those of a sexual or aggressive nature; (2) it persuades the ego to attend to moral rather than realistic goals and thus presumably accounts for various types of self-sacrifice and altruism; and (3) it directs the individual toward the pursuit of perfection.

Prior to Freud's treatment of the subject, internal restraints on one's actions of the kind we call ethical or moral were presumed to come from a "still, small voice" which had been provided by God (Brown, 1965). Freud argued that moral conscience is not inherited and, in fact, that quite the reverse is true. Neonates have no concern for the welfare of others and are interested only in their own immediate satisfactions. Moral concerns must somehow be acquired after birth.

The development of the superego involves "taking in" or incorporating the values of one's parents in a way analogous to the incorporation of food from the outside world into the body. This process begins about the fourth year of life and is closely related to the solution of the Oedipus complex. Through defensive identification with the same-sexed parent, the child acquires the parent's moral values as well as appropriate sex-role behavior. Identification with both parents occurs through another process, called *anaclitic identification,* in which children come to value their parents (and, by association, the standards and ideals of their parents) because of the love, warmth, and comfort that the parents provide.

A note on the validity of the three agencies of the mind

If Freud was correct in believing that it is useful to view personality as a joint function of three agencies—id, ego, and superego—then this should be evident in behavior. Although casual observation reveals that there are desiring (id), rational (ego), and ideal (superego) aspects in much of human behavior, there has been little empirical investigation of Freud's hypothesis. Again, it appears that difficulty in providing adequate research definitions for the concepts is the major obstacle.

Some tentative findings by Cattell and his associates (Cattell, 1957; Pawlik & Cattell, 1964) suggest the possibility of using factor analysis to investigate the role of id, ego, and superego functions in behavior. Basically, factor analysis is a research strategy (see Chapter 10) that involves giving a large sample of subjects many different tests and then examining their performances to see whether these can be explained by a small number of basic traits which the subjects possess. Using a series of laboratory tasks to study motivation, Pawlik and Cattell (1964) found that three main factors summarized the relationships of the subjects' performances on the various tasks. These factors were described as "high self-assertion," "immature self-centered temperament," and "restrained acceptance of external norms." Pawlik and Cattell conclude, "Although we did not start our studies with any predilections for psychoanalytic theory, it is a striking fact that the psychoanalytic descriptions of Ego, Id and Superego would fit very well the three major patterns found in this research" (p. 16).

To briefly summarize the development of the aspects of personality, recall that, at birth, only the id exists. Later, in response to the demands of reality, the ego develops out of the id. Finally, the superego develops as an outgrowth of the ego and serves as the societal or moral representative in the personality. When all three aspects have developed, the psychic energy which once belonged solely to the id is divided among the id, ego, and superego and fluctuates among them. As depicted in Figure 5–2, the ego serves as a mediator among the three basic forces acting upon an individual—the demands of the id, the requirements of reality (of the external environment), and the limitations imposed by the superego. It is therefore the task of the ego to see that instinctual needs are met in a realistic and, at the same time, socially approved manner.

An intrapsychic *conflict* occurs when the direction and discharge of energy demanded by one aspect of the personality are at odds with the requirements of one or both of the other aspects. All of the possibilities for conflict are presented in Table 5–1. In principle, conflicts could be resolved by the complete elimination of a drive, the redirection of the drive from its original aim (e.g., incestuous goals), or the expression of the drive in undiluted form. In psychoanalytic theory, the first alternative is assumed never to occur. A drive can be banished from conscious

The relationships among the id, ego, and superego

FIGURE 5–2
The ego as the mediator of personality

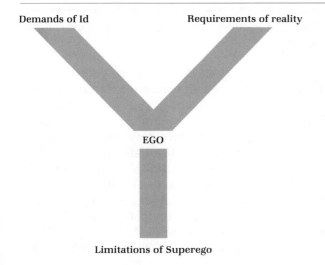

Demands of Id   Requirements of reality

EGO

Limitations of Superego

TABLE 5–1
Possible conflicts among the aspects of personality

Conflict	Example
Id versus Ego	Choosing between a small immediate reward and a larger reward which requires some period of waiting (i.e., delay of gratification).
Id versus Superego	Deciding whether to return the difference when you are overpaid or undercharged.
Ego versus Superego	Choosing between acting in a realistic way (e.g., telling a "white lie") and adhering to a potentially costly or unrealistic standard (e.g., always telling the truth).
Id and Ego versus Superego	Deciding whether to retaliate against the attack of a weak opponent or to "turn the other cheek."
Id and Superego versus Ego	Deciding whether to act in a realistic way that conflicts both with your desires and your moral convictions (e.g., the decision faced by devout Roman Catholics as to the use of contraceptive devices).
Ego and Superego versus Id	Choosing whether to "act on the impulse" to steal something you want and cannot afford. The ego would presumably be increasingly involved in such a conflict as the probability of being apprehended increases.

awareness but not from the total personality. The battle, then, is between redirection and unbridled expression of the drive.

Redirection of a drive involves arbitration among the forces acting within and upon the personality, and this requires the expenditure of psychic energy. Since a person has only a fixed amount of psychic energy, the more successfully the ego minimizes intrapsychic conflicts, the more energy will be "left over" for positive cathexes and higher mental functions of the ego, such as problem solving. If redirection of an impulse is not possible, then the ego is likely to be overwhelmed with excitation and the person will feel intense anxiety. However, this rarely occurs in adults because anxiety serves as a signal for the ego to defend itself.

EGO PSYCHOLOGY: EXPANDING THE FUNCTIONS OF THE EGO

Although Freud divided personality functioning into three aspects—id, ego, and superego—these aspects by no means share equally in guiding behavior. For Freud, not only is the id the original part of the personality, from which all other aspects develop, but it is also the dominant force. The ego (and to some degree the superego) must constantly struggle to keep id impulses in control, and the primary function of the ego is to prevent the personality from being overwhelmed by the instinctual desires of the id (see below). Although the aims of all three aspects of the personality can be in conflict (in various combinations, as illustrated in Table 5–1), most often, intrapsychic conflict erupts because of id demands which are pressing for immediate satisfaction.

With the development of psychoanalysis, it became clear to many psychoanalysts that this view of the dynamics of personality was limiting. An id-dominated, conflict-ridden personality was a reasonable explanation of the development of psychopathology (abnormal behavior), but it was an inadequate base for the study of the normal, adaptive personality. From this perceived deficit, there arose a new branch of psychoanalysis called *ego psychology*.

Anna Freud was among the first of orthodox psychoanalysts to stress ego functioning. Ego psychology was born with the 1936 publication of Anna Freud's book, *The Ego and the Mechanisms of Defense* and spurred on by Heinz Hartmann's 1939 book, *Ego Psychology and The Problem of Adaptation*. Anna Freud's interest was mainly in unconscious ego processes; we will discuss her ideas about defense mechanisms in the next section. Hartmann's contribution was rooted in the belief that certain functions of the ego develop and remain partially independent of the id. Without denying the existence and, indeed, the necessity for conflict between the ego and the id or the defensive operations of the ego, ego psychologists maintain that there is also a "conflict-free ego-sphere" (Hartmann, 1951) and focus their theorizing and study on such conflict-free personality processes as perception, thinking, language, creative production, attention, memory, and other cognitive, *adaptive* functions. In this way, Hartmann sought to turn psychoanalysis into a complete theory of psychology, encompassing the full range of psychological processes.

The task of ego psychology is to investigate "how psychological conflict and 'peaceful' internal development mutually facilitate and hamper each other" (Hartmann, 1951, p. 368). In emphasizing adaptive or coping functions of personality, even the defensive aspects of the ego, which reside outside the conflict-free ego-sphere, are sometimes responsible for personal growth (see, for example, A. Freud, 1966). (We will return to this issue at the end of our discussion of ego defense mechanisms later in this chapter.)

In a similar vein, fantasy (daydreaming) is a secondary process which can have definite adaptive features. Hartmann (1951) contends that "fantasy can be fruitful even in scientific thinking, which is the undisputed domain of rational thinking" (p. 372). Kris (1950) makes clear that the role of fantasy in creative and artistic thinking can be fully explained only if the ego is considered to be an autonomous part of the personality which can freely make and relinquish its own cathexes (investments of psychic energy).

The experience of anxiety is all too well known to each of us. In his early theorizing (during the 1890s), Freud viewed anxiety as the result of repressed libido which was transformed into anxiety. Some 30 years later he revised his theory to state that the reverse was true—

ANXIETY AND DEFENSE

anxiety led to repression. Freud's later formulation, which was published in 1926 in a short book entitled *Inhibitions, Symptoms, and Anxiety,* held that anxiety was a *signal* of impending danger. Although the source of the danger could be either external or internal, Freud, not surprisingly, thought that it was usually the result of an id impulse seeking expression. Due to the intense id impulse, the ego is in danger of being overwhelmed by stimulation (tension) which it cannot master or discharge.

This *signal anxiety* originates in early childhood. During the period when the infant is incapable of delaying gratification (i.e., before the ego develops), the infant is occasionally overwhelmed by the tension of an id impulse seeking expression, as when there is no one around to satisfy the infant's hunger drive. This trauma is accompanied by intense stimulation which is called *primary anxiety.* Later, children learn to anticipate the danger (e.g., when they see their mother leaving the room) and to react with anxiety. However, now the anxiety is less intense than that which accompanied the actual traumatic experience and serves as a warning to the ego to somehow prevent the recurrence of the trauma and the accompanying overwhelming stimulation. The ego is "motivated" to deal with the danger because the signal anxiety is unpleasant.

Freud made a distinction among three types of anxiety which occur in adulthood.

Neurotic anxiety results from an id-ego conflict in which the id seeks to discharge an impulse, and the ego tries to place reality restraints on the impulse. Consistent with the dynamic aspects of his theory (see p. 69f), Freud believed that neurotic anxiety arises out of transformed libido, a process he likened to wine turning to vinegar. In claiming that sexual desires and anxiety were closely linked, Freud noted the physical similarities between the experience of anxiety and the experience of sexual arousal: accelerated breathing, palpitations, and sweating occur in both.

Moral anxiety is generated by an id-superego conflict in which the id impulse (e.g., to shoplift) is in opposition to the moral and ideal standards of society (e.g., "Thou shalt not steal") and is experienced by the individual as guilt or shame.

Objective anxiety is produced when a realistic, external threat is present, such as a fire or a mugger.

Note that in each case, anxiety is a signal of impending danger. In objective anxiety, the danger is external and can be dealt with by taking realistic steps to eliminate or reduce the actual threat. Neurotic and moral anxiety, however, are due to an impending intrapsychic danger, and they must be coped with by internal means, namely, the defense mechanisms of the ego.

Defense mechanisms refer to *unconscious* processes of the ego which keep disturbing and unacceptable impulses from being expressed directly. They are very resistant to change through ordinary experience. Although it is helpful for didactic purposes to distinguish among specific ego defense mechanisms, people rarely defend themselves against anxiety with a single mechanism. An individual's characteristic modes of defense are typically a combination of different defense mechanisms. Furthermore, as will become apparent in the following examples, there is considerable overlap in the way the defense mechanisms operate to protect the ego from overwhelming anxiety.

Sublimation

The process of *sublimation* alters unacceptable impulses by changing them to completely acceptable, and even admired, social behaviors. Sublimation deprives an impulse of its primitive character while, at the same time, allowing it some expression. Freud believed that our highest virtues have grown up, as sublimations, out of our lowest dispositions. The surgeon, for example, may be regarded as having found a socially acceptable outlet for aggressive impulses, and the gynecologist and the movie censor as having sublimated their sexual drives. More common ways of sublimating aggression include engaging in or even observing competitive contact sports, such as boxing and football. Common sublimations of sex are said to be painting and creative writing.

Sublimation is the only truly successful defense mechanism because it succeeds in permanently redirecting undesirable impulses. All other defense mechanisms are to some degree unsuccessful in that they require a continual warding off of the threatening impulses.

Repression

Repression is the process whereby a dangerous impulse is actively and totally excluded from consciousness. As a solution to conflict it is characterized by a continual struggle to contain primitive desires. Psychoanalytic theory acknowledges that repression may occur in "healthy" individuals but contends that, unlike sublimation, repression exacts a severe price.

> Many impulses in the healthy personality are thus permanently banned from awareness, but at the expense of being excluded from the development of the total personality. It is as if the ego had slammed the door against a dimly perceived threatening intruder, but once the door has been shut, the ego will never know whether the intruder was indeed as threatening as he was believed to be, or, whether it is worth spending

energy in keeping him out. . . . Once this energy is used for repressive purposes, it cannot be used as "free" energy in the task of adaptation. (Strupp, 1967, p. 51)

In Freud's early writing, "repression" was used as a general term, synonymous with "ego defense." In a sense, then, other defense mechanisms may be construed as types of repression.

Experimental evidence for repression.   Repression has been the subject of numerous laboratory investigations (e.g., D'Zurilla, 1965; Worchel, 1955; Zeller, 1950, 1951). The typical experimental paradigm, which is outlined in Table 5–2, can be divided into three phases. In the first phase, experimental and control subjects learn a list of words and then are tested for their recall of the words (Recall Test 1). Since subjects have been treated in the same way to this point, no differences between the recall of experimental and control subjects are expected. During the second phase, experimental subjects are exposed to an ego-threatening situation, such as taking a personality test and receiving negative feedback (e.g., "The test indicates that you may be prone to spells of anxiety"). The control subjects are exposed to a similar, but nonthreatening, situation, such as taking a personality test but receiving neutral feedback.

Next, the subjects' recall of the words is assessed again (Recall Test 2), and this time it is predicted that experimental subjects who have been ego threatened will recall fewer words than will control subjects. It is assumed that the words have become associated with

TABLE 5–2
Experimental paradigm for demonstrating the existence of repression

	Procedures		*Prediction*	*Interpretation*
	Experimental subjects	*Control subjects*		
Phase 1	Learn list of words Recall Test 1	Learn list of words Recall Test 1	No differences between experimental and control subjects	Groups have been treated identically
Phase 2	Ego-threatening task Recall Test 2	Neutral task Recall Test 2	Experimental subjects recall less than control subjects	Ego-threat and resultant anxiety lead experimental subjects to repress words associated with threat
Phase 3	Debriefing (threat removed) Recall Test 3	Debriefing Recall Test 3	No differences between experimental and control subjects	When threat is removed, repression is lifted and memory of repressed words becomes conscious again

the ego threat for the experimental group, since both occurred in the same situation and in close temporal proximity, and that the words which elicit anxiety due to the threat have therefore been repressed.

The theory of repression would also predict that, if the threat were removed and anxiety were thus reduced, the repressed material would return to consciousness. To test this conceptual hypothesis, in the third phase of the study subjects are debriefed (by telling them that they have been given *false* feedback) and then tested once more for their recall of the list of words (Recall Test 3). Now it is expected that there will be no differences in recall between the experimental and control subjects.

In general, studies have obtained results consistent with the predictions based on psychoanalytic theory. Ego threat leads to lowered recall in Test 2, and removal of the threat restores recall to its pre-threat level in Test 3. These results have been interpreted to support the concept of repression.[4]

Reaction formation

One way of warding off an unacceptable impulse is to overemphasize its opposite in thought and behavior. A man threatened by his desire to dominate and be aggressive in social situations might think of himself as a timid and shy person, act passively, and be unable to refuse requests made of him no matter how unreasonable they were. Timidity and passivity would be a *reaction formation* against a strong aggressive drive.

It is often difficult to tell whether a given act is an undisguised manifestation of an impulse or a manifestation of its opposite. An important hallmark of reaction formation is the persistence or excess of the behavior ("going overboard"). As Shakespeare (in *Hamlet*), who antedated Freud and the concept of reaction formation by some 300 years, observed: "The lady doth protest too much." So, too, the apparently puritanical person, particularly one who responds to sexual advances with numerous gasps, may well be seething with erotic desire and sexuality. Similarly, an individual's avowed love for a sibling or spouse may sometimes be interpreted as profound, but disguised, hate.

Undoing

The aim of *undoing* is to make retribution for the harm caused by an unacceptable act or the potential harm inherent in the thought of the unacceptable act. Brenner (1957) used the example of a child who

---

[4] Other studies (e.g., Holmes, 1972; Holmes & Schallow, 1969) have suggested that there are equally plausible alternative explanations which will account for these experimental findings.

defends himself against unconscious hostile wishes toward a younger brother by finding injured animals and nursing them back to health. The act of healing sick animals (the animals are symbols of the child's brother) unconsciously undoes the harm that the hostile impulses might cause the brother. Adults who are unscrupulous in their business dealings may undo their disreputable "nine-to-five" behavior by being very active in civic and charitable organizations at night and on weekends. Undoing frequently involves a ritualistic act that symbolically compensates for an id impulse which is threatening to the ego. In a classic example of undoing, Lady Macbeth compulsively washed her hands as if to cleanse her self of the blood she had spilled as a party to murder.

Projection

The defense mechanism of *projection* involves attributing one's own unacceptable and disturbing impulses or wishes to someone or something else. Freud used the example of the jealous husband who called his wife unfaithful when, in fact, it was the husband who had the impulse but could not face it in himself.

Experimental evidence for projection. Two types of projection are recognized in the psychological literature. *Classical projection* occurs when an individual is *unaware* of possessing a negative characteristic and, to defend against awareness, attributes the characteristic to someone else, usually a *disliked* other. (Scape-goating is thought by psychoanalysts to be projection on a mass scale.)

Attributive projection, in contrast, is involved whenever a person projects a characteristic which he or she is *aware* of having onto another individual. Attributive projection is not a Freudian concept, and early studies which endeavored to demonstrate classical projection were criticized for having shown attributive projection instead (Holmes, 1978).

Several recent experiments have provided evidence that the psychoanalytic or classical concept of projection can and does occur under some circumstances. In a particularly well-designed study, Halpern (1977) asked undergraduate men and women to complete a questionnaire designed to tap their sexual defensiveness. The questionnaire asked the subjects to respond true or false to simple statements such as "I never have sexual fantasies" or "I never have dreams with sexual content." Inasmuch as these are common experiences almost everyone has had, subjects choosing a large number of "true" responses to these statements were presumed to be relatively more sexually defensive. Halpern began by telling his subjects that participation in the study would involve filling out a number of questionnaires and performing several tasks. Next, Halpern showed his subjects six photographs of college students taken at a university library, explained that part of the study involved determining students' ability to make personality judgments from pictures, and asked the subjects to rank the photographs from most favorable to least favorable as personalities. At this point, the experience of the subjects depended upon whether they had been assigned to the experimental or the control group. Subjects in the experimental group were shown a set of pornographic pictures (which would presumably instigate a degree of sexual arousal) and told that they would be asked about the pictures later. Control subjects were not shown any pictures. Then, as a final measure, subjects rated themselves and the least favorable person whom they had picked from the photographs on a personality scale containing a number of "filler" items and one critical item, a rating of *lustfulness*. The critical prediction derived from psychoanalytic theory is that subjects who are highly sexual defensive, when presented with material that would sexually stimulate them, would deny the feelings in themselves by projecting them onto the disliked other. Thus, highly defensive subjects in the experimental group should project more lust onto the disliked other than would low-defensive subjects in the experimental group. In contrast, in the control group, there should be little or no difference between high and low sexually defensive subjects. This is exactly the result which emerged.

In another study demonstrating the operation of classical projection, Sherwood (1979) presented female undergraduates with false information from a personality test indicating that they showed a tendency toward "neuroticism." The women were then asked to rate both a favorable and an unfavorable target person on neuroticism. As expected from the psychoanalytic theory of projection, women who denied the higher level of neuroticism in themselves tended to attribute neuroticism to the unfavorable target person, whereas those who accepted the psychologist's claim that they were neurotic tended to attribute neuroticism to a favorable other. Thus, the study provides a demonstration of the operation of both classical and attributive projection.

Displacement

Whereas projection involves attributing one's impulse to another person, *displacement* involves shifting an impulse which is directed toward an unacceptable and threatening object (or person) to a more acceptable and less threatening object. A common example of displacement involves employees who, rather than express hostility toward the superior who has bawled them out on the job, which is obviously a threatening and unadaptive strategy, redirect their anger toward their family when they arrive home. Displacement is the primary mechanism involved in phobias. According to the psychoanalytic viewpoint, a phobia, or irrational fear, originates with a realistic or unrealistic fear of some person or object which is difficult to avoid. In order to reduce the intense anxiety which repeated contact with the feared object induces, the individual displaces the fear to another object which can easily be avoided and is symbolically related to the originally feared object.

Regression

One frequently used method of coping with frustration and anxiety is to escape to a mode of behavior that is more satisfying and pleasant. *Regression,* according to psychoanalytic theory, involves such a retreat to an earlier period of development, which, for adults, is a pregenital psychosexual stage. Common examples of regression include sleeping, dreaming, smoking, fingernail biting, talking baby talk, getting drunk, overeating, breaking the law, and losing one's temper. Hall (1955) interestingly notes that "some of these regressions are so commonplace that they are taken to be signs of maturity" (p. 96).

The potential importance of regression as an adaptive mode of behavior in people with malfunctioning kidneys has been discussed by psychoanalysts (Viederman, 1974; von Euen, 1974). Patients whose kidneys do not perform their normal function of cleansing the blood of waste materials undergo a procedure called hemodialysis which involves being attached to a dialysis machine that artificially extracts waste products. Usually, hemodialysis must be performed for five to eight hours two or three times a week. Without such treatment (or a successful kidney transplant), the patient will die. The parallel between hemodialysis and the mother-child relationship during the oral stage is easy to see.

> The machine represents the mother through its life-giving potential, through its umbilical-like connections, through the bath and water which may symbolize the womb and birth processes. It is a demanding and restricting mother, permitting only brief periods of separation before reunion is required. It can easily be perceived as a bad mother since it frustrates orally, is always threatening to break down (ruptured coils occur with considerable frequency), and often leaves the patient feeling ill (weak, with muscle cramps, hypotension, etc.). (Viederman, 1974, p. 69)

On the basis of case studies of patients undergoing hemodialysis, Viederman (1974) concludes that success in adapting to the highly stressful treatment depends upon the patients' ability to regress to the oral stage and to deal with their infantile-oral conflicts. Similar reasoning has been advanced in discussing the severe dietary restrictions that are also a part of the treatment of kidney patients. Von Euen (1974) interpreted patients' noncompliance with the prescribed low-protein diet as resisting being deprived of oral gratification, which is symbolic of early arbitrary parental demands.

Rationalization

After performing an unacceptable act or thinking a threatening thought, people frequently alleviate the anxiety or guilt which ensues by finding a "perfectly reasonable" excuse for their behavior. *Rationalization,* as this defensive strategy is called, is often used as a mechanism for maintaining one's self-esteem. When we are "stood up" by a date, we may tell ourselves and friends that we "really" didn't want to go out with the creep. Such a rationalization has been colloquially labeled "sour grapes," after the fable of the fox who was unable to reach some grapes and therefore concluded that they were sour. Rationalization is an *unconscious* process, as are all of the ego defense mechanisms, and should not be confused with consciously making up an excuse.

Denial

Still another way to handle painful experiences and thoughts is to deny their existence. Sometimes a person will refuse to believe that a loved one has died and will continue to behave as if the deceased person were still alive. A more common form of *denial,* which most people engage in from time to time, involves fantasy or play. People may find temporary relief from reality by daydreaming about how things would be if some unpleasant circumstance had not occurred. Children deny their inferiority through play, as when a young boy assumes the role of a strict father while playing "house."

As Freud conceptualized the ego defense mechanisms, their major purpose is to defend the ego from id impulses. Ego psychologists believe that the mechanisms of defense can also have a more positive, adaptive role in the personality. Hartmann (1951) makes this point in regard to the defensive operations of denial and avoidance: ". . . avoidance of the environment in which difficulties are encountered—and its positive correlate, the search for one offering easier and better possibilities for action—is also a most effective adaptation process" (p. 373). For example, though putting off studying for a final examination indefinitely is far from adaptive for a student, it is often useful to *temporarily* forget the upcoming test (denial) and engage in some diverting, recreational activity (avoidance) before resuming studying.

Psychoanalytic theory is quite complicated, and it has also undergone a continuing process of evolution since Freud and his early followers first charted the course of psychoanalysis. There are four broad directions which can be identified in the evolution and, partly by way of summary, we shall briefly describe these post-Freudian trends.

TRENDS IN THE EVOLUTION OF PSYCHOANALYTIC THEORY

Acknowledging the social determinants of personality

For Freud, human motivation is a product of biological forces and impulses. While not denying the importance of biology, many post-Freudians have noted and emphasized the social and interpersonal factors that shape personality.

Expanding the time frame of personality development

Closely related to the shift toward social and interpersonal factors is the notion that personality develops in significant and important ways throughout the life span, rather than being virtually complete by age five. Jung was the first to recognize the midlife crisis, which has begun to receive considerable attention. Also, even more orthodox analysts are beginning to acknowledge further personality development in adulthood. One team of psychoanalysts described their new understanding this way:

> Whereas the formation of psychic structure in a child is like broad strokes painted on a bare canvas, the evolution of psychic structure in adulthood is equivalent to fine, nearly invisible strokes on a complicated background. . . . (Colarusso & Nemiroff, 1979, p. 62)

From this viewpoint, adulthood is no longer seen as a relatively stable or finished state, but rather as just a broad span of time in the ongoing, dynamic process of psychological development that occurs for each individual. Similarly, Shane (1977), another analyst who has abandoned the older idea of adulthood as static in favor of a life span developmental orientation, has contended to his colleagues that "the analytic patient, regardless of age, is considered to be still in the process of ongoing development as opposed to merely being in possession of a past that influences his present conscious and unconscious life" (pp. 95–96).

Parenting is also increasingly thought to be a role which engages and alters the basic personality structure. Psychoanalyst Therese Benedek said of motherhood that "it channelizes the primarily introverted, narcissistic tendencies into many psychic qualities designated 'feminine,' such as responsiveness, empathy, sympathy and the desire to do, to care for others etc." (1950, p. 20). Not long thereafter, Rangell (1953) wrote on the role of the parent in the Oedipus complex, noting that the experience, as described in Freud's writings, could obviously have an intensity for parents that matched its importance for their children.

An important implication of this change in time frame is that the present and future become psychologically quite important, in contrast to Freud's single-minded focus on the past. Present conflicts and difficulties, for example, have a significance of their own according to many contemporary analysts (Gedo, 1979).

For Freud, the personality is almost completely dominated by unconscious processes which are instinctual and animal-like in nature—primarily sex and aggression (id processes which seek immediate release of tension and, hence, pleasure gratification). Post-Freudians have focused on the conscious realm of personality and personality functions related to reality and higher mental processes, such as thinking and problem solving (ego processes).

In Freud's theory, it is conflict among intrapsychic aspects of the personality (id, ego, superego) which determines behavior. There is a constant struggle for predominance among instinctual drives (id), reality demands (ego), and the moral restraints of society (superego). This struggle frequently causes psychological and behavioral disturbances (neuroses), and much of Freudian theory relates to such psychopathology—its origins, manifestations, and treatment. Post-Freudians (especially ego analysts) have examined the other side of the coin—the conflict-free part of personality which enables people to remain relatively healthy by coping successfully with the inner and outer forces that shape their personalities.

Psychoanalysis began outside of traditional academic circles. Although Freud liked to be called "the Professor," he never had a regular academic appointment and had some difficulty with the adjunct position he finally secured. Also, his writings (on such matters as the interpretation of dreams) did not deal with the sort of basic processes which academic and research-minded psychologists felt were important. Since the 1930s, however, there have been numerous attempts to relate psychoanalysis to theories and research in the mainstream of academic psychology. When Pavlov's work on conditioning drew international attention, some writers noted the relationship between Pavlovian conditioning and the formation of anxiety. When drive-based learning theory became a dominant force in experimental psychology, psychoanalysis was translated into learning theory terms.

Today, the major trend in academic psychology is toward the examination of cognitive processes, and many psychologists are vigorously pursuing the possible ties between cognitive psychology and psychoanalysis. The clearest link so far is in the conclusion of cognitive psychologists that humans systematically process and "edit" environmental input or stimuli during one or more initial stages that are unconscious but nonetheless highly active (Erdelyi, 1974; Motley & Baars, 1978; Neisser, 1976; Nisbett & Wilson, 1977; Posner, 1973). Psychoanalysts have been insisting that there are unconscious processes for almost 100 years.

Recognizing significant processes that do not involve unconscious conflict

Relating psychoanalysis to basic theory and research in academic psychology

6 | *The psychoanalytic strategy*

Assessment and personality change

The previous chapters explored the major theoretical propositions of psychoanalysis. This chapter is devoted to a discussion of the assessment and modification of personality from the psychoanalytic perspective. Because psychoanalysis assumes that most of personality is unconscious, it must employ indirect means of assessment. Several indirect techniques have already been discussed: the analysis of slips of the tongue, forgetting, the loss of objects, and "accidental" mistakes. The present chapter begins with dream interpretation, the method of personality assessment which Freud thought most useful for examining intrapsychic events. Then projective techniques are discussed. Finally, we consider the psychoanalytic method of personality change, relating it back to our discussion of theory.

One third of our lives is spent sleeping, and dreams are the only processes occurring during sleep of which we have more or less direct knowledge. It is no wonder, then, that people have long been fascinated with their dreams and the dreams of others.

DREAMS: THE ROYAL ROAD TO THE UNCONSCIOUS

Technically a dream is:

What is a dream?

> a mental experience, occurring in sleep, which is characterized by hallucinoid imagery, predominately visual and often vivid; by bizarre elements due to such spatiotemporal distortions as condensation, discontinuity, and acceleration; and by a delusional acceptance of these phenomena as "real" at the time that they occur. Strong emotion may or may not be associated with these distinctive formal properties of the dream, and subsequent recall of these mental events is almost invariably poor unless an immediate arousal from sleep occurs. (Hobson & McCarley, 1977, p. 1336)

The above definition is theoretically neutral and does not answer the question of whether dreams have any psychological significance or meaning. One ancient view, illustrated in Joseph's famous dream interpretations in the Bible, is that every dream has a secret meaning which can be interpreted by a sufficiently skilled person who listens to the dreamer's recollection. Other famous ideas about the meaning of dreams include the belief that they represent wishes in disguised form and that they come about by the condensation and reorganization of the experiences and ideas of waking life.

Freud's dream theory

Although Freud was not the first to call attention to the psychological meaning of dreams, his theory was the first comprehensive account of dreaming. Moreover, Freud believed that dreaming obeys the same underlying psychological laws as all other mental functioning, and, thus, his theory of dreams is an integral part of his overall theory of the mind.

The major expression of Freud's dream theory, *The Interpretation of Dreams,* is based in substantial measure on Freud's analysis of his own dreams.[1] Freud updated this book regularly and considered it the most important contribution of his career.

Freud believed that dreams are highly significant mental products, resulting from the interaction of unconscious wishes and the censoring mechanisms of the ego. Dreams are *compromise formations of intrapsychic conflict,* and, properly understood, they reveal the secret methods of the mind. Although the dream itself occurs in sleep, the origins and preparation of the dream reflect all aspects of the dreamer's psychological experience. Dreams, for Freud, are carefully constructed camouflages under which there is always a concealed wish and a true meaning. Despite their superficial brevity, dreams are subtle and profound reflections of intrapsychic processes. (Freud likened a dream to a firework, "which takes hours to prepare but goes off in a moment.")

Manifest versus latent content of dreams

Freud was interested in dreams because of what he thought their content revealed about an individual's personality, particularly its unconscious aspects. He made a clear distinction between two levels of dream content: the *manifest content* is what a person can remember about a dream, whereas the *latent content* refers to the underlying intrapsychic events which led to the manifest content. The latent content of a dream consists primarily of unconscious thoughts, wishes, fantasies, and conflicts which are expressed in disguised form in the manifest content. Because of their unacceptable or threatening nature, these unconscious events are prevented from entering consciousness

---

[1] Indeed, a good deal of psychoanalytic theory arose from the discoveries Freud felt he made through his own self-analysis. (The thrust of Freud's self-analysis occurred between 1895 and 1900, but Freud also tried to continue the process through his whole life.)

directly. They can, however, be expressed incognito, and the manifest content represents the dressed-up version of the disreputable determinants of the dream. Latent content becomes manifest through two basic processes, dream work and symbolization.

Dream work

Dream work refers to the ways in which the latent dream content is transformed into the manifest content. *Condensation* is a type of dream work wherein separate thoughts are compressed and combined into a single, unified thought. The process involves borrowing elements from a number of different sources to form a compound which is far less extensive than the sum of the latent elements from which it was derived. In this way, threatening latent content is disguised so that its threat is not apparent in the manifest dream. An example of condensation would be a husband dreaming of being affectionate with his wife who, in the dream, appeared as his mother. The wife and mother were condensed into a single person. In such a process, the manifest content is said to be *overdetermined*—that is, it is the result of more than one latent source.

Sometimes an important element of the latent content may appear as only a trivial aspect of the manifest content, or vice versa. This process is known as *displacement* and can be illustrated by the example of a woman who receives a telegram which says that her son has been killed in battle and who dreams of merely receiving a telegram without any reference to its contents.

If the woman had dreamt that the telegram said her son had been found alive after having been missing in action, this would be an example of the dream-work process called *opposites*. (When Freud dreamt of being recognized as an honest man, he concluded that the dream reflected his concerns about being considered dishonest and a plagiarizer.)

The similarity between displacement and opposites as dream work and displacement and reaction formation as defense mechanisms should be noted. Both dream work and defense mechanisms serve to keep unacceptable and threatening material from becoming conscious.

Upon awakening from a dream and trying to reconstruct it, we sometimes find that the parts of the dream do not fit together logically. According to Freud, this is the result of the dream work which has taken place. Dream work is a type of primary process and therefore does not follow the laws of logic. In reconstructing the dream, the dreamer attempts to fill in the missing elements and otherwise create a coherent overall picture of the dream. In doing so, the dreamer changes the dream content even further, and this process is referred to as *secondary elaboration*.

Symbolism

Freud believed that there were two ways to decipher a dream. One is to motivate the dreamer to provide private associations about various elements of the dream and to synthesize these pieces of information into a coherent interpretation. However, Freud also believed that there were certain widely used dream symbols and that, up to a point, these symbols could be helpful in decoding a dream.

Whereas dream work changes unacceptable latent content into acceptable manifest content, *symbolism* serves to bring the latent element directly into the manifest content, but in such a form as to be unrecognizable and therefore unthreatening to the ego. *Symbols* are objects or ideas which stand for something else, and, in psychoanalysis, symbols typically substitute for something unconscious and threatening. One aspect of dream interpretation involves translating the symbols in the manifest dream. This task is facilitated by the fact that some symbols have universal meanings and therefore represent the same thing in all dreams. Freud believed that these universal symbols first came to be connected with their referents in prehistoric times (cf. Jung's archetypes; see Chapter 5).

Symbols are not the exclusive domain of dreams, and Freud and many others have examined symbolism in myths, fairy tales, literature, and colloquial speech. Some common symbols and their meanings according to psychoanalytic theory are presented in Table 6–1. It is apparent from the table that most of the symbols refer to sexual objects and activities, which is in keeping with the central psychoanalytic pos-

TABLE 6–1
Common psychoanalytic symbols and their latent meanings

Symbol	Latent meaning
House	Human body
Smooth-fronted house	Male body
House with ledges and balconies	Female body
King and queen	Parents
Little animals	Children
Children	Genitals
Playing with children	Masturbation
Beginning a journey	Dying
Clothes	Nakedness
The number three	Male genitals
Elongated object (e.g., snake, stick, gun, tree trunk, necktie, pencil)	Penis
Balloon, airplane	Erection
Woods and thickets	Pubic hair
Room	Woman
Suite of rooms	Brothel or harem
Box	Uterus
Fruit	Breast
Climbing stairs or ladder	Sexual intercourse
Baldness, tooth extraction	Castration
Bath	Birth

tulate that human motivation is primarily sexual in nature. Although there are many symbols, according to Freud, only a few subjects are symbolized.

A final note of caution is in order. Despite the fact that he offered these relatively simple examples, Freud explicitly warned that it was impossible to accurately interpret a dream without taking into account its full clinical context.

What evidence exists for sexual symbolism? Do people connect the sexual symbols with sexual objects, as psychoanalysis proposes? One line of research which has dealt with these questions involves having individuals classify psychoanalytic symbols of male and female genitals as either masculine or feminine. In general, these studies have confirmed that adults, and sometimes children, are able to categorize sexual symbols according to the gender predicted by psychoanalytic theory at a better-than-chance level (Kline, 1972).

It would be possible to argue that, although the symbols were classified in accordance with psychoanalytic theory, the principles which the subjects used to make the classifications were based on cultural differences. This would be the case when psychoanalytic and cultural symbolism coincide. A gun, for example, is a masculine symbol both in psychoanalysis and in our culture. Lessler (1964) examined the possible influence of both psychoanalytic theory and cultural stereotypes on the classification of sexual symbols. Lessler found that the cultural stereotype was used to assign gender when the symbols had cultural referents, but that the symbols were classified according to psychoanalytic theory where no cultural bias existed. These results show that cultural sexual stereotypes, as well as psychoanalytic sexual symbolism, influence people's classification of symbols into masculine and feminine categories. Lessler argued that the results are completely in accord with psychoanalytic theory. Because sexual objects are usually threatening, if a cultural gender referent for the symbol exists, people are more likely to choose it instead of the psychoanalytic sexual meaning (e.g., calling a rolling pin feminine). On the other hand, if no cultural gender meaning is obvious, then people "must" and do use the psychoanalytic sexual meaning (e.g., classifying a cane as masculine).

In another major line of research aimed at validating psychoanalytic symbolism hypotheses, differences between the dreams of men and women have been examined. A good example of such research is Hall and Van de Castle's (1963) study of the effect of the masculine and feminine Oedipal situations on the respective dreams of men and women, which was described in Chapter 4.

The functions of dreaming

Why do people dream? Freud talked about three interrelated functions of dreaming: (1) *wish fulfillment,* (2) *the release of unconscious tension,* and (3) *the guarding of sleep.* He believed that wishing and unfulfilled desire is behind all thought processes, and that every dream is an attempt to fulfill a wish. The wish may be a conscious desire which is not fulfilled during the day (e.g., a person desires to be out sailing rather than at the office working) or an unconscious desire which is a more direct expression of a repressed drive (e.g., murdering a friend). Frequently, dreams represent a combination of the two. Thoughts from the day, called *day residues,* combine with an unconscious impulse to produce the dream. In effect, the unconscious impulse provides the psychic energy for the enactment of the day residues in the form of a dream. The result is that each of the three functions of dreaming is satisfied.

First, the wish is fulfilled in the dream. Recall that nocturnal dreams are primary processes in which the mental representation of the object or activity required to satisfy a wish is not distinguished from the actual object. Thus, when a wish "comes true" in a dream, it is as if it were actually fulfilled. This theoretical proposition is in keeping with the common observation that when we are dreaming we believe that the events are really happening.

Second, the unconscious impulse is allowed expression, albeit in a disguised and acceptable form, due to dream work and symbolism. This allows dreams to serve as a safety valve for tensions which have built up in the unconscious.

Third, the individual remains asleep even though unconscious threatening impulses are becoming conscious in the manifest dream. In a waking state, if threatening impulses began to become conscious, anxiety would be generated. If such anxiety were to be present during dreaming, the person would be awakened. However, through dream work and symbolism, the threatening aspects of the latent material are removed. The result is that anxiety is not generated, and the person can continue sleeping without interruption.

An example of dream interpretation

The interpretation of dreams, the primary method of studying dreams within psychoanalysis, involves examining the manifest content of a reported dream as well as the subject's free associations about the dream, to arrive at an understanding of its latent content. Knowledge of symbolism and dream work helps the psychoanalyst make interpretations. These procedures are illustrated in the following dream interpretation by Freud. The dreamer, a patient of Freud's, was a woman who was still quite young but had been married for a number of years. She had recently received news that a friend of hers, Elise L., a person of about her own age, had become engaged to marry. Shortly thereafter, she had the following dream.

She was at the theatre with her husband. One side of the stalls [theater boxes] were completely empty. Her husband told her that Elsie L. and her fiancé had wanted to go too, but had only been able to get bad seats—three for 1 florin 50 kreuzers—and of course they could not take those. She thought it would really not have done any harm if they had. (Freud, 1961, p. 415)

Freud began his discussion of this rather brief dream report by analyzing the symbolic meaning of the monetary units. This particular symbol was partially determined by an unimportant event of the previous day. The dreamer had learned that her sister-in-law had recently been given a gift of 150 florins (exactly 100 times the amount dreamt of) and had hastened to spend this gift on jewelry. Freud notes that *three* tickets are mentioned in the dream, whereas Elise L. and her fiancé would only have required two tickets for themselves. Examination of previous statements made by the dreamer revealed a connection: ". . . her newly engaged friend was the same number of months— *three*—her junior" (p. 415).

That one side of the stalls was entirely empty is important. Recently, when the patient had wished to attend a play, she had rushed out to purchase tickets days ahead of time and, in doing so, had incurred an extra booking fee. When the patient and her husband arrived at the theater, they in fact found that one half of the house was almost entirely empty. This bit of information accounts in part for the appearance of the "empty stalls" in the dream. More important in terms of psychoanalytic theory is the underlying meaning of the empty stalls. In the patient's actual life, her experience with the theater tickets could clearly lead to the conclusion that she had been excessively hasty about running out to buy tickets and therefore had had to pay an additional, unnecessary price. Freud assumed that the same *meaning* may be hidden with respect to her feelings about her own marriage and that, in symbolic form, these feelings are revealed by the dream. Thus, the following final interpretation of the dream is offered:

"It was *absurd* to marry so early. There was *no need for me to be in such a hurry.* I see from Elise L.'s example that I should have got a husband in the end. Indeed, I should have got one a *hundred times* better" (a *treasure*) "if I had only *waited*" (in antithesis to her sister-in-law's *hurry*). "My money" (or dowry) "could have bought *three* men just as good." (p. 416)

There have been a number of significant developments in our understanding of dreams since Freud's classic work was done. Virtually all research on dreaming makes some mention of psychoanalytic theory, but the research has increasingly suggested that substantial modifications of Freud's original position are required.

Post-Freudian developments in dream research

We will consider the physiology of sleep and dreaming, research on the manifest content of dreams, and the modern psychoanalytic concept of dreams as attempts at problem solving and information processing.

The physiology of sleep and dreaming

Some remarkable techniques for objectively studying dreams and other sleep-related phenomena have been developed. The two most important of these are the continuous recording of brain-wave patterns of sleeping subjects and the parallel recording of eye movements.

Brain waves are recorded by an instrument called an *electroencephalograph* which produces an *electroencephalogram* (EEG), a tracing, plotted against time, of the frequency and potential (voltage) of electric currents emitted by the brain (see Figure 6–1). The frequency of the electric currents from the brain is measured horizontally on the EEG, so that the closer together the tracings are, the greater is the frequency. The electric potential is measured vertically on the EEG, so that the greater the amplitude, or height, of the tracings, the greater is the electric potential. EEG recordings are made by placing electrodes directly on the scalp, a procedure which is painless and noninjurious to the subject, and does not appear to disturb sleep.

Eye movements have been measured during sleep primarily by plac-

FIGURE 6–1
Sample EEG patterns for the waking state and the four stages of sleep

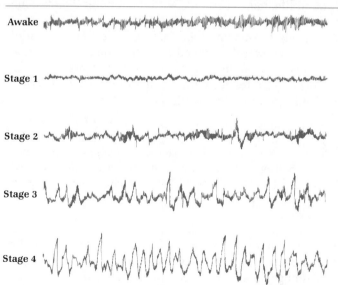

Source: Dement, W. C. An essay on dreams: The role of physiology in understanding their nature. In *New directions in psychology*. Vol. 2. New York: Holt, Rinehart & Winston, 1965.

ing small electrodes around the orbits of the eyes and measuring the differences in electric potential produced by displacement of the eyeballs. Figure 6–2 shows a subject wearing both brain-wave and eye-movement electrodes.

Stages of sleep and dreaming. It has been known for some time that sleep is not a uniform state but rather consists of various stages. EEG recordings during sleep reveal four basic stages of sleep which can be distinguished from the waking state. Figure 6–1 illustrates that, as sleep progresses from Stage 1 to Stage 4, there is a progressive development of high-amplitude, low-frequency waves. Originally, this was thought to be correlated with reduction in neural activity and responsiveness as the person went from "light sleep" in Stage 1 to "deep sleep" in Stage 4. More recent evidence makes it clear that, although the stages of sleep can be roughly placed on a quantitative continuum of depth, there is a very important exception. Indeed, this exception, which occurs during Stage 1 sleep, is so striking that it has been the primary focus of sleep researchers.

FIGURE 6–2
A sleeping subject with EEG and eye-movement electrodes

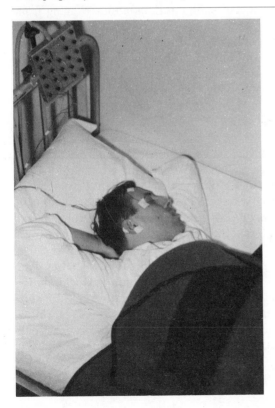

In 1953, Aserinsky and Kleitman at the University of Chicago were studying the sleep patterns of infants and inadvertently discovered the occurrence of occasional periods of rapid movements of the eyes during sleep. Such *rapid eye movement* (REM) activity has been shown to occur only during Stage 1 sleep, although not all of Stage 1 is characterized by REMs.[2] Much research has been directed toward elucidating the characteristics of REM sleep. During this phase in the cerebral cortex there is a considerable amount of neural activity which is similar to that found in the waking state. The autonomic nervous system is activated, as manifested in the presence of an irregular heart beat, irregular breathing, and penile erection. These physiological correlates of REM sleep give the impression of "light sleep." At the same time, REM sleep is associated with considerable muscular relaxation. People in REM sleep are relatively insensitive to external stimulation, and when they are awakened they frequently report that they they have been in "deep sleep."

Is REM sleep "light" or "deep"? The best available answer seems to be that it is both and neither, which is to say that it is a unique neurophysiological stage which is qualitatively different from the other stages of sleep. This *paradoxical sleep,* as it is sometimes called, is found in humans of all ages and in subhuman mammals ranging from the opossum (Snyder, 1965) to the monkey (Weitzmann, 1961). In adult humans, REM sleep occupies slightly more than 20 percent of total sleep time (about 50 percent in infants). It usually occurs in regularly occurring cycles of approximately 90 minutes each, as shown in Figure 6–3. Successive REM periods become progressively longer, with the final period lasting from 25 to 45 minutes. Of course, these are only average figures, and they vary somewhat from individual to individual and from night to night.

The most important psychological aspect of REM sleep is that this is when most dreaming occurs. When Aserinsky and Kleitman discovered the periodic occurrence of REMs, they believed that it might be related to dreaming. To test this hunch, they awakened adult subjects during REM and NREM *(nonrapid eye movement)* periods and asked them whether they had been dreaming. Of the subjects awakened from REM sleep, 74 percent indicated that they had been dreaming; of those awakened from NREM sleep, only 7 percent indicated that they had been dreaming (Aserinsky & Kleitman, 1955). This finding was of major significance because it was the first time that a reliable relationship had been found between an objective measure of a sleep variable (REM) and recall of dreams. Although the percentage of dream recall for REM and NREM awakenings has varied in different studies, the

---

[2] REMs occur in almost all Stage 1 sleep except the initial period of Stage 1 when the person first falls asleep.

FIGURE 6–3
Sleep cycles as they relate to stages of sleep

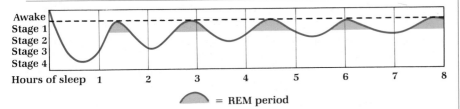

general finding that REM periods are associated with substantially more dream reports than are NREM periods has been upheld in numerous investigations (Van de Castle, 1971).

Continuing with this work, Dement and his associates reasoned that, if dreams actually occur during REM sleep, then the subjective duration of the dream should be proportional to the duration of rapid eye movement observed prior to awakening the subject. The results were very positive.

> In one series of trials, subjects were awakened either 5 minutes or 15 minutes after the onset of REMs and were asked to choose the correct interval on the basis of whatever dream material they recalled. A correct choice was made in 92 of 111 instances. In another series, high correlation coefficients were obtained between the number of words in the dream narratives and the number of minutes of REMP [REM period] preceding the awakenings. (Dement, 1965, p. 172)

Besides being an objective indication that there is a high probability that dreaming is occurring, REMs seem able to yield information about the content of dreams. It appears that dreamers scan their dream images in much the same way that they would visually scan similar events in a waking state and that their eyes move accordingly. Studies performed in different laboratories have found that more frequent individual eye movements were associated with reports of active dreams (e.g., running or fighting), while less frequent individual eye movements were related to reports of passive dreams (e.g., staring at a distant object) (Berger & Oswald, 1962; Dement & Wolpert, 1958). Furthermore, when REMs were vertical, subjects tended to report dreams of vertical movement, such as looking up and down a flight of stairs; when the rapid eye movements were horizontal, the dream reports tended to contain horizontal imagery, such as two people throwing a ball back and forth (Dement & Kleitman, 1957).

Dream deprivation. A corollary to Freud's hypothesis concerning the release of repressed psychic energy through dreaming is that, if such an outlet is not provided, then the individual should exhibit signs of abnormal behavior. Studies of dream deprivation have shed some light on this issue. The procedure involves depriving subjects in a sleep laboratory of REM periods. A subject is awakened just as he or she is beginning to enter a REM period, and then is allowed to fall back to sleep. There are large individual differences in reaction to dream deprivation (Cartwright & Ratzel, 1972). However, after a review of the relevant studies, Webb (1975) concluded that there have been no clear-cut cases in which REM deprivation resulted in abnormal behavior, either in normal or psychotic subjects. Nonetheless, some interesting effects have been observed and can be interpreted as supporting Freud's basic hypothesis. Thus, Fisher and Greenberg argue:

> True, the disturbance following dream deprivation is not of the extreme magnitude that the original investigators of this matter thought it to be. It is also true that marked individual differences exist in mode of adaptation to the deprivation. But there is a discernible average trend for signs of disturbance to a person following limitation of dreaming that fit in with the idea that dreams somehow serve as an outlet or channel for tension reduction. (1977, p. 61)

Dreaming as a response to central nervous system desynchronization.   Hobson and McCarley (1977) have proposed a physiological theory of dreaming. Their theory is rooted in the current neurophysiological view that the central nervous system may be in any of three states: waking, synchronized sleep, and desynchronized sleep (the only state in which REM and dreaming occur). During desynchronized sleep, the brain, because of its disinhibited state, spontaneously activates a variety of systems. These activations do not lead to much coordinated overt motor activity, but they do lead to activation of somewhat disorganized thought, experienced as dreaming. Thus, within this view, the primary causal events of dreaming are seen to be physiological rather than psychological.

Research on the manifest content of dreams

Freud placed little theoretical importance on the overt, manifest content of dreams,[3] but modern psychoanalytic researchers have found that much can be learned from listening to the manifest content of their patients' dreams. Research reviewed by Fisher and Greenberg (1977) suggests strongly that *people tend to dream about matters which concern them,* implying that the manifest content of dreams, i.e., what we remember dreaming about, is of considerable psychological significance. To cite a few examples from the wide array of findings: Pregnant women are significantly more likely than other women to report dreams

---

[3] Despite his blanket dismissal of the manifest content of dreams in his theoretical writings, Freud actually relied quite a bit on the manifest dream content of his patients in many of his published dream interpretations.

involving babies or children. Men are more likely than women to have dreams involving aggression. Women are more likely to have dreams relating to sex or hostility during their menstrual periods than at other times. Older people (those over 65) are more likely than other individuals to report dreams involving loss of resources and strength or death-related topics. Finally, studies of sleep and dreaming conducted in sleep laboratories reveal that first-night dreams of subjects often bear directly on how the dreamer is experiencing the sleep laboratory. (Interestingly, when the laboratory personnel are male, male subjects' dreams tend to focus on issues of attack and getting hurt, whereas female subjects respond to the male laboratory assistants by having dreams that tend to involve sexual exploitation.)

Dreaming as problem solving

Some post-Freudian writers have turned toward the view that dreaming can serve the important ego function of problem solving and planning for future actions (e.g., Erikson, 1954; French & Fromm, 1964). Adler was an early proponent of this position, believing that "the dream attempts to bring a present problem to a solution" (1973, p. 214). Grieser, Greenberg, and Harrison (1972) investigated the general hypothesis that "dreaming serves to integrate current stressful experiences with similar experiences from the past, thus enabling the individual to use his basic coping mechanisms (defenses) to deal with the current stressful situation" (p. 281). College students were given anagrams to solve, following which they were told which anagrams they had solved and which they had failed to solve. Failure was made ego-threatening by informing the subjects that the task was a test of intelligence in which the average college student was able to do quite well. It was predicted that subjects who were permitted to dream following the experimental task would remember the failed anagrams better than subjects who were prevented from dreaming. This hypothesis follows from the view that dreaming is a period in which the person copes with a stressful situation, such as failure. By coping with the failure, a person presumably makes it less ego-threatening. The person will therefore have less need to repress the events leading to the failure (i.e., the unsolved anagrams) and will be more likely to remember them.

Grieser et al. (1972) found that subjects who were awakened during NREM periods, and thus were able to dream during REM sleep, recalled significantly more failed anagrams than did subjects who were awakened during REM periods, and thus were "dream deprived." These results were interpreted as supporting the view that dreams have an adaptive function which enables the dreamer to cope with ego-threatening material.

If dreaming involves planning for the future, then it should be related to memory functions. Thus Jones (1970) has suggested that dreaming plays a critical role in problem solving, representing "computations" which relate present experience to the individual's permanent memory structure. Similarly, based on his psychoanalytic observations, Palombo (1978) claims that dreams "are not the insignificant odds and ends that Freud thought them to be . . . but precisely those experiences whose novelty of meaning and associated affect make them worth preserving for future reference" (p. 15).

PROJECTIVE TECHNIQUES

The psychoanalytic approach to personality places a heavy emphasis on unconscious factors in the determination of behavior. Since the individual is, by definition, not directly aware of these factors, indirect methods of assessment are necessary to uncover the unconscious determinants of behavior. This section explores the use of *projective techniques* in assessing unconscious motives and feelings.

The nature of projective techniques

All projective techniques are based on the assumption, called the *projective hypothesis,* that when individuals are forced to impose meaning or order on an ambiguous stimulus, their responses will be projections or reflections of their feelings, attitudes, desires, and needs. The principle is similar to the defense mechanism of projection.

There are a variety of existing projective techniques, with a wide range of stimulus materials and responses required of the subject. Some projective techniques require that the subject make *associations* to stimuli such as inkblots or words. Some involve the *construction* of stories about pictures which are open to a variety of interpretations (e.g., the Thematic Apperception Test [TAT]). Other projective techniques require the subject to *complete* sentences (such as "I often feel . . .") or stories. In still other projective techniques, subjects must *express* themselves through drawings (e.g., the Draw-a-Person Test) or by acting out a loosely specified role (as in psychodrama). Finally, there are projective techniques in which subjects *choose* among a variety of stimuli, indicating those they like best and least (e.g., in the Szondi Test the stimuli are photographs of psychiatric patients with different diagnoses). Table 6–2 summarizes the most common types of projective techniques.

Although there is considerable variety in the type of stimuli presented to the subject and the type of response required, all projective techniques share several important characteristics.

1. The stimulus material, be it an inkblot, a picture, or the first part of a sentence, is relatively unstructured and ambiguous. This forces the subject to impose some order or structure.

TABLE 6–2
Common types of projective techniques

Type of task	Stimulus materials	Instructions	Example
Association ..	Word (e.g., man)	"After hearing each word, say the first word that comes to mind."	Word association
Construction..	Picture	"Tell a story about the picture."	Thematic Apperception Test (TAT)
Completion ...	Sentence stem (e.g., "I want . . .")	"Complete the sentence."	Incomplete sentences
Expression ...	Paper and pencil	"Draw a picture of yourself and a person of the opposite sex."	Draw-a-Person Test
Choice	Photographs of diagnosed psychiatric patients	"Choose the picture you like best and the picture you like least."	Szondi Test

2. The subject is usually not told the purpose of the test and how responses will be scored or interpreted.
3. The subject is told that there are no "right" or "wrong" answers.
4. Each response is considered to reveal a true and significant aspect of the subject.
5. The scoring and interpretation of projective methods of personality assessment are generally lengthy and relatively subjective procedures.

Technique versus test

It should be noted that our discussion thus far has referred to projective *techniques* rather than projective tests. Although some projective techniques may appear quite similar to assessment procedures which are commonly called tests (sentence completion techniques, for example, are reminiscent of "fill-in-the-blank" items used in school examinations), others are substantially different from the usual kinds of tests. Additionally, and of more significance, most projective techniques do not meet the generally agreed upon psychometric standards of a test. For example, they are not standardized.

Two projective techniques will be described in some detail—the Rorschach inkblots and the Holtzman Inkblot Technique. The Thematic Apperception Test will be discussed in Chapter 12.

The use of inkblots to reveal something about an individual, such as imaginativeness, was not a new idea when Hermann Rorschach,

The Rorschach inkblots

a Swiss psychiatrist, began his experiments in the early part of the 20th century. Rorschach, however, was the first to make a systematic attempt to assess personality by the use of a standard set of blots. His efforts began with experiments on a variety of geometric forms in different colors. Later, Rorschach shifted his interest to less structured inkblots. The results of his work were first published in his 1921 monograph titled *Psychodiagnostik*, which was subtitled "Methodology and results of a perceptual-diagnostic experiment (interpretation of accidental forms)." Regrettably, Rorschach died the year after the publication of his monograph, and it was left to others to elaborate on the basic procedures he had outlined.

Description of the inkblots

The Rorschach Inkblot technique (usually called simply "the Rorschach") consists of 10 nearly symmetrical inkblots, 5 of which have some color and 5 of which are in black and white. The blots are printed and centered on pieces of white cardboard about 7 inches by 10 inches in size. Figure 6–4 presents inkblots similar to the kind used in the Rorschach. The blots were originally made by spilling ink on a piece of paper and then folding the paper in half.

Administration

The Rorschach is usually administered to a subject individually, and the administration is typically divided into two basic phases. In the *performance proper*, the examiner gives the subject instructions such as the following: "I am going to show you a number of inkblots, and I want you to tell me what you see in each of them." The examiner records *what* the subject relates about each blot. If the subject asks whether it is permissible to turn the card, how many responses should

FIGURE 6–4
Inkblots similar to those employed by Rorschach

Source: Kleinmuntz, B. *Personality measurement: An introduction,* Homewood, Ill.: Dorsey Press, 1967.

be made for each blot, or similar questions, the examiner tries to respond in such a way as to leave the decision up to the subject.

When the subject has finished responding to all 10 inkblots, the second phase of the administration, the *inquiry,* begins. Starting with the first card again, the examiner reminds the subject of each of his or her responses and inquires both *where* and *how* the subject saw each response (i.e., what about the inkblot made it look like it did).

Scoring and interpretation

A number of different systems for scoring and interpreting responses to the Rorschach have been developed. In one of the more widely used systems (Klopfer & Davidson, 1962), each response is scored for five major characteristics.

1. *Location*—where on the card the concept was seen.
2. *Determinant*—the qualities of the blot that led to the formation of the concept.
3. *Popularity-originality*—the frequency with which particular responses are given by subjects in general.
4. *Content*—the subject matter of the concept.
5. *Form-level*—how accurately the concept is seen and how closely the concept fits the blot.

While scoring the Rorschach is a detailed procedure, interpretation is even more complex. Most often, the responses are subjected to a formal analysis in which the way they were arrived at is examined. Table 6–3 presents examples of possible interpretations of responses. It is important to keep in mind that a given response or set of responses is always viewed in relation to the other responses made by the subject and in relation to how other subjects typically respond. The latter criterion can be thought of as "informal norms" which each Rorschach examiner keeps in mind (they are rarely written down) from experience using the Rorschach. Interpretations of Rorschach responses are actually hypotheses. Their validity or usefulness varies with the purpose of the assessment and the individual case. A common way of checking the validity of interpretations based on Rorschach responses is to compare them with interpretations derived from other projective techniques to see whether the interpretations are consistent with one another.

As noted earlier, one criticism of projective techniques is that they cannot be scrutinized by the same psychometric standards as other personality tests. Cognizant of this limitation, Holtzman and his associates (Holtzman, Thorpe, Swartz, & Herron, 1961) developed what they described as "a completely new approach to inkblot testing, one which

**The Holtzman
Inkblot Technique**

TABLE 6–3
Examples of scoring and interpretation of the Rorschach inkblots

Scoring characteristic	Examples of scoring category	Sample responses	Examples of interpretations*
Location	Whole	Entire blot used for concept	Ability to organize and integrate material
	Small usual detail	Small part which is easily marked off from the rest of the blot	Need to be exact and accurate
Determinant	Form	"The outline looks like a bear"	Degree of emotional control
	Movement	"A flying hawk"	Level of ego functioning
Popularity-originality	Popular	Response which many people give	Need to be conventional
	Original	Response which few people give and which fits blot well	Superior intelligence
Content	Animal figures	"Looks like a house cat"	Passivity and dependence
	Human figures	"It's a man or a woman"	Problem with sexual identity
Form-level	High form-level	Concept fits blot well	High intellectual functioning
	Low form-level	Concept is a poor match to blot	Contact with reality tenuous

* Interpretations would be made only if the type of response occurred a number of times (i.e., not just once). See text for further precautions regarding interpretations of Rorschach responses.

is designed from its inception to meet adequate standards of measurement while preserving the uniquely valuable projective quality of the Rorschach" (p. 10). They administered a large number of inkblots to samples of normal college students and psychiatric patients. The criteria for the selection of inkblots were: (1) the ability of an inkblot to reliably differentiate between the normal and abnormal samples, and (2) maximum *interrater reliability* (agreement among scorers) on the categories for which the inkblots were being scored. Two parallel (equivalent) sets of 45 inkblots were eventually selected. Parallel sets make it possible to use the technique twice with the same subjects without having their second responses contaminated by the fact that they have seen the inkblots previously. For example, personality changes measured by the Holtzman can be assessed before and after an experimental treatment or psychotherapy. *Retest reliability,* which measures the stability of a test over time, can be assessed with the Holtzman inkblots because parallel sets exist.

Subjects are shown each of the 45 inkblots and asked to give *one* response to each. This makes an important variable, response productivity, constant for all people and facilitates comparisons among people and the development of norms. Each response is scored for 22 variables, including all those for which the Rorschach inkblots are scored and such other variables as pathognomic (deviant) verbalization, integration, anxiety, and hostility.

The observations which led Freud to his elaborate theory of personality were made in the context of his clinical practice. In the latter half of the 19th century, the science of neurology was making little progress in treating mental disorders. One of the exceptions to this general state of affairs was the work of Jean Charcot in Paris, with whom Freud studied for about a year. Charcot used hypnosis in his treatment of hysteria, more commonly called conversion reaction today. In hysteria, the patient suffers from seemingly physical ailments, such as a paralyzed limb or a defective sense organ, for which no physical cause can be found. Charcot hypnotized his hysteric patients and then directly ordered them (hypnotic suggestion) to renounce their symptoms. The orders were generally effective as long as the patient remained in the hypnotic state. However, when the patient awoke, the hysteric symptoms almost inevitably returned. This peculiar and intriguing combination of success and failure seemed extremely important to Freud, who was eager to find procedures which would make the hypnotic cure both more enduring and more understandable.

Shortly after returning from his studies with Charcot, Freud opened his private medical practice in Vienna and became associated with Josef Breuer, a prominent Viennese physician who also used hypnosis in treating hysteria. In the book *Studies in Hysteria* (1895), based on their collaboration, Breuer and Freud concluded that hysteric patients have repressed painful memories and emotions in an unconscious region of the mind. The painful memories and experiences nonetheless make themselves felt as the bodily symptoms of hysteria.[4] Freud and Breuer described the *cathartic method*,[5] whereby repressed emotions can finally be expressed and released, with the release itself being called *abreaction*. Rather than directly willing a hysteric patient's symptoms away, Breuer had asked the hypnotized patient to vividly recall the traumatic experiences which had caused the hysteria. The patient's reenactment of the trauma which produced the neurosis was accompanied by a great emotional release, in the form of tears and

PSYCHOANALYTIC PSYCHOTHERAPY

---

[4] The problem which occupied Freud and Breuer, hysteria, has become very rare today, while depression has become much more common. Interestingly, according to psychoanalytic theory, depression arises as a result of hostile wishes felt toward another which are then defensively turned toward the self.

[5] *Catharsis* is the Greek word for purification.

words, and seemingly led to a cure. Unlike the changes in Charcot's patients, these changes persisted after the patient awakened. Breuer and Freud hypothesized that it was the recollection of the events and the resulting discharge of dammed-up emotions (later to be called libido by Freud) which led to the alleviation of the symptoms and the cure of the neurosis.[6]

Meanwhile, though, Breuer was experiencing the embarrassing difficulty that his hysterical patients (virtually all of whom were female) tended to display a strong erotic attachment to him. This upset Breuer greatly, and he decided to abandon his work with hysterics. For the more daring and less prudish Freud, however, these misplaced erotic interests were grist for the theoretical mill, ultimately leading to the concept of transference, about which we shall have more to say shortly.

Initially, Freud treated his patients, who were almost exclusively hysterics, by hypnosis. He rejected Charcot's method of direct influence in favor of Breuer's more indirect *hypnocatharsis*. But Freud was not always successful in hypnotizing his patients, and soon he substituted the technique of asking nonhypnotized patients to concentrate on recalling past events that were associated with their neuroses. He found that, given sufficient freedom, patients wandered in their thoughts and recollections and that this led to a superior understanding of the patients' unconscious processes. Freud called this technique *free association*, and it became the fundamental technique of psychoanalysis.

In free association, the patient is told not to censor any thoughts, to say whatever comes to mind without regard to social convention, logic and order, seeming importance or triviality, and any feelings of embarrassment or shame. To facilitate free association, Freud had the patient recline on a couch while he sat behind and out of view of the patient (see Figure 6–5). The reclining position, reminiscent of sleep, is thought to bring a person closer to unconscious primary processes and to stimulate fantasy and memory. With the therapist out of view, the patient is not constantly reminded of the therapist's presence, and free association is thereby made easier.

There was another important way in which Freud parted company with Breuer—in Freud's final conception of hysteria. Freud and Breuer had found that many hysterical patients reported sexual encounters as part of their abreaction, suggesting that the neuroses were rooted in actual childhood seductions. However, Freud came to realize from his own clinical observations that these reports referred to fantasies and not to actual past events.

Finally, mention should be made of Freud's conclusions about the

---

[6] "Neurosis" is a psychological disorder characterized by much anxiety with which the person has difficulty coping and by abnormal behavior, such as irrational fears (phobias), obsessional thoughts, and, as in hysteria, physical complaints.

FIGURE 6–5
Freud's consulting room in Vienna, with his chair and patient's couch. Truly it may
be said psychoanalysis was born here.

Edmund Engelman

nature of neurotic symptoms. Freud came to believe that neurosis always reflects unresolved conflicts which may be manifest in any of an array of neurotic symptoms (anxieties, compulsions, phobias, depression, and hysterical paralysis, to name a few). However, all neurotic symptoms, like all dreams, have a hidden meaning. Specifically, Freud suggested that the neurotic symptom is a compromise born out of both unconscious wish fulfillment and ego defense. Neurotic symptoms thus came to be viewed as the product of inhibition, being "substituted satisfactions for what is missed in life" (Roazen, 1975, p. 111). A person's "choice of neuroses" is determined by both environmental and constitutional factors, and a person may be freed of one symptom only to be overcome by another if treated superficially, that is, without getting at the root of the person's conflict. The appearance of new symptoms under these circumstances is referred to as *symptom substitution*.

Psychoanalytic practice

Freud viewed all mental illness as a manifestation of repressed conflicts and dammed-up libido seeking expression. However, because of the traumatic or culturally taboo nature of these conflicts, they cannot become conscious. Thus, Freud reasoned that the goal of psychotherapy must be to bring unconscious wishes, thoughts, and emotions, which have long since been repressed, into the conscious part of the mind.

Free association is the initial step in penetrating the unconscious, but free association is not sufficient in and of itself. Unconscious material comes to the conscious surface only in disguised or symbolic form during free association, just as it does in dreams. It is the task of the analyst to translate the symbolism and *interpret* the unconscious material for the patient. Interpretations are also made of dreams, symptoms, behavior in and out of therapy, the patient's relation to the analyst, and past experiences. The analyst's interpretations help to reconstruct childhood experiences which led to the conflict producing the neurosis. In Freud's own words, this process

> resembles to a great extent an archaeologist's excavation of some dwelling-place that has been destroyed and buried. . . . The two processes are in fact identical, except that the analyst works under better conditions and has more material at his command to assist him, since what he is dealing with is not something destroyed, but something that is still alive. . . . But just as the archaeologist builds up the walls of the building from the foundations that have remained standing, determines the number and position of the columns from the depressions in the floor and reconstructs the mural decorations and paintings from the remains found in the debris, so does the analyst proceed when he draws his inferences from the fragments of memories, from the associations and from the behavior of the subject of analysis. (cited in Wolman, 1968, pp. 168–69)

Insight

From the analyst's interpretations, the patient gains *insight* into the nature and origin of the neurosis. According to Freud, it is vital that individuals actually believe that they have found the correct interpretation of aspects of their own lives. Merely giving lip service to the analyst's suggestions would be an empty achievement. Neither is insight merely an intellectual understanding of one's personality and its inner conflicts and drives. Rather, it is an *emotional experiencing* of parts of the personality which have been unconscious.

Finally, insights cannot be forced upon patients, but rather the individual must work through inner resistances and work through the ways in which they continue to repeat themes of the past. This is a sort of understanding and acceptance that develops slowly and gradually, and perhaps in a distinctive way for each person.

Resistance and transference

Early in his treatment of neurotics, Freud observed that patients often resisted being cured. *Resistance,* as Freud came to call these impediments to successful treatment, can be conscious or unconscious. In the former case, the patient is aware of impeding the progress of analysis. For example, a patient who does not want to talk about a dream or thought which comes to mind is consciously resisting. In unconscious resistance, the patient is not aware of "fighting" the treatment. For example, the ego defense mechanisms may keep unconscious material from coming out in free association, or the patient may forget to come to a therapy session (unconsciously motivated forgetting). Unconscious resistance is more difficult to overcome than its conscious counterpart, but at the same time it is more significant since it is another manifestation of the patient's unconscious strivings.

The most important form of unconscious resistance is known as *transference.* Transference refers to all the feelings that the patient experiences toward the analyst which are *distorted displacements* from significant figures in the patient's past.[7] For example, patients may act *as if* the analyst were their father or mother. Transference can be both positive, involving feelings of love, respect, and admiration, or negative, involving such emotions as hatred, jealousy, and disgust.

Transference is an impediment to psychoanalysis because it is an *inappropriate* reaction. The analyst is not really the patient's father. At the same time, the inappropriateness of these feelings serves to point out to patients the significance of their early experiences. An integral part of psychoanalysis is the interpretation of instances of transference. Relative to other feelings about which the patient is expected to gain insight, the patient's feelings toward the analyst are easily seen as inappropriate in the therapy situation (i.e., the analyst gives the patient no provocation for either love or hate) but pertinent in another, past situation (i.e., some significant relationship in the patient's childhood). Thus, transference is both a form of resistance and a road to the patient's past experiences and unconscious representations of the past. In fact, Freud believed that, for psychoanalysis to be successful, the patient had to experience transference, which was then worked through as part of the treatment.

---

[7] The analyst may also experience feelings toward the patient which are distorted displacements from his or her own past, and this is known as *countertransference.* In order to minimize the adverse effects of countertransference on the therapy (e.g., a reduction in the analyst's objectivity), psychoanalysts are themselves psychoanalyzed as part of their training. By having insight into their own unconscious processes and conflicts, they are better able to understand and deal with countertransference.

The psychoanalytic session

It is difficult to capture the exact nature of the psychoanalytic session, but certainly it is one of Freud's most remarkable innovations. Today, many types of psychotherapy involve a verbal interchange between patient and therapist. But almost a century ago, when Freud began to practice psychoanalysis, verbal psychotherapy was virtually unknown. Even more startling was the revolutionary change in the patient-therapist relationship which Freud advocated in the treatment of psychological disturbances. Hitherto, patients had played only a passive role in their cure, while the physician had actively treated them. Freud's new therapeutic procedures reversed these roles. Now it became the patient's job to work (to free associate and to reenact important childhood experiences) and the therapist's task to act as a compassionate but neutral observer who occasionally made significant interpretations of the origin and nature of the patient's intrapsychic conflicts. Many of Freud's contemporaries reacted in astonishment to this new psychotherapy and remarked indignantly that Freud *listened* to his patients! And Freud was a most astute listener. He hovered over the patient's words, he questioned suggestively and sought the meaning of every response. Hesitations, pauses, slight excesses of emotion in the voice might be picked up and pursued by the first psychoanalyst.

Freud believed strongly that neutrality was the only proper attitude for the psychoanalyst during a session. He recommended that analysts maintain "evenly suspended attention" while at the same time being somewhat distrustful of what the patient was saying. Freud urged analysts to model themselves after the surgeon, "who puts aside all his feelings, even his human sympathy, and concentrates his mental forces on the single aim of performing the operation as skillfully as possible" (cited by Roazen, 1975, p. 133).

Freud saw his own patients for 55-minute sessions five or six times a week, recommending that they not talk about their analysis with anyone. Though he believed that some patients require lifelong treatment (and that, in some sense, all analyses are lifelong), he generally felt that treatment required between six months and three years. (Interestingly, Freud performed the analysis of one of his students, Wilhelm Stekel, in only nine sessions.)

Requirements and training for being considered a psychoanalyst

Freud was deeply committed to what has been called "the medical model." He referred to psychoanalytic practitioners as physicians in his writings, and referred to his subjects as patients. He saw psychological problems as illnesses to be cured, and he saw the difficulties people presented in the consulting room as no more than symptoms of underlying disorders which had to be routed out. Nonetheless, Freud envisioned some nonmedical practitioners, referred to as "lay analysts." (Freud's daughter Anna was not medically trained and thus would be considered a lay analyst.)

Psychoanalytic theory indicates that analysts must be sufficiently aware of their own personality dynamics to keep these from interfering with therapy. Therefore, to be recognized as a psychoanalyst by other analysts, one must have undergone a successful training analysis, typically at a psychoanalytic institute. During training, the prospective analyst is referred to as a "candidate" who may or may not be admitted into the ranks depending on the training analyst's judgment of the candidate's suitability and progress. Thus, the basic technique of psychoanalytic research and therapy, the ability to conduct a psychoanalysis, is learned in apprenticeship fashion through what remains largely an oral tradition.

Besides expanding and modifying Freud's theory of personality, some analysts have also made some changes in psychoanalytic psychotherapy. While there are many forms of post-Freudian therapy (e.g., Adlerian, Jungian, Sullivanian, Eriksonian), it is possible to abstract some common trends to parallel the general overview of post-Freudian approaches to personality presented in Chapters 4 and 5. In fact, as we shall see, post-Freudian therapy techniques have been consistent with post-Freudian personality theory.

Post-Freudian modifications of psychoanalytic psychotherapy

In neoanalytic therapy (as the practice of post-Freudians may be called) the patient's present behavior—current functioning and adjustment—is examined as are significant aspects of the patient's past. Neoanalysts consider it important to explore the ways in which the patient is functioning effectively as well as the problem behaviors which bring the patient to therapy. The individual's strengths are used to devise a plan of therapy to deal with the individual's weaknesses. There is an emphasis on the patient's interpersonal relations, and situational stresses are considered along with intrapsychic conflicts.

Neoanalysts assume a more active role in therapy. They tend to talk more and to be more directive, and they may give advice to their patients (which orthodox psychoanalysts usually do not do). They also make interpretations, but in contrast to those made in orthodox analysis, neoanalytic interpretations are likely to be psychosocial as well as psychosexual in nature, and may be more concrete and practical and less abstract and theoretical.

In general, post-Freudian approaches to psychotherapy are more flexible. The interaction between therapist and patient is less formal and restrictive. To begin with, the patient usually sits facing the therapist, rather than reclining on a couch with the therapist out of sight. The patient-therapist interactions are examined as one example of the patient's style of interpersonal behavior, and interpretations of these interactions are viewed as indicating more than transference. The emphasis in therapy can be supportive as well as uncovering (of early childhood and intrapsychic conflicts). The therapy can be briefer than orthodox psychoanalysis (e.g., fewer sessions per week and fewer total sessions). Compared with orthodox psychoanalysis, neoanalytic therapy is likely to be customized to the individual client's needs and less likely to follow standard procedures or stages which guide the treatment of all patients (e.g., experiencing and successfully working through transference).

Freud viewed transference rather narrowly in that he considered all transference to be a reliving of the patient's Oedipus complex. This viewpoint is consonant with Freud's conception that all neurosis has its origin in an unsuccessful resolution of the Oedipus complex. He maintained that persons suffering from non-neurotic disorders, such as psychotic disorders[8] and character disorders,[9] were not amenable to psychoanalytic treatment. These people were presumed either to have regressed to (in psychotic disorders) or to have been fixated at (in character disorders) prephallic stages of psychosexual development. In both cases, this meant that much of their psychic energy was invested in earlier conflicts and therefore was unavailable for transference. But as early as 1920, post-Freudians began to broaden the definition of transference to include the reenactment of feelings toward significant adults which occurred in any stage of psychosexual development. The view that persons manifesting non-neurotic disorders could form a transference relationship with the analyst led a number of psychotherapists to begin treating such patients by psychoanalysis (e.g., Sullivan with schizophrenics and Reich with persons suffering from character disorders).

Efficacy of psychoanalytic therapy

How effective is psychoanalytic psychotherapy? The question has proved to be a thorny one throughout the history of psychoanalysis. At first, Freud was quite optimistic about psychoanalysis as therapy. He believed that for suitable patients, that is, verbal and intelligent neurotics, uncovering their secrets was the sufficient goal of therapy. Exposure of the mind's underlying conflicts would lead to insight which would lead to recovery. Later, after the practice of psychoanalysis

---

[8] *Psychotic disorders* refer to psychological disorders in which the person's behavior seems to be out of contact with objective reality and is sometimes bizarre in nature (e.g., hearing voices, thinking illogically). Most patients in psychiatric or mental hospitals are diagnosed as psychotic.

[9] *Character disorders* refer to psychological disorders involving long-standing maladaptive patterns of living.

had begun to flourish, Freud felt obliged to emphasize the significance of his theories over his therapeutic methods. In a paper published in 1933 he wrote:

> I have told you that psychoanalysis began as a method of treatment, but I did not want to commend it to your interest as a method of treatment but on account of the truths it contains, on account of the information it gives us about that which concerns human beings most of all—their own nature—and on account of the connections it discloses between the most different of their activities. (Freud, 1964, pp. 156–157, as cited by Fisher & Greenberg, 1977, p. 283)

As regards Freud's changing feelings about psychoanalytic therapy, Fisher and Greenberg (1977) offer the following observation: "It has become clear, as we traced his thoughts concerning psychoanalytic therapy, that Freud never specified the necessary and sufficient conditions for achieving a therapeutic effect" (p. 394). There is also increasing agreement among Freud scholars that over his lifetime Freud became "more and more convinced that the true significance of psychoanalysis was not as therapy but as an understanding of man and the unconscious mind" (Brooks, 1980, p. 26).

Freud's own ultimate conclusions were really quite pessimistic. On his 80th birthday, he declared: "Constitution is everything." At about the same time he also announced to one of his students: "My discoveries are not primarily a heal-all. My discoveries are a basis for a very grave philosophy. There are very few who understand this, *there are very few who are capable of understanding"* (cited by Sulloway, 1979, p. 439, italics in original).

The gravity Freud spoke of has made itself felt. Studies (e.g., Houts, 1981; Strupp, 1958b) show that psychoanalytic therapists are less positive and less optimistic in their expectations for patient improvement than are other therapists.

Still, there remains the important question of goals. Seward (1962–63) found that psychoanalysts do not agree among themselves as to the goals of therapy, but tend *not* to think of such factors as better relationships with people or greater self-realization as the goals. Some contemporary psychoanalysts believe the test of successful psychoanalytic therapy is whether or not the patient comes to know and accept the "truth" about him- or herself.

Such knowing inevitably leads to at least a degree of acceptance of one's self and one's fate, but no "improvement" or "cure" in the usual sense is contemplated or necessarily expected. Many consider psychoanalysis an educational rather than a therapeutic process, and it is certainly widely agreed upon that psychoanalysis is not for everyone. What analysts implicitly claim is that a certain depth and kind of understanding about oneself can be achieved through psychoanalysis that is not attainable in any other way.

7 *The psychoanalytic strategy*

Liabilities

Several of the often heard criticisms of the psychoanalytic strategy will be mentioned in this chapter; each has proved to be a liability for the strategy, or at least a source of controversy. They are: (1) the vague, nonspecific nature of many psychoanalytic concepts; (2) the failure of psychoanalysts to make several important logical distinctions in presenting evidence to support psychoanalytic theory; (3) the sources of bias which enter into psychoanalytic case studies; (4) the untestability of much of psychoanalytic theory; (5) the low reliability and validity of projective techniques; and (6) the questionable efficacy of psychoanalytic psychotherapy.

In general, psychoanalytic terminology is poorly and ambiguously defined. For example, Freud (1965) defines the "unconscious" as any mental event the existence of which we must assume but of which we have no knowledge. This definition gives us no information. The definitions of other phenomena, such as "reaction formation," are somewhat clearer yet do not provide sufficient guidelines for us to be able to ascertain when the phenomena are occurring. Under what conditions, for example, is affection toward another person a manifestation of underlying hate as opposed to love? The vagueness of psychoanalytic terminology is partly a function of the style of language in which the theory is written—that is, in narrative form, much like a story, which easily lends itself to the use of metaphorical language.

Psychoanalytic theory can be interpreted on at least two levels, the literal and the metaphorical. For instance, the id is spoken of *as if* it were a little person inside us. Here it is fairly clear that Freud did not expect others to interpret his writing literally. What, however, of the description of the Oedipus complex? Did Freud literally mean that every four-year-old boy wants to have sexual intercourse with his mother? Or was the description of the Oedipal situation to be taken as an analogy of a complex rivalry between children and their parents (cf. Fromm and other post-Freudians [Mullahy, 1948])?

As a result of the imprecise terminology, many critical questions cannot be answered because there is no way to measure or quantify

PSYCHOANALYTIC CONCEPTS ARE VAGUELY DEFINED

such relevant concepts as libido, cathexis, fixation, conflict, resistance, and transference. How much libido must be invested at the oral stage for a person to be considered an oral character? How much threat of castration must children experience in order to repress sexual desire for their same-sexed parent?

Another level of definition of theoretical concepts involves finding reliable and valid measures for research. Much of psychoanalytic theorizing involves unconscious content and processes of which, by definition, the subject has no awareness. Although it is to the credit of psychoanalytic researchers that they have attempted to develop acceptable measures of "elusive" concepts, the task is extremely difficult, and to date such efforts have been relatively unsuccessful.

Consider two of the studies cited as evidence concerning the Oedipus complex discussed in Chapter 4. Johnson's (1966) finding that more women than men hoarded pencils, which could be construed as evidence for women's penis envy, is probably best viewed as a cute demonstration. Yet, the number of pencils—pencils are a clear-cut phallic symbol according to psychoanalytic theory—is at least an objective and reliable dependent variable. Most correlational and experimental investigations of psychoanalytic theory have employed dependent variables which require subjective judgments of one or more raters (Kline, 1972), and frequently agreement among raters (interrater reliability) is disappointingly low. If the obvious flaws in Johnson's experiment are ignored,[1] the major question then becomes whether pencil hoarding is a *valid* measure of penis envy. And this is the crux of the problem with which psychoanalytic researchers must contend. It is an issue in Sarnoff and Corwin's (1959) investigation of castration anxiety and the fear of death, one of the few controlled experiments involving psychoanalytic concepts (Kline, 1972; Silverman, 1976). Sarnoff and Corwin's findings are valid only if one accepts fear of death as a legitimate measure of fear of being castrated.

PSYCHOANALYSTS FAIL TO MAKE IMPORTANT LOGICAL DISTINCTIONS

When presenting the evidence for psychoanalytic theory, psychoanalysts often do not make three important logical distinctions. First, usually no distinction is made between observation and inference. The Oedipus complex is a prime example. Freud observed that at around age four, boys are affectionate toward and seek the attention of their mothers and, to some degree, avoid their fathers. To explain these *observations,* Freud conjectured that the boy's feelings for his mother were due to sexual desires and that his feelings for his father must

---

[1] At a minimum, Johnson could have controlled for hoarding behavior per se (which, interestingly, would be considered indicative of anal, rather than phallic, problems), as by passing out round or square erasers, which could not be considered phallic symbols, along with the pencils.

be related to the rivalry created by this sexual attachment and the implicit threat of castration. This *inference* has the status of a hypothesis, one alternative explanation, and nothing more. Thus, to say that four-year-old boys experience an Oedipus complex is, in effect, *replacing the observation with the inference.* It would, of course, be a different matter to say that four-year-olds exhibit behavior *consistent with* the Oedipus complex which Freud postulated. The fallacy of presenting inferences as observations when they represent nothing more than a possible explanation is especially acute because there is good evidence that theories other than those of psychoanalysis can provide at least as good and often better explanations of the observed facts (e.g., Sears, 1943).

Second, there is a confusion in psychoanalysis between correlation and causation. It is legitimate to report the observation that during the first year of life children engage in many behaviors involving the mouth (e.g., eating, sucking, crying) and are also dependent on other people for most of their needs. Oral behavior and dependency occur concurrently, and therefore they can be said to be correlated. However, on the basis of this observed relationship, it is not legitimate to conclude that dependency is based on orality (see Chapter 2 for a discussion of correlation and causation).

Psychoanalysis employs many analogies in describing its principles (e.g., troops left in battle, dammed-up libido, a mental censor of ideas), and herein lies a third logical error. Analogy is not proof. Although an analogy may help to describe a new or complex concept, it should not be alluded to as independent verification of the concept, which is frequently done in psychoanalytic writing. That military troops may be permanently lost for future battles in a difficult skirmish does not in any way validate the principle that libido is fixated at a stage in which the child has trouble resolving the relevant conflict.

PSYCHOANALYTIC CASE STUDIES ARE BIASED

The primary method of personality research in the psychoanalytic strategy is the case study, usually of a patient in psychoanalysis. The limitations of the case-study method have already been discussed in Chapter 2; in this section, some specific sources of bias which affect psychoanalytic case studies will be mentioned.

The psychoanalytic interview, essentially a private discussion, is inherently subject to bias. One of the earliest criticisms of Freud's work, provoked by his initial publications with Breuer, is that the confessions of patients in psychoanalysis may merely be responses to suggestions made by the analyst rather than reflecting the patient's private experiences.

Sherwood (1969) has provided a succinct description of the methodological problems that plague the psychoanalytic case study:

In such records dangers of distortion have been compounded. First, there is the analyst's influence upon patient's own statements, which remains a completely unassessable factor since verbatim records are not available. Second there is the selective nature of the analyst's recollections of the case and the possibility of his reconstructing earlier materials in the light of later observations. Thus the psychoanalyst's theoretical commitment can influence both the patient's utterances themselves and the manner in which they are organized, written up, and interpreted. Finally, almost all psychoanalytic case histories, in contrast to those standard for physical medicine, do not differentiate between exposition of the case—including chief complaint, present illness, and personal history—and diagnosis, etiology, pathogenesis, and prognosis. (p. 71)

Houts (1981) found that psychoanalytically oriented therapists were more likely to be "totally committed" to their theoretical viewpoints than either cognitive or behavior therapists. This commitment may make analysts especially susceptible to some of the distortions mentioned by Sherwood. The evidence certainly suggests that practicing psychoanalysts overrate their ability to make certain kinds of judgments. For example, Hall and Closson (1964) had experienced psychoanalysts listen to recorded segments of psychoanalytic sections and judge whether they believed the patient was seated or on the couch. The analysts expressed confidence that they had successfully discriminated between the two situations, but, in fact, their performance did not exceed chance.

There is, in fact, evidence to suggest that analytically oriented therapists are somewhat more likely to succumb to observer bias than are therapists of other persuasions (Langer & Abelson, 1974; Weiss, 1972). For example, Langer and Abelson (1974) conducted an experiment in which clinicians with different orientations interviewed "patients" and "job applicants." The analysts were significantly more likely than the behaviorists to vary their clinical observations based on the labels alone, finding the "patients" more disturbed than the "job applicants."

Psychoanalytic evidence is also biased in the sense that it is based on a small and atypical sample of individuals, namely, those that have undergone analysis. Indeed, psychoanalysis is avowedly based on Freud's discoveries as a result of his own self-analysis (between 1895 and 1900), even though self-analysis was rejected by Freud as a technique for others. In all of his writings, Freud describes only 12 cases in any detail; and, at a theoretical level, he considered very few people suitable for analysis. Among the requirements, as Freud saw them were: maturity, courage, education, good character, and "a normal psychical state from which the pathological material can be mastered" (cited by Roazen, 1975, p. 137). Freud only saw people who met his requirements; his generalization to other groups is sheer speculation, not even based on psychoanalytic evidence!

Among those psychoanalyzed today, dramatic biases can be noted. They are typically young or middle-aged white adults with relatively high incomes (private psychoanalysis can easily cost $10,000 or more per year) who are considerably above average in intelligence and highly articulate. They are typically Jewish or Protestant, and almost never Catholic. They are also unusually psychologically minded. In a study of 100 people applying for analysis, fully half were themselves workers in mental-health fields (Knapp, Levin, McCarter, Wermer, & Zetzel, 1960). Furthermore, observation of this highly restricted sample is very limited. The subjects are observed in a psychoanalyst's office, stretched out on a couch, free-associating for 50 minutes. How typical is that of human behavior?

Psychoanalytic case studies usually contain a wealth of information about a patient, but rarely is any attempt at independent verification made. Either conscious or unconscious lying by the patient is certainly a possibility, not to mention the varying degrees of distortion due to forgetting, secondary elaboration, condensation, and similar mental processes which affect one's retrospective reports. Interestingly, the possibility of such erroneous or distorted data is less of a problem within the psychoanalytic strategy than in other personality strategies. This is because one of the basic assumptions of psychoanalysis is that all behavior is determined and has meaning. Theoretically, then, it should be possible to ferret out the truth from whatever the patient reports. Practically, however, this may not be done, and the result can be a major misinterpretation of the data. We have already mentioned the classic example of this, which occurred when, early in Freud's career, his patients reported that they had been sexually seduced as children. Initially, Freud took these reports at face value and based his theory of neurosis on them. Later, Freud realized that the seductions were fantasies, and this led to a major change in his theory.

If psychoanalytic investigations are based mainly on uncontrolled observations, then it is crucial that the analysis of the observations be reliable. For instance, two or more independent analysts scrutinizing the same data should arrive at similar interpretations. As it turns out, such agreement is infrequent. Dream interpretation is a prime example in that the same dream will often be interpreted in different ways by independent, highly competent psychoanalysts (e.g., Lorand, 1946; Schafer, 1950). The low reliability of psychoanalytic interpretations is partially due to the qualitative nature of the data and the interpretations. If these were quantified, even in the rudimentary sense of categorization, it might be possible to obtain more agreement.

The most severe critics have accused psychoanalysis of having a cult-like character, a condition which insulates it from the evidence and ensures the perpetuation of biases. Freud's followers have been called "a sect, with all of the prominent features of one, including a fanatical degree of faith, a special jargon, a sense of moral superiority, and a predilection for marked intolerance of opponents" (Sulloway, 1979, p. 460).

Certainly psychoanalysis is unique among personality theories in its zeal, and many analysts take the position that psychoanalysis cannot be properly grasped by those who have not themselves been psychoanalyzed. Freud explicitly advised his followers to treat their scientific critics as they would patients displaying resistance. He also was given to dramatizing the mission of psychoanalysis in a world hostile to the truths he had revealed. In 1912, Freud went so far as to form a secret committee of his most intimate associates; he gave each a specially made gold ring on which had been mounted engraved seals from his private collection of Greek antiques.

PSYCHOANALYTIC THEORY IS UNTESTABLE

One of the first criticisms to be leveled at psychoanalysis was that it "involves so many arbitrary interpretations that it is impossible to speak of proof in any strict sense of the term" (Moll, 1912, p. 190). Psychoanalysis was conceived as a reconstruction of the past based on clues gathered and analyzed in the present. It is retrospective, and, after the fact, all findings can be interpreted within psychoanalysis as substantiating the theoretical proposition being tested. Psychoanalysis has been called a "rubber sheet theory" because it can be stretched to cover any outcome. Suppose that the hypothesis under investigation is that people who are fixated at the oral stage are dependent in their relationships with others. If the results of the study show that oral characters are dependent, the hypothesis is obviously confirmed. If the study reveals that oral characters are independent, the hypothesis is also confirmed, because independence can be a defense (i.e., a reaction formation) against dependence. Finally, if oral characters are found to be both dependent and independent, then the hypothesis still can be said to receive support, because the behavior is a compromise between the drive and its defense.

Similarly, Freud postulated that all dreams serve to fulfill a hidden wish, yet not infrequently dreams are unpleasant and disturbing, and it is difficult to understand how such dreams can be wish fulfilling. Freud (1961) explained that these are counterwish dreams which are, at the same time, wish fulfillments in that they satisfy the person's masochistic inclinations. Present-day psychoanalytic researchers are no less guilty of such logically indefensible practices. For example, when Cooperman and Child (1971) failed to replicate some previous laboratory investigations on characteristics of oral and anal character types, they concluded: "Our finding . . . though *opposite* in direction to the findings of earlier studies, seems to be what the theory used in those studies would predict" (p. 59; italics added).

Some of the problems with projective techniques stem from the lack of standardization of procedures for administration, scoring, and interpretation. Subtle changes in the manner in which a projective technique is presented to the subject, including the relationship between the examiner and the subject, can lead to differing performance (e.g., Masling, 1960). In many cases, the scoring of projective techniques involves some subjective judgment on the part of the examiner, even when scoring consists of placing responses in already designated categories. Considerably more subjectivity goes into the interpretation of the responses once they have been scored, and it is not surprising that interpretations of projective techniques vary widely with the skill and experience of the examiner as well as between examiners of comparable ability. This implies that projective techniques may be as much a projection of the examiner's own biases, hypotheses, favorite interpretations, and theoretical persuasion as an indication of the personality characteristics of the subject (Anastasi, 1968). The existence of well-developed norms for use in the scoring and interpretation of projective techniques would certainly help with this problem, but few adequate sets of norms are available.

Several thousand studies (Buros, 1965, 1972) have been performed to assess the reliability and validity of projective techniques. However, there are few adequate studies which support their reliability. Agreement among scorers and internal consistency (agreement among the items or stimuli used with a given technique) is usually low. Reliability over time (retest reliability) has been shown to be equally poor when comparisons are made of an examinee's responses or of the themes based on those responses in two separate administrations. As an example of the latter finding, Lindzey and Herman (1955) gave the same subjects the TAT twice, but for the second administration they instructed subjects to write different stories. If the TAT were effectively assessing the subjects' personality dynamics, then the *themes* of the stories should have been the same for each subject in the two administrations even though the stories were different. However, no support for this hypothesis was obtained.

The case for the validity of projective techniques is also largely unsubstantiated by research. The findings of validity studies of techniques such as the Rorschach and the TAT have not been all negative, however. The predictive accuracy of a projective technique appears to be highest when the technique is being used to measure a particular personality characteristic (e.g., achievement motivation with the TAT; see Chapter 12) rather than to generate a general personality description. Nevertheless, a majority of the studies have produced inconsistent and inconclusive findings due to a host of methodological (e.g., Anastasi, 1968; Kleinmuntz, 1967) and statistical (e.g., Cronbach, 1949) problems. In one of the more common types of validity studies, experienced clinicians write personality descriptions about subjects based on the

PROJECTIVE TECHNIQUES HAVE LOW RELIABILITY AND VALIDITY

subjects' responses to a projective technique such as the Rorschach. The judges are "blind" with respect to any other information about the subjects. Not only has the agreement between the judges' descriptions been found to be low, but often the descriptions are so general as to be applicable to almost anyone.[2]

Projective techniques are used extensively in personality research and in applied clinical settings for appraisal and diagnostic purposes (Lubin, Wallis, & Paine, 1971). How is this possible, one might well ask, in light of our brief summary of the negative evidence regarding their reliability and validity? The continued popularity of projectives among personality researchers, particularly clinicians, has several possible explanations. Perhaps the simplest of these can be summarized in one word: *Tradition!* Projective techniques have the longest history and have received the most attention of all personality assessment instruments. It is difficult to discard such a huge investment of time and effort. Moreover, projective techniques are used primarily to measure unconscious motives, conflicts, and ideas, and, to date, few alternatives for assessing the unconscious have been developed. Thus, personality psychologists interested in studying the unconscious must rely on projective techniques as a major source of data. Since most of the negative evidence regarding projective techniques has been based on examinations of the criteria established for psychometric tests, the argument (noted in Chapter 6) that projectives are *techniques* rather than tests must be kept in mind. Related to this argument is the fact that there are certainly individual clinicians who can use projective data to make accurate predictions about a client's behavior. However, in these instances, the clinicians using the projective responses, and not the responses per se, account for the accuracy of the predictions (cf. Sarbin, Taft, & Bailey, 1960). Thus, the value of projectives "as clinical tools is proportional to the skill of the clinician and hence cannot be assessed independently of the individual clinician using them" (Anastasi, 1976, p. 586).

As a final criticism of projective techniques, there is some evidence that casts doubt on the basic assumption of the techniques, namely, the projective hypothesis (i.e., a person's responses to ambiguous stimuli will be a projection of his or her enduring personality characteristics). Rather than assessing underlying personality dynamics and motivational dispositions, projective techniques may be measuring perceptual and cognitive factors. Even if it could be demonstrated empirically that a relationship exists between responses to an inkblot and overt behavior, such as sexual activity, this would not necessarily mean that an underlying sexual drive is being measured and is the

---

[2] The description would include statements like those appearing in Demonstration 1–1.

cause of the sexual activity. An equally plausible explanation of the relationship, which has been supported by research findings (e.g., S. Epstein, 1966; Klinger, 1966; Murstein, 1963), would be that people who engage in more sexual behavior have more sexual thoughts.

We pointed out in Chapter 6 that, over his career, Freud felt his discoveries concerning the mind were much more important than his contributions to healing as a psychiatrist. According to Fisher and Greenberg (1975), "Freud never presented any data, in statistical or case study form, that demonstrated that his treatment was of benefit to a significant number of the patients as he himself saw" (p. 285). Nonetheless, since Freud's time, most psychoanalysts depend on their art for their livelihood, and so the question of the therapeutic efficacy of psychoanalysis continues to be hotly debated.

Psychotherapy research can be classified into two major categories: studies of the *process* (the procedures employed to bring about change) and studies of the *outcome* (the success of the procedures in bringing about change). There are very few quantitative studies of the essential elements of the psychoanalytic process, such as transference and interpretation (Luborsky & Spence, 1971). At least one investigation of psychoanalysts' interpretations of their patients' statements casts doubt on the necessity for interpretations in psychoanalysis (Paul, Gill, Simon, Fink, & Endicott, 1969, as cited in Luborsky & Spence, 1971). After listening to tape-recorded excerpts of patients' statements during psychoanalysis and then to the analysts' interpretations of the statements, judges rated the "goodness" of the interpretations. Although the judges were found to agree with one another as to the quality of interpretations, their agreement did not substantially decrease when the ratings were made of the interpretations alone—that is, without the patients' statements about which the interpretations were made! This finding does not negate the importance of interpretation in psychoanalysis; the study is only concerned with agreement on what good interpretations are. The finding does suggest, however, that if interpretations were shown to be a critical factor in psychoanalysis, then the interpretations need not be related to the content of the patients' verbalizations. This is in keeping with the common observation that people feel relieved when they are given an explanation for their problems, no matter what that explanation happens to be. That the therapist's interpretation is irrelevant to the patient's problem is at variance with the psychoanalytic assumption that interpretations *are* relevant.

Eysenck's (1952, 1961) classic summary of outcome studies of psychotherapy (which were predominantly psychoanalytic in nature) revealed that there is no substantial evidence that psychotherapy is more effective than no treatment at all. That is, the proportion of people

THE EFFICACY OF PSYCHOANALYTIC THERAPY IS QUESTIONABLE

who are rated by the therapists as improved (about two thirds) is no higher than the proportion of people who recover from their psychological problems without psychotherapy (a phenomenon called *spontaneous remission*). A more recent study of exclusively psychoanalytic therapy has also found that about two thirds of patients improve when therapists' ratings are the dependent variable (Feldman, 1968). Some writers (e.g., Bandura, 1969a) have pointed out that the two-thirds improvement rate for treated persons may actually be inflated because "dropouts" from therapy serve to restrict the sample of treated persons to those who are more likely to improve and because therapists are apt to overestimate their successes. At present, it appears that no evidence exists for the effectiveness of psychoanalysis over and above spontaneous remission rates. The present state of affairs is no different today than it was the year Freud died, when Myerson (1939) wrote: "The neuroses are 'cured' by . . . osteopathy, chiropractic, nux vomica and bromides, benzedrine sulfate, change of scene, a blow on the head, and psychoanalysis, which probably means that none of these has yet established its real worth" (p. 641).

It is true that some people are helped by psychoanalysis, and this fact raises the issue of the efficiency of the process. "Successful" psychoanalysis often takes *years* of intensive effort[3] (involving as many as four or five sessions per week), and it is not at all clear that such an expenditure of time (not to mention money) is worth the results obtained.

PSYCHOANALYSIS AND SCIENCE

The criticisms leveled against psychoanalysis in the present chapter have been made primarily from the standpoint of rigorous and generally accepted scientific standards. The possibility exists that psychoanalysis should not be judged according to such criteria. In fairness to Freud and his followers, it may be applicable to paraphrase the words (used in a different context) of Kenneth Clark (1970): "They care passionately for the truth, but their evidence is different from ours." Furthermore, Freud often considered calling psychoanalysis "metapsychology" (meaning that it goes beyond psychology), thereby removing it from psychology as the science of behavior. Indeed, in 1900 Freud wrote:

> I am not really a man of science. . . . I am nothing but by temperament . . . an adventurer . . . with the curiosity, the boldness, and the tenacity that belongs to that type of being. Such people are apt to be treasured if they succeed, if they have really discovered something; otherwise they are thrown aside. And that is not altogether unjust. (quoted in Jones, 1953, p. 348)

---

[3] The great length of time required for psychoanalysis may account in part for reports of favorable outcomes since spontaneous remission rates increase with the passage of time.

The dispositional strategy

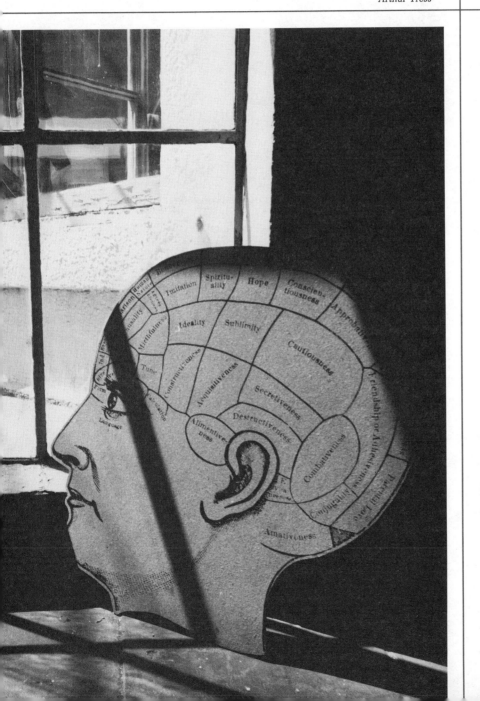

8 | *The dispositional strategy*

Introduction

"[He] has a special personal charm, a fine courage that dominated his physical weakness, great gifts as a conversationalist and a persistent gaiety that made for him warm friends" (Nisenson & DeWitt, 1949, p. 139). Reading this description gives us the feeling that we know something about the man described. There is a hint of the enduring qualities which set him apart from others and which might help us to identify him or what he will do in different situations. The description is of Robert Louis Stevenson. It might, of course, be applicable to many other people as well, and there is much that it does not tell us about Stevenson's personality. Still, we feel that it has told us something about his basic characteristics and about the way he was usually *disposed* to behave in social interactions.

This section considers the dispositional strategy for studying and understanding human personality. The major idea behind the strategy is that there are *enduring, stable personality differences which reside within the person.* One person differs from another in the way each is disposed to behave, according to this strategy. Put another way, people differ in what they are basically like. Perhaps it should come as no surprise that most writers view this as the oldest of the strategies, for describing people, groups, and even nations in dispositional terms seems almost to "come naturally." Therefore, before proceeding further, you may wish to try Demonstration 8–1. In it, you will be able to explore some of your own dispositional notions about human behavior and personality.

DESCRIBING PEOPLE IN DISPOSITIONAL TERMS

Demonstration 8–1

We are all accustomed to using dispositional notions in describing and attempting to explain people's behavior. These usually take the form "So-and-so is a _____ person" or "So-and-so acts that way because he or she is _____." For example, we might say that "Harry is a **meek** person" or that "Susan acts that way because she is **proud**."

The purpose of this Demonstration is to give you an opportunity to describe in dispositional terms people whom you know. It will allow you to compare the way in which you use dispositions to the way in which psychologists use the dispositional strategy. It will also serve as an introduction to some of the methods, predictions, and general findings of the dispositional strategy.

PROCEDURE

1. Take six sheets of lined paper and write one of the letters "A" through "F" at the top of each sheet. Then make a copy of the work sheet in Table 8–1 (this will be used later in the Demonstration).

2. You will need to designate a particular person of your **own sex** for each of the categories listed below. Write each of their names at the top of the appropriate sheet of paper.

A. Your same-sexed parent or, if you have never known this person, a close biological relative of the same sex (i.e., a "blood relative").
B. A close friend who is not related to you.
C. Someone with whom you are somewhat friendly (i.e., with whom you have a more casual relationship than with person B above).
D. Someone whom you know only in one specific context (e.g., a high school or college teacher).
E. A historical figure whom you admire.
F. Yourself.

3. Beginning with your same-sexed parent (i.e., person A), list all the adjectives you can think of that describe him or her. Write down as many or as few adjectives as seem necessary to describe the person fully. You need not put the adjectives down in any particular order. Repeat this procedure for the persons in categories B through F, in that order.

4. Starting with person A, look over the adjectives to see whether any of them are similar or redundant. (For example, "clumsy" and "awkward" have similar meanings.) When you are unsure, double-check with a standard thesau-

TABLE 8–1
Work sheet for Demonstration 8–1

Rank	Name	Number of adjectives used	Almost always 4	Fairly fre-quently 3	Occa-sionally 2	Rarely 1	Percent of similarity
				Pervasiveness			
	Self						
Know best 1st							
2d							
3d							
4th							
Know least 5th							
"∑" = Sum(total)		$\sum =$	$\sum =$	$\sum =$	$\sum =$	$\sum =$	
"M" = Mean		M =	%	%	%	%	

rus. *Condense any redundant adjectives either by eliminating one or more of the adjectives or by combining them* (e.g., clumsy-awkward). Repeat this procedure for persons B through F, in that order.

5. Starting again with person A, now rate each of the adjectives or adjective combinations according to the degree to which each is characteristic of the person. Use the following scale:

> 4 = *Almost always* characterizes the person.
> 3 = *Fairly frequently* characterizes the person.
> 2 = *Occasionally* characterizes the person.
> 1 = *Rarely* characterizes the person.

Write the scale number which is most applicable next to each of the adjectives or adjective combinations. Repeat this procedure for persons B through F, in that order.

6. *Rank* the people A through E (excluding yourself) in terms of how well you know them. The person whom you feel you know best should be given the "1st" rank, the person whom you feel you know second best should be assigned the "2d" rank, and so on until the person whom you feel you know least well has received the "5th" rank. Write the rank in the upper right-hand corner of each sheet.

7. In the first column of the work sheet (which you copied in step 1), write the names of the five people *other than yourself* (i.e., persons A through E) in order of the degree to which you feel you are familiar with them (see step 6). The person whom you ranked "1st" (i.e., the one you feel you know best) should be listed first, the person whom you ranked "2d" should be listed next, and so on.

8. On the work sheet, in the "Number of Adjectives Used" column, put the total number of adjectives or adjective combinations you have used to describe each of the persons (A through F).

Then, at the bottom of the column, put the total number of adjectives or adjective combinations used to describe all of the people *other than yourself* (i.e., sheet A through E). Divide this total by five to obtain the mean number of adjectives which you used to describe the other people and enter this in the appropriate space at the bottom of the work sheet.

9. In the "Pervasiveness" columns of the work sheet, record the number of adjectives for each person (A through F) which fall in each of the four categories. These are the numbers you wrote next to the adjectives in step 5.

Then, at the bottom of the column, put the total number of adjectives in each of the four pervasiveness categories for the five persons *other than yourself.*

Next, compute and record at the bottom of the work sheet the percentage of adjectives which fall into each of the pervasiveness categories. To do this, divide the total number of adjectives for each category by the total number of adjectives used to describe the other persons (i.e., combined across all categories) and then multiply by 100.

10. Looking at all of the sheets on which you have listed adjectives (i.e., A through F), check to see whether any of the adjectives are similar or redundant across persons. For example, if you described yourself as generous and

your parent as giving, these should now be condensed to one adjective, either by changing "generous" to "giving" or vice versa or by hyphenating the two adjectives where they both appear (e.g., "generous-giving"). Note that this step is similar to step 4, and a thesaurus may help you. On sheets A through E (i.e., every sheet except the one for yourself) *circle each adjective or adjective combination which is the same as one you have used to describe yourself* (on sheet F).

11. Compute the *percentage* of adjectives used for each of the other people (A through E) which corresponds to your own, and record it in the "Percent of Similarity" column (i.e., divide the number of adjectives which are the same for yourself and the other person—the ones you have circled—by the total number of adjectives used to describe the other person, and then multiply by 100).

DISCUSSION

You may have already noticed a number of interesting features and patterns in your use of dispositional descriptions for others and yourself. To lend some further order to your inspection of what you have done, we shall mention a few of the findings of dispositional psychologists which are related to the Demonstration and will be discussed in detail later in Section 3.

Number of descriptive adjectives used.   Gordon Allport was one of the first to examine the range of dispositional terms, or "trait names," which people use to describe others. He found that we often use a large number of adjectives for this purpose, but that many of them are synonymous. The number can therefore be reduced. To the extent that your own experiences in this Demonstration parallel Allport's findings, you would have been able to reduce the size of your initial lists of descriptive adjectives.

After condensing redundant adjectives, Allport found that most people actually use a fairly small number of adjectives in describing people they know, the usual range being between 3 and 10. Does your mean number of adjectives fall within this range? How does the number of adjectives you used to describe yourself compare with the mean number of adjectives you used to describe other people?

Dispositions and genetics.   Dispositional psychologists who take a biological view have found evidence suggesting that certain dispositions are transmitted genetically. Evidence of genetic dispositions might show up in this Demonstration in the degree of similarity between yourself and your parent ("Percent of Similarity" column of the work sheet). Is this similarity greater than the similarity between yourself and a close friend? A more casual acquaintance?

Relationship to people.   Many people believe that the closer one's relationship to someone, the "better" they know that person. Yet there is some evidence from psychological studies that we often feel more comfortable assigning dispositional adjectives to people whom we know less well.

Examine the relationship between the number of adjectives you used to describe a person and how well you feel you know that person. Since the five people other than yourself are listed on the work sheet in descending order of familiarity, you can look down the "Number of Adjectives Used" column to see whether a pattern emerges. Is "secondhand" information such as that which you used to describe the historical figure whom you admire sufficient to adequately characterize the person? How well were you able to describe the person you know in only a single context?

Generality of dispositions. Dispositional psychologists believe that there is a good deal of generality in human characteristics so that a person who acts in certain ways in one situation will also tend to act in those ways in other situations. One measure of whether you view people from a dispositional perspective is the number of adjectives you used to describe the person whom you know in only one context. Did you feel that you were able to describe this person's overall characteristics? Or did you feel that there were probably many characteristics of which you were unaware? In the former case, you would probably have used about the same number of adjectives as you did to describe a close friend.

Pervasiveness. Allport and others have noted that dispositions vary in the degree to which they seem to pervade a particular personality. Not very many people have dispositions which pervade all that they do and dominate their entire personality ("almost always" category), and we are not likely to ascribe characteristics to people which occur "rarely."

Other issues. You may find it useful to save these materials and to inspect them again as you read the chapters in this section. Even now, you might wish to consider some further analyses of your own. What are the qualitative differences among the adjectives you use to describe various individuals you know? What differences would you expect if you repeated the Demonstration, but described people of the opposite sex? Examining questions like these will help you to better understand the dispositional strategy for the study of personality.

Most people find Demonstration 8–1 an easy one, in the sense that we do often think of others in dispositional terms. One reason is that disposition labels serve lay people, just as they serve psychologists, as organizing concepts that may explain a person's voluntary behavior in a variety of diverse situations. Stagner (1976) gives this example:

> If a young man refuses an invitation to a party, drops a course that requires group discussion, and takes his vacation hiking alone in the mountains, we begin to get the idea that there is an inner consistency that involves the avoidance of situations that require close contact with other human beings. . . . The concept of a trait of seclusiveness, it seems to me, makes better sense as a unifying concept here than any situation-specific kind of interpretation. (p. 112)

The use of dispositional concepts to organize and explain the actions of others has been employed in one form or another for thousands of years. It is therefore both useful and interesting to take a brief look at some of the early dispositional ideas before describing in detail the approaches which make up the contemporary dispositional strategy.

EARLY DISPOSITIONAL CONCEPTS

Early dispositional views assumed that human beings could be divided into a relatively small number of *types,* according to their personalities, and that by knowing an individual's type, one could predict with reasonable accuracy the way in which that person would behave in a variety of circumstances. The ancient Hebrews used this perspective to conduct what may have been the first formal effort at personality assessment. In the following quotation from the Old Testament, it is apparent that this perspective was dichotomous, with the goal of describing only two types of people, those who could be ferocious fighters and those who lacked this quality.

> And the Lord said unto Gideon, The people that are with thee are too many for me to give the Midianites into their hands. . . . Now therefore go to, proclaim in the ears of the people, saying, Whosoever is fearful and afraid, let him return and depart early from Mount Gilead. And there returned of the people twenty and two thousand; and there remained ten thousand.
>
> And the Lord said unto Gideon, The people are yet too many; bring them down unto the water, and I will try them for thee there. . . . So he brought down the people unto the water: and the Lord said unto Gideon, Every one that lappeth of the water with his tongue, as a dog lappeth, him shalt thou set by himself; likewise every one that boweth down upon his knees to drink. And the number of them that lapped putting their hand to their mouth, were three hundred men: but all the rest of the people bowed down upon their knees to drink water. And the Lord said unto Gideon, By the three hundred men that lapped will I save you, and deliver the Midianites into thine hand: and let all the other people go every man unto his place. (Judges 7:2–7)

A second ancient view, the *theory of the four temperaments,* is closely akin to several contemporary theories and to a goodly number of everyday conceptions of personality. The position has as its basis the Greek hypothesis that the physical universe can be described in terms of four basic elements: air, earth, fire, and water. Hippocrates, often called the "father of medicine," extended this argument to people themselves by suggesting that the body is composed of four corresponding "humors": blood, black bile, yellow bile, and phlegm. Galen later postulated that an excess of any of these humors led to a characteristic temperament, or "personality type": sanguine (hopeful), melancholic (sad), choleric (hot tempered), or phlegmatic (apathetic). Although this ancient psychophysiological theory of personality is no longer taken seriously, the four temperaments have survived to this day as part of our language.

Conspicuous even to the ancients, however, was the fact that there are clearly more than four types of people. Thus, extensive catalogs of types emerged. The notion of identifying types of people continued, with only minor changes, as the popular conception of personality for thousands of years. Among the most striking of the modifications that did appear was the hypothesis that one could guess a person's behavior and personality from his or her physical appearance. In William Shakespeare's play *Julius Caesar,* for example, Caesar advises Marcus Antonius:

> Let me have men about me that are fat;
> Sleek-headed men, and such as sleep o' nights.
> Yond Cassius has a lean and hungry look;
> He thinks too much: such men are dangerous.
>
> (act 1, scene 2)

The belief advanced by Shakespeare's Caesar is still rather popular today; for instance, many people believe that they can identify a "criminal type" by physical appearance.

ASSUMPTIONS OF THE DISPOSITIONAL STRATEGY

Three major assumptions are common to all of the theories and viewpoints that fall within the dispositional strategy. They are that dispositions are relatively stable and enduring within the individual, that dispositions have at least a degree of consistency and generality, and that individuals differ in their dispositions.

Relative stability of dispositions

If persons are truly disposed to act or respond in particular ways, then personalities should display at least some stability over time. However, dispositional psychologists often caution that this assumption must be understood in the light of several further distinctions.

For one thing, most dispositional psychologists distinguish between an individual's enduring dispositions (for example, *traits*) and various temporary dispositions, or *states,* that result from such transient conditions as fatigue, stress, or sudden changes in fortune. In the case of anxiety, for example, Spielberger (Spielberger, 1966; Spielberger & Gorsuch, 1966) draws a distinction between trait anxiety, or A-trait, "the disposition to respond [with anxiety] to situations that are perceived as threatening," and the state of anxiety, "a condition of the organism characterized by subjective feelings of apprehension and heightened autonomic nervous system activity" (Spielberger & Gorsuch, 1966, p. 33). Trait anxiety is therefore anxiety proneness, but a person high in A-trait will not necessarily be anxious all the time, and a person low in A-trait may exhibit state anxiety under highly stressful conditions.

Equally important, dispositional psychologists point out that a disposition is a higher-order abstraction or general mode of functioning which may take different concrete behavioral forms as the individual matures or as new skills develop and old ones fall into disuse or take on different functions. Thus, before determining whether or not an individual's behavior has remained "stable" over time (and therefore supports a dispositional view of the person), one must know what kind of stability to look for. Dispositions are not merely habits; they reflect instead a kind of inner consistency that may escape a simplistic analysis of overt acts.

This point is well illustrated in an article by Lewis (1967) titled "The Meaning of a Response, or Why Researchers in Infant Behavior Should Be Oriental Metaphysicians." Briefly, Lewis was interested in the consistency of infants' responses to frustration, which he measured in a group of babies at 1 month of age and then again when his subjects were 12 months old. At 1 month, the frustration experience involved removing a nipple from the infants' mouths for 30 seconds; at 12 months, a physical barrier blocked the youngsters from reaching either their mothers or some attractive toys. On the "obvious" measure of response to frustration, crying, it was found that responses to the two situations were negatively related. The babies who cried at 1 month were *not* the ones who cried at 12 months. However, as Lewis points out, this inconsistency should not allow a deeper consistency to be masked, namely, that some of the babies were consistently *active* and others consistently *passive* in their response to the two frustrating experiences. At one month, when its motor skills are not yet developed, the active baby can do nothing but cry—which it does. But at 12 months, at which age crying is a relatively passive response, the active babies did not cry; they took some physical action to try and change the situation.

Consistency and generality of dispositions

A second assumption of the dispositional strategy, related to the first, is that dispositions have *some* consistency and generality within the person. The terms *consistency* and *generality* both refer to the assumed breadth of the effect of dispositions on behavior. A man who is ambitious in his work is also likely to be ambitious and striving in his play (e.g., at golf or sailing) and will probably have high ambitions for his children as well. On the other hand, it is important to note that though the dispositional strategy expects some consistency and generality, it does not expect perfect consistency.

One reason that dispositions are not expected to manifest themselves all the time or in every situation is that a person has many dispositions and characteristics, and a somewhat different set may be brought into play, depending on task demands and circumstances. That is, one disposition can serve as a "moderator" for another. Kipnis (1971), for example, found that the effects of impulsiveness on academic performance was moderated by the person's intellectual ability. Among those with above-average intelligence, persons who were impulsive appeared to do less well academically because of their impulsiveness, but impulsiveness was unrelated to academic performance among those below the average in intellectual ability.

As we shall see, one of the major criticisms of the dispositional strategy has focused on the lack of empirical evidence demonstrating that personality traits are stable over time and across situations. At the forefront of this group of critics stands Walter Mischel (1968, 1969), who has argued that "the behaviors which are often construed as stable personality trait indicators actually are highly specific and depend on the details of the evoking situations and the response mode employed to measure them" (1968, p. 37). Dispositional theorists have since cast considerable doubt on Mischel's conclusions, however. Block (1977) has demonstrated, for example, that many of the studies chosen by Mischel as demonstrating inconsistency were in fact flawed by inadequate methodological construction. More recently, Atkinson (1981) has suggested that these criticisms can be adequately handled by a more sophisticated motivational approach. As will become clear in Chapter 13, however, this problem still remains one of the greatest liabilities of the dispositional approach.

From the time they are born, infants differ in the vigor and tone of their responses to the environment, both frustrating and rewarding (Diamond, 1957; Marquis, 1943). Similarly, one can see clear differences in abilities, interests, and social responses even among adults who come from the same background or group. A major assumption of the dispositional strategy is that these individual differences arise from the fact that persons differ in the strength, the amount, and even the number of the dispositions they possess. Thus, the most fascinating and important fact about human beings—that we do not all think or act alike—is explained by saying that we differ in what we *are,* or at least that it is useful to view things that way.

Individual differences

Human behavior can be ordered and divided on a nearly infinite number of dimensions. We can speak of someone as a happy person, an aggressive person, a person who needs to be loved, a benevolent person, a stingy person, and so on. Which of these dimensions are important? Which are most likely to meet the assumptions of the dispositional strategy?

Although, as Demonstration 8–1 reveals, most people tend to describe themselves and others with a relatively small number of dispositions, the total number of traits, types, motives, needs, and characteristics that have been suggested as human dispositions is truly vast. Modern dispositional psychologists have therefore been searching for a set of

IDENTIFYING PERSONALITY DISPOSITIONS

underlying personality dimensions from which all the other trait-like characteristics of a person can be derived and on which one person can be compared with another.

The search is not unlike one undertaken in years past by psychologists interested in visual perception and color vision. These earlier investigators sought to identify the "primary colors" from which all others could be derived by appropriate combinations and mixtures. It is now known that just three colors of light—red, green, and blue—can be used to produce any one of the vast array of colors that can be seen by a normally sighted person. Many dispositional psychologists believe that personality can also be cast into a small set of primary, or underlying dimensions from which all the others can be derived, though, of course, there will not necessarily be three of them. For example, the ancient type theories, which assumed that there are a small number of types, each having a number of more specific characteristics associated with it, constitute an early effort at this kind of simplifying, reducing approach. A number of more modern theories have done the same, as we shall see.

In principle, there are three possible ways to go about identifying the dimensions of personality which are most likely to be significant psychological dispositions. Such dimensions can be anticipated from a theory, distilled from common lore, or searched for empirically. Generally, dispositional psychologists have not begun with theories telling them which dimensions to look for; only a few dispositionalists, such as Gordon Allport, have tried to take advantage of common lore. Instead, most dispositional psychologists have favored the empirical approach, carefully searching for dispositions, like prospectors sifting for a find.

Even with this empirical emphasis, however, there are two decisions made by dispositional theorists largely on the basis of their own preferences or intuitions. One decision is to differentiate between dispositions that are *expressive*, that is, characteristic of the individual (e.g., he *is* submissive), and those that are *dynamic*, arising from forces or motivations within the individual that direct his or her thoughts and actions (Hogan, DeSoto, & Solano, 1977; Liebert & Spiegler, 1974). In Chapters 9 and 10 we shall describe the search for expressive dispositions in human personality. Then, in Chapter 12, after a discussion of personality testing (Chapter 11), we shall turn to the dynamic approach to dispositions, which is based on the concepts of need and motive.

The other decision is to search either for a large number of limited components of personality or for a smaller number of *typical* dispositional clusters that occur frequently. The former approach gives rise to *trait* theories, and the latter to *type* theories. One convenient way to think about the distinction is that people can have a number of traits but can fit only one type. In either case, however, the disposition will retain the scientific status of an abstraction, synthesized and inferred from diverse sources of information about persons.

Regardless of whether a dispositional psychologist proposes a type, a trait, a need, or a motive, some fairly clear indicators, or criteria, can be used to test whether a given dimension, a prospective psychological disposition, will be useful. One such indicator involves meeting the assumptions of consistency and generality. But consistency and generality are not sufficient. The dimension must also clearly discriminate between or among people. If everyone were happy (or aggressive or ambitious), then this dimension would be of little use as a psychological disposition, for we could not use it to predict or explain any of the *differences* in behavior among people. Dispositional approaches are, in fact, very much psychologies of "amount," and dispositions which do not make it possible to say that people have more or less of some durable characteristic add no predictive power.

The dispositional strategy has employed almost all of the major personality assessment techniques. For example, interviews as well as projective and situational tests of various sorts have been used to identify the presence of various characteristics. However, one general type of assessment, written reports and descriptions of behavior, has played a central role in most dispositional assessment enterprises. It includes a wide range of "paper-and-pencil" self-report tests (see Chapter 11) and also "reputational" reports in the form of descriptions provided by an assessee's friends, acquaintances, and, sometimes, his or her biographers.

Because dispositions are theoretical constructs, it is not possible to measure them directly. Instead, the personality researcher who adopts the dispositional strategy must devise measures of behavior, often self-report inventories, which yield signs or indicators of various underlying dispositions. At the same time, it is presumed that there is no one "absolute measure" of a disposition: in fact, there should be several different indices. The dispositional psychologist

> explains the behavior of an individual by the values assigned him on dimensions considered relevant to the behavior in question. These values may be expressed numerically as scores on a test, or they may be represented by labels that stand for different positions on the dimension. A psychologist might, for example, explain an individual's pattern of deference to certain people and hostility to others in terms of authoritarianism, by saying that he is an authoritarian type of person. Or the psychologist might predict a person's success as a business executive from his scores on measures of intelligence, aggressiveness, and sociability. The use of

DISPOSITIONAL PERSONALITY ASSESSMENT

these and other dimensions implies that the values obtained on them by individuals have consequences over a fairly wide realm of behavior and that these dimensions exist independently of any single method of measurement. Therefore, although a particular test may be the one most frequently used in the measurement of some dimension, it is assumed that there may be other, equally valid measures. Like other theoretical constructs, dimensions are inferred; their definition rests not on any single set of operations but on the *convergence* of a set of operations. (Levy, 1970, p. 200)

A related characteristic of the dispositional approach to assessment is that it assumes an *additive* model of personality (cf. the nonadditive model of the psychoanalytic strategy; see Chapter 3). The strength of various dispositions is assumed to be the "sum" of various individual response tendencies. For example, a person who likes to meet strangers, easily approaches teachers to dispute grades on examinations, *and* is often outspoken in class discussions would be considered somewhat more extroverted than a person who likes to meet strangers and argue about grades but prefers not to play a prominent role in large-group discussions.

A good example of what is meant by using trait indexes additively to infer a disposition is found in the work by Robins (1966), who used a combination of aggressive symptoms in childhood to predict adult criminal behavior. Robins found that adding up all the early signs and symptoms suggesting the child's disposition toward aggression predicted later criminal behavior considerably better than did the occurrence of any single aggressive or delinquent act during childhood.

Convergent and discriminant validity

The foregoing remarks are related closely to some of the more formal criteria for measuring the adequacy of an assessment procedure. Specifically, since the appearance of a classic article by Campbell and Fiske (1959), the ultimate criterion for dispositional measurement has been the development of instruments having both *convergent* and *discriminant* validity. The terms are technical, but the idea itself is straightforward. Even if measures of what is presumably the same disposition are quite different in form (e.g., paper-and-pencil, projective, situational), they should *converge* and thus correlate highly with one another; on the other hand, tests designed to measure different dispositions should *discriminate* between them and thus *not* be highly correlated.

As a final remark about dispositional assessment, it should be noted that dispositional psychologists typically believe that their measuring instruments are imperfect and thus will include error, or "noise," as well as true information about the disposition which is being measured. Part and parcel of this belief is the assumption that estimates of the stability and generality of dispositions, based as they are on imperfect measurements, probably *under*estimate the actual stability and generality of the underlying dispositions.

Dispositional personality research is concerned with four major problems. One, as we have just implied, involves an effort to identify the underlying dimensions of personality. A second is the origin of various individual differences, especially as these may be found in the individual's genetic endowment or early life experiences. Third, dispositional researchers try to determine the reliability and validity of various personality and ability tests and to determine the usefulness of such instruments for purposes of prediction. Finally, a recent trend in dispositional research is to recognize that all dispositions are modulated by "the sociocultural framework, immediate situational demands and opportunities, the individual's changing skills, interests, moods, and so on" and therefore to try to understand more fully the nature of the interaction between the situation and the person (Inkeles & Levinson, 1969, p. 426).

Recall that, in discussing the psychoanalytic strategy, we noted how the approach had dictated that the predominant method of research would be the case study. The dispositional strategy also dictates that one method of research will predominate—the correlational method. The dispositional researcher is interested in how well various behaviors go together, for only when a number of different behaviors are related can one speak of an underlying personality disposition which may be controlling them.

Unlike the other three personality strategies discussed in this book, the dispositional strategy has little to say about personality change and is not associated with any form of therapy. There are at least two reasons why this is so. First, it follows logically that any psychologist who emphasizes the stability of personality would view personality change as a difficult—if not impossible—enterprise. Second, many of the psychologists associated with the dispositional strategy have had their strongest links with the academic world rather than with clinical endeavors. The practical contributions of dispositional psychologists have focused on the measurement and prediction of behavior rather than on its control. That is, the dispositional psychologist often uses measurement to find a situation for which the person is already well suited, rather than using psychotherapy to modify the person to fit the situation he or she is in. If people are disposed to be very aggressive, it may be wiser to keep them away from aggression-provoking situations than to try to change them into people who turn the other cheek when provoked.

DISPOSITIONAL RESEARCH

DURABILITY OF DISPOSITIONS AND THE POSSIBILITY OF PERSONALITY CHANGE

While the dispositional strategy has not itself been associated with efforts to change personality, some of the individual psychologists discussed in this section have been actively interested in personality change techniques based on one of the other strategies. The dispositionalist David McClelland, for example, has developed an imaginative program for altering one disposition, the need to achieve (see Chapter 12).

9 *The dispositional strategy*

Biological views of personality

A person's psychological dispositions might come from many sources. The theoretical viewpoints and investigations described in this chapter all try to draw some link between biological aspects of the person, such as genes, physical constitution, or other bodily attributes, and his or her personality and behavior. In this sense, the chapter is directly concerned with the biological underpinnings of personality. It should be noted clearly at the outset, however, that *almost no one thinks that all of personality can be explained in biological terms alone*. The question, instead, is whether any significant portion of personality can be explained in biological and/or constitutional terms. When the answer to this question appears to be yes, as has often been the case for, say, a person's genes, then the personality psychologist turns to a series of follow-up questions. To what extent does a particular biological factor account for personality? What processes explain the link between biology and personality? Do biological factors limit the degree to which an individual personality can be changed, and, if so, what is the nature and extent of these limitations?

THE LOGIC OF THE BIOLOGICAL APPROACH

The basic argument underlying the biological approach to personality is that *there are differences in the physical constitution of individuals, and that often these differences cause differences in behavior*. It is apparent that the assertion, if viable, has far-reaching consequences for both predicting and understanding individual differences in personality.

The essence of this view was concisely set forth by Williams (1967) in an essay on "The Biological Approach to the Study of Personality." His argument consists of five main points.

First, there are obviously *interspecies* (comparison of one species to another) biological differences, which suggests the existence of *intraspecies* (within the species) differences.

> It is beyond dispute, of course, that dogs, cats, rats, and monkeys, for example, show species differences with respect to their patterns of conditionability. Stimuli which are highly effective for one species may be of negligible importance for another. If hereditary factors make for inter-

species differences, it is entirely reasonable to suppose that intra-species differences exist for the same reason. (p. 22)

Second, intraspecies differences have regularly been found in experimental work with animals. Ivan Pavlov, in his pioneering animal experimentation, placed great emphasis on conditioning behavior. Williams argues, however, that a major aspect of Pavlov's findings is the pervasive suggestion of constitutional differences among his dogs, an aspect of his research rarely cited by behavioral psychologists.

> Pavlov found as a result of extensive study of many dogs that they often exhibit innate tendencies to react differently to the same stimulus. He recognized in his dogs four basic types: (1) excitable, (2) inhibitory, (3) equilibrated, and (4) active, as well as intermediate types. (p. 21)

Third, there is an impressive battery of evidence that humans show intraspecies differences in their biological and hereditary makeup. For example:

> normal stomachs vary greatly in shape and about six-fold in size. . . . Arising from the aortic arch are two, three, four, and sometimes five and six branch arteries. . . . each person exhibits a distinct breathing pattern as shown in the spirograms of different individuals under comparable conditions. . . . The morphology of the pituitary glands which produce eight different hormones is so variable, when different healthy persons are compared, as to allow for several fold differences in the production of individual hormones. . . . the male sex glands vary in weight from 10 to 45 grams in so-called "normal" males. (p. 23)

Fourth, behavioral indexes of these physiological differences also exist and frequently show up in basic research on the ability of humans to discriminate between stimuli.

> Investigations involving "cold spots," "warm spots," and "pain spots" on the skin indicate that each individual exhibits a distinctive pattern of each. In a relatively recent study of pain spots in 21 healthy young adults, a high degree of variation was observed. . . . One young man, "A," showed 7 percent of the area tested to be "highly sensitive," while in another, "B," the right hand showed 100 percent "highly sensitive" areas. On A's hand, 49 percent of the area registered "no pain" under standard pain-producing test conditions. On B's hand, however, there was no area which registered "no pain." (pp. 23–24)

Fifth, Williams concludes that there should be a greater integration of this pattern of findings and reasoning into psychological research.

> It seems indefensible to assume that people are built in separate compartments, one anatomical, one physiological, one biochemical, one psychological, and that these compartments are unrelated or only distantly related to each other. Each human possesses and exhibits unity. Certainly anatomy is basic to physiology and biochemistry, and it may be logically presumed that it is also basic to psychology. (pp. 22–23)

The biological-type approaches to personality which will be discussed next are in agreement with this conclusion.

In 1921, Ernst Kretschmer, a German psychiatrist, published a volume titled *Physique and Character.* In it were found the rudiments of the first modern biological-type approach to personality. Instigated by observations made in his clinical practice, Kretschmer investigated the relationship between physique and mental disorder. He proposed three fundamental types of physique: the *asthenic,* a fragile, narrowly built physique type, the *athletic,* a muscular type, and the *pyknic,* which was characterized by plumpness. Other, more unusual types were lumped together in the *dysplastic* category (see Figure 9–1). After examining approximately 400 psychiatric patients, Kretschmer and his colleagues concluded that, while persons of pyknic build are most likely to be diagnosed as manic depressive (i.e., to experience alternating periods of elation or sadness), the remaining types were more likely to be schizophrenic (i.e., to suffer from thought disorders). Some of the data reported by Kretschmer are summarized in Table 9–1.

Following Kretschmer's lead, an American psychologist named William Sheldon (1942) attempted to relate physique to behavior falling within the normal range. Sheldon's first step was to develop taxonomies of physique and temperament. Like Kretschmer, he identified three components of body structure which he chose to call *endomorphy* (the plump type), *mesomorphy* (the muscular type), and *ectomorphy* (the frail type) (see Figure 9–2). Unlike Kretschmer's approach, however, Sheldon's scheme did not classify persons as one type or the other. Rather, he developed a system of somatyping through a seven-point rating system, with each individual being rated for the presence of all three body types. In somatyping, the first numeral refers to endomorphy, the second to mesomorphy, and the last to ectomorphy. Thus, a muscular, powerful person might approach the somatype 1–7–1, whereas an individual of average build might be somatyped 4–4–4.

Sheldon further identified three components of temperament, *viscerotonia, somatotonia,* and *cerebrotonia,* each of which was composed of 20 traits. The nature of these components can be seen in the short form, having 10 traits for each component, of Sheldon's Scale of Temperament, which is reproduced in Table 9–2 (page 178).

After developing taxonomies of physique and temperament in this manner, Sheldon sought to determine the nature of the relationship between the two. Two hundred white males were selected as subjects and were somatyped, after which they were rated for the three components of temperament for a five-year period. The results were striking. Each of the three body types was positively related to one and only one of the temperamental components and negatively related to the

**THE EARLY WORK
OF KRETSCHMER
AND SHELDON**

FIGURE 9–1
The four body types identified by Kretschmer

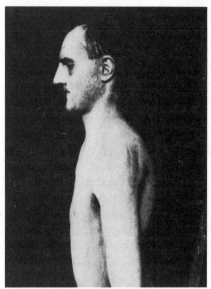

Asthenic

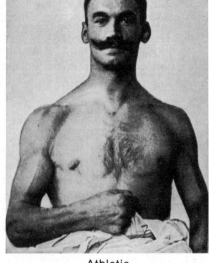

Athletic

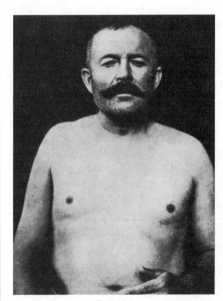

Pyknic

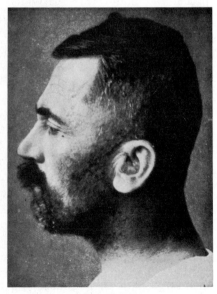

Dysplastic

Source: Kretschmer, E. *Physique and character: An investigation of the nature of constitution and of the theory of temperament* (W. J. H. Sprott, Trans.). New York: Harcourt, 1926.

TABLE 9–1
The relationship between physique and psychiatric diagnosis

	Schizo-phrenic (%)	Manic-depressive (%)	Total (%)
Asthenic and athletic	91.2	8.8	100.0
Pyknic	6.5	93.5	100.0

Source: Adapted from Kretschmer, E. *Physique and character: An investigation of the nature of constitution and of the theory of temperament* (W. J. H. Sprott, Trans.). New York: Harcourt, 1926.

FIGURE 9–2
A comparison of a predominant endomorph, mesomorph, and ectomorph with a man of average physique

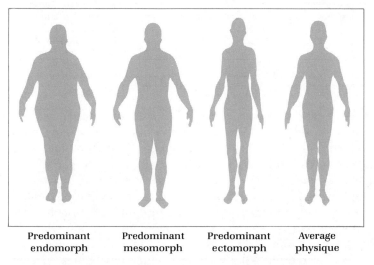

| Predominant endomorph | Predominant mesomorph | Predominant ectomorph | Average physique |

Source: Drawn from Sheldon, W. H. *The varieties of temperament: A psychology of constitutional differences.* New York: Harper & Row, 1942.

others: Endomorphy was associated with viscerotonia, mesomorphy was related to somatotonia, and ectomorphy was positively correlated with cerebrotonia. Sheldon therefore concluded that this strong association between physique and personality was probably due to the fact that they were both expressions of essentially common components.

If the value of a theory is to be inferred from the amount of research activity it generates, then the early theories of Kretschmer and Sheldon are quite valuable indeed. The search for relationships between body type and personality features was continued for many years. Shortly after Sheldon's work was published, Sanford, Adkins, Miller, and Cobb

Developments following Sheldon's work

TABLE 9–2
A short form of Sheldon's scale of temperament

I	II	III
Viscerotonia	*Somatotonia*	*Cerebrotonia*
Relaxation in posture and movement	Assertiveness of posture and movement	Restraint in posture and movement, tightness
Love of physical comfort	Love of physical adventure	Overly fast reactions
Slow reaction	The energetic characteristic	Love of privacy
Love of polite ceremony	Need for and enjoyment of exercise	Mental overintensity, hyperattentionality, apprehensiveness
Sociophilia	Love of risk and chance	Secretiveness of feeling, emotional restraint
Evenness of emotional flow	Bold directness of manner	Self-conscious motility of the eyes and face
Tolerance	Physical courage for combat	Sociophobia
Complacency	Competitive agressiveness	Inhibited social address
The untempered characteristic	The unrestrained voice	Vocal restraint, and general restraint of noise
Smooth, easy communication of feeling, extroversion of viscerotonia	Overmaturity of appearance	Youthful intentness of manner and appearance

Source: Adapted from Sheldon, W. H. *The varieties of temperament: A psychology of constitutional differences.* New York: Harper & Row, 1942.

(1943) compared school performance and personality tendencies in a group of normal children, finding that while tall, narrow body types did well in school and tended to suffer from guilt and remorse, wide, heavy children tended to be more secure. Others (Davidson, McInnes, & Parnell, 1957; Parnell, 1957), using Sheldon's somatypes, found ectomorphs to be meticulous and fussy as children and more likely to require psychiatric care, on the average, as adults. In their comparison of the predominant somatypes of a group of delinquent and a group of nondelinquent boys, Glueck and Glueck (1950, 1956) found that a much larger percentage of mesomorphs and a much smaller percentage of ectomorphs were delinquent than would be expected by chance (see Figure 9–3).

Another series of investigations dealt with the relationship between physique and occupation, and produced a good deal of objective evidence that physique is related to the type of occupation one pursues, as well as one's success in it. Students of engineering, dentistry, and medicine are more mesomorphic and less ectomorphic than are students who pursue physics and chemistry (Parnell, 1953); officer cadets are considerably more mesomorphic and less endomorphic than university students (Tanner, 1955); and, in one study, research workers were found to be more ectomorphic and less mesomorphic than were factory workers in the same organization (Garn & Gertler, 1950). Civilian air pilots are more mesomorphic than the general population is (McFarland, 1953), and the most successful wartime aviators seem to be the most mesomorphic (Damon, 1955).

FIGURE 9–3
A portion of Glueck and Glueck's comparison of the somatotypes of matched pairs of delinquent and nondelinquent boys. Among the delinquents there are more mesomorphs and fewer ectomorphs than would be expected by chance, a finding consistent with Sheldon's constitutional theory.

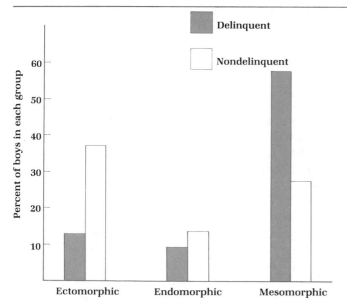

Source: From data published in Glueck S., & Glueck, E. *Unraveling juvenile delinquency.* New York: Commonwealth Fund, 1950.

What accounts for these associations? Tanner (1955) suggested four possibilities: (1) social background and early environment, (2) career selection along the lines of one's dispositions, (3) institutional selection, and (4) physical changes that occur in the person after beginning a particular career. Background and postjob changes do not seem to account for very much, however, and Tanner concluded that career selection and institutional selection are probably the most important factors. When a person seems to be "cut out" for a particular occupation by virtue of physical strength or even appearance, he or she may be attracted to that type of employment and may also be seen as attractive by relevant selection officers and employers.

What conclusions, then, can be drawn about these correlational studies of the relationship between physique and personality? Rees (1961) has summed it up this way:

> one might say that the evidence suggests that there are tendencies for different types of physique to be associated with certain psychological characteristics . . . but the majority of investigations do not report any correlations as high as those reported by Sheldon. . . . The available evidence suggests that the correlations between physical characteristics

and personality traits . . . are nearly always too small to be trusted for the needs of diagnosis. (p. 377)

It is thus clear that an individual cannot be psychologically "sized up" by body type with any degree of accuracy, although *on the average,* people with different body types do tend to show recognizable patterns of personality characteristics.

THE EXPERIMENTAL APPROACH

Almost all of the studies we have discussed so far in this section have been correlational, and they have disclosed little about any of the processes that may relate physique and behavior. We will now turn to the more systematic attempts to explore these processes through the experimental method, illustrated by the work of Stanley Schachter and his students and by investigators working in the area of the Type A behavior pattern.

Obesity and personality

Schachter first became interested in the relationship between obesity and personality after reading an early article by Stunkard and Koch (1964) which reported a high correlation between hunger and gastric contractions in normal, but not in obese individuals. For Stunkard and Koch the significance of this finding was clinical; reports of hunger by fat people are "biased," and physicians must be wary of taking them at face value. However, for Schachter, the finding had considerable theoretical significance, revealing not bias but basic differences in the degree to which gastric contractions are associated with feeling hungry in obese and normal individuals. But what was the meaning of the correlation? Did it reflect a more basic or more general type of individual difference among people? To answer these questions, Schachter and his students turned to the experimental method.

In one of the earliest experiments, Schachter, Goldman, and Gordon (1968) manipulated the variable of gastric contractions by asking both obese and nonobese individuals to skip a meal prior to their participation. In order to reduce the contractions, as well as other physiological hunger messages, half of the subjects were given roast beef sandwiches upon arrival at the lab, while the remainder were given nothing. The subjects were then asked to evaluate the taste characteristics of five types of crackers, each made available in abundance. Actually, the critical dependent measure in the study was not concerned with cracker ratings at all, but with how many crackers each subject ate. The results are shown in Figure 9–4, from which it can be seen that persons of normal weight consumed considerably more crackers when their stomachs were empty than when they were full. In marked contrast, "preloading" with roast-beef sandwiches did not reduce the number of

FIGURE 9–4
The effects of "preloading" with roast-beef sandwiches on the number of crackers eaten by Schachter, Goldman, and Gordon's normal and obese subjects. Note that the normal subjects, unlike the obese subjects, ate considerably more crackers when their stomachs were empty than when they were full.

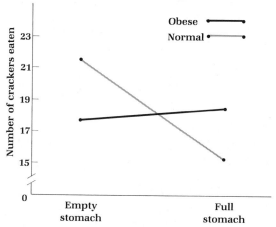

Source: Schachter, S. Some extraordinary facts about obese humans and rats. *American Psychologist*, 1971, *26*, 129–44.

crackers eaten by obese people; in fact, they ate slightly more when their stomachs were full!

In the years that followed, Schachter's group conducted a provocative series of experiments which explored this phenomenon further. One block of experiments involved manipulating time variables, and it was typically found that the eating behavior of overweight subjects was influenced more than that of normal people by the passage of time or by the amount of time that was thought to have passed (Rodin, 1975). These studies implied that while normal subjects ate only when they were hungry, overweight subjects were more reliant on external cues such as the time of day. Other researchers investigated the effects of the taste and sight of food on eating behavior, and found overweight individuals to be more responsive to these dimensions than were their normal peers (Nisbett, 1968; Price & Grinker, 1973). Nisbett (1968) further demonstrated that the number of visual food cues present differentially affected normal and overweight individuals, with obese subjects eating more as the number of cues increased.

On the basis of these and related studies, Schachter and Rodin (1974) proposed a dichotomy between internal and external control as explaining differences between overweight and normal people. In their view, fat people were seen as predisposed to the control of external stimulation of all kinds, while persons of normal weight were responsive to internal stimuli. This external responsiveness was clearly demonstrated by experiments such as those described above. The eating behavior of fat people was repeatedly found to be controlled by external cues, such as the sight, smell, and taste of food, while those of normal weight were not consistently affected by these variables.

Of course, this is not to imply that external responsiveness alone can fully explain obesity. As pointed out in a number of recent reviews (Leon & Roth, 1977; Rodin, 1980, 1981), the differences between obese and normal individuals are far more complex. For example, rather than demonstrating that overweight people are more responsive to external cues than are individuals of normal weight, the majority of recent studies have instead revealed that there are people in *all* weight categories who are highly responsive to these external stimuli (Rodin, 1980). Each of us can provide support for this finding from our own experience: consider the last time you walked by a bakery and were enticed by the smell of freshly baked bread. And yet, not all of us are obese. Clearly, other factors must be involved.

Most researchers currently working in the area of obesity therefore examine a number of variables in addition to external responsiveness. As pointed out by Rodin (1981), for example, recent studies have suggested that internal and external cues interact in the regulation of eating in ways that have yet to be clearly explicated. Krantz (1978) has suggested that what appears to be external responsiveness may in fact reflect attempts by the obese to behave in ways considered "socially appropriate," thereby pointing out the importance of social factors in obesity. Schachter and his colleagues therefore only touched the tip of the iceberg in demonstrating some of the external conditions that can lead to overeating and weight gain. Current researchers have begun to investigate the importance of other variables, as well, and now "generally see food-relevant behavior as a multiply regulated process that is influenced by interactions among physiological, cognitive, social, and cultural variables" (Rodin, 1981, p. 362).

The Type A behavior pattern

Clinicians have long noted that the personalities of people afflicted with coronary disease differ from those without heart problems, but it wasn't until the late 1950s that attempts were made to systematically examine the contribution of psychological and behavioral variables to the development of such problems. At that time two cardiologists, Meyer Friedman and Ray Rosenman, sent out a questionnaire to 150 businesspeople in the San Francisco area, asking them to indicate what complex of behaviors they had seen as preceding a friend's heart attack. More than 70 percent of those who responded claimed that "excessive competitive drive and meeting deadlines" were the most prominent characteristics of heart disease victims they had known. These and subsequent findings led Friedman and Rosenman to propose a complex of emotional reactions, which they labeled the Type A behavior pattern, as a major cause of coronary artery and heart disease (Friedman & Rosenman, 1974).

The Type A syndrome has since received considerable empirical validation. While the initial questionnaire survey by Friedman and Rosenman produced results of a strictly correlational nature, the major thrust of these early findings has since been supported and extended by a number of independent prospective and retrospective investigations. One of the earliest and most ambitious prospective studies, the Western Collaborative Group Study, followed the progress of over 3,500 men over a 15-year period (Rosenman, Friedman, Straus, Wurm, Kositchek, Haan, & Werthessen, 1964; 1970; Rosenman, Jenkins, Brand, Friedman, Straus, & Wurm, 1975). Using a structured interview procedure that has since been shown to be highly reliable, each individual's vocal response style and motor behavior, as well as the content of his responses, were scored to produce a behavior type rating. Reports of the incidence of coronary problems in those individuals who were unafflicted at the start of the investigation were subsequently obtained after periods of 4½, 6½, and 8½ years. The results have been quite compelling: those judged as evidencing the Type A behavior pattern at the study's start were 1.7 to 4.5 times more likely to suffer from coronary disease than were men judged to possess a more relaxed and easygoing behavior pattern (labeled Type B). Subsequent studies have replicated these findings (Bruhn, McCrady, & du Pleissis, 1974; Jenkins, Rosenman, & Zyanski, 1974).

The picture of the Type A individual that has emerged from the above studies has recently been summarized by Rosenman (1978):

> We conceive of Type A behavior pattern as being a particular action-emotion complex which is possessed and exhibited by an individual who is engaged in a relatively chronic and excessive struggle. More often than not this struggle is to obtain a usually unlimited number of things from the environment in the shortest possible period of time and/or against the opposing efforts of other persons or things in the same environment. . . . Major facets of Type A behavior are a chronic sense of time urgency and a striving, either by preference or necessity, to accomplish more and to be ever more involved in both vocational and avocational pursuits, despite an ever increasing lack of time. Type A's have an enhanced aggressiveness and drive that are usually associated with or evolve into competitive hostility. Type A behavior occurs when these traits are "activated." Thus it depends on the nature of the environmental stimuli, challenges and demands that confront susceptible individuals, and on both their interpretation and response to these environmental phenomena. (p. xv)

In contrast, the Type B individual is seen as having a relaxed approach to life situations and is rarely harried by desires to get or do more (although he or she may be ambitious). In short, the Type B behavior pattern is the psychological opposite of the Type A pattern (Friedman & Rosenman, 1974).

A number of experiments have confirmed the existence of many of these differences among individuals judged on the basis of interview or questionnaire responses to be Type A or Type B. Most notable in this area is the work of David Glass (1977a) who, for example, empirically demonstrated the existence of time urgency in Type A individuals by examining performance on a reaction-time task, during which he manipulated the length of the intervals between trials. Lengthy intervals were expected to arouse impatience in As, with consequent fidgeting and distraction from the task at hand. As Type A individuals responded more slowly than Type Bs when the intervals were long, while responding more quickly than Bs when the intervals were short, Glass interpreted the behavior of the Type A subjects as reflecting time urgency.

Glass (1977a) also confirmed the hostility component of the Type A pattern in another experiment. In this case, subjects were given the opportunity to administer what they thought to be electric shocks to individuals who had either ridiculed their efforts to perform a difficult task ("Instigation" condition), or to individuals whom they had never met. While, under the instigation condition, the Type A individuals reliably delivered higher levels of shock than they did under the no instigation condition, no such difference in shock intensity was found for Type B individuals. Thus, the aggressiveness mentioned by Friedman as characterizing the Type A individual was experimentally validated, and was elicited under the types of arousing conditions Friedman specified, as well.

The precise mechanisms through which Type A behavior leads to an increased risk of coronary disease have yet to be clearly specified, although several interesting models have been generated. Friedman and Rosenman (1974) reported following the serum cholesterol level of a group of accountants from January to June, with the finding that, as the April 15 tax deadline approached (and, presumably, as their sense of time urgency increased), so did their levels of serum cholesterol. They therefore proposed that Type A behavior induces biochemical changes that predispose the individual to coronary artery and heart disease. Williams and co-workers (Williams, Friedman, Glass, Herd, & Schneiderman, 1978) have reviewed evidence suggesting that both the lipid metabolism and neuroendocrine responses of Type A individuals differ from those of Type B individuals, implying that these differences may lead to increased risk of coronary difficulties. Alternatively, Glass (1977b) has conducted a number of studies suggesting that, while Type A individuals initially respond to uncontrollable stress with increased levels of catecholamines (compounds which are related to autonomic nervous system activity), they are also prone to give up frequently and intensely. Glass has proposed that this cycle of hyperreactivity and hyporeactivity may result in an increased likelihood of coronary problems.

But what of the origins of this behavior? Friedman and Rosenman (1974) originally suspected that there may be genetic influences at play in the development of this behavior pattern, possibly through the inheritance of an aggressive drive to achieve. Analyses of twin studies have not confirmed this suspicion, however, and it is currently believed that Type A behavior is not inherited (Cohen, Matthews, & Waldron, 1978; Rosenman et al., 1975). As pointed out by Glass (1977b), however, while Type A behavior itself does not show a strong genetic basis, it correlates about .50 with measured activity level. As we shall see later on in this chapter, activity level does have a strong hereditary component, so it may be that the behavior labeled Type A reflects a more basic genetic predisposition.

The suggestion that an individual's personality dispositions (as well as his or her physical characteristics) can be transmitted "through the blood" is well known. Is there support for such a belief? The ways of answering this question that at first seem "obvious" are fraught with difficulties.

Suppose that a man who is very capable verbally *and* very aggressive has three children. If all three of them were also verbal and aggressive, it would be commonly inferred that they had inherited these dispositions from their father. Yet it is equally possible that the transmission was social rather than biological; the children may have been exposed to a large vocabulary, books, and socially aggressive behavior and thus have *learned* these characteristics during the early years of life. To sort out the relative effects of heredity and environment, circumstances would somehow have to "hold one of them constant" so that the effects of the other could be detected. The *twin study method* of research appears to do just this.

Out of every 85 births, 1 is a multiple birth producing 2 children. Approximately two thirds of all twins are "fraternal," or, technically, *dizygotic,* meaning that they developed from separate ova and sperm. Fraternal twins share only a birthday with their "womb mates" and are otherwise no more alike genetically than are siblings born separately. The smaller remaining group, the "identical," or *monozygotic,* twins, consists of twins who have developed from the same ovum and sperm and consequently have the same genetic endowment. Identical twins have held a fascination for many people, both in and out of science, not only because of their statistical rarity but also because

THE GENETIC APPROACH

The twin study method

of their tremendous potential for helping us to investigate the extent to which hereditary factors influence behavior.

Twin research in personality involves two major assumptions. First, identical twins are genetically alike, whereas fraternal twins are not. Second, the social and environmental experiences of twins reared together are alike. Therefore, greater similarity on measures of personality between identical twins, as compared with fraternal twins, is a consequence of genetic contribution. Given this reasoning, the research strategy is one of selecting a good dependent measure of personality and determining the degree of *concordance* (similarity) among many pairs of twins who are either identical or fraternal.

Twin studies of abnormality and deviance

Perhaps the greatest accumulation of literature in this area has focused on the heritability of schizophrenia. One of the pioneers in this regard was Franz Kallman, a German psychiatrist who examined large samples of persons diagnosed schizophrenic and determined the percentage of twins also diagnosed schizophrenic (Jackson, 1960). His finding that concordance, or similarity in diagnosis, for schizophrenia was significantly higher for monozygotic than for dizygotic twins has since been replicated by a number of different researchers in the area (Fischer, 1973; Gottesman & Shields, 1966; Hoffer & Pollin, 1970). In a recent summary of available twin studies, Davison and Neale (1978) noted that reported concordance rates ranged from 2 to 14 percent for dizygotic twins, while the corresponding rates for monozygotic twin pairs ranged from 0 to 86 percent. Despite the fact that results have been somewhat variable, then, the suggestion that schizophrenia does have *some* genetic component is fairly compelling.

Investigators working in other areas have produced similar results. In his summary of the available studies of incidence of neurosis in the co-twin of neurotic individuals, for example, Rosenthal (1970) found a concordance rate of 53 percent in monozygotic twins as compared to 40 percent in dizygotic twins. In the area of depression, Zerbin-Rüdin (1968) found that when one monozygotic twin suffered from bipolar depression (characterized by episodes of both mania and depression), his or her co-twin also suffered from depressive illness in 70 percent of the cases. Price (1968), however, found a concordance rate of only 23 percent for depression in dizygotic twin pairs, suggesting that bipolar depression is in part genetically determined. As is the case with the studies of schizophrenia, however, none of the studies has reported concordance rates of 100 percent for abnormality in monozygotic twins, indicating that environmental influences are also significant in the development of these disorders.

Eysenck's (1964) investigation of the heritability of deviant tendencies also used the twin study method. Eysenck studied over 200 monozygotic and dizygotic twin pairs, and compared the degree of similarity within the twin pairs for different types of "social deviations." As indicated by Table 9–3, the monozygotic pairs were more likely than the dizygotic pairs to share a number of "deviant" characteristics, suggesting a strong hereditary influence in their development. Particularly striking was the finding that, without exception, homosexuality in one monozygotic twin was accompanied by a similar tendency in the other, while only 12 percent of the dizygotic twins were both homosexual. As with all of the findings produced with the twin study method, however, this finding is at best only suggestive. Perhaps the monozygotic twins, by virtue of their identical appearances, are raised in a more similar fashion than are dizygotic twins, thereby resulting in a greater degree of similarity. Perhaps homosexuality reflects certain child-rearing practices to which only the monozygotic twins were exposed. As these arguments apply to all the investigations described in this section, it is clear that while there appears to be some genetic component to various forms of abnormality and deviance, these findings alone are suggestive rather than definitive.

TABLE 9–3
Similarity of monozygotic and dizygotic twins for five different types of "social deviation," as reported by Eysenck. The data are based on 107 monozygotic twin pairs and 118 dizygotic twin pairs.

	Percentage similar	
	Monozygotic	*Dizygotic*
Adult crime	71	34
Juvenile delinquency	85	75
Childhood behavior problem	87	43
Homosexuality	100	12
Alcoholism	65	30

Source: Data reported in Eysenck, H. J. *Crime and personality*. Boston: Houghton Mifflin, 1964.

Twin studies of personality within the normal range

An early twin study of "normal" personality, hallmarked by the fact that it was more sensitive to methodological problems than were its predecessors, was reported by Gottesman in 1963. Gottesman began by enumerating *all* of the same-sexed twins enrolled in public high schools in the Minneapolis–Saint Paul area, thereby drawing his twin sample from a population of over 31,000 children. Voluntary cooperation of more than half of the twin pairs in this sample was then secured. Gottesman legitimately noted that his sample "compares favorably in size with the majority of twin studies reported in the psychological literature. In representativeness, it is superior to the majority" (p. 4).

The next problem was to determine with high certainty which of the pairs were monozygotic and which dizygotic. Previous researchers had failed to acknowledge that, despite the fact that a twin pair appears to be identical, the possibility remains that they are in fact dizygotic. To separate monozygotic from dizygotic twins, Gottesman therefore used the combined criteria of blood typing on nine blood groups, fingerprint ridge count, height and weight, and judgments by geneticists, psychologists, and artists. The probability of a chance likeness on all of these characteristics given that the twins were actually dizygotic, is about 1 in 200. Thus, Gottesman's procedure resulted in a high probability that he had successfully distinguished between monozygotic and dizygotic pairs. Furthermore, the 68 pairs were found by this assessment procedure to consist of 34 monozygotic pairs and 34 dizygotic pairs, precisely the estimate which would be made from prior knowledge of twin frequencies.[1]

The personality measures Gottesman used in his study were derived from three paper-and-pencil tests. The first was the Minnesota Multiphasic Personality Inventory (MMPI), which consists of 550 statements about oneself which must be answered true or false. The MMPI is typically scored for 10 clinical scales, each representing a personality trait (e.g., depression, social introversion-extroversion, and so on). The second test used was Cattell's High School Personality Questionnaire (HSPQ), which was specifically developed for use with persons between the ages of 12 and 17. Its 280 forced-choice items form 14 scales (also representing personality traits), which are said to "cover all the major dimensions involved in any comprehensive view of individual differences in personality" (Gottesman, 1963, p. 7). Finally, subjects' IQ scores were available.

On 5 of the 10 MMPI scales and on the IQ measure monozygotic twins were significantly more alike than were dizygotic twins. Paradoxically, though, this pattern did not hold up for the HSPQ where, in fact, the dizygotic twins were somewhat more alike. Overall, Gottesman's results seem to suggest *some* hereditary component on *some* measures of personality, and support for this view has continued to grow.

Loehlin and Nichols (1976) conducted one of the most extensive twin studies done to date. These investigators compared 514 pairs of monozygotic twins with 336 relatively comparable same-sexed dizygotic twins. The twin pairs were identified from the roster of almost 600,000 persons who, as high school students, had taken the National Merit Scholarship test in 1962, and included both opposite-sexed and

---

[1] Of the total population of twins, one third would be monozygotic and two thirds dizygotic. However, among the latter, *half* would be opposite-sexed. Thus, an equal number of monozygotic twins (who are, by definition, same-sexed) and same-sexed dizygotic twins would be expected.

same-sexed pairs. Each subject was administered a wide variety of personality, attitude, and interest tests and questionnaires, and the National Merit Scholarship test scores of the subjects were also available. What is most impressive about the sample, however, is that it represents the entire United States, rather than a single geographic region or ethnic group, and that it includes more than 5 percent of the entire U.S. twin population of the age group studied.

The major results of the study are shown in Table 9–4. As can be seen, Loehlin and Nichols' (1976) results support numerous earlier studies in that monozygotic twins were found to be more alike than dizygotic same-sexed pairs on a wide variety of measures of personality and ability. In addition, though this is not shown in Table 9–4, the same general pattern held for both male pairs and female pairs.

TABLE 9–4
Resemblance of monozygotic and dizygotic twin pairs in Loehlin and Nichols' study of 1,700 twins. The data shown are correlation coefficients.

Area measured	Monozygotic twins	Dizygotic twins
General ability	.86	.62
Special abilities	.74	.52
Personality scales	.50	.28
Self-concept clusters	.34	.10

Source: From data reported in Loehlin, J. C., & Nichols, R. C. *Heredity, environment, and personality.* Austin, Tex.: University of Texas Press, 1976.

Nonetheless, monozygotic twins are often treated more similarly than are dizygotic twins (Smith, 1965; von Bracken, 1934), a finding which is also true of this study. But Loehlin and Nichols (1976) were able to deal with this issue, at least in part, by performing an ingenious additional analysis. Specifically, they used information from parents and the subjects on similarity of treatment to ask two questions:

1. Were the monozygotic twins who were treated more similarly more alike than other monozygotic twins treated less similarly?
2. Were the dizygotic twins who were treated more similarly more alike than other dizygotic twins treated less similarly?

The answer to these questions was, in both instances, a clear no, which led the investigators to conclude:

> our data do indeed suggest that identical-twin pairs are subjected to environments that are in many respects more similar than those of fraternal pairs. But, in those same respects, variations in environmental similarity show negligible ability to predict personality resemblances *within* the two twin groups. Thus, either it is their greater genetic similarity that makes identical twins alike or it is environmental factors that are largely independent of such traditional ones as dressing alike, playing

together, being treated alike by parents, and so forth. (Loehlin & Nichols, 1976, p. 89)

Before concluding that personality bears a strong hereditary component, however, one must acknowledge that the findings of both of the investigations reported above were based solely on the results of self-report questionnaires. More recently, Robert Plomin and his colleagues attempted a behavioral genetic analysis of personality using more objective measures (Plomin, 1981). Plomin and Rowe (1979), in their comparison of monozygotic and same-sex dizygotic infant twin pairs, measured social behavior through the use of judges rating different observable components of this behavior across a variety of standardized situations. While none of the infants' social behavior toward the mother showed evidence of a genetic component, social behavior toward strangers appeared to display strong genetic influence.

Plomin and Foch (1980) further investigated differences in personality across 5 to 10-year-old twin pairs, using a broader range of objective measures of behavior. In this study, twins were brought into a laboratory and participated in a series of games and tasks, all of which were videotaped for later scoring from behind a one-way mirror. Comparison of the similarity on these measures across mono- and dizygotic twins suggested that, while some behaviors appear to be influenced by heredity (for example, activity level and fidgeting), others (aggressive behavior, selective attention, and vigilance) are not. Plomin (1981) therefore concluded that "although more research will be needed to verify these findings, the results of these studies of objectively assessed behaviors indicate the determinants of personality development are more complex than suggested by the results of using self-report questionnaires" (p. 140).

Aspects of personality most susceptible to genetic influence

While there is not yet clear agreement that some aspects of personality have a stronger hereditary component than others, it is clear that some characteristics show up as "heritable" much more reliably than others. Summarizing numerous studies, Vandenberg (1967) concluded that three aspects of human personality—introversion-extroversion, emotionality, and overall activity level—are almost certain to be influenced in part by genetic factor. More recent evidence has, if anything, lent further support to Vandenberg's claim.

Introversion–extroversion

The introversion-extroversion continuum refers to two rather opposite styles in dealing with one's social environment. At one extreme, introverts would be shy and anxious in all novel social situations and would much prefer to withdraw from people than to approach them.

Extroverts, in contrast, would be distinguished by an unusual ease among people, great friendliness, and a marked ability and willingness to introduce themselves and seek out people. It has been found that friendly infants tend to become friendly teenagers, whereas cold infants are also somewhat unfriendly as adolescents (Schaefer & Bayley, 1963). What is more, the genetic evidence suggests that monozygotic twins are more alike than dizygotic twins in this dimension (Buss, Plomin, & Willerman, 1973; Freedman & Keller, 1963; Scarr, 1969; Vandenberg, 1966).

Temperament (or emotionality)

A modern dictionary (Random House, 1969, p. 1461) defines temperament as "a natural disposition; the individual peculiarity of physical organization by which the manner of thinking, feeling and acting of every person is permanently affected." The word *temperament* derives from the same root as *temperature,* and refers to the internal emotional climate in which the personality operates. It is for this reason that people are sometimes spoken of as being "cool," "lukewarm," or "hot-headed." And it is for this reason that emotionality and temperament are equated by some (though not all) dispositional psychologists.

A growing amount of evidence suggests that a person's temperament, especially the degree to which a person is emotionally reactive, has a hereditary component. There is, for example, evidence that children differ in temperament almost from birth (Birns, 1965; Thomas, Chess, & Birch, 1970; Thomas & Chess, 1977). The findings of Thomas and his associates are illustrative. Thomas et al. have been following the development of a sample of 141 children longitudinally since 1956, conducting interviews with each youngster's parents every three months during the first year, every six months until age five, and every year thereafter. Furthermore, behavioral data were obtained through teacher interviews, direct classroom observation, during psychometric testing done at ages 3, 6, and 9, and through a direct interview with each child at ages 16 to 17. The data revealed both that persons show well-established individuality in temperament by the time they are two or three months old—as seen, for example, in their responses to unfamiliar objects—and that this temperament is substantially determined by the individual's genetic endowment. These findings are in close accord with earlier studies of newborns which showed sizable individual differences in the intensity with which infants respond to various situations, even in the first few days of life (Birns, 1965; Schaffer & Emerson, 1964).

A more recent study of the inheritance of temperament, employing the twin study method, was reported by Buss, Plomin, and Willerman (1973). These investigators obtained extensive questionnaire informa-

TABLE 9–5
Similarity of emotionality in Buss, Plomin, and Willerman's study of monozygotic and dizygotic twin pairs as rated by their mothers. The data are correlation coefficients.

Boys		Girls	
Monozygotic	Dizygotic	Monozygotic	Dizygotic
.63	.00	.73	.20

Source: From data reported in Buss, A. H., Plomin, R., & Willerman, L. The inheritance of temperaments. *Journal of Personality*, 1973, *41*, 513–24.

tion from the mothers of 127 pairs of twins, including monozygotic and same-sexed dizygotic pairs of both sexes, by soliciting volunteer mothers from the Mothers of Twin Clubs in eight states. The age of the twins at the time of the study ranged from 4 months to 16 years, and the emphasis was clearly upon a pattern of heritability in childhood. A portion of Buss et al.'s results are shown in Table 9–5, from which it can be seen clearly that ratings of similar emotionality were higher for monozygotic than for dizygotic twins and that this was true for both males and females.

Activity level

A person's overall level of activity—what Buss et al. (1973) have referred to as "the sheer amount of response output" of the individual—also seems to be influenced by genetic factors. For example, two studies of hyperactive children have shown that such youngsters may be as much as 10 times more likely than nonhyperactive, control-group children to have had hyperactive parents (Cantwell, 1972; Morrison & Stewart, 1971).

A number of studies lend further support to the suggestion that activity level is heritable (Buss & Plomin, 1975; Plomin & Foch, 1980; Scarr, 1966; Willerman, 1973) and that the effect is present for both sexes. The most impressive pattern of results, however, was obtained by Willerman and Plomin (1973), who found significant correlations between the rated activity levels of normal children and the activity levels of both parents when the parents themselves were children.

EVOLUTION AND BEHAVIOR: THE SOCIOBIOLOGICAL APPROACH

Perhaps the most controversial of the biological approaches to personality, sociobiology seeks to apply evolutionary theory to the social behavior of all animals, including humans. The consolidation of the discipline was marked by the publication of E. O. Wilson's *Sociobiology: The New Synthesis* in 1975, in which much of the data and theory from evolutionary genetics, ethology, and ecology were combined to form a framework for the scientific study of social systems. Although initial reaction to the book was largely favorable, it has since generated heated criticism and debate over both its scientific status and its political implications.

As described by E. O. Wilson (1978a), even though about 90 percent of the available publications dealing with sociobiology concern its application to animals, over 90 percent of the attention given to sociobiology by nonscientists focuses on its application to *human* social behavior. In addition, scientists have recently turned to the study of the sociobiological bases of human behavior in increasing numbers (cf. DeFries, 1980; Freedman, 1979; Gregory, Silvers, & Sutch, 1978; E. O. Wilson, 1978b; to name a few), with some promising implications for a theory of personality. As an understanding of evolutionary theory is central to the sociobiological approach, it is here that we will begin.

Contrary to popular belief, the concept of evolution was in existence long before Darwin's treatise (1859/1964) on the subject (Eiseley, 1958). According to Barash (1977), Darwin's most significant contribution is his notion of *natural selection,* through which the mechanism whereby organisms evolve is explicated. Barash has described Darwin's notion of natural selection as emerging from the following assumptions:

The basic tenets of Darwin's theory of evolution

1. All living things have a tendency to overproduce. In order to maintain the population at a constant size, each set of parents would by necessity produce two offspring. In actual fact, however, animals of all species tend to produce more than two offspring.
2. Even with this persistent capacity to overproduce, populations tend to remain remarkably stable in size from generation to generation.
3. There is considerable variability among individuals within a species, and to some extent these individual differences are passed on to offspring.
4. Given the stability of populations from one generation to the next, it is evident that some individuals are more successful than others in producing offspring. Furthermore, it is apparent that some offspring are more successful than others in surviving through adulthood. Implicit here is the notion of competition and survival of the fittest. Essentially, this means that those individuals having characteristics that increase the likelihood of survival and reproduction will do so, and will therefore be better represented in the next generation than will those individuals who are less fit. This process of differential reproduction among individuals is what is meant by natural selection.
5. Finally, since the process of natural selection results in differential reproductive rates among individuals within a species such that

some individuals are better represented than others in successive generations, a gradual change in the makeup of each species results. This gradual change is termed evolution.

While Darwin assumed that individual differences are passed on to offspring, he did so without any evidence of underlying genetic mechanisms. The differences in individual characteristics observed by Darwin are currently referred to as *phenotypes,* or the outward manifestation of genes. We now know that the form that any characteristic or phenotype will take is determined by the *genotype,* which is the individual's genetic endowment. This distinction is an important one in evolutionary theory, because natural selection can lead to evolutionary change only when the observed differences that make some individuals more fit than others reflect some degree of underlying genetic difference.

When certain genes produce phenotypes that are more successful than others in dealing with existing environmental conditions, they are therefore better represented in subsequent generations. This reproductive success has been labeled *fitness,* and is measured by comparing the frequency of a gene or genotype from one generation to the next. The measure of fitness most commonly used is the proportion of the gene frequency in one generation that is represented in the following one. Thus, if one population is composed of 25 X individuals and 25 Y individuals (where X and Y are different genotypes), and the next generation has 75 X's and 25 Y's, then the fitness of X is 75/25, or 3, while the fitness of Y is 25/25, or 1. From this example, it is clear that genes having a fitness of one do not increase their frequency in the next generation. On the other hand, fitnesses of less than one mean that the frequency of genes has decreased from one generation to the next, while fitnesses of more than one signify an increase in the representation of genes.

One final notion of evolutionary theory implicit in the preceding discussion is that of adaptation. Any characteristic that increases the fitness of an organism is considered to be adaptive. One popular example of the adaptive significance of evolutionary change is found in Kettlewell's work on industrial melanism in moths (1956). During the Industrial Revolution in England, there was a curious increase in the frequency of dark-colored moths and a corresponding decrease in the frequency of light-colored forms. By definition, the darker color was adaptive in that moths with this trait reproduced more successfully (that is, they were more fit), but to what were the moths adapting? It seems that the change evolved as a result of the deposition of soot on trees which occurred as a by-product of increased industrialization. The discoloration of the trees rendered the lighter moths more conspicuous to predators than were the dark forms, thereby resulting in an increased frequency of dark moths in successive generations.

According to Barash (1978), two basic assumptions underlie the sociobiological approach. The first assumption, labeled the *central theorem of sociobiology* (Barash, 1977), holds that if a behavior is at least in part genetically determined, then animals ought to behave so as to maximize their *inclusive fitness.* The notion of inclusive fitness differs from Darwinian fitness in that the emphasis in the former is on genes rather than on individuals per se. This important modification recognizes gene frequency as reflected in all relatives, rather than restricting it to the production of offspring. Thus, the central theorem predicts that organisms will behave in such a way as to ensure that their genes will be represented as much as possible in future generations. While this is most often achieved by increasing the number of successful offspring produced, other means are also available, as our discussion of altruism will demonstrate.

Sociobiology's second assumption holds that all observable characteristics (phenotypes) result from the interaction of heredity and environment. As mentioned previously, natural selection operates only when observed differences among individuals reflect differences in underlying genetic endowment. As genes specify the organization of the nervous system, behavior is assumed to be a product of a similar interaction. Barash (1978) has provided a superb explanation of the sociobiological position:

> Consider behavior as analogous to the sound produced by a drummer playing drums: The sound is not the product of the drums (genotype) alone; but neither is it produced by the drummer (environment) alone. Rather, it arises from the interaction of the two. Change the drums or the drummer, and the sound changes as well. Continuing the analogy, the *differences* between the sounds produced by different drums (genotypes) exposed to identical drummers (environments) are due to the differences between the drums, just as differences between the behavior of different species in identical environments are attributable to the genotypic differences between the species but not to the genotype of either, acting alone. A similar argument applies to switching drummers on the same drum (different environments experienced by the same genotype can induce different behaviors). In either case, the message should be clear: No behavior is produced by genotype acting alone, and, similarly, no behavior is produced by environment alone. (p. 24)

Altruism

In the broadest sense, altruism is a label applied to any behavior which involves sacrifice for the benefit of another, without hope of reciprocation. Under sociobiological theory, however, if any behavior results in harm to the self, such behavior would be selected against relative to more selfish alternatives, unless there are some benefits to the performer which will ultimately outweigh the initial cost. "Insofar as animals possess genetically mediated tendencies to behave for the benefit of another, the logic of evolution demands that these tendencies be grounded in underlying selfishness. Otherwise they would not persist" (Barash, 1977, p. 70). The sociobiological view of altruism therefore strays somewhat from our original definition, and accounts instead for behavior that *appears* to involve sacrifice. In a sociobiological analysis, the occurrence of "true" altruism would at best be rare and adventitious.

Sociobiologists tend to distinguish between two separate forms of altruism, and provide different mechanisms to account for the evolution of each. E. O. Wilson (1978b) has labeled altruism most commonly directed toward relatives as "hard-core" altruism, and describes it as being irrational and directed at others without a desire for equal return. Although there are several competing explanations for this behavior, the most compelling one is grounded in *kin selection theory*. This approach capitalizes on the notion of inclusive fitness, and holds that altruistic behavior toward an individual will occur in direct proportion to one's degree of relatedness to that individual. According to this view, then, hard-core altruism should be more common among closely related than among distantly related individuals—that is, it should decrease as the number of shared genes decreases. Field observations have provided some support for this prediction (Brown, 1975).

While assistance may be less likely to occur in the absence of genetic relatedness, it nevertheless does occur. E. O. Wilson (1978b) calls this form of altruism "soft-core"; others (Barash, 1977; Trivers, 1971) have labeled it "reciprocal altruism." This position states that we should be willing to help our nonkin only to the extent that they are likely to reciprocate our aid such that the ultimate benefits exceed the cost of the original act. E. O. Wilson (1978b) describes soft-core behavior in this way:

> The "altruist" expects reciprocation from society for himself or his closest relatives. His good behavior is calculating, often in a wholly conscious way, and his maneuvers are orchestrated by the excruciatingly intricate sanctions and demands of society. The capacity for soft-core altruism can be expected to have evolved primarily by selection of individuals and to be deeply influenced by the vagaries of cultural evolution. Its psychological vehicles are lying, pretense, and deceit, including self-deceit, because the actor is most convincing who believes that his performance is real. (p. 162)

Wilson believes that soft-core altruism based on expected reciprocation is the key to human society.

Aggression

Sociobiology views our species as innately aggressive; that is, human beings are envisioned as having a strong hereditary predisposition to respond to external threat with hatred and hostility. Unlike competing conceptualizations (e.g., Fromm, 1973), however, sociobiology does not claim that humans are the most violent of animals. E. O. Wilson (1975; 1978b) has pointed out that among many species, including hyenas, lions, and langur monkeys, the rates of lethal fighting, infanticide, and cannibalism far exceed our own.

According to E. O. Wilson's (1978b) analysis, despite aggressive behavior's hereditary component, it is still one of the most labile of traits and can take a variety of different forms. While the actual range of possible forms is limited by each species' genetic endowment, which forms actually do develop within a species depends upon the culture in which they are immersed. The cultural evolution of aggression appears to incorporate the requirements of the environment in which the species finds itself with the previous history of the group, which leads the species to favor one innovation over another. Thus, while the particular forms of violence that characterize a species are not inherited, the predisposition to behave aggressively is (E. O. Wilson, 1978b).

But what of the adaptive significance of aggression? As stated previously, sociobiology holds that, in order for a phenotype to evolve, it must confer some selective advantage on those bearing it. E. O. Wilson (1975; 1978b) sees aggression in humans as having great adaptive significance for the survival and reproduction of the individual, especially when the individual is faced with competition for limited resources, such as food or shelter. As crowding increases, these resources grow scarcer, so that aggression and competition increase. This, in turn, leads to a decrease in population growth, which might itself be adaptive. Thus, aggressive behavior serves at least two functions: it ensures that the individual gets an adequate share of scarce resources, and it serves as a density-dependent means of controlling population size. Both functions presumably enhance the inclusive fitness of the aggressive individuals.

Prospects and limitations

As the sociobiological approach has engendered an enormous amount of criticism and debate, a thorough discussion of this controversy is beyond the scope of this text (see Ruse, 1979, for a comprehensive treatment of the major issues). Broadly speaking, there are two major blocks of criticism: the scientific and the sociopolitical (Kaplan, 1976). Representatives of the former school have found fault with the discipline's conceptual and methodological base, and have produced arguments of the form that the theory cannot be disproved and is consequently of no utility (Allen et al., 1977; Burian, 1977; Sahlins, 1976), and that it does not adequately account for available anthropological data (Sahlins, 1976). Critics of the approach's sociopolitical implications have accused it of offenses ranging from racism to sexism to promoting biological determinism as a justification for the status quo (Allen et al., 1977; Sahlins, 1976). Despite opposition, however, sociobiology has continued to flourish. Many have adopted the attitude espoused by Ruse (1979): "Human sociobiology should be given the chance to prove its worth. If it cannot deliver on its promises, it will collapse soon enough. . . . but if it does prove viable, then its success could pay scientific dividends of the highest order" (p. 214).

10 | *The dispositional strategy*

Trait and type approaches

In contemporary writing, both popular and scientific, the terms *trait* and *type* have come to be used in several different ways. Sometimes "type" and "trait" are used as summary labels for observed differences in behavior. To say of a friend "At parties he is usually the shy type" is merely to conveniently summarize our observations. In the same vein, Guilford (1959) defined a trait as *"any distinguishable, relatively enduring way in which one individual varies from others"* (p. 6). Used in this way, the terms have no necessary theoretical implications and serve merely to facilitate communication.

Alternatively, traits and types have been considered by many personality psychologists to be real psychological entities. Gordon Allport (1897–1967), acknowledged by his colleagues to be one of the founders of modern trait theory, described this latter approach as *heuristic realism*. The word *heuristic* derives from Greek and Latin roots meaning "to find out or discover," and Allport meant to convey by his term that "the person who confronts us possesses inside his skin generalized action tendencies (or traits) and that it is our job scientifically to discover what they are" (Allport, 1966, p. 3). Allport did not believe, of course, that traits existed as physical entities, like glands or organs: what he did believe was that psychological traits are real attributes of persons in the sense that they serve to *explain* behavior rather than merely to describe it.

Suppose, for example, that a 5-year-old girl and a 25-year-old woman are given a 50-pound barbell to lift. It is a safe bet, assuming that both subjects are motivated, that the woman will succeed at this task but that the girl will fail. Why? Many people would say that the reason is because the woman is stronger than the girl. The difference in strength does not merely describe the fact that one individual was able to lift the weight, whereas the other was not. The difference in strength, an attribute of the persons involved, explains *why* one succeeded and the other failed. In much the same way, trait and type theorists believe that it is legitimate to say that an individual behaves aggressively *because* she has an aggressive trait or because he is an aggressive type. Allport, Raymond Cattell, and Hans Eysenck, the three theorists whose work is considered in this chapter, believe that traits and types

Gordon Allport

Harvard University News Office

determine, and therefore explain a good deal about, individual differences in personality.

ALLPORT'S TRAIT APPROACH

Allport spent virtually his entire professional career trying to understand human personality, and his significant writings span more than 35 years. Throughout this period, Allport adhered to the philosophy of heuristic realism, which we have already mentioned, and insisted that the job of finding out "what the other fellow is really like" should not be shunned despite the difficulties involved. A year before his death, Allport published an article titled "Traits Revisited" which contained this warning to other psychologists:

> The incredible complexity of the structure we seek to understand is enough to discourage the realist, and to tempt him to play some form of positivistic gamesmanship. He is tempted to settle for such elusive formations as: "If we knew enough about the situation we wouldn't need the concept of personality"; or, "One's personality is merely the way other people see one"; or, "There is no structure in personality but only varying degrees of consistency in the environment." Yet the truly persistent realist prefers not to abandon his commitment to find out what the other fellow is really like. (Allport, 1966, p. 3).[1]

Given this attitude, it should not be surprising that Allport, perhaps more than any other modern personality theorist, attempted to treat personality in its entirety. He emphasized not only the importance of the whole, living person, but also the importance of integrating every bit of available biological and psychological reserach into this perspective. Thus, he spoke of the importance of learning, the meaning of private experience and selfhood, and the truths to be found in psychoanalysis. And he fashioned from all of this a more or less cohesive picture of personality.[2]

A definition of personality

Allport (1961) defined personality as *"the dynamic organization within the individual of those psychophysical systems that determine his characteristic behavior and thought"* (p. 28). He went on to explain what he wished to emphasize by each of the key concepts. The phrase *dynamic organization* is used to stress the high degree of integration in personality and to indicate that the opposite condition, disintegration of personality, is also possible. *Psychophysical* is an important term in the definition because it reminds us that personality does not refer to the mind or the body alone, but to the "inextricable unity" of mind

---

[1] Here Allport is criticizing both the phenomenological and the behavioral strategies.

[2] Allport even felt obliged to raise the question of whether animals have personalities. He concluded, guardedly, that they do (see Allport, 1961, p. 29).

and body. The word *determine* is very important in Allport's definition, and he elaborated on the significance of the term at length:

> Personality *is* something and *does* something. The latent psychophysical systems, when called into action, either motivate or direct specific activity, and thought. All the systems that comprise personality are to be regarded as *determining tendencies*. They exert a directive force upon all the adjustive and expressive acts by which the personality comes to be known. (Allport, 1961, p. 29)

Finally, the phrase *behavior and thought* is openly used as "a blanket to designate anything whatsoever an individual may do."

In the introduction to his book *Pattern and Growth in Personality,* Allport (1961) insisted that "psychology should not be content with studying an artificial man, but should describe and explain a real one" (p. ix). But how can one go about studying personality? "Look for the real person" is not enough of a guideline. We must further decide what units to employ.

    What are the specific structures for which we search? Allport's answer is that we are looking for *traits*. His original statement of the characteristics of traits appeared in 1931, and Allport still judged it to be defensible in 1966. His eight assertions are:

Traits as the units for studying personality

1. *Traits have more than nominal existence.* They are not just summary labels of observed behavior. Rather, traits exist within the person.
2. *Traits are more generalized than habits.* Brushing one's teeth, Allport notes, may well be a habit, but it is not properly called a trait (although an underlying trait—for example, cleanliness—might account for it).
3. *Traits are dynamic, or at least determinative, in behavior.* Traits direct action and are not mere structural artifacts. And unlike the intrapsychic structures posited by Freud, they do not require energizing from somewhere else.
4. *Traits may be established empirically.* Allport was steeped in the tradition of experimental psychology and acknowledged unequivocally that theorists must finally defer to their data.
5. *Traits are only relatively independent of other traits.*
6. *Traits are not synonymous with moral or social judgments.*
7. *Traits may be viewed either in the light of the personality which contains them (i.e., idiographically) or in the light of their distribution in the population (i.e., nomothetically).*
8. *Acts, and even habits, that are inconsistent with a trait are not proof of the nonexistence of the trait.*

The dimensions of traits: Pervasiveness within a personality

Allport had proposed that an individual's traits may be classified in terms of the degree to which they pervade his or her personality. Allport distinguished among three levels of traits, although he acknowledged that "these three graduations are arbitrary and are phrased mainly for convenience of discourse" (1961, p. 365).

The most pervasive traits are referred to as *cardinal dispositions.* A cardinal disposition dominates the individual's entire existence. It cannot remain hidden, and it often makes its possessor famous. The proper names of historical and fictitious characters which became trait adjectives in our language, such as *quixotic, machiavellian,* and *lesbian,* suggest what is meant by a cardinal disposition, as does the use of the proper names themselves (e.g., "He is a real Beau Brummel"). According to Allport, few persons have cardinal dispositions.

Central dispositions refer to the relatively small number of traits which tend to be highly characteristic of the individual. They might be thought of as those characteristics which one would enumerate when writing a detailed letter of recommendation. Given this sort of definition and the further suggestion that all persons can be characterized by central dispositions, a vital question becomes: How many central dispositions does the average person have? To answer this question, Allport (1961) asked 93 students "to think of some one individual of your own sex whom you know well" and "to describe him or her by writing words, phrases, or sentences that express fairly well what seem to you to be the essential characteristics of this person" (p. 366). Most students listed between 3 and 10 essential characteristics. The average number was 7.2.

Secondary dispositions are those characteristics of the individual which operate only in limited settings. Preferences for particular kinds of food, fairly specific attitudes, and other "peripheral" or situationally determined characteristics of the person would be placed in this category.

The dimensions of traits: Comparison with other personalities

Allport argued that traits may be viewed either as characteristics which allow us to compare one person with another (as we might compare body weights) or as unique characteristics of the individual which need not invite, or even permit, comparison with those of others.

Common traits

Trait comparisons across people involve the assumption of *common traits* and have often been referred to as part of the psychology of "individual differences" (cf. Willerman, 1975). Life situations continually require us to compare people. Business executives must choose between prospective candidates for a secretarial position; colleges must identify the best applicants for higher education; and in most situations where the job or role is fixed, someone is required to identify the personality or person who "fits." While most of us make such rough and approximate comparisons between persons daily, the researcher committed to discovering common traits must formalize both the criteria for identifying a common trait and the procedures for measuring it.

This task is exemplified in a classic study by Allport and Allport (1928) in which the investigations were interested in finding a common trait which they labeled *ascendance-submission*. They developed a scale with which individuals responded to a variety of situations where the alternatives for action could be characterized as either dominating another (ascendance) or being dominated oneself (submission). For example:

> Someone tries to push ahead of you in line. You have been waiting for some time, and can't wait much longer. Suppose the intruder is of the same sex as yourself, do you usually:
> Remonstrate with the intruder _____
> "Look daggers" at the intruder or make clearly
> audible comments to your neighbor _____
> Decide not to wait, and go away _____
> Do nothing _____
>
> (Allport, 1961, p. 338)[3]

For Allport, the proof of the trait's existence lies in its *reliability*. The reliability of a measure (test) refers to its consistency or repeatability and is customarily expressed as a correlation coefficient. If a test has high *retest reliability* (consistency between administrations) when the same test (or an equivalent form) is given to the same persons at a later time, each person should place about the same on the scale on both occasions. Here the correlation is between test administrations. If a test has high *internal reliability,* most of the items in the test tend to be measuring the same thing, and the correlation is between items or groups of items.

Trait theory requires that an individual who is ascendant in one situation should also tend to be so in other situations. Allport reported that the test for ascendance-submission has a retest reliability of $+$ .78 and an internal reliability of $+$ .85, thereby indicating a moderately high degree of reliability for the trait in question.

Common traits, according to Allport, when scaled for the population at large, often have a *normal distribution*. That is, the scores of a large sample, when plotted on a graph, appear to produce a continuous

---

[3] According to Allport, "remonstrate with the intruder" is a moderately ascendant response and is scored $+$ 2, " 'look daggers' at the intruder . . ." and "do nothing" are moderately submissive responses and scored $-$ 2, and "decide not to wait and go away" is an even more submissive response and is scored $-$ 3.

bell-shaped curve, with the majority of cases piling up as average scores in the middle and the number of high and low scores tapering off at the more extreme positions. Allport's test for ascendance-submission appears to be distributed in this way. As seen in Figure 10–1, most people are slightly submissive, but a few are very submissive or very ascendant.

FIGURE 10–1
The distribution of scores from a test measuring ascendance-submission

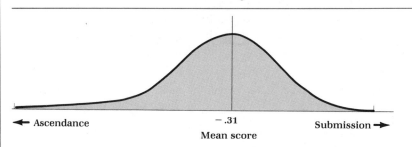

◄— Ascendance   − .31   Submission —►
                                      Mean score

Source: Allport, G. W. *Pattern and growth in personality.* New York: Holt, Rinehart & Winston, 1961.

"Patterned individuality" and the nature of individual traits

Allport not only acknowledged but expounded upon the merits of comparing personalities along common dimensions (the nomothetic approach), yet he himself insisted that we can really understand others only by coming to grips with the uniqueness of personality. Each of us, Allport believed, has a unique inner organization of motives, traits, and personal style that results in a "patterned individuality" that will never again be exactly repeated.

Personality psychologists who favor a nomothetic approach and seek universal laws often argue that this uniqueness merely reflects the combination of common traits in varying strength. Allport took issue with this line of reasoning and claimed that a person's traits always interact to form a unique pattern that cannot be explained fully by its separate parts. As an example, he invites us to compare a molecule of water with a molecule of peroxide. They "have the same universals—hydrogen and oxygen; they differ only quantitatively (H_2O vs. H_2O_2) but a small quantitative difference leads to totally unlike products. Try them on your hair and see" (Allport, 1961, p. 10).

Allport used the term *individual traits* to refer to those important characteristics of the individual which do not lend themselves to comparison across persons. Although most of Allport's research focused upon common traits (nomothetic research), he often stated that such studies can offer only approximations of what persons are really like and that *all* of an individual's behavior and thought is unique to that person. "Even the acts and concepts that we apparently 'share' with others," he wrote, "are at bottom individual. . . . It is true that some acts and concepts are more idiosyncratic than others, but none can be found that lacks the personal flavor" (Allport, 1961, p. 29).

Elsewhere he insisted that "the key-qualities which we seek must . . . be *personal,* not universal," adding:

> I am not repudiating the use of nomothetic factors, nor of test-scales, ratings and dimensions. More of my own research and writing has been devoted to this type of approach to personality than to any other. The resulting "common traits," I find, have utility for *comparative* purposes, for approximations to the modes of adjustment that similarly constituted individuals in similarly constituted societies can be expected to acquire. . . . What I argue is that . . . we must acknowledge the roughness and inadequacy of our universal dimensions. Thereby shall we enhance our own ability to understand, predict and control. By learning to handle the individuality of motives and the uniqueness of personality, we shall become better scientists, not worse. (Allport, 1960, p. 148)

This task is accomplished, according to Allport (1966), by searching "for the natural cleavages that mark an individual life" (p. 7), a procedure illustrated in his *Letters from Jenny* (1965). This lengthy case study was based on the personal letters of Jenny Grove Masterson, which

> tell the story of a mother-son relationship and trace the course of a life beset by frustration and defeat. . . . Between the ages of fifty-eight and seventy she wrote a series of 301 letters to two young friends, a married couple living and teaching in an eastern college town. The tie of friendship extended back to the time when the husband . . . had been the roommate of Jenny's son . . . at college, about ten years before the beginning of the correspondence. . . . The correspondence begins in earnest in March, 1926, and continues without interruption for eleven and a half years, until Jenny's death in October, 1937. (Allport, 1965, p. v)

The letters were evaluated by 36 judges, who read them in sequence and assigned a total of 198 descriptive adjectives to Jenny based on their overall impression of her personality. Many of the adjectives were synonymous, though, and when they were combined, eight central traits emerged.

It was also possible to compare the impressionistic description with one derived from a more systematic method of analysis. The procedure involved a determination of the frequency with which various key words in the letters were used in conjunction with one another. The resulting data were combined statistically by the method of factor analysis (to be discussed later in this chapter), yielding seven traits. When the traits derived from the two divergent methods (one impressionistic and the other statistical) were compared, there were differences in terminology, but a marked similarity of description was nevertheless apparent, as can be seen in Table 10–1.

TABLE 10–1
Evaluation of Jenny's personality from her letters based on impressionistic and factor-analytic assessment

Impressionistic traits	Factorial traits
Quarrelsome-suspicious	
Aggressive	Aggression
Self-centered (possessive)	Possessiveness
Sentimental	Need for affiliation
	Need for family acceptance
Independent-autonomous	Need for autonomy
Esthetic-artistic	Sentience
Self-centered (self-pitying)	Martyrdom
(No parallel)	Sexuality
Dramatic-intense	("Overstate")

Source: Adapted from Allport, G. W. Traits revisited. *American Psychologist*, 1966, *21*, 1–10.

Allport (1966) interpreted the similarity of the two analyses as evidence for the validity of the conclusions about Jenny's personality and at the same time construed the disparities found as confirming the utility of the idiographic approach:

> the judges, it seems, gain much from the running style of the letters. Since the style is constant it would not appear in a factorial analysis. . . . The common-sense traits *cynical-morbid* and *dramatic-intense* are judgements of a pervading expressive style in Jenny's personality and seem to be missed by factoring procedure. (p. 8)

But is not the assignment of a list of traits to Jenny a mere variation on the nomothetic or comparative approach? Allport argues that it is not. The idiographic approach is not necessarily characterized by an absence of either labels or statistics. It is characterized by the positive quality of letting the behavior of the person under study, rather than an existing battery of tests, measuring instruments, or common traits, dictate the description which will emerge.

FACTOR ANALYSIS AND MULTIVARIATE RESEARCH

Raymond B. Cattell (1905–   ), a prominent dispositional psychologist, has quipped that "the trouble with measuring traits is that there are too many of them!" (1965, p. 55). Cattell was referring to the procedure, central to most trait research, "to fancy some particular trait . . . and to concentrate on its relations to all kinds of things" (1965, p. 55). This procedure, Cattell argued, has many disadvantages, the most salient being that trait researchers cannot compare or integrate their findings with one another's, or agree on what is a referent for such commonly researched traits as "anxiety." If a common method were employed, which allowed for interrelating the various findings of trait research and the simultaneous examination of many traits, this problem would be solved. A statistical technique with these properties is available and has come to be called *factor analysis*. In this section, we shall examine the basic assumptions and principles of factor analysis and consider some research which has been based on this technique.

Cattell and most other researchers who have used factor-analytic techniques believe that natural, unitary structures in personality underlie the various trait names and behaviors which have traditionally been examined. Freud, it will be recalled, assumed the existence of three structures in all persons, while Allport assumed that each individual had a unique (trait) structure. Cattell (1965), in contrast to both, believes that there is a common structure across personalities which must be determined *empirically*:

> The problem which baffled psychologists for many years was to find a method which would tease out these functionally unitary influences in the chaotic jungle of human behavior. But let us ask how, in the literal tropical jungle, the hunter decides whether the dark blobs which he sees are two or three rotting logs or a single alligator? He watches for movement. *If they move together*—come and disappear together—*he infers a single structure.* Just so, as John Stuart Mill pointed out in his philosophy of science, the scientist should look for "concomitant variation" in seeking unitary concepts. (p. 56; italics added)

In the "jungle" of human behavior, however, perfect covariation is rarely to be found. Psychological variables do not seem to *always* go together. We may get a fleeting glimpse of some strong covariations but never the perfect data generated by Cattell's alligator. The correlational method allows for the evaluation of degrees of relationship which are not perfect, and it is the statistical correlation coefficient which is at the heart of factor-analytic procedures. However, factor analysis deals not with one or two correlations, but with the entire *array of intercorrelations* among many variables. Although factor analysis was first developed in 1904 by Charles Spearman, a British psychologist and statistician, its recent popularity is a result of the availability of high-speed computers, without which much of the current work using the technique would be virtually impossible.

Let us suppose that an investigator wishes to find out something about the structure of college students' patterns of academic performance, in order to determine what underlying skills are involved. If factor analysis were chosen as the research tool, the investigation would proceed in five steps.

The logic of factor analysis

Raymond B. Cattell

Courtesy of Raymond B. Cattell

A hypothetical example of a factor analysis

Data collection

The first step in factor analysis is data collection. In our hypothetical example, the investigator might obtain the test scores for a large number of students (subjects) in each of a large number of different courses (measures).

Determining the relationship of each variable to every other: The correlation matrix

The next step involves producing a so-called *correlation matrix,* showing the exact relationship between each measure and every one of the others. Consider, for example, the hypothetical correlation matrix in Table 10–2. It contains the correlations of each of seven measures with every other measure. What this matrix tells us is that there is a high positive relationship between *a* and *b* (+.70), *a* and *c* (+.80), *a* and *d* (+.80), *b* and *c* (+.90), *b* and *d* (+.70), *c* and *d* (+.80), *e* and *f* (+.80), *e* and *g* (+.70), and *f* and *g* (+.70), and virtually no systematic relationship (i.e., correlation coefficients in the vicinity of 0) between *a* and *e* (−.10), *a* and *f* (.00), *a* and *g* (.00), *b* and *e* (+.10), *b* and *f* (+.10), *b* and *g* (.00), *c* and *e* (−.10), *c* and *f* (−.10), *c* and *g* (−.10), *d* and *e* (.00), *d* and *f* (−.10), and *d* and *g* (.00).

Factor extraction

Despite the rather clear-cut nature of the hypothetical correlation matrix in Table 10–2 and the relatively small number of measures included (it is not uncommon for 100 or more variables to be correlated with one another in factor-analytic studies), the complexities and sheer time needed to summarize and interpret the data contained in the matrix should be apparent from the enumeration of results just presented.

TABLE 10–2
Hypothetical correlation matrix

Measure	*a*	*b*	*c*	*d*	*e*	*f*	*g*
a	+1.00	+.70	+.80	+.80	−.10	.00	.00
b		+1.00	+.90	+.70	+.10	+.10	.00
c			+1.00	+.80	−.10	−.10	−.10
d				+1.00	.00	−.10	.00
e					+1.00	+.80	+.70
f						+1.00	+.70
g							+1.00

One of the major functions of factor analysis is to reduce large sets of data, most often in the form of correlation matrices, to manageable units. By means of complex mathematical formulas, the data are reduced to small numbers of relatively homogeneous dimensions, called *factors*. At this point in the procedure, some theoretical decisions must be made about the number and type of factors to be extracted. These theoretical decisions will in turn guide several mathematical decisions about the precise type of factor analysis to be performed (see, for example, Comrey, 1973, *A First Course in Factor Analysis*), but details of the process are not important for our discussion here.

Determining factor loadings

As a result of the factor extraction, the investigator will have the information necessary to construct a so-called *factor matrix*. The factors in the matrix are hypothetical entities which, taken together, "account for" the myriad of relationships in the original correlation matrix. The correlation between each of the original measures and each of the factors reflects the *loading* of the measure on the particular factor in question. Thus, a specific measure is said to "load" on a factor to the extent that it is correlated with that factor.

Any given factor matrix can be expressed in several different forms which are mathematically equivalent in the sense of accounting equally well for the original correlation matrix. These alternatives are the possible "rotations" of the factor matrix. For purposes of our highly simplified explanation here, it is sufficient to know that, when a factor matrix is mathematically transformed (rotated), a different set of measures tends to load highly on each factor, or to load in a different pattern.

Factor naming

Factor naming is the last step in a factor analysis, and it is the point at which inference and subjective judgment enter the picture. Experts in the area continually advance such warnings as "when we do not know beforehand what the primary dimensions are, it is difficult to justify the belief that factor analysis will somehow magically point them out to us" (Overall, 1964, p. 273), or "the correctness of interpretations based on factor-analytic results must be confirmed by evidence outside the factor analysis itself" (Comrey, 1973, p. 11).

To illustrate the meaning of these cautionary notes concretely, let us return to the hypothetical correlation matrix in Table 10–2. Suppose that the measures were aptitude tests for academic fields, where a = English, b = fine arts, c = history, d = French, e = mathematics, f = physics, and g = engineering. Among these seven measures (a through g) there is a distinct pattern to be found. Specifically, a, b, c, and d

seem to "go together." They are highly correlated with one another but show little or no relationship (i.e., near 0) to the other three measures. Similarly, *e, f,* and *g* are highly related to one another but not to the other measures. Thus, two units or *factors* emerge from the seven measures. These might be labeled, sterilely, factor X and factor Y. Factor X would then consist of English, fine arts, history, and French, and factor Y would consist of mathematics, physics, and engineering. Or we could inspect the several related measures for their common qualities and provide a more meaningful name than X or Y for the two factors. However, the naming itself would be a *subjective judgment* and not a logical consequence of the statistical procedures involved. Some people might insist that factor X represents a "literary" aptitude and factor Y a "scientific" aptitude; others might say that factor Y involves the understanding of inanimate forces, whereas factor X involves the understanding of people and their products; and so on. This is why it is well to remember that "there is nothing in the factor-analytic methods themselves that can demonstrate that one factor solution is more scientifically useful than another" (Comrey, 1973, p. 11).

A summary of the five steps involved in factor analysis, distinguishing the points at which judgments and opinions enter, is shown in Figure 10–2.

A number of personality psychologists have turned to factor analysis

FIGURE 10–2
The five steps involved in factor analysis. The purpose of the procedure is to reduce the information available about a large number of measures (variables) to manageable size, and to interpret the pattern that emerges.

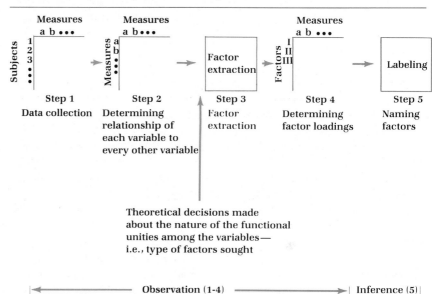

as a strategy for directing their research. We shall discuss two of the more prominent of these dispositionalists, Cattell and Eysenck.

Cattell (1965; 1979; Cattell & Kline, 1977) proposed that there should be three broad sources of data about personality, which he labeled *L*-data, *Q*-data, and *T*-data. *L-data* refer to information which can be gathered from the life record of the individual and are usually taken from ratings made by observers as to the frequency and intensity of occurrence of specific kinds of behavior.

CATTELL'S TRAIT APPROACH

Q-data consist of information gathered from questionnaires and interviews. The common feature of *Q*-data is that the individual answers direct questions about him- or herself, based on personal observations and introspection (e.g., "Do you have trouble making and keeping friends?").

Data gathered from so-called objective tests are referred to as *T-data*. Teachers and educators might well be tempted to call questionnaire and essay data (i.e., *Q*-data) "objective" whenever these are scored in some standardized way so as to lead two or more examiners to exactly the same conclusions. However, Cattell argued that these procedures are often not objective in another sense, since the individual may "take on airs" or otherwise attempt to fabricate or distort responses. Cattell (1965) defined an objective test as one in which "the subject is placed in a miniature situation and simply acts . . . [and] *does not know on what aspect of his behavior he is really being evaluated"* (p. 104). Cattell and Warburton (1967) have published a compendium of more than 600 tests that meet these criteria of objectivity.

According to Cattell, the three sources of data can and must be integrated to capture the full complexity of human personality. Traditionally, psychologists have looked at only one slice at a time and their experiments have been *univariate*—that is, experiments which vary one (independent) variable and examine its effects on one other (dependent) variable. In contrast, the *multivariate* approach has the advantage that "with sufficient analytical subtlety we can tease out the connexions from the behavior of the man in his actual life situation—without the false situation of controlling and manipulating" (Cattell, 1965, p. 20). Cattell calls such research "multivariate experiments," but by the more usual definition (see Chapter 2) they are not really *experiments* at all, for the very reason that they eschew systematic variation and control. They are correlational studies.

Cattell asserts that

the development of beautiful and complex mathematicostatistical methods like factor analysis has enabled us to take natural data, much as the clinician has long done—except that normals are now included—

and to find laws and build sound theories about the structure and functioning of personality. (1965, p. 23)

What evidence exists for this assertion?

Three traits of personality derived from *L*- and *Q*-data

In one of Cattell's studies, several hundred young men and women were rated by people who knew them well on 50 different *trait elements,* the elements from which the traits are factor-analytically derived. A sample of four of these trait elements appears in Table 10–3.

TABLE 10–3
Four (of 50) trait elements on which young men and women were rated

1. *Adaptable:* flexible; accepts changes of plan easily; satisfied with compromises; is not upset, surprised, baffled, or irritated if things are different from what he expected — vs. *Rigid:* insists that things be done the way he has always done them; does not adapt his habits and ways of thinking to those of the group; nonplussed if his routine is upset.

2. *Emotional:* excitable; cries a lot (children), laughs a lot, shows affection, anger, all emotions, to excess. — vs. *Calm:* stable, shows few signs of emotional excitement of any kind; remains calm, even under-reacts, in dispute, danger, social hilarity, etc.

3. *Conscientious:* honest; knows what is right and generally does it, even if no one is watching him; does not tell lies or attempt to deceive others; respects others' property. — vs. *Unconscientious:* somewhat unscrupulous; not too careful about standards of right and wrong where personal desires are concerned; tells lies and is given to little deceits; does not respect others' property.

4. *Conventional:* conforms to accepted standards, ways of acting, thinking, dressing, etc.: does the "proper" thing; seems distressed if he finds he is being different. — vs. *Unconventional, eccentric:* acts differently from others: not concerned about wearing the same clothes or doing the same things as others; has somewhat eccentric interests, attitudes, and ways of behaving; goes his own rather peculiar way.

Source: Cattell, R. B. *The scientific analysis of personality.* Baltimore: Penguin Books, 1965.

When a set of correlations among the ratings on the 50 trait elements was subjected to a factor analysis, Cattell found that a number of factors, perhaps as many as 20, emerge.[4] Although 20 factors summarize the personality ratings better than 50 trait elements do, 20 bits of information are still not exactly an easily comprehensible summary. Therefore, the next step is to determine the relative importance of each of the 20 factors. For this purpose, they are placed in hierarchical order in terms of the degree to which each factor "explains" or "accounts for" all of the trait elements as a group. At the top of the hierarchy

---

[4] The number of factors which adequately summarize a given set of data depend upon the nature of the data and the specific mathematical procedures (type of factor analysis) employed.

would be the factor which represents the greatest single summary of all the data. This factor is assigned the letter *A;* the letter *B* is assigned to the factor which accounts for the next greatest amount of variance of all the trait elements; and so on. Cattell (1965) suggested that this last procedure permits one to look at the obtained patterns of results "without prejudice from earlier clinical notions or traditional popular terms" and noted, as an aside, that "the investigators of vitamins did just the same, in a parallel situation, where the entities could be identified in terms of their *effects* before truly interpretive chemical labels could be attached to them" (p. 65).

In summarizing his work in *The Scientific Analysis of Personality,* Cattell (1965) indicated that 16 personality traits have been scientifically derived with factor-analytic and related procedures and that these represent the major dimensions of differences in human personality. These traits are listed in Table 10–4. As the names in parentheses show, Cattell has a penchant for exotic labels (e.g., *harria* versus *premsia* or *praxernia* versus *autia*). One critic has said:

> If you think you are having difficulty getting the meaning of these factors, picture poor Cattell having to interpret and name them! He concluded that the best thing to do, by and large, was to give them names out of his imagination, along with a few adjectives indicating the flavor of the thing, waiting for future research to clarify their psychological meaning. (Maddi, 1972, p. 422)

Let us consider the three most important factors (i.e., *A, B,* and *C*) which Cattell consistently found. As part of the factor analysis, the ratings for each of the 50 trait elements on which the subjects were

TABLE 10–4
The 16 major factors in Cattell's analysis of personality. Some of the terms in parentheses are labels that Cattell invented.

Low-Score description	Factor		Factor	High-Score description
Reserved (sizothymia)	$A-$	vs.	$A+$	Outgoing (affectothymia)
Less intelligent (low 'g')	$B-$	vs.	$B+$	More intelligent (high 'g')
Emotional (low ego-strength)	$C-$	vs.	$C+$	Stable (high ego-strength)
Humble (submissiveness)	$E-$	vs.	$E+$	Assertive (dominance)
Sober (desurgency)	$F-$	vs.	$F+$	Happy-go-lucky (surgency)
Expedient (low superego)	$G-$	vs.	$G+$	Conscientious (high superego)
Shy (threctia)	$H-$	vs.	$H+$	Venturesome (parmia)
Tough-minded (harria)	$I-$	vs.	$I+$	Tender-minded (premsia)
Trusting (alaxia)	$L-$	vs.	$L+$	Suspicious (protension)
Practical (praxernia)	$M-$	vs.	$M+$	Imaginative (autia)
Forthright (artlessness)	$N-$	vs.	$N+$	Shrewd (shrewdness)
Placid (assurance)	$O-$	vs.	$O+$	Apprehensive (guilt-proneness)
Conservative (conservatism)	Q_1-	vs.	Q_1+	Experimenting (radicalism)
Group-tied (group adherence)	Q_2-	vs.	Q_2+	Self-sufficient (self-sufficiency)
Casual (low integration)	Q_3-	vs.	Q_3+	Controlled (high self-concept)
Relaxed (low ergic tension)	Q_4-	vs.	Q_4+	Tense (ergic tension)

Source: Adapted from Cattell, R. B. *The scientific analysis of personality.* Baltimore: Penguin Books, 1965, p. 365.

rated were correlated with each of the factors which had been found. The resulting correlations are technically called *factor loadings*. The elements which loaded (correlated) most highly (both in a positive and a negative direction) with factor *A* are listed in Table 10–5.

TABLE 10–5
Elements (ratings) which load on source trait A; Affectothymia versus sizothymia

A+ (positively loaded)		A– (negatively loaded)
Good-natured, easygoing	vs.	Critical, grasping
Cooperative	vs.	Obstructive
Attentive to people	vs.	Cool, aloof
Softhearted	vs.	Hard, precise
Trustful	vs.	Suspicious
Adaptable	vs.	Rigid

Source: Cattell, R. B. *The scientific analysis of personality*. Baltimore: Penguin Books, 1965.

Source traits

Cattell calls factor *A* (as well as factors *B* and *C*) a *source trait*, indicating that it is an underlying variable which is a source or determinant of overt behavior. He views source traits as the building blocks of personality and maintains that they can be discovered only by factor analysis.

Surface traits are the products of the interaction of source traits. They are clusters of overt behavior which seem to go together, even to the casual observer. However, the behaviors which make up a surface trait do not always vary together and may not have a common cause. For example, success in politics and success in business ventures are sometimes observed to occur in the same people, and their relationship would constitute a surface trait. This surface trait, though, might be caused by a combination of independent source traits, such as affectothymia and shrewdness.

Relative to surface traits, there are only a small number of source traits, and source traits tend to be more stable. Surface traits are primarily descriptive, whereas source traits are explanatory and causal. The distinction between surface and source traits is parallel to Freud's distinction between manifest and latent dream content.

Let us return to our discussion of factor *A*, affectothymia-sizothymia. If it is a source trait, we would expect that the same pattern of results that emerged from the *L*-data (i.e., the ratings on the 50 trait elements) would appear in *Q*-data. That is, if a trait is really an underlying dimension of personality, it should be reflected in all measures of personality. Sample questionnaire responses which load high on factor *A* are given in Table 10–6. Considering the *Q*-data, which are summarized in Table 10–6, and referring back to the *L*-data, Cattell (1965) concluded: "The warm sociability at one pole, and the aloofness and unconcern with people at the other are as evident here as in the observers' ratings" (p. 71).

TABLE 10–6
Factor A in questionnaire responses

1. I would rather work as:
   (a) An engineer
   (b) *A social science teacher*
2. I could stand being a hermit
   (a) True
   (b) *False*
3. I am careful to turn up when someone expects me
   (a) *True*
   (b) False
4. I would prefer to marry someone who is:
   (a) A thoughtful companion
   (b) *Effective in a social group*
5. I would prefer to read a book on:
   (a) *National social service*
   (b) New scientific weapons
6. I trust strangers:
   (a) Sometimes
   (b) *Practically always*

Note: A person who selects all the italicized answers has a highly affectothyme temperament, whereas selection of all the nonitalicized responses indicates sizothymia. Most people, presumably, would fall between these extremes.
Source: Cattell, R. B. *The scientific analysis of personality*. Baltimore: Penguin Books, 1965.

With respect to the ratings on the 50 trait elements (i.e., *L*-data), Cattell (1965) concluded that the second largest source trait, factor *B*, "looks like nothing less than general intelligence, and correlates well with actual test results" (p. 72).

Concerning the third largest source trait, factor *C*, he noted:

> The essence of *C* factor appears to be an inability to control one's emotions and impulses, especially by finding for them some satisfactory realistic expression. Looked at from the opposite or positive pole, it sharpens and gives scientific substance to the psychoanalytic concept of "ego strength," which it [factor *C*] has come to be called. (1965, pp. 73–74)

To illustrate the nature of the source trait "ego strength," exemplary *L*- and *Q*-data are presented in Table 10–7 (page 218).

Cattell's dispositional approach to personality is empirical and relatively untheoretical. While he conducted his research without stated preconceived theoretical notions as to the nature of the traits which would emerge from the factor-analytic procedures, his findings are not as free from bias as is often assumed. Rather than a "discovery" of the traits which compromise personality, it appears more likely that Cattell's findings were largely determined by the preconceptions and stereotypes regarding personality organization that his raters brought with them to his studies.

The role that the raters' conceptual categories play in determining the factors that later "emerge" was well demonstrated by Warren Norman and his colleagues (1961; 1963). As was done in earlier investigations (Tupes & Christal, 1958; 1961), Norman used the factor-analytic approach to peer ratings across a number of diverse groups of people, and consistently found that a stable set of the same five factors emerged. In a related study, however, Passini and Norman (1966) later

TABLE 10–7
L- and Q-data for source trait C

Behavior ratings which load on C

C+ *(positively loaded)*		C– *(negatively loaded)*
Mature	vs.	Unable to tolerate frustration
Steady, persistent	vs.	Changeable
Emotionally calm	vs.	Impulsively emotional
Realistic about problems	vs.	Evasive, avoids necessary decisions
Absence of neurotic fatigue	vs.	Neurotically fatigued (with no real effort)

Factor C questionnaire responses

Do you find it difficult to take no for an answer even when what you want to do is obviously impossible?
  (a) Yes   (b) *No*

If you had your life to live over again, would you
  (a) *Want it to be essentially the same?*   (b) Plan it very differently?

Do you often have really disturbing dreams?
  (a) Yes   (b) *No*

Do your moods sometimes make you seem unreasonable even to yourself?
  (a) Yes   (b) *No*

Do you feel tired when you've done nothing to justify it?
  (a) *Rarely*   (b) Often

Can you change old habits, without relapse, when you decide to?
  (a) *Yes*   (b) No

Note: A person who selects all the italicized answers has high ego-strength, whereas selection of all the nonitalicized responses indicates low ego-strength.
Source: Adapted from Cattell, R. B. *The scientific analysis of personality.* Baltimore: Penguin Books, 1965.

found that very similar factors emerged when they had students rate classmates with whom they were previously unacquainted, without even allowing them to speak with each other. As these students could not possibly have known the ratees' attributes along the dimensions in question, Passini and Norman suggested that perhaps the trait ratings reflected the concepts of the judges about personality (for example, about what traits seem to go together) more than they do the organization of these traits in the rated persons.

Still, given his contributions toward a system of personality measurement and description, Cattell's importance should not be underestimated. In the next section, the approach taken by H. J. Eysenck, another prominent dispositional psychologist, will be considered. Like Cattell, Eysenck attempted to discover the basic components of personality and relied heavily on factor analysis to accomplish this goal.

TYPES AS DIMENSIONS OF PERSONALITY: EYSENCK'S VIEW

Perhaps the most fundamental difference between the dispositional approaches espoused by Cattell and Hans Eysenck (1916–   ) lies in the level at which each chose to look for the basic dimensions of personality. Cattell's research has revealed a relatively lengthy list of source traits. In contrast, Eysenck's investigations have focused on discovering a small number of basic personality *types*.

In Eysenck's view, types are not categories that a few people fit; rather, types are dimensions on which persons differ. They tend to be normally distributed, as do traits (see Figure 10–1), with most people around the average mark. This difference between the ancient type theories and Eysenck's conception of types in modern personality theory is suggested in Figure 10–3.

H. J. Eysenck

FIGURE 10–3
A graphic representation of the difference between ancient type theories (A) and Eysenck's view of types as continuous dimensions on which personalities differ (B)

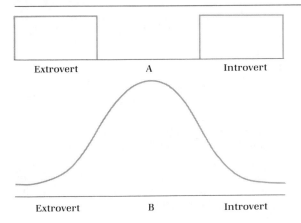

Courtesy of H. J. Eysenck

Like many other theorists, Eysenck envisioned a structural model of personality. Types are at the pinnacle of the personality structure, and therefore they exert the most commanding influence. Types are composed of traits; traits are composed of habitual responses; and, at the most particular level, specific responses are the elements out of which our habits are made. This overall view of personality is depicted in Figure 10–4.

Using factor-analytic procedures, Eysenck and his colleagues have performed dozens of studies over a period of more than 30 years. (As far back as World War II, for example, Eysenck applied factor-analytic procedures to a multitude of ratings and classifications of approximately 10,000 soldiers.) In this time he has marshaled an impressive body of evidence suggesting that there are two major dimensions on which personality can be cast: *introversion-extroversion* and *stability-instability*.[5] In the third edition of *The Structure of Human Personality*, Eysenck (1970) states that many

---

[5] In his earlier writings, Eysenck referred to the stability-instability dimension as "neuroticism" and favored the spelling *"extraversion"* over *"extroversion."*

FIGURE 10–4
Eysenck's hierarchical model of personality

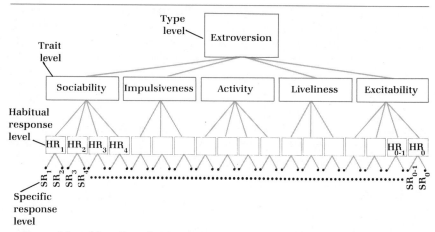

Source: Adapted from Eysenck, H. J. *The biological basis of personality.* Springfield, Ill.: Charles C Thomas, 1967.

independent sets of investigations all support very strongly the thesis that two orthogonal [independent] personality factors, extraversion–introversion and emotionality–stability, are omnipresent in empirical studies and analyses, and account for a large and important portion of the total variance, for children as much as for adults, and for mentally ill as well as mentally normal people. (p. 425)

How are extroversion-introversion and stability-instability related? Eysenck (1975) presented a graphic representation of each individual's personality as being positioned somewhere within a circle bisected by each of the two dimensions, so that four quadrants result. Of this model, reproduced in Figure 10–5, Eysenck says: "The trait names inside the circle may serve to give an idea of the behavior patterns characteristic of extroverts and introverts, labile and stabile people—remembering always that extremes in either direction are rare, and that most people are somewhere intermediate" (1975, p. 190). Having entered this caveat, Eysenck (1975) proceeded to point out that various deviances, such as neurosis and criminality, can be understood in part as extreme cases in the normal distribution of the two major personality dimensions. He concluded that a person who has both high emotionality and strong introversion will tend to be clinically neurotic, whereas a combination of high emotionality and high extroversion tends to produce criminality (Eysenck, 1977).

A third aspect of personality which weaves its way in and out of Eysenck's writings is *psychoticism*. His most recent view is that the underlying dimension is best labeled *P* and that it includes both a disposition toward being psychotic and a degree of psychopathy (characterized by an absence of real loyalties to any person, group, or code).

FIGURE 10–5
The two major dimensions of personality suggested by Eysenck's factor-analytic studies. An individual personality can fall in any of the four quadrants.

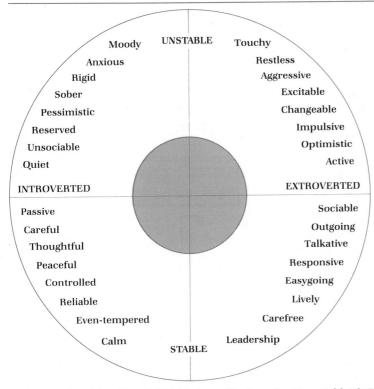

Source: Adapted from Eysenck, H. J. *The inequality of man*. San Diego, Calif.: Edit Publishers, 1975.

Unlike extroversion-introversion and stability-instability, P is not a dimension with polar opposites; rather, P is an ingredient which is present to varying degrees in individual personalities. High P scorers, according to Eysenck (1975, p. 197), are characterized by 11 dispositions:

1. Solitary, not caring for people.
2. Troublesome, not fitting in.
3. Cruel, inhumane.
4. Lack feeling, insensitive.
5. Sensation-seeking, underaroused.
6. Hostile to others, aggressive.
7. Like odd, unusual things.
8. Disregard danger, foolhardy.
9. Like to make fools of other people, upsetting them.
10. Opposed to accepted social customs.
11. Engage in little personal interaction; prefer "impersonal" sex.

Eysenck (1975) reports that P is higher in men than in women, is heritable, is higher in prisoners than in nonprisoners (and highest in those imprisoned for sexual or aggressive offenses), and is lower in psychiatric patients who have improved than in those who have not.

Origins of personality differences

In Eysenck's earlier writings (e.g., Eysenck, 1952), he remained uncommitted regarding the causes of personality. Later, Eysenck (1961, 1964) hypothesized that underlying all the differences that distinguish introversion from extroversion is a difference in "conditionability" (the forming of stimulus-response associations on the basis of experience). Specifically, Eysenck believes that introverts condition much more rapidly than do extroverts and that this explains (among other things) why persons in the former group seem so "sensitive." He also believes that the brains of extreme introverts are too easily aroused so that they shy away from stimulation, whereas extreme extroverts must seek stimulation to keep up their brain activity levels and thus avoid the feeling of boredom. "Extroverts," Eysenck writes, "tend to have a level [of arousal] which is too low much of the time, unless environment can provide excitement and stimulation; hence they tend to be stimulus-hungry and sensation-seeking" (1975, p. 194).

In his book *Crime and Personality* (1977), Eysenck provides a review of the literature supporting a relationship between extroversion and antisocial behavior. Along these lines, Eysenck, (1964) and other investigators (Lykken, 1957; Schachter & Latané, 1964) have reported that antisocial individuals do not easily form conditioned avoidance responses. For example, in Lykken's (1957) experiment, the subjects were penitentiary inmates judged to have *sociopathic personalities* (characterized by selfishness, lack of guilt feelings, and an inability to display loyalty), inmates judged not to be sociopaths, and college students. The task involved learning through trial and error to avoid pressing a lever that produced electric shocks for the subject. This experimental task is one that everyone learns with experience, but the college students learned to avoid shocks more quickly, thereby suggesting at least some relationship between personality and conditionability. Eysenck has interpreted these and similar findings as demonstrating an association between the need for stimulation and the difficulty in learning social inhibitions that characterize extroversion, and a tendency toward criminal behavior.

In his later writings, Eysenck (1967, 1975) has gone further in suggesting that much of personality is fixed and of a constitutional or genetic origin. "However we look at the facts," argues Eysenck (1975) after summarizing 40 years of research, "heredity plays a very important part in the cause of these many different types of conduct and . . . behavior, and is responsible for a good proportion of the individual differences observed in our type of society" (p. 201).

11 *The dispositional strategy*

Self-report personality inventories, ratings, and related issues

As we saw in the last chapter, many psychologists who study the structure of personality from a trait or type approach have relied heavily on *self-report inventories* for their data. (Self-report inventories are also employed in other personality strategies.) Self-report inventories usually consist of a large number of statements or questions to which the subject is asked to respond in terms of a limited number of fixed alternatives, such as "yes-no," "true-false," and "agree-disagree" (occasionally there is a "cannot say" alternative). Typical items are of the following sort:

I often get mad when things don't turn out as planned.

I enjoy music and dancing.

Are you afraid of high places?

Do you have trouble falling asleep at night?

The items are usually printed in a booklet with separate answer sheets so that the tests can easily be administered to many subjects at once. The use of such procedures is extremely widespread; perhaps as much as two thirds of the American population will take some sort of self-report personality inventory at some time in their lives (cf. Fiske, 1967, 1971).

We have seen that most dispositional psychologists regard traits or types as being composed of more specific habits, response tendencies, and ways of reacting to situations. Thus it would seem that, given a specification of what a person with a particular disposition should feel and do, an adequate self-report inventory need only sample these feelings and behaviors. For example, an item which reflects the disposition toward depression might be: "I am often sad." If the domain of habits and "symptoms" of the dispositions it intends to measure are adequately sampled, a personality inventory would have *content validity*.

CONSTRUCTION OF PERSONALITY INVENTORIES

The *content validation approach* to inventory construction has a number of difficulties. First, content validity does not speak to the issue of whether a test actually works for the intended purpose. To

Content validation and its problems

determine the degree to which the test is successful in classifying individuals into categories, some means of *external* validation is necessary. For example, the classification obtained by using the test could be compared with that obtained by the independent clinical judgments of psychologists. If individuals cannot be classified properly from the way they respond to the items, there is little solace in knowing that the test inquired about the full range of behavior in every category. As we shall see shortly, a test with high content validity can fail to work because examinees are responding not to the content of the items but rather to some aspect of the test-taking situation.

Second, an inventory constructed on the basis of content validity may have insufficiently subtle test items. Early test constructors paid little attention to this problem (e.g., the Woodworth Personal Data Sheet; Woodworth, 1920), reasoning that a test item which was to measure something ought to "look like" it was doing so. More recently, psychologists have tended to gravitate to the other extreme, maintaining that a test item should be constructed so that the respondent is unaware of what it purports to measure. One of the principal arguments for the use of subtle test items is that obvious items allow the subject to fake answers, make a good impression, or otherwise distort his or her "real" personality. The contemporary use of more subtle items in psychological tests has contributed to the public denunciation in recent years of psychological testing as an invasion of privacy (e.g., investigations by Congress; cf. American Psychological Association, 1965).

Empirical keying: An alternative to content validation

Sensitive to the limitations of constructing self-report inventories by content validation, many research-minded test makers have employed *empirical keying,* a procedure which makes few theoretical assumptions about the type of items that will be required to make a valid test. To illustrate the procedure, we will describe the development of the Minnesota Multiphasic Personality Inventory (MMPI).

The MMPI was developed by S. R. Hathaway, a clinical psychologist, and J. C. McKinley, a neuropsychiatrist, in 1942 in response to a need for a practical and valid test which could classify patients into the existing diagnostic categories of abnormal behavior. Hathaway and McKinley began with a pool of 1,000 self-descriptive statements collected from various psychiatric examination forms and procedures, psychiatric textbooks, and previously used inventories. Then they administered the 1,000-item inventory to groups of diagnosed psychiatric patients (so classified on the basis of clinical judgments) and groups of normal (nonpatient) subjects. For each of the diagnostic groups and the normal sample, the frequency of endorsement of (agreement with) each item was tabulated. Only those items which clearly differentiated between a diagnostic group and the normal group was retained for the final inventory. For instance, a statement became an item on the Depression scale if, and only if, patients diagnosed as having a depressive disorder endorsed the statement significantly more often than did normal persons. Thus, using empirical keying, it is possible for an item which had little content validity (e.g., "I sometimes tease animals") to be included on the Depression scale, or any other scale, of the MMPI.

The MMPI is the most widely used personality inventory (Edwards & Abbott, 1973). It consists of 550 statements which deal with such matters as attitudes, educational information, general physical health, sex roles, mood, morale, vocational interests, fears, and preoccupations. There are 4 validity scales and 10 basic clinical scales for which the MMPI is scored. The characteristics and labels of these scales are presented in Table 11–1. (Note that the labels are often misleading and fail to give an accurate impression of how the scale is actually interpreted.) The function of the validity scales is to provide information concerning the validity of the respondent's answers on the clinical scales. For example, an elevated Lie (L) scale indicates that the respondent is attempting to answer the items so as to present her- or himself in a favorable light.

THE MINNESOTA MULTIPHASIC PERSONALITY INVENTORY

The scoring of the MMPI is straightforward. Scoring keys indicate the items which appear on each scale and the scored direction of each item (i.e., true or false). The test can be scored by hand in less than 10 minutes and in considerably less time by computer. Interpretation of the scores is not as simple. To arrive at a clinical diagnosis, the *pattern* of scores on the 10 clinical scales is examined. This pattern is often presented graphically, as in Figure 11–1, in what is called a *psychogram,* or *personality profile.* A number of MMPI atlases provide assistance in interpreting profiles (e.g., Marks & Seeman, 1963). These books contain typical profiles and descriptive information about samples of subjects producing each profile. For example, along with a list of typical and atypical symptoms and behaviors for people with a given profile, there may be information about the most common diagnostic category of these people, their personal histories, courses of treatment, and so on. While it is rare to find a perfect match of profiles (i.e., identical scores on all the scales), a series of criteria which must be met for two profiles to be considered similar help the examiner to find the "typical" profile in the atlas which will be most like that of the respondent.

Although the MMPI was originally designed to aid in the diagnosis of psychiatric patients and still serves this function, it has also been used extensively in personality research. For this latter purpose, several hundred additional experimental scales using the basic 550 items have been developed. In many cases, the MMPI items which make up an

TABLE 11–1
The validity and clinical scales of the MMPI

Scale name	Symbol	Sample item	Interpretation
Cannot say	?	No sample. It is merely the number of items marked in the "cannot say" category or left blank.	This is one of four validity scales, and a high score indicates evasiveness.
Lie	L	I get angry sometimes. (False)*	This is the second validity scale. Persons trying to present themselves in a favorable light (e.g., good, wholesome, honest) obtain high L-scale scores.
Frequency	F	Everything tastes the same. (True)	F is the third validity scale. High scores suggest carelessness, confusion, or "fake bad."
Correction	K	I have very few fears compared to my friends. (False)	An elevation on the last validity scale, K, suggests a defensive test-taking attitude. Exceedingly low scores may indicate a lack of ability to deny symptomatology.
Hypochondriasis	Hs	I wake up fresh and rested most mornings. (False)	High scorers have been described as cynical and defeatist.
Depression	D	At times I am full of energy. (False)	High scorers are usually shy, despondent, and distressed.
Hysteria	Hy	I have never had a fainting spell. (False)	High scorers tend to complain of multiple symptoms.
Psychopathic deviate	Pd	I liked school. (False)	Adjectives used to describe some high scorers are adventurous, courageous, and generous.
Masculinity-femininity	Mf	I like mechanics magazines. (False)	Among males, high scorers have been described as esthetic and sensitive. High-scoring women have been described as rebellious, unrealistic, and indecisive.
Paranoia	Pa	Someone has it in for me. (True)	High scorers on this scale are characterized as shrewd, guarded, and worrisome.
Psychasthenia	Pt	I am certainly lacking in self-confidence. (True)	Fearful, rigid, anxious and worrisome are some of the adjectives used to describe high Pt scorers.
Schizophrenia	Sc	I believe I am a condemned person. (True)	Adjectives such as withdrawn and unusual describe Sc high scorers.
Hypomania	Ma	At times my thoughts have raced ahead faster than I could speak them. (True)	High scorers are called sociable, energetic, and impulsive.
Social introversion-extroversion	Si	I enjoy social gatherings just to be with people. (False)	High scorers: modest, shy, and self-effacing. Low scorers: sociable, colorful, and ambitious.

* The true or false responses within parentheses indicate the scored direction of each of the items.
Source: Psychological Corporation. Reproduced by permission. Copyright 1943, renewed 1970 by the University of Minnesota. Published by The Psychological Corporation, New York, N.Y. All rights reserved.

FIGURE 11–1
Sample MMPI profile (psychogram)

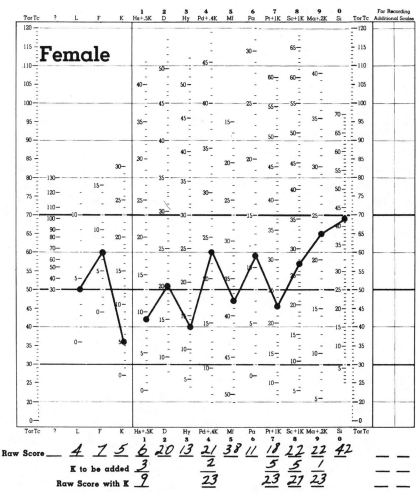

The Minnesota Multiphasic Personality Inventory

Starke R. Hathaway and J. Charnley McKinley

experimental scale are used alone, as is the case, for example, with the Taylor Manifest Anxiety Scale (Taylor, 1953), which has been used widely in research on anxiety.

Several studies also show that MMPI scores can be used to predict the long-range performance of persons. Hathaway and Monachesi

(1952), for example, were able to predict delinquent behavior that occurred two years later by using a combination of their subjects' Pd (psychopathic deviate) and Ma (hypomania) scales. In a more recent study, Harrell (1972) found that speed of advancement in business and income 10 years later were predictable at well above chance level from the Ma scale of several hundred Stanford University graduate students in business.

THE CALIFORNIA PSYCHOLOGICAL INVENTORY

Another example of an empirically keyed self-report personality inventory is the California Psychological Inventory (CPI), which was devised by Harrison Gough (1956) as an MMPI-like scale intended for use with a normal population. Careful research went into its construction, including a validation sample of 13,000 normal subjects.

The CPI contains almost 500 true-false items, about half of which come from the MMPI. Administered, scored, and profiled in much the same way as the MMPI, the CPI contains 3 validity scales and scales for 15 personality traits, including dominance, tolerance, self-control, achievement via conformance and achievement via independence, self-acceptance, sense of well-being, responsibility, socialization, and flexibility. The scales discriminate well on *non*psychiatric criteria, such as leadership, and there is much favorable evidence for their validity (Cronbach, 1959; Kleinmuntz, 1967). For example, one scale of the CPI is designed to measure the tendency to seek achievement via conformance (the *Ac* scale). Validation studies show that *Ac* is a better predictor of students' grade-point averages than is IQ (Gough, 1953) and that it can discriminate between achieving and underachieving high school students even when they are matched on IQ (Gill & Spilka, 1962; Gough, 1964; Pierce, 1961a).

The CPI socialization scale

To illustrate the validation research that underlies the CPI, we will discuss the socialization *(So)* scale in some detail. The *So* scale is based on the assumption that persons differ in their ability to sense and interpret the subtler aspects of the social situations in which they find themselves and thus differ in the degree that they control their own behavior in social situations. A person's *So* score is intended to reflect his or her position on a continuum "ranging from behaviors of greater waywardness and recalcitrance at one end, through an intermediate zone of partial balance and adaptation, to an extreme of archetypal virtue and probity [integrity]" (Gough & Sandhu, 1964, pp. 544–45).

Below are a few of the items on the CPI that are "diagnostic" for *So.* You will probably be able to guess the direction of the more socialized "answer."

Before I do something I try to consider how my friends will react to it.

I have often gone against my parents' wishes.

If the pay was right I would like to travel with a circus or carnival.

I find it easy to "drop" or "break with" a friend.

I often think about how I look and what impression I am making upon others.

Gough (1960) demonstrated the validity of the *So* scale in a massive study involving 41 research samples and over 20,000 subjects. His basic logic was that "a scale of measurement for 'socialization' should position individuals in the 'asocial,' 'normal,' and 'supernormal' zones of the continuum in general accordance with the verdict which the socio-cultural environment has handed down concerning them" (1960, p. 23). Gough (1960) administered the *So* scale to samples of persons representing groups whom society considered to be "exemplary," or socialized to a supernormal degree (such as individuals who had been nominated as "best citizens" of their high schools), as well as those judged to be "asocial" (such as persons with records of high school delinquency or, more seriously, persons who were prison inmates), and to a number of groups whom society judged to be socialized more or less within the normal range (high school students, psychology graduate students, airline hostesses, and machine operators). The scale would be valid to the extent that the supernormals scored higher on it than the normals, who in turn scored higher than those whose status is considered asocial. A portion of Gough's (1960) actual findings is shown in Figure 11–2. It can be seen plainly that the *So* scale received strong validation; the more "socialized" the group, the higher its mean *So* score. Note, too, that virtually the same pattern is found for both females and males.

Another inventory that is currently gaining in popularity is the Jackson Personality Inventory, or the JPI (Jackson, 1976). Like the California Psychological Inventory, the JPI was developed as a measure of personality in nonclinical populations of average or above-average intelligence. The format of the JPI is similar to that of the CPI. It consists of 320 true-false items divided equally into 16, 20-item scales, with one being a validity scale. When it comes to methods of scale construction and interpretation, however, the two inventories clearly part company.

Jackson (1970, 1971, 1978) has argued that the empirical scale construction based on differentiation among criterion groups which characterized both MMPI and CPI development often results in scales loaded with response bias and lacking in usefulness. Rather than employing empirical keying, as was done with the MMPI, Jackson used a content validation approach. After selecting the constructs to be included in

THE JACKSON PERSONALITY INVENTORY

FIGURE 11–2
Mean scores on the CPI *So* scale in Gough's (1960) study

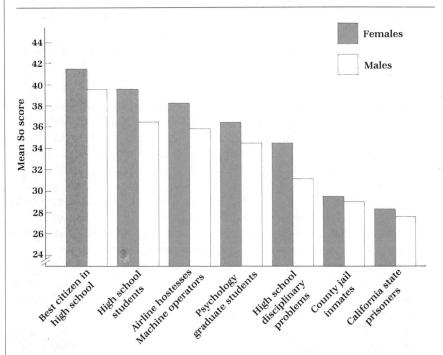

the scale, his first step was to broadly, yet explicitly, define each concept to be measured and to carefully write a large number of items that represented the concept in question, but which also avoided extreme levels of evaluative bias. (The importance of the latter concern will become evident in a later section of this chapter.) He next employed a number of empirical item-selection strategies in order to select items for each scale that not only measured the same construct (i.e., which ensured *scale homogeneity*) but which also measured only the constructs that they were supposed to measure, without tapping into other scale dimensions as well. This was achieved in part by administering the items to large samples of respondents and subjecting their responses to sophisticated statistical analyses. On the basis of this and other procedures, the final items were selected, and the process of validating and providing performance norms was begun.

The resultant inventory taps personality variables such as anxiety, breadth of interest, energy level, conformity, risk taking, and tolerance. But how is a person's pattern of scores on these scales interpreted? On the basis of further investigations, Jackson and his students identified five modal personality profiles for each sex, with each profile reflecting a specific pattern of personality scores. An individual's responses on the JPI are therefore analyzed and the profile type best approximated by his or her overall performance is identified. It is hoped that knowledge of one's modal profile type will eventually permit the tester to make useful predictions about the respondent. At present, though, the ability of the JPI to predict behavior in different situations on the basis of modal types has yet to be clearly demonstrated, although there is some evidence in that direction (Skinner, Jackson, & Rampton, 1976; Strasburger & Jackson, 1977).

When used for purposes of personnel selection, personality inventories determine whether a potential employee's personality structure or attributes fit those believed to be important for successful performance of the job in question. More frequently, however, they are used in an attempt to screen out individuals from highly stressful or responsible positions because of poor mental health or adjustment difficulties. While it is generally accepted that the MMPI is an inadequate inventory for the former purpose, studies have demonstrated that the test fairly reliably detects psychopathology in job applicants. It is therefore sometimes used as an exclusion criterion for critical occupations requiring a strong sense of responsibility and personality stability (Butcher, 1979).

Recently, however, use of the MMPI in this manner has generated considerable controversy and even litigation (Dahlstrom, 1980). In the summer of 1977, five men sued two officials of the Jersey City, New Jersey government along with the Stevens Institute of Technology, which is affiliated with the Laboratory of Psychological Studies (LPS) and which conducted psychological screening for the emotional fitness of aspiring fire fighters. In this civil suit (which was later joined by several civil-liberties organizations), two firemen, two applicants for a position in the fire department, and one unsuccessful candidate charged that the use of psychological tests like the MMPI required the applicants to disclose personal information and therefore constituted an invasion of privacy. As some of the items from the MMPI allude to sexual practices and to religious and political beliefs, the men further charged that the testing violated their rights of freedom of belief as protected by the 1st and 14th amendments to the Constitution.

After an extremely lengthy trial, Senior Judge James A. Coolahan issued his opinion (*McKenna* v. *Fargo*, 451 F. Supp. 1355 [1978]). He envisioned the heart of the case as involving the fact of "involuntary disclosure" that accompanied responding to the MMPI and to the projective techniques in the test battery. As the job applicant did not always know exactly what his responses to specific items were revealing about his personality, his privacy was being invaded on some level. Nevertheless, Judge Coolahan dismissed the allegation that the applicants' constitutional right of freedom of belief was violated. It did not appear that the applicants were being tested for their beliefs or values, as the fire department received a testing summary rather than seeing the raw scores of the tests that showed how applicants responded to specific items. Further, as the judge saw the occupation of fireman as entailing life-threatening risks to the applicant and the public, he recognized the need for the state to protect its interests by hiring only those emotionally fit.

Judge Coolahan therefore decided "that the constitutional protection afforded privacy interests is not absolute. State interests may become sufficiently compelling to sustain State regulations or activities which burden the right to privacy." He further determined that psychological evaluation was an acceptable selection procedure, largely because of the major role that psychological factors play in the role of fire fighting. This decision has since been upheld by the Circuit Court of Appeals in Philadelphia (June 1979).

ALTERNATIVES TO TRADITIONAL SELF-REPORT INVENTORIES

Recent years have seen several scathing critiques of dispositional personality assessment procedures, and several writers (Krasner & Ullmann, 1973; Mischel, 1968) have concluded that, in most cases, self-report and similar measures are not able to predict the actual behavior of individual persons with sufficient precision to make them useful. Not surprisingly, proponents of the dispositional view have found fault with a number of the critics' specific arguments and conclusions (e.g., Bowers, 1973; Jaccard, 1974). But the recent attacks on traditional personality tests have also led to some critical reappraisal of personality assessment and assessment research (cf. Hogan, DeSoto, & Solano, 1977).

Ratings and nominations

Perhaps the most obvious alternative to self-reports of personality is to observe the person directly in many situations and thereby to determine objectively whether he or she "gets mad often" or "tires easily" or whatever. (Recall from Chapter 10 that Cattell urged the collection of such information, referring to it as *L*-data.) However, in most assessment efforts, the psychologist will be unable to observe the person directly over a range of situations and a length of time sufficient to make an adequate dispositional rating possible.[1] Therefore, the only way to obtain *L*-data is through the reports of those who

---

[1] Dispositional assessment, it will be recalled, is based on the assumption of the *additivity* of individual observations (see page 168); and many dispositional psychologists explicitly denounce the idea that even a person's most basic dispositions will necessarily show up in every situation. For these reasons, the dispositional strategy requires a good deal of assessment information.

know the person well. Assessment data obtained in this way are given the general name *ratings*.

Ratings of one kind or another enjoy extremely wide use, and almost everyone has been a rater and been rated by others. Ratings are often used, for example, in letters of recommendation by one's former employers and teachers, and they may also be used in reports made by mental-health workers about a client's behavior or progress. More formal rating scales are used widely in personality assessment and research. Typically, the psychologist will ask a person who knows the subject well (such as a teacher, friend, or mate) to rate the subject on *whether* he or she has a particular characteristic, or will ask for a number (say, from 0 to 10) that indicates *how much* of a given characteristic the subject has.

However, a strong word of caution needs to be injected about ratings. Unless rating scales are designed very carefully, they are open to a number of serious biases and distortions. These biases reside within the rater, and they distort the picture that he or she provides about the subject of the assessment. Several of the major types of bias that have been identified are shown in Table 11–2.

TABLE 11–2
Possible sources of bias in personality rating scales

Source of error	Explanation
Error of leniency	When raters know a person well, as they must in order to offer an informed evaluation, they tend to rate the person higher (or sometimes lower) than they should.
Error of central tendency	Raters are often reluctant to use the extreme ends of a rating scale even when these are appropriate, preferring to stick closer to the middle range of descriptions. (We all do this when we describe a very ugly person as "not being that attractive.")
Halo effect	Raters tend to permit their *general* impression of a person to influence their ratings for most of the person's specific characteristics, just as a halo casts a pleasant, diffuse light over an angel or a cherub.
Contrast error	Raters often describe others as being less like themselves than is actually the case. A relatively submissive rater, for example, may see others as being considerably more dominant than they really are.
"Logical" error	Raters often assume that two characteristics should be related ("it seems logical") and bias their evaluations accordingly. For example, a rater who believes that *hostility* and *abrasiveness* go together may rate people who are abrasive as being more hostile than they really are.
Proximity error	When a standard rating form is used, characteristics that are near one another on the list often receive similar ratings just because they are close together. This is a type of "response set" problem.

Source: Based on the analysis offered by Guilford, J. P. *Psychometric methods.* 2d ed. New York: McGraw-Hill, 1954.

In contrast to evaluations by one or two raters, *nominations* based on observations made over extended periods of time by a number of observers who see the person from a variety of perspectives and with whom the person has had an array of relationships provide the single best source of assessment data available (Neale & Liebert, 1980; Smith, 1967). In a longitudinal project of Neale and Weintraub (1977), for example, peer nominations are being obtained for a large number of children of schizophrenic parents, and each of these subjects has at least one matched control child from a more normal family background. The subjects in the Neale and Weintraub study are being assessed in part by a 35-item peer nomination procedure developed by Pekarik and his associates (Pekarik, Prinz, Liebert, Weintraub, & Neale, 1976). The procedure involves distributing the 35-item Pupil Evaluation Inventory to all of the children in the subject's classroom. The inventory asks the children to name (nominate) other children in the class who possess various characteristics (e.g., "Those who can't sit still," "Those who are liked by everyone," and "Those who make fun of people"). The subject's score for any category is his or her percentage of the possible nominations in that category; thus, a child in a class of 50 who was nominated by 10 classmates as among "those who can't sit still" would receive a score of 20 (10/50 = 20 percent), whereas a child in a class of 25 who was nominated by 20 classmates would receive a score of 80. The usefulness of the procedure has been clearly demonstrated (Pekarik et al., 1976), but the cost is high because the inventory must be administered to an entire classroom in order to assess a single child. In fact, for assessment of a single individual, gathering data through an adequate nomination technique is often out of the question except in the assessment of school children.

The "composite profile" approach to assessment

Rather than relying on one method of personality measurement, some investigators have proposed that a multimethod approach be used to ensure that one's findings are statistically sound (Campbell, 1960; Campbell & Fiske, 1959). By using as many disparate measures of the same trait as possible, it is assumed that the measurement error associated with any one method will be less likely to distort the final measure in a given direction. In the measurement of generosity, for example, it may well be the case that individuals are inclined to present themselves in a favorable light, and so may overestimate their generosity when filling out a self-report questionnaire. Clearly, the resultant measures will differ from the "true" measure of generosity in the respondents. If, however, one asked peers to rate these individuals for the trait in question, a more accurate picture will emerge when the two different measures are combined.

Using this sort of rationale, Harris (1980) has proposed that three methods of assessment should be used together to approximate an individual's "true" personality profile. He suggests starting with a carefully constructed personality inventory which objectively assesses formally defined variables. In addition to personality inventory measures, both peer and self-report ratings on the same variables as those assessed by the inventory should be obtained. The three separate configurations of personality variables that result should then be averaged to produce a composite profile.

Harris (1980) has demonstrated that composite profiles derived in this manner are considerably more stable over time than are single-method profiles, and further, that such profiles provide quite valid measures of personality. So long as one's time and budget are sufficient, then, Harris' three-method approach may offer a viable alternative to traditional personality assessment.

Another new approach to dispositional personality assessment begins with an analysis of the differences between ability tests (which are generally quite good as predictors) and personality tests. Table 11–3 lists six of these differences, all of which suggest that the superiority of the ability test very likely stems from its clarity and lack of ambiguity. With this notion in mind, Willerman, Turner, and Peterson (1976) set out to ask for subjects' self-reports of what their typical and maximal performances would be like in an anger-producing and an elation-producing situation. Subsequently, the subjects were asked to imagine that someone had made them angry or that something had made them elated, and to act out what their typical and their most extreme (maximal) responses would be.

> The "abilities" approach to personality testing

TABLE 11–3
Basic differences between ability and personality tests

	Ability	Personality
Instructions	Subject told to do his or her best	Subject told to "be honest"
Questions	Usually clear	Vary from ambiguous to clear
Answers	Right and wrong answers	No correct answers
Set	Subject knows what is expected	Subject often unaware of examiner's expectations
Motivation	Subjects highly motivated	Motivation of subjects may vary considerably
Goals	Examiner wants *maximal* performance	Examiner usually interested in modal or *typical* performance

Source: Willerman, L., Turner, R. G., & Peterson, M. A. A comparison of the predictive validity of typical and maximal personality measures. *Journal of Research in Personality*, 1976, *10*, 482–92.

Both the subjects' self-reports and their subsequent behavior were quantified on a carefully constructed scale, permitting Willerman and his associates to determine whether the two types of tests differed in their ability to predict actual behavior. For anger, they clearly did.

Table 11–4 shows the correlations between each of the tests (i.e., subjects' self-reports of how they would typically express their anger or their self-reports of how angry they would be *capable of becoming*) and the subjects' actual displays of behavior. To obtain the behavioral measure, subjects were given the following instructions:

> you are to imagine that some person has made you very angry. Now we would like you to imagine that the Bobo doll [an inflatable plastic "punching bag" about four feet high] here is that person, and you are to express your anger to it. In addition, imagine that you are in your own home. We are going to take two measures of your anger. One will ask you to show us how angry you typically get, and the other will show us *how angry you're capable of being,* that is, we are interested in this case in your maximal expression of anger. First, we would like to see how you typically respond to someone who has made you angry. (Willerman et al., 1976, p. 485)

As can be seen from Table 11–4, a person's behavioral expression of anger was predicted better by the ability-oriented self-report than by the "typical me"–oriented one, *even when the prediction referred to typical behavior.* Though this investigation is only the beginning of an ability-based conception of dispositional assessment, Willerman and his associates are certainly correct in noting the immediate significance of their finding:

> Perhaps one of the most interesting implications for the present study concerns its application to clinical assessment. . . . When the clinician

TABLE 11–4
Correlations between ability and personality test self-reports and subjects' actual performance of aggression in the laboratory. The results suggest that, especially for males, ability-oriented self-reports provide the superior prediction of individual behavior.

	Behavioral measure	
Self-report	Typical	Maximal
Males		
"Typical for me"	.27	.01
"My maximal ability"	.51†	.69†
Females		
"Typical for me"	.35	−.14
"My maximal ability"	.42*	.43*

$* p < .05$
$† p < .01$
Source: Data from Willerman, L., Turner, R. G., & Peterson, M. A. A comparison of the predictive validity of typical and maximal personality measures. *Journal of Research in Personality,* 1976, *10,* 782–92.

is so often asked to make predictions about the potential violence of a client, it appears that he is treading on dangerous ground using only typical performance tests for making such predictions. It might be better that maximal performance tests be devised for that purpose. (Willerman et al., 1976, p. 491)

We have been talking a lot about self-report personality inventories, and it's time to try one out firsthand. Most of the major inventories (e.g., the MMPI and the CPI) would be inappropriate for this sort of trial because special training and a technical manual are required to interpret personality profiles meaningfully. But Willerman (1975) has published a short inventory that can yield some interesting insights, as seen in Demonstration 11–1.

FIRSTHAND EXPERIENCE WITH A SELF-REPORT PERSONALITY INVENTORY

Demonstration 11–1

PROCEDURE

1. Before reading further, complete the personality inventory below by selecting the number from 1 to 5 that best describes how true each item is of you. Since there are 15 items, you may wish to list the numbers 1 through 15 on a separate piece of paper and to write down your numerical answer as you read each item.

Item	Hardly at all				A lot
			How true is this of you?		
1. I make friends easily.	1	2	3	4	5
2. I tend to be shy. (R)	1	2	3	4	5
3. I like to be with others.	1	2	3	4	5
4. I like to be independent of people. (R)	1	2	3	4	5
5. I usually prefer to do things alone. (R)	1	2	3	4	5
6. I am always on the go.	1	2	3	4	5
7. I like to be off and running as soon as I wake up in the morning.	1	2	3	4	5
8. I like to keep busy all of the time.	1	2	3	4	5
9. I am very energetic.	1	2	3	4	5
10. I prefer quiet, inactive pastimes to more active ones. (R)	1	2	3	4	5
11. I tend to cry easily.	1	2	3	4	5
12. I am easily frightened.	1	2	3	4	5
13. I tend to be somewhat emotional.	1	2	3	4	5
14. I get upset easily.	1	2	3	4	5
15. I tend to be easily irritated.	1	2	3	4	5

2. Before you can score the inventory, items 2, 4, 5, and 10 (which have an R after them) need to be reversed. In other words, if you indicated "5," change it to "1." Similarly, change "4" to "2," "2" to "4," and "1" to "5." ("3" remains unchanged.)

3. To score the inventory, group your answers into three clusters: items 1–5, 6–10, and 11–15. Sum your answers to obtain a total score for each of the three clusters.

4. You are now ready to evaluate the inventory. Items 1–5 pertain to sociability, items 6–10 to activity level, and items 11–15 to emotionality. (You may recall from Chapters 9 and 10 that some psychologists believe these three dispositions to be partly inherited.)

5. Most self-report personality inventories can only be understood with respect to group norms, and this one is no exception. Willerman (1975) reports that 68 percent of University of Texas at Austin students score within the ranges given below, and adds: "If your score falls below or above these ranges, you may regard yourself as exceptionally high or low [in that disposition]" (p. 35).

	Males' average range	Females' average range
Sociability	13–19	15–20
Activity	13–19	13–20
Emotionality	9–16	11–18

6. Several other considerations regarding the Demonstration have to do with the utility of the measure. For example, did you feel that you knew what the questions were "getting at" as you answered them? Do you think you purposely (or unwittingly) biased your answers in any way? Could someone else use a copy of your answers to actually predict your *behavior* from them? And, somewhat more technically, were your responses influenced by the form of the question (reversed or not) or by possible social judgments of its content (e.g., our culture does not admire those who are easily frightened)? These are the sorts of issues to which the text now turns.

PROBLEMS WITH SELF-REPORT AND RATING DATA

Years ago Richard LaPiere (1934), a sociologist, reported on the outcome of a study in which he wrote letters to 250 hotels and restaurants across the United States, asking: "Will you accept members of the Chinese race as guests in your establishment?" A majority of the proprietors answered LaPiere's letter, and almost all of the respondents (more than 90 percent) replied that they would *not* serve Chinese guests. Perhaps this should not have been surprising, inasmuch as there was a good deal of anti-Chinese sentiment in the United States during the middle 1930s. What was surprising was that the proprietors didn't mean it, as LaPiere well knew. Six months earlier he had toured the country with a Chinese couple, stopping at each of the 250 establishments to which he had written, and *the Chinese couple had in fact been served in 249 of them, for the most part with very pleasant treatment!* More recent studies have repeatedly confirmed LaPiere's basic finding, that people's stated attitudes or intentions may tell us little or nothing about how they will behave. A "law-and-order" political attitude does not go along with adherence to certain municipal laws (Wrightsman, 1969); church attendance cannot be predicted from expressed attitudes toward the church (Wicker, 1971); and it is almost impossible to predict how often individual students will cut classes from their attitudes toward their professors (Rokeach & Kliejunas, 1972). The general point underlying all of these findings is that the "answers" we get in personality assessment will often depend on the method of inquiry or test we use; many innkeepers who might have been labeled harsh bigots on the basis of their written sentiments would have been perceived as fair-minded and unbiased on the basis of their observed actions. And aren't there people who follow a pattern that is opposite to the one shown by LaPiere's innkeepers, people who continually express egalitarian attitudes but whose private lives are filled with racially or ethnically biased actions? Of course, we might still believe that some innkeepers are more prejudiced than others, regardless of what method of assessment is used, but the burden of proof regarding the validity of both the disposition we are trying to measure ("prejudice") and the method of measurement used lies with the theorist and researcher and is never "obvious" enough to be taken on faith. This is why many investigators have tried to identify and ferret out the weaknesses in personality inventories.

People taking tests such as the MMPI have devised various schemes for falsifying their answers (e.g., in order to make a "good impression" when applying for a job or a "bad impression" when being tested for sanity in connection with a murder trial). How successful are these conscious efforts to achieve a desired impression?

Faking on personality inventories

Some "fakers," particularly those who overdo it, are likely to be detected by one or more of the validity scales built into most inventories. Still, there appears to be little doubt that, on the average, people can get "better scores" on self-report personality inventories when told to simulate a "nice personality," although there are wide individual differences in the degree to which people succeed in faking good or faking bad (Edwards & Abbott, 1973). There are, moreover, certain other kinds of test-taking attitudes—response sets—which may distort the personality picture presented by self-report inventories such as the MMPI and the CPI.

Psychologists who use self-report personality inventories often assume that the individual's response to any given item reflects his or her disposition toward the *content* of the item. For example, it may be important to assume that a person who responds "true" to the state-

Response sets

ment "I like parties" attends social functions frequently. Are there sources of distortion which can weaken or invalidate this assumption? The answer appears to be yes, since it has been found that respondents with particular test-taking attitudes may not be answering the items in terms of their content. *Response sets,* as these reactions to the test situation are called, are characteristic and consistent ways of respond-ing to a test regardless of what the items say. *Response acquiescence* is the tendency to agree with items, no matter what their content. *Response deviation* is the tendency to answer items in an uncommon direction.

Social desirability as a response set

One response set which has received much attention in recent years is *social desirability,* which is characterized by answering items in the most socially accepted direction, irrespective of whether such an-swers are correct for the respondent. For example, an individual who prefers to be alone and dislikes social gatherings might answer "true" to the statement "I like parties" because he or she feels that it is socially desirable to enjoy parties.

Several methods have been devised for controlling the influence of social desirability. One approach is to measure the respondent's tendency to answer items on a self-report inventory in the socially desirable direction and then to adjust his or her score on the inventory to take the degree of this tendency into account.

Another approach involves employing neutral items with respect to social desirability (i.e., statements which are rated in the middle of the social desirability-undesirability scale), as, for example, "I am easily awakened by noise." However, it often proves difficult to find or rewrite items which meet the requirement of neutrality and simulta-neously convey the necessary content. It is hard to imagine how one could rewrite the statement "Most of the time I wish I were dead" (an MMPI item which is rated as extremely undesirable; Hanley, 1956) so as to make it more socially desirable without changing the meaning substantially.

A third approach for controlling the effects of social desirability is to use a *forced-choice inventory.* All of the statements appearing in the inventory are first scaled for social desirability and then paired according to their scale values. The members of each pair have approxi-mately the same social desirability scale value but different content. Therefore, when respondents choose the statement in each pair which is more characteristic of them, the choices cannot be based on social desirability. Edwards (1953a) constructed his Personal Preference Schedule in this way to control for the influence of social desirability. The Personal Preference Schedule is a self-report personality inventory

TABLE 11–5
Examples of items from the Edwards Personal Preference Schedule

Alternatives	Items
A B	A: I like to tell amusing stories and jokes at parties. B: I would like to write a great novel or play.
A B	A: I like to have my work organized and planned before beginning it. B: I like to travel and see the country.
A B	A: I feel like blaming others when things go wrong for me. B: I feel that I am inferior to others in most respects.
A B	A: I like to avoid responsibilities and obligations. B: I feel like making fun of people who do things that I regard as stupid.

Source: Edwards, 1953a. Reproduced by permission. Copyright 1953 by the Psychological Corporation, New York, N.Y. All rights reserved.

developed for use in counseling and research with nonpsychiatric persons. Examples of items appearing on it are presented in Table 11–5.

Response styles: An alternative view of the data

Fiske and Pearson (1970) note that people can judge the intended domain of a personality test rather accurately and point to the complex implications of this fact. "Like other reactions," they write, "reactions to tests and to test tasks have their personality correlates" (p. 68). In other words, an examinee's response to the fact that he or she is taking a test may itself be a personality disposition, one which may alter the person's responses to the particular items on the test. Thus, while some psychologists have endeavored to rid self-report inventories of the distorting influence of response sets, other psychologists have observed that these characteristic modes of responding might not be sources of error at all. This latter group has suggested that it would be more fruitful to look at test-taking attitudes as personality traits than as situation-specific reactions. That is, the salient measures of personality in self-report inventories might be *how* an individual responds rather than *what* is responded to (i.e., the content of the items).

Because an examinee's response tendencies can be viewed either as a source of distortion or error in personality assessment or as an indication of personality dispositions, it is useful to assign different terms to describe each situation. The former are referred to as response *sets*, and the latter are called response *styles* (Jackson & Messick, 1958).[2] We have already examined social desirability as a response set; now,

---

[2] Some response tendencies probably fall between these categories. Response acquiescence, for example, "may be an internally consistent disposition, [but] it is not a generalized disposition, and occurs more readily when items are weak in content . . . or when subjects are uncertain" (Fiske & Pearson, 1970, pp. 71–72).

we shall consider the evidence for its being a response style—that is, a true personality disposition.

Social desirability as a response style: Edwards' approach

In order to measure a person's inclination to respond to self-descriptive statements in the socially desirable direction, Edwards (1953a) developed a Social Desirability (SD) scale. He selected 150 items from the MMPI and asked 10 judges to respond to each of the items in the socially desirable direction. The judges agreed perfectly on 79 of the 150 statements, and these 79 items formed the first SD scale. Later, Edwards reduced the SD scale to 39 items by selecting those items which showed the greatest differentiation between subjects who had high and low total scores.

Edwards hypothesized: "If the SD scale does provide a measure of the tendency of subjects to give socially desirable responses to statements in self-description, then the correlations of scores on this scale with other personality scales, given under standard instructions, should indicate something of the extent to which the social desirability variable is operating at the time" (1957, pp. 31, 33). A number of studies by Edwards and other investigators (e.g., Edwards, 1953a, 1957; Merrill & Heathers, 1956) have provided evidence supporting this hypothesis. Scales measuring socially desirable traits, such as dominance, responsibility, status, cooperativeness, agreeableness, and objectivity, have been found to be positively correlated with the SD scale. In contrast, scales measuring socially undesirable traits, such as social introversion, neuroticism, hostility, dependency, insecurity, and anxiety, have been found to be negatively correlated with the SD scale (cf. Edwards, 1970).

One possible implication of the correlations found between Edwards' SD scale and other personality scales is that the traits which these scales are measuring are, despite their names (e.g., dominance and social introversion), only different aspects of social desirability. Perhaps it would be more fruitful from the standpoint of predictive and explanatory power and parsimony to view the various traits which have been found to correlate strongly with the SD scale as if they were measures of social desirability. However, several important points should be kept in mind. First, correlation does not mean identity. Height and weight are known to be highly correlated, for example, but it is clear that the two concepts are not interchangeable. Similarly, the fact that Drake's Social Introversion Scale (Merrill & Heathers, 1956) and Edwards' SD scale are strongly related (−.90) means only that one can be predicted from the other with a high degree of accuracy. Second, although the relationship *may* occur because both scales measure social desirability, it may also occur because both measure a disposition that is better thought of as social introversion or because of some third variable that is tied to both (see Chapter 2).

In addition, it appears that the social desirability of an *item* (as averaged across many subjects) does not reflect its social desirability for most people considered as individual examinees. Fiske (1971) observes:

> When correlations are computed for each subject between his own [social desirability] ratings and his endorsements [of personality test items] the values are much lower than the ones for group averages reported by Edwards. Even with these lower but positive relationships for individuals, what is the direction of the influence? Perhaps subjects tend to rate as desirable whatever characteristics they perceive in themselves, rather than to attribute to themselves those characteristics they deem to be socially desirable. (p. 216)

Despite these limitations, proponents of different response styles have endeavored to subsume a variety of traits measured by self-report personality inventories under the rubric of a single response style. Edwards, who has championed the trait of social desirability, is no exception. Consider the persuasive argument he has made for interpreting the trait being measured by the Taylor Manifest Anxiety (MA) Scale as social desirability-undesirability.

The MA scale has been found to be negatively correlated with the SD scale,[3] which means that high anxiety tends to be associated with low social desirability, and low anxiety tends to be associated with high social desirability. This finding is not surprising when one examines the items that make up the MA scale. Statements such as "I am a very nervous person," "I am certainly lacking in self-confidence," and "I cry easily," which appear on the MA scale, are unquestionably socially undesirable characteristics in our general society. Thus, high scores on the MA scale can be viewed as a function of endorsing these and other socially undesirable statements, whereas low scores on the MA scale would be a function of denying socially undesirable characteristics. (It is interesting to note that for certain subgroups of our culture—such as the residents of mental hospitals or homes for the aged—these socially undesirable characteristics are less undesirable and may even be construed as socially desirable—for example, because they foster attention and care.)

---

[3] Edwards (1957) reports a correlation of −.84 between the MA scale and the 39-item SD scale and a correlation of −.60 between the MA scale and the 79-item SD scale. The negative relationship between the MA and SD scales, as well as the substantially higher correlation obtained with the shorter SD scale, could be accounted for by the 22 overlapping items on the 39-item SD scale and the MA scale. On the basis of further statistical analyses, Edwards concludes that the negative correlation between the SD scale and the MA scale cannot be accounted for "merely in terms of the item overlap between the two scales" (1957, p. 88 n.).

The MA scale has been used in numerous experimental studies investigating the effect of anxiety on performance to select subjects with high and low anxiety. One finding[4] has been that, for certain kinds of verbal learning (such as verbal maze, paired-associate, and serial nonsense-syllable learning), low-anxiety subjects make fewer errors and reach a stage of learning faster (in fewer trials) than do high-anxiety subjects (e.g., Montague, 1953; Ramond, 1953; Taylor & Spence, 1952). Edwards (1957) attempts to explain these results in terms of social desirability in the following way.

> I believe it possible . . . to describe the low group on the Taylor scale as those who desire to make a good impression on others and the high group as those who are less interested in what others may think of them. I would predict that the group desiring to make a good impression on the Taylor scale, that is to say, those with low scores, might also desire to make a good impression in terms of their performance on the learning task. They are, in other words, perhaps more highly motivated by the desire to "look good," not only in their responses to the Taylor scale, but also in their performance in the learning situation itself. Surely, to be able to learn fast is, in our society, a socially desirable characteristic. If a subject has a strong tendency to give socially desirable responses in self-description, is it unreasonable to believe that he may also reveal this tendency in his behavior in a learning situation where he is aware of what would be considered socially desirable, namely to learn fast, to do his best? The high group, on the other hand, being less interested in making a good impression, showing less of a tendency to give socially desirable responses in self-description, caring less about how others may value them, does not have equal motivation with the low group in the learning situation. (p. 89)

Evaluation of response sets and response styles

Our discussion of response sets and response styles has focused on social desirability and has presented the evidence *for* their importance and validity. While the arguments favoring a response-style or response-set interpretation of self-report inventories are impressive, they have certainly not gone unchallenged. In fact, several investigators (Block, 1965; Rorer, 1965) have argued that the tendency to respond to items on the basis of characteristics other than content may in fact be of minimal signifiance. Block (1965) went so far as to develop an MMPI scale that consisted of only those items that were rated as neutral in social desirability value and administered the scale to nine diverse samples of subjects. As he found that the factor structure of the MMPI did not change, even with this modification, he concluded that the influence of social desirability on MMPI responding is insignificant.

---

[4] The relationship between level of anxiety and performance is rather complex, depending to a large degree on the nature of the performance task (see Spence & Spence, 1966).

Nevertheless, the response set versus content distinction remains a salient one. Currently, it is taken for granted that psychologists avoid the confounding influence of response sets in test construction, using methods like those described above (e.g., using forced-choice inventories). This is not to suggest that responses be interpreted in terms of content alone, however. As pointed out by Wiggins (1973), all behavior, including test-taking behavior, is multiply determined and cannot be adequately explained in terms of item content or response styles alone. Rather, he argues that a complete understanding of test responses and their interpretation requires consideration of several hypothetical components that interact to determine such responses, which include the strategy under which the test was constructed, the test-item characteristics, response-style biases, and the content of the items. The controversy between a response-set or style and a content interpretation of self-report inventories, despite its historical importance, therefore appears naive in light of recent developments.

The polarization which has tended to characterize the debate between the content and response-style interpretations of self-report personality inventories is typical of many controversies in psychology. Psychologists often take extreme stands on issues rather than look for the middle ground between them. (One consequence of this fact is that it becomes possible to classify approaches to personality into opposing strategies, as has been done in this book for heuristic purposes.) Yet all personality psychologists would no doubt agree that behavior is multiply determined. Therefore, on purely common sense grounds, it would seem more enlightening to search for the interactions among the multiple sources of personality (e.g., traits *and* situational influences rather than traits *versus* situational influences). The approach taken by Henry A. Murray and described in the next chapter is a partial attempt to view personality as an interaction of enduring dispositions within the person and external situational forces that press in from the environment.

12 The dispositional strategy

Needs and motives

The idea that people can be understood and their behavior predicted by knowing something of "what drives them"—that is, their motivational structure—has enormous appeal. However, raising the question of the motivational forces behind personality brings with it a host of more specific questions. Is there a set of common human motives that can be measured in almost everyone? Do these motives exert a pervasive and general influence on our behavior? Can evidence of our personal motivations be found in the incidental things we say and do, such as our favorite metaphors of speech and the kinds of stories we tell? These questions would all be answered "yes" by the dispositional psychologists to whose work we now turn. In their view, the needs which people have differ in both kind and amount. In turn, these differences motivate people to think about different things and take different courses of action. Thus, needs supply motives which lead to thought and action, as shown in Figure 12–1.

The work on motives to be discussed in this chapter differs in some very fundamental ways from the more static, attributive dispositional theories discussed in Chapters 9 and 10. One difference is that motivational theorists have been influenced heavily by several psychoanalytic ideas, especially (1) the importance of driving, impelling forces within the person for explaining behavior, and (2) the belief that information about personality can be extracted from a person's projective test responses and other elicited fantasies. Despite these ties with the psychoanalytic strategy, however, all of the need and motive theorists discussed in this chapter have worked within the fundamental framework of the dispositional strategy. They assume (1) that there are measurable individual differences among people (in this case, in the relative strength of their needs and motives); (2) that these individual differences manifest themselves in a wide range of actions and are relatively durable over time; and (3) that motives and needs, as dispositions within the person, provide the basis for predicting, explaining, and understanding behavior. While the psychoanalytic strategy emphasizes the *similarity* in the motivations of all people, the motive theorists discussed in the pages that follow have all emphasized the dispositional strategy's basic approach: to identify and elaborate the *differences* that exist among individuals in terms of the strength of their motives and the ways in which those motives are manifested.

FIGURE 12–1
The relationship between needs and motives, showing how the motive influences both thought and action

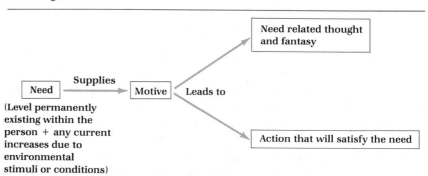

WINTER'S

THE CONCEPT OF MOTIVE

Winter (1973) has provided an exceptionally lucid analysis of the concept of motive. He suggests that the modern concept of *motive* involves six related points.

First, the concept of motive is invoked to explain changes in behavior. Motivation-type issues arise whenever we ask a "why" question, such as "Why did John cross the street?" While some answers refer to external causes (for example, a barricade blocked the sidewalk), most refer to explanations that *are within John.* For instance, "John crossed the street because he wanted to get a newspaper" is a motivational explanation of John's behavior, as is "John crossed the street to keep from slipping on the ice ahead." Thus, Winter (1973) observes that " 'motive' is a way of explaining those changes in behavior that cannot readily be explained by external forces alone" (p. 21).

Second, a motive-based explanation typically connects a specific behavior to a more general disposition. If John wants a newspaper today, he has probably wanted one in the past and will probably want one in the future as well. We must say that John "likes to," "tends to," or "often does" buy the newspaper.

Third, a motive explanation of behavior usually implies a *goal* and the possession of knowledge about certain means-ends relationships. John must know that newspapers exist, what they are, and how and where to go about buying one if he is crossing the street to get a newspaper.

Fourth, and very important, the motive explanation gives rise to predictions of how the person will behave in other situations. It also defines the limits of the behavior that has been observed. If John has already bought or read the newspaper today, we can predict that he probably will *not* cross the street to buy one.

Fifth, under some circumstances, a motive explanation enables us to anticipate an entire sequence of behavior. If, having crossed the street, John finds that the newspaper stand is out of papers, he may "go out of his way" to another newsstand or be more likely to tune in the news on his car radio that evening.

Sixth, a motive explanation leaves habit and stylistic factors totally unspecified. "We do not know whether John will walk, run, jump, or perhaps even use a pogo-stick to get across the road," writes Winter. "We do not know whether he will cross the road at a right angle or take a diagonal course directly to the front of the newstand. To answer those questions, we would ask about his *habits*" (1973, p. 22).

A person has a particular psychological (psychogenic) need to the extent that he or she is interested in need-related behavior and finds the area of functioning to be *meaningful* or salient in his or her own experience. One component of this preoccupation involves the positive, or *approach tendencies* associated with any need or motive. Thus, a person may strive for achievement or power and may seek the approval of others or affiliation with them. But *avoidance tendencies* may also be the dominant aspect of a person's motivation. While some people are driven by their achievement concerns to approach success, others are motivated to avoid failure (Atkinson & Litwin, 1960); while some people hope for power, others fear it (Winter, 1973). Personality psychologists have not yet reached agreement on exactly how to conceptualize the two faces of motivation, but some aspect of the approach-avoidance element of motivations and needs is noted by virtually every theorist.

Approach and avoidance: The two faces of motivation

The father of the modern need theory of personality is certainly Henry A. Murray (1893–   ). The approach constructed by Murray and his associates[2] beginning in the 1930s deals with "directional forces within the subject, forces which seek out or respond to various objects or total situations in the environment" (1962, p. 24). Positing such forces was not a unique venture. Impelling passions and drives had been suggested by many earlier writers, and the dynamics of Freud's theory were already well known. But Murray sought to do more than acknowl-

MURRAY'S PERSONOLOGY[1]

---

[1] Murray and his co-workers defined their area of interest as *personology,* arguing that the phrase " 'the psychology of personality' [is] a clumsy and tautological expression" (1962, p. 4).

[2] Murray's original formulation and his approach was published in 1938 in a volume of more than 700 pages titled *Explorations in Personality.* Its 1962 reprint is the primary source of information for this section.

Henry A. Murray

Harvard University News Office

Primary constructs

edge these forces. He wished to identify and catalog them, to assess them in persons, to determine their relationship to one another, and to take the bold step of writing a comprehensive theory. Recognizing that they did not have "sufficient" data to justify their stand, Murray and his colleagues noted:

> for the present the destiny of personology is best served by giving scope to speculation, perhaps not so much as psycho-analysts allow themselves, but plenty. Hence, in the present volume we have checked self-criticism, ignored various details, winked a little at statistics, and from first to last have never hesitated to offer interpretative hypotheses. Had we made a ritual of rigorous analysis nothing would have filtered through to write about. Speech is healthier than silence, even though one knows that what one says is vague and inconclusive. (1962, p. 22)

Murray believes that the individual and her or his environment must be considered together as a person-environment interaction. However, to begin an analysis of this interaction, forces within the individual and forces from the environment are temporarily separated. The former are referred to as *needs* and the latter as *press*. (Note: The plural of "press" is *press*, not presses.)

Needs

A need *(n)* is a theoretical construct, a convenient fiction which is useful only insofar as it helps the psychologist to deal with facts. It is "an organic potentiality or readiness to respond in a certain way under given conditions. . . . it is a noun which stands for the fact that a certain trend is apt to recur" (Murray, 1962, p. 61). So defined, needs are identified with particular effects or temporary end states (e.g., the need for sex is identified with orgasm). A need must be distinguished from an *actone,* which is a pattern of action (a behavior) that may serve to satisfy a need. An actone may become associated with a need if it is regularly associated with its end state. For example, verbal "threats" are actones which may function well in the service of a need for power. A given actone can often be used to satisfy a number of different needs (getting married, for example, may directly or indirectly satisfy a person's need for security, sex, and food). Therefore, it is not always possible to identify someone's active needs by observing his or her behavior. (We shall return to the problem of assessing needs in a later section.)

Murray believed that there were 39 human needs in all. This number can be broken down into the *primary,* or *viscerogenic,* needs and the *secondary,* or *psychogenic,* needs. The viscerogenic needs are best thought of as representing the physical requirements of the organism. There are said to be 12 of them: *n* Air, *n* Water, *n* Food, *n* Sex, *n* Heatavoidance, *n* Lactation, *n* Urination, *n* Defecation, *n* Harmavoidance, *n* Noxavoidance (avoidance of noxious stimuli), *n* Sentience (consciousness), and *n* Coldavoidance. While Murray uses an occasional novel term, there is general agreement that this list represents universal, biological requirements of the organism. Further, it is relatively easy to obtain agreement on the external or internal conditions which will engender one of these needs (e.g., a seductive mate for *n* Sex or increased carbon dioxide for *n* Air). There is less agreement about Murray's enumeration of the 27 psychogenic needs (listed in Table 12–1), which, among other things, are not entirely independent of one another.

TABLE 12–1
Murray's list of psychogenic needs

Major category	Need	Behavioral example
Ambition	*n* Achievement	Overcoming obstacles
	n Recognition	Boasting
	n Exhibition	Making efforts to shock or thrill others
	n Acquisition	Acquiring things by work or stealing
	n Conservance	Repairing possessions
	n Order	Tidying up
	n Retention	Hoarding
	n Construction	Organizing or building something
Defense of status	*n* Inviolacy	Maintaining psychological "distance"
	n Infavoidance	Concealing a disfigurement
	n Defendance	Offering explanations or excuses
	n Counteraction	Engaging in acts of retaliation
Response to human power . .	*n* Dominance	Dictating to or directing others
	n Deference	Cooperating with others
	n Similance	Imitating others
	n Autonomy	Manifesting defiance of authority
	n Contrariance	Taking unconventional or oppositional views
	n Aggression	Assaulting or belittling others
	n Abasement	Apologizing, confessing, or surrendering
	n Blamavoidance	Inhibiting unconventional impulses
Affection between people . . .	*n* Affiliation	Joining groups
	n Rejection	Discriminating against or snubbing others
	n Nurturance	"Mothering" a child
	n Succorance	Crying for help
	n Play	Seeking diversion by "having fun"
Exchange of information	*n* Cognizance	Asking questions
	n Exposition	Lecturing to, or interpreting for, others

Source: Adapted from Murray, H. A. *Explorations in personality.* New York: Science Editions, 1962.

Press

Murray and his associates reasoned that needs were but one half of the interactional process that determines behavior and selected the term *press* to represent the complementary, and equally important, directional forces provided by objects, situations, or events in the environment. Some common examples of press appear in Table 12–2. Murray distinguished two types of press: *alpha press* and *beta press*. The former represents an objective description of environmental situations (e.g., a certain grade-point average is required for admission to medical school), while the latter represents significant environmental influences as they are perceived by the individual (e.g., "If I don't make the required grade-point average for medical school, I have been a total failure"). For people to function adequately in an interaction with the environment, there must be reasonable correspondence between their alpha press (objective experience) and their beta press (subjective experience) of the same situation. The case in which alpha press and beta press sharply diverge would be called delusion.

TABLE 12–2
Common examples of press

Press	Example
p Achievement	Others getting good grades
p Order	A messy desk
p Counteraction	Being attacked (verbally or physically)
p Autonomy	Overprotective parents
p Abasement	Doing something wrong
p Affiliation	Friendly companions
p Play	Saturday night
p Cognizance	Not understanding a lecture

Murray's approach to personality assessment

Murray and his colleagues assumed that needs are sometimes *manifest* (observed in overt behavior), sometimes *latent* (inhibited, covert, or imaginal), and that the strength of a need must be measured in both of its forms.

The assessment of manifest needs

The four major criteria for estimating the strength of manifest needs from overt action are: (1) frequency of action, (2) duration of action, (3) intensity of action, and (4) readiness to act. Frequency and duration are simple to measure because they require only a calendar and a watch. When we say that a friend "needs a lot of sleep," our inference is usually based on these measures and instruments. The third criterion, intensity, may be measured by a graded scaling of responses to a given situation. For example, Murray (1962) suggested the following gradation for *n* Aggression: "criticism given with a smile, a laugh at the O's [other's] expense, a mild insult, a severe accusation, a violent push, a blow in the face, murder" (p. 254). Finally, readiness to act may be measured by the latency of a response (e.g., "I was asleep as soon as my head touched the pillow") or the appropriateness of the object to which it is directed (e.g., it takes a rather hungry individual to eat scraps from the garbage).

The assessment of latent needs

Dealing with needs which are not objectified in action is more complicated. Consider the theoretical nature of latent needs:

> The chief differences between an imaginal need and an overt need is that the former enjoys in reading, or represents in fantasy, in speech or in play what the latter objectifies in serious action. Thus, instead of pushing through a difficult enterprise, an S [subject] will have visions of doing it or read books about others doing it; or instead of injuring an enemy, he will express his dislike of him to others or enjoy playing an aggressive role in a play. . . . The term "imaginal need" is convenient for the expression "the amount of need tension that exhibits itself in thought and make-believe action." (Murray, 1962, p. 257)[3]

The logic of assessment of latent needs follows from this description. A strong latent need "is apt to perceive and apperceive what it 'wants.' . . . an S [subject] under the influence of a drive has a tendency to 'project' into surrounding objects some of the imagery associated with the drive that is operating" (Murray, 1962, p. 260). This reasoning gave rise to the development of a now widely used projective technique, the Thematic Apperception Test (TAT).

The TAT materials consist of a set of 20 pictures, with separate sets for males and females and for children. Most of the pictures show at least one person, thus providing someone with whom the respondent can presumably identify. The subject is given the following instructions:

> This is a test of your creative imagination. I shall show you a picture and I want you to make up a plot or story for which it might be used as an illustration. What is the relation of the individuals in the picture? What has happened to them? What are their present thoughts and feelings? What will be the outcome? Do your very best. Since I am asking you to indulge your literary imagination you may make your story as long and detailed as you wish. (Murray, 1962, p. 532)

One of the TAT pictures appears in Figure 12–2. (To better understand the discussion which follows, it may be helpful for the reader

---

[3] Apart from interest in imaginal or latent needs as phenomena in their own right, Murray (1962) notes: "Also, what is imaginal today may be objectified tomorrow" (p. 257).

to respond to the picture according to the preceding instructions.) Subjects' responses to the TAT cards, which the examiner usually records verbatim, can be scored for the presence of needs and press. Both the use of the test and an example of how other data are used to assess personality in terms of Murray's personology can be illustrated through a brief examination of a case study (Murray, 1962).

The case of Virt

Virt was a Russian immigrant who came to the United States when he was 11 years old. As a Russian Jew living near the German border during World War I, he had suffered religious persecutions in childhood. Virt's autobiographical account of his childhood experiences is scored (in parentheses) for various press and needs.

> Recollections of those persecutions . . . still prey on my mind: dead bodies with torn limbs dragged in heaps to the cemetery; my uncle forced to dig his own grave before my eyes; my aunt shot in cold blood at my hand; bombs thrown a few feet before me (*p* Aggression). . . . Suddenly the door [to a cellar in which he and his mother had been trapped without water (*p* Lack: Water, Food)] was blown open. . . . my mother and I stood quite near. I at once ran out to the next building, intent on procuring food and drink. . . . I darted across through the bullets and shrapnel and forced open the door of the next building. Imagine the fright of the inmates. They refused to let me go back (*p* Dominance: Restraint: Enforced Separation from Mother). (Murray, 1962, p. 535)

Another persistent recollection which Virt reported concerned the time, when he was eight, that his mother left him alone (*p* Insupport: Separation from Mother) in a Warsaw hotel while she went to get their passports.

> "Tired of staying at home, I ventured out," he writes. "I determined in some way or other to go to her" (*n* Succorance for Mother). He happened to pick up a transfer, took the first car and eventually found his mother. "Lucky for me it was the right car. Otherwise I would have been lost in a strange large city. The surprise of my mother was great when she saw me." (Murray, 1962, p. 535)

Virt was given part of the TAT, and his response to Picture Number 11 (Figure 12–2) follows:

> Mother and boy were living happily. She had no husband (Oedipus complex). Her son was her only support (*n* Nurturance for Mother). Then the boy got into bad company and participated in a gang robbery, playing a minor part. He was found out and sentenced to five years in prison. Picture represents him parting with his mother. Mother is sad, feeling ashamed of him. Boy is very much ashamed. He cares more about the harm he did his mother than about going to prison. He gets out for good

FIGURE 12-2
Example of a TAT picture

behaviour but the mother dies. He repents for what he has done but he finds that his reputation is lost in the city. No one will employ him. He again meets bad companions and in despair he joins them in crime. However, he meets a girl with whom he falls in love. She suggests that he quit the gang. He decides to quit after one more hold-up. He is caught and sent to prison. In the meantime, the girl has met someone else. When he comes out he is quite old and spends the rest of his life repenting in misery. (Murray, 1962, pp. 537–39)

The story is scored for p Dominance ("bad influences" and the externalization of blame), n Acquisition (robbery), p Aggression (the punishment of prison), p Loss (mother's death), n Abasement (the remorse which the boy feels), and p Rejection (the girl friend's preference for a rival). The complex theme regarding the boy's mother is repeated with his girlfriend (i.e., *p* Rejection is substituted for *p* Loss). Murray (1962) argues that the fantasy meaningfully reflects Virt's personality; that is, the boy in the story *is* Virt.

> The subject presents the Son-Lover thema followed by the death of the mother, and later the Love thema followed by desertion. In neither case is union between the lovers achieved. We also find a conflict between mother and son over the question of crime and gang robberies. Since the subject's desire for achievement and marriage are much restricted by poverty, and since his much-respected mother was a smuggler in Russia, we may suppose that temptations to rob and cheat have at times occurred to him.
>
> The conflict of the hero with the mother brings to mind some incidents mentioned by the subject when giving his childhood memories. He said that he had occasionally quarrelled with his mother because she nagged him. Once when he was thirteen he ran away and got a job in Pittsburgh. Another time he ran away to Newport News on account of a romantic longing he had for adventure. In regard to the repentance theme in the . . . story the subject said in his introspections: "That's the way I would feel. If I took my car and stayed out all night I would be ashamed for having hurt my mother (*n* Nurturance for Mother), not for anything I might have done. We are really close to each other. She confides everything to me (*p* Succorance). She doesn't get on well with my father." The subject's conscience is a personal one. It prohibits him from hurting the woman he loves. He is not guided by an impersonal ethical standard. (p. 539)

On the basis of Virt's response to TAT Picture Number 11, his responses to four other TAT pictures, and the autobiographical material, Murray (1962) finds "a reverberation of actual experiences and fantasies which occurred in childhood" (p. 544) and suggests that they reflect an underlying theme of "Tragic Love."

THE NEED TO ACHIEVE

Prominent among the lasting accomplishments of Murray's dispositional approach to personality is the large amount of research which it has stimulated. A prime example is the work of David C. McClelland (1917–   ) and his colleagues on the achievement motive. For more than 25 years, McClelland investigated the need to achieve (i.e., Murray's *n* Achievement) both theoretically and, more recently, from an extremely practical vantage point. While Murray and McClelland share a common bias concerning the nature of human personality, their basic strategies of attacking similar problems differ. Murray chose to catalog and study a large number of needs, whereas McClelland chose to focus his attention on a single need. McClelland justifies his approach in the following way:

concentration on a limited research problem is not necessarily narrowing; it may lead ultimately into the whole of psychology. In personality theory there is inevitably a certain impatience—a desire to solve every problem at once so as to get the "whole" personality in focus. We have proceeded the other way. By concentrating on one problem, on *one motive,* we have found in the course of our study that we have learned not only a lot about the achievement motive but other areas of personality as well. (McClelland, Atkinson, Clark, & Lowell, 1953, p. vi)

The first step in studying the achievement motive, or any motive or personality variable for that matter, is to develop a way of defining and measuring it. The strategy for defining and measuring motives devised by McClelland and his colleague John Atkinson (Atkinson, 1958; Atkinson & McClelland, 1948; McClelland, Atkinson, Clark, & Lowell, 1953) underlies most of the research that will be discussed in the remainder of this chapter.

In brief, the McClelland-Atkinson strategy involves the following steps. First, groups of subjects are exposed to a motive-arousing experience (e.g., being told that they are taking an important examination to arouse the achievement motive, or watching a stirring political film to arouse the power motive) or to a "neutral" experience that presumably does not arouse the motive in question. Then subjects in both groups write TAT-type stories about standard pictures, and the difference in imagery produced by the aroused and nonaroused group is taken to be evidence of the motive. Thus, a

> person who has a strong motive can be thought of as being in a more or less continuous state of arousal, or as being more likely to be in this state of arousal at any one time. In other words, he customarily reacts to (or assigns meaning to) the stimulus picture-cues in the way that most people do only under special, strong, externally induced conditions. (Winter, 1973, p. 37)

Initial experimentation in measuring the strength of a primary need, n Food, showed that sailors who had been deprived of food for varying lengths of time could be reliably differentiated on the basis of their fantasy responses to Murray's TAT (Atkinson & McClelland, 1948). Following this success, it was decided to try measuring a psychogenic need, n Achievement, by the same technique.

Male students[4] who were exposed to various experimental conditions were asked to write stories about four TAT-type pictures. The instructions were very similar to those which Murray used with the

The McClelland-Atkinson strategy for defining and measuring motives

David C. McClelland

Harvard University News Office

---

[4] Most of the research on the achievement motive has been done with male subjects. The few studies which have investigated n Achievement in females are summarized in a later section of this chapter.

TAT, and thus the test was presented to the students as one of creative imagination. However, McClelland and Atkinson introduced some new pictures especially pertinent to *n* Achievement, and they employed a group testing procedure in which subjects wrote their stories with an imposed time limit.

The experimental conditions consisted of various achievement-arousing situations (subjects were given success or failure experiences) and non–achievement-arousing situations (the experimental tasks were presented in a casual, relaxed atmosphere). The stories were scored for a number of different categories related to achievement motivation, and those scoring categories which successfully differentiated subjects who had been exposed to varying degrees of achievement arousal were defined as measures of *n* Achievement. A summary of the basic logic of this assessment approach, suggesting how the individual's *n* Achievement score is multiply determined, is shown in Figure 12–3.

FIGURE 12–3
Determinants of the *n* Achievement score derived from a single story

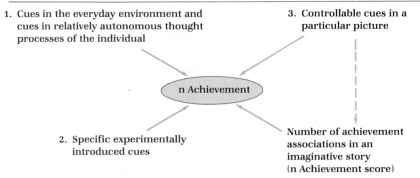

1. Cues in the everyday environment and cues in relatively autonomous thought processes of the individual

2. Specific experimentally introduced cues

3. Controllable cues in a particular picture

n Achievement

Number of achievement associations in an imaginative story (n Achievement score)

Source: McClelland, D. C., Atkinson, J. W., Clark, R. A., & Lowell, E. I. *The achievement motive.* New York: Appleton-Century-Crofts, 1953.

Research on achievement motivation

McClelland and his associates validated the use of achievement imagery as a measure of achievement motivation within the person by contrasting those with high and low achievement imagery scores. They reported:

> In general, people with a high achievement imagery index score complete more tasks under achievement orientation, solve more simple arithmetic problems on a timed test, improve faster in their ability to do anagrams, tend to get better grades, use more future tenses and abstract nouns in talking about themselves, . . . and so on. (McClelland et al., 1953, p. 327)

Subsequently, the basic technique of measuring achievement motivation by fantasy was used by McClelland and others in a wide variety of investigations. The antecedents and development of achievement motivation have been studied, and it appears that the origins of *n* Achievement (abbreviated *n* Ach) are

> rooted in early training for independence, subsequent harnessing of the dispositions so acquired for socially defined achievement situations, support of the n Ach by warm but demanding parental models, and considerable experience with emotional satisfaction in achievement situations. Certainly such a pattern does suggest that the n Achiever should be experienced in maximizing payoffs, relatively free from anxiety about failure, and therefore, efficient at those tasks he chooses to attempt. (Birney, 1968, p. 878)

The modified TAT fantasy measure of the achievement motive has made possible a unique type of psychological investigation. Since the scoring system for TAT stories is applicable to any prose material, McClelland has been able to study *n* Achievement in individuals and groups of individuals who lived in the past but left written accounts of their lives. For example, McClelland and his associates (McClelland et al., 1953) have studied the relationship between independence training and achievement motivation in a number of North American Indian tribes by scoring their folktales for *n* Achievement.

An even more ambitious task in the same vein has involved McClelland's (1967) attempt to "search for the broadest possible test of the hypothesis that a particular psychological factor—the need for Achievement—is responsible for economic growth and decline" (p. vii). Specifically, McClelland tried to "predict" the economic growth of 23 countries over the period 1929–50 on the basis of the amount of achievement imagery in children's stories in those countries in the preceding decade, 1920–29. He found a moderately high positive correlation (+.53) between the achievement emphasis of a given nation's children's stories and an index of that nation's economic growth. The evidence suggests that a society's achievement aspirations may well be found in the stories which it offers its children, and that the stories may have influenced those who heard them as children. The latter possibility is supported further by a more recent experimental study (McArthur & Eisen, 1976) in which preschool children's efforts to complete an achievement-related task increased after the children were read a story detailing the achievement-related behavior of another child of their own sex.

McClelland (1978) has reviewed the recent research on achievement motivation in an attempt to demonstrate the potential of psychological research in this area for improving the human condition. While this may sound immodest, the evidence he presents is, in fact, quite compelling. Through various programs aimed at increasing achievement motivation, experimenters have managed to raise the standard of living of the poor (McClelland, 1965), to enhance the benefits derived from a compensatory education program (DeCharms, 1976), to aid in the control of alcoholism (McClelland, 1977), and to make business management more effective (McClelland & Burnham, 1976). We will now describe the type of program able to achieve such striking results in greater detail.

A program for developing achievement motivation

McClelland's (1965; McClelland & Winter, 1969) formal course to increase the achievement motivation of individuals (particularly businesspeople) was based on evidence that entrepreneurs require high *n* Achievement in order to function successfully. Realizing that most psychologists have considered the acquisition of motives in adulthood to be difficult or impossible, McClelland (1965) says:

> we were encouraged by the successful efforts of two quite different groups of "change agents"—operant conditioners and missionaries. . . . The operant conditioners have not been encumbered by any elaborate theoretical apparatus; they do not believe motives exist anyway, and continue demonstrating vigorously that if you want a person to make a response, all you have to do is elicit it and reward it. . . . Like operant conditioners, the missionaries have gone ahead changing people because they have believed it possible. . . . common-sense observation yields dozens of cases of adults whose motivational structure has seemed to be quite radically and permanently altered by the educational efforts of the Communist party, Mormon, or other devout missionaries. (p. 322)

The supposition that an individual's motivational structure can change in adulthood has several implications for revising traditional theories of motivation. Perhaps the most important of these revisions, according to McClelland, is the proposition that *all human motives are learned;* even motives of biological origin (e.g., hunger or sex) cannot be observed until some learning has occurred so that they are associated with cues which can indicate their presence or absence.

The program

McClelland's (1965) courses for developing *n* Achievement were typically taught to groups of from 9 to 25 businesspeople over a short, but highly concentrated period (the optimal period has been found to be somewhere between 6 and 14 days, 12 to 18 hours per day). Most of the courses have been taught in India, but courses have also been held in the United States, Japan, Mexico, and Spain. As a result of the experience gained from these initial courses, McClelland (1965) abstracted 12 theoretical propositions or guidelines for motive change. Although these principles evolved from a program designed to increase a particular motive, McClelland believed that they should be applicable to the development of motivational dispositions in general.

The first thing one must do in any motivational development program is create confidence that the program will work. Proposition 1 states: *"The more reasons an individual has in advance to believe that he can, will, or should develop a motive, the more educational attempts designed to develop that motive are likely to succeed."* McClelland invoked the scientific authority of research, the prestige of Harvard University (where he was chairman of the Department of Social Relations), and all of the suggestive power which experimenter enthusiasm can produce in "selling" the program and setting high expectations for the participants before the actual training began.[5]

In Proposition 2, the importance of rational arguments in introducing the purpose of the course is stressed: *"The more an individual perceives that developing a motive is consistent with the demands of reality (and reason), the more educational attempts designed to develop that motive are likely to succeed."*

Proposition 3 provides the first hint of what the training program itself entails. *"The more thoroughly an individual develops and clearly conceptualizes the associative network defining the motive, the more likely he is to develop the motive."* With this principle in mind, it is easy to understand why McClelland chooses an explanation of the meaning of achievement motivation as one of the first steps in training. All participants are asked to take the fantasy test of *n* Achievement at the outset and are taught to score it for themselves. McClelland (1965) says: ". . . we point out that if they think their score is too low, that can be easily remedied, since we teach them how to code and how to write stories saturated with *n* Achievement; in fact, that is one of the basic purposes of the course: to teach them to think constantly in *n* Achievement terms" (p. 325).

The next step is to tie changes in thought to changes in action, as seen in Proposition 4: *"The more an individual can link the newly developed network to related actions, the more the change in both thought and action is likely to occur and endure."* Earlier work by McClelland had shown that persons high in achievement motivation: (1) like challenges in their work and prefer moderate risk situations; (2) seek concrete feedback as to how well they are doing; and (3) like to take personal responsibility for achieving work goals. In order to develop these characteristics in the course participants, McClelland makes use of a specially designed business game which allows the participants to learn achievement-oriented actions by both playing the game and observing others play.

The game is designed to mimic real life: they must order parts to make certain objects (e.g., a Tinker Toy model bridge) after having estimated

---

[5] It is interesting to note that what many experimenters consider "error" and try to exclude, McClelland purposely built into his program.

how many they think they can construct in the time allotted. They have a real chance to take over, plan the whole game, learn from how well they are doing (use of feedback), and show a paper profit or loss at the end. While they are surprised often that they should have to display their real action characteristics this way in public, they usually get emotionally involved in observing how they behave under pressure of a more or less "real" work situation. (McClelland, 1965, p. 326)

Behavior developed in the game situation must then be generalized to actual business situations. Accordingly, Proposition 5 states: *"The more an individual can link the newly conceptualized association-action complex (or motive) to events in his everyday life, the more likely the motive complex is to influence his thoughts and actions outside the training experience."* In this regard, examples of career development are explored by means of actual case studies which the group discusses.

However clear it may become to a participant that an achievement orientation is applicable to actual business experience, each participant must be convinced that he or she, as an individual, is suited to such a way of life. This point is made in Proposition 6: *"The more an individual can perceive and experience the newly conceptualized motive as an improvement in the self-image, the more the motive is likely to influence his future thoughts and actions."* The importance of candid self-appraisal is emphasized to the participants by telling them of an incident which occurred in one of the courses. A participant decided that he did not wish to become an achievement-oriented person. This honest self-evaluation led the man to leave the course, quit his managerial position, and subsequently retire and become a chicken farmer. (This case is the exception rather than the rule, however, since most participants come to view achievement motivation as desirable.) Participants are aided in their evaluation of the influence of increased achievement motivation on their self-images through such techniques as individual counseling, group-dynamics sessions, and silent group meditation.

Just as participants must reconcile increased achievement motivation with their self-concepts, so, too, must they come to feel that their increase n Achievement is in line with, or an improvement on, the existing popular or traditional cultural values of their own country. Proposition 7 states: *"The more an individual can perceive and experience the newly conceptualized motive as an improvement on prevailing cultural values, the more the motive is likely to influence his future thoughts and actions."* After having examined their personal values with regard to achievement motivation, the course participants engage in an analysis of the values of their culture with regard to achievement by analyzing children's stories, myths, popular religion, customs, and so on. In the United States, for example, participants discuss the way in which high achievement motivation can interfere with a person's popularity. Besides rational discussions of such problems, role playing is employed to help the participants understand and accept their new motivational sets in relation to their cultural values.

At the end of the course, each participant writes an essay outlining his aspirations and plans for the next two years. Emphasis is placed on describing one's future realistically and on setting moderate (rather than inordinately high) goals. The essay not only serves to assist participants in making use of the practical implications of the course but also provides a basis for further evaluation of the candidates and the program. During the two-year follow-up period, questionnaries are sent to the course participants every six months, both to remind them of the goals they have set for themselves and to assess their progress. These procedures have led to the formulation of Propositions 8 and 9: *"The more an individual commits himself to achieving concrete goals in life related to the newly formed motives, the more the motive is likely to influence his future thoughts and actions,"* and *"The more an individual keeps a record of his progress toward achieving goals to which he is committed, the more the newly formed motive is likely to influence his future thoughts and actions."*

As mentioned previously, McClelland and his associates have found it helpful for the course instructors (consulting psychologists) to be warm, rewarding, and somewhat nondirective in their dealings with the participants, a result consistent with an earlier study which showed that fathers of high *n* Achievement boys were warmer, more encouraging, and less directive than fathers of boys low on this measure (Rosen & D'Andrade, 1959). Proposition 10 states: *"Changes in motives are more likely to occur in an interpersonal atmosphere in which the individual feels warmly but honestly supported and respected by others as a person capable of guiding and directing his own future behavior."*

The course is structured as a retreat for self-study. Whenever possible, the sessions are conducted in an isolated resort hotel to enhance concentration and exclude outside interference. Furthermore, there is considerable evidence to show that changes in people's opinions, attitudes, or beliefs are greatly facilitated if they join new reference groups. In addition to fostering the emergence of a new reference group by having participants study and live together for the duration of the course, McClelland provides signs of identification with the group, such as knowledge of the *n* Achievement coding system and membership certificates. Moreover, he tries to have all participants in a group come from the same community so that, after leaving the course, the new reference group will remain physically intact and will help maintain the newly acquired motivation. These procedures are reflected in Propositions 11 and 12: *"Changes in motives are more likely to occur the more the setting dramatizes the importance of self-study and lifts it out of the routine of everyday life,"* and *"Changes in motives are more likely to occur and persist if the new motive is a sign of membership in a new reference group."*

Results of the program

How successful have McClelland's achievement motivation courses been? On a number of concrete, economic measures, it appears that businesspeople who participated in the courses increased their achievement motivation substantially more than did businesspeople who applied for admission but were not accepted (i.e., control subjects). As can be seen in Table 12–3, course participants and controls were similar in the two-year period before the course. Following the course, however, significantly more participants than controls were rated as engaging in a high level of business activity (i.e., actions which directly improve business), working longer hours, starting new businesses, and employing more workers in their businesses (McClelland & Winter, 1969).

Additionally, it is interesting to examine a case study which illustrates the potential impact of the course.

> A short time after participating in one of our courses in India, a 47-year-old businessman rather suddenly and dramatically decided to quit his excellent job and go into the construction business on his own in a big way. A man with some means of his own, he had had a very successful career as employee-relations manager for a larger oil firm. His job involved adjusting management-employee difficulties, negotiating union contracts, etc. He was well-to-do, well thought of in his company, and admired in the community, but he was restless because he found his job increasingly boring. At the time of the course his original n Achievement score was not very high and he was thinking of retiring and living

TABLE 12–3
Examples of the economic effects of McClelland's achievement motivation courses

		Before course (1962–1964)	*After course (1964–1966)*
1. Rated at highest business activity level*	Participants	18%	51%
	Controls	22%	25%
2. Working longer hours	Participants	7%	20%
	Controls	11%	7%
3. Starting new business	Participants	4%	22%
	Controls	7%	8%
4. Employing more people at end of two-year period	Participants	35%	59%
	Controls	31%	33%

* Subjects' business activity was rated on a four-point scale, with the highest level being exemplified by an action which directly resulted in an improvement in a business venture (e.g., increased profit).

Source: Data from McClelland, D. C. & Winter, D. G. *Motivating economic achievement.* New York: Free Press, 1969.

in England where his son was studying. In an interview, 8 months later, he said the course had served not so much to "motivate" him but to "crystallize" a lot of ideas he had vaguely or half consciously picked up about work and achievement all through his life. It provided him with a new language (he still talked in terms of standards of excellence, blocks, moderate risk, goal anticipation, etc.), a new construct which served to organize those ideas and explain to him why he was bored with his job, despite his obvious success. He decided he wanted to be an n-Achievement-oriented person, that he would be unhappy in retirement, and that he should take a risk, quit his job, and start in business on his own. He acted on his decision and in 6 months had drawn plans and raised over $1,000,000 to build the tallest building in his large city, to be called the "Everest Apartments." He is extremely happy in his new activity because it means selling, promoting, trying to wangle scarce materials, etc. His first building is partway up and he is planning two more. (McClelland, 1965, p. 332)

Unfortunately, there is neither a systematic theory nor a consistent body of data about achievement motivation in women. This is due mainly to the scarcity of achievement studies of women until quite recently. Here is what one critic said, in retrospect, about McClelland's 1961 book, *The Achieving Society*.

Achievement motivation in women

> He talks about achievement motivation in the Quakers, the Turks, the ancient Greeks, the Apaches and the Commanches, the Saudi Arabians, and the Vikings of Iceland. He describes achievement motivation in Poland, Argentina, Pakistan, Bulgaria, Australia, and the USSR. He finds expression of achievement strivings in vases, in flags, in the Peloponnesian War, in Russian children's readers, in the use of motors, in Zen Buddhism, and in doodles. But there is not a single reference to achievement motivation in women. (Lesser, 1973, p. 202)

With the acknowledgment that the data are limited and that achievement motivation may have a different form of expression for different types of women (different class background, ethnic group, or age), we will review some findings that seem to shed a bit of light on achievement motivation in women. One of the few consistent themes in these data is that from childhood males and females have very different experiences as regards the cultivation and expression of achievement strivings.

Maternal attitudes and achievement motivation

One very consistent finding has been that mothers of high *n* Achievement girls tend to be hostile toward their daughters. Kagan and Moss (1962) found that one of the best predictors of child and adult intellectual achievement in girls was early maternal hostility during the ages 0 to 3. For boys, on the other hand, maternal protectiveness predicted achievement. In contrast to the highly protective mothers of achievement-oriented boys, mothers of achieving girls tended to be aggressive and competitive women who were critical of their daughters. Another study (Crandall, Dewey, Katkovsky, & Preston, 1964) found that mothers of academically successful elementary school girls were less affectionate and less nurturant toward their daughters than were mothers of less competent girls. Completing the negative picture with high school subjects, Pierce (1961b) described the mothers of high-achieving girls as stricter, more authoritarian, and more controlling than the mothers of low-achieving girls.

In a nationwide study of the consequences of different home backgrounds, Veroff, Atkinson, Feld, and Gurin (1960) found different results for women and men. Their results, shown in Figure 12–4, indicate that women whose parents have been divorced or separated are more likely to have high *n* Achievement scores than are women from intact homes or women whose parents had died. The reverse was true for men.

FIGURE 12–4
Relationship of various home backgrounds to the frequency with which men and women show above-average *n* Achievement

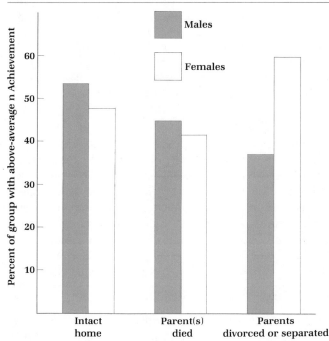

Source: Data from Veroff, J., Atkinson, J. W., Feld, S. C., & Gurin, G. The use of thematic apperception to assess motivation in a nationwide interview study. *Psychological Monographs,* 1960, *74.*

Veroff and his associates (1960) interpret the findings and the differences between men and women as follows:

> A boy, having lost his masculine model for achievement, may become highly involved in avoiding failure. In doing so, his achievement motivation, his positive motivations for success, become weakened. On the other hand, girls living with a divorced mother have a readily available model for achievement identification. Resentment of the father can reinforce the need for feminine independence and self-reliance in a masculine world. The fact that her mother is apparently self-sufficient further enhances an image of the achievement orientation of women. (p. 27)

Social acceptability as a factor in women's achievement motivation

Another clear theme appearing in studies of women is that n Achievement seems more closely tied to social acceptability in women than in men. Two studies (Crandall, Katkovsky, & Preston, 1962; Sears, 1962) found that the achievement needs of girls in elementary school are directly related to girls' desire for adult approval and affection, while disclosing that this pattern does not hold for boys. Perhaps this is why, in most studies, achievement motivation scores have been unrelated to girls' academic achievement, but do predict girls' social relations skills (Fadiman, 1960). In this regard, it is interesting that, though females usually fail to show the expected increases in n Achievement scores when exposed to arousal conditions that stress intelligence and leadership ability[6] (McClelland et al., 1953), they do respond with increases in these scores when presented with arousal conditions involving social acceptance (Field, 1951).

Some studies with adult women have supported the finding that achievement in female children is closely tied to social acceptability. Women college-faculty members described desirable colleagues and good students as their chief job satisfactions, whereas men mentioned independence and opportunities for research (Eckert & Stecklein, 1959). However, this study was conducted well before the influence of the feminist movement as were some others mentioned here, and profound changes may have occurred.

Nuttall (1964) found that high-n-Achievement black women tended to join racial protest movements, whereas high-n-Achievement black men did not. Nuttall interprets these findings as indicating a "social orientation" in the achievement needs of women; women, in this view, express their achievement orientation through attempts to help the entire group, whereas men strive for more personal advancement.

---

[6] Exceptions to this finding indicate that social role models make a difference among females. See Lesser (1973) for more on this subject.

Anxiety about achievement: The motive to avoid success

Evidence has been available for some time to suggest that women, more than men, experience conflict over the role that achievement strivings should play in their lives (French & Lesser, 1964; Lesser, 1973; Lesser, Krawitz, & Packard, 1963). In fact, discussion of the possible negative consequences of success for women—competition with men, loss of femininity, the possibility of social rejection by peers—can be found in some of the classic writings of Freud (1965) and Mead (1949).

Horner (1973) has theorized that this kind of conflict causes anxiety for women in achievement-oriented situations and that women's anxiety about success may be one of the major factors underlying the sex differences reported in research on achievement motivation and performance. Horner (1973) calls anxiety that is caused by negative consequences associated with success the *motive to avoid success,* which she views as "a stable personality predisposition within the person acquired early in life in conjunction with sex role standards" (p. 224).

To test her hypothesis, Horner (1973) asked females and males to write a story following a verbal lead designed to elicit a disposition or motive to avoid success. The females in Horner's study were given the lead:

> *After first-term finals, Anne finds herself at the top of her medical school class.*

The lead for males was identical, except that the name of the story character was changed:

> *After first-term finals, John finds himself at the top of his medical school class.*

Scores for motive to avoid success were based on the presence of negative imagery related to success (e.g., concern about success or the consequences of success, denial of success, and bizarre responses to the situation). As Horner had predicted, the responses of the women were strikingly different from those of the men. More than 65 percent of the women in the sample had high fear of success, whereas less than 10 percent of the men did!

In Horner's study, the most frequently occurring responses of women were those emphasizing negative social consequences of success, such as rejection by others, loss of friendship, reduced chances for marriage, or just loneliness. The second-largest category of responses to the Anne lead involved remarkable denials. Here are some examples:

> Anne is a code name for a non-existent person created by a group of med students. They take turns taking exams and writing papers for Anne.

> Anne is really happy she's on top, though Tom is higher than she—though that's as it should be. . . . Anne doesn't mind Tom winning.

Anne is talking to her counselor. Counselor says she will make a fine nurse. She will continue her med school courses. She will study very hard and find she can and will become a good nurse.

It was luck that Anne came out on top of her med class because she didn't want to go to med school anyway. (Horner, 1973, p. 226)

Another type of response that occurred quite frequently tended to propel Anne out of the conflicting situation—and out of medical school. Here is one that Horner (1973) describes as a "typical female story."

Anne has a boyfriend Carl in the same class and they are quite serious. Anne met Carl at college and they started dating around their soph years in undergraduate school. Anne is rather upset and so is Carl. She wants him to be higher scholastically than she is. Anne will deliberately lower her academic standing the next term, while she does all she subtly can to help Carl. His grades come up and Anne soon drops out of med-school. They marry and he goes on in school while she raises their family. (p. 227)

Finally, some of the stories that Anne's situation elicited from otherwise normal women are bizarre. Below is an excerpt from one such response.

She starts proclaiming her surprise and joy. Her fellow classmates are so disgusted with her behavior that they jump on her in a body and beat her. She is maimed for life. (Horner, 1973, p. 226)

Although the times have unquestionably changed since Horner's data were actually collected (in 1968), it is likely that many women still experience the deep conflict and anxiety about success that were revealed so dramatically in Horner's pioneering work. In addition, more recent work has revealed that men may experience as strong a motive to avoid success as women, but apparently for a different reason (e.g., Hoffman, 1974). Specifically, men usually question the value of achievement (rather than being concerned with social rejection).

In Murray's list of psychogenic needs (see page 253), there is no direct mention of a need for power. The systematic study of power motivation was begun by Veroff (1955, 1957) and has been continued most notably by David Winter (1967, 1968, 1972, 1973).

As he explains in the first line of his book, *The Power Motive,* Winter sees "the striving for power as one important motive or disposition in individuals" (1973). Winter defines power as *the ability or capacity of one person to produce intended effects on the behavior or emotions of another person,* and indicates that his task has been "to determine whether there are differences in the extent to which people want power, or strive to affect the behavior of others according to their own intentions; to measure these differences; and to determine their further conse-

POWER: THE ANATOMY OF A MOTIVE

quences and associated characteristics" (1973, p. 5). In fact, Winter and a number of other investigators have amassed an enormous amount of evidence that there are individual differences in power motivation (or *n* Power).

Borrowing from the work of Murray and McClelland on the measurement of motives, and from Veroff's pioneering work, Winter devised (1967) and then refined (1972) a relatively simple projective measure of *n* Power. *The Power Motive* (Winter, 1973) is concerned primarily with the consequences and associated characteristics of high power motivation, and thus discloses the anatomy of psychological power.

The measurement and meaning of power motivation

According to Winter (1973), the goal of the power motive is the *status of having power*. He elaborates on what he means by the power motive.

> By the power motive, I mean a disposition to strive for certain kinds of goals, or to be affected by certain kinds of incentives. People who have the power motive, or who strive for power, are trying to bring about a certain state of affairs—they want to feel "power" or "more powerful than. . . ." Power is their goal. We would expect that they tend to construe the world in terms of power and to use the concept of "power" in categorizing human interaction, but they do more than that. Not only do they categorize the world in terms of power, but they also want to feel themselves as the most powerful. (p. 18)

Winter used six TAT-like pictures to measure *n* Power; each picture was selected to cover one or more general themes related to power motivation. In one of the pictures, for example, soldiers in field dress are seen pointing to a map or chart. The pictures, together with a fairly sophisticated scoring system, were selected and developed along the same broad lines that were used by McClelland and Atkinson in their studies of achievement motivation. That is, the sample consisted of two otherwise comparable groups, one of which was aroused by power-related experiences (e.g., by viewing certain kinds of power-inspiring films), while the other responded to the pictures without prior arousal. Differences in the imagery generated by the two groups became the basis for identifying themes that would be "diagnostic" of naturally high levels of *n* Power.

What types of responses constitute evidence of a high power motive? According to Winter (1973), there are three types: responses containing imagery of strong, vigorous actions expressing power, responses containing imagery of actions that produce strong emotional reactions in others, and responses containing statements expressing explicit concern about a person's reputation or position.

The hope and fear of power

The use of power-related themes in projective stories does not always imply a hope of power. Sometimes, one encounters power-related themes in which the power goal is expressed for someone other than the subject, and sometimes the reaction to power expressed in such themes seems riddled with conflict or doubt. Winter belives that there are two aspects to the power motive—Hope of Power and Fear of Power. *Hope of Power* and the overall power motive show high positive correlations (see Table 12–4). Therefore, Hope of Power and *n* Power will be treated as roughly equivalent in our discussion. Hope of Power and Fear of Power bear a slightly negative relationship to each other; people with high Hope of Power tend to have low Fear of Power, and vice versa.

TABLE 12–4
The correlations between Hope of Power and total *n* Power in five samples. The data show that the two scores can be considered almost interchangeable for many research purposes.

Sample	Correlation coefficient
Total sample of Wesleyan students ($n = 325$)	.80*
Upper middle-class American executives ($n = 22$)	.71*
Harvard class of 1964 students ($n = 225$)	.91*
Oxford University students ($n = 58$)	.86*
German engineering students ($n = 96$)	.80*

* $p < .01$.
Source: Data reported in Winter, D. G. *The power motive*. New York: Free Press, 1973.

Fear of Power: A closer look

Fear of Power can be defined as a simultaneous interest in and concern about power, especially when the individual wants to avoid power. For example, to investigate the relationship between Fear of Power and attitudes toward academic work among college students, Winter (1973) gave over 200 freshmen an extensive questionnaire, which included the following questions:

> Which of the following statements
> comes closest to your views?
> > There are bodies of knowledge to
> > be learned, and college faculty are
> > more competent than the student
> > to direct the student's course of
> > study through required courses,
> > prerequisites, etc.

> *College students should be given*
> *great freedom in choosing their*
> *subjects of study and in choosing*
> *their own areas of interest within*
> *their subjects.*

Would you prefer to have your
academic work organized to allow:
  A predominance of class work,
    class assignments, regular exam-
    inations, etc.
  A predominance of independent
    reading, writing, and research.

In the average humanities or social
sciences course, do you generally
prefer:
  Objective examinations (e.g., true-
    false, multiple choice).
  Essay examinations.

If class size permitted, which type of
instruction would you prefer?
  All or mostly lectures.
  All or mostly discussions. (Winter, 1973, p. 150)

Most of the students displayed some preference for the less structured
alternatives (those printed in italics), but students high in Fear of Power
were significantly more likely than others to insist on almost absolute
autonomy.

> One interpretation of these results is that the autonomy concerns of men
> high in Fear of Power derive from a fear of structure, especially structure
> that is imposed by someone else of high status or power (e.g., a professor
> or university administrator). Specified programs, assigned work, lectures,
> and "objective" examinations are all constraints on behavior that origi-
> nate from the "outside." Fearing the structure that someone else imposes
> is thus one manifestation of a fear of the potential power of other people.
> (Winter, 1973, p. 149)

This interpretation receives additional support from two further studies
which show that sudents high in Fear of Power are more likely than
are other students to hand in major term papers late in the face of
warnings (e.g., that the papers would be graded down for lateness)
and are also more likely to take "incompletes" in their courses.

There is the clear implication in this work that Fear of Power is
often unadaptive, and Winter has other evidence that also points in
this direction. For example, those high in Fear of Power tend to have
more automobile accidents than do other students and are also relatively more inefficient when thrust into a competitive bidding game.
When "their" power is threatened, those with high Fear of Power seem
to become debilitated.

A major component of Winter's research strategy has been to look for what he refers to as the "action correlates" of persons who display high n Power—that is, the overt behavioral manifestations of the power motive.

Presentation of self

Two studies (Winter, 1968, 1972) have shown that persons with high n Power tend to have more "prestige possessions" than do those with low n Power, even when income or spending money is held constant. Students high in n Power are also more likely to put their names on the doors of their dormitory rooms and to report their college grades in a "favorable" light. For example, Winter (1973) found that when students were asked to indicate the lowest final grade they had received thus far in college, those high in n Power tended to report their lowest grade as higher than it really was.

Among both male college students and middle-class businessmen, those who wear beards or mustaches tend to be higher in n Power than do those who are clean shaven. Working-class men who are high in n Power are more likely to pay for their purchases with credit cards than are working-class men who are low in n Power (Davis, 1969). This last finding, as well as those described above, helps to put the self-presentation aspect of the power motive into perspective. The person high in n Power is an individual who acquires or displays the trappings of prestige, power, and potency. These adornments are presumably satisfying because of the effects they have on the behavior or reaction of others toward the individual motivated by power.

There is a bit more to the picture, though. Winter (1973) asked middle-class business executives and college students what automobile they would most like to have and found that those high in n Power tended to prefer *not* the most expensive cars, but the cars that were most maneuverable and handled best. This was true of both the students and the executives, and held for both those who chose American cars and those who chose foreign cars.[7]

It therefore becomes apparent that *control* (of people, possessions, and situations) is of central concern to the person motivated by n Power. Such control may be gained through force, prestige possessions, or the embellishment of one's products. Here is an interesting example:

> At Wesleyan University as elsewhere, students submit term papers in a great variety of formats, bindings, and conditions of neatness. Some hand in a few ragged sheets of paper full of typing mistakes and bound

---

[7] Winter constructed a maneuverability scale for automobiles based on their track-to-wheelbase and horsepower-to-weight ratios. Interested readers should see Winter (1973, pp. 130–33).

precariously with a paper clip. Others submit neatly typed, carefully proofread papers which are impressively bound in colored plastic covers with plastic grips running along the left margin. To the extent that professors judge a paper by its cover—a misleading but human tendency— the paper that is neatly and impressively bound will fare a little better or at least get a favorable first reaction. In a small way, such bindings use prestige to enhance reputation—they are an "impressive show." In one introductory psychology course, those 13 students who bound their term papers in colored plastic or colored paper binders were significantly higher in Hope of Power than those 50 students who turned in ordinary papers. (Winter, 1973, p. 133)

In a related vein, Veroff (1957) found that college men high in *n* Power tended to be argumentative in class and to be eager to convince their instructors or fellow students of their point of view. This may be why men high in *n* Power do well in college courses that require classroom participation (McKeachie, 1961).

Selection of friends

Winter (1973) found that students high in *n* Power tend to prefer as their friends individuals who are not popular or well known. Winter (1973) explains:

> To a power-motivated person, such friends are attractive because they are presumably not a threat, since they do not compete for power and prestige. Being less well known, such friends are also more disposed to form strong ties of friendship, regard, and support for the power-motivated "leader." (p. 114)

One of the most remarkable characteristics of individuals high in *n* Power is that they cultivate a group of followers to whom they turn a generous and understanding face, while at the same time displaying a competitive stance toward those who are outside the circle. In one of Winter's studies, students were asked: "Do you generally like to do things in your own way and without regard for what other students around you may think?" A majority of those who were *low* in power motivation answered yes to this question, whereas a majority of those who were high in power motivation answered no. To be powerful you must have a following, and to maintain a following you must display consideration toward those who follow you. Or so it seems.

On the other hand, persons high in *n* Power have a rough-and-ready attitude toward those who oppose them. For example, Winter (1973) asked students: "If you could say one sentence—any sentence—to *anyone,* anywhere in the world, in person and without fear of reprisal, what would you say . . . ?" Students high in *n* Power were significantly more likely to say something with a strong negative effect, usually something obscene, than were those low in *n* Power.

Relative indifference to time and risk

Winter believes that persons high in *n* Power are relatively indifferent to time and risk. In the autumn of 1967, when most college men in the United States faced the serious likelihood of being drafted into the Army, Winter questioned 145 men as to whether they would enlist after college (thus ensuring admission to the branch of their choice but committing themselves to some form of military service) or risk the possibility of conscription and take their chances. Men high in *n* Power were significantly more likely than other men to take their chances. "Thus they are prepared to gamble about military conscription," observes Winter, "just as they also like to gamble when they play ordinary games" (1973, p. 181). In another study, Winter examined the *n* Power scores of 35 undergraduates who kept calendars of some sort in their rooms, and found that these scores were significantly lower than the *n* Power scores of an otherwise comparable group of 35 students who had no calendar. It is uncertain whether the latter students felt that they didn't need to know what day it was, or whether they felt that they didn't need to be reminded by an "external" source. In either event, though, the message is clear. "I'm not worried," says the person with high power motivation. "It's all under control."

Moderator variables in the expression of the power motive

The power motive does not express itself in the same way in all environments, and its expression is also influenced by the person's other dispositions. In other words, *moderator variables* seem to exert an enormous influence on the forms power motivation will (or can) take. These variables seem to include social class, gender, race, and geographical or national origin.

In one study, Greene and Winter (1971) found that black students high in *n* Power tended to hold office in black organizations and to participate in black theater groups. But in working for social change, power-motivated black students who grew up in the North shunned "the system" and tended to work exclusively with the black community; in contrast, power-motivated black students who grew up in the South tended to be "pragmatic" and to deal with what were viewed as establishment institutions when it seemed advantageous to do so.

In a different vein, Davis (1969) found that working-class men high in *n* Power reported that they were likely to throw books, magazines, and so on around the room; fail to show up for a day's work "just because they didn't feel like it"; and take towels from a motel or hotel room. Among middle-class men, power motivation does not reveal itself in these impulsive forms of temporary power (Winter, 1973), presumably because they have other means of obtaining power of a more durable and socially valued kind.

Sexual behavior and power

Winter argues that sexual behavior and power have been closely related themes both in literature and in psychological discussion. His own research indicates that the suggested link has some basis in fact. Male students who report having had sexual intercourse before college have appreciably higher *n* Power scores than do those who report that they did not have intercourse before entering college; the trend is in the same direction through the sophomore year but not thereafter. Power-motivated men either have sexual intercourse at an earlier age than do other men, or are inclined to report that they did. Winter's findings are shown in Figure 12–5.

FIGURE 12–5
Mean *n* Power scores of men reporting that they did and did not have sexual intercourse at various periods. The data suggest that a desire for early sexual experience is associated with power motivation.

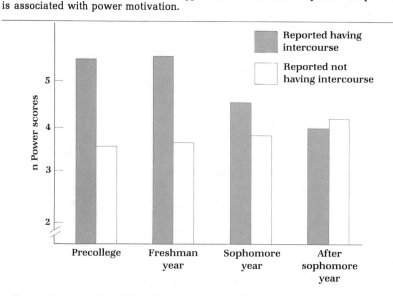

Source: Data reported in Winter, D. G. *The power motive.* New York: Free Press, 1973.

In a related study, Winter found that college men high in *n* Power were more likely than other men to say that they considered an "ideal wife" to be a woman who was dependent rather than independent. Winter (1973) explains:

> While a dependent wife may interfere with her husband's power, she probably enhances his *feelings* of power; presumably he then thinks that *he* is not dependent on *her.* Thus this combination of qualities is attractive to high *n* Power men because it gives them . . . feelings of superiority. (p. 178)

Alcoholism and power

McClelland and his colleagues (1972) have proposed that the need for power plays a major role in the onset and continuance of problem drinking. As a result of a 10-year research program, these investigators not only found that men increased in feelings of power after drinking alcohol, but that those who had an intense need for power to begin with drank even more to satisfy that need, particularly if they were low in self-control. The investigators therefore concluded that it is the dependence on alcohol to satisfy one's need for power, rather than achieving increased power through instrumental behavior, that distinguishes alcoholics from nonalcoholics.

Further empirical support for this formulation has recently emerged from an investigation of the usefulness of a power-motivation training program (PMT) as an adjunct to a standard VA hospital therapy program for alcoholism (McClelland, 1977). Cutter, Boyatzis, and Clancy (1977) developed a program which provided feedback to the participants on their need for power and the way alcohol satisfied that need, along with training in more appropriate alternatives for doing so. Analysis of the results of the therapy program found that only 25 percent of the alcoholics receiving the standard treatment alone remained rehabilitated one year after the treatment terminated. On the other hand, nearly 50 percent of the alcoholics treated with the standard therapy and the power-motivation training program remained rehabilitated at follow-up, supporting the hypothesis that the need for power plays a role in alcoholism. This program is currently being evaluated on a national scale.

High blood pressure and power

In a recently reported longitudinal study, McClelland (1979) has implicated the *inhibited power motive syndrome* in elevated blood pressure and the later emergence of hypertensive pathology. By measuring the need for power relative to the need for affiliation as an index of one's tendency to be either assertive or angry, as well as analyzing the tendency to inhibit activity (by counting the frequency of "nots" used in imaginative stories), McClelland was able to identify the pattern that was most predictive of high blood pressure and associated problems. The results were strikingly similar across three diverse groups of subjects. Those who exhibited a higher need for power relative to the need for affiliation, coupled with a strong tendency to inhibit the overt expression of this need (i.e., the inhibited power-motive syndrome) at age 30 had diastolic and systolic blood pressure levels that averaged 9 points higher at age 50 than did men with other motive patterns at age 30. Furthermore, 61 percent of the men so classified at age 30 showed definite signs of hypertensive pathology in their 50s as compared to only 23 percent of the men who did not exhibit the syndrome at age 30. Apparently, the need for power can have a deleterious impact on one's health when coupled with the tendency to suppress expression of this need.

Substitutes for power

According to Winter (1973), the goal of the power-motivated person is to create "an inner feeling of power" (p. 137). This inner feeling does not always have to come from the exercise of real power; substitute and vicarious activities may also satisfy the power motive. Winter found that persons high in *n* Power, especially Hope of Power, consume more alcohol and enjoy gambling more than do those low in *n* Power. Those high in Hope of Power also tend to watch more sports events and to read more "vicarious power magazines" (e.g., *Playboy, Sports Illustrated*) than do those low in Hope of Power.

How do these vicarious experiences and substitutes relate to the seeking and exercising of "real" power, that is, socially objective power? One suggestion made by Winter is that individuals high in *n* Power will be especially likely to seek out substitute forms of power when they are very young or very old or are otherwise blocked from objective power. The teenage boy doing hundreds of push-ups a day and the grandparent reciting tales of battles fought 20 years before are prime examples of high *n* Power people trying to satisfy an inner need as best they can. Power-motivated people will try to feel strong through whatever means are at hand. Vicarious forms of power, then, are attractive to everyone who is high in power motivation, but are especially attractive to such people when real social power is unavailable to them (e.g., by virtue of social barriers) or is declining (by virtue of age or the loss of previously enjoyed fame and fortune). According to Winter, this is why leaders of a collapsed military regime or a crumbling political empire so often "retire" to sex, gambling, drinking, and so on. By the same token, persons born to advantaged positions may, as youths, lead lives spiced with power substitutes. Shakespeare's Prince Hal occupies himself in whoring and drinking with Falstaff and a lusty crowd. But when Hal assumes the crown, he is transformed into Henry V who, as he promised soon after his coronation, "rises with so full a glory as to dazzle all the eyes of France" and wins the Battle of Agincourt (*Henry V,* act 1, sc. 2). This is precisely the pattern to be expected of a person high in power motivation.

13 *The dispositional strategy*

Liabilities

In its strongest form, an attack on the dispositional strategy would dismiss it as a mere catalog of labeled relationships that have been used to describe and predict behavior without any notable success. Specifically, critics have argued that the dispositional strategy (1) "borrows" its theory from other views; (2) places excessive reliance on the self-report inventory, an assessment tool which has serious weaknesses for measuring some aspects of personality; (3) rests many of its contentions on subjective decisions masked as "scientific" conclusions; (4) cannot predict individual behavior, though it is relied on heavily for that purpose; (5) deals only with the static individual; and (6) fails to provide any useful causal analyses.

Rather than beginning the quest for critical dimensions of personality from a theoretical base, dispositional psychologists typically search for traits, types, or needs in a "shotgun," empirical fashion. The dispositional strategy has, in fact, given rise to very few theoretical constructs of its own. Instead, dispositional psychologists have had to borrow theoretical ideas from other strategies in order to explain and make sense of orderly patterns uncovered in their research. We saw, for instance, that Cattell used the term *ego strength,* borrowed from psychoanalytic theory, to both label and help us understand what he had found in "source trait *C.*"

Even the term *trait* itself was borrowed (from genetics), and how much similarity is intended between the biological and the psychological concept still remains unclear in most dispositional discussions. Both Allport and Williams, for example, borrow the facts as well as the concepts of biology to argue for a dispositional approach to personality.

When terms such as *ego strength* and *introversion* are employed, empirical findings do in fact find a "theoretical home" and can more easily be associated with other personality variables. The theory employed, however, is not itself a dispositional one; rather, the data have been placed in a "foster home." Although dispositional psychologists employ theoretical notions in their work, for the most part they have not developed their own theories of personality and are therefore dependent on other strategies for theoretical progress.

THE DISPOSITIONAL STRATEGY LACKS ITS OWN THEORETICAL STRUCTURE

THE DISPOSITIONAL STRATEGY HEAVILY RELIES ON SELF-REPORT INVENTORIES

Each of the strategies uses self-report inventories in some form or other. However, these are relied on most heavily in dispositional assessment, and there is evidence that such reliance may not be justified. Self-reports, while clearly useful to some extent, are more limited than dispositional psychologists recognize.

Faking

In any personality assessment procedure, the assessee can probably succeed to some extent in faking—that is, presenting himself or herself in a different (and usually, but not always, more favorable) light than "the truth" would justify. Self-report inventories, however, are particularly susceptible to dissimulation inasmuch as the absence of an examiner lends a somewhat more impersonal and distant character to the evaluation. The assessee need not fear, for example, that facial expressions or other signs of "nervousness" will give him or her away because the inaccurate or misleading response can be made by simply checking a category or circling a number.

There have been numerous demonstrations that such faking can be quite successful (e.g., Anastasi, 1968; Noll, 1951; Wesman, 1952). Further, as Anastasi (1968) points out, the problem is compounded because persons of lower educational or intellectual level may be less able to fake. Various corrections, such as the Lie scale on the MMPI, may fail to detect faking by brighter or more insightful assessees while still generally, but unevenly, improving an instrument's validity.

Situational and set variables

Test scores of the sort obtained on self-report inventories have been shown repeatedly to be influenced by a wide variety of situational variables, including characteristics of the examiner (e.g., race, age, and sex), the testing conditions, and the stated or presumed purpose of the test.

Closely related to situational influences on self-report assessment are the response sets and styles which were discussed in Chapter 11. While it can be argued that a tendency to give the socially desirable response may itself be a personality disposition, a test that correlates highly with a social desirability scale is not measuring the theoretical construct it was originally designed to measure. Nor is it the case that these aspects of personality are the only viable personality dispositions. Rather, they may simply be the only ones that can be measured by self-report inventories.

The "test-trait" fallacy

Tryon (1979) has argued that the basic assumptions of dispositional theorists working within the area of personality testing are faulty. He has labeled the problem the "test-trait fallacy," and views it as originating in the mistaken assumption that test scores are actually trait measures. Adding to this the second assumption that trait measures are basic properties of the individual, dispositional psychologists reason that test scores therefore reflect these basic properties. Tryon, however, claims that what tests actually provide are performance measures which enable the tester to predict how the individual will respond to similar, but naturally occurring, stimuli. He therefore concludes that, in reifying such measures and scores into causal forces, dispositional theorists are misinterpreting test measures and going dangerously beyond the information that the test scores actually provide.

In our discussion of factor analysis, we mentioned that the naming of factors is invariably a subjective decision and that the number and kinds of factors extracted from such an analysis will depend on the particular mathematical procedure chosen. Put another way, Eysenck finds two factors and Cattell finds 16 or more because of the type of statistical analysis they have chosen to do. Obviously, then, Eysenck has not discovered that there are a small number of types, but has made subjective decisions that cause his findings to take on that character, and the same is true for Cattell.

THE DISPOSITIONAL STRATEGY ULTIMATELY RESTS ON SUBJECTIVE DECISIONS

This problem is by no means limited to the factor analysts. Arguments about the definition of achievement, power, aggression, and a host of other classes of behavior that have become trait names abound in the dispositional literature. Consider, for example, the striking difference between Murray's idea of *n* Achievement and McClelland's. Although they both use the same term (and it is a novel and technical-sounding term at that), they are referring to very different concepts. By *n* Achievement Murray meant a permanent characteristic set down in childhood and operating almost unconsciously. McClelland, on the other hand, has in mind a conscious attitude and orientation that can be readily taught to adults. What is more remarkable, both researchers used the same basic measuring instrument, the TAT. But for Murray, a person who wrote achievement-saturated stories in response to TAT cards would be displaying the latent need for *n* Achievement, of which the person was probably not even aware. The value of the TAT, Murray (1951) wrote, "is its capacity to reveal things that the patient is unwilling to tell or unable to tell because he is unconscious of them" (p. 577). In contrast, McClelland used the TAT to teach people to become achievement-oriented. McClelland did not do this because he discovered through research that Murray was wrong about the difference between latent and manifest needs. He changed the meaning of *n* Achievement because he decided that the new concept would be more "fruitful" than the old one was. It is not even clear that the McClelland meaning is as useful as was hoped. It has proven difficult to predict actual school grades for either children or college students from McClelland *n* Achievement scores (Crandall, 1967; Holmes & Tyler, 1968).

THE DISPOSITIONAL STRATEGY CANNOT PREDICT INDIVIDUAL BEHAVIOR

No one doubts that the dispositional strategy has produced many statistically significant and intriguing relationships, for example, between physical appearance (being fat, sporting a beard or mustache) and personality. Nor does anyone seriously doubt that there is *some* consistency in the way people behave. But the dispositional strategy provides almost no basis for predicting the behavior of a single individual with a high degree of accuracy. For example, many people with delicate builds love action and adventure (despite the general tendency for this group to be somewhat introverted and bookwormish), and many powerful leaders refrain from using alcohol or engaging in sexual exploits and drive cars that would hardly be found at the grand prix: Ralph Nader is a good example.

To illustrate the problem, let us consider a somewhat exaggerated hypothetical example. Suppose that an investigator observes informally that some people seem to be more intrusive than others and, to reflect this idea, defines intrusiveness as "a tendency to provide unsolicited information or advice to other persons, to present oneself uninvited, and to examine and employ the belongings of others without permission or request." Next, the investigator devises a broadly based assessment procedure to measure intrusiveness (including peer ratings, self-report measures, and fantasy measures) which is found to produce reliable intrusiveness scores and considerable individual differences among people.

At this point, the investigator begins to compare the backgrounds of those who are high (i.e., above average) and those who are low (i.e., below average) in intrusiveness. One finding is that high intrusives tend to report that their parents used to leave the doors to their rooms—and even their homes—unlocked, apparently worrying little about privacy. Persons low on intrusiveness, in contrast, report that their parents locked their doors and emphasized everyone's "right to privacy."

Now suppose that, having heard of this outcome, you meet a person who happens to mention his or her parents always leave the doors unlocked at home. You would certainly be tempted to assume (or at least to think it quite likely) that your new acquaintance will tend to be intrusive. This is *not* sound logic, and there is a very good chance that your assumption will be wrong.

Part of the reason can be seen from Figure 13–1, which displays our hypothetical intrusiveness data. We have assumed that intrusiveness is normally distributed, a common assumption among modern dispositional theorist (see Chapter 10). We have also shown a difference between the "locked door" and the "unlocked door" group that is large enough to be statistically significant with moderate sample sizes. In other words, Figure 13–1 represents the magnitude of difference that is typically obtained between "trait-high" and "trait-low" people in dispositional personality research.

FIGURE 13–1

Hypothetical distributions of scores for the disposition "intrusiveness," showing that a significant difference between the average trait scores of two groups (here, "locked door" versus "unlocked door" backgrounds) does not ordinarily provide the basis for predicting what a single individual will be like.

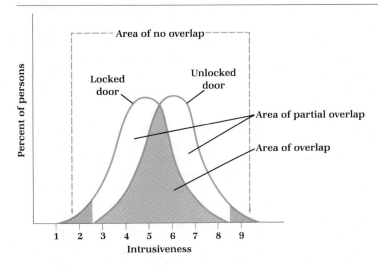

Three areas of the figure deserve comment. The lightly shaded area, called the "area of overlap," accounts for more than half of the area under the curves, showing that *most people will tend to get an average intrusiveness score, whether or not the doors in their homes were locked.* The two unshaded areas are areas of "partial overlap," meaning that some members of both groups obtain scores in this range, but that one group predominates in each area. We can also see from the figure that some persons from "locked door" and "unlocked door" backgrounds obtained an intrusiveness score of "4," but that the preponderance of those who did so were in the "locked door" group. Finally, the heavily darkened areas, the "areas of nonoverlap," are those in which only one group is represented. In the figure, the only people with intrusiveness scores as low as "2" came from homes where the doors were locked and the only people with intrusiveness scores as high as "9" came from homes where the doors were unlocked. The most important thing to note about the area of nonoverlap is how small it is; only a tiny percentage of people fall into these extreme ranges.

With this analysis in mind, we can ask: What conclusion can we draw about an individual person's intrusiveness from the knowledge that that person comes from a home where the doors were never locked? We certainly do not want to conclude that the person must be highly intrusive, because even among people from "unlocked-door" homes the majority are only about average in intrusiveness. As a matter of fact, our new acquaintance could be less intrusive than average—maybe even very *un*intrusive—and still come from a home where the doors were left unlocked. In this case at least, to reach any other conclusion would be a kind of stereotyping of the individual.

Of course, this does not mean that the data presented in the preceding chapters were wrong. Rather, it means that the dispositional strategy has, to date, given us assessment procedures that improve our guessing (above chance) as to what other people will be like or do, but that do not elevate us above the level of still *guessing*.

Mischel (1968), in a now-classic critique of the dispositional strategy, made the point this way:

> It is important to clearly distinguish between "statistically significant" associations and equivalence. A correlation of .30 easily reaches statistical significance when the sample of subjects is sufficiently large, and suggests an association that is highly unlikely on the basis of chance. However, the same coefficient accounts for less than 10 percent of the relevant variance [i.e., what the variables share in common]. Statistically significant relationships of this magnitude are sufficient to justify personality research on individual and group differences. It is equally plain that their value for making statements about an individual are severely limited. Even when statistically significant behavioral consistencies are found, and even when they replicate reliably, the relationships usually are not large enough to warrant individual assessment and treatment decisions except for certain screening and selection purposes. (p. 38)

Bolles (1978) has also pointed to the inadequacy of motivational concepts in this regard, and, in fact, has gone so far as to claim that the whole concept of motivation as impelling the organism to action is no longer a viable one. As a result of advances in the behavioral sciences, humans are now generally viewed as intrinsically active and goal directed. Furthermore, Bolles argues that we are now able to account for behavior in terms of laws which do not require that motivational concepts be invoked. Since motives were originally used to account for behavior that could not be explained under a view of people as passive structures of stimulus-response associations, Bolles holds that such constructs are no longer necessary. Rather, he claims that we are now better able to predict behavior without invoking motives.

Underestimation of the importance of situational factors

A related liability of the dispositional strategy is that it tends to underestimate (or, sometimes, overlooks entirely) the role of the situation and circumstances in determining what a person becomes. For example, for years psychologists, psychiatrists, and others sought to determine what traits make a person a leader. Ultimately, however, it was recognized that, in most groups, a leader is selected on the basis of how well he or she can facilitate attainment of the group's goals. As Hollander (1964) pointed out:

What was overlooked . . . in the view that leaders are uniquely endowed
. . . was the actual fact of daily life, that is, that persons function as
leaders in a particular time and place, and that these are both varying
and delimiting conditions; that there are several pathways to leadership,
sometimes from higher authority, other times from group consent. . . .
Indeed, if any point stands forth in the modern day view of leadership
it is that leaders are made by circumstances. . . . The leader's emergence
or waning of status is . . . inextricably linked to the prevailing situation.
(pp. 4–5, 15)

Recall the last of Allport's eight assumptions of a dispositional approach: "Acts, and even habits, that are inconsistent with a trait are
not proof of the nonexistence of the trait." The intent of this assumption
is clear: people do not always act consistently, but Allport does not
want that fact to vitiate a trait approach. At some point, though, the
argument is stretched to absurdity. If *all* of a person's acts are inconsistent with a trait, surely that is proof that the person does not possess
the disposition in question. Otherwise we can describe people in any
dispositional way we like, without regard to their behavior. An example
would be to say that a minority group has the trait of dishonesty despite
the fact that you have always known its members to behave honestly.
How much inconsistency can a dispositional approach endure?

Critics (e.g., Bandura & Walters, 1963; Mischel, 1968; Rotter, 1954)
have repeatedly challenged the assumption that human behavior is
consistent enough across situations to justify a dispositional view of
personality, and they have been able to muster both empirical evidence
from psychological investigations and compelling everyday examples
to support their argument. It is clear, for instance, that the aggressive
and forward man at the office may be a milquetoast at home, completely
dominated by his wife and children. Overstated, the criticism becomes
unfair. Allport's point was that dispositional psychologists do not necessarily claim, for example, that a person with the trait of hostility
will be hostile in every situation. But if a hostile person is not hostile
in every situation, it is essential to know *when* the characteristic is
likely to be operative. A fundamental deficiency of the dispositional
strategy is its failure to provide a useful way of describing or predicting
in which situations a disposition will and will not be manifest.

As much as any other strategy, the dispositional view has given
rise to longitudinal data—that is, the characteristics of people have
been measured at various points in time (e.g., in childhood and again
in adulthood), and similarities and differences have been noted. While
these data certainly indicate some of the consistency in behavior predicted by the dispositionalist, changes over time are also apparent
for most individuals. The dispositional strategy has paid little attention

**Failure to specify
when dispositions
will be manifest in
behavior**

**THE
DISPOSITIONAL
STRATEGY FAILS
TO EXPLAIN
PERSONALITY
DEVELOPMENT**

to these changes and has hardly concerned itself with the *processes* that might underlie the initial development or the changing complexion over time of a person's traits, types, or needs. When and how do source traits develop? Why does one behavior pattern emerge and not another? Such questions are not simply unanswered from the dispositional perspective: the strategy does not even call upon the investigator to ask them.

A closely related point is that the dispositional strategy has contributed almost nothing to the important question of how to devise intervention procedures so that undesirable aspects of personality can be changed. Some individuals whose names are associated with the dispositional strategy (e.g., Murray, Eysenck, and McClelland) have been involved in personality-change work, but their personality-change approaches, like many of their basic theoretical concepts, have been borrowed from other views. Murray, whose approach to personality is based on needs, practiced as a therapist in the Harvard Psychological Clinic using procedures influenced primarily by psychoanalysis; Eysenck, a major advocate of the type approach based on factor analysis, is also one of the most ardent proponents of personality change procedures associated with the behavioral strategy (see Section 5); and McClelland's program to foster and increase people's need to achieve is based on principles derived from psychoanalytic, phenomenological, and behavioral personality theories.

In sum, the dispositional strategy tries to capture and describe a *static* person, and ignores the dynamics of development, growth, and change which are also important aspects of personality.

THE DISPOSITIONAL STRATEGY FAILS TO DISTINGUISH DESCRIPTION FROM EXPLANATION

When certain consistencies or regularities are observed, whether in people's behavior or in nature, it is often convenient to summarize the observation with a descriptive label. Thus "introversion" is a label chosen to describe an observed pattern of behavior or set of relationships. This labeling process is perfectly legitimate if our purpose is description, but the label obviously does not explain in any meaningful way the observations which gave rise to it. Yet the error of confusing description with explanation is repeatedly made by dispositionalists (cf. parallel error made by psychoanalysts; pages 144–45).

Below is an example given by Skinner (1953) many years ago. By substituting appropriately, you can see how Skinner's argument applies to introversion, achievement motivation, or any of the other labels that have been invented to describe behavior.

> When we say that a man eats *because* he is hungry, smokes a great deal *because* he has the tobacco habit, fights *because* he has the instinct of pugnacity, behaves brilliantly *because* of his intelligence, or plays the piano well *because* of his musical ability, we seem to be referring

to causes. But on analysis these phrases prove to be merely redundant descriptions. A single set of facts is described by the two statements: "He eats" and "He is hungry." A single set of facts is described by the statements "He smokes a great deal" and "He has the smoking habit." A single set of facts is described by the two statements: "He plays well" and "He has musical ability." The practice of explaining one statement in terms of the other is dangerous because it suggests that we have found the cause and therefore need search no further. (p. 31)

This liability cannot be escaped by those who claim that dispositions are only meant as descriptions. In that case, critics could say that the dispositional strategy, by its own admissions, does not provide an *explanation* of behavior.

The phenomenological strategy

14

The phenomenological strategy

Introduction

If a tree falls in a forest, but no one is there to hear it fall, does it make any sound as it falls? This philosophical and epistemological question addresses the fundamental issue of whether physical phenomena have reality of their own, or whether they must be perceived in order to be real or exist. Psychology, too, is interested in the reality of physical events from the point of view of the perceiver. In fact, questions about the nature of subjective human experience were among the first to be asked by psychologists (James, 1890).

How people react to events in their physical or interpersonal world depends to some degree on the *meaning* that the various events have for them. Suppose that someone were standing close to the proverbial tree as it fell and heard the loud, cracking sound that precedes the fall. If the person were a lumberjack, the sound would undoubtedly be familiar, and it is likely that the lumberjack would hastily retreat to a safe distance from the impending crash. However, the same sound might have no special meaning to a lawyer from the "big city" who had never heard it before, and the lawyer might not react to the sound (other than to look around curiously for its source). Note that, in fact, the lumberjack reacts not to the sound itself, but to an interpretation of the sound, just as the lawyer fails to react because the lawyer has no interpretation of the sound.

What has been illustrated in the preceding example is the *phenomenological* view of personality which, in brief, holds that the reality of phenomena is solely a function of the way in which they are observed. What is real to an individual is that which is in that person's *internal frame of reference,* or subjective world, and this includes everything that the person is aware of at a particular point in time. There is nothing intrinsically brown, round, or large about a basketball; one must look to the reacting individual to find out the color, shape, and relative size of the object.

From the standpoint of predicting behavior, phenomenological psychology says that effective reality is *reality as it is perceived.* Two people observing the "same" set of circumstances may perceive two very different occurrences, as is so often the case with "eyewitnesses" in traffic accidents.

The importance of the way things are perceived and experienced subjectively is well illustrated in an experiment by Geer, Davison, and Gatchel (1970). These investigators hypothesized that the amount of stress a person experiences in various situations will be determined not only by the objective characteristics of the situation (such as its severity or the person's ability to influence what happens), but also by whether the person *believes* he or she can control what is happening. To test this hypothesis, Geer and his associates devised an experiment in which all subjects received a series of identical electric shocks over which they had no control whatsoever, but some of the subjects believed that they could control the shocks, whereas others believed they could not.

The experiment was presented to the subjects as a study of reaction times and was conducted in two phases. During Phase I, all subjects were treated alike; they were given a series of painful electric shocks, each of which lasted six seconds, and were asked to press a switch— as a measure of reaction time—as soon as the shock began. During this period, every subject's level of physiological arousal to the shocks was measured as a baseline. During Phase II, half the subjects were assigned to a *perceived control* condition and were told that they could cut the duration of the next 10 shocks in half if their reaction times in pressing the switch were "quick enough" (but the necessary speed was left undefined); the remaining subjects were assigned to a *perceived noncontrol* condition and were just told that the next 10 shocks would be shorter in duration. Actually, all of the subjects received shocks of three seconds' duration while their physiological arousal was again measured. The question then became: Would the perceived control subjects experience less arousal during Phase II than the perceived noncontrol subjects because of their belief that they could influence the situation? As seen in Figure 14–1, the answer is a clear yes. Geer and his associates noted the following implication of their finding:

> Man creates his own gods to fill in gaps in his knowledge about a sometimes terrifying environment, creating at least an illusion of control which is presumably comforting. Perhaps the next best thing to being master of one's fate is being deluded into thinking he is. (1970, pp. 737–38)

Adopting a phenomenological orientation for studying personality implies that a person's behavior can only be understood from the person's own point of view. The important object of study is a person's subjective experiences, for it is these experiences that direct behavior. Subjective experience may or may not coincide with "objective reality," a point which is well illustrated by the following example, drawn from the writings of George A. Kelly, whose psychology of personal constructs will be considered in detail in Chapter 17.

FIGURE 14–1

The effects of perceived control on the amount of arousal subjects experienced while awaiting electric shocks in Geer et al.'s experiment. During Phase I, all subjects received shocks of six seconds' duration, whereras during Phase II, all subjects received shocks of three seconds' duration. Subjects in the perceived control group believed that the shorter shocks were a result of their own quick reaction times, whereas subjects in the perceived noncontrol group believed that shock duration was unrelated to their responses and therefore not within their control.

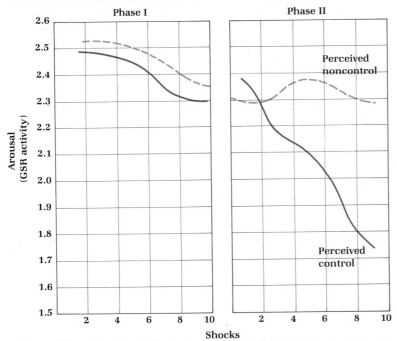

Source: Adapted from Geer, J. H., Davison, G. C., & Gatchel, R. I. Reduction of stress in humans through nonveridical control of aversive stimulation. *Journal of Personality and Social Psychology*, 1970, *16*, 731–38.

A man construes his neighbor's behavior as hostile. By that he means that his neighbor, given the proper opportunity, will do him harm. He tries out his construction of his neighbor's attitude by throwing rocks at his neighbor's dog. His neighbor responds with an angry rebuke. The man may then believe that he has validated his construction of his neighbor as a hostile person.

The man's construction of his neighbor as a hostile person may appear to be "validated" by another kind of fallacy. The man reasons, "If my neighbor is hostile, he will be eager to know when I get into trouble, when I am ill, or when I am in any way vulnerable. I will watch to see if this isn't so." The next morning the man meets his neighbor and is greeted with the conventional, "How are you?" Sure enough, the neighbor is doing just what was predicted of a hostile person. (Kelly, 1955, pp. 12–13)

However, there are instances in which objective reality is much less clear and, for all practical purposes, what a person perceives, his or her subjective experience, determines the ultimate reality of the situation for the person. Consider the example of eight-year-old Beth, whose family has just moved to a new city. After her first day at the new school, her parents inquire, "How was school today?" "I hated it," says Beth. "The kids are really unfriendly. When I came into the class, all the kids stared at me. They were grinning and thought I was funny looking. Only two kids in the whole class even talked to me at lunch." Now consider how Beth might have *perceived* the same objective situation differently and reported, "I liked it. The kids are really friendly. When I came into the class, they were all interested in me. The kids were looking at me and smiling. And two kids, who I didn't even know, came over to talk to me at lunch!" It is possible that the same objective situation could have led Beth to have either of these two very different subjective experiences.[1]

From a philosophical standpoint, no practical problems are presented by phenomenology's exclusive concern with subjective knowledge—those things which each individual person knows. But when phenomenology is brought into the realm of psychology, a scientific endeavor which purports to deal with objective knowledge, a dilemma arises. Objective knowledge comes from observations upon which others can agree, whereas subjective knowledge involves only a single person's experiences, of which that person alone has direct knowledge. The solution to this predicament, which has been adopted by phenomenological psychologists, has been to seek what Carl Rogers (1964) has called *phenomenological knowledge*—that is, an understanding of a person as viewed from the person's own internal frame of reference.

The phenomenological position is often implicit in "everyday psychology." Such common expressions as "Beauty is all in the eye of the beholder," "One person's meat is another person's poison," and "Try stepping into the other person's shoes" emphasize the salience of subjective knowledge in determining one's actions and the importance of gaining phenomenological knowledge when trying to understand and predict someone else's behavior. The failure to see things as other people see them gets us into interpersonal difficulties, as when someone makes a joke about an incident which another person takes seriously.

To illustrate the phenomenological strategy for the study of personality, we shall examine two somewhat different approaches. First we discuss the self-actualization approaches of Carl Rogers and Abraham

---

[1] Another important point which could be gleaned from this example is that Beth's perception of her new classmates affected her behavior, which, in turn, influenced how they reacted to her, thereby changing the nature of the objective situation in subsequent interactions.

Maslow, both of which emphasize the importance of understanding an individual's personality and behavior in terms of that person's unique biological and learned inclinations to develop and change in particular directions. Then we turn to George Kelly's psychology of personal constructs which deals with how people interpret and come to understand what is going on in their lives and in doing so develop unique personalities. These positions differ considerably in their theoretical assumptions about the nature of human personality, the concepts that they employ, and the techniques for changing personality that they advocate. Nevertheless, they share some basic suppositions about personality theory, assessment, research, and change, which serve as guides for the scientific and practical endeavors that are derived from them.

PHENOMENO-LOGICAL PERSONALITY THEORY

Both Rogers and Kelly have proposed broad theories of personality which, at least hypothetically, can account for all our diverse behaviors. Each of these theories grew, in part, out of the clinical experiences Rogers and Kelly had in dealing with abnormal behavior, and it is therefore no wonder that the theories include both the "healthy" and "sick" sides of personality.

In contrast, Maslow's theorizing has been much more delimited. Rather than formulate a comprehensive theory of personality, he focused on theoretical explanations of a few different aspects of human behavior. As a personality theorist, Maslow stands virtually alone in having attended almost exclusively to the positive, healthy side of personality. For example, believing that every individual has a vast potential for growth, Maslow explored the optimal or fully functioning person, the individual who is close to all he or she is capable of becoming.

The theories of Rogers, Maslow, and Kelly all focus on "higher" human functions. Rogers' and Maslow's work deals with self-actualization, and Kelly's personal construct theory is concerned with the way in which people assign explanations and interpretations to their experiences. These emphases should be contrasted with the "lower" functions, such as drives and reflexes, which are the focus of other approaches to personality. Each of the phenomenological positions to be discussed takes into account the fact that essential biological needs have to be met, but its theorizing about human personality commences at the point where these have been satisfied.

Another common theme running through all these approaches is that humans are active, reacting beings. In making this assumption, phenomenologists partially circumvent the basic problem of explaining how behavior is motivated. If humans are conceived of as inert objects which must be compelled to action, then it becomes necessary to posit some special force, such as a drive or a trait to account for behavior.

Each of the phenomenological positions to be discussed views the human being as an active organism rather than a passive object—each sees the person as reacting *with* his or her biological makeup and immediate environment, rather than being compelled to action *by* them.

Phenomenologists are also concerned with the direction human behavior takes (e.g., goals). On a broad scale, why do some people spend much of their lives accumulating money while others seek prestige and fame? In the more narrow sphere of day-to-day endeavors, what factors determine Janet's spending an evening listening to music while her roommate Janice cleans their apartment? To explain the direction which behavior takes, a general principle is advanced. Rogers and Maslow posit that all people have a tendency to actualize themselves so as to approach their own unique potential. Kelly theorizes that people act in those ways which lead to their being able to predict the events in their lives most accurately. The specifics of how either of these broad principles operates to direct a person's behavior vary with each individual.

The phenomenological approaches to personality not only view people as active, but also see them as changing constantly. As Rogers (1961) put it: "Life, at its best, is a flowing, changing process in which nothing is fixed" (p. 27). This dynamic conception of the person is wholly consistent with the phenomenological emphasis on the "here and now." In other words, behavior is determined by the individual's phenomenal field at any given point in time. Although the phenomenologists certainly acknowledge that past experiences influence present behavior, they view the past only in terms of how it affects present perceptions. Phenomenological theories pay little attention to stable, enduring characteristics of the individual, which are the focus of the dispositional strategy, and to lifelong patterns of action which have originated in early childhood, which are the core of the psychoanalytic strategy.

Does this mean that human behavior is totally inconsistent and unpredictable? Certainly not. In fact, consistency is an important theme running through the theories of Rogers, Maslow, and Kelly. These theories can be called *holistic* in that they view and explain each of a person's specific acts in terms of his or her entire personality. For example, Rogers stresses the importance of consistency between how people view themselves and how they would like to be.

The concept of self

The phenomenological strategy, more than any of the others, stresses the importance of the idea of *self*. Thus Epstein (1973) observes that:

> those self-theorists identified as phenomenologists consider the self-concept to be the most central concept in all of psychology, as it provides the only perspective from which an individual's behavior can be understood. From such a position, behavioristic attempts [see Chapters 19–

23] to develop an objective, scientific psychology that does not include a self-concept can represent nothing more than a futile exercise in mimicking the physical sciences. (p. 404)

Ruth Wylie (1968) has suggested that the self can be viewed as a complex structure of interrelated aspects. In Wylie's view, we can speak of a *generic self-concept,* that is, an all-inclusive concept of self which incorporates all of the following features:

1. The person's experiencing himself or herself as a distinct entity which can be differentiated from others.
2. A sense of continuing to be the same person over time.
3. A person's physical characteristics *as experienced by the person.*
4. A person's past behaviors as experienced and remembered, especially those that are perceived as having been executed voluntarily or as having been under the control of the person.
5. The experiencing of a degree of organization or unity among the various aspects of the generic-self concept.
6. Evaluations, thoughts, and memories.
7. Varying degrees of consciousness or unconsciousness.

In addition, the generic-self concept can be subdivided into the *actual-self-concept* and the *ideal self-concept,* the former dealing with what we are and the other with what we would like to be. And, finally, there is an important difference between the way we see ourselves and the way we present ourselves, just as there is a difference between the way we see ourselves and the way we think others see us. The actual self-concept is therefore subdivided into concepts of the social self and private self, while the ideal self-concept comprises our own ideal self-concepts and our concepts of what others think would be ideal for us. The entire analysis is shown schematically in Figure 14–2.

FIGURE 14–2
Wylie's analysis of the self-concept as used by most phenomenological self theorists

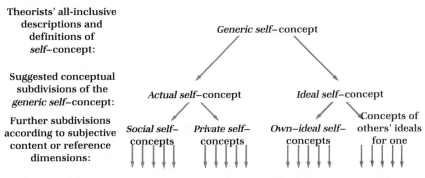

Source: Wylie, R. C. The present state of self theory. In E. F. Borgatta & W. W. Lambert (Eds.), *Handbook of personality theory and research.* Chicago: Rand McNally, 1968.

Existential psychology and the phenomenological approach

The phenomenological approach to personality has close ties with the existential movement in psychology. As Rollo May, a prominent champion of existential psychology, has pointed out, existential psychology is "an *attitude,* an approach to human beings, rather than a special school or group. . . . it is not a system of therapy but an attitude toward therapy, not a set of new techniques but a concern with the understanding of the structure of the human being and his experience" (1967, p. 245).

The existential attitude, according to May, requires an intimate understanding or experiencing of what another person is going through. The attitude requires that the psychologist try to *know* people rather than merely know *about* them. This emphasis on the existing person is the philosophical basis for phenomenological personality change.

Each individual's existence is assumed to include both a unique pattern of potentialities and the ability to actualize them, given proper circumstances. Thus, an important contribution of the existential attitude to the phenomenological strategy is its relative stress on the free will and opportunity for choice available to each person. The person can and must affirm his or her existence by making choices, while the therapist's role is to support rather than guide or direct. As we will see in the chapters that follow, this theme of nondirectiveness and a belief in voluntary choice is a central one in all phenomenological therapies.

The phenomenological strategy, more than any other, assumes that the person is *rational* and that an individual's actions will be a "sensible" response to the world as that individual perceives it. What is more, there is a necessary emphasis on "consciousness," and *conscious experience* is assumed to play a causal role in social behavior—in fact, to control it.

PHENOMENO-LOGICAL PERSONALITY ASSESSMENT

Personality assessment presents difficulties for the phenomenological strategy. How can other persons' thoughts be known, when all we have is their word for what their phenomenological reality is like? Even putting issues of trust and accuracy aside, how can you be sure that the experience you hear another person describing is even remotely like the one that the person has in mind? Think of how many different meanings a nonemotional phrase such as *casual attire* can have, and you begin to get a hint of what the odds are against your knowing exactly what people mean when they say that they are terribly afraid or that they love you.

Because the phenomenological strategy is concerned with the subjective experiences of persons, phenomenological personality assessment necessitates gaining knowledge of private events. Recall that this is also the essential task of psychoanalytic personality assessment. In both the phenomenological and psychoanalytic strategies, behavior is neither the basic unit of personality nor the exclusive means used to get at personality. Consider the student who does not speak up in a class discussion. What can we infer from this behavior? Would it be a good hunch that the student has not read the assignment for the day and therefore is not prepared to participate in the discussion? Or is the student thoroughly familiar with the background reading but reluctant to venture forth in the discussion because he or she is afraid to be considered a show-off? The student's behavior on any given day will not answer these questions, because the same behavior can have vastly different *meanings* for the same person on different occasions. Within broad limits, behavior can yield information about an individual's personality; but for more specific information, the meaning of the behavior for the person must be assessed. In fact, all of phenomenological personality assessment could be said to be aimed at the assessment of *meaning,* for it is the meaning of experiences for people which constitutes their personalities and determines their actions.

Seeing the world as another person does is different from making inferences about that person's behavior, which are projections, in the psychoanalytic sense, of the assessor's own view of things rather than an accurate picture of the other person's perspective. This is illustrated by the case of a college student who tells his college-educated parents that he wants to drop out of school because he does not believe he is learning anything worthwhile. His parents reply that they "understand" exactly how he feels. When they were in college, his parents recall, there were times when they were tired and wanted to quit; so why doesn't he take a few days off at the lake and relax, and then he will be ready to complete the semester. Obviously, what the parents "understand" is how *they* felt and not how their son feels. Phenomenological knowledge is a matter of *what the experience means for the person* and not what it means for the assessor or for people in general.

The salience of "here-and-now" experiences in the phenomenological strategy contrasts sharply with psychoanalytic personality assessment. Phenomenological assessment techniques focus on the present. An individual's subjective experiences of the past are important only insofar as they clarify present perceptions. In practice, Rogerian personality assessment almost completely eschews the past and Kellian assessment techniques deal with the past sparingly.

Phenomenological personality assessment is relatively straightforward, again in contrast to the largely inferential tack employed in the psychoanalytic strategy. The subjective experience itself is taken as the basic datum from which a picture of the individual's total personality is constructed. Of course, subjective experience can never be known fully by anyone but the person having the experience. The basic strategy, then, is to gain phenomenological knowledge—that is, to try to understand another person's subjective experience from his or her perspective (which is only an approximation of another's subjective experience).

Most techniques of personality assessment used within the phenomenological strategy involve self-report measures, especially verbal self-report. These reports of subjective experience are accepted more or less at face value. They are not considered signs or indications of some inferred psychological state (e.g., an intrapsychic conflict) or some underlying disposition (e.g., trait). The assessment remains on the level of phenomenological knowledge. For example, conscious experiences are taken as direct evidence of important personality functions and are not necessarily viewed as indicators of underlying unconscious processes.

A basic assumption of the phenomenological strategy is that people are generally aware of their subjective experiences. In fact, it is the awareness of these events which is presumed to direct their behavior and is the subject matter of phenomenology. The position of the phenomenological strategy with regard to experiences outside one's awareness (i.e., unconscious) is that they do exist but that they do not constitute the major determinants of normal behavior. It should be noted, however, that within both Rogers' and Kelly's approaches, unconscious processes begin to play a greater role as a person's behavior becomes more abnormal or psychologically deviant.

Phenomenological assessment may set up conditions in which people will be most likely to be open about their experiences. One example of this approach is Rogers' client-centered therapy, in which the therapist attempts to establish an accepting, warm, threat-free atmosphere for the client. The essence of phenomenological personality assessment involves the assessor's attempt to understand the communication of subjective experiences from the internal frame of reference of the person relating such experiences. This primarily involves what is called *empathy,* understanding a person's experiences in terms of what they mean for that person. It necessitates, among other things, abandoning one's own connotations for the words and phrases the other person uses and one's own interpretation of the experiences related.

Demonstration 14–1

PERCEIVING FROM ANOTHER'S INTERNAL FRAME OF REFERENCE

The reader is invited to try to understand another person's subjective experiences from his internal frame of reference. Below are a series of statements made by a 30-year-old man at the beginning of a therapy session. Assume that you were counseling this man and wanted to let him know by your comments that you were understanding what he was telling you *from his perspec-tive.* Read each statement made by the client and then write down a sentence or two describing the response you would make to each of the client's state-ments. In other words, describe the attitudes or thoughts you have concerning the statement as *you assume the internal frame of reference of this client.*

1. "I thought I'd have something to talk about—then it all goes around in circles. I was trying to think of what I was going to say. Then coming here it doesn't work out. . . . I tell you, it seemed that it would be much easier before I came."
2. "I tell you, I just can't make a decision; I don't know what I want. I've tried to reason this thing out logically—tried to figure out which things are important to me."
3. "I thought that there are maybe two things a man might do; he might get married and raise a family. But if he was just a bachelor, just making a living—that isn't very good."
4. "I find myself and my thoughts getting back to the days when I was a kid, and I cry very easily. The dam would break through."
5. "I [was] in the Army 4½ years. I had no problems then, no hopes, no wishes. My only thought was to get out when peace would come."

Now compare your attitudes and thoughts with those in Table 14–1 to see what success you had at adopting the client's internal frame of reference. While your thoughts do not have to be identical with those given in the table, they should be of the same general flavor as those in the left-hand column. Rogers (1965) explains why the attitudes in the right-hand column are represen-tative of an external frame of reference by noting that "these are all attitudes which are basically sympathetic. There is nothing 'wrong' with them. They are even attempts to 'understand,' in the sense of 'understanding about,' rather than 'understanding with.' The locus of perceiving is, however, outside of the client" (p. 33).

TABLE 14–1
Attitudes and thoughts representing internal and external frames of reference*

Internal frame of reference	*External frame of reference*
1. It's really hard for you to get started.	1. Should I help you get started talking? Is your inability to get under way a type of dependence?
2. Decision making just seems impossible to you.	2. What is the cause of your indecisiveness?
3. You want marriage, but it doesn't seem to you to be much of a possibility.	3. Why are you focusing on marriage and family? You appear to be a bachelor. I didn't know that.
4. You feel yourself brimming over with childish feelings.	4. The crying, the "dam," sound as though you are repressing a great deal.
5. To you the Army represented stagna-tion.	5. You're a veteran. Were you a psychiat-ric patient? I feel sorry for anybody who spent 4½ years in the service.

*Statements quoted or paraphrased from Rogers, C. R. *Client-centered therapy.* Boston: Houghton Mifflin, 1965, pp. 33–34.

maybe a major a general question

PHENOMENOLOG-ICAL RESEARCH

All three of the basic methods of personality research—experimental, correlational, and case study—have been used within the phenomenological strategy, and examples of each will be given in the next three chapters. What characterizes the various types of research endeavors is the focus on subjective experiences and the way people perceive events.

There is a heavy emphasis on idiographic research in the phenomenological strategy. This is in keeping with the idea of conceiving of an individual's personality processes in terms of the subjective phenomenal world, of that which is real to that one person and that person alone. Such idiographic research, of which Maslow's investigations of the self-actualizing person are a prime example, most frequently utilizes the case-study method. The data from these studies are detailed, qualitative descriptions of subjective, intensely personal experiences, and they yield rich, in-depth portraits of single personalities. By studying subjects with particular characteristics (e.g., self-actualization), the researcher can combine the data to produce a composite picture of the nature of that personality characteristic. Thus, what begins as an idiographic investigation, a detailed study of a single individual, can also be used to supply nomothetic information which will be applicable to a great many people.

As in the case in the psychoanalytic strategy, phenomenological research is often related to and done in conjunction with psychotherapy. Historically this is probably due to the fact that phenomenological psychologists such as Rogers, Maslow, and Kelly were clinical psychologists who were actively engaged in psychotherapeutic endeavors as they developed their approaches. Additionally, phenomenological approaches to personality have tended to emphasize the application of their theoretical principles to practical human problems.

PHENOMENO-LOGICAL PERSONALITY CHANGE

If personality is a function of one's perceptions and subjective evaluations of the events in one's life, then it follows that in order to modify personality, it is these private experiences which must be changed. In general, this entails a process whereby the person becomes more aware of his or her subjective experiences and their influence on her or his behavior. The basic assumption is that, when individuals' perceptions of their life experiences are altered, their behavior will change.

In phenomenological personality-change procedures the client[2] assumes the major responsibility for modifying his or her personality, a fact which evolves directly from phenomenological personality theory. Since human beings are seen as active organisms, it follows that clients

---

[2] Phenomenological psychologists use the term *client* more frequently than the term *patient.*

themselves play a major role in altering their own personalities. It is assumed that people have the capacity to change their own personalities and behavior. Although the specific procedures employed in psychotherapy to encourage self-modification vary with the particular approach, the basic theme of self-determination runs through all phenomenological personality-change procedures. Furthermore, clients know themselves and their own subjective experiences far better than anyone else could. Therefore, the client, rather than the therapist, should direct the change process.

Phenomenological personality change is primarily present oriented, and often "present" involves what is going on immediately, in the *here and now.* This means the events taking place in therapy—including all of the feelings and thoughts the client has during the therapy session—become the focus of the therapeutic procedures (e.g., the interactions of the client and therapist or among clients in group therapy). There is also a sense in which phenomenological personality change deals with the future in that expectations, beliefs, and predictions about the future (but which are obviously occurring in the present) are frequent topics in therapy.

The encounter-group movement

In recent years, there has been a proliferation of techniques aimed at changing personality within groups. Some of the better-known techniques have been called "T-groups," "encounter groups," and "sensitivity training." The formal origin of these groups dates back more than 30 years. In the late 1940s, Kurt Lewin, a noted social psychologist at MIT, and his associates were experimenting with training (the meaning of *T*) groups aimed at developing the interpersonal interaction skills of industrial managers and executives.

> The T group started informally, almost accidentally. Lewin originally scheduled it as a casual discussion by group leaders of events occurring in the afternoon workshop. Some group members also attended. This led to direct confrontations, as leaders and participants disagreed in their perceptions of what had occurred in the workshop sessions. The argument moved on to more personal and immediate ground, to what was happening in the "here and now." The group attempted to develop new structures for handling problems as they arose. Out of this developed a new approach to training, an unstructured group centered on the study of its own dynamics. The focus of the group was on the way members interacted in the process of organizing themselves into a group. (Schloss, Siroka, & Siroka, 1971, p. 4)

The initial T-groups focused on organizational and human relations skills. In the late 1950s, a second type of group emerged, which shifted the emphasis to the personal growth of the group members. These groups are more likely to be called encounter groups or sensitivity training. They are closer to psychotherapy than were the earlier T-groups, though many of them purport to be designed for "normal" people who are interested in growth experiences, in becoming more aware of themselves and others, and in developing their full potential as human beings.

Some of the general goals of T-groups, according to Aronson (1972), are the following:

1. To develop a willingness to examine one's behavior and to experiment with new ways of behaving.
2. To learn more about people in general.
3. To become more authentic and honest in interpersonal relations.
4. To become better able to work cooperatively with people other than in an authoritative or submissive manner.
5. To develop the ability to resolve conflicts by using logical and rational problem solving rather than by means of coercion or manipulation.

The encounter-group movement, which is part of a larger movement referred to as "humanistic psychology"[3] has a number of ties with the phenomenological strategy, particularly in its aims. In encounter groups or sensitivity training, for example, emphasis is placed on subjective experiences and feelings, understanding others from their perspective, increasing self-awareness and self-acceptance, developing wholeness and consistency within one's personality, and being in the "here and now." The content of the group discussion comes from the spontaneous interaction of the group members and steers away from the past.

The main technique used in group therapy involves open and frank feedback to individuals from other group members and the trainer. Vicarious learning also takes place. For example, when one member who is socially anxious tries to deal with the problem, others with similar difficulties may learn from watching the encounter (Aronson, 1972). Group pressure is another effective technique. It may be easy to reject a message from one person, even a therapist, but if three or four people claim that someone is hostile, that person is forced to examine the charge more carefully. There are also a host of "action" techniques, such as body contact, to heighten one's awareness of bodily sensations, and physical games to develop trust. An example of the latter is having a group member lean over backward until he or she is off balance and has to be caught by another group member. Bindrim (1968) has used nudity as an aid to lowering defenses, and weekend

---

[3] Maslow (1962) speaks of humanistic psychology as the "third force" in psychology—a reaction and alternative to psychoanalysis on the one hand and to behavioral approaches on the other.

encounter groups or marathon-type sessions (Bach, 1966; Mintz, 1967; Stoller, 1968) may allow little or no sleep in the expectation that fatigue and long exposure will weaken the defenses of the participants and allow them to be more open. The main goal of such techniques is to encourage people to "loosen up" and express their feelings frankly. With this emphasis on openness, people may feel pressured to reveal more about themselves than they would like to, but an individual's right to privacy need not be violated. A competent group leader will direct the conversation away from those who indicate that certain areas are private.

Because of the popularity of encounter-type experiences, people frequently ask what goes on in them (see, for example, Rogers, 1970; Schutz, 1967). Aronson (1972) describes how a group session may get started:

> He [the leader] . . . falls into silence. Minutes pass. They seem like hours. The group members may look at each other or out the window. Typically, participants may look at the trainer for guidance or direction. None is forthcoming. After several minutes, someone might express his discomfort. This may or may not be responded to. Eventually, in a typical group, someone will express annoyance at the leader: "I'm getting sick of this. This is a waste of time. How come you're not doing your job? What the hell are we paying you for? Why don't you tell us what we're supposed to do?" There may be a ripple of applause in the background. But someone else might jump in and ask the first person why he is so bothered by a lack of direction—does he need someone to tell him what to do? And the T-group is off and running. (p. 241)

The actual experiences of group members depend upon how the situation is perceived by each individual, which is the essence of the phenomenological position.

Despite the close connection between many of the aims and some of the techniques of sensitivity training and the phenomenological strategy, the theoretical underpinnings of encounter groups are diverse. They include Gestalt therapy (e.g., Perls, 1969), Rogers' client-centered therapy, variations on psychoanalysis (e.g., Berne's [1961, 1964] transactional analysis), as well as the self-actualization approach to personality discussed in the next two chapters.

Currently, there is little controlled research evidence demonstrating any beneficial effects of encounter groups. However, positive outcomes have been reported by therapists and many participants. Rogers says:

Evaluation of encounter groups

> I have known individuals for whom the encounter experience has meant an almost miraculous change in the depth of their communication with spouse and children. Sometimes for the first time real feelings are

shared. . . . I have seen teachers who have transformed their classroom . . . into a personal, caring, trusting, learning group, where students participate fully and openly in forming the curriculum and all the other aspects of their education. Tough business executives who described a particular business relationship as hopeless, have gone home and changed it into a constructive one. (1970, p. 71)

On the negative side, there have been reports of T-group "casualties" (Yalom & Lieberman, 1971). A person who has been told by another group member that he or she has a serious deficiency in dealing with others may leave the group feeling worse if the group leader then allows the discussion to shift away from that person rather than deal with the problem (Serber, 1972a). It appears that much of the effectiveness of encounter-type groups depends on the skill of the group leader; there is no guarantee that the impact of the encounter group will always be beneficial.

15 | *The phenomenological strategy*

Rogers' self-actualization theory

It has been said that each person has, at most, one seminal idea in his or her life, and all of one's work is an expansion, elaboration, and extrapolation on that fundamental idea. That is certainly true for Carl Rogers (1902–   ). His seminal idea is simply this: Each individual has within him- or herself a unique potential to develop, grow, and change in inherently healthy and positive directions; given the right psychological climate, which is essentially free of externally imposed influences or constraints, that potential will guide all of the person's behavior. This central theme has directed and pervaded Carl Rogers' theorizing, research, and counseling over more than 50 years. His seminal idea, which is called *self-actualization,* has had a major impact on the field of personality psychology. In reflecting on the possible reasons for the enormous impact that his work has had, Rogers (1974) concluded that he had formulated an idea whose time had come. The field of personality psychology was ready, and indeed probably in need of, such a new central theme.

Carl Rogers

Courtesy of Carl Rogers, photo by Nozizwe S.

When Rogers began his career in 1927, personality psychology was essentially equivalent to the psychoanalytic strategy; there were no other approaches with any significant impact on the field. It is not difficult to see that Rogers' self-actualization principle was in direct conflict with the prevailing strategy, psychoanalysis. For instance, at a very basic level, Rogers' principle of self-actualization, in contrast to Freud's psychoanalysis, expresses a distinctly *optimistic* outlook of humans' ability to develop and enhance themselves in positive and healthy ways. Rogers' thinking, like that of many of the personality psychologists after Freud, was a reaction to psychoanalysis. However, only a handful of theoretical ideas have become major alternatives to psychoanalysis, and Rogers' self-actualization approach unquestionably numbers among those select few. In fact, Rogers' theory was the first major alternative to psychoanalysis.

Rogers, like Freud, began as a clinician, treating persons with various abnormal behaviors, and he used his experiences in therapy as both a source of hypotheses about human personality and an arena for testing, refining, and revising these hypotheses. Also like Freud's, Rogers' ideas were initially considered heretical. Rogers had a strong personal belief in the validity of his basic theoretical notions, and he persisted in his efforts to develop, test, and elaborate them as well as to extrapolate them beyond personality to a variety of human endeavors, including interpersonal relations, education, and the development and survival of cultures.

PERSONALITY DEVELOPMENT

The actualizing tendency

Rogers (1959) postulated that all behavior is governed by the *actualizing tendency*, "the inherent tendency of the organism to develop all its capacities in ways which serve to maintain or enhance the organism" (p. 196). At a very basic, organic level this inborn tendency involves the maintenance of the individual by meeting fundamental needs, such as the need for oxygen, water, and food, and the enhancement of the person by providing for the development and differentiation of the body's organs and functions and its continual growth and regeneration. But of more importance to human personality is the motivation which the actualizing tendency provides for increased autonomy and self-sufficiency, for expanding one's repertoire of experiences, and for creativity.

The actualizing tendency guides the person toward generally positive or healthy behaviors (e.g., independence and self-regulation) rather than toward negative or unhealthy behaviors (e.g., dependence and self-destruction). In discussing this specific directionality, Rogers (1980) described an analogous process which has been demonstrated in biological research.

> One example, replicated with different species, is the work of Hans Driesch with sea urchins many years ago. Driesch learned how to tease apart the two cells that are formed after the first division of the fertilized egg. Had they been left to develop normally, it is clear that each of these two cells would have grown into a portion of a sea urchin larva, the contributions of both being needed to form a whole creature. So it seems equally obvious that when the two cells are skillfully separated, each, if it grows, will simply develop into some portion of a sea urchin. But this assumption overlooks the directional and actualizing tendency characteristic of all organic growth. It is found that each cell, if it can be kept alive, now develops into a whole sea urchin larva—a bit smaller than usual, but normal and complete.
>
> I have chosen this example because it seems so closely analogous to my experience in dealing with individuals in one-to-one therapeutic relationships, in facilitating intensive groups, in providing "freedom to learn" for students in classes. In these situations, I am most impressed with the fact that each human being has a directional tendency toward wholeness, toward actualization of his or her potentialities. I have not found psychotherapy or group experience effective when I have tried to create in another individual something that is not already there; I have found, however, that if I can provide the conditions that allow

growth to occur, then this positive directional tendency brings about constructive results. The scientist with the divided sea urchin egg was in the same situation. He could not cause the cell to develop in one way or another, but when he focused his skill on providing the conditions that permitted the cell to survive and grow, the tendency for growth and the direction of growth were evident, and came from within the organism. I cannot think of a better analogy for therapy or the group experience, where, if I can supply a psychological amniotic fluid, forward movement of a constructive sort will occur.

I would like to add one comment which may be clarifying. Sometimes this growth tendency is spoken of as though it involved the development of all the potentialities of the organism. This is clearly not true. As one of my colleagues pointed out, the organism does not tend toward developing its capacity for nausea, nor does it actualize its potentiality for self-destruction, nor its ability to bear pain. Only under unusual or perverse circumstances do these potentialities become actualized. It is clear that *the actualizing tendency is selective and directional—a constructive tendency, if you will.* (pp. 119–21; italics added)

The actualizing tendency serves as the criterion by which all experiences[1] are evaluated. The *organismic valuing process* is the term Rogers used to describe the process (or mechanism) through which the actualizing tendency operates to evaluate experiences. Those experiences which are perceived as maintaining or enhancing are evaluated positively and are sought. Such positive experiences give the person a feeling of satisfaction. In contrast, experiences which are perceived to be in opposition to the maintenance or enhancement of the person are evaluated negatively and are avoided.

The most important aspect of the actualizing tendency from the standpoint of personality is the tendency toward *self-actualization.* Self-actualization involves all movement of a person in the direction of maintenance and enhancement of the *self.*

The development of the self

In early infancy, the child perceives all experiences, whether they are produced by bodily sensations or by external agents (such as the behavior of parents), as unitary. The infant makes no distinction between what is "me" and what is "not me." However, as part of the actualizing tendency's process of differentiation, the child soon begins to distinguish between that which is directly part of him or her and that which is external. It is this differentiation, which leads to the development of the self. The *self,* or *self-concept* (Rogers uses the terms

---

[1] "This term is used to include all that is going on within the envelope of the organism at any given moment which is potentially available to awareness. It includes events of which the individual is unaware, as well as all the phenomena which are in consciousness. . . . It is to be noted that experience refers to the given moment, not to some accumulation of past experience" (Rogers, 1959, p. 197).

synonymously), refers to "the organized, consistent conceptual gestalt [whole] composed of perceptions of the characteristics of the 'I' or 'me' and the perceptions of the relationships of the 'I' or 'me' to others and to various aspects of life, together with the values attached to these perceptions" (Rogers, 1959, p. 200). In line with Rogers' holistic approach, the self is viewed as a consistent organized whole, which implies that all aspects of the self must be in agreement with one another. For example, a woman could think of herself as being both dominant and submissive if, and only if, these two contrasting characteristics could be reconciled. One way to do this would be for the woman to perceive some situations as being appropriate for domineering behavior and other situations as being appropriate for submissiveness. If a reconciliation were not possible, as would be the case if the woman felt that one or the other type of behavior was always proper, then the wholeness and consistency of her self-concept would be threatened. The meaning of threat to the self-structure and the defensive response which naturally follows will be discussed later.

The self-concept of persons includes not only their perception of what they are actually like but also what they think they ought to be and would like to be. The latter aspect of the self is called the *ideal self.*

Measuring the self-concept via the Q-sort

While it is true that a person's self-concept can only be fully known by the person, it is possible to gain some understanding of the way individuals view themselves. Rogers and his associates have used a technique called the *Q-sort* to gain information about an individual's self-concept. The Q-sort allows people to make comparative judgments about self-descriptive statements and is particularly useful for assessing changes in these judgments over time. For example, Rogers observed that, during the course of psychotherapy, a client's self-concept generally underwent change. Usually, at the beginning of therapy, there was much divergence between the way in which clients actually viewed themselves and the way they would have liked to be (i.e., their ideal self). During psychotherapy, these two aspects of the self came closer together. This observation has been amply documented by studies employing the Q-sort.

In a typical study, before entering counseling,[2] clients are given the task of sorting a large number of self-referent statements (e.g., "I am lazy"; "I don't like to be with other people"; "I am generally happy"; "I am a domineering person"). These statements, which are printed on cards, are placed in a series of piles, each corresponding to a point

---

[2] Rogers uses the words *counseling* and *psychotherapy* synonymously.

FIGURE 15–1
Example of a forced Q-sort distribution of self-referent statements

	Very characteristic					Neutral					Not characteristic
Pile number	0	1	2	3	4	5	6	7	8	9	10
Number of statements	2	4	6	12	14	20	14	12	6	4	2

on a continuum ranging from "very characteristic of me" to "not at all characteristic of me." Usually, the client must sort the statements according to some fixed distribution, placing a specific number of statements in each pile, as illustrated in Figure 15–1.

Clients first sort the statements under directions to describe themselves as they see themselves at the present moment. After this *self-sort* is completed, clients are asked to sort the same statements again. This time, however, they aim to describe their ideal self, the kind of person they would most like to be. This second sort is called the *ideal sort*. The two Q-sorts are then compared by correlating the ratings. Each statement is assigned two numbers, one representing the pile number for the self-sort and the other the pile number for the ideal sort, and it is these numbers that are correlated. The closer each pair of numbers, the more congruent are the perceived self and the ideal self. A positive correlation is indicative of congruence and a negative correlation of divergence between the perceived self and the ideal self; in each case, the size of the correlation coefficient is an index of the degree of congruence or divergence. Correlation coefficients not significantly different from zero indicate that there is no systematic relationship between the perceived self and the ideal self. Clients are asked to perform self- and ideal sorts again at several intervals during counseling and at the completion of counseling, and each time the correlation between the two sorts is calculated. It thus becomes possible to determine whether there is a change in the relationship between a client's perceived self and ideal self over the course of counseling by comparing the correlations between the two sorts.

THE Q-SORT

Demonstration 15–1

To get a better understanding of the Q-sort, the reader is invited to perform two Q-sorts of his or her interests.

PREPARATION

1. First, write the name of each of the interests or activities listed in Table 15–1 along with its number on separate 3 × 5 index cards (or any small pieces of paper).

TABLE 15–1
List of activities for Q-sort Demonstration 15–1

1. Basketball	14. Sewing or knitting
2. Camping or hiking	15. Shopping
3. Card games	16. Singing
4. Dancing	17. Social drinking
5. Dining out	18. Swimming
6. Drawing or painting	19. Talking with friends
7. Going to movies	20. Tennis
8. Going to parties	21. Travel
9. Hunting or fishing	22. Visiting museums or art galleries
10. Listening to music	23. Walking
11. Playing a musical instrument	24. Watching television
12. Politics	25. Writing letters
13. Reading for pleasure	

2. Next, referring to Table 15–2, number nine cards (1–9). On each card, write the description of the corresponding degree of interest and the required number of activities, which must be sorted into the pile. The first three columns of Table 15–2 provide the descriptions for the nine cards. On a desk or other flat surface, place these cards in numerical order (from left to right), thereby forming a nine-point scale. You are now ready to perform the first Q-sort.

TABLE 15–2
Outline for Q-sort Demonstration 15–1

Pile number	Degree of interest	Required number in each pile	Rank
1	Very strong interest	1	1.0
2	Strong interest	2	2.5
3	Moderate interest	3	5.0
4	Slight interest	4	8.5
5	Ambivalent (neutral)	5	13.0
6	Slight lack of interest	4	17.5
7	Moderate lack of interest	3	21.0
8	Strong lack of interest	2	23.5
9	Very strong lack of interest	1	25.0

FIRST Q-SORT

3. To help you sort the activities into nine piles, first divide the 25 activity cards into three broad categories: those activities in which you are **definitely interested** at present, those activities in which you are **definitely not interested** at present, and those activities about which you are **ambivalent**.

4. You have just sorted the activities into the three gross categories of definitely interested, ambivalent, and definitely not interested. The Q-sort involves

TABLE 15–3
Sample recording sheet for Q-sort Demonstration 14–1

Activity number	First sort rank	Second sort rank	Difference	Difference squared
1				
2				
3				
4				
5				
6				
7				
8				
9				
10				
11				
12				
13				
14				
15				
16				
17				
18				
19				
20				
21				
22				
23				
24				
25				
Sum of difference squared =				

sorting the activities on the nine-point scale which you have set up. Start with the "definitely interested" category, and distribute these cards where you feel they belong (i.e., according to how interested you are in the activities *at the present time*). Be sure to adhere to the required number of activities for each pile. Next, do the same with the "definitely not interested" category, and finally, sort the "ambivalent" category.[3]

5. Check each pile to see that it contains the correct number of cards.

6. Check the Q-sort to be sure that each activity is in the pile you think it ought to be in.

7. It is now possible to rank the activities from the ones you are most interested in to the ones you are least interested in. The ranks for each pile are given in the last column of Table 15–2.[4] Make a copy of the "Recording Sheet" in Table 15–3 on a piece of lined paper and record the rank of each activity in the column designated "First Sort Rank."

---

[3] In this way you will be working for the most part from the extremes to the middle of the scale. This is generally the optimal strategy because more extreme preferences are usually easier to classify than are less extreme ones.

[4] The activity in pile number 1 will be assigned the rank of "1." The next most preferred activity would receive the rank of "2," except that two activities are designated in pile number 2. Unless activities are ranked within each of the nine categories (a tedious

By examining the Q-sort you have just produced, you can get an idea of what your present interests are, just as a therapist can gain some understanding of a client's self-concept by looking at the client's Q-sort of self-referent statements. However, usually more than one Q-sort is made, and, indeed, one of the most useful features of the Q-sort is that comparisons between sorts are possible.

SECOND Q-SORT

8. To make such a comparison, repeat steps 2 through 7, but now sort the activities with respect to your interests sometime *in the past,* say, five years ago. (One alternative would be to have a friend perform the Q-sort of her or his present interests.) Record the rank of each activity in the column designated "Second Sort Rank" on your Recording Sheet.

COMPARISON OF Q-SORTS

9. You are now ready to compare the two Q-sorts. Although this can be done by visual inspection alone, correlating the rankings of the activities on the two sorts is a more exact and potentially more meaningful method of comparison. This is easily and quickly done by means of the **rank-order correlation** method, which is outlined in the following simple, step-by-step fashion.[5]

a. For each pair of ranks (i.e., for each activity), calculate the difference between the ranks. The smaller value can always be subtracted from the larger, disregarding algebraic signs (since these values will be squared). Record the differences in the "Difference" column on your Recording Sheet.

b. Now square each difference and record the squared differences in the last column of the Recording Sheet.

c. Add all the squared differences found in step *b.*

d. Multiply the sum obtained in step *c* by 6.

e. Divide the product obtained in step *d* by 15,600.

f. Subtract the quotient obtained in step *e* from 1.00. This number is the rank-order correlation coefficient, which is designated by the Greek letter **rho.**

If **rho** is positive, your interests have tended to remain the same. The closer **rho** is to +1.00, the greater is the similarity between your interests in the two sorts. If **rho** is negative, then your interest now tend to be different from those you had in the past. The closer **rho** is to −1.00, the more dissimilar are your present interests from your past interests.

---

and time-consuming task which, because of the fine discriminations required, may be only arbitrary at best), it must be assumed that the activities within categories are equally preferable. The solution is to assign the average (mean) of the tied ranks. In the case of the two activities in pile number 2, the second and third ranks are tied, which means that each of the activities in this pile will receive the rank of "2.5" (as shown in Table 15–2).

[5] Lest the reader think that the steps in calculating the rank-order correlation coefficient *(rho)* have been magically rather than mathematically determined, the formula is:

$$rho = 1 - \frac{6\Sigma D^2}{N(N^2 - 1)}$$

where D = differences in ranks of each pair and N = number of pairs of ranks (in the present example $N = 25$).

Having discussed the development of the self, a central theoretical construct in Rogers' personality theory, and how it can be assessed empirically by the Q-sort, we now turn to a second important concept in Rogers' theory, the need for positive regard.

Rogers postulated that all persons have a basic need to experience attitudes such as acceptance, respect, sympathy, warmth, and love from significant people in their lives. This *need for positive regard* may be inborn or learned, and although Rogers tends to favor the latter explanation, he stated that its origin is irrelevant to his theory. An important characteristic of positive regard is its reciprocal nature; that is, when a person becomes aware that he or she is satisfying another's need for positive regard, the person's own need is also satisfied.

The need for positive regard

Most often, we receive positive regard for specific things we do, and in this sense positive regard is *conditional* and is similar to reinforcement (e.g., praise or attention). It is possible, however, to give or receive positive regard irrespective of the worth placed on specific aspects of a person's behavior. This means that the person, as a whole, is accepted and respected. Such *unconditional positive regard* is most frequently seen in a parent's love for a child when, regardless of the child's specific behavior, the child is loved and accepted. It is similar to what Erich Fromm (1963) has called "motherly love," which, in contrast to conditional "fatherly love," is given to the child "because it is her child, not because the child has fulfilled any specific condition, or lived up to any specific expectation" (p. 35).[6] Unconditional positive regard may be given even though all of the recipient's specific behaviors are not valued equally. A parent, for instance, may love and comfort a child who has misbehaved even though the parent disapproves of the child's misbehavior.

The concept of unconditional positive regard, like most concepts in Rogers' personality theory, was developed in the context of psychotherapy. Rogers contended that one of the major requisites for successful psychotherapy is that the therapist "prize" the whole person of the client. The therapist must feel and show unconditional positive regard for clients who are frightened or ashamed of their behavior, as well as for clients who are excited about or satisfied with their behavior. When this occurs, clients will become more accepting of all their experiences. This makes them more whole, or congruent, persons who consequently are able to function more effectively.

Positive self-regard develops from the positive attitudes shown toward a person by others. However, rather than coming from other

---

[6] The terms *motherly love* and *fatherly love* denote particular types of love and may be given by persons of either sex.

people, the positive regard for one's experiences comes directly from the self. It is as if the self had become a significant other. The development of positive self-regard is another step toward autonomy, which is part of the tendency toward self-actualization. When persons perceive their whole self as worthy of positive regard, independently of how they evaluate specific aspects of their behavior, they are said to experience *unconditional positive self-regard.*

Conditions of worth

It is difficult for significant others to regard all of a child's behavior equally. *Conditions of worth* thus develop "when the positive regard of a significant other is conditional, when the individual feels that in some respects he is prized and in others not" (Rogers, 1959, p. 209). Conditions of worth are the equivalent of internalized values which form the basis of the superego in psychoanalytic theory. It is from this differential assignment of positive regard that children learn to differentially evaluate their own behavior.

Because the need for positive regard, both from significant others and from oneself, is extremely powerful, it can come to supersede the organismic valuing process. That is, independently of whether an experience itself is in any way maintaining or enhancing the organism, an experience may be valued as positive or negative and subsequently either approached or avoided. And this state of affairs will have negative consequences for the individual's personality growth because conditions of worth substitute for and interfere with the organismic valuing process, thereby preventing the person from functioning freely and with maximum effectiveness. When conditions of worth become more influential in directing the person's behavior than is the organismic valuing process, nature is being tampered with, so to speak.

The experience of threat and the process of defense

When the self is first formed, it is governed by the organismic valuing process alone, which uses as criteria of evaluation the principles of self-actualization. However, as the need for positive regard becomes important to the individual and conditions of worth become part of the self, conflicts arise between the self and experience. Where unconditional positive regard exists, all experiences are admitted to the individuals' awareness and symbolized accurately; if no experience is more or less worthy of positive regard than any other, there is no reason to exclude any experience from awareness. However, if conditions of worth are embodied within the self, awareness of experiences will vary to the extent that they are valued (e.g., mother says it is better to eat oatmeal than ice cream and cake for breakfast). Those experiences which are consistent with the self and its conditions of worth, and thus are valued positively, are allowed to enter awareness and are perceived accurately. Experiences which conflict with the self and its conditions of worth, and therefore are valued negatively, represent a danger to the self-concept and are kept from entering awareness and being accurately perceived.

Consider the case of Charles F., a young man who had been taught by his parents that people have an obligation to be loyal to their country and had come to feel that this was how he should behave. While in college, he was exposed to points of view which were opposed to unconditional support of one's country. Charles F. was about to be drafted into the army to fight in the Vietnam War. Because he felt that his country was engaged in this war unjustly, he decided to leave the country rather than be drafted. This experience was in direct opposition to his self-concept which included a high value for patriotism (a condition of worth), and it was therefore threatening to him.

For Rogers, *threat* exists when a person perceives an incongruity between some experience and his or her self-concept.[7] The person experiences threat as vague uneasiness and tension, which is commonly labeled anxiety. Incongruence between one's self-concept and experience is threatening because the individual's personality is no longer a consistent whole. In our example, Charles F.'s behavior was no longer regulated by a unitary force, the actualizing tendency, but instead was governed by several different standards. Rogers (1959) speaks of this division in the following way:

> This, as we see it, is the basic estrangement in man. He has not been true to himself, to his own natural organismic valuing of experience, but for the sake of preserving the positive regard of others has now come to falsify some of the values he experiences and to perceive them only in terms based upon their value to others. Yet this has not been a conscious choice, but a natural—and tragic—development in infancy. The path of development toward psychological maturity, the path of therapy, is the undoing of this estrangement in man's functioning, the dissolving of conditions of worth, the achievement of a self which is congruent with experience, and the restoration of a unified organismic valuing process as the regulator of behavior. (pp. 226–27)

It is impossible to conceive of an individual completely devoid of conditions of worth actually existing in the world as we know it. The absence of conditions of worth and the presence of a unified organismic valuing process as the sole regulator of behavior are only goals toward which a person can strive in order to achieve better psychological adjustment. However, to understand how Charles F. was threatened

---

[7] Incongruity between experience and self-concept need not be perceived at a conscious level. Indeed, Rogers postulated that, most frequently, the individual is able to discriminate an experience as threatening without the threat being symbolized in awareness.

as a result of the presence of conditions of worth, it would be constructive to consider, hypothetically, how things would have been different had his conditions of worth been absent.

If Charles F. had been reared in an atmosphere in which all his feelings were accepted and prized, he would have come to value all of his experiences equally, and his behavior would be guided by his organismic valuing process. Under these circumstances, his parents' attitude, and subsequently his own, about patriotism might have been of the following sort: "We all have an obligation to be loyal to our country, but we also have an obligation to follow our consciences in matters of right and wrong. Sometimes these two obligations are in conflict, and we must make a choice between the two. But choosing one does not permanently exclude the other as a course of action at a different time and under other circumstances. Nor does such a decision make one mode of behavior any more worthy than the other. Sometimes it is possible to satisfy one urge, and sometimes the other." By using his own organismic valuing process of experiences, he could achieve a balance between the two modes of behavior, and his whole, consistent self would remain intact.

Charles F. was not fortunate enough to have grown up in such utopian circumstances (nor is any person), and so we must turn from the completely hypothetical situation to the more practical one which confronted him. Having made the choice to leave his country rather than serve in the army, he was potentially vulnerable to disorganization of his personality resulting from the incongruity between his self-concept and his experience. Accordingly, Charles F. would have been experiencing anxiety.

Anxiety is the emotional response to threat. It serves as a signal that the unified self-concept is in danger of being disorganized if the discrepency between it and the threatening experience is symbolized accurately—that is, if the person becomes aware of it.

The process of defense

People defend themselves against this type of danger by a process which attempts to maintain the self as it exists at that time. "This goal is achieved by the perceptual distortion of the experience in awareness, in such a way as to reduce the incongruity between the experience and the structure of the self, or by the denial to awareness of an experience, thus denying any threat to the self" (Rogers, 1959, pp. 204–5).

Rogers' two basic defensive behaviors, *perceptual distortion* and *denial,* can be illustrated in the various alternatives Charles F. could have used to defend himself against his threatening experience, namely, leaving the country to avoid serving in the army. Rationalization is a good example of perceptual distortion: "I didn't really leave my country to avoid being drafted. Actually, there are many good opportunities for getting ahead in this new country." Fantasy is also a mechanism of defense primarily involving distortion: "I am serving my country by looking after its interests in another country." Reaction formation involves both distortion and denial: "I didn't want to serve my country in the first place. I've always felt that a man owes nothing to his country." Projection also is a composite of the two basic defensive responses to threat: "Look at all those men who have left their country to avoid serving in the army! I'm glad I'm not like them." The ultimate defense would be pure denial that the experience ever occurred: "I've never been called to serve in my country's army." In each case, the defensive behavior serves to keep Charles F. from becoming fully aware of the actual threatening experience, either by distorting the experience so that it is no longer incongruent with his self-concept, or by not allowing any aspect of the experience to enter his consciousness.

Rogers viewed psychological adjustment in terms of the degree of congruence between the self and experience. People who are psychologically well adjusted perceive themselves and their relation to people and objects in their environment as they "really" are (i.e., as an objective observer would see them). At first glance, the preceding statement may appear inconsistent with the salience of subjective experience in the phenomenological strategy. In Rogers' approach it is still subjective experience which is critical, but psychological adjustment requires a close correspondence between subjective experience and external reality. When this is the case, a person is *open to experience* rather than threatened by it because experience is in agreement with the perception the person has of it. When an experience is in conflict with the perceptions of the self, the threatening experience is prevented from being accurately symbolized by perceptual distortion or denial.

These theoretical notions have received support in a study by Chodorkoff (1954). The study examined the following hypotheses about the relationships among self-perception, perceptual defense, and personal adjustment.

1. The greater the agreement between the individual's self-description and an objective description of him, the less perceptual defense he will show.

2. The greater the agreement between the individual's self-description and an objective description of him, the more adequate will be his personal adjustment.

3. The more adequate the personal adjustment of the individual, the less perceptual defense he will show. (Chodorkoff, 1954, p. 508)

To test these hypotheses, Chodorkoff had male undergraduate students describe themselves via a Q-sort of 125 self-descriptive statements. These self-descriptions were compared with another Q-sort of the same statements, made for each subject by two clinically experienced judges. The judges' Q-sort description, which served as the objective description of each individual, was based on information about the subject gleaned from projective techniques, including a word-association test, and a biographical inventory.

In the word-association test, each subject was presented with 50 emotional words (e.g., whore, bitch, penis) and 50 neutral words (e.g., house, book, tree), and his reaction time to each word was recorded. For each subject, the 10 emotional words having the longest reaction time and the 10 neutral words having the shortest reaction time were used in the perceptual defense test. These 20 words were flashed on a screen in random order by means of a tachistoscope, a device for visually presenting material for brief, controlled durations (e.g., 1/100 second). The exposure time for each word was increased until the word was accurately reported, and this reaction time became the recognition score for each word.

Perceptual defense is a theoretical construct which has been used to denote an unconscious mechanism which resists allowing threatening material to enter consciousness (cf. Erdelyi, 1974). It was experimentally defined in Chodorkoff's study as the difference between the recognition thresholds for emotional and neutral words. The higher this difference is, the greater is the degree of perceptual defense.

The third variable of interest in Chodorkoff's study, personal adjustment, was rated, from the projective techniques, by the clinically experienced judges.

The hypotheses were evaluated by performing the appropriate correlations. The first hypothesis compared the accuracy of self-description with recognition thresholds, and it was found that the two variables were negatively correlated: high accuracy of self-description tended to be associated with low recognition thresholds for threatening words. The second hypothesis compared accuracy of self-description and personal adjustment ratings and found them to be positively correlated: high accuracy in self-description was associated with good psychological adjustment. To test the third hypothesis, personal adjustment ratings were compared with recognition thresholds; these variables were negatively correlated: greater psychological adjustment was associated with lower thresholds of recognition. Thus, all three hypotheses received support, and Chodorkoff (1954) concluded:

> In a group of Ss [subjects] who show varying degrees of adjustment and defensiveness, one finds that the more inaccurate and faulty the individual's perception of his environment, the more inaccurate and faulty is his perception of himself; and the more inaccurate and faulty the individual's perceptions of himself and his environment, the more inadequate is his personal adjustment. (p. 511)

The process of breakdown and disorganization

The discussion of Rogers' theory of personality has focused thus far on "normal" personality development. Even the most psychologically well-adjusted individuals are occasionally threatened by an experience which is inconsistent with their self-concept and forces them to distort or deny the experience. Doubtless most people experience anxiety as part of their daily living. But their anxiety is at a moderate, and therefore tolerable, level because the inconsistency between self and experience is correspondingly moderate and their defenses are adequate. When experiences become more than moderately incongruent with the self, or when the incongruent experiences occur frequently, the person feels a level of anxiety that is distinctly unpleasant and may actually interfere with daily activities. Such individuals are typically labeled "neurotic" and may seek assistance in reducing their anxiety via psychotherapy. However, the neurotic's defenses are still capable of keeping incongruent experiences out of conscious awareness, thereby allowing the self to remain as a whole, if somewhat tenuous, process.

If the inconsistency between self and experience becomes very great, the individual's defenses may be incapable of distorting or denying the experience. The result is that, in this defenseless state, the incongruent experience is accurately symbolized in awareness and the consistent, whole self is shattered. A person in such a disorganized state is typically labeled "psychotic" and may exhibit behaviors which, to an objective observer, seem odd, irrational, or even bizarre. On closer inspection the behaviors may prove to be congruent with the previously denied experiences. The behaviors are odd only insofar as they are incongruent with the way in which the person is seen by *others*. For example, a woman who has rigidly controlled her aggressive tendencies, denying that they were part of her self, may openly display hostility toward people. The woman's friends may view the hostility as alien to her personality, whereas, in fact, it was very much a part of her personality, albeit an aspect of which she was unaware.

One of the factors which may result in the disorganization of personality observed in psychotic patients is that these individuals feel that they are not understood, that there is no consensual validation (affirmation from other people) for their views of the world. Rogers (1980) believes that when a person tries

> to share something that is very personal with another individual and it is not received and not understood, this is a very deflating and a very lonely experience. I have come to believe that such an experience makes some individuals psychotic. It causes them to give up hoping that anyone can understand them. Once they have lost that hope, then their own inner world, which becomes more and more bizarre, is the only place

where they can live. They can no longer live in any shared human experience. I can sympathize with them because I know that when I try to share some feeling aspect of myself which is private, precious, and tentative, and when this communication is met by evaluation, by reassurance, by distortion of my meaning, my very strong reaction is, "Oh, what's the use!" At such a time, one knows what it is to be alone. (p. 14)

The process of reintegration

While successfully operating defenses are certainly preferable to a disorganized personality, one always pays a price for keeping incongruent experiences from being accurately symbolized in awareness (cf. the psychoanalytic concept that libido used for defense mechanisms is not available for other ego functions; Chapter 5). An individual who distorts or denies certain experiences must constantly defend himself or herself against having these experiences come accurately into consciousness. People who are colloquially described as "always on the defensive" illustrate the detrimental consequences of the defensive process. Such people question the meaning and sincerity of even the most innocuous comments made by other people and are quick to respond as if the comments were derogatory toward them. But from their internal frame of reference, the innocent remark of another person *is* derogatory, because it has been perceived in a distorted form.

A person who inaccurately perceives his or her experiences is not able to function fully and is not completely open to experience. Thus he or she misses or must avoid those aspects of life which are potentially threatening. Consider the young woman in college who, due to a self-concept which condones only success, is threatened by any situation in which she might fail. By distorting her view of such an event from one which *could* lead to failure to one which is undesirable, she successfully avoids it. Rather than seek admission to graduate school, she "decides" that she can do just as well with a bachelor's degree (and, anyhow, she might as well be making money while her friends in graduate school take out loans).

Discrepancies between one's self-concept and one's experiences can be reduced through a process of reintegration within the personality. This is achieved by reversing the process of defense; that is, the individual becomes clearly aware of hitherto distorted or denied experiences and, *under certain specific conditions,* is able to make these experiences part of his or her self-concept. The student who was threatened by situations in which she might fail could, in the course of reintegration, come to realize that she might not be admitted to graduate school, but this possibility could become acceptable by integrating it into her self-concept. Her self-concept would now include a notion such as:

"It is not necessary for me to succeed at everything I try," thereby making her less likely to find such situations threatening.

Rogers maintains that this reintegrative process is possible only when there is *a reduction in the person's conditions of worth and an increase in unconditional positive self-regard.* This can occur if the individual is exposed to and perceives the unconditional positive regard of another person. However, unconditional positive regard can only be communicated if *empathy* is occurring—that is, another person must be accurately perceiving the internal frame of reference of the individual. To be empathic, one must feel as if he or she were the individual, but without losing the "as if" quality.

> To be with another in this way means that for the time being, you lay aside your own views and values in order to enter another's world without prejudice. In some sense it means that you lay aside your self; this can only be done by persons who are secure enough in themselves that they know they will not get lost in what may turn out to be the strange or bizarre world of the other, and that they can comfortably return to their own world when they wish. (Rogers, 1980, p. 143)

Rogers (1959) explains why empathy is necessary for unconditional positive regard:

> If I know little or nothing of you, and experience an unconditional positive regard for you, this means little because further knowledge of you may reveal aspects which I cannot so regard. But if I know you thoroughly, knowing and empathically understanding a wide variety of your feelings and behaviors, and still experience an unconditional positive regard, this is very meaningful. It comes close to being fully known and fully accepted. (p. 231)

Persons who acquire conditions of worth begin to value one experience more than another, and their self-concept comes to include experiences which are valued positively and to exclude experiences which are valued negatively. Those experiences which have been excluded from the self must be kept from awareness in order to maintain the self as a consistent whole. Thus, the person becomes aware only of the experiences which are regarded positively. If, however, all experiences were regarded equally, there would be no conditions of worth. In a state of unconditional positive regard, the existing conditions of worth lose their significance and power to direct the person's behavior. The individual becomes open to more experiences, since without conditions of worth all experiences are consistent with the self. For example, a man who values restraint positively and aggression negatively is unable to accurately perceive his need to be aggressive on some occasions. Aggressive behavior is inconsistent with his self-concept "I am a restrained person," which *ipso facto* makes restraint good. If this condition of worth were dissolved, restraint and aggression would have the same unconditional positive regard, and they could exist harmoniously within a unified self. Sometimes the man would behave with restraint and at other times aggressively. There is, in effect, no value placed on either mode of behavior, since neither is valued more or less than the other.

As a consequence of the unconditional positive regard shown by another individual, one experiences an increase in one's own unconditional positive *self*-regard which makes it possible to maintain an openness to experience and a lack of defensiveness when the other person is no longer present. Increased unconditional positive self-regard and the concomitant decrease in conditions of worth are the prerequisites for the reintegration of one's personality. Receiving unconditional positive regard from someone else is not the only way to achieve this, although it is the process by which client-centered therapy is postulated to work.

Before we turn to a discussion of client-centered therapy, a word or two should be said about the many minor personality reintegrations which occur in our daily lives. Such reintegrations are possible without the unconditional positive regard of a significant other *if there is an absence of threat to the self*. Typically, when we are left alone we are able to face minor, inconsistent experiences and to restructure our self-concept to assimilate these experiences. Rogers (1965) gives the following example:

> the child who feels that he is weak and powerless to do a certain task, to build a tower or repair a bicycle, may find, as he works rather hopelessly at the task, that he is successful. This experience is inconsistent with the concept he holds of himself, and may not be integrated at once; but if the child is left to himself he gradually assimilates, upon his own initiative, a revision of his concept of self, that while he is generally weak and powerless, in this respect he has ability. This is the normal way in which, free from threat, new perceptions are assimilated. But if this same child is repeatedly told by his parents that he is competent to do the task, he is likely to deny it, and to prove by his behavior that he is unable to do it. The more forceful intrusion of the notion of his competence constitutes more of a threat to self and is more forcefully resisted. (p. 519)

Rogers (1965) maintained that reintegration which occurs without the help of another person is not effective when the inconsistency between the self and experience is large: "It appears possible for the person to face such [large] inconsistency only while in a relationship with another in which he is sure that he will be accepted" (p. 519). The relationship to which Rogers alludes is that found in client-centered therapy.

The essence of client-centered therapy[8] is contained in the meaning of its name. Rogers (1965) explained the use of the term *client* in the following way:

> What term shall be used to indicate the person with whom the therapist is dealing? "Patient," "subject," "counselee," "analysand," are terms which have been used. We have increasingly used the term client, to the point where we have absorbed it into the label of "client-centered therapy." It has been chosen because, in spite of its imperfections of dictionary meaning and derivation, it seems to come closest to conveying the picture of this person as we see it. The client, as the term has acquired its meaning, is one who comes actively and voluntarily to gain help on a problem, but without any notion of surrendering his own responsibility for the situation. It is because the term has these connotations that we have chosen it, since it avoids the connotation that he is sick, or the object of an experiment, and so on. (p. 7)

In keeping with Rogers' phenomenological position, psychotherapy is *centered* on the client. It is the client's unique problems, feelings, perceptions, attitudes, and goals which are dealt with in therapy. Therapy can only proceed from the vantage point of the client's internal frame of reference. While the therapist can only hope to gain an incomplete knowledge of the client's subjective experiences, the therapist must, through empathic understanding, try to learn as much as possible about the way the client views his or her particular experiences.

Rogers hypothesized that there are certain necessary, but not always sufficient, conditions which must be met before the therapeutic process can begin. First, clients must be experiencing some inconsistency between their self-concept and their experiences. One source of evidence in support of this hypothesis is a study which revealed that less anxious clients have difficulty becoming involved in therapy and consequently tend to drop out (Gallagher, 1953).

Second, the therapist's self-concept and his or her experiences *in relation to the client* must be congruent. The therapist need not be open to all experiences in life, but while taking part in the therapeutic relationship, the therapist should be relatively free of threatening experiences. Rogers (1959) thinks that the therapist can be most effective when "completely and fully himself, with his experience of the moment being accurately symbolized and integrated into the picture he holds of himself" (p. 215). Such a fully functioning therapist is capable of experiencing unconditional positive regard for the client as well as the third prerequisite, empathic understanding of the client's internal

---

[8] Client-centered therapy has alternatively been called *nondirective therapy*, since it is the client, not the therapist, who directs the course of treatment.

CLIENT-CENTERED THERAPY

The meaning of "client-centered"

Minimal conditions for the therapeutic process

frame of reference. These essential requirements serve to foster a situation which is free of threat and therefore is maximally conducive to reintegration of the client's personality.

A fourth prerequisite for the therapeutic process is that the client perceive, at least to some degree, the therapist's unconditional positive regard and the therapist's empathic understanding of his or her outlook. This last condition reemphasizes the importance of viewing the client through the client's internal frame of reference, since it would not matter how much unconditional positive regard or empathic understanding the therapist experienced for the client if the client did not perceive it.

Rogers (1975) considered a high degree of empathy to be the most potent factor in creating personality change. Much research has addressed the role of empathy in a variety of types of psychotherapy (i.e., not just client-centered therapy) and some of the more important findings are summarized below.

1. *The ideal therapist is, first of all, perceived as empathic* (Fiedler, 1950b; Raskin, 1974). For example, Raskin (1974) asked 83 practicing psychotherapists of at least eight different orientations to describe the ideal therapist—the type of therapist they would like to be. Empathy was considered the most important quality.

2. *Empathy is positively correlated with client self-exploration and progress in therapy* (e.g., Bergin & Strupp, 1972; Kurtz & Grummon, 1972; Tausch, Bastine, Friese, & Sander, 1970).

3. *Empathy early in therapy predicts later success in therapy* (Barrett-Lennard, 1962; Tausch, 1973). The degree of empathy a therapist shows for a client can be identified as early as the second session, and such early measurements are positively correlated with later success in therapy.

4. *Therapists offer more empathy than caring friends* (van der Veen, 1970), a finding which reinforces the notion that empathy is a skill which is acquired with training and experience (see below).

5. *Experienced therapists tend to offer more empathy than inexperienced therapists* (Barrett-Lennard, 1962; Fiedler, 1950a; Mullen & Abeles, 1972). In an early study, Fiedler (1950a) compared the relationship established between expert and novice therapists and their clients in three different types of psychotherapy: client-centered, traditional psychoanalytic, and neoanalytic (post-Freudian). Four judges listened to recordings of the therapy sessions, and, for each session, they sorted 75 statements descriptive of the therapeutic relationship (e.g., "Therapist treats patient with much deference"; "Therapist is sympathetic with patient") on a seven-category Q-sort ranging from most characteristic to least characteristic of the session. The results showed that experienced therapists of all

three orientations tended to create a relationship in which they demonstrated an understanding of the client's communications from the client's point of view.

6. *Therapists who are better integrated (well-adjusted) show a higher degree of empathy for their clients* (Bergin & Jasper, 1969; Bergin & Solomon, 1970). Not surprisingly, being relatively free of personal problems and feeling confident in interpersonal relationships is associated with the ability to empathize with another person.

7. *Empathy can be learned, especially from empathic persons* (Aspy, 1972; Aspy & Roebuck, 1974; Guerney, Andronico, & Guerney, 1970). This is an important finding because it means that therapists can acquire empathic understanding and need not be born with it. Having this skill modeled by one's teachers, supervisors, and parents appears to be a prime means of learning to be empathic oneself.

How do a psychological climate, therapist congruence, unconditional positive regard, and empathy facilitate personality change in the client?

> Briefly, as persons are accepted and prized, they tend to develop a more caring attitude toward themselves. As persons are empathically heard, it becomes possible for them to listen more accurately to the flow of inner experiencings. But as a person understands and prizes self, the self becomes more congruent with the experiencings. The person thus becomes more real, more genuine. These tendencies, the reciprocal of the therapist's attitudes, enable the person to be a more effective growth-enhancer for himself or herself. There is a greater freedom to be the true, whole person. (Rogers, 1980, pp. 116–17)

The process of client-centered therapy

In client-centered therapy, the major responsibility for the therapeutic process falls to the client. Rogers' basic philosophy in this regard is that, given the proper circumstances, the client will have the capacity to begin to resolve his or her problems. This position is directly in keeping with Rogers' view of the development of behavioral disorders. Behavioral disorders are a consequence of conflict between a person's two fundamental evaluative processes, one based on the self-actualization tendency—the organismic valuing process—and the other based on the values of other people—conditions of worth. Rogers firmly believes that no behavior disorders would develop if the person were guided solely by the organismic valuing process. It is necessary in client-centered therapy to create a situation in which clients feel free from conditions of worth and which allows their behavior to be guided by their organismic valuing process. This goal can be achieved in a nonthreatening situation in which the client feels understood (empathic understanding) and accepted as a whole person (unconditional positive regard). Under these conditions, clients can accurately examine those experiences which have been inconsistent with their self-concepts and of which they were previously unaware because the experiences were either perceived in a distorted fashion or not at all. How, then, does the therapist create these ideal conditions?

Client-centered therapy proceeds by means of a verbal interchange between the client and the therapist. The therapist shows unconditional positive regard for the client by accepting what the client says without either approval or disapproval. The therapist accepts equally and without evaluation all of the client's feelings and behavior. Typically, this is done by responding to the client's statements with such relatively neutral comments as "Yes," "I see," and "Mm-hmm."

The therapist communicates empathic understanding of the client's internal frame of reference primarily on an emotional level and attempts to clarify the client's feelings by synthesizing or reorganizing the feelings which the client has expressed directly or indirectly. This is called *clarification of feeling.* Secondarily, the therapist restates on a cognitive or intellectual level the ideas expressed by the client, without any attempt to reorganize the client's statements, so that the feelings involved are clarified. This is called *restatement of content.* The major difference between the two basic responses client-centered therapists offer their clients is whether the focus is on the clients' emotions (clarification of feelings) or thoughts (restatement of content).

Both types of responses are illustrated in the following excerpt from an actual record of a client-centered therapy session. The client is a 20-year-old college woman whose right hand is malformed. See whether you can tell which of the therapist's comments involve clarification of feeling and which involve restatement of content (see footnote 9 for the correct identification).

> **Client (C):** After I left here last time—that night during dinner the student dean in our house asked to speak to my roommate. My roommate told me about it afterwards—Miss Hansen asked if I would be embarrassed as hostess at the table. She said she didn't want to hurt me! These darn student deans who think that they must guard us! The other student dean I had before never raised the issue. It makes me so mad!
>
> **Therapist (T):** You feel that this incident helped to accentuate the difficulty.
>
> **C:** That was the first time with a student dean. Really though, it struck me very funny. She watches us like a hawk. We can't make a move but she knows it.
>
> **T:** You resent her activity.
>
> **C:** I just don't like it on general principles. Oh, I suppose that she was trying to save me embarrassment.
>
> **T:** You can see why she did that.

C: I think that she is really afraid of us—she's queer. I don't know, but so far as I am concerned, I'm pretty indifferent to her.

T: You feel that she doesn't affect you one way or the other.[9]

(Snyder, 1947, p. 278)

For either type of response to be considered *empathic* understanding, the therapist must experience the cognition or affect from the client's internal frame of reference. This is not easy to do because we are accustomed to viewing others from an *external* frame of reference, as objective, outside observers. It is necessary for the therapist to actively try to stay within the client's subjective world.

It is important to note that the client-centered therapist does not make any interpretations of the client's statements, behaviors, or displays of emotion and does not give the client advice. Interpretations are inappropriate because they represent an external frame of reference, and the meaning of a client's behavior is only relevant from the perspective of the client's internal frame of reference. Advice is inappropriate in client-centered therapy because the therapist proceeds under the assumption that the client's organismic valuing process is the optimal source of guidance for the client. Thus, the best that the therapist can hope to do for the client is to provide a warm, accepting atmosphere which is most conducive to the operation of the client's organismic valuing process.

A case example of personality growth and change

The following letter was written to Carl Rogers (Rogers, 1980) by a young woman who was in therapy; Rogers knew neither the woman nor her therapist.

Dear Dr. Rogers,

I don't know how to explain who I am or why I am writing to you except to say that I have just read your book, *On Becoming a Person,* and it left a great impression on me. I just happened to find it one day and started reading. It's kind of a coincidence because right now I need something to help me find *me.* I do not feel that I can do much for others until I find me.

I think that I began to lose me when I was in high school. I always wanted to go into work that would be of help to people but my family resisted, and I thought they must be right. Things went along smoothly for everyone else for four or five years until about two years ago. I met a guy that I thought was ideal. Then nearly a year ago I took a good look at us, and realized that I was everything that *he* wanted me to be and nothing that *I* was. I have always been emotional and I have

---

[9] The therapist's first two comments are clarification of feeling, while the last two are restatement of content.

had many feelings. I could never sort them out and identify them. My fiancé would tell me that I was just mad or just happy and I would say okay and leave it at that. Then when I took this good look at us I realized that I was angry because I wasn't following my true emotions.

I backed out of the relationship gracefully and tried to find out where all the pieces were that I had lost. After a few months of searching had gone by I found that there were many more than I knew what to do with and I couldn't seem to separate them. I began seeing a psychologist and am presently seeing him. He has helped me to find parts of me that I was not aware of. Some parts are bad by our society's standards but I have found them to be very good for me. I have felt more threatened and confused since going to him but I have also felt more relief and more sure of myself.

I remember one night in particular. I had been in for my regular appointment with the psychologist that day and I had come home feeling angry. I was angry because I wanted to talk about something but I couldn't identify what it was. By eight o'clock that night I was so upset I was frightened. I called him and he told me to come to his office as soon as I could. I got there and cried for at least an hour and then the words came. I still don't know all of what I was saying. All I know is that *so much hurt* and *anger* came out of me that I *never really knew existed*. I went home and it seemed that an *alien* had taken over and I was hallucinating like some of the patients I have seen in a state hospital. I continued to feel this way until one night I was sitting and thinking and I realized that this alien was the *me* that I had been trying to find.

I have noticed since that night that people no longer seem so strange to me. Now it is beginning to seem that life is just starting for me. I am alone right now but I am not frightened and I don't have to be doing something. I like meeting me and making friends with my thoughts and feelings. Because of this I have learned to enjoy other people. One older man in particular—who is very ill—makes me feel very much alive. He accepts everyone. He told me the other day that I have changed very much. According to him, I have begun to open up and love. I think that I have always loved people and I told him so. He said, "Were they aware of it?" I don't suppose I have expressed my love any more than I did my anger and hurt.

Among other things, I am finding out that I never had too much self-respect. And now that I am learning to really like me I am finally finding peace within myself. Thanks for your part in this.

Rogers comments on this letter by paraphrasing what he considers to be the critical statements concerning the woman's feelings and attitudes. His remarks provide a good summary of his view of personality development, growth, and change.

I was losing me. Her own experiences and their meanings were being denied, and she was developing a self that was different from her real experienced self, which was becoming increasingly unknown to her.

My experience told me the work I wanted to go into, but my family showed me that I couldn't trust my own feelings to be right. This phrase shows how a false concept of self is built up. Because she accepted her parents' meanings as her own experience, she came to distrust her own organismic experience. She could hardly have introjected her parents' values on this subject had she not had a long previous experience of introjecting their values. As she distrusted more and more of her own experience, her sense of self-worth steadily declined until she had very little use for her own experience or herself.

Things went along smoothly for everyone else. What a revealing statement! Of course things were fine for those whom she was trying to please. This pseudoself was just what they wanted. It was only within herself, at some deep and unknown level, that there was a vague uneasiness.

I was everything he wanted me to be. Here again she was denying to awareness all her own experiencing—to the point where she no longer really had a self and was trying to be a self wanted by someone else.

Finally my organism rebelled and I tried to find me again but I couldn't, without help. Why did she finally rebel and take a good look at her relationship with her fiancé? One can only attribute this rebellion to the actualizing tendency that had been suppressed for so long but that finally asserted itself. However, because she had distrusted her own experience for such a long period and because the self by which she was living was so sharply different from the experiences of her organism, she could not reconstruct her true self without help. The need for help often exists when there is such a great discrepancy.

Now I am discovering my experiences—some bad according to society, parents, and boyfriend, but all good as far as I am concerned. The locus of evaluation that formerly had resided in her parents, in her boyfriend, and others, she is now reclaiming as her own. She is the one who decides the values of her experience. She is the center of the valuing process, and the evidence is provided by her own senses. Society may call a given experience bad, but when she trusts her own valuing of it, she finds that it is worthwhile and significant to her.

An important turning point came when a flood of the experiences that I had been denying to awareness came close to the surface. I was frightened and upset. When denied experience comes close to awareness, anxiety always results because these previously unadmitted experiences will have meanings that will change the structure of the self by which one has been living. Any drastic change in the self-concept is always a threatening and frightening experience. She was dimly aware of this threat even though she did not yet know what would emerge.

When the denied experiences broke through the dam, they turned out to be hurts and angers that I had been completely unaware of. It is impossible for most people to realize how completely an experience can be shut out of awareness until it does break through into awareness. Every individual is able to shut out and deny those experiences that would endanger his or her self-concept.

I thought I was insane because some foreign person had taken over in me. When the self-concept is so sharply changed that parts of it are completely shattered, it is a very frightening experience, and her description of the feeling that an alien had taken over is a very accurate one.

Only gradually did I realize that this alien was the real me. What she was discovering was that the submissive, malleable self by which she had been living, the self that had been guided by the statements, attitudes, and expectations of others, was no longer hers. This new self that had seemed so alien was a self that had experienced hurt and anger and feelings that society regards as bad, as well as wild hallucinatory thoughts—and love. As she goes further into self-discovery, it is likely that she will find out that some of her anger is directed against her parents. The hurts will have come from various sources; some of the feelings and experiences that society regards as bad but that she finds good and satisfying are experiences and feelings that probably have to do with sexuality. In any event, her self is becoming much more firmly rooted in her own gut-level experiences. Another person put something of this in the phrase "I am beginning to let my experience *tell me* what it means instead of *my* trying to *impose* a meaning on it." The more the individual's self-concept is rooted in the spontaneously felt meanings of his or her experiencing, the more he or she is an integrated person.

I like meeting me and making friends with my thoughts and feelings. Here is the dawning of the self-respect and self-acceptance of which she has been deprived for so long. She is even feeling affection for herself. One of the curious but common side effects of this change is that now she will be able to give herself more freely to others, to enjoy others more, to be more genuinely interested in them.

I have begun to open up and love. She will find that as she is more expressive of her love she can also be more expressive of her anger and hurt, her likes and dislikes, and her "wild" thoughts and feelings (which will turn out to be creative impulses). She is in the process of changing from psychological maladjustment to a much healthier relationship to others and to reality.

I am finally finding peace within myself. There is a peaceful harmony in being a whole person, but she will be mistaken if she thinks this reaction is permanent. Instead, if she is really open to her experience, she will find other hidden aspects of herself that she has denied to awareness, and each such discovery will give her uneasy and anxious moments or days until it is assimilated into a revised and changing picture of herself. She will discover that growing toward a congruence between her experiencing organism and her concept of herself is an exciting, sometimes disturbing, but never-ending adventure. (Rogers, 1980, pp. 208–14)

Toward a person-centered way of being: Beyond client-centered therapy

Carl Rogers' career as a psychologist spans more than half a century, and he is still active professionally at age 80. Although Rogers has broadened his interests and professional endeavors considerably in the past two decades, his basic view of personality has remained essentially unchanged. That view can be stated succinctly as a deep faith in the inherent capability of each person to develop, grow, and change in basically healthy ways when the person is guided by her or his unique self-actualizing tendency.

Much of Rogers' career has been devoted to discovering the conditions under which a person's unique resources will be allowed expression. Rogers has found that there are three basic conditions which must be present in order for a climate to be growth producing. A person must experience from another individual (1) congruence, genuineness, or realness—an openness or transparency in which the other individual is being totally what he or she is in the relationship with no holding back and no facades; (2) unconditional positive regard—a nonpossessive caring, acceptance, or prizing of the person no matter what the person is doing or feeling at the time (including objectively negative actions or emotions); and (3) empathic understanding—being accurately perceived by the other person. These conditions are those which are required for effective client-centered therapy, but Rogers believes that they are not restricted to individual therapy. Rather, they ". . . apply whether we are speaking of the relationship between therapist and client, parent and child, leader and group, teacher and student, or administrator and staff. The conditions apply, in fact, in any situation in which the development of the person is a goal" (Rogers, 1980, p. 115). Rogers (1980) even boldly asserts that these conditions might

> be effective in situations now dominated by the exercise of raw power—in politics, for example, especially in our dealings with other nations. I challenge, with all the strength I possess, the current American belief, evident in every phase of our foreign policy, and especially in our insane wars, that "might makes right." That, in my estimation, is the road to self-destruction. I go along with Martin Buber and the ancient Oriental sages: "He who imposes himself has the small, manifest might; he who does not impose himself has the great, secret might." (p. 45)

In recent years, Rogers has turned his attention to discovering and creating psychological climates which facilitate growth and enhancement in such human endeavors as encounter groups (Rogers, 1967; 1970), general education (Rogers, 1969), humanizing medical education (Rogers, 1980), and interracial and intercultural harmony, including an attempt to ease tensions between Catholics, Protestants, and the English in Belfast, Northern Ireland (McGaw, Rice, & Rogers, 1973).

Rogers' most far-reaching speculation concerns the future of humankind. He is keenly aware of a number of contemporary trends which he believes are counter to human beings' self-actualizing, to growing and enhancing themselves according to their natural inclinations. They include: "advances in computer intelligence and decision-making; 'test-tube' babies. . . ; new species of . . . life being created through recombinant work with the genes; cities under domes, with the whole environment controlled. . . ; completely artificial environments permitting human beings to live in space: these are some of the new technologies that may affect our lives. They have in common the fact that each removes humankind further from nature, from the soil, the weather, the sun, the wind, and all natural processes" (Rogers, 1980, pp. 342–43). But as has been characteristic of his theorizing throughout his career, Rogers continues to be optimistic in his view of humankind.

Rogers (1980) believes that there are "many new developments today that alter our whole conception of the potentialities of the individual; that change our perceptions of 'reality'; that change our ways of being and behaving; that alter our belief systems" (p. 343). As examples he cites: increased interest in various forms of meditation which points to a recognition and use of our "inner energy resources"; a growing appreciation and use of intuition as a potent tool; many people experiencing altered states of consciousness which may increase human capabilities; the vast potential of biofeedback training; holistic health concepts and practices, which include the increasing recognition that we may be able to cure or alleviate physical diseases, such as cancer, through the "intentional use of our conscious and nonconscious minds" (cf. Siminton et al., 1980). Rogers' optimism is based, ultimately, on a conviction that, to survive in a world which is characterized by increasing technology and artificiality, human beings will have to become interpersonally oriented and natural—that is, more *person-centered*. Rogers (1980) enumerates 12 qualities which he thinks will be characteristic of the "survivors" in our future world: (1) an openness to experience; (2) a desire for authenticity; (3) a skepticism regarding science and technology; (4) a desire for wholeness; (5) a wish for intimacy; (6) being process persons (always changing); (7) a caring for others; (8) a feeling of closeness to nature; (9) being anti-institutional; (10) a trust in inner authority and distrust of external authority; (11) an indifference to material things; (12) a yearning for spirituality (pp. 350–52). Obviously, no single individual will possess all of these qualities. Interestingly, these hypothesized optimal characteristics of persons of tomorrow closely parallel the qualities which Maslow has identified as characteristic of fully self-actualized individuals, as we shall see in the next chapter.

As his career progressed, Rogers has increasingly devoted his attention to expanding the horizons of psychology and tried to bring psychology itself a step closer toward self-actualization. He has pointedly

> raised the question as to whether psychology will remain a narrow technological fragment of a science, tied to an outdated philosophical conception of itself, clinging to a security blanket of observable behaviors only; or whether it can possibly become a truly broad and creative science, rooted in subjective vision, open to all aspects of the human condition, worthy of the name of a mature science. (Rogers, 1973, p. 387)

Specifically, Rogers is concerned that psychology

for all its thousands of experiments, its multitude of white rats, its vast enterprises involving laboratories, computers, electronic equipment, highly sophisticated statistical measures, and the like, is . . . slipping backward as a significant science. We have failed dismally to heed Robert Oppenheimer's (1956) warning, addressed to the APA, when he pointed out that the worst thing psychology might do would be "to model itself after a physics which is not there anymore, which has been outdated." (Rogers, 1973, p. 379)

In place of the narrow view of science which Rogers thinks pervades psychology, he suggests a more open approach, based on careful observation, particularly of inner cognitive processes, and most importantly, a science that does not "push the individual into some contrived situation to investigate some hypothesis we have imposed . . ." on the person (Rogers, 1973, p. 380). Instead, Rogers advocates that psychologists open their minds as well as their "whole selves" to learning *from* the individual. An example of this openness would be the investigation of mysterious, and possibly personally threatening, phenomena which have been classified as parapsychology (e.g., ESP, telepathic communication, and other so-called psychic experiences). Rogers (1973) makes it clear that he "is not suggesting that we 'know' there is a separate reality (or realities) . . . ," but that psychologists would not demean themselves by becoming "open-minded to such a possibility and started investigating it . . ." (p. 386). In keeping with his personality theory, Rogers believes that by being open and nonjudgmental about all experiences, psychology will "move closer toward . . . enhancement, deepening, enrichment" by taking the profession "a step closer to self-actualization" (Rogers, 1973, p. 387). The question in Rogers' mind, however, is whether psychologists will dare to accept this challenge. One psychologist who dared was Abraham Maslow, to whose work we turn next. Maslow investigated areas of personality that are not amenable to rigid experimental controls and statistical analyses, but which are, nonetheless, important to study and understand.

16 *The phenomenological strategy*

Maslow's theory of human motivation

Abraham Maslow (1908–1970), in contrast to Carl Rogers, did not develop a major theory of personality. Instead he concentrated his efforts on understanding the factors which motivate people, and he was especially interested in those motives which direct the lives of fully functioning individuals.

In our discussion of Rogers in the previous chapter, the *fully functioning person* was mentioned several times. Such persons are fully self-actualizing; their behavior is regulated by their organismic valuing process. Fully functioning people are open to all experiences; their self-concepts are whole and consistent with their experiences; and they are free of threat and anxiety and therefore have no defenses. In short, the fully functioning person epitomizes psychological health or adjustment. Actually, the type of person we have just described is an ideal, and such a (living) specimen has yet to be found. However, some individuals come close to the goal of complete self-actualization.

Shortly we shall take a fascinating peak (sic) at what self-actualization would be like, but first it is necessary to understand how people reach the stage at which their self-actualization motives begin to dominate their lives. In other words, we shall take several steps backward (downward) to see how Maslow conceptualized motivation in the average person.

Before reading any further, take a few minutes to do Demonstration 16–1. It is directly related to our discussion of Maslow's hierarchy of needs, and you may find it useful to briefly examine some of your own needs before learning what Maslow theorized about human motivation.

Abraham Maslow

Courtesy of Bertha G. Maslow,
photo by Marcia Roltner

AN ASSESSMENT OF YOUR PRESENT NEEDS

Demonstration 16–1[1]

As we have seen in previous chapters, personality psychologists have identified various basic needs which motivate our behavior. Table 16–1 lists five categories of needs, which Maslow believed were essential for all individuals,

---

[1] This demonstration is adapted from Grasha (1978).

TABLE 16–1
Maslow's categories of needs with examples (for Demonstration 16–1)

Self-actualization needs

Examples:
  Living up to your potential
  Accepting your strengths and limitations
  Accepting other people for whom and what they are
  Being spontaneous
  Acting creatively
  Acting independently (of other's opinions)

Esteem needs

Examples:
Self-esteem	*Esteem from others*
Achievement	Recognition
Confidence	Appreciation
Mastery	Attention
Strength	Status
	Reputation

Social needs

Examples:
  Love
  Affection
  Belonging (to family, group)
  Friendship
  Spending time with other people

Safety needs

Examples:
  Physical security
  Dependence
  Stability, order, structure
  Freedom from fear

Physiological needs

Examples:
  Food and water
  Rest and sleep
  Exercise
  Health
  Sexual behavior

along with specific examples of each. After reading over the list, **write down three significant examples of activities in which you have engaged in the past month that fit into each category.** The activities can be either overt actions or covert behaviors, such as thoughts or fantasies. (Note that if you have to spend a lot of time thinking of an example, it probably has not been very important in your life this past month.) You may find it convenient to use a worksheet like the sample in Table 16–2.

Now that you have an idea of the activities in which you were involved recently that correspond to each of the five categories of needs, **estimate the percentage of time you spent meeting each of the five need categories.** (This should add up to 100 percent.) Next think about how content or satisfied you are that you have been able to meet the needs in each category. This will

TABLE 16–2
Sample worksheet for Demonstration 16–1

Need category	Examples of recent behavior	Percent of time spent meeting needs in category	Satisfaction rating
Self-actualization	1. 2. 3.	%	
Esteem	1. 2. 3.	%	
Social	1. 2. 3.	%	
Safety	1. 2. 3.	%	
Physiological	1. 2. 3.	%	
		Total = 100%	

be very much an individual matter. Using the scale below, **rate the degree to which you are satisfied that your needs have been met in each category.** Write the scale number next to the percentage of time you spent meeting the needs for that category.

1 = totally unsatisfied
2 = generally unsatisfied
3 = slightly unsatisfied
4 = slightly satisfied
5 = generally satisfied
6 = totally satisfied

As you read about Maslow's theory regarding the five categories of needs, you will have a chance to observe how well your individual behavior with respect to these needs fits with his theory. To briefly preview what we shall shortly discuss in detail, Maslow arranged the five categories of needs in a hierarchy of importance, with it being important to satisfy needs lower in the hierarchy before higher needs are satisfied. The need categories in Table 16–1 are listed in descending order with self-actualization needs being the highest (and last to be fulfilled) and physiological needs being the lowest (and first to be fulfilled). Generally, our satisfaction in meeting our needs decreases the higher the need (e.g., we tend to be most content with how we meet our physiological needs and least content with how we meet our self-actualization needs; see, for example, Graham & Balloun, 1973).

Obviously, this Demonstration may have some practical implications for you. Assessing how well you are fulfilling various needs can be revealing and may suggest changes you'd like to make in your priorities. For instance, you may not have been aware of the amount of time you tend to devote to one set of needs compared to others, and this information may suggest some reordering of priorities of your time and efforts. Whatever personal use you may make of the information you gleaned from doing Demonstration 16–1, keep in mind that this assessment of your needs is very broad and superficial and therefore it should only be used as a rough guideline to point to **possible** personal implications which should be checked out further.

A HIERARCHICAL THEORY OF MOTIVATION

The instinctoid nature of needs

Maslow conceptualized human motivation in terms of a hierarchy of instinctoid needs. *Instinctoid* is a term that Maslow coined in order to distinguish human needs which have a biological basis from the biologically-based needs of other animal species. This is an important distinction because Maslow firmly believed that humans are only minimally influenced by biological instincts. Instinctual motivation, Maslow (1970) held, tends to disappear as animals proceed up the phylogenetic scale:

> For instance, in the white rat it is fair to say that, by our definition, there are found the hunger instinct, the sex instinct, the maternal instinct. In the monkey the sexual instinct has definitely disappeared, the hunger instinct has clearly been modified in various ways, and only the maternal instinct is undoubtedly present. In the human being, by our definition, they have all three disappeared, leaving in their place conglomerations of hereditary reflexes, hereditary drives, autogenous learning, and cultural learning in the motivated behavior and in the choice of goal objects. . . . Thus if we examine the sexual life of the human being we find that sheer drive itself is given by heredity but that the choice of object and the choice of behavior must be acquired or learned in the course of the life history. (p. 27)

Like instinctual needs, the instinctoid needs which Maslow identified as critical for development and growth are present in *all* human beings which is the reason for labeling them as biologically rooted (i.e., instinctoid). However, in contrast to instinctual needs, the behaviors which follow from and fulfill instinctoid needs are individually determined for each person—according to his or her unique biological makeup and environmental experiences—rather than being essentially the same for all members of the species.

There are some important ways in which Maslow's conception of needs differs from the views of needs held by most of the dispositional psychologists whom we discussed in Section 3. Recall that needs and other dispositions such as traits and types are generally considered relatively stable (and sometimes even permanent) personality characteristics of the individual, with the clear implication that they are not expected to change very much over time or in different situations. In contrast, Maslow thought that the instinctoid needs of a given person could and probably would vary in their influence on the person's behavior at different periods in the person's life. Furthermore, whereas dispositionalists tend to view needs as static entities, Maslow (1970) conceived of needs as *dynamic* processes. Specifically, he believed that people are incessantly seeking satisfaction of needs. When they are successful in satisfying one set of needs, they turn to another set of as yet unfulfilled and *higher* needs (or goals). Consistent with the basic assumptions of the phenomenological strategy, Maslow's theory of human motivation is predicated on the view of human beings as active striving organisms rather than passive, reactive ones. This position is inherent in Maslow's hierarchy of instinctoid needs.

Maslow postulated that there are five levels of basic human needs that can be ordered in a hierarchy of potency, as depicted in Figure 16–1. These levels, in order of decreasing strength, are: (1) basic physiological needs (e.g., food); (2) safety needs (e.g., shelter); (3) belongingness and love needs (e.g., companionship); (4) esteem needs (e.g., feeling competent); (5) self-actualization needs (e.g., creativity). We shall discuss each of these levels of needs in detail below.

The nature of the need hierarchy

FIGURE 16–1
Schematic representation of Maslow's hierarchy of instinctoid needs. The higher the need in the hierarchy, the weaker is the need in terms of motivating human behavior.

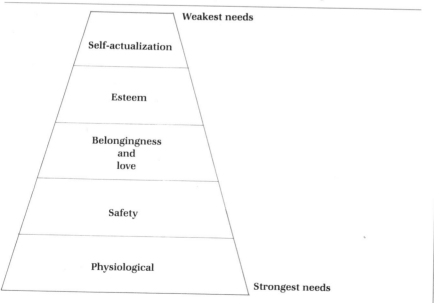

The lower a need is in the hierarchy, the more powerful it is, and the more intrusive it is on our behavior. The higher a need is in the hierarchy, the weaker it is in terms of its potential influence on behavior, but the more distinctly human it becomes. In other words, humans definitely share lower physiological and safety needs with other animals; humans may share needs of belongingness and love with higher species; and it is assumed that humans alone possess higher needs of esteem and self-actualization.

Maslow believed that, as the needs at one level in the hierarchy were satisfied, a person progressed to the next level of needs which then became the focal point of behavior until those needs were reasonably met at which point the person progressed to the next level. In general, one does not become concerned with meeting higher needs until lower needs have been at least partially satisfied. There are some notable exceptions to this rule. One exception is relatively rare and occurs with individuals who defy "normal" social customs. For example, some highly creative people lead a life of physical hardship including eating poorly and living in squalor in order to pursue their creative interests (e.g., writing). Another exception would be dedicated political activists who choose to forsake their personal safety (as well as some of their basic physiological needs) to protest what they consider to be social injustices. Examples include the civil rights advocates in the 1950s who risked being beaten or even killed while marching in the Deep South of the United States to help desegregate public transportation and schools; or, more recently, IRA prisoners who starved themselves to death protesting the British government's policies concerning Ireland.

A more common exception to the rule of hierarchical movement with regard to meeting our needs periodically occurs for most of us. At various points in our lives, it is inevitable that some of our basic needs may be frustrated temporarily. When this occurs, we move to a lower level of the hierarchy and concentrate our efforts on fulfilling those needs before returning to the higher level which had been the focal point of our behavior. An ordinary example is when we become physically ill and literally cannot perform our daily functions, including our work and social activities. Until we have sufficiently recovered from our illness, our life is focused on taking care of very basic physiological needs while higher social and esteem needs are, by necessity, placed "on a back burner." (At such times, we become aware of the fact that there are few things in this world that we *must* do. However, under normal circumstances, we often live as if certain commitments, such as to work, cannot be put aside.) Thus, no matter how far an individual has progressed up the need hierarchy, when more basic needs are not being met, the individual must temporarily engage in behavior which will satisfy the basic needs before the higher needs once again can be attended to.

Another example of this important principle occurred with a successful, unmarried business executive in his early 30s whose life was currently dominated by esteem needs. He described the following experience which he had one evening while working late in his office.

> I was very much enjoying my work, going over the draft of a marketing report I had written the previous week. I liked what I had written and so it was gratifying to put the finishing touches on it before it was to be typed and distributed. I felt good working—the work was going well and I was enjoying doing it. I felt very content to be working at my desk late at night, a kind of "all's well with the world" sensation except . . . except that something was missing to make it complete, to make it perfect. At first I couldn't figure out what could be missing. I had a good secure job which I enjoyed, and I had been getting a lot of the right kind of exposure in the field. My boss openly expressed his pleasure about what I had been doing, and my co-workers seemed to like me and, especially important, seemed to respect my abilities. I was making enough money, I was healthy, and I had interesting recreational activities to keep me occupied when I wasn't working. What more could I want? Finally I realized that all this good life I was having was solely mine and that I did not share it with anyone else. I apparently was missing sharing good things with a close, loved one. I had not had much social life recently but did not miss it at this time in my life since I was very much into my work. But the more I thought about it, the more I realized that I would have felt more content, more full, if there were a woman in my life with whom I could have shared my otherwise very positive life.

How would this man's feelings be explained in terms of Maslow's hierarchy of needs? The man was primarily functioning at the esteem need level, which consists of needs that are satisfied by the recognition of other people for one's accomplishments as well as feelings of self-worth (self-esteem) about one's abilities. From his own report, these esteem needs appeared to have been well met. However, his needs relating to belongingness and love, which are at a lower level, were not being satisfied. These lower needs must have been gratified at one time in his life in order for him to have progressed to dealing with higher level esteem needs. But apparently his single-minded devotion to his work (to esteem needs) created a temporary void in his life that called for a return to a lower level to satisfy his unmet social needs.

Physiological needs

Physiological needs are those which are directly related to survival. They are the most obvious of our needs, and they are the most powerful needs we have. They include the need for food, water, oxygen, elimina-

The five levels
of needs

tion, rest, and sex. When one of these basic needs is not met, it will consume the person's life until it is satisfied. An individual who is in a chronic and extreme state of hunger is convinced that Utopia is a place where food is always available and that he or she will be totally satisfied with life, never desiring anything else, as long as food is plentiful. Food becomes the central focus of the hungry person's life, behavior, thoughts, dreams, and so on. Such a person would be said to live by bread alone (Maslow, 1970). However, at least in our society and most of the Western world, there are few people who find themselves in such a situation with respect to hunger or any of the other physiological needs. Thus, under normal circumstances, physiological needs play an insignificant role in human motivation, and needs higher in the hierarchy (and less potent) dominate most people's lives. Before examining these higher needs, it should be pointed out that Maslow did not hold that any set of needs had to be totally satisfied before an individual was capable of dealing with the next highest set of needs. When lower needs are substantially and consistently fulfilled, the person is free to devote time and energy to higher needs.

Safety needs

When physiological needs have been substantially met, safety needs emerge as the motivating force in human beings. Safety needs include security, protection, dependency, stability, order, structure, limits, and freedom from fear, anxiety, and chaos. In essence, when our safety needs have been met, we feel that our world is secure and free from danger. (As we shall see in the next chapter, George Kelly's theory of personality is based on people's attempts to reduce uncertainty in their lives, to be able to predict future events accurately.)

The safety needs of most adults in our culture are largely satisfied. "The peaceful, smoothly running, stable, good society ordinarily makes its members feel safe enough from wild animals, extremes of temperature, criminal assault, murder, chaos, tyranny, and so on" (Maslow, 1970, p. 41). Thus, for adults under normal circumstances, safety needs are not active motivators. The dominance of safety needs are most easily observed in the behavior of children and neurotic adults.

"Infants," for example, "will react in a total fashion and as if they were endangered, if they are disturbed or dropped suddenly, startled by loud noises, flashing light, or other unusual sensory stimulation, by rough handling, by general loss of support in the mother's arms, or by inadequate support" (Maslow, 1970, p. 39). The urgency of safety needs can be readily seen when a child suffers from illness or injury.

> At such a moment of pain, it may be postulated that, for the child, the whole world suddenly changes from sunniness to darkness, so to speak, and becomes a place in which anything at all might happen, in which

> previously stable things have suddenly become unstable. Thus, a child
> who because of some bad food is taken ill may for a day or two develop
> fear, nightmares, and a need for protection and reassurance never seen
> . . . before. . . . (Maslow, 1970, p. 40)

Still another indication of children's heightened safety needs is evident
in their preference for some predictable, undisrupted routine in their
lives (e.g., having meals at a set time).

Adult neurotic behavior is frequently similar, in many respects, to
the unsafe child's desire for safety. The world may be perceived as
hostile, threatening, and overwhelming. The neurotic adult may behave
"as if a great catastrophe were almost always impending . . . usually
responding as if to an emergency" (Maslow, 1970, p. 42). This is most
clearly seen in obsessive-compulsive neurotic behavior.

> Compulsive-obsessives try frantically to order and stabilize the world
> so that no unmanageable, unexpected, or unfamiliar dangers will ever
> appear. They hedge themselves about with all sorts of ceremonials, rules,
> and formulas so that every possible contingency may be provided for
> and so that no new contingencies may appear. (Maslow, 1970, p. 42)

But for most of us, safety needs are generally well satisfied in the
course of our normal existence, and they take a back seat to higher
needs. Common vestiges of our safety needs include our buying insur-
ance policies (e.g., medical, theft, liability) and having savings accounts
as well as our preference for jobs which are secure and tenured.

Belongingness and love needs

Needs related to affiliation, affection, and love emerge when physiological and safety needs have been gratified. When this occurs, we
become motivated by deep feelings of loneliness when friends, family,
and loved ones are missing. We long for affectionate relationships and
a secure place in primary groups (e.g., family). When belongingness
and love needs predominate, people are keenly aware and upset by
feelings of ostracism, rejection, friendlessness, rootlessness, and ano-
mie.

Maslow, along with other personality psychologists (e.g., Fromm,
1963), believed that the failure of belongingness and love needs to be
met for many people is a major contemporary problem in the United
States and other Western societies. The popularity in recent years of
encounter groups and other personal-growth groups may in part be
due to

> this unsatisfied hunger for contact, for intimacy, for belongingness and
> by the need to overcome the widespread feelings of alienation, aloneness,
> strangeness, and loneliness, which have been worsened by our mobility,

by the breakdown of traditional groupings, the scattering of families, the generation gap, the steady urbanization and disappearance of village face-to-faceness, and the resulting shallowness of American friendship. My strong impression is also that *some* proportion of youth rebellion groups—I don't know how many or how much—is motivated by the profound hunger for groupiness, for contact, for real togetherness in the face of a common enemy, *any* enemy that can serve to form an amity group simply by posing an external threat. The same kind of thing was observed in groups of soldiers who were pushed into an unwonted brotherliness and intimacy by their common external danger, and who may stick together throughout a lifetime as a consequence. Any good society must satisfy this need, one way or another, if it is to survive and be healthy. (Maslow, 1970, p. 44)

Esteem needs

If a person's first three levels of needs have been adequately satisfied, then the person becomes concerned with meeting esteem needs. Maslow (1970) distinguished between two types of esteem needs: self-esteem and esteem from others. Self-esteem involves a desire for competency, mastery, achievement, strength, adequacy, confidence, independence, and freedom. When these needs are met, one feels worthwhile, confident, capable, and useful and necessary in the world. Should these needs be frustrated, one is apt to feel inferior, weak, and helpless. Esteem from significant other people in our lives involves a desire for recognition, appreciation, attention, prestige, reputation, status, and fame. In short, we have a need to feel respected by others for what we can do, a desire that others recognize and make note of our worth.

Maslow thought that self-esteem was more essential than esteem from others, although the former is partially a result of the latter (cf. Rogers' positive regard and positive self-regard). However, he emphasized that enduring and healthy self-esteem is based on the *deserved* respect of others, recognition that has been earned through a person's efforts, rather than being based on status or fame.

Self-actualization needs

Most individuals spend their lives attempting to fulfill their physiological, safety, love, and esteem needs and never completely accomplish this task. A small number of persons, however, succeed at fairly well gratifying their needs in the first four levels of Maslow's hierarchy, and these people then become motivated by self-actualization needs. Maslow (1970) defined *self-actualization* as "the desire to become more and more what one idiosyncratically is, to become everything that one is capable of becoming" (p. 46). Only by being all that one is "destined for" can a person's needs ever be truly satisfied and can the person feel truly content.

Self-actualization is a goal that is never fully attained by any person although a few people—Maslow estimated about one percent of the population—come close to reaching it. For several reasons, movement toward self-actualization is by no means automatic or easy, even for people who have been successful at fulfilling their lower needs.

First, self-actualization needs are at the top of the hierarchy which means that they are the weakest of the instinctoid needs. "This inner nature is not strong and overpowering and unmistakable like the instincts of animals. It is weak and delicate and subtle and easily overcome by habit, cultural pressure, and wrong attitudes toward it" (Maslow, 1968, p. 4).

Second, Maslow believed that people frequently are afraid of the kind of self-knowledge that is necessary for self-actualization. Accurate self-knowledge can be threatening because it may change one's self-concept and because inevitably it involves giving up the certainty of what one has long known, believed, and trusted for new concepts, the unknown, and uncertainty. This choice is more readily made by people who feel secure. For example, Maslow observed that children from secure, nurturing families are more likely to select experiences that result in personal growth than are children from insecure, cold families.

Third, self-actualization generally requires an environment where one is free to express oneself, to explore, to choose one's behavior without restriction (within the normal bounds of not harming others), and to pursue such intrinsic values as truth, justice, and honesty. Few people are fortunate enough to live in such (ideal) circumstances. For instance, our culture generally inhibits the genuine spontaneity which tends to characterize self-actualized persons through its established social customs about the proper and polite expression of one's feelings, especially in public.

The specific nature of self-actualization needs varies considerably from person to person, in contrast to considerable similarity in the form that lower needs take in different individuals. It is important to note that self-actualization does not necessarily involve special talent or creative and artistic activities, such as we attribute to Bach or Picasso. As we shall see shortly in our description of the characteristics of self-actualizers, self-actualization may be manifest in any human activity (e.g., farming, athletics, mechanics, parenting).

GROWTH MOTIVATION (VERSUS DEFICIT MOTIVATION)

Although Maslow placed self-actualization needs at the top of the hierarchy of human motives, there is a sense in which self-actualization needs do not fit on the hierarchy because they are distinctly different from the basic needs which comprise the first four levels. We have already indicated that most people never satisfy their lower needs sufficiently to become motivated by self-actualization needs. A more telling difference between lower needs (i.e., physiological, safety, love, and esteem) and higher needs (i.e., self-actualization) is that the former motivate people in terms of deprivation while the latter do so in terms of growth (Maslow, 1955).

We are most familiar with *deficit motivation* in which an individual's behavior is energized by and directed (i.e., motivated) toward reducing tension or filling a temporary lack of a particular need. We drink because we are thirsty and drinking relieves our thirst, just as we seek the company of friends because we are lonely and being with them eliminates our loneliness. Needs in the first four levels of Maslow's hierarchy operate through deficit motivation, although this tends to be more the case for physiological and safety needs and somewhat less the case for belongingness-love and esteem needs. A deficit motive is characterized by five criteria (Maslow, 1968):

1. When it is absent, illness occurs (e.g., in the case of hunger, a person who does not eat will get sick).
2. When it is present, illness is prevented (e.g., eating properly prevents certain illness).
3. When it is restored, illness is cured (e.g., illness caused by malnutrition is often cured by proper eating).
4. Under special, complex free-choice situations a deprived individual will prefer gratification of a deficit motive to other gratifications (e.g., a starving person will be more interested in food than in compliments from friends).
5. It is essentially inactive in a healthy person (e.g., healthy people tend to be sufficiently well fed so that hunger is not an active drive for them).

Growth motivation, in contrast to deficit motivation, is oriented toward enhancing an individual's life in line with the person's unique self-actualizing tendencies. Maslow used a variety of terms in writing of the motives associated with growth motivation, including *growth motives, being* or *B-motives* (as opposed to *deficiency,* or *D-motives*), *metamotives,* and *metaneeds.* "Meta" means beyond or after, and metaneeds thus designate motives that are a step beyond basic needs or come after one's basic needs have been satisfied. Metaneeds are the self-actualization motives and are "intrinsic values" such as beauty, truth, justice, perfection, and self-sufficiency. Growth motivation is aimed at increasing one's experiences (i.e., leading to inner growth) and thus might be considered "tension increasing" as opposed to the tension-reducing aim of deficiency motivation.

The two styles of perceiving associated with deficiency and being motivation illustrate an important difference between these two life orientations. Jourard (1974) characterizes *D-perception* as "a highly focused search-light darting here and there, seeking the objects which will satisfy needs, ignoring everything irrelevant to the need" whereas he sees *B-perception* as "a more passive mode of perceiving. It involves letting oneself be reached, touched, or affected by what is there so that the perception is richer" (p. 68).

One further illustration of the difference between B- and D-motivation involves a contrast between "B-love (love for the Being of another person, unneeding love, unselfish love) and D-love (deficiency-love, love need, selfish love)" (Maslow, 1968, p. 42). Maslow (1968) lists the following characteristics of B-love, which implicitly contrast it to D-love.

1. B-love is completely enjoyed and is nonpossessive.
2. B-love can never be satisfied, and it usually increases rather than decreases over time. The opposite is true for D-love.
3. B-love is often likened to an aesthetic or mystic experience.
4. B-love can have a deep, therapeutic effect.
5. B-love is a richer, higher, and more valuable experience than is D-love.
6. B-love involves no anxiety-hostility component such as is always present to some degree with D-love.
7. B-lovers are less dependent on each other, less jealous, less needful, less invested in the other person than are D-lovers. At the same time, B-lovers are more eager to help their partner self-actualize and tend to be prouder of the other's accomplishments than are D-lovers.
8. B-love involves the truest, most penetrating perception of the other, whereas D-love is often "blind."
9. Receiving B-love fosters personal growth, self-acceptance, and feelings of self-worth. In fact, Maslow (1968) questioned "whether the full development of the human being is possible without it" (p. 43).

In Maslow's (1970) later theorizing, he suggested that metaneeds are instinctoid and must be gratified for a person to remain psychologically healthy and to fully self-actualize.[2] Each of the 15 metaneeds which Maslow (1971) identified has associated with it a specific *metapathology* (meta-illness) which results from the deprivation of the metaneed. These metapathologies "have been discussed through the centuries by religionists, historians, and philosophers under the rubric of *spiritual or religious shortcomings,* rather than by physicians, scientists, or psychologists under the rubric of psychiatric or psychological or

---

[2] This position is obviously contradictory to Maslow's (1955) earlier view that B-motivation did not involve deprivation which had to be alleviated. Unfortunately, Maslow's untimely death in 1970 has left this theorizing in a controversial and unfinished stage.

biological 'illnesses' " (Maslow, 1971, pp. 316–17; italics added). Maslow (1971) suggested that television, and especially television advertising provides "a rich source of metapathologies of all types, i.e., of the vulgarization or destruction of all instrinsic values . . ." (p. 310). The number of advertisements on television dealing with body odor, bad breath, dandruff, hemorrhoids, loose dentures, etc. clearly illustrates Maslow's contention. Table 16–3 lists the metapathologies that will occur if specific metaneeds are not sufficiently satisfied.

Maslow theorized that metaneeds, such as those listed in Table 16–3, are of equal value and thus are not arranged in hierarchical order as are basic needs. Furthermore, because metaneeds all involve intrinsic values and their fulfillment is in the service of the common goal of enhancement or growth, metaneeds can be readily substituted for one another depending upon the present circumstances in a person's life. When people are motivated by metaneeds, even their routine work is on a higher plane. For example,

> "the law" is apt to be more a way of seeking justice, truth, goodness, etc., rather than financial security, admiration, status, prestige, dominance, masculinity, etc. When I ask the questions: Which aspects of your work do you enjoy most? What gives you your greatest pleasures? When do you get a kick out of your work? etc., such people are more apt to answer in terms of intrinsic values, of transpersonal, beyond-the-selfish, altruistic satisfactions, e.g., seeing justice done, doing a more perfect job, advancing the truth, rewarding virtue and punishing evil, etc. (Maslow, 1971, p. 310)

Metaneeds play a very small role in most people's lives. However, occasionally nonself-actualized individuals are motivated by intrinsic B-values. This may occur at special times in their lives. One example might be when we are temporarily in a situation that demands extraordinary behavior (e.g., a crisis in one's community) with the result that we temporarily postpone the gratification of basic needs and rise above them to the realm of metaneeds (e.g., performing feats of courage or self-sacrifice). Under normal circumstances, however, only people who would be classified as self-actualizers are motivated by metaneeds.

A DESCRIPTION OF SELF-ACTUALIZING PERSONS

Maslow (1972) describes the origin of his studies of the self-actualizing person in the following words:

> My investigations on self-actualization were not planned to be research and did not start out as research. They started out as the effort of a young intellectual to try to understand two of his teachers whom he loved, adored, and admired and who were very, very wonderful people. It was a kind of high-IQ devotion. I could not be content simply to adore, but sought to understand why these two people were so different from the run-of-the-mill people in the world. These two people were Ruth

TABLE 16–3
Metaneeds and the metapathologies that result from deprivation of these needs

Metaneed	Specific metapathology
1. Truth	Disbelief; mistrust; cynicism; skepticism; suspicion.
2. Goodness	Utter selfishness; hatred; repulsion; disgust. Reliance only upon self and for self. Nihilism; cynicism.
3. Beauty	Vulgarity; specific unhappiness, restlessness, loss of taste, tension, fatigue. Philistinism; bleakness.
4. Unity; wholeness	Disintegration; "the world is falling apart." Arbitrariness.
4A. Dichotomy-transcendence	Black-white thinking, either/or thinking. Seeing everything as a duel or a war, or a conflict. Low synergy. Simplisitc view of life.
5. Aliveness; process	Deadness; robotizing; feeling oneself to be totally determined. Loss of emotion. Boredom (?), loss of zest in life. Experiential emptiness.
6. Uniqueness	Loss of feeling of self and of individuality. Feeling oneself to be interchangeable, anonymous, not really needed.
7. Perfection	Discouragement (?); hopelessness; nothing to work for.
7A. Necessity	Chaos; unpredictability. Loss of safety; vigilance.
8. Completion; finality	Feelings of incompleteness with perseveration. Hopelessness. Cessation of striving and coping. No use trying.
9. Justice	Insecurity; anger; cynicism; mistrust; lawlessness; jungle world-view; total selfishness.
9A. Order	Insecurity; wariness. Loss of safety, of predictability. Necessity for vigilance, alertness, tension, being on guard.
10. Simplicity	Overcomplexity; confusion; bewilderment, conflict, loss of orientation.
11. Richness; totality; comprehensiveness	Depression; uneasiness; loss of interest in world.
12. Effortlessness	Fatigue, strain, striving, clumsiness, awkwardness, gracelessness, stiffness.
13. Playfulness	Grimness; depression; paranoid humorlessness; loss of zest in life. Cheerlessness. Loss of ability to enjoy.
14. Self-sufficiency	Dependence upon (?) the perceiver (?). It becomes his responsibility.
15. Meaningfulness	Meaninglessness; despair; senselessness of life.

Source: Adapted from Maslow, A. H. *The farther reaches of human nature.* New York: Viking Press, 1971, pp. 318–19.

Benedict and Max Wertheimer.[3] They were my teachers . . . and they were most remarkable human beings. My training in psychology equipped me not at all for understanding them. It was as if they were not quite

---

[3] Ruth Benedict was an anthropologist at Columbia University whose main field of interest was the American Indian. Max Wertheimer taught at the New School for Social Research and was one of the founders of Gestalt psychology.

people but something more than people. My own investigation began as a prescientific or nonscientific activity. . . . When I tried to understand them, think about them, and write about them . . . I realized in one wonderful moment that their two patterns could be generalized. I was talking about a kind of person, not about two noncomparable individuals. There was wonderful excitement in that. I tried to see whether this pattern could be found elsewhere, and I did find it elsewhere, in one person after another. (pp. 41–42)

Maslow's investigation of self-actualizing persons relies heavily on the case study method and is based on data from a relatively small and select group of subjects, including both living persons and historical figures (cf. McClelland's study of achievement motivation in past societies discussed in Chapter 12). Ethical considerations regarding confidentiality precluded divulging the names of the living subjects studied. However, the historical persons whom Maslow studied are known and included: Jane Addams, Sholom Aleichem, Martin Buber, George Washington Carver, Pablo Casals, Albert Einstein, Ralph Waldo Emerson, Benjamin Franklin, Aldous Huxley, William James, Thomas Jefferson, Abraham Lincoln, John Muir, Eleanor Roosevelt, Albert Schweitzer, Adlai Stevenson, Baruch Spinoza, Harriet Tubman, and Walt Whitman. It is interesting to note that many of the living subjects had to be studied "indirectly, indeed almost surreptitiously" because "possible subjects, when informed of the purpose of the research, became self-conscious, froze up, laughed off the whole effort, or broke off the relationship" (Maslow, 1970, p. 151).

In his report of the research, which was first published in 1950, Maslow justified his unorthodox approach in the following way:

I consider the problem of psychological health to be so pressing, that *any* suggestions, *any* bits of data, however moot, are endowed with great heuristic value. This kind of research is in principle so difficult—involving as it does a kind of lifting oneself by one's axiological bootstraps—that if we were to wait for conventionally reliable data, we should have to wait forever. It seems that the only manly thing to do is not to fear mistakes, to plunge in, to do the best that one can, hoping to learn enough from blunders to correct them eventually. At present the only alternative is simply to refuse to work with the problem. Accordingly, for whatever use can be made of it, the following report is presented with due apologies to those who insist on conventional reliability, validity, sampling, etc. (Maslow, 1963, p. 527)

In keeping with this philosophy, Maslow's research focused primarily on making observations rather than testing hypotheses, and the resulting observations are admittedly subjective in nature. With this type of qualitative data, the ability of the investigator to accurately and graphically summarize his or her impressions (the basic units of the data) greatly enhances the usefulness of the report. Maslow has a distinct talent in this regard. Accordingly, the present explication of Maslow's 15 most salient characteristics of self-actualizing persons relies heavily on direct quotations of Maslow's (1963) highly expressive and communicative language.

To begin with, self-actualizing people can be characterized by their *efficient perception of reality.*

> The first form in which this capacity was noticed was an unusual ability to detect the spurious, the fake, and the dishonest in personality, and in general to judge people correctly and efficiently. . . . As the study progressed, it slowly became apparent that this efficiency extended to many other areas of life—indeed *all* areas that were tested. In art and music, in things of the intellect, in scientific matters, in politics and public affairs, they seemed as a group to be able to see concealed or confused realities more swiftly and more correctly than others. Thus an informal experiment indicated that their predictions of the future from whatever facts were in hand at the time seemed to be more often correct, because [they were] less [likely to be] based upon wish, desire, anxiety, fear, or upon generalized, character-determined optimism or pessimism. (p. 531)

Maslow observes that fully functioning individuals are characterized by *acceptance* of themselves, of others, and of nature.

> They can accept their own human nature in stoic style, with all its shortcomings, with all its discrepancies from the ideal image without feeling real concern. It would convey the wrong impression to say that they are self-satisfied. What we must say rather is that they can take the frailties and sins, weaknesses, and evils of human nature in the same unquestioning spirit with which one accepts the characteristics of nature. One does not complain about water because it is wet, or about rocks because they are hard, or about trees because they are green. As the child looks out upon the world with wide, uncritical innocent eyes, simply noting and observing what is the case, without either arguing the matter or demanding that it be otherwise, so does the self-actualizing person look upon human nature in himself and in others. (p. 533)

Although self-actualizing people are *spontaneous,* they are not necessarily the most unconventional people in society.

> Their behavior is marked by simplicity and naturalness, and by lack of artificiality or straining for effect. This does not necessarily mean consistently unconventional behavior. . . . It is his impulses, thought, consciousness that are so unusually unconventional, spontaneous, and natural. Apparently recognizing that the world of people in which he lives could not understand or accept this, and since he has no wish to hurt them or fight with them over every triviality, he will go through the ceremonies and rituals of convention with a good-humored shrug and with the best possible grace. Thus I have seen a man accept an honor he laughed at and even despised in private, rather than make an issue of it and hurt the people who thought they were pleasing him. (p. 535)

Maslow's subjects are *problem-centered* in the sense that they are

> ordinarily concerned with basic issues and eternal questions of the type that we have learned to call philosophical or ethical. Such people live customarily in the widest possible frame of reference. They seem never to get so close to the trees that they fail to see the forest. They work within a framework of values that is broad and not petty, universal and not local, and in terms of a century rather than the moment. In a word, these people are all in one sense or another philosophers, however homely. (p. 537)

Self-actualizers appear to have a greater *affinity for solitude and privacy* than the average person and also show a tendency to be *independent from their culture and environment.*

> Self-actualizing people are not dependent for their main satisfactions on the real world, or other people or culture or means to ends or, in general, on extrinsic satisfactions. Rather they are dependent for their own development and continued growth on their own potentialities and latent resources. Just as the tree needs sunshine and water and food, so do most people need love, safety, and other basic need gratifications that can come only from without. But once these external satisfiers are obtained, once these inner deficiencies are satiated by outside satisfiers, the true problem of individual development begins . . . self-actualization. (p. 539)

Fully functioning persons exhibit a *continued freshness of appreciation* for even the most ordinary events in their lives. They have

> the wonderful capacity to appreciate again and again, freshly and naïvely, the basic goods of life, with awe, pleasure, wonder, and even ecstasy, however stale these experiences may have become to others. . . . any sunset may be as beautiful as the first one. . . . For such people, even the casual workaday, moment-to-moment business of living can be thrilling, exciting, and ecstatic. These intense feelings do not come all the time; they come occasionally rather than usually, but at the most unexpected moments. (pp. 539–40)

They are also likely to experience what Maslow calls *"the oceanic feeling."* This phrase refers to feelings of

> limitless horizons opening up to the vision, the feeling of being simultaneously more powerful and also more helpless than one ever was before, the feeling of great ecstasy and wonder and awe, the loss of placing in time and space with, finally, the conviction that something extremely important and valuable had happened, so that the subject is to some extent transformed and strengthened even in his daily life by such experiences. (p. 541)

Such *peak-experiences,* as these oceanic experiences are more commonly known, do not only occur in self-actualizing persons (though self-actualizers tend to have them more frequently than most people), and Maslow considered them " 'a transient moment of self-actualization' of the ordinary people" (Chiang & Maslow, 1977, p. 259). Maslow gathered written examples of peak experiences from 190 college students at Brandeis University (where he was chairperson of the Department of Psychology) by giving them the following instructions:

> *I would like you to think of the most wonderful experience or experiences of your life; happiest moments, ecstatic moments, moments of rapture, perhaps from being in love, or from listening to music or suddenly "being hit" by a book or painting, or from some great creative moment. First list these. And then try to tell me how you feel in such acute moments, how you feel* differently *from the way you feel at other times, how you are at the moment a different person in some ways.* (Maslow, 1968, p. 71)

(Following those instructions would make an interesting and informative exercise for the reader.) As an example of a peak experience, consider the following description.

It was to be the last and most difficult climb of our brief climbing trip. Being the novice of the group, Richard and Christopher briefed me on what lay above, giving special attention to the overhang in the third and last pitch [segment of the climb]. Some 50 feet below the summit there was a five-foot horizontal outcropping (i.e., at a right angle to the face of the cliff and parallel to the ground). Quite simply, to proceed to the summit, a climber would, for a brief time, be in a position with his or her back parallel to the ground as the overhang was negotiated. I had never done anything like that before, but my more experienced team members assured me that it was within my capabilities.

The first two pitches were relatively uneventful as was most of the third. Then there was a short traverse to the left along a narrow ledge, and I found myself directly below the overhang. I was being belayed [protected from a fall by a rope] from above by Christopher who, because of the overhang, was out of sight and sound. Fortunately, Richard was below me and gave me detailed instructions as to how to negotiate the overhang. It would involve jamming [wedging] both feet in a large crack in the vertical wall while my right hand gripped the underside of the overhang at about the position of my right knee and my left hand made a small but secure finger jam in a crack on the underside of the overhang at about the level of my shoulder. In fact, it was easier to get into this position than the description might sound, and because it was a secure position, I felt relatively safe to rest in it for the moment. However, the next and critical move would require me to let go of my secure right grip, straighten my legs, and reach up and around the overhang to blindly feel for a large hand hold on the top side of the overhang.

That was easier explained than done. My right hand must have started its assigned journey a dozen times in the next five minutes, only to quickly retreat to its secure hold each time. Finally, it was time to risk. My right hand quickly found the crack on the top, and it was not difficult to then move my left hand into the same crack, release my legs from their supports, and mantle [raise oneself by pressing downward with the arms] to the top of the overhang.

I was exhilarated, triumphant, almost giddy with joy. As I climbed the last bit to the top, I had to keep reminding myself that I'd better pay attention lest I fall on this relatively easy final ascent.

Safely on top, I told Christopher, "Off belay," and we proceeded to embrace each other. I asked him if he wanted me to belay Richard to the top; he said no, that he was fine and that I should rest. So I walked along the summit and shortly came to a magnificent overlook, displaying the entire lush green valley to the southeast. As I stood there, glowing in the warmth of the afternoon sun and my own energy, I had the following thoughts, which I shall never forget.

I was surely not ready to die. I may never have felt more alive, that life was so full and worth living, than at that moment. But, if I had to die, I was more ready to—because I had lived.

Self-actualizing people usually have a *genuine desire to help the human race,* although they tend to have *deep ties with relatively few individuals.* As one of Maslow's subjects noted: "I haven't got time for many friends. Nobody has, that is, if they are to be *real* friends" (Maslow, 1963, p. 542).

Maslow describes self-actualizers as being *democratic* in the deepest sense. Besides being free of prejudice with regard to superficial characteristics of people, such as race or political beliefs, they tend to respect all persons. For example, they are willing to learn from anyone who is able to teach them something. At the same time, Maslow says that his subjects do not indiscriminately equalize all human beings. Rather, self-actualizing people, "themselves elite, select for their friends elite, but this is an elite of character, capacity, and talent, rather than of birth, race, blood, name, family, age, youth, fame, or power" (1963, p. 544).

Fully functioning individuals show a keen *ability to discriminate between means and ends.* While they usually focus on ends rather than means, their ends are frequently what most people consider means. That is, they are "somewhat more likely to appreciate for its own sake, and in an absolute way, the doing itself; they can often enjoy for its own sake the getting to some place as well as the arriving. It is occasionally possible for them to make out of the most trivial and routine activity an intrinsically enjoyable game or dance or play" (1963, p. 545).

Maslow's subjects tend to have a *philosophical sense of humor.* Whereas the average person often enjoys humor that pokes fun at some individual's inferiority, that hurts someone, or that is "off-color," the self-actualizing person finds humor dealing with the foolishness of humans-in-general appealing. Such thoughtful, philosophical humor typically elicits a smile rather than a laugh.

Not surprisingly, Maslow finds that, without exception, his subjects are characterized by *creativeness*. However, the creativeness manifested by self-actualizing persons is different from unusual talent or genius. Rather, Maslow (1963) likens it to the

> naïve and universal creativeness of unspoiled children. It seems to be more a fundamental characteristic of common human nature—a potentiality given to all human beings at birth. Most human beings lose this as they become enculturated, but some few individuals seem either to retain this fresh and naïve, direct way of looking at life, or if they have lost it, as most people do, they later in life recover it. (p. 546)

The special creativeness characteristic of self-actualizers is, in fact, merely another way of describing in terms of consequences, the heightened freshness and efficiency of perception of self-actualizing persons.

Self-actualizing persons tend to *resist enculturation*. Outwardly, in their dress, speech, and manner of behaving, they remain within the limits of convention. At the same time, they "maintain a certain inner detachment from the culture in which they are immersed" (Maslow, 1963, p. 547). Furthermore, although they are not among those in the forefront of social action, they may be committed to social change, as Maslow points out in the following example.

> One of these subjects, who was a hot rebel in his younger days, a union organizer in the days when this was a highly dangerous occupation, has given up in disgust and hopelessness. As he became resigned to the slowness of social change (in this culture and in this era) he turned finally to education of the young. All the others show what might be called a calm, long-time concern with culture improvement that seems to me to imply an acceptance of slowness of change along with the unquestioned desirability and necessity of such change. (1963, p. 548)

Finally, Maslow makes it clear that self-actualizing persons are indeed "fully functioning" in the sense that, like all of us, they are not perfect.

> They too are equipped with silly, wasteful, or thoughtless habits. They can be boring, stubborn, irritating. They are by no means free from a rather superficial vanity, pride, partiality to their own productions, family, friends, and children. Temper outbursts are not rare. Our subjects are occasionally capable of an extraordinary and unexpected ruthlessness. It must be remembered that they are very strong people. This makes it possible for them to display a surgical coldness when this is called for, beyond the power of the average man. The man who found that a long-trusted acquaintance was dishonest cut himself off from this friendship sharply and abruptly and without any pangs whatsoever. Another woman who was married to someone she did not love, when she decided on divorce, did it with a decisiveness that looked almost like ruthlessness. Some of them recover so quickly from the death of people close to them as to seem heartless. (1963, pp. 550–51)

People who are classified as self-actualizers, such as the subjects of Maslow's research, tend to have made significant contributions or produced notable achievements which account for their being so identified. It is intriguing to speculate as to whether there may be more people than Maslow realized that are quietly and privately living to their full potential—undistinguished in the public eye, but distinctive in their being as fully human as members of our species are capable of being.

Readers familiar with the movie *Being There*[4] should reflect on the degree to which Chance (played by the late Peter Sellers) might be considered a self-actualizing person. Chance would be labeled a "simpleton," a man of low intelligence, illiterate, and uneducated. His life consists of watching television and gardening (he apparently is fairly competent at the latter). His basic needs are provided for by virtue of his being a permanent "guest" of a rich old man whose maid serves Chance all of his meals. When his benefactor dies, Chance, by a quirk of fate, becomes the temporary guest of another rich and influential man, named Ben Rand, who is quickly taken by Chance's fresh appreciation of life, his complete candor and spontaneity, his genuineness and total lack of pretense, and his acceptance of his life for what it is. Chance has undoubtedly become everything that he is capable of becoming (and, in some sense, even more). The irony, and the source of the story's humor, is that intellectually Chance's potential is rather limited, yet most people do not realize that. Even the President of the United States, whom he meets through Ben Rand, mistakes (?) Chance's objectively very simple pronouncements about the inevitable change of seasons (made in the context of gardening) as having some deep significance concerning a change in the nation's economic state. In fact, given Chance's minimal intellectual skills, his ideas about seasonal changes might well be considered profound from a phenomenological viewpoint (i.e., looked at from Chance's internal frame of reference).

ASSESSING SELF-ACTUALIZATION: THE PERSONAL ORIENTATION INVENTORY

Not surprisingly, one of the major criticisms of Maslow's research on self-actualizing individuals is that the criteria for identifying self-actualizers are highly subjective, being based almost entirely on the clinical impression of Maslow and his co-workers. One response to this criticism has been the development of an objective test of values and behaviors related to self-actualization.

The Personal Orientation Inventory (POI), devised by Everett Shostrom, consists of 150 two-choice comparative value and behavior judgments (Knapp, 1976; Shostrom, 1963, 1964, 1974; Shostrom, Knapp, &

---

[4] The Hal Ashby movie is based on Jerzy N. Kosinski's 1970 novel of the same name.

TABLE 16–4
Items and instructions similar to those appearing on the Personal Orientation
Inventory

Instructions: After reading each pair of statements, decide which one
is most consistently true for you.
1. *a.* I enjoy listening to dirty stories.
    b. I rarely enjoy listening to dirty stories.
2. *a.* When I get something new, I like to use it right away.
    b. When I get something new, I like to save it for a special time.
3. *a.* I am afraid of expressing my emotions.
    b. I am not afraid of expressing my emotions.
4. *a.* Daydreaming about the future can be harmful.
    b. Daydreaming about the future is always good.
5. *a.* I have a lot of bad memories.
    b. I have very few bad memories.
6. *a.* People are naturally friendly.
    b. People are naturally hostile.

Knapp, 1976). The POI is self-administered; respondents merely record
which of the two statements for each item more consistently applies
to them. Table 16–4 contains several examples of the type of items
found on the POI.

The items are scored twice, first for two scales which measure fundamental personal orientations with respect to whether the person is
present versus past and future oriented (time ratio) and whether the
person is self versus other oriented (support ratio). Then the 150 items
are rescored for 10 subscales which measure important elements of
self-actualization. A brief description of each of these 12 scales appears
in Table 16–5. The time and support ratio scores will be discussed in
some detail to illustrate how traditionally subjective, abstract, and
even esoteric concepts related to self-actualization have been made
operational in the POI.

The time scale measures the extent to which a person lives primarily
in the present as opposed to primarily focusing on the past and future.
Scores on this scale are presented as a ratio (proportion) between
time incompetence (past and future focus) and time competence (present focus) because one's time orientation is relative rather than absolute
(i.e., no one is entirely oriented in one time frame). *Time competency*
involves living "primarily in the present with full awareness, contact
and full feeling reactivity" while *time incompetency* is characterized
by living "primarily in the past, with guilts, regrets, and resentments,
and/or in the future, with idealized goals, plans, expectations, predictions and fears" (Shostrom, 1974, p. 4).

The self-actualizing person is primarily time competent, meaning
that his or her focus is on what is happening in the present. Time-
competent individuals are not oblivious to or independent of the past

TABLE 16–5
The scales of the Personal Orientation Inventory

	Scale name	Description
I. Ratio scores		
	Time ratio	The ratio of time incompetence to time competence indicates the degree to which a person lives in (is oriented toward) the past and future versus the present, respectively.
	Support ratio	The ratio of other to inner indicates the degree to which a person relies primarily on social or external factors versus internalized factors, respectively, to guide behavior.
II. Subscales*		
Valuing	Self-actualizing value	Measures extent to which person holds values of self-actualizing people.
	Existentiality	Measures degree of flexibility in applying principles to one's life.
Feeling	Feeling reactivity	Measures sensitivity to one's own feelings and needs.
	Spontaneity	Measures one's ability to express feelings behaviorally, to be oneself, to be uninhibited.
Self-perception	Self-regard	Measures ability to like oneself because of one's strengths and worth.
	Self-acceptance	Measures ability to like oneself in spite of one's limitations and weaknesses.
Awareness	Nature of man	Measures the extent to which a person views people as essentially good.
	Synergy	Measures the ability to view opposites in life as meaningfully related (e.g., viewing work and play as not really different).
Interpersonal sensitivity	Acceptance of aggression	Measures ability to accept one's anger or aggression as natural and to not deny such feelings.
	Capacity for intimate contact	Measures the ability to make meaningful, close relations with other people.

* The subscales can be grouped into complementary pairs—valuing, feeling, self-perception, awareness, and interpersonal sensitivity—representing the balancing which is important for self-actualization.

and future, however; such persons are "able to tie the past and the future to the present in meaningful continuity" (Shostrom, 1974, p. 13). They are able to usefully reflect on the past as it relates to the present and to realistically tie long-range aspirations to current, on-going goals. Time-competent individuals are optimistic about the future without being overly idealistic. In contrast, nonself-actualizers tend to be relatively time incompetent, basing their current lives on regrets and guilt from their past and unrealistic future goals and pessimism about the future. People who are primarily time incompetent have essentially split off their past and future from their present. They have difficulty meaningfully using what they have done previously and can potentially do at some later time in their current lives. These two contrasting styles are diagrammed schematically in Figure 16–2.

The support scale measures the extent to which a person is characteristically other or outer oriented as compared to self or inner oriented (cf. Reisman, Glazer, & Denney, 1950). The scale's score is presented as a ratio between other and inner orientation; as with the time scale, the ratio indicates that people use both orientations in their lives and thus it is most meaningful to view their support orientation as the extent to which they are other oriented relative to inner oriented. An *inner,* or self, *orientation* is characterized by one's behavior being governed primarily by internalized principles and motives; inner directedness is associated with autonomy, self-support, individuality, and freedom. An *other orientation* is characterized by one's behavior primarily being influenced by social norms and pressures and other external factors; other directedness is associated with dependence, conformity, and desire for approval and acceptance.

Self-actualizers tend to have a mixture of both support orientations although, as would be expected, they tend to be more inner directed than other directed, in a ratio of about 3 : 1. This contrasts with the close to an even balance between inner and other orientation in nonself-actualizers (i.e., approximately a 1 : 1 ratio).

Interpretation of POI involves examining the pattern of scores obtained on the 12 scales. As with the MMPI, a profile is plotted on a psychogram. Often the subscales are grouped into complementary pairs to facilitate interpretation. These pairs, which are identified in Table 16–5, represent characteristics of self-actualization that tend to be synergistic (work together) and represent a balance which is critical to self-actualization. For example, acceptance of aggression and capacity

FIGURE 16–2
Schematic representation of the difference between time competence (living in the present), which is characteristic of self-actualizers, and time incompetence (living in the past and future), which is characteristic of nonself-actualizers.

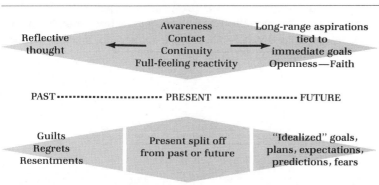

Source: Adapted from Shostrom, E. L. *Manual for the Personal Orientation Inventory.* San Diego: EdITS, 1974, p. 14.

for intimate contact may be viewed as complementary qualities. "It is possible to be either assertive and aggressive or warm and loving in human contacts. Both are expressions of good interpersonal contacts and both may be considered to reflect the general area of interpersonal sensitivity" (Shostrom, 1974, p. 18). Adequate interpretation of the POI requires an understanding of the inventory and its rationale as well as familiarity with the theoretical concepts of self-actualization.

One of the major uses of the POI has been in the evaluation of encounter-group experiences in which the fundamental goal is usually related to increasing participants' self-actualization. The availability of an objective measure such as the POI to assess a significant aim of encounter groups clearly represents a forward step because encounter-group research has had a history of subjectivity (as well as of methodologically flawed studies). In the typical study, participants are administered the POI before and after their encounter-group experience, and sometimes these pre-post changes are compared to parallel changes in a control group of subjects. For example, Guinan and Foulds (1970) investigated the changes in self-actualization qualities among "normal" college students who volunteered for a 30-hour weekend marathon experience, and compared them to changes in a control group of students who volunteered to participate in "an experiment." Comparison of the pre- and post-POI scores indicated that the students who participated in the marathon group showed significant changes in the direction of self-actualization on 7 of the 12 POI scales, whereas there were no significant changes for the control group students. However, some caution in interpreting these results is necessary because of an interesting finding that, as a group, the students who volunteered for the marathon experience tended to be less self-actualized, as measured by the POI, than the students who volunteered for the experiment. Specifically, the marathon subjects were more other directed, less spontaneous, had lower self-regard and self-acceptance, and had greater difficulty developing interpersonal relationships than did control subjects. Thus, the failure to obtain any significant pre-post changes in the direction of self-actualization among the control subjects may have been due to a ceiling effect (i.e., because they were higher on the POI scores, there was less chance of increasing their scores).

The psychology of personal constructs

The third phenomenological theory of personality we shall discuss, George A. Kelly's (1905–1967) *theory of personal constructs,* differs in a number of respects from Rogers and Maslow's self-actualization approaches. Nonetheless, Kelly's theory shares many of the same philosophical roots and is clearly a representative example of the phenomenological strategy.

After receiving his degree in experimental psychology from the University of Iowa in 1931, Kelly had planned to pursue his interests in physiological psychology. But, at the time, the country was in the midst of its greatest economic depression, and there was a vast need for psychologists to deal with the myriad psychological problems associated with these hard times. Accordingly, Kelly began his career as a "clinical" psychologist with very little background in personality or abnormal psychology (which may be one of the factors that led to his distinctly unique theory of personality).

Relying on the pragmatism which he had acquired during his youth on a midwestern farm, Kelly experimented with a variety of therapy and assessment procedures in his early years as a "converted" clinical psychologist, adopting those that worked and discarding those that did not. A significant example involved his use of traditional Freudian interpretations to help his clients. Although Kelly was having some success using them, he began to feel that their accuracy was less important in helping his clients change than was the fact that the interpretations allowed his clients to view themselves and their problems in a different way. To test out this hunch, Kelly (1969) tried an informal experiment which he describes as follows:

> I began fabricating "insights." I deliberately offered "preposterous interpretations" to my clients. Some of them were about as un-Freudian as I could make them—first proposed somewhat cautiously, of course, and then, as I began to see what was happening, more boldly. My only criteria were that the explanation account for the crucial facts as the client saw them, and that it carry implications for approaching the future in a different way. (p. 52)

Eventually Kelly came to the conclusion that therapist interpretations were unnecessary because all persons have their own interpretations—

George A. Kelly

National Library of Medicine

which he called personal constructs—and behavioral changes in therapy could be effected by helping clients change these interpretations (i.e., helping them view their worlds somewhat differently).

As a psychologist, Kelly was in the business of attempting to predict and control human behavior. In the midst of this endeavor, he found something paradoxical about the way personality psychologists studied people. It was as if the psychologist stood in another world looking down on alien beings who were the subject of investigation, examining these foreign specimens systematically, generating hypotheses about their behavior, and then testing these hypotheses in research. The psychologist went about this business in an intellectual, rational fashion. The people being studied, however, were supposed to be neither rational nor intellectual; rather, they were assumed to be impelled by dark, mysterious forces which were entirely irrational.

But it is elitist, at the very least, to think that psychologists have more of a special claim on intellectual and rational powers than have any other human beings. Furthermore, all persons have a need to predict events, especially interpersonal events—what other people will do or say, or how they will react in particular situations. Thus, it is not unreasonable to hypothesize, as Kelly eventually did, that all people, in their daily interactions with other persons and in the events in their lives, might behave in much the same way as personality psychologists do in their work. In other words, it may be that we all think (theorize) about events, advance predictions (hypotheses) about those events which affect us, and test out these predictions (albeit in a much less formal way than is the case for psychologists).

Consider that a young boy who has not received the second helping of ice cream he wants and, in an effort to secure it, cuddles up with tearful eyes to a visiting grandparent can be viewed as a scientist at work. The child is acting on the theory, however implicit it may be, that grandparents are likely to be beguiled by affection and also that they tend to be more lenient with second portions of dessert than parents are. His hypothesis might be: "I have a better chance of getting that ice cream if I play on grandpa's sympathy." He could then proceed to test this prediction by tearfully snuggling up to his grandfather. If it turns out that grandpa somehow succeeds in securing the ice cream for him, then the hypothesis is confirmed and the theory receives some support. In the future the child will be more confident in using this theory. If, however, grandpa is not as soft as his grandson thought he was or is not capable of convincing the parents that a second helping would do no harm, then the hypothesis is not supported. In this case, the child may very well try a new strategy the next time ice cream is served for dessert.

The observation that humans are constantly involved in the prediction and control of events in their lives led Kelly to view people *as if they were scientists*. All people, like scientists, have many theories about the nature of events in the real world, and it is through these theories that they deal with their environment. (Recall the discussion of implicit theories of personality in Chapter 1.) Kelly has assumed, it should be noted, that events in the real world actually have existence. That is, they do not exist just in the mind. At the same time, people's theories, or concepts, of these real events also have existence, and can be the subject of scientific investigation.

Kelly (1955) suggested that "man looks at his world through transparent patterns or templets which he creates and then attempts to fit over the realities of which the world is composed" (pp. 8–9). Kelly called these templets *constructs.* A construct is a representation of some event in the person's environment, a way of looking at something which is then tested against the reality of the environment. Constructs are not abstracted from existing realities; rather, they are imposed *upon* real events: *a construct comes from the person who uses it, not from the event it is being used to construe.*

Examples of constructs include "just vs. unjust," "stable vs. changing," "liberal vs. conservative," "healthy vs. sick," "flexible vs. dogmatic," "warm vs. aloof," and "friendly vs. hostile." It is important to note that Kellian constructs always take the form of one characteristic versus another (often opposite) characteristic. In Kelly's terms, constructs are *bipolar* (i.e., they have two poles or ends) and *dichotomous* (i.e., they are divided into two elements), which implies that when a construct is used, only one pole is being applied. This will be discussed in detail later in the chapter.

Everyone has his or her own set of unique *personal constructs*. It is only because of the inability of our language to express subtle nuances of meaning that constructs, when they are made explicit in speech or writing, appear to be the same for many different people. For example, most of us use a construct that we would label "good vs. bad," but that construct has a slightly different meaning for each person. Thus it is necessary to understand a person's constructs from that individual's unique perspective (which is the crux of the phenomenological strategy).

Constructs are used to *construe,* or place an interpretation or meaning on, events. The term *event* is used by Kelly to refer to anything going on in a person's life, and essentially has the same meaning as "experience" has for Rogers (see Chapter 15). In construing an event, a person hypothesizes that a particular construct will adequately fit the event and then puts this hypothesis to the test by interacting with

PERSONAL CONSTRUCTS: THE BASIC UNITS OF PERSONALITY

the event, be it interpersonal or material in nature, in the manner dictated by the construct. The little boy in the previous example acted in accordance with his construct "Grandparents are benevolent" by first making a specific prediction from this construct (i.e., that he would get a second helping of ice cream by cajoling grandpa) and then acting upon the prediction to test its validity. If a prediction is confirmed, the construct from which it was derived receives support and is therefore maintained as useful. If the construct leads to incorrect predictions, then it is likely to undergo some revision or it may even be discarded altogether. The measure which is used to assess the validity of a construct is its *predictive efficiency*. The more successful a construct is in anticipating events, the greater is its predictive efficiency.

Constructive alternativism: Freedom from one's biography

Kelly's psychology of personal constructs is based on the philosophical position of *constructive alternativism:*

> there are always some alternative constructions available to choose among in dealing with the world. No one needs to paint himself into a corner; no one needs to be completely hemmed in by circumstances; no one needs to be the victim of his biography. (Kelly, 1955, p. 15)

This position, one of free will, strikingly contrasts with the deterministic views of Freud, who saw each person as having an unchangeable, partially universal "construct system." According to Freud, people are very much victims of their biological endowments (i.e., they are born with universal drives) and their experiences in the first few years of life. Kelly, on the other hand, believed that each person has a unique system of constructs and always has the option of changing these ways of construing the world. In fact, according to Kelly, our outlooks (constructs) rarely are the same today as they were yesterday. The inevitable failure of our constructs from time to time to successfully anticipate future events makes their revision necessary if we are to construe the world with high predictive efficiency. The constructs that undergo the most frequent modification are those that make predictions concerning events in the near future and therefore result in rapid feedback concerning their ability to anticipate.

Although events have reality in and of themselves, they do not belong to any construct in particular. In line with constructive alternativism, the same event can be viewed from a variety of different perspectives. One interesting example of how different a situation becomes when it is construed from a different construct involved a patient in a psychiatric hospital (Neale, 1968). The patient's behavior was among the most deviant on the ward, as evidenced by her unintelligible speech, extremely poor personal habits, ludicrous behavior in the presence of other patients and visitors, and occasional violent outbursts. One day the aides dressed the patient in an attractive outfit, including nylon stockings, high heels, lipstick, and makeup, and took her to the beauty parlor to have her hair styled and set. When she returned to the ward several hours later, the patient no longer showed any of the blatantly abnormal symptoms which had become her trademark. Yet, she was still a patient in a psychiatric hospital, and in every other respect her circumstances remained unchanged. It was obvious from her behavior that the way she construed herself had definitely changed, if only temporarily, and her new self-concept resulted in new behavior.

Each of our constructs is useful for construing a particular set of events. This *range of convenience,* as these particular events are called, puts a limit on the usefulness of the construct. The construct "religious vs. not religious" can be used to construe a variety of human behaviors, but it is hardly applicable for talking about the relative merits of American and European sports cars. It is often tempting to generalize beyond the range of convenience of a construct, but inevitably this results in lowered predictive efficiency.

Although all constructs have a limited range of convenience, the breadth of the range may vary substantially from construct to construct. The construct "good vs. bad" can be used to construe most events in which evaluation is possible, and thus it has a wide range of convenience. Contrast this with the construct "brave vs. cowardly," which is considerably narrower in its scope of application.

Each construct also has a *focus of convenience,* which is the point in the construct's range of convenience at which it is maximally predictive. For example, the focus of convenience of the construct "religious vs. not religious" might be the customs and ceremonies of a church. Although cheating on an examination could be construed as "not religious," it would be more efficiently construed by the construct "honest vs. dishonest." Cheating is an event that is within the *range* of convenience of both constructs, but it is the *focus* of convenience only of the latter construct. If we wanted to anticipate Fred's future behavior in a variety of situations, it would be more useful to construe his using concealed class notes during a final examination via the construct "honest vs. dishonest" than via the construct "religious vs. not religious." Using the construct "religious vs. not religious," it would be difficult to predict the frequency of Fred's church attendance from his behavior during the final examination. Presumably, however, using the construct "honest vs. dishonest" would make it easier to anticipate whether Fred would use his brother's old term paper if he needed an "A" in a course.

Constructs also vary on a dimension of *permeability*. A permeable construct is one that is able to admit newly encountered events to

Properties of constructs

its range of convenience. An impermeable construct is one that has already been used to construe all the events in its range of convenience and therefore is closed to construing new experiences. One person's construct of "good vs. bad symphonic music" might be sufficiently permeable to account for any new piece of music heard. For example, on hearing music produced by a Moog synthesizer for the first time, the person could construe it as either "good" or "bad." Another person's construct of "good vs. bad symphonic music" might be impermeable to any sounds other than those made by traditional orchestral instruments and therefore could not be used to construe Moog-synthesized music.

There are relative degrees of permeability; constructs range from those which can very easily construe new events to those which virtually exclude any new events. In actuality, few constructs are completely impermeable; the exception would be a completely concrete construct which, "if there were such a thing, would not be permeable at all, for it would be made up of certain specified events—those and no others" (Kelly, 1955, p. 79). Furthermore, the notion of permeability is relevant only to events in the range of convenience of the construct because, by definition, a construct is impermeable to any event outside its range of convenience. For instance, the range of convenience of "intelligent vs. stupid" includes some animals, ideas, and perhaps computers, and thus this construct is potentially permeable to animals, ideas, and computers. However, rocks and trees are not in the construct's range of convenience, which implies that it is impermeable to rocks and trees.

THE FUNDAMENTAL POSTULATE AND ITS COROLLARIES
The Fundamental Postulate

Kelly's theory is presented in the form of a basic postulate and a series of corollaries which follow from it.

Kelly's (1955) *Fundamental Postulate* states that: *"A person's processes are psychologically channelized by the ways in which he anticipates events"* (p. 46). The first two words of Kelly's fundamental postulate indicate that his theory is *holistic,* dealing with the whole individual and not with particular aspects which make up a person or groups of persons. The theory of personal constructs focuses on *processes* rather than on inert substances. Kelly believed that traditional concepts of motivation, which postulate various internal and external forces that either push or pull an individual, are redundant. Instead, he viewed the object of his study, human beings, as already behaving (motivated) organisms. Kelly's system is *psychological* and therefore limits its range of convenience to the investigation of human behavior. The word *channelized* denotes the stability of behavior; behavior remains relatively stable across time and situations because it is directed by means of the constructs *(ways)* a person uses to predict *(anticipate)* actual happenings *(events)* in the future. Although Kelly rejected the traditional psychological view of motivation, it appears that his Fundamental Postulate is actually a motivation-like statement. As Kelly construed human behavior, the "motive" to predict future events is what directs people's activities.

The Construction Corollary

The *Construction Corollary* says: "A person anticipates events by construing their replications" (Kelly, 1955, p. 50). In other words, we predict future events by viewing them in terms of *recurrent themes* (replications) which we have come to expect with regard to similar events in the past. No two events are ever exactly the same (e.g., according to the old adage, one can never step into the same river twice), but events can be very similar. More importantly, our construction (interpretation) of similar events can, and indeed must, be the same (Kelly, 1970). Otherwise, we would live in an utterly chaotic world where nothing would be predictable. If we did not construe most of the events in our daily lives as similar to past events, we would be in the untenable situation of having to "start from scratch" in dealing with hundreds of events each day. To realize just how unlivable this would be, think about the occasions in which you have been faced with what seemed like a totally new event and were at a complete loss as to how to deal with it. In fact, this may never have occurred in your life; if it has, it was no doubt very upsetting. Perhaps the most common examples of such an occurrence, albeit still relatively rare, involve catastrophies such as returning home one evening to find one's house and all of one's possessions totally destroyed by fire. Since nothing similar to that is likely to ever have occurred previously, the person has no way of knowing how to react. In Kellian terms, the person has no constructs to construe the events.

Fortunately, under normal circumstances, new events can be dealt with by construing them using the same constructs which were used to construe similar events in the past. One's task is to search for those themes or characteristics of the events which remain relatively stable over time and circumstances. We then anticipate events by construing those aspects of the events that do recur consistently.

The process of construing involves perceiving not only the similar features which an event has over time, but also those features which are *not* characteristic of it. That is, a construct must specify both similarities and contrasts. If you think of some of your own personal constructs, you may not immediately see that differences are implied along with similarities. Constructs such as "good people," "pretty girl," "happy occasion," and "funny movie" appear at the outset to be referring only to similarities among events. However, the contrasts (i.e., "bad people," "homely girl," "sad occasion," and "serious movie") are implicitly there, and must be there, for the construct to be at all useful in anticipating events. In the example of the little boy who wanted more ice cream, the construct was actually "grandpa is benevolent vs. grandpa is not benevolent," although the opposite pole ("grandpa is not benevolent") remained implicit.

Although the *contrast* is often implicitly present when we employ a construct, it is a *sine qua non* and therefore must be capable of being made explicit. Consider the constructs "happy vs. sad" and "good vs. bad" in relation to "happy vs. euphoric" and "good vs. non-Christian." To state only one of the construct's poles is insufficient; in the present examples, the second set of constructs is as legitimate as the first. The opposite of a concept often differs with the way a person construes things.

The verbal label one puts on a construct should not be confused with the construct itself. The former is generally necessary when a person needs to communicate the construct to others. But all of us have many *nonverbal constructs* to which labels in the form of communicable language cannot be applied. Although this may be because the constructs are not well specified, more often than not it is due to the limitations of our language. Children's constructs are frequently at a preverbal level, though they may be no less predictively efficient than those of adults. Furthermore, the fact that two constructs have the same label does not necessarily mean that they are equivalent, just as the fact that two constructs are given different labels does not necessarily mean that the constructs are different.

The Individuality Corollary

In the *Individuality Corollary,* which states that "persons differ from each other in their construction of events" (1955, p. 55), Kelly emphasized that each person has a set of unique personal constructs. As shown schematically in Figure 17–1, no two people observing the same event will have exactly the same interpretation of it. All qualities, not just beauty, are in the eyes of the beholders. Is it any wonder that interpersonal communication is often so difficult and that there is so much disagreement among persons?

> Examples abound. Consider the traditional differences of opinion between political liberals and conservatives on such issues as welfare, military spending, abortion, taxation, forced racial integration, pornography, and capital punishment. Or reflect on why students may disagree with professors, professors with department chairpersons, department chairpersons with deans, and everybody with college presidents. Or what

FIGURE 17–1
The same life events are viewed somewhat differently by different persons because they are perceived through unique individual constructs which are analogous to variously hued spectacles.

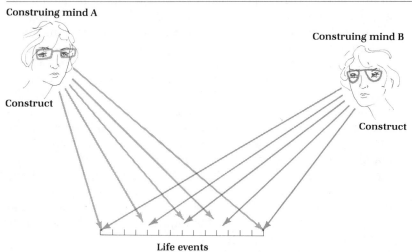

Construing mind A

Construct

Construing mind B

Construct

Life events

Source: Adapted from Rychlak, J. The psychology of personal constructs. In *Introduction to personality and psychotherapy.* Boston, Houghton Mifflin, 1973.

is popularly called the "generation gap"—the fundamental differences of viewpoint between parents and their offspring—a situation which, in Kelly's theory, might more properly be labeled a "personal construct gap." (Hjelle & Ziegler, 1981, p. 333)

The Dichotomy Corollary

The *Dichotomy Corollary,* which says, "A person's construct system is composed of a finite number of dichotomous constructs" (Kelly, 1955, p. 59), emphasizes the *bipolar* and *dichotomous* nature of personal constructs. A construct must specify both similarity and difference in order to be able to construe the replication of events.

The necessity of having a contrast or opposite to a concept for the concept to have meaning was mentioned earlier. If this is not readily apparent, consider the fact that your appreciation and even knowledge of physical health is only possible because you are occasionally sick (and observe others' illnesses).

Because a construct always indicates how some events are like or different from other events, a minimum of three events are required to construe any event: the event being construed, a second event which is similar to it (i.e., which it replicates), and a third event which is different from the first two. For example, Paul takes a bite of pizza and declares it (construes it as) "tasty." To make this interpretation,

Paul is implicitly comparing the pizza to at least one other pizza (or similar food) which he considered "tasty" and contrasting it to at least one other pizza (or similar food) which he considered "bland." His concept of "tasty" pizza would have no meaning without both the comparison (replication) and contrast. If he had never tasted a pizza or similar food before, then he would not have been able to consider it "tasty." Furthermore, if he had only had pizza which he considered tasty, then he could not make any comparison with bland pizza which would mean that he could only have used a construct such as "pizza vs. not pizza."

One pole of a construct indicates similarity and is called the *emergent pole,* and the other pole indicates difference and is called the *implicit pole.* In the previous example, "tasty" was the emergent pole and "bland" was the implicit pole of the construct "tasty vs. bland." If Paul had considered the pizza "bland," then the poles would have been reversed, with "bland" being the emergent pole and "tasty" being the implicit pole. Thus, the emergent pole is the one that is being used directly to construe the event, and the implicit pole is the one that is being used indirectly as a contrast.

Kelly considered the poles of a construct to be discrete or mutually exclusive. Thus, a construct is bipolar but it is *not* a continuum. Practically, if a construct is relevant to a particular event (i.e., if the event is in its range of convenience), then the event must be construed at *either* one pole of the construct *or* the other—and not somewhere in between. The dichotomous nature of constructs is perhaps the most controversial aspect of Kelly's formal propositions. The notion that human thought is dichotomous rather than continuous is at variance with most contemporary theories of thinking.

No problem arises with employing a dichotomy in the case of a construct in which the difference between the poles is unequivocal, as is usually the case with "male vs. female." But although things may be either black or white, they are most often a shade of gray (i.e., neither black nor white). Kelly (1955) was aware of this problem and explained how constructs, which are composed of mutually exclusive alternatives, can be used relativistically: ". . . dichotomous constructs can be built into scales, the scales representing superordinate constructs [see discussion of the Organization Corollary below] which are further abstractions of the separate scalar values. Thus, *more grayness vs. less grayness* is a further abstraction of the construct *black vs. white*" (p. 66).

The implicit pole of a construct includes only contrasting events and *not,* as in classical logic, both irrelevant events and contrasting events. In other words, events which are placed at the implicit pole must be in the construct's range of convenience. Suppose one were using the construct "friendly vs. unfriendly" and "friendly" were the emergent pole. The implicit pole "unfriendly" could be used to construe people, pets, and some places (e.g., a friendly atmosphere), but it would not make sense to use it to construe luggage, linen, and lollipops because the latter are not within the range of convenience of the construct.

The Range Corollary

Not only do people have a *finite* number of constructs, but, according to the *Range Corollary,* "a construct is convenient for the anticipation of a finite range of events only" (Kelly, 1955, p. 68). That a construct's range of convenience is finite implies that people may encounter events which they are not able to construe, and this may occur for one of two reasons. Either a person has no applicable construct to interpret the event, or the person's existing constructs are too impermeable to admit the new event. When we cannot construe an event, we experience anxiety.

Anxiety. The vague feeling of helplessness which we commonly denote as anxiety can be viewed as a result of being unable to anticipate an event because one's available constructs do not apply. When this occurs, the person cannot fully comprehend what is happening because the event exists without a reference point or meaning. Hence, although anxious individuals feel apprehensive or afraid, they are unable to "put their finger" on why they feel that way.

The prevalent view of neurotic behavior holds that anxiety is a major causative factor (e.g., Freud's position, Chapters 5 and 6). If we accept this view as valid, it is interesting to see how the notion is translated into the concepts of the psychology of personal constructs. Anxious persons, rather than being the victims of inner conflicts and dammed-up energy (the psychoanalytic interpretation of neurosis), are overwhelmed by happenings in life which they cannot understand (anticipate). From that perspective, psychotherapy then becomes a process in which the patient acquires new constructs which will successfully predict the troublesome events or make already existing constructs more permeable so as to admit the new events. This process will be discussed more fully in a later section.

The Organization Corollary

For Kelly, the units of personality are personal constructs. The structure or organization of personality is determined by the relationship of the constructs to one another. This point is presented in the *Organization Corollary:* "Each person characteristically evolves, for his convenience in anticipating events, a construct system embracing ordinal relationships between constructs" (1955, p. 56). People not only differ in the constructs they use, but, perhaps even more important, they differ in the way they organize their constructs. It is possible for two people to have similar personal constructs yet have extremely different personalities because their constructs are ordered differently.

Within one's personal construct system, constructs are arranged in a hierarchical structure, with most constructs being both subordinate to some constructs and superordinate to others. This type of organization makes it possible for an individual to move from one construct to another in an orderly fashion and to resolve conflicts and inconsistencies among constructs. Consider the relationships among three of David's constructs which are depicted in Figure 17–2. The construct "loving vs. unloving" is superordinate to the constructs "giving vs. selfish" and "pleasant vs. unpleasant," which, for David, are on the same hierarchical level. David has planned to spend the day at the beach with his friends and is faced with the dilemma of deciding whether to take along his younger brother as his mother requested. If his brother should go with them, David would construe himself as "giving" but the day at the beach as "unpleasant." On the other hand, if he chooses to leave his brother at home, David would construe himself as "selfish" but the day as "pleasant." To resolve this conflict between two of his constructs, David uses the superordinate construct "loving vs. unloving" to construe the situation. Both "giving" and "pleasant" are subsumed under the "loving" pole of the superordinate construct, which makes it possible for David to construe the event as both "giving" and "pleasant."

In the example of David's personal construct hierarchy, one of the poles of each of the subordinate constructs was subsumed under one of the poles of the superordinate construct (see Figure 17–2 and the text). Another possible hierarchical structure would be for both poles of a subordinate construct to be subsumed under one of the poles of a superordinate construct. Both possibilities are illustrated in Figure 17–3.

A construct system—the ordinal relationships among constructs—is somewhat more permanent than individual constructs, but it can change. Sometimes there is even a reversal of superordinate and subordinate constructs. In the previous example, "giving vs. selfish" might become superordinate to "loving vs. unloving." Since a person's construct system develops for his or her convenience in anticipating events,

FIGURE 17–2

An example of a hierarchical structure among three personal constructs

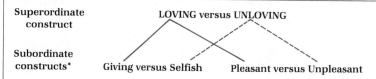

Superordinate
   construct

Subordinate
   constructs*

FIGURE 17–3
Examples of two types of hierarchical structures of personal constructs: *(a)* two poles
of the same construct are subsumed under one pole of a superordinate construct;
and *(b)* both poles of the same subordinate construct are subsumed under one pole
of a superordinate construct.

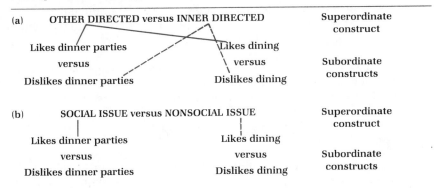

predictive efficiency is the criterion which determines the relative merit
of one hierarchical order of constructs over another.

The Choice Corollary and elaboration of a construct system

To predict a person's behavior, it is necessary to know not only
what construct the person will use to construe the relevant events
but also which of the two poles of the dichotomous construct will be
employed. Kelly (1970) dealt with this latter problem in his *Choice
Corollary:* "A person chooses for himself that alternative in a dichoto-
mized construct through which he anticipates the greater possibility
for the elaboration of his system" (p. 15).

There are two basic ways in which people can elaborate their construct system and thereby enhance its ability to anticipate events—
by defining it more precisely and by extending its range of convenience
to new events. The meaning of definition and extension of a construct
system can be understood in terms of two different kinds of wagers
with respect to the anticipation of events. "Definition" involves a relatively safe wager with a modest payoff, while "extension" involves a
riskier bet but with a more substantial payoff.

In the case of *definition*, the person chooses the pole of the construct
that has in the past led to the more accurate prediction of events similar
to the present one and therefore has the higher probability of predicting
the present event. If the prediction is accurate, the construct becomes
more explicit or precise by virtue of its having made an additional
successful prediction.

Extension involves choosing the alternative which has the greater
probability of expanding the construct so as to include new events

(i.e., increasing its range of convenience). In extension, the construct is being used either to anticipate a new event or to anticipate a familiar event in a new way, and therefore the probability of success is less than it is when definition is the goal. However, if the prediction proves to be correct, then the construct becomes more comprehensive.

Kelly (1955) spoke of the difference between definition and extension as one between security and adventure.

> Internal conflict . . . is often a matter of trying to balance off the secure definiteness of a narrowly encompassed world against the uncertain possibilities of life's adventure. One may anticipate events by trying to become more and more certain about fewer and fewer things or by trying to become vaguely aware of more and more things on the misty horizon. (p. 67)

The difference between definition and extension can be seen with respect to a college professor's use of the construct "intellectual vs. emotional." Not surprisingly, the professor has most frequently dealt with events in her life intellectually rather than emotionally, and she has been relatively successful in anticipating events using the "intellectual" pole of the construct. Behaviorally, this has meant that she evaluates events in terms of how useful or valuable in the long-run they might be rather than dealing with events on an emotional level by responding in terms of her "gut-level" impressions, what feels good or right at the time. Thus, when an event falls within the range of convenience of her construct "intellectual vs. emotional," using the "intellectual" pole to construe the event will probably result in anticipating the event with a high degree of precision as well as making her feel comfortable and confident because she is "in familiar territory." At the same time, she is not likely to gain much new experience construing the event in a way with which she is quite familiar and is already proficient. (The issue of "experience" will be discussed in the next section.) By way of contrast, construing an event via the "emotional" pole could add substantially to her experience, since she would be viewing the event differently than she is accustomed to. However, there is a greater chance that she will poorly anticipate the event and that she will feel uneasy and hesitant because the "emotional" pole is the less tried and proven one.

Suppose the professor were asked out for a date by a man she happened to meet while waiting to have her car repaired. In the course of a quite pleasant conversation, she learned that the man was a construction worker and a semiprofessional athlete. Although neither of these two facts was compatible with her academic and sedentary life (obviously an intellectual evaluation), she felt very much at ease with the man and found herself very attracted to him (an emotional reaction). If the professor uses her construct "intellectual vs. emotional" to construe the date (i.e., to anticipate the future event), she is faced with the choice of which pole to use. It is likely that an intellectual evaluation, which would involve definition, will result in an accurate prediction: namely that the man is not an appropriate date for her (e.g., no long-term, serious relationship could result). Choosing to construe the date emotionally would involve extension, and following her feelings certainly would be the riskier alternative, because she has less experience using that pole of the construct. On the other hand, she just might have a wonderful time and be pleased that she accepted the date and/ or she might learn something about new activities and find that she was more interested in them than she had ever realized.

Kelly's theory does not specifically address the issue of when people choose to define and when they choose to extend their construct systems, nor has any empirical research been specifically directed toward this important question. It is reasonable to speculate, however, that extension is more likely to occur when prediction of future events has been relatively successful and definition is more likely to occur when prediction has been relatively unsuccessful. For example,

> a young man is more likely to consider asking the new girl in town for a date when he has been relatively successful in his experiences with the old ones, and he is more likely to ask her when the proposed date is for a relatively familiar function. (Sechrest, 1963, p. 221)

Another hypothesis which follows from Kelly's theory is that, when people are anxious, they are more likely to define and when people are bored they are more likely to elaborate (Sechrest, 1977).

It is also possible that people may have characteristic styles, so that one person may typically prefer the conservative definition route while another may choose the riskier elaboration approach in most situations. Or it is possible that the same person may prefer definition in construing some aspects of his or her life (e.g., with respect to finances) but choose extension in other areas (e.g., with respect to recreation and relaxation).

Both definition and extension serve to elaborate a construct, and neither alternative is *ipso facto* the better choice. Elaboration of one's construct system frequently involves both definition and extension, allowing the individual to experiment (extension) in life and at the same time remain within a safe distance of proven constructs (definition). This strategy for elaboration protects the person from the threatening experience of having one's construct system undergo a major change and is analogous to making a moderately risky wager. Whichever path to elaboration is chosen, a person will use that pole of the personal construct which is more likely to elaborate the construct and enhance its efficiency in predicting future events.

Elaboration of one's construct system may come about when natural choice points or dilemmas present themselves. Or individuals may actively seek experiences which will elaborate their predictive system. The student who does extra work, takes more or unusual courses, asks questions and expresses opinions in large classes, and spends much time after class discussing material with teachers would exemplify active elaboration. So, too, would the woman who goes out of her way to meet men, to engage attractive males in conversation, and to arrange for her own dates rather than wait to be asked. In both cases the behavior is likely to be viewed as *aggressive*.

Aggression. For Kelly, aggression refers to the *active* elaboration of one's construct system. Aggression need not be hostile or antisocial in nature. In fact, aggression commonly has two distinct meanings—one involving hostility and attack and the other concerning assertiveness, boldness, and enterprise. Kelly viewed aggression in the latter sense, and, seen in this way, aggression can have definite positive and adaptive features. In the business world, for example, aggressiveness is the mark of a successful person or one who is labeled as a "comer."

In the course of actively pursuing the elaboration of one's construct system, a person may not take other people's welfare into account and, if that is the case, aggression may have injurious consequences. For instance, the student who talks to the instructor "endlessly" after class may be infringing on other students' opportunity to engage in similar discussions.

Active elaboration, or aggression, requires setting up choice points in one's life, making decisions, and taking action. Not infrequently, other people become inadvertently swept into this whirlwind of action and uncertainty with the result that they are threatened. Specifically, *threat,* in Kelly's theory, is the awareness that a major change in one's construct system is imminent.

> The aggressive person—for example the "social pusher"—keeps plunging himself and his associates into ventures which unduly complicate their well-ordered lives. The very fact that he insists on construing himself as belonging to the social group is threatening to those who are already identified with the group. They see, in their impending reciprocal identification with him, a major shift coming up in their own core structures. (Kelly, 1955, pp. 509–10)

The Experience Corollary: How a construct system changes

The purpose of a construct system is to anticipate future events as well as possible. If there were no problems in predicting events, then there would be no reason for making changes in one's construct system. But problems in prediction inevitably arise, particularly when new events must be construed. The more novel an event, and thus the less similar the event to previously construed events, the less likely it is that the new event can be effectively construed using one's existing constructs. To construe new events, it is often necessary to modify existing constructs (e.g., by making them more permeable), to rearrange the hierarchical order of one's constructs, or to add new constructs.

Kelly (1955) dealt with the change of a construct system in his *Experience Corollary:* "A person's construct system varies as he successively construes the replications of events" (p. 72). Like hypotheses derived from scientific theories, predictions made using constructs are tested to see how well they anticipate events. Constructs which make accurate predictions are typically retained in their existing form, whereas those which fall short of accurate prediction are modified or eliminated. This tends to be an ongoing process for most people, because life is full of novel events which must be anticipated. Thus, minor changes are occurring within our construct systems all the time. Only people who tend to have little variation in their daily lives have relatively stable construct systems (e.g., some elderly people who spend most of their time at home and lead highly structured, routine lives).

Experience had a special meaning for Kelly (1955), involving "successive construing of events. It is not constituted merely by the succession of events themselves" (p. 73). Emphasizing that humans are active, reacting organisms, Kelly (1955) observed:

> A person can be a witness to a tremendous parade of episodes and yet, if he fails to keep making something out of them, or if he waits until they have all occurred before he attempts to reconstrue them, he gains little in the way of experience from having been around when they happened. It is not what happens around him that makes a man experienced; it is the successive construing and reconstruing of what happens, as it happens, that enriches the experience of his life. (p. 73)

Applying Kelly's concept of experience, a teacher who delivers the same lectures year after year for eight years can only claim one year of teaching experience (rather than eight years).

An important implication of the Experience Corollary is that learning is a process (active) rather than an outcome (static). Learning is constantly going on as long as we are reconstruing events, as long as we are experiencing. For Kelly, learning is not a special process; like motivation, it comes with the person, so to speak. "It does not happen to a person on occasion; it is what makes that person in the first place" (Sechrest, 1977, p. 215).

The Modulation Corollary: When a construct system changes

The *Modulation Corollary* specifies the conditions under which change in a construct system can take place: "The variation in a person's construction system is limited by the permeability of the constructs within whose range of convenience the variants lie" (Kelly, 1955, p. 77). Permeability, it will be recalled, refers to the degree to which a construct is open to the interpretation of new events. The more permeable a person's constructs are, the greater is the change which can occur within the system. The Modulation Corollary specifically addresses itself to an even more basic idea: not only must persons construe the new event, but they must also be able to construe the change itself. The alteration of a construct or a group of constructs is an event, and thus, for the change to have any influence on people's behavior, they must already possess a superordinate construct which is capable of construing the change.

> At the present time, to point to an instance, many people in our society are undergoing a change of construction with respect to homosexuality, which has for a long time been construed largely in terms of such evaluative constructs as *good-bad, moral-immoral, strong-weak, and healthy-sick*. Now, however, different constructions are being applied, and, while it is difficult to specify both poles of the constructs, homosexuality is being construed as tolerable, nonthreatening, a matter of lifestyle, and as "normal" for certain people. For such changes in construction to occur, the Modulation Corollary states that there must be permeable constructs capable of making sense out of the change. One such construct might be something like *legitimate concerns of the public–legitimate private concerns*. If matters of morality or immorality are reconstrued from being public concerns to private concerns, then it may also be possible to reconstrue homosexuality as a private and tolerable lifestyle for some people and as not especially threatening to the lifestyles of other persons. Another superordinate construct within which change might be construed is *things people choose to be–things people become*. If evaluative constructs such as *good-bad* and *moral-immoral* make sense only when applied to people's chosen behaviors, and if homosexuality comes to be seen as a state of being rather than as a choice, the change from evaluative to nonevaluative constructions may be possible. (Sechrest, 1977, p. 215)

The Commonality Corollary

If, as was indicated by the Individuality Corollary, differences among people are due to differences in the way they construe events, it follows that similarity between people is a function of similarity in construing events. The *Commonality Corollary,* the Individuality Corollary's counterpart, states: "To the extent that one person employs a construction of experience which is similar to that employed by another, his processes are psychologically similar to those of the other person" (Kelly, 1970, p. 20). This corollary asserts that people's behaviors are governed by their constructs and that two people are likely to behave in similar ways to the extent that they construe events in similar ways.

It is important to make clear that we have not said that if one person has experienced the same events as another he will duplicate the other's psychological processes. . . . One of the advantages of this position is that it does not require us to assume that it would take identical events in the lives of two people to make them act alike. Two people can act alike even if they have each been exposed to quite different phenomenal stimuli. It is in the similarity in the construction of events that we find the basis for similar action, not in the identity of the events themselves. (Kelly, 1955, pp. 90–91)

An interesting implication of the Commonality Corollary concerns the nature of a culture. As the term *culture* is generally used, it refers to a group of people who exhibit similar behavior. Typically, the common behavior is thought to be the result of similarities in their upbringing and their environment. Kelly (1955) went several steps further: "People belong to the same cultural group, not merely because they behave alike, nor because they expect the same things of others, but especially because they construe their experience in the same way" (p. 94).

The Sociality Corollary

The *Sociality Corollary* sets forth the basic requirement for an interpersonal relationship: "To the extent that one person construes the construction processes of another, he may play a role in a social process involving the other person" (1955, p. 95). For Kelly, playing a role with respect to another person involves construing how the other person views events—that is, the role player must be attempting to understand part of the other person's construct system. Specifically, the role player is interested in how the other person views the role which is being played. For instance, a woman who wants to play the role of "student" in relation to her teacher must predict how the teacher construes "student behavior" and then act in accord with the predicted expectations. If the student thought that her teacher considered asking a lot of questions part of the student role, then she would presumably ask questions.

Interestingly, what is critical to Kelly's notion of role is that the role player is *attempting* to infer the other person's view of the world, and not that the role player is necessarily successful (Sechrest, 1977). Of course, the more accurate the role player's understanding of the other person's constructs, the more effective the role player will be in enacting the role. However, the role player need not construe events as the other person does; the role player must only have an understanding of the other's outlook.

The fact that two or more people are together, are conversing, are working on a mutual task is not sufficient to constitute an interpersonal relationship, according to Kelly. An interpersonal relationship requires that at least one of the parties is construing the other's perspective—

that is, playing a role with respect to the other person. However, role playing need not be reciprocal. Indeed, there are numerous one-sided relationships in our society (e.g., employee-employer, therapist-client, athlete-coach). An optimal relationship, of course, usually involves understanding of one another's views. This understanding may be limited in scope, as in the case of a student-professor relationship which is confined primarily to academic matters; or it may be extremely broad, covering most of each person's construct system, as in a good marital relationship.

People need not have the same constructs in order to be able to subsume the other's constructs within their own systems. As the Commonality Corollary suggests, it is, no doubt, easier to understand the way another person thinks if both share similar outlooks, but this is certainly not a requirement for effective role playing.

We play many different roles in our lives—friend, adversary, customer, colleague, student, teacher, lover, playmate. The majority of the roles we play are peripheral in the sense that they have little significance to what is really important to us. For instance, most of us frequently play the role of "customer," but with the exception of professional buyers, how well we play that role generally makes little difference. However, each of us plays a few roles which are central to our lives, roles which are at the core of our identity and essential to our self-concept. Kelly called these *core roles,* and how well we perform them does have important consequences for us.

Guilt.   When people become aware that they are deviating from one of their core roles, they experience *guilt,* according to Kelly. At the outset, this definition of guilt may seem quite odd and may not make any sense. To understand Kelly's notion of guilt, think about times that you have felt guilty. What made you feel guilty? Your answer is apt to be that you were doing something "wrong." One way to construe what was "wrong" is that you were not acting as you think you should have been or, more accurately, as you think someone else thought you should have been. In other words, you were not playing a particular role. Unless that role was important to you, you are not likely to have experienced guilt. Thus, feeling guilty can be viewed as a consequence of not behaving in accord with one of your core constructs. A person who considers his or her role as a "student" important (i.e., a core role) will feel guilty when he or she cuts classes, turns in assignments late, and studies insufficiently, because these behaviors are inconsistent with the "student role." Similarly, a young woman who considered herself a "good daughter" experiences guilt when she does not write to her parents, when she moves to a distant city, or when she brings home a male friend they don't approve of—all behaviors which deviate from her parents' expectations about how a "good daughter" should act.

Defining guilt in this nontraditional manner has the advantage of setting an important human experience apart from conventional notions of evil and punishment which are absolute, value-laden concepts. In personal construct theory, whether or not people feel guilty depends upon their core-role structure rather than upon some absolute standard of proper conduct (be it religious or cultural).

By now, it must be obvious to the reader that Kelly's definitions of such traditional personality concepts as guilt, aggression, and anxiety are very different from the definitions employed by other personality psychologists as well as from the common dictionary definitions. (Kelly's unique definitions of personality concepts are a good illustration of how people can vary in their views of the same phenomenon, and we may assume that his definitions represent what, for Kelly, were the most efficient ways to predict behavior.) The uniqueness of his definitions is partially due to their conspicuous independence from value judgments. This absence of evaluation, in combination with Kelly's insistence on understanding the personality of others by construing their constructs, is the essence of the phenomenological strategy.

THE ASSESSMENT OF PERSONAL CONSTRUCTS: THE ROLE CONSTRUCT REPERTORY TEST

If personality consists of one's personal construct system, then personality assessment must involve a description of personal constructs. Although personal constructs determine behavior, directly observing people's behavior may not yield valid information about how they are construing the relevant events. People may engage in the same behaviors despite their construing events in very different ways. Take the example of three men who play golf together on Saturday mornings. One of the men views golf as a competitive sport, and each week he looks forward to improving his score and beating his two opponents. For the second man the game of golf is more a means of socializing than an athletic event. The third man construes the Saturday morning golf games as an opportunity to be outdoors and get some exercise. It would be difficult to accurately predict each man's construction of the events taking place from observing his behavior alone.

It is important to digress briefly to stress an issue which is fundamental to the psychology of personal constructs. Of what practical use is knowledge of an individual's personal constructs, over and above knowledge of the individual's behavior? If our interest were only in predicting what each man in the previous example would probably be doing on the next Saturday morning, the behavioral observation might serve us well. However, knowing the way in which each man construes the Saturday golf game may enable us to predict how he would behave in other situations. For instance, we might predict that the first man would be competitive in his work as well as on the golf course if he uses the same construct to construe both work and golf.

Besides behavioral observation, another way to assess people's personal constructs would be to ask them directly. But constructs cannot always be communicated in words; when they can be, the meanings of the words are often too broad to give the assessor much specific information about the individual's personal constructs. Furthermore, people are usually not accustomed to communicating their personal constructs.[1]

Kelly devised a technique for the assessment of personal constructs which surmounts some of the problems associated with behavioral observation and direct inquiry. Called the *Role Construct Repertory Test (Rep Test)*, the technique elicits the constructs which persons use to construe the important people in their lives. (A *role construct*, as one might infer from the previous discussion of roles, is a construct that an individual uses to understand another's views and expectations.) A good way to learn about the Rep Test is to actually use the technique, as indicated in Demonstration 17–1, to explore some of your own personal constructs.

Demonstration 17–1

THE ROLE CONSTRUCT REPERTORY TEST

In the Rep Test you will be comparing and contrasting (a process called **sorting**) people (called **figures**) in your life in order to elicit the constructs which you use to construe them.

DESIGNATING FIGURES

Figure 17–4 is the "grid form" used for the Rep Test. First, draw on a large sheet of paper the grid form exactly as it appears in Figure 17–4. Note that each row of the grid has three circles; check to be sure that you have placed the circles for each row in the correct columns.

Next, turn to Table 17–1 which contains 15 role definitions. Read each definition carefully and then write, in the appropriate diagonal space at the top of your grid form, the first name of the person who best fits that role in your life. If you cannot remember the name of the person, put down a word or brief phrase that will bring the person to mind. Do *not* repeat any names; if some person has already been listed, simply make a second choice. Thus, next to the word **Self** write your own name. Then next to the word **Mother** put your mother's name (or the person who has played the part of a mother in your life; see Table 17–1). Continue until all 15 roles have been designated with the name of a specific individual.

---

[1] You may wish to ascertain the difficulty of this task by attempting to make a list of *your* personal constructs. It should be noted that you are in a substantially better position to do this than most people, since you have already had an introduction to the nature of personal constructs which included numerous examples of such constructs.

FIGURE 17–4
Sample grid form of the Rep Test for Demonstration 17–1.

Sort No.	Self 1	Mother 2	Father 3	Brother 4	Sister 5	Spouse 6	Pal 7	Ex-Pal 8	Rejecting Person 9	Pitied Person 10	Threatening Person 11	Attractive Person 12	Accepted Teacher 13	Rejected Teacher 14	Happy Person 15	EMERGENT POLE	IMPLICIT POLE
1									⊘	O		O					
2		O	O	O													
3				⊘								O		O			
4		O				O						⊘					
5	⊘								O		O						
6				O			O						O				
7			O				O			O							
8					O					O				O			
9						O	O				O						
10	O			O	O												
11		O	O							O							
12						O			O					O			
13	O					O	O										
14	O	O	O														
15				O					O					O			

SORTING FIGURES

Now look at the first *row* of the grid form. Note that there are circles in the squares under *columns* 9, 10, and 12. These circles designate the three people whom you are to consider in Sort No. 1 (i.e., Rejecting Person, Pitied Person, and Attractive Person). Think about these three people, and decide how *two of them are alike* in some important way that *differentiates them from the third person.* When you have decided the most important way in which two of the people are alike but different from the third person, put an "X" in each of the two circles which correspond to the two persons who are alike. Do *not* place any mark in the third circle; leave it blank.

Next, in the column marked "Emergent Pole," write a word or short phrase that tells how the two people are alike. Then, in the column marked "Implicit Pole," write a word or short phrase that explains the way in which the third person is different from the other two.

Finally, consider each of the remaining 12 persons and think about which of them, in addition to the two you have already marked with an "X," also have the characteristic you have designated under the "Emergent Pole." Place an "X" in the square corresponding to the name of each of the other persons who has this characteristic. When you have finished this procedure for the first row (Sort No. 1), go to the second row (Sort No. 2). The process should

TABLE 17–1
Definition of roles for Demonstration 17–1

1. *Self:* Yourself.
2. *Mother:* Your mother or the person who has played the part in your life.
3. *Father:* Your father or the person who has played the part in your life.
4. *Brother:* Your brother who is nearest your own age or, if you do not have a brother, a boy near your own age who has been most like a brother to you.
5. *Sister:* Your sister who is nearest your own age or, if you do not have a sister, a girl near your own age who has been most like a sister to you.
6. *Spouse:* Your wife (or husband) or, if you are not married, your closest present girlfriend or boyfriend.
7. *Pal:* Your closest present friend of the same sex as yourself.
8. *Ex-pal:* A person of the same sex as yourself whom you once thought was a close friend but in whom you were badly disappointed later.
9. *Rejecting person:* A person with whom you have been associated who, for some unexplained reason, appeared to dislike you.
10. *Pitied person:* The person whom you would most like to help or for whom you feel most sorry.
11. *Threatening person:* The person who threatens you the most or the person who makes you feel the most uncomfortable.
12. *Attractive person:* A person whom you have recently met whom you would like to know better.
13. *Accepted teacher:* The teacher who influenced you most.
14. *Rejected teacher:* The teacher whose point of view you have found most objectionable.
15. *Happy person:* The happiest person whom you know personally.

Source: Kelly, G. A. *The psychology of personal constructs.* New York: W. W. Norton, 1955.

be repeated until it has been carried out for each of the rows. In summary, the steps to be followed for each of the 15 rows (sorts) are:

1. Consider the three people who are designated by circles under their names. Decide how two of them are alike in an important way, and different from the third.
2. Put an "X" in the circles corresponding to the two people who are alike and leave the remaining circle blank.
3. In the "Emergent Pole" column, write a brief description of the way in which the two people are *alike.*
4. In the "Implicit Pole" column, write a brief description of the way in which the third person is *different* from the two who are alike.
5. Consider the remaining 12 persons and place an "X" in the squares corresponding to those who can also be characterized by the description in the "Emergent Pole" column.

DISCUSSION

By the time you have completed the Demonstration Rep Test, a number of its characteristics should be apparent. Think about how the Rep Test has elicited your constructs. What is the range of convenience of the constructs? Which constructs are relatively permeable, and which relatively impermeable? What relation do these constructs have with one another? Do the sorts compare people randomly, or is there a rationale behind each sort? Finally, you might ask yourself whether the Rep Test has given you any insights into the way you construe your interpersonal world.

The procedure of the Rep Test is similar to a concept-formation task. However, instead of sorting objects, respondents sort persons (figures) who play important roles in their lives. The particular sorts which the examiner asks the client to make will depend upon the purpose of the assessment procedure. The following are examples of sorts used in Demonstration 17–1, with a brief explanation of each (Kelly, 1955, pp. 275–76).

Sort no. 1

Valency sort. The client is asked to compare and contrast a person whose rejection of him he cannot quite understand, a person whom he thinks needs him, and a person whom he does not really know well but whom he thinks he would like to know better. All three of these are somewhat phantom figures, and one may expect that in interpreting them the client relies heavily upon projected attitudes.

Sort no. 3

Sister sort. This is an invitation to construe a Sister figure. It provides an opportunity to see the Sister as like the Accepted Teacher and in contrast to the Happy Person, like the Happy Person and in contrast to the Accepted Teacher, or in contrast to both of them.

Sort no. 5

Need sort. The Self is compared and contrasted with the Pitied Person and the Attractive Person. This gives the clinician an opportunity to study the relative subjective and objective reference which the client gives to personal needs.

Sort no. 7

Threat sort. The client has an opportunity to construe threat in the context of the Brother, Ex-Pal, and Threatening Person.

Sort no. 11

Parental preference sort. The Mother and Father are placed in context with the Threatening Person.

In the *grid form* of the Rep Test (e.g., Demonstration 17–1), a grid, or matrix, is constructed with significant people in the client's life on one axis and the constructs used to construe them on the other axis. At the intersection of each row and column (of each construct and role title) the client indicates whether the emergent pole (i.e., that pole which was emergent for the sort) of the construct applies to that person by placing an "X" there if it does. The absence of an "X" at a particular intersection indicates that the implicit pole is applicable. Each intersect then becomes either an *incident* (i.e., an "X" indicates that the emergent pole applies) or a *void* (i.e., a blank indicates that the implicit pole applies). The requirement that *either* one pole *or* the other apply to a figure is a direct consequence of the dichotomous nature of constructs. Because one of the basic assumptions of the Rep Test is that every construct applies to every figure, the client examines all of the figures and indicates whether or not the emergent pole can be used to construe each of them.

Several limitations of the Rep Test should be noted. First, the constructs elicited by the Rep Test are those which the person uses to construe the behavior of others. If the goal is to predict the behavior of the person taking the test, then it is necessary to ascertain whether the constructs the client applies to others apply to his or her own behavior as well (Sechrest, 1963).

Second, though the Rep Test requires that constructs be set down in words, constructs need not be verbalizable. Therefore, it cannot be assumed that the constructs elicited by the test represent all, or even the most important of the constructs the person uses to construe individuals in her or his life.

Third, even when people make their constructs more or less explicitly known by means of verbal labels which appear to have generally accepted meanings, one cannot be sure that the labels do, in fact, have common referents. Constructs such as "successful vs. unsuccessful," "attractive vs. unattractive," and "difficult vs. easy" have highly personalized meanings. Here it is critical to examine how the person uses constructs, as by looking at the pattern of incidents and voids in the grid form.

EVIDENCE FOR THE PSYCHOLOGY OF PERSONAL CONSTRUCTS

In this section, the nature of the evidence for several of the theoretical propositions of the psychology of personal constructs will be illustrated. We shall examine a few representative studies in order to exemplify the kinds of investigations which have arisen from Kelly's theory.

The Individuality Corollary

Kelly asserted, in his Individuality Corollary, that people differ from one another because, besides having had experience with different events, they construe events differently. Each person, then, has a set of *personal* constructs. It is legitimate to ask how stable or permanent persons' construct systems tend to be. To answer this question, Fjeld and Landfield (1961) asked subjects to take the Rep Test twice. The second time the test was administered, the subjects were instructed not to use the same figures they employed in the first Rep Test, and the trio of role titles which they compared also differed in the two administrations. Still, the constructs that subjects used in the two different Rep Tests tended to be the same, as evidenced by high retest reliability (correlation coefficient of +.79). Thus, there is some evidence that an individual's constructs are not only stable across time but are also relatively independent of the particular events being construed.

If each person has a unique set of constructs, then it follows that the optimal way to predict people's behavior would be to understand the individual's personal constructs as opposed to the constructs which other people use to describe them. To test this hypothesis, Payne (1956) had subjects, in groups of three, predict how the other two people in the triad would complete a questionnaire about social behavior. Each subject was given a list of 15 personal constructs of one of the partners and 15 constructs *about* the other partner from peer descriptions. Payne found that subjects were significantly more accurate at predicting how another person had responded to the questionnaire when they had access to the individual's *personal* constructs.

The Experience Corollary says that a person's views of the world change as the person reconstrues events over time. The corollary makes sense intuitively, and few psychologists, including those skeptical about personal construct theory, would doubt its validity. (This does not mean, however, that such obvious statements do not need to be tested empirically.) The real value of the Experience Corollary (and of the Individuality Corollary) is that it has stimulated research which has led to important extensions of the corollary. Three investigations which elucidate some of the conditions for construct change and the nature of that change will be discussed.

In a study of interpersonal perception, Bieri (1953) showed that social interaction between people will produce a change in the way they construe each other. In accordance with the standard design of studies of interpersonal perception, the subjects were first asked to fill out a questionnaire describing an aspect of their behavior. Then they were asked to predict another subject's answers to the questionnaire both before and after a discussion with the other subject. As predicted, subjects came to view the other person as more like themselves after their short social interaction.

Lundy (1952) provided an interesting explanation and extension of Bieri's findings in an investigation of the effect of increased social interaction on the perception of others. The subjects were six patients who were participating in group therapy over a period of four weeks. Each patient predicted the responses of the other five individuals on a questionnaire administered before and after the first session and once a week for the remaining three weeks. Lundy reasoned that before any social interaction occurred, the subjects could only guess how

The Experience Corollary

the others would answer the questionnaire. After a minimal amount of interaction, they would assume that the other persons were similar to themselves (Bieri's finding) in an effort to gain some structure. Only after the subjects had gotten to know one another better would they attempt to construe the others differently from themselves. The results supported these hypotheses.

A final illustration of research related to Kelly's theory is a study of changes during individual psychotherapy. Tippett (1959) used as subjects patients who had been in therapy at least three months between two administrations of the Rep Test. Tippett's results are particularly enlightening with regard to the predominant topics of discussion during therapy. When the therapist concentrated on the patient's past, the constructs which underwent the most change were those which were predominantly used to construe figures who are generally associated with a person's early life (e.g., parents). When the emphasis was on the present, constructs which were used to construe figures who are usually important to a person later in life (e.g., spouse) tended to be altered. The changes in constructs were evidenced both in the verbal labels applied to the constructs and in the pattern of application of the constructs to the figures.

PERSONALITY CHANGE

People seek help in making personality changes when they are dissatisfied with the way in which they are acting or feeling. From the point of view of personal construct theory, people are likely to become involved in some sort of psychotherapeutic process when they are having difficulty anticipating events in their lives. Such difficulty may take several forms.

One possibility is that people do not have constructs which can effectively construe new events. This frequently occurs when someone is thrust into a new life situation with little or no knowledge about how to act. Common examples would include going off to college (especially if this is one's first extended period of time away from home), starting on a new job, moving to a new town, getting married or divorced, and having a close relative die. In these cases, the individuals might have to develop new constructs which are appropriate to and capable of anticipating the new events in their lives.

In other instances, it may be sufficient to modify existing personal constructs to make them more predictively efficient. Often a person's views of events are too narrow, which results from using impermeable constructs. John earned good grades in high school with only a few hours of studying per week and construed "good grades with minimal studying" at the "bright" pole of his construct "bright vs. dumb student." When he finds that he is having to spend many more hours studying in college and is still not doing as well as he did in high school, he is confused. The new event, "lower grades and more studying," cannot be subsumed under the "bright" pole of the construct as he has defined it; at the same time, he does not consider himself to be a dumb student. The result is that he feels frustrated, becomes depressed when he thinks that he may not be as bright as he thought he was, and starts avoiding his schoolwork because he becomes anxious when he thinks about it. These "symptoms" are the by-product of an impermeable construct. Using his personal construct "bright vs. dumb student," he is not able to construe the new event in his life, namely, his doing less well academically and studying more hours than previously. However, instead of developing a completely new construct to anticipate his academic behavior, it may be sufficient to make his existing construct more permeable so that it will be capable of including his present behavior.

Sometimes constructs are inefficient because they are too permeable. This is likely to be the case when a person continues to use an obsolete construct which anticipated events in the past but is no longer appropriate in the present. For instance, construing one's parents as people whose wishes must be acceded to at all times may have been a useful construct when the person was 5 years old, but at age 25 the construct is likely to interfere with other events in one's life (e.g., demands of employer, spouse, friends). One solution to this not uncommon dilemma would be to make a construct such as "blind obedience vs. disrespect" less permeable by considering it appropriate for use only by five-year-old children. Since the individual can never be five years old again, this has the effect of "embalming a construct in literalistic impermeability" (Kelly, 1955, p. 592).

In keeping with the basic philosophical position of constructive alternativism, Kelly viewed psychotherapy as a future-oriented process. In general terms, the aim of psychotherapy is to help clients develop personal construct systems which will enable them to follow their own natural developmental process, much as Rogers advocates. Personality change is conceived as a continuing process of modification as opposed to a terminal state of well-being or an optimal static construct system. The therapist's role is to set the stage for such an ongoing program of construct revision by directly and indirectly providing the client with the model of a scientist who formulates hypotheses about future events, tests them, and then revises the theory (construct) in order to increase its predictive efficiency.

The personality change procedures which Kelly advocated do not attempt to change personal constructs directly. Rather, Kelly's general approach to modifying constructs involves effecting *changes in behavior* which, in turn, will lead to a reconstruction of events. According to Kelly, new behaviors which clients perform provide evidence of movement within their construct system; that is, new behaviors indicate that the clients are viewing the events in their lives somewhat differently. When this occurs, therapeutic progress has been made. Interestingly, Kelly's assumption that changes in behavior must occur before there can be lasting changes in personality (i.e., in one's construct system) is very much in keeping with the psychotherapeutic approach of the *behavioral* strategy discussed in Section 5.

Fixed-role therapy

The basic principle of changing behavior in order to modify one's construct system is illustrated by *fixed-role therapy,* a specific technique developed by Kelly. In fixed-role therapy, the client is asked to play the role of a fictitious person whose behavior is consistent with a construct system which the therapist believes would be beneficial for the client to adopt. The client first writes a self-characterization sketch and completes a number of self-descriptive personality tests, such as incomplete sentences and a Q-sort. On the basis of this information and knowledge of the client's problems, a panel of therapists writes a fixed-role sketch that describes the new role the client is asked to enact. The following is a fixed-role sketch written for a male client who characterized himself as *passive, self-conscious, shy, and occasionally interpersonally boring and who was having difficulties with his sex-role identity.*

> Dick Benton[2] is probably the only one of his kind in the world. People are always just a little puzzled as to how to take him. About the time they decide that he is a conventional person with the usual lines of thinking in religion, politics, school, etc., they discover that there is a new side to his personality that they have overlooked. At times, they think that he has a brand-new way of looking at life, a really *fresh* point of view. Some people go through an hour of conversation with him without being particularly impressed; while others find that afterwards they cannot get some of his unusual ideas out of their minds. Every once in a while he throws an idea into a discussion like a bomb with a very slow fuse attached. People don't get it until later.
>
> At times he deliberately makes himself socially inconspicuous. Those are the times when he wishes to listen and learn, rather than to stimulate other people's thinking. He is kindly and gentle with people, even on those occasions when he is challenging their thoughts with utterly new ideas. Because of this, people do not feel hurt by his ideas, even when they seem outrageous.
>
> He is devoted to his wife and she is the only person who always seems to understand what is going on in his mind.
>
> His work in college is somewhat spotted and the courses are interesting to him only to the extent that they give him a new outlook.

---

[2] Each fixed-role character is given a name in order to make the character more credible and to facilitate reference to the fixed role as opposed to the client's customary role.

All in all, Dick Benton is a combination of gentleness and intellectual unpredictability. He likes to take people as they are but he likes to surprise them with new ideas. (Kelly, 1955, p. 121)

The fixed role usually deals with only a few of the clients' constructs and thus is not aimed at making major personality changes. As a matter of fact, the fixed role often includes some of the client's positive attributes in order to bolster her or his efficient constructs and make the role easier and more realistic to enact.

Clients are not asked to be the person described in the fixed-role sketch, nor are they required to adopt the role as their own. They are merely requested to try *acting* the role for a period of time. What frequently occurs, though, is that clients stop thinking of their new behavior as a role and begin to consider it as their own, "natural" way of behaving. Clients often adjust their fixed role so that it is more consistent with their other behavior. The result of fully "getting into" the fixed role is that clients begin to adopt the constructs which underlie the fixed-role behavior.

In order to get a "feel" for what fixed-role therapy entails for the client, you may wish to do Demonstration 17–2.

A DEVIL'S ADVOCATE ANALOGUE TO FIXED-ROLE THERAPY

Demonstration 17–2

Formal debating involves supporting arguments that are either for or against a particular proposition. Competitive debaters must be able to defend a position whether they agree with it or not, and frequently they are assigned to argue for a proposition that is very alien to their own views. This situation is analogous to what a client is asked to do in fixed-role therapy, namely, behave in a manner consistent with a **new** set of constructs.

To do this Demonstration, first write down on index cards five propositions about important social issues with which you **strongly agree.** The more strongly you agree with the propositions and the more personal investment you have in them (e.g., as shown in your actions regarding them), the better able you will be to do this Demonstration. Each proposition should be written so that your position on the issue is clear. For example, if you believe that marijuana possession should not be illegal, you should write a statement such as "Possession of marijuana should be legalized" and **not** just "Marijuana laws" (which does not specify what your position on the issue is).

Next, shuffle the cards and "blindly" choose one of them.

Now, write down as many arguments as you can think of **against** the proposition you have stated. This may not be easy, particularly if it is a proposition about which you feel very positively. You may find it difficult to think of negative arguments, but keep trying. Or you may find yourself countering each of the negative arguments you write down; avoid this temptation. Instead, make every effort to assume a "devil's advocate" position and argue as strongly **against** the idea as you would prefer to argue for it.

An alternative way of doing this Demonstration is to actually debate the issue—arguing vehemently against it—with a friend who strongly agrees with the position (as you actually do).

In order to get a good "feel" for what a client experiences in fixed-role therapy, you should randomly select at least one more of the remaining issues you have written down for the Demonstration and devise arguments against it. Keep in mind that, in contrast to a client in fixed-role therapy, you are only verbalizing, not acting, in accord with new or alien constructs, and you are doing this for only a brief time, rather than consistently over the course of several days or weeks.

18 *The phenomenological strategy*

Liabilities

In this chapter we will discuss five broad criticisms of the phenomenological strategy. Critics have argued that (1) the phenomenological strategy is limited in the scope of the phenomena it studies; (2) phenomenological personality assessment places unjustified credence on self-reports; (3) phenomenological personality theory is more descriptive than explanatory; (4) phenomenological personality theory does not adequately explain the development of personality; and (5) the phenomenological approach is romantically naive.

The phenomenological strategy focuses on the person's conscious experiences of the moment and, in this emphasis, comes close to dealing with those aspects of human behavior which lay persons most often think should be the focus of psychological investigations—namely, their subjective experiences. Thus, the phenomenological strategy "makes sense intuitively" and is consistent with "common-sense" notions of personality.

However, concentrating on people's conscious, subjective experiences excludes from study any events of which a person is not immediately aware. Can a person's behavior be predicted accurately by knowing only what is in that person's phenomenal field? Can actions be explained without reference to past experiences and influences on which the person is not concentrating at the moment? Consider all the rules and principles we have learned in the past, rules about how we should act, what is considered acceptable behavior, when it is appropriate to act in particular ways. They influence our present behavior even though we are not aware of them at the time, and they are common examples of how events outside one's momentary phenomenal field influence behavior. Psychoanalysts would argue even more strongly that events which are out of a person's immediate awareness (i.e., unconscious), perhaps permanently, form the core of personality and play a crucial role in determining behavior.

The phenomenological strategy is limited by almost totally ignoring the influence of the past, focusing, as it does, on immediate, subjective experiences. Obviously, this is an extreme point of view and contrasts

THE PHENOMENOLOGI-CAL STRATEGY IS LIMITED IN SCOPE

with the psychoanalytic strategy which, at least in its traditional Freudian approach, is at the other extreme by placing almost complete credence on one's past. Neither perspective seems viable because each clearly disregards important variables in other time frames. Of course, phenomenologists realize that the past does affect a person's immediate experiences, but they do not account for it or explain the nature and extent of the influence. Furthermore, no attempt is made to examine an individual's past experiences even when they might be directly related to that person's present experiences. The assumption is that, if something in a person's past is important in the present, it will not only be salient in the person's present experiences, but the form it assumes in the present is all that is germane to an understanding of the individual's current personality functioning.

Phenomenological personality theories are also limited in their ability to predict specific behaviors. This is particularly true of personal construct theory which, on the surface, appears ironic in that the central theme of Kelly's theory is the prediction of future events. However, the theory deals more with persons anticipating other people's behavior than with their anticipating their own. Furthermore, in order to predict how an individual will behave in a given situation, it would be necessary to know not only what his or her constructs were but also which construct(s) the person would use to construe the ongoing events. Nowhere in his theory does Kelly address that critical issue. Rogers' self-actualization theory also presents problems in predicting specific behaviors because, in order to do so, it is necessary to have a reasonably comprehensive understanding of the individual's unique self-actualizing tendencies, which determine the direction the person's behavior will take. Maslow's self-actualization position makes prediction of the direction of one's behavior somewhat easier because his need hierarchy is relevant to people in general. By knowing which of a person's basic needs have been satisfied, the level at which the individual is currently functioning is known, and this allows for some prediction of a person's behavior.

Besides the limited scope of the phenomenological strategy in general, two of the major phenomenological approaches which we considered, those of Rogers and Kelly, have specific limitations which result from their particular emphases. Rogers' phenomenological approach tends to focus on the feeling or emotional aspects of human functioning while largely ignoring the intellectual, thinking aspects. Interestingly, the bias of Kelly's psychology of personal constructs is exactly opposite; Kelly emphasizes cognitive processes and pays little attention to emotions. As Bruner (1956) pointed out in a review of Kelly's theory, Kelly was so perturbed by those in the psychoanalytic, dispositional, and behavioral camps who regarded human beings as irrational animals that he overreacted and turned *Homo sapiens* into a race of superrational college professors. Say Bruner (1956) of Kelly's analysis:

> Here is an example of the folly: "No matter how obvious it may be that a person would be better off if he avoided a fight . . . , such a source of action would seem to him personally to limit the definition and extension of his system as a whole." *I rather suspect that when some people get angry or inspired or in love, they couldn't care less about their "system as a whole."* (p. 356)

Phenomenological psychologists often criticize colleagues of other theoretical persuasions for presenting an oversimplified, mechanical view of personality. Yet in many ways it is the phenomenologists themselves who have been narrow and simplistic. Wylie (1968) put it this way:

Phenomenological analysis offers a simplistic view of personality

> . . . at the same time that they criticize other psychologists for oversimplifying their analysis of man, the typical alternative [offered by phenomenologists] is a single, overriding motive (e.g., self-actualization, enhancement of the phenomenal self). Such an alternative, if taken literally, provides too few parameters to account for complex behaviors. Some *ad hoc* way must be found to stuff many diverse observations into one or two pigeonholes, yielding serious distortions and omissions. (pp. 731–32)

As we have stated at several points in the preceding three chapters, the fundamental premises of all three phenomenological approaches we have examined can be easily stated in a sentence or two. This is especially true for Rogers and Kelly who each had a single core idea about the nature of personality which they expanded into an entire theory of personality. While this may facilitate understanding of their positions and foster internal consistency in their theories, it also may result in a simplification that is inappropriate for the study of such a complex and multifaceted topic as human personality. Furthermore, phenomenologists have tended to dismiss as unimportant or trivial some of the psychological processes which a majority of personality psychologists have considered essential to the study of personality but with which phenomenological theories cannot deal. A prime example is the concept of motivation, which is a central issue for most personality theories but is casually passed over by Rogers and Kelly who assume that people are inherently motivated and that this "fact" requires no explanation and is not worthy of study.

In a related vein, the phenomenological strategy may also be faulted for rarely, if ever, coming to grips with the real complexity of one of its central concepts, the self. To be sure, several useful assessment techniques, such as the Rep Test and the Q-sort, have been developed.

But these instruments can only provide pale reflections of the underlying experience they seek to elucidate.

> An individual's conception of himself is ordinarily many-sided and internally contradictory. To determine and interrelate its many facets is no small undertaking. We need to know which facets of the self conception are unconscious; which facets are conscious and how they are regarded (for example, with pride, resignation, guilt, or casual acceptance); what the person thinks he is, what he would like to be, and what he expects, eagerly or anxiously, to become. Pervading the overall conception of self will be the individual's concepts of masculinity and femininity; his values, in the form of both moral prohibitions and ideals; and his modes of dealing with inner dispositions and with external opportunities and demands. (Inkeles & Levinson, 1969, p. 450)

PHENOMENOLOGISTS PLACE UNJUSTIFIED CREDENCE ON SELF-REPORTS

The goal of phenomenological personality assessment is to gain knowledge about a person's subjective experiences, to understand behavior from someone's internal frame of reference. Since, by definition, the individual alone has direct knowledge of these phenomena, phenomenological personality assessment relies on the self-reports of the assessee. The basic assumption of this approach is that people are both willing and able to accurately describe their phenomenological experiences when asked to do so. There are, however, a number of considerations which cast doubt on this assumption and on the credence which phenomenologists place in self-reports.

Abundant evidence exists both from psychological research and everyday observations to suggest that people's self-reports are often distorted in systematic ways. People tend to report those aspects of themselves which they want others to know about, and usually this means that they will distort their personality picture so as to be seen favorably by others. Recall, for example, the influence of response sets, such as social desirability, on self-report inventories (see Chapter 11).

The problem of people being unwilling to fully reveal their private experiences, assuming that they are aware of them and have the resources (usually language related) to do so, is not unique to the phenomenological strategy. As we have seen, psychoanalytic and dispositional personality assessment attempt to circumvent this dilemma by employing indirect procedures so that the respondent is not fully aware of what is being assessed (e.g., projective techniques and empirically keyed personality inventories). But such an indirect approach would be contrary to a basic theme of straightforwardness or openness that implicitly permeates the phenomenological strategy. Whereas subjective experiences are used for inferring basic personality processes in the psychoanalytic and dispositional strategies, subjective experiences *are* the basic units of personality in the phenomenological strategy.

As we shall see in the next section of the book, the behavioral strategy handles the problem of people's reluctance to reveal their subjective experiences by placing less emphasis on the importance of private events and more emphasis on public events—namely, overt behavior. This, too, is not a viable option in the phenomenological strategy because overt behavior is considered only indirectly related to the subjective experiences which constitute the core of personality. Thus, the effectiveness and validity of phenomenological personality assessment is limited to the extent that people are reticent to be fully open about their subjective experiences.

Even if a person is willing to report his or her experiences and feelings honestly to someone else, there still remains the problem of whether the person has the ability to report them accurately. Phenomenological personality assessment is based on the premise that people are aware of ("in touch with") those private experiences which directly influence their behavior. The limitations of this view have already been pointed out above.

There is also the issue of whether or not people are capable of providing information about their subjective experiences in a form that will be both meaningful and useful to the assessor. We are all aware of the frustrating experience of trying to tell someone else how we are feeling. We struggle ineptly with words such as: "I'm kind of depressed but not really depressed. It's more like I'm . . . Oh, I don't know . . . I just can't describe it." A major reason for this failure to communicate resides in the limitations of language.

For language to be useful in allowing an individual to convey information to another person, the words and phrases must have commonly agreed upon and understood referents. However, private experiences frequently do not easily translate themselves into words which fully describe them and, at the same time, communicate that description to another person. What often happens is that the words are understood but the meaning is lost. When language is too imprecise and general, observers can base their understanding of words only on their own experiences and perspective, and this does not result in phenomenological knowledge.

A major criticism of phenomenological approaches to personality is that they provide more of a description than an explanation of behavior. Key theoretical concepts such as the self and personal constructs are viewed by some critics (e.g., Skinner, 1964) as only partial explanations. To say that George behaves in a particular manner because of the construct he uses to construe the relevant events or that Carl acts the way he does as a result of his self-actualizing tendency does not explain the person's actions unless the construct or the self-actualizing tendency is, in turn, accounted for. "Personal constructs" and "self-actualizing tendencies" are theoretical constructs which only have the

PHENOMENOLOGI-CAL PERSONALITY THEORY IS MORE DESCRIPTIVE THAN EXPLANATORY

status of what Skinner (1964) has called "mental way stations." They leave unanswered the question of what conditions are responsible for one's personal constructs or one's self-actualizing tendency.

Prediction becomes difficult, if not impossible, when a theory provides behavioral descriptions without specifying the conditions which determine the behavior described (or without designating the variables that influence the theoretical constructs which are hypothesized to be most directly responsible for the behavior). The self-actualization approaches of Rogers and Maslow are particularly vulnerable in this regard. Aside from serving to physically sustain life, the nature of the self-actualizing tendency differs from person to person. Each of us has a different basic nature, and our behavior is guided by it. Given this strategy, "explanations" of behavior take the forms of "Phylis is what she is," which is, of course, merely a tautology *(A = A)* and tells us nothing.

In studying self-actualizing individuals, Maslow ran headlong into this problem. How can self-actualization for a given individual be defined? Is living up to one's potential a sufficient definition (assuming, that is, that one's potential could be measured accurately)? If so, this gives rise to such questions as: Are all people with high IQs who do not attend college nonself-actualizers? Is it possible for fully actualized persons to function at less than their capacity?

Maslow never adequately solved the basic dilemma of definition. A priori, he defined certain individuals as self-actualizing; then he studied such people and, from what he learned about them, further described the characteristics of self-actualizers. But this circular strategy is no different from making such meaningless statements as: "Anxious people are more anxious than nonanxious people." Mere reiteration of one's definition does not elucidate a phenomenon.

To a lesser degree, Kelly's psychology of personal constructs also suffers from the limitation of being more descriptive than explanatory. Kelly's basic statement about the factors which determine behavior is contained in his Fundamental Postulate: "A person's processes are psychologically channelized by the ways in which he anticipates events." Knowing that people constantly strive toward accurate prediction of events gives us little information about the *direction* of behavior since, as Kelly fully acknowledges in his advocacy of constructive alternativism, a person has available a multitude of alternative ways of anticipating events.

The phenomenological strategy posits arbitrary inborn tendencies

A concrete example of the phenomenological strategy's failure to provide real explanations for personality phenomena can be found in its introduction of various inborn tendencies as "explanations" of behavior. Specifically, the phenomenological strategy rests on the assumption that there are inborn tendencies (to construe events, to actualize one's potentialities) which direct and explain behavior. However, none of the theorists has specified the origins of these tendencies, and the tendencies have not been identified by emerging research findings. Thus, as Maddi (1976) points out, neither Maslow nor Rogers "gives us enough formal theoretical basis for determining what the assumed inherent potentialities are so that we can avoid the circular position of deciding that everything that the person has done must have stemmed from some potential of his" (p. 104).

The inner tendency is simply said to exist (e.g., "The organism has one basic tendency and striving—to actualize, maintain, and enhance the experiencing organism" [Rogers, 1965, p. 487]), and, thereafter, the tendency becomes an all-purpose explanation of behavior. Writings of the phenomenological theorists often give the impression that the constructs these theorists favor were not so much discovered (e.g., through systematic research or logical deduction) as revealed by some unspecified process of insight or inspiration.

The self as a homunculus

A close examination of phenomenological theories discloses that most of them advance arguments that explain nothing, but rather relegate the problem of explanation to a freewheeling "self" or similar entity within the personality. The self is portrayed as a *homunculus* (a miniature person within the person) which can feel, think, distort, evaluate, accept and reject facts, and so on. These tendencies are simply imputed to the self by pronouncement (e.g., an actualizing tendency or an inborn and universal bent for anticipating future events). In the last analysis, explaining personality on the basis of hypothesized self-tendencies is reassuring double-talk, not explanation.

PHENOMENOLOGICAL PERSONALITY THEORY DOES NOT ADEQUATELY EXPLAIN PERSONALITY DEVELOPMENT

A major weakness of Kelly's psychology of personal constructs is the absence of discussion of how personality develops. Kelly certainly did not believe that anyone is born with constructs, since constructs develop in order to predict one's experiences, which, it is reasonable to assume, do not begin until birth. But beyond the simple assertion that constructs are learned, there is little in Kelly's theory which speaks to the issue of how they develop. The psychology of personal constructs is applicable only to an already-construing person, a person who has developed a set of templets through which to view his or her experiences. How does a child develop a construct? What factors determine the hierarchical order of a child's constructs? Are there stages of development in which constructs and the construct system have particular characteristics? Do nonverbal constructs become verbal when the child learns to speak? These and similar questions pertinent to personality development are left unanswered by personal construct theory.

In contrast to Kelly's theory, Rogers' theory includes some discussion of the development of personality (e.g., in relation to the self-concept and conditions of worth). However, the developmental *process* is not spelled out explicitly. For example, according to Rogers, the self-concept develops as part of the actualizing tendency's process of differentiation. But other than indicating that the actualizing tendency is responsible for differentiating psychological functions (presumably by parceling out "energy" from the actualizing tendency to various functions), Rogers' theory says little about how the process operates.

Another, more serious problem presented by Rogers' theorizing about personality development is that it is no more than theorizing, since there is no empirical evidence to support his notions. Although Rogers has conducted and inspired a large body of research concerning personality change, there have been no parallel efforts to accumulate evidence regarding the development of the actualizing tendency, the self-concept, conditions of worth, and other key constructs. Thus, Rogers' theory of personality development is somewhat vague and unspecified and remains untested.

It is interesting to speculate about the reasons for the relative lack of emphasis given to developmental issues by both Kelly and Rogers. One possibility is that interest in how personality characteristics develop is not in keeping with the phenomenological perspective's emphasis on the individual's present ("here and now") experiences and her or his momentary interpretation of them as the primary means of understanding personality.

THE PHENOMENOLOGICAL APPROACH IS ROMANTICALLY NAIVE

A frequently heard criticism of the phenomenological strategy is that it expresses a naive and rather romantic notion of human beings. Millon (1967) summarized this concern forcefully:

> Particular exception is taken to [the phenomenologists'] idealistic conception of man's inherent nature. The notion that man would be a constructive, rational, and socially conscious being, were he free of the malevolent distortions of society, seems not only sentimental but invalid. There is something grossly naive in exhorting man to live life to the fullest and then expecting socially beneficial consequences to follow. What evidence is there that one's inherent self-interest would not clash with the self-interests of others? There is something as banal as the proverbialism of a fortune cookie in the suggestion "be thyself." Conceiving man's emotional disorders as a failure to "be thyself" seems equally naive and banal. (p. 307)

The *romantic attitude,* as we are using the term, refers to the general belief that another person's experiences can be known with sufficient certainty to admit this knowledge into the realm of psychological discourse. The concern expressed by Millon in the preceding quotation is that, by virtue of its announced subject matter, the phenomenological strategy cannot meet the requirements of scientific psychology.

That conclusions should be able to withstand and overcome all reasonable doubt is an idea which lies at the heart of science. In order to do this, all scientific theories and investigations must adopt what Smith (1950) has called the *observer's frame of reference*. As Smith notes, "[theoretical] constructs framed in terms of the 'private world' of the behaving individual remain constructs, and as such must ultimately be rooted in data accessible to the observer's frame of reference" (p. 518). Obviously that would be antithetical to the basic tenets of the phenomenological strategy.

In other words, as we emphasized in Chapter 1, it is agreement among observers and the repeatability of findings that distinguishes the psychological approach to the human condition from religious, philosophical, and literary approaches. Psychology does not attempt to describe the total life space and experience of the individual, nor would it be possible to do so. The psychological approach is one vantage point (the religious, philosophical, and literary approaches being other examples). Those who insist on abandoning the scientific criterion of agreement about observations in favor of plausibility, common sense, or a romanticized vision of what human beings can become, propel themselves out of science entirely, for then only shared faith with others can protect them from disagreements which can never be resolved (cf. comments on the scientific status of the psychoanalytic strategy in Chapter 7).

section **5**

The behavioral strategy

Jean-Claude Lejeune

19

The behavioral strategy

Introduction

All strategies for the study of personality begin with an examination of overt behavior, although in most strategies directly observable behavior is not what is of ultimate interest. A psychoanalytic psychologist collects a subject's dream reports, which can be considered, in and of themselves, a type of overt and relatively objective behavior. If the subject speaks in a clear, audible manner, then any number of observers listening to the subject's report should be able to record the same dream content. However, a psychoanalyst is not interested in the dream report per se, but rather in what the dream content will reveal about the individual's intrapsychic processes, such as unconscious wishes and personality conflicts. In much the same way, a dispositional psychologist concerned with people's need to achieve will be interested in their performance in a business game as an expression of this need rather than as a sample of how they will act in similar business situations. And what a phenomenological psychologist is most interested in is the congruence between a subject's self and ideal self rather than the way in which he or she sorts self-referent statements into categories.

In contrast to the psychoanalytic, dispositional, and phenomenological strategies, the behavioral strategy is directly and ultimately concerned with *behavior* for its own sake. Behavioral personality assessment techniques employ the basic strategy of sampling relevant behavior in an effort to predict similar behavior. A dream report *could* be used to predict the types of dreams the person is likely to have (or be willing to describe); performance in a simulated business task *could* give the behavioral psychologist information about how the person would probably act in an actual business situation; and the way in which individuals sort statements about themselves *could* be used in behavioral personality assessment to predict similar categorizing behavior. The basic unit of personality in the behavioral strategy is *behavior*.

Although behavioral psychologists infrequently use the term *personality*, in fact, for them, personality is the summation and organization

WE ARE WHAT WE DO

417

of an individual's behavior. Personality and behavior are closer to being synonymous in the behavioral strategy than in any of the other three strategies.

Behavior can be *overt*—external and more or less directly observable—or *covert*—internal, private, and not directly observable. To take the example of what you may be doing right now, your overt behavior may include sitting at a desk, underlining the words in this book, and turning the pages; your covert behavior may include reading, thinking, memorizing, or daydreaming. The former overt behaviors can be seen by others, whereas the latter covert behaviors can only be inferred from overt behaviors. "Reading," for example, might be inferred from a test on the material in the book. If you *said* you were fantasizing about being at the beach, this verbal report, an overt behavior, could be taken as an indication of "daydreaming."

The place of overt and covert behavior in the behavioral strategy

John Broadus Watson

The Ferdinand Hamburger, Jr., Archives, The Johns Hopkins University

Historically, the behavioral strategy grew out of the school of psychology called *behaviorism* founded by John Broadus Watson (1878–1958) in the early years of the 20th century. Watson supported two distinct forms of behaviorism, one dealing with the subject matter of psychology and the other with its methods and procedures of inquiry. *"Radical" behaviorism* (or metaphysical behaviorism), so-called because of the extreme nature of its propositions, is concerned with the phenomena that should be studied in psychology. In brief, Watson (1914, 1919) believed that psychology was the science of *behavior*—by which he most emphatically meant only *overt* behavior—and not of consciousness, which could only be studied subjectively by introspection (i.e., by subjects' verbally reporting their thoughts and feelings). A few excerpts from Watson's first book, *Behavior* (1914), will give the flavor of behaviorism as its founder saw it.

> Psychology as the behaviorist views it is a purely objective experimental branch of natural science. Its theoretical goal is the prediction and control of behavior. . . . The behaviorist attempts to get a unitary scheme of animal response. He recognizes no dividing line between man and brute. The behavior of man, with all of its refinements and complexity, forms only a part of his total field of investigation. . . . It is possible to write a psychology, to define it as . . . the "science of behavior" . . . and never go back upon the definition: never to use the terms consciousness, mental states, mind, content, will, imagery, and the like. . . . Certain stimuli lead . . . organisms to make . . . responses. In a system of psychology completely worked out, given the responses the stimuli can be predicted; given the stimuli the responses can be predicted. (pp. 1, 9, 10)

Watson also espoused a second form of behaviorism called *methodological behaviorism* which is alluded to in the quotation above when Watson speaks of "a purely objective experimental branch of natural science." In brief, methodological behaviorism emphasizes objectivity, direct observation of phenomena, precise definitions, and controlled experimentation in the study of human behavior. Methodological behaviorism does *not* specify what is legitimate to investigate, merely what are the legitimate ways of going about scientific inquiry in psychology.

From its inception and through the present, behavioral psychology has adhered to the basic postulates of methodological behaviorism. Until relatively recently, psychologists of this school have, to a large extent, also subscribed to radical behaviorism. However, a current trend within the behavioral strategy has been to study covert events such as cognitions and mental images. This work deals with the role which overt behavior plays in determining covert events (e.g., our actions toward someone influence our attitudes about that person) as well as the use of covert events to induce certain changes in overt behavior (e.g., mentally rehearsing how we will perform in a difficult situation). This *cognitive-behavioral* approach represents a break from radical behaviorism but is very much in keeping with methodological behaviorism. Two important factors tend to distinguish the study of covert events within the behavioral strategy from their study in other personality strategies (Spiegler, 1982). First, covert behaviors are defined explicitly and unambiguously in terms of the procedures or operations used to measure them. Second, whenever possible, the covert events are defined or anchored in terms of observable events. To cite an example of this practice which is familiar to readers, in school, "learning," a covert behavior, is usually defined in terms of performance on an examination, which is an overt and directly observable behavior.

Besides the focus on behavior, another unifying factor of the behavioral strategy is the emphasis on learning. A basic assumption is that behavior develops and is modified primarily, though not exclusively, in accordance with principles of learning rather than through heredity and biological determination. Behavioral approaches differ, however, with respect to the form of learning that is emphasized.

The *classical conditioning*, or *respondent*, approach (Chapter 20) focuses on learning new responses through a process of *association*. For example, a male college professor who wears jeans to a faculty party to which most of his male colleagues wear suits may have learned to do so because the look and feel of tight denim trousers have been associated with very pleasant experiences in the past, such as being out with attractive women. According to the *operant conditioning*, or *instrumental learning*, approach (Chapter 21), behavior is learned as a result of the *consequences* which people receive when they act. From this perspective, the college professor might be said to have developed

BEHAVIOR IS LEARNED

the habit of wearing jeans to parties because jeans often bring him compliments and always attract the attention of others (which he likes). In the *observational learning* approach (Chapter 22), learning occurs by observing the *behavior of others* and its consequences for them. Applying this third approach to learning, the professor may have learned to wear jeans to parties by observing that his students did so, and they were obviously more comfortable than men in business suits, starched collars, and ties. These three explanations reflect three different learning processes, and, in real life, most complex behavior is acquired and sustained by a combination of observational, operant, and respondent learning.

Emphasis on the external environment

Closely related to the assumption about the primacy of learning in personality is the emphasis the behavioral strategy places on the external environment, which includes interpersonal events, as key determinants of behavior (both overt and covert). This latter position is based on two interrelated factors. One is that there is abundant evidence that environmental variables significantly influence human behavior, a point which will be repeatedly illustrated in the chapters that follow. The other, and in many ways the more salient, issue is that environmental variables can be directly observed and controlled, thereby rendering them more amenable to objective, scientific investigation. This is much less the case for biological factors, for example. In the behavioral strategy, biological factors and genetic endowment are viewed as primarily setting limits on one's abilities and the behaviors one will be able to learn. Within these limits, which are often broad, an individual's personality develops as a result of learning experiences. To borrow George Kelly's phrase, the focus of convenience of the behavioral strategy is the external environment, just as the foci of convenience of the psychoanalytic strategy are intrapsychic events, of the dispositional strategy are enduring characteristics, and of the phenomenological strategy are subjective experiences.

The situational specificity of behavior

An important corollary of the emphasis placed on environmental factors within the behavioral strategy is an adherence to the *situational specificity* of behavior. All personality theories must account for the relative consistency of people's behavior, and behavioral theories hold that this consistency is primarily a function of environmental cues and consequences. In other words, people behave the way they do in response to the demands and characteristics of the particular situation they are in at the moment, including their past experience in similar situations, and therefore their behavior is said to be situation specific. A college student sits quietly in lectures, engages in casual conversation during meals at the dorm cafeteria, and becomes hoarse from yelling at basketball and football games. In each case, the student's verbal behavior is determined by the requirements and restrictions of the situation. The student's behavior is *consistent within a given situation,* though not necessarily in different situations.

The situational specificity position contrasts sharply with the generality-consistency assumptions of the dispositional strategy. For instance, rather than simply being aggressive or acquiescent, workers may well be aggressive with their subordinates but courteously passive with their boss.

Increasing recognition of person variables

In recent years, there has been a growning recognition within the behavioral strategy that a fully adequate description of the causes of a person's behavior must take into account more than just external circumstances because

> obviously behavior is not entirely situation specific; we do not have to relearn everything in every new situation, we have memories, and our past predisposes our present behavior in critically important and complex ways. Obviously people have characteristics and overall "average" differences in behavior between individuals can be abstracted on many dimensions and used to discriminate among persons for many purposes. Obviously knowing how a person behaved before can help predict how he will behave again in similar contexts. Obviously the impact of any stimulus depends on the organism that experiences it. No one suggests that the organism approaches every new situation with an empty head . . . . (Mischel, 1973b, pp. 261–62)

Walter Mischel (1930–   ), a prominent cognitive-behavioral psychologist, has theorized about the important *person variables* that interact with situation variables to determine how people behave. Specifically, Mischel (1973b) has identified five broad person variables. First, there are behavioral and cognitive *competencies* which refer to the range and quality of overt and covert behaviors a person is capable of engaging in when the circumstances call for them. Second, we have individual *encoding strategies and personal constructs,* specific ways of sorting out and categorizing the interpersonal and physical events we encounter. The third person variable is the *expectancies* (probability estimates) a person has about the outcome of particular courses of action in specific situations. Fourth, people place *values* on the outcomes of various courses of action they might take. Although two people may have similar expectancies about the outcome of a particular behavior, they will behave differently if they differ in the value they place on the outcome. Two men may both expect a hangover the morning after a night of heavy drinking, but one may consider that a "price" worth paying

Walter Mischel

Courtesy of Walter Mischel

for the "pleasures of the night," whereas the other may not consider the "price" worth it. The fifth person variable is the *self-regulatory systems and plans* that each of us brings to a situation. These are important because we are not just influenced by extrinsically imposed conditions. Our behavior is also influenced by self-imposed goals (standards of acceptable performance we establish for ourselves) and self-produced consequences (rewards we give ourselves for reaching our goals).

It is important to differentiate between Mischel's person variables and the broad and general personality dispositions that were discussed in Section 3. Person variables are posited to interact with the specific situation variables present in each circumstance, whereas traditional personality dispositions are considered consistent in diverse situations. Note, for example, that the way one chooses to view events or the expectancies one has about the outcomes of courses of action are likely to be highly variable in different situations. Thus, in order to predict a person's behavior, one must have information about three factors: (1) the demands and restrictions inherent in the situation; (2) the individual's person variables; and (3) the particular manner in which the situation and person variables interact, or, to put it another way, the specific way that the person variables mediate the effects of the situation.

BEHAVIORAL PERSONALITY THEORY

Of the four aspects of the study of personality, theory is given the least attention in the behavioral strategy. Furthermore, the amount of theorizing tends to be uneven across the varied approaches to personality within the behavioral strategy. For instance, there is considerably more theorizing done within the observational learning approach than within the operant conditioning approach.

However, there are common characteristics of behavioral personality theory, including its being relatively parsimonious, minimizing the use of theoretical constructs, and minimizing inferences. It is important to note that each of these characteristics must be viewed *relative to the other three strategies* for the study of personality.

Parsimony

Behavioral theories of personality usually make relatively few basic assumptions and therefore can be said to be parsimonious. Within a given learning approach, a single set of principles is used to explain a variety of different behaviors. The behavioral explanation of "unexpressed" (inhibited) behavior is a case in point. "Unexpressed behavior" refers to acts which a person is capable of performing but which are not being performed at present. An example would be the failure to recall a fact which one knows (as evidenced by its being recalled when the appropriate cues are available). In some approaches to personality, particularly the psychoanalytic strategy, unexpressed behavior is explained by assuming first that there are levels of awareness (consciousness), and second that conscious responses are made unconscious by a defensive process, such as repression. Behavioral approaches deal with unexpressed behavior without recourse to *additional* assumptions (e.g., assumptions over and above those invoked to explain expressed behavior). For example, Bandura (1969a) holds that an unexpressed response "does not have a qualitatively different nature from any response that has been superseded by an alternative pattern of behavior" (pp. 592–93). On a broader scale, within the behavioral strategy, normal and abnormal behavior are postulated to develop, be maintained, and change according to identical principles of learning (e.g., Ullmann & Krasner, 1975). In effect, there is nothing special about abnormal behavior from the standpoint of understanding its basic nature.[1]

Compared with the other three personality strategies, relatively few theoretical constructs are employed within the behavioral strategy. Note that this is a *relative* statement because behavioral personality theory is by no means free of theoretical constructs, as will be apparent in the chapters that follow.

Behavioral theories do, however, specifically avoid explanations via recourse to special entities within the person. For example, behavioral theories do not posit any kind of unifying force or structure for personality. There are no behavioral equivalents of an ego or self. Instead, each aspect of personality is viewed semi-independently of all other aspects, which is consistent with the view that behavior is determined primarily by external rather than internal factors. As another example, a behavioral psychologist is more likely to study "avoiding talking about painful past experiences" than repression.

Because theoretical constructs often serve as shorthand summaries of personality phenomena, the fact that their use in the behavioral strategy is minimized means that behavioral descriptions of personality phenomena tend to be lengthy and complex. For instance, it is simpler to use the theoretical construct "repression" to describe "avoiding talking about painful past experiences." At the same time, a detailed description has the advantage of greater precision and specificity.

Minimum of theoretical constructs

---

[1] What is "special" about behavior which is labeled "abnormal" is the consequences which accrue to it (e.g., reactions of other people, the limitations the abnormal behavior may place on the person, and the legal ramifications of some abnormal behaviors). For a comprehensive account of the behavioral view of abnormal behavior see Ullmann and Krasner (1975).

**Minimum of
inferences**

Because it is behavior per se which is observed and studied in the behavioral strategy, it follows that inferences are minimized. Of course, inference is involved whenever one event is used to yield information about another event. If it is predicted that Mary will arrive at work at 8:00 a.m. on Thursday on the basis of her having arrived at that time on Monday, Tuesday, and Wednesday, then Mary's arrival time on Thursday is inferred from her previous behavior in the same situation. What is inferred, however, is on the same level of abstraction (i.e., the level of "behavior") as the data from which it is inferred. Future *behavior* is being predicted on the basis of past *behavior*. This one-level inferential process should be contrasted with predicting (inferring) future *behavior* from a *nonbehavioral* source, as would be the case if Mary's punctuality on Thursday were predicted on the basis of Mary's being a compulsive type of person or on the basis of Mary's superego compelling her to be on time. Behavioral predictions are typically one-level inferences and therefore involve less of an inferential leap than do predictions stemming from multilevel inferences, which are frequently made in the other three strategies (cf. Mahoney, 1974, Chapter 3).

**BEHAVIORAL
PERSONALITY
ASSESSMENT**

Assessment of personality in the behavioral strategy can be characterized as being direct, present oriented, and circumscribed.

Direct

Inasmuch as all personality assessment begins with observations of behavior, and because in the behavioral strategy these observations themselves are of central interest, behavioral personality assessment can be considered *direct*. Unlike indirect approaches to assessment, which *infer* the units of personality (e.g., traits) from observed behavior, the behavioral strategy regards observed behavior itself as the basic unit of personality. To learn how a person is likely to act when confronted with a stressful situation, the behavioral psychologist observes the person in one or more stressful situations, or, when this is not possible, inquires how the person has behaved in stress-evoking circumstances in the recent past.

When self-report measures are used as part of behavioral assessment, the focus is on *direct* assessment of the phenomenon being investigated. The maxim of behavioral self-report measures is: If you want to know something, ask about it directly (cf. phenomenological assessment). For example, the behavioral psychologist studying people's fears might use the Fear Survey Schedule (Wolpe & Lazarus, 1966), a self-report inventory which asks people to rate the degree of fear they have of a number of different situations and objects. (Contrast this approach, for example, with asking a person to describe what they see in an inkblot and then inferring fear on the basis of the person having ignored certain aspects of the blot that are considered symbolic of the feared stimuli.) As with all self-report measures, subjects' responses to the Fear Survey Schedule are likely to be influenced by response sets and other extraneous variables and are, at best, only moderately correlated with actual overt behavior. Nevertheless, direct self-reports often prove to be a more valid measure of actual behavior than do indirect assessment methods, such as projective techniques (e.g., Mischel, 1968).

In predicting future behavior, the behavioral psychologist relies most heavily on the individual's present and *recent* past behavior as a guide. Consistent with the situational specificity hypothesis, there is little reason to explore an adult's childhood personality in order to assess her or his present personality. Events in the remote past, as in childhood for an adult, no doubt have had an influence on present personality, but this influence is considered minimal in the behavioral strategy for two important reasons. First, the influence is, at the present time, indirect. Although the habit of crying as a reaction to frustrating events in one's life may have been learned by observing one's mother react in this way, that habit will persist in adult life only if it continues to be reinforced (e.g., by a close friend's sympathy). Second, the influence of events in one's remote past is obscure, and there is no way to reliably assess these events and the nature of their influence. At best, correlations between past and present personality variables can be obtained, but such relationships are not likely to yield information about causation. Adult obsessive behavior may be correlated with severity of toilet training, but such a relationship does not tell us whether the difficulties one had with appropriate sphincter control have resulted in running one's business affairs in a precise and orderly fashion.

Present oriented

Behavioral personality assessment proceeds by examining relatively small aspects of an individual's total personality. For instance, it would be feasible within the behavioral strategy to study the interpersonal relationships of individuals without delving into their sexual relationships. Sometimes two or more aspects of personality are closely related, and it is therefore necessary to consider them simultaneously in order to fully understand one of them. However, the behavioral approach to personality does not assume, a priori, that there is a necessary interdependence among different aspects of personality. This may be contrasted with the holistic approach, espoused by the phenomenological strategy, which maintains that each component of personality must be viewed in relation to one's total personality. The circumscribed

Circumscribed

approach of behavioral assessment has important implications for both behavioral research and personality change. Specific personality phenomena tend to be studied in greater depth, and efforts are made to change particular behaviors rather than to modify the individual's total personality.

Demonstration 19–1

THE OBSERVATION AND RECORDING OF BEHAVIOR

The detailed direct observation and recording of behavior are an essential part of behavioral personality assessment. This Demonstration will give you some practice in observing some of your own behavior, recording it, and then plotting its frequency.

OUTLINE OF PROCEDURES

The following steps are involved.

1. *Select a target behavior that you will observe and record.*
2. *Define the unit of behavior* (e.g., number of pages read or cigarettes smoked).
3. *Define the unit of time* (e.g., hours, days).
4. *Make a convenient recording device* (e.g., a 3 × 5 index card marked off in time units). You may also want to keep brief notes on your daily activities.
5. *Observe and record the target behavior.*
6. *Plot the frequency of responses each day.*

SELECTING A TARGET BEHAVIOR

The first step is to choose a response. Table 19–1 contains a list of behaviors which are particularly applicable to the purposes of the Demonstration, but you can select another response (perhaps one suggested by the examples in the table) as long as it has several features important for this Demonstration. The response should be relatively easy to observe and record without disrupting

TABLE 19–1
Example of target behaviors to observe and record (Demonstration 19–1)

Behavior	Unit of behavior	Unit of time
Reading	Pages	Day or hour
Writing	Lines	Day or hour
Body weight	Pounds (lost or gained)	Week
Jogging	¼ miles	Day
Swimming	Laps in a pool	Day
Tardiness	Times late for an appointment	Day
Daydreaming	Minutes spent	Day or hour
Talking on the telephone	Minutes spent on phone calls	Day or hour
Swearing	Curse words	Day or hour
Foreign language vocabulary	Words learned	Day
Studying	Minutes spent	Day
Bull sessions	Minutes spent	Day
Drinking		Day or hour
(a) Coffee	(a) Cups	
(b) Beer	(b) Ounces	
Smoking	Cigarettes	Day or hour

the behavior and without taking very much of your time. If the response occurs at too rapid a rate, it may prove difficult to record (e.g., eye blinks). On the other hand, it should occur with reasonable frequency in your life so that it can be observed and recorded. (Buying a new car or getting married would, for most people, not occur often enough to be used in this Demonstration!)

You may find it helpful to select a behavior which you actually wish to increase or decrease, although this is not mandatory. (All of the examples in Table 19–1 have this feature.) Working with some behavior you want to modify has the advantage that, directly or indirectly, it may help you make the change you desire. The purpose of this Demonstration is *not* to teach you desirable habits or to have you get rid of undesirable ones. Nonetheless, recording of behavior one wishes to modify often changes the frequency of the behavior in the desired direction (e.g., Lindsley, 1966). (Although this is not a problem when behavior change is the psychologist's primary goal, it does interfere with obtaining accurate baseline measures for research purposes.)

Indirectly, the record you make of your behavior may help you to analyze it, which, in turn, may lead you to think of ways of modifying it. Suppose that you choose reading as your target behavior because you find that you do not read as much as you need to for your work. You may note that, on certain days of the week, your reading rate is higher than on other days, and thus you may find it desirable to make a systematic effort to read more on some days. In this regard, it will be helpful to keep a brief diary of the events in your life over the course of your recording in order to help you isolate the events which are associated with a change in response rate.

OBSERVATIONS AND RECORDING

After selecting a target behavior, the next step is to observe it and keep a record of its frequency. This can easily be done by marking off a 3 × 5 index card in time intervals, and then simply making a tally mark each time you perform the behavior, as is shown in Figure 19–1. At the end of each

FIGURE 19–1
Example of an index-card record of pages read in a week (Demonstration 19–1)

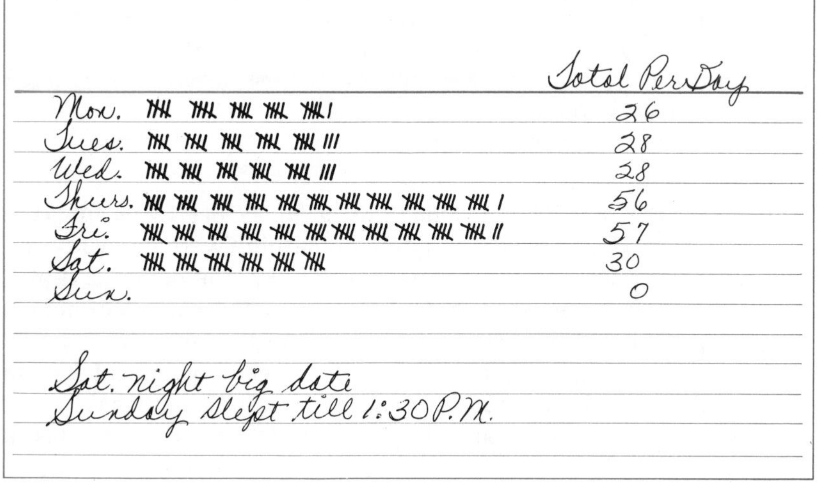

		Total Per Day
Mon.	ⅢⅢ ⅢⅢ ⅢⅢ ⅢⅢ ⅢⅢⅠ	26
Tues.	ⅢⅢ ⅢⅢ ⅢⅢ ⅢⅢ ⅢⅢ Ⅲ	28
Wed.	ⅢⅢ ⅢⅢ ⅢⅢ ⅢⅢ ⅢⅢ Ⅲ	28
Thurs.	ⅢⅢ ⅢⅢ ⅢⅢ ⅢⅢ ⅢⅢ ⅢⅢ ⅢⅢ ⅢⅢ ⅢⅢ ⅢⅢ ⅢⅢ Ⅰ	56
Fri.	ⅢⅢ ⅢⅢ ⅢⅢ ⅢⅢ ⅢⅢ ⅢⅢ ⅢⅢ ⅢⅢ ⅢⅢ ⅢⅢ ⅢⅢ ⅡⅠ	57
Sat.	ⅢⅢ ⅢⅢ ⅢⅢ ⅢⅢ ⅢⅢ ⅢⅢ	30
Sun.		0

Sat. night big date
Sunday slept till 1:30 P.M.

FIGURE 19–2
Graph of a week's reading behavior (Demonstration 19–1)

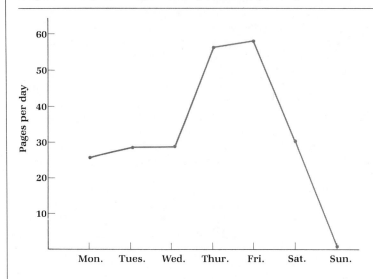

day (or other unit of time you are using), the total number of tally marks is calculated, and this becomes your rate for the day (e.g., 26 pages read per day).

GRAPHING THE RESULTS OF OBSERVATION

Each day's rate should then be plotted on a graph to facilitate inspection of the data. As is illustrated in Figure 19–2, the horizontal axis of the graph is marked off in time intervals, such as days or hours. The vertical axis represents the number of responses per unit of time.

As can be seen from the graph, the person read approximately the same number of pages (i.e., between 26 and 28) for the first three days. On Thursday, the number of pages nearly doubled, and it remained the same on Friday. On Saturday the number of pages dropped to approximately the Monday-through-Wednesday rate, perhaps because of the interference of the individual's Saturday evening social engagement. And on the seventh day no pages were read (perhaps because the person rested).

BEHAVIORAL RESEARCH

The historical roots of the behavioral strategy are to be found in the laboratories where animal and human learning were being investigated. By way of comparison, recall that the psychoanalytic and phenomenological strategies grew primarily out of observations of human behavior, particularly in a clinical setting, and that the dispositional strategy was an outgrowth of studies of the components of human behavior. The behavioral strategy is a descendant of the behavioristic approach to learning; it is partially an attempt to apply principles of learning developed in the laboratory to problems of human personality. Examples include the classical conditioning of attitudes, which is a direct outgrowth of Pavlov's well-known work on the conditioning of salivation of dogs (see Chapter 20) and complex procedures for teaching language to children and adults who do not speak, which were derived from principles developed with pigeons pecking a target (see Chapter 21). These investigations were steeped in the tradition of methodological behaviorism with its emphasis on objectivity and empirical verification of theoretical propositions. It is no wonder, then, that well-controlled empirical research, particularly that performed in the psychology laboratory (where rigorous controls are possible), is an essential element of the behavioral strategy.

The experimental method is most frequently used in behavioral personality research because it is especially suited to the study of specific behaviors under controlled conditions. Rather than examine personality as a single entity, behavioral research investigates small aspects of personality intensively. The research is predominantly nomothetic, although idiographic studies of single subjects often are part of behavioral personality-change techniques. However, such detailed study of single cases focuses on specific behaviors (e.g., inability to work, difficulties relating to people in authority positions) as opposed to the individual's total personality or global dispositions.

The dependent variables employed in behavioral experimentation tend to be *samples* of the actual behavior of interest. For example, in behavioral experiments dealing with the factors leading to aggression, the measures of aggression are direct samples of aggressive behavior, such as administering a painful electric shock to another person.

BEHAVIORAL PERSONALITY CHANGE

The generic terms most frequently used to denote personality-change or therapy techniques arising from the behavioral strategy are *behavior therapy* and *behavior modification*. Although many forms of behavior therapy owe their conceptual origins to principles of learning developed with laboratory animals, contemporary behavior therapy is based more on practical considerations of treating clients' problem behaviors (Spiegler, 1982). This pragmatic, and often atheoretical, approach has led to many potent procedures for personality change, as we shall see in Chapters 20–22.

Learning and relearning

There are many different types of behavior therapy techniques, but they are all based on the premise that behavior, be it adaptive or maladaptive in nature, is learned. Thus, problematic or abnormal behavior which necessitates therapeutic intervention is dealt with by having the person develop new or unpracticed adaptive behaviors to replace the maladaptive abnormal behaviors.

Target behaviors

Since personality is viewed in terms of specific behaviors and not in a holistic fashion, it follows that personality change is aimed at modifying specific behaviors rather than the individual's whole personality. Toward this end, behavior therapy works on changing selected *target behaviors.* Typically, people come to therapy of any orientation with more than one problem and define their difficulties in vague, general terms. The behavior therapist first helps the client to specify the problems so that they can be worked with on a behavioral level. For example, clients frequently report feeling "anxious and 'uptight' " much of the time. Through behavioral assessment techniques the therapist will attempt to find the *overt behavioral referents* of the client's report of anxiety and "uptightness." For one client, the subjective experience of anxiety may result in avoiding certain situations (e.g., dates), and for another it may lead to poor performance (e.g., on examinations).

The fact that behavior therapy treats specific target behaviors sometimes leads to the *erroneous* conclusion that it cannot deal with complex and multifaceted problems, and that it changes only simple, relatively straightforward problem behaviors (e.g., snake phobias!). Target behaviors form the components of highly complex human behavioral problems. For instance, complicated marital difficulties may necessitate working on such component target behaviors as anxiety about sexual matters, interpersonal skills, emotional sensitivity, dependency behavior, and so on. Behavior therapy deals with one or a few target behaviors at a time and, when the desired behavior change has taken place, then proceeds to tackle other target behaviors. In practice, behavior therapy techniques frequently bring about behavior change in a relatively short period of time—often in as few as a dozen sessions. One of the implications of this efficiency is that when a client has more than one problem, they can be dealt with sequentially.

Maintaining conditions

The task of behavior therapy is to assess those conditions which are currently maintaining the behavior to be changed (the target behavior) and then to modify the maintaining conditions so as to bring about the desired change. Although the target behavior may have originated many years in the past, knowledge about its origin, say in childhood, is not necessary unless the conditions which brought it about initially are the same conditions which account for its present persistence. (Frequently the conditions which first led to the behavior and the factors which are currently maintaining it are different—see the previous discussion of the present orientation of behavioral assessment.)

The factors which are maintaining a target behavior can be grouped broadly into two major categories: antecedent and consequent conditions. *Antecedent conditions* refer to all the stimuli which are present before the target behavior occurs, including situational cues (e.g., where the target behavior occurs and what is going on at the time), temporal cues (e.g., time of day), and interpersonal cues (e.g., who is present and what they are doing). *Consequent conditions* refer to everything that happens after the target behavior is performed and include both the immediate and the long-range consequences to the individual performing the behavior, as well as to other people and even the physical environment.

To illustrate what is meant by antecedent and consequent conditions, consider the behavior of overeating which Ann would like to change. On the antecedent side of the overeating might be such stimuli as: Ann is at home alone in the evening; she is bored or frustrated; the refrigerator is well stocked with "treats." The consequences of Ann's overeating include: Ann enjoys the treats; she feels guilty; she gains weight; she cannot wear some of her most attractive clothes; her best friend calls her "chubs." Depending on the specific behavior therapy technique employed to deal with Ann's overeating, the emphasis would be on changing the antecedent or the consequent conditions or both.

Consistent with the recent trend within the behavioral strategy to pay increasing attention to covert, cognitive events, behavioral psychologists have developed techniques of *cognitive behavior modification* (i.e., procedures for modifying a person's thoughts and images as an intermediary or mediating step in modifying the person's overt behavior). In the following chapters we shall describe a number of procedures that are forms of cognitive behavior modification.

Cognitive behavior modification

In this introductory chapter, we have alluded to a recent trend in the behavioral strategy which can be succinctly described as a *cognitive-behavioral approach.* This approach grew out of the discontent of some behavioral personality psychologists with the limitations of radical behavioral approaches. In particular, these psychologists (e.g., Bandura, 1977a, 1977b; Mahoney, 1974; Meichenbaum, 1977; Mischel, 1979) believed that the behavioral approach was "missing the boat" by failing to study phenomena that were not directly observable but that were nonetheless essential aspects of human personality. The primary examples are various cognitive processes, such as thinking and imagining, that make humans unique among other animals. (Recall that Watson [1914] believed in a "unitary scheme of animal response" and in there being "no dividing line between man and brute.") Accordingly, a number of behavioral psychologists have begun to study cognitive and other covert processes. In doing so, they have obviously departed

THE CURRENT STATUS OF THE BEHAVIORAL STRATEGY

from the tradition of radical behaviorism, but they are still operating within the tradition of methodological-behaviorism by adhering to rigorous standards of scientific investigation.

While cognitive-behavioral psychologists view their efforts as an extension of the traditional behavioral approaches to personality, a number of (traditional) behavioral psychologists consider them as being outside the purview of the behavioral strategy (e.g., Rachlin, 1977; Wolpe, 1978a, 1978b). The result is a major controversy within the behavioral strategy which appears to be a long way from being resolved. In fact, given the history of controversy in psychology (and most other fields of study), it is doubtful that either camp will "triumph" over the other and take over as the legitimate resident of the behavioral strategy. More likely, the cognitive-behavioral approach will either be accepted as a "neobehavioral" approach, analogous to neoanalytic (post-Freudian) approaches, or it will become a separate strategy (cf. Liebert & Spiegler, 1970). However, this is only speculation, and, for the present, the behavioral strategy for the study of personality is clearly composed of somewhat different viewpoints.

Thus, it is appropriate that we present the behavioral strategy from both perspectives. Chapter 20 will deal with the earliest behavioral personality work stemming directly from the classical conditioning research of Ivan Pavlov and the writings of Watson, the father of radical behaviorism. The tradition of radical behaviorism was continued and expanded by proponents of the operant conditioning approach, and we shall discuss this work, based primarily on B. F. Skinner's pioneering efforts to precisely predict and control behavior, in Chapter 21. Then, in Chapter 22, we shall consider the "new" behavioral approach which is based, to some degree, on the earlier and more traditional classical and operant conditioning approaches but also includes and emphasizes observational learning. Furthermore, in the observational learning approach there is a definite interest in covert, cognitive events which are hypothesized to govern observational learning by forming links (or mediating) between what a person observes from various models in the environment and how the person subsequently behaves as a result of this observation. Finally, in Chapter 22 we shall specifically cover some of the recent cognitive-behavioral contributions to the study of personality.

20 *The behavioral strategy*

The classical conditioning approach

During the early part of the 20th century, the seeds of modern personality psychology were being sown. Freud's position was just gaining prominence, Gestalt psychology (which may be considered a grandparent of the phenomenological approaches) was born, and the behavioristic movement in psychology was announced with enthusiasm and denounced with vigor.

In America, the predominant psychology in the early 1900s was the science of conscious experience. During this period, research with animals was only on the fringes of the prevailing psychology, since it had been generally accepted (from Descartes on) that consciousness in subhuman species could not be logically proved to exist. However, one psychologist, John Broadus Watson, inspired in part by the writings of the Russian physiologist Ivan Pavlov, was conducting experiments with animals and humans which disavowed the importance of consciousness and paved the way for a behavioristic psychology of learning.

During the late 19th century, Pavlov was investigating the digestive processes of dogs. To Pavlov's dismay, the results of his studies of the flow of digestive juices were often disrupted by a then unexpected phenomenon which was to become one of the cornerstones of the psychology of learning. Specifically, the dogs often appeared to anticipate the food (meat powder), which Pavlov used to induce salivation, even *before* the salivary flow had been directly stimulated. Initially Pavlov considered these "psychic secretions"[1] a nuisance which should be eliminated.

Upon further consideration, however, Pavlov decided to study the phenomenon on which he had accidentally chanced. His first approach was introspective, involving an effort to imagine the situation from the dog's point of view. This strategy led up blind alleys (his assistants could not agree on what the dog ought to think or feel) rather than to objective results and was subsequently banned from Pavlov's labora-

HISTORICAL ANTECEDENTS: PAVLOV AND WATSON

Pavlov's experiments

---

[1] The term is Pavlov's.

FIGURE 20–1
Schematic diagram of the classical conditioning process

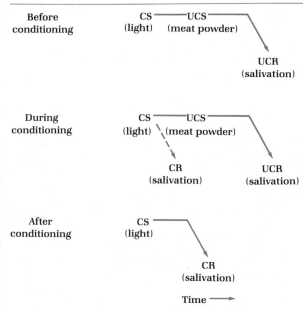

tory (Hyman, 1964). Turning next to a more objective and verifiable approach, Pavlov reasoned that, since the salivation occurred with some regularity, as he began each experiment, the animal's natural, or reflexive, tendency to respond to the meat powder in its mouth with salivation had somehow also come to be evoked by the mere sight of this food. This latter reaction was not an innate one. It had to be *conditioned,* or acquired, by environmental events which were potentially under experimental control. Pavlov began to investigate the manner in which such conditioned responses are formed.

The experiments conducted by Pavlov followed a paradigm now referred to as *classical conditioning.* The order of events in a typical classical conditioning experiment is described below and is illustrated in Figure 20–1.[2] The reader may find it useful in understanding the examples of classical conditioning discussed throughout this chapter to refer back to Figure 20–1, substituting the relevant stimuli and responses.

First, a *conditioned stimulus* (CS), such as a light, is presented, which

---

[2] While this order is the most effective one for showing a conditioning effect, others have been the subject of experimentation (e.g., trace conditioning involves the termination of the conditioned stimulus before the unconditioned stimulus is presented). Interested readers should consult learning texts such as Kimble's (1961) *Hilgard and Marquis' Conditioning and Learning.*

does not initially produce the relevant response (salivation in Pavlov's work). Very shortly thereafter (a fraction of a second to no more than a few seconds), a stimulus known to reflexively produce a certain response is introduced. This stimulus is referred to as the *unconditioned stimulus* (UCS), and the response which it produces is the *unconditioned response* (UCR). In Pavlov's studies, the meat powder served as the UCS and salivary flow was the UCR. Upon repeated contiguous presentations of the CS and UCS (each presentation being referred to as a *trial*), the CS (light) began to produce salivary flow even before the UCS (meat powder) was presented. The salivary flow in this latter condition is referred to as the *conditioned response* (CR). Although the UCR and the CR are usually similar, they are not identical. (For example, the amount of salivation may be slightly, but reliably, different.) The entire process appeared to be an extremely simple and objective way to study the process of learning.

Pavlov's research revealed that a CR is not only developed through the association of the CS and the UCS, but that it must also be maintained by occasional trials in which this association occurs again. The pairing of a CS and a UCS is known as *reinforcement*.

Although an established CS will continue to produce the CR if the UCS is absent for a number of trials (i.e., no reinforcement), ultimately the CR is likely to weaken or disappear completely. Both the failure to provide reinforcement and the actual decrease of the response are referred to as *extinction*.

The form of conditioning described above would have limited use for understanding behavior if the *exact* CS used in training were required in order to produce the CR at a later time. However, this restriction often does not hold. Instead, stimuli which are similar to (but not identical with) the original CS may also evoke the CR. This basic phenomenon is known as *generalization,* and the greater the similarity between the new stimulus and the original stimulus, the greater will be the degree to which the new stimulus can be substituted for the original stimulus. The concept of generalization can be used to understand and predict complex human behavior in novel situations. For example, we are accustomed to seeing and dealing with U.S. police officers. Mexican police officers wear different uniforms and act somewhat differently than do their U.S. counterparts. Yet, on our first trip to Mexico, we are likely to react and behave appropriately to traffic directions being given by a police officer.

Discrimination may be thought of as the opposite of generalization. If the experimental situation is correctly arranged, the subject will learn to respond only to a particular stimulus and not to others that are similar to it. One of Pavlov's most intriguing experiments illustrates how this may occur. The basic procedure was to always reinforce one CS, a luminous circle, but never to reinforce an ellipse with an axes ratio of 2:1. This discrimination was easily formed, so that the dog salivated when the circle was presented but not when the ellipse was presented. Pavlov then proceeded to make the ellipse more and more like a circle (less egg shaped and more round), and the dog responded remarkably well—up to a point. Finally, however, the two stimuli were so similar (a ratio of 9:8) that the dog could no longer make the discrimination.

> After three weeks of work upon this differentiation not only did the discrimination fail to improve, but it became considerably worse, and finally disappeared altogether. At the same time the whole behaviour of the animal underwent an abrupt change. The hitherto quiet dog began to squeal in its stand, kept wriggling about, tore off with its teeth the apparatus for mechanical stimulation of the skin, and bit through the tubes connecting the animal's room with the observer, a behaviour which never happened before. On being taken to the experimental room the dog now barked violently, which was also contrary to its usual custom; in short it presented all the symptoms of a condition of acute neurosis. On testing the cruder differentiations they were also found to be destroyed. (Pavlov, 1927, p. 291)

These observations appear to have implications for human behavior. For instance, it has been suggested that overaspiring parents who push their children beyond their capabilities for top grades or other superlative accomplishments, may foster abnormal behavior in their children analogous to the problems encountered by Pavlov's dog. The process of discrimination certainly has many positive and adaptive ramifications for human behavior. When we are served poor-tasting food in a restaurant, for example, we may not return to that particular eating establishment, but we don't give up eating out altogether.

In the foregoing discussion, we have described the basic principles of classical conditioning and implied that they may be extended to some aspects of human behavior. Watson was perhaps the first psychologist to take this possibility seriously.

Watson's application of classical conditioning to humans

Watson was familiar with Pavlov's work, and he was very much aware of its implications for human behavior. He had established a psychological laboratory for the study of human, as well as animal, behavior. Watson (1919) stressed the importance of a detailed and thorough analysis of the individual's observable behavior, especially as part of controlled experiments in the laboratory. This strategy is illustrated by the (in)famous case of "little Albert" (Watson & Rayner, 1920). Albert, an 11-month-old apathetic child, appeared to be afraid of nothing except the loud sound made by striking a steel bar. In order to induce another fear in Albert, Watson and Rayner placed a white rat in front of him and at the same time produced the loud sound he disliked. After a series of seven such presentations, the rat, which had not previously elicited fear in Albert, came to elicit a fear, or avoidance, reaction (e.g., crying, attempts to escape from the situation). Unfortunately, the facts of this classic case have been distorted by literally dozens of writers (including Watson himself in subsequent reports of the experiment), especially by exaggerating Albert's fear as well as the degree to which it generalized to other furry animals and similar objects (Harris, 1979). Furthermore, early attempts to replicate the study were unsuccessful (e.g., Bregman, 1934; Valentine, 1930). Thus, it appears that Watson and Rayner's (1920) study left us with historically " 'interesting but uninterpretable results' " (Harris, 1979, p. 158). Finally, Watson and Rayner never extinguished Albert's fear of rats (although why they didn't is unclear).

However, there is, in effect, a sequel to the case of little Albert. Three years later, Mary Cover Jones (1924b), "with the advice of Dr. John B. Watson," successfully eliminated a child's fear. Jones's subject, Peter, who "seemed almost to be Albert grown a bit older," came to the laboratory already afraid of white rats and other furry objects. When Peter was 2 years and 10 months of age, his fear was quite severe. "Peter was put in a crib in a play room and immediately became absorbed in his toys. A white rat was introduced into the crib from behind. . . . At sight of the rat, Peter screamed and fell flat on his back in a paroxysm of fear" (Jones, 1924b, p. 309).

Peter was even more afraid of a rabbit, and Jones decided to focus on reducing fear of it. Initially, Peter was exposed to fearless peer models during a daily play period in the laboratory. During these sessions, Peter played with three other children who were completely unafraid of furry rodents, and a rabbit was merely present during a part of each play period. Peter's progress was regularly assessed by exposing him to the rabbit from time to time in the absence of his playmates. Jones (1924b) noted impressive improvement "by more or less regular steps from almost complete terror at sight of the rabbit to a completely positive response with no signs of disturbance" (p. 310). After seven treatment sessions, Peter contracted scarlet fever and was taken to the hospital for two months. When he came back to the laboratory, most of his earlier fear had returned. A nurse reported an incident which may have contributed to the apparent relapse.

> As they were entering a taxi at the door of the hospital, a large dog, running past, jumped at them. Both Peter and the nurse were very much frightened, Peter so much that he lay back in the taxi pale and quiet. . . . This seemed reason enough for his precipitate descent back to the original fear level. Being threatened by a large dog when ill, and in a strange place and being with an adult who also showed fear, was a terrifying situation against which our training could not have fortified him. (Jones, 1924b, p. 312)

This setback gave Jones an opportunity to examine another novel form of treatment in conjunction with exposure to fearless peer models which had proved successful in Peter's initial treatment. Based on classical conditioning principles, *counterconditioning* involves simultaneous pairing of a pleasant event (e.g., eating a favorite food) with exposure to the feared situation (e.g., presence of a rabbit). In her laboratory notes, Jones (1924b) describes a typical session using this procedure:

> Lawrence and Peter sitting near together in their high chairs eating candy. Rabbit in cage put down 12 feet away. Peter began to cry. Lawrence said, "Oh, rabbit." Clambered down, ran over and looking in the cage at him. Peter followed close and watched.
>
> Peter with candy in high chair. Experimenter brought rabbit and sat down in front of the tray with it. Peter cried out, "I don't want him," and withdrew. Rabbit was given to another child sitting near to hold. His holding the rabbit served as a powerful suggestion; Peter wanted the rabbit on his lap, and held it for an instant. (p. 313)

Not until many years later did procedures (and results) similar to those reported by Jones find their way into the mainstream of psychology.

THE CLASSICAL CONDITIONING OF COMPLEX BEHAVIOR

Since Pavlov's and Watson's pioneering work, numerous investigations have been designed to ascertain whether complex human behavior might develop by classical conditioning. To illustrate this line of research, we shall discuss the development of attitudes and emotional reactions through such learning processes.

The classical conditioning of attitudes

A wide array of stimuli are known to elicit evaluative reactions, or attitudes, in humans including the names of certain subgroups, such as cops, jocks, and politicians, particular proper names, such as those with special ethnic origins, various situations and events, such as New Year's Eve, and even inanimate objects, as the following newspaper item illustrates:

> Dear Abby:
>
> My friend fixed me up with a blind date and I should have known the minute he showed up in a bow tie that he couldn't be trusted. I fell for him like a rock. He got me to love him on purpose and then lied to me and cheated on me. Every time I go with a man who wears a bow tie, the same thing happens. I think girls should be warned about men who wear them. (cited in Bandura, 1968, pp. 306–7)

Despite the humorous element in this account, there is no reason to doubt the letter writer's sincerity. She may indeed have specific reactions to men who wear bow ties. It is a reasonable hypothesis that many attitudes may have been produced through classical conditioning, by a process whereby a neutral stimulus (one which initially elicits no particular evaluative response) is paired with a stimulus that elicits a definitive evaluative reaction. Much advertising is based on the assumption that this associative process will influence potential customers. Famous or prestigious people who have no connection whatsoever with a product, are paid enormous fees to endorse it. Several years ago, Muhammad Ali was chosen by an advertising firm to put across a message about a giant double-decker cheeseburger being introduced by a large fast-food chain. According to the agency's president, Ali was selected because a survey had found him to be the most recognized person in the world.

What is the evidence that attitudes can be acquired through classical conditioning? Two early studies by Razran (1938, 1940) tested the hypothesis that attitudes could be modified by association with pleasant or unpleasant stimuli. In the first of Razran's studies (1938), 100 judges (whose composition was distributed to correspond to the U.S. adult population in racial and national background, religion, and education) rated photographs of 30 college women as to their beauty, intelligence, character, entertainingness, ambition, and the degree to which they would be generally liked. Two weeks later, the judges were asked to rate the photographs of the women again, and this time they were ostensibly told their names. Of the surnames chosen, 15 corresponded to ethnic minorities—5 Jewish, 5 Irish, and 5 Italian—while the remaining 15 were selected from the Social Register and signers of the Declaration of Independence. As expected, liking for the photographs of the women with minority group names decreased, as did evaluations of their character and beauty. Among other changes observed, Jewish names produced higher intelligence and ambition ratings, while there were decrements in the intelligence ratings of the Irish- and Italian-named photographs. These biases largely disappeared, however, when the photographs were presented a third time together with a distinctly pleasant stimulus. (Note that this is an example of counterconditioning.) Specifically, the judges rated the photographs while eating a free lunch, thereby presumably conditioning the names to a positive experience. This procedure has come to be known as the *luncheon technique*. In a second study, Razran (1940) demonstrated that ratings of sociopolitical slogans would change depending on whether the raters evaluated the slogans while enjoying a free lunch or while inhaling unpleasant odors.

The luncheon technique may be applied in a variety of practical ways. Many business executives, for instance, make it a practice to hold important negotiations over a pleasant meal. To demonstrate the luncheon technique to students in his class on personality, one of the authors distributed candy, which had been left over from Halloween trick-or-treat, to the students. He started the bag of candy in the last row of the class and told the students to pass it across each row. When the candy had been passed among approximately half the students, the author reclaimed the remaining candy, ostensibly to save for his other classes. About an hour later, the students were asked to evaluate how the class was progressing, it being midsemester, using a simple five-point scale. After this rating had been written on an index card, the students were asked to indicate whether or not they had had the candy passed to them. Impressively, students who had merely been offered candy rated the class significantly more favorably than students who had not been offered candy (Spiegler, 1970).[3]

That attitudes can be classically conditioned in childhood has been dramatically shown in a series of studies by Nunnally and his associates (Nunnally, Duchnowski, & Parker, 1965; Parker & Nunnally, 1966; Wilson & Nunnally, 1971). In one such study (Nunnally et al., 1965), elementary school children were asked to play a spin-wheel game. Three nonsense syllables appeared randomly on the 18 possible stopping points on the wheel (see Figure 20–2). Each child was asked to spin the wheel 30 times, receiving a different consequence depending on where the wheel stopped: one of the syllable stopping points was associated with a reward (two pennies), another with no consequences, and the third with a negative outcome (the loss of a penny). The question was whether, through this association, the individual nonsense syllables (which were known to be neutral before the game) would take on conditioned meaning or value. The answer was a clear yes.

After playing the game, each participant was shown three stick figures with blank faces; one of the three nonsense syllables—previously associated with a positive, a neutral, or a negative event—appeared below each figure. It was explained to the child that each nonsense syllable was the name of the "boy" above it. The child was read a list of complimentary and derogatory adjectives and asked to attribute each to one of the boys (e.g., "Which is the *friendly* boy?" or "Which is the *mean* boy?"). The results were striking: an average of 4.7 (out of a possible 5) positive evaluations were assigned to the boy whose name had been associated with a reward, while *no* positive evaluations were assigned to the boy whose name had been associated with a negative outcome. Similar findings have been obtained in experimental studies with adults (e.g., Staats & Staats, 1958).

These experimental findings certainly have implications for the development of ethnic, racial, and religious prejudice as well as both the positive and the negative feelings and attitudes we have toward

---

[3] To control for the possibility that students who had been passed the candy might have been more favorably disposed to the class, the candy was distributed to the students sitting in the back half of the lecture hall. Typically, more interested students (as well as those who tend to get higher grades in a course) sit in the front half of a classroom.

FIGURE 20–2
A child playing the spinning wheel game in Nunnally's classical conditioning research

Courtesy Professor Jum C. Nunnally

particular individuals. In turn, these attitudes may have a strong influence on the way we *behave* toward others. In one experiment, Berkowitz and Knurek (1969) first classically conditioned a negative attitude toward a critical name, Ed or George. Then the subjects participated in a group discussion with two other people (both experimental confederates), one of whom bore the critical name. The subjects acted with more hostility toward the confederate named Ed or George than toward the confederate with a neutral name. Furthermore, prior to the group discussion, half of the subjects had deliberately been made angry by one of the experimenters. In contrast to subjects who had not received this additional treatment, the angered subjects were significantly less friendly toward the confederate with the critical name than toward the confederate with the neutral name.

There is ample evidence that a variety of emotional reactions can be produced by classical conditioning procedures. In one example of this phenomenon, Geer (1968) used color photographs of victims of violent and sudden death as unconditioned stimuli. The photographs were presented to college students five seconds after the presentation

The classical conditioning of emotional reactions

of a tone, an initially neutral stimulus. After 20 such pairings, the previously neutral tone produced galvanic skin responses indicating heightened emotional arousal.

Geer included a "random association" group whose subjects experienced occasional but unpredictable pairings (instead of continuous and reliable pairings) of the tone with the photographs of the dead bodies. The random procedure had particularly strong effects in producing emotional arousal in subjects, a finding that may have far-reaching implications.

> One could speculate that oppressed groups within a society function in an environment that delivers unpredicted noxious stimuli and that such conditions may result in extensive emotional disturbance. . . . Individuals in long-term stressful conditions characterized by lack of prediction or control may experience considerable disturbance. . . . Certain behavior disorders [may be] states in which the individual is unable to predict the occurrence of noxious stimuli. (Geer, 1968, p. 155)

Asthma as a classically conditioned response

Laboratory studies of asthma have suggested that this disorder may be produced through *aversive classical conditioning*—the pairing of a neutral stimulus and one that elicits an unpleasant, or aversive, response. Dekker, Pelser, and Groen (1957) studied two subjects who suffered from severe bronchial asthma. The patients repeatedly inhaled an allergen (UCS) to which they were highly sensitive. This produced an automatic asthmatic attack (UCR). Although the neutral solvent (CS) in which these allergens were dissolved did not initially produce any asthmatic symptoms, after repeated trials it came to elicit attacks of asthma (CR) by itself. Moreover, the inhalation of pure oxygen and even the presence of the inhalation mouthpiece (both of which would not have produced any reaction *initially*) were now able to evoke severe attacks of asthma that were difficult to distinguish from those which were produced by the allergen itself.

Also consistent with a classical conditioning explanation of asthma is Dekker and Groen's (1956) report that asthma patients, when encouraged to talk freely about the cause of the attacks, list a variety of causative factors, including the sight of dust, watching someone swallow an aspirin, knitting, and sunshine. Such stimuli can also elicit asthma attacks in the laboratory.

> Patient L had told us that she got an asthmatic attack from looking at a goldfish. After a base line had been obtained, a goldfish in a bowl was brought into the room. . . . Under our eyes she developed a severe asthmatic attack with loud wheezing, followed by a gradual remission after the goldfish had been taken from the room. During the next experiment the goldfish was replaced by a plastic toy which was easily recog-

nized as such . . . but a fierce attack resulted. . . . Upon this she told the investigator the following dream, which she had had after the preceding investigation.

> In her home stood a big goldfish bowl. On a shelf high up near the window were her books. In one of them she wanted to read why goldfishes cause asthma. She climbed on a chair and reached for the book, but it was too high. She lost her balance and fell into the goldfish bowl. She gasped for breath behind the glass. The fishes swam around her. Her neck was caught in a streak of water weed. She awoke with an attack of asthma. She also remembered suddenly how when she was a child her mother threw away her bowl of goldfish, which she loved so much. The patient had saved her pocket-money to buy them. Mother threw the fishes into the water closet and flushed them through. (Dekker & Groen, 1956, p. 62)

Dekker and his associates were largely unsuccessful in their efforts to treat their asthmatic patients with traditional methods of psychotherapy and called for the development of "a more specific deconditioning therapy that makes the conditioning disappear in the same way in which it came" (Dekker et al., 1957, p. 107). As we shall see shortly, such therapeutic techniques have been developed.

Anxiety as a classically conditioned response

Joseph Wolpe (1958) believes that anxiety is an inappropriate fear response to situations and events that carry no objective threat to the individual and that it is learned by classical conditioning (cf. Freud's view of anxiety). Specifically, a neutral cue (CS) which is present at the same time that another stimulus (UCS) elicits a fear or anxiety response (UCR) comes to elicit a similar response (CR) on future occasions. This learning paradigm and the central role it plays in the development and maintenance of neurotic behavior is illustrated in the following prototypical example.

> The child places his hand on the big, black, hot coal stove. He quickly withdraws the painful hand, tearful and fearful. His mother comforts him, but later notes that he keeps away from the stove and seems afraid of it. Clearly, the child has developed a beneficial habit of fearing and avoiding an actually harmful object.
>
> But in some cases the experience also has another and less favorable consequence. Suppose in the mother's bedroom there is a large black chest of drawers. The child may have become afraid of this too—purely on the basis of its *physical resemblance* to the stove— . . . [that is,] generalization. Fear of the chest of drawers is neurotic because there can be no harm in touching it. It can have several undesirable implications. In the first place, the very presence of an unpleasant emotion like fear is objectionable where it is not appropriate. Secondly, the child is now forced to make a detour if the chest of drawers is in his path; and

thirdly, he no longer has easy access to any delectable contents of the drawers, such as candy. In these features of this child's case, we have the model of all neurotic fear reactions. (Wolpe & Lazarus, 1966, pp. 17–18)

PERSONALITY CHANGE THROUGH CLASSICAL CONDITIONING

Classical conditioning procedures have been used in three basic ways to modify behavior (cf. Spiegler, 1982). First, when the goal of therapy is to elicit and increase an adaptive behavior, an appropriate stimulus (CS) may be conditioned to the adaptive behavior (CR). For example, one component of a standard treatment for insomnia (e.g., Bootzin & Nicassio, 1978; Coates & Thoresen, 1977) involves pairing various environmental and internal stimuli, such as being in bed and feeling tired, with sleep, the desired CR, and with no other responses, thereby establishing a classically conditioned discrimination.

Second, when the goal is to eliminate an undesirable behavior, extinction may be employed. This involves repeatedly exposing the person to the CS without the UCS occurring, thereby removing reinforcement. This procedure is commonly employed to reduce and prevent subsequent prolonged negative emotional reactions resulting from traumatic experiences. For instance, people who have been in a serious automobile accident may be advised to drive or ride in a car as soon as possible after the accident so that they will experience being in the car (CS) without an accident occurring (UCS).

Third, classical conditioning can be used to substitute a more desirable behavior or eliciting stimulus for a less desirable CR or CS. This form of therapy is typically applied with three different types of problems. In one case, a situation or event (CS) is eliciting a maladaptive response (CR), as when a person is prevented from taking long trips because of an excessive fear of flying. Here the aim of therapy would be to substitute a more adaptive CR, such as feeling relaxed, to the CS (flying in airplanes).

With another type of problem, the CR is desirable, but the condition (CS) which elicits it is inappropriate or otherwise undesirable. In this case the focus would be on changing the CS. For example, this approach has been used with adults who are sexually aroused by children so that the pleasures of sexual arousal can be elicited by more appropriate stimuli.

Finally, in some instances, the object is to substitute an unpleasant, but ultimately more adaptive, CR, as would be the case if a person wished to stop drinking alcohol. Here alcohol consumption (CS) could be paired with an aversive response, such as feeling nauseated, which would become a substitute for the usual CR (e.g., relaxation, lowered inhibitions, and euphoria).

In the following sections, we will discuss classical conditioning procedures for changing behavior which fit into each of the categories just described. In clinical practice, these applications of classical conditioning are often employed in combination with one another as well as with other behavioral personality change procedures which will be discussed in subsequent chapters.

Enuresis is the inability of persons older than three to voluntarily control urination; it most frequently occurs during sleep, in which case it is called nocturnal enuresis or simply bedwetting. Viewed in learning terms, the problem of nocturnal enuresis is that the child (most enuresis occurs in children) has not learned to awaken before urination occurs because the stimulation of bladder tension does not produce the necessary response of awakening. Mowrer and Mowrer (1938) developed and tested a classical conditioning therapy to establish the awakening response by pairing bladder tension (CS) with the ringing of a bell (UCS), a stimulus which inevitably awakens (UCR) the child and permits the child to reach the toilet in time.

The treatment of enuresis by classical conditioning procedures

To test the effectiveness of this treatment, 30 children ages 3–13 slept on a specially prepared pad, consisting of two pieces of bronze screening separated by heavy cotton fabric (see Figure 20–3). When urination occurred, the urine seeped through the fabric and closed an electrical circuit, which, in turn, sounded a bell. Through such repeated pairings, bladder tension alone was able to awaken the child before urination occurred. Bedwetting was eliminated in all 30 cases, with the maximum period of treatment being two months. Furthermore, the Mowrers reported accompanying improvements:

> Personality changes, when they occurred as a result of the application of the present method of treating enuresis, have uniformly been in a favorable direction. In no case has there been any evidence of "symptom substitution."[4] Our results, therefore, do not support the assumption, sometimes made, that any attempt to deal directly with the problem of enuresis will necessarily result in the child's developing "something worse." (Mowrer & Mowrer, 1938, p. 451)

Since Mowrer and Mowrer's (1938) original work, a number of studies have demonstrated the effectiveness of the bell-and-pad technique for controlling enuresis (Yates, 1970). A bell-and-pad apparatus is available commercially for less than $50, and the technique can be used by parents without professional counseling. (A similar classical conditioning procedure has been developed for the treatment of constipation [Quarti & Renaud, 1964].)

---

[4] *Symptom substitution* refers to the notion that when a symptom is eliminated without eliminating its underlying cause (e.g., an intrapsychic conflict), another symptom will replace it.

FIGURE 20–3
A schematic diagram of the bell-and-pad apparatus used to treat nocturnal enuresis

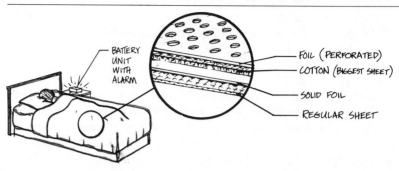

Wolpe (1958) has developed a technique for alleviating anxiety called *systematic desensitization,* which he based on the theoretical concept of *reciprocal inhibition:* "If a response antagonistic to anxiety can be made to occur in the presence of anxiety-evoking stimuli so that it is accompanied by a complete or partial suppression of the anxiety responses, the bond between these stimuli and the anxiety responses will be weakened" (p. 71). Recall that one of the techniques Jones (1924b) employed to eliminate Peter's fear of rabbits began with Peter's eating a food which he liked. Then the feared stimulus (a caged rabbit) was gradually brought closer and closer to Peter, without disturbing his eating. In this case, the eating response was antagonistic to the anxiety response in that it is difficult to simultaneously enjoy eating and experience the discomfort we call anxiety.

The technique of systematic desensitization involves three sets of operations. First, the anxious individual must be taught a response which is antagonistic to anxiety. Second, specific details of the client's anxiety must be assessed and an *anxiety hierarchy* constructed. Desensitization involves the repeated pairing of the response which is antagonistic to anxiety with anxiety-evoking stimuli. Each of these operations will be illustrated in the following sections.

Deep muscle relaxation

The response most frequently employed as an antagonist to anxiety is deep muscle relaxation.[5] The physiological concomitants of anxiety (increased heart rate, perspiring, shaking, and so on) are, for the most part, incompatible with a state of deep muscle relaxation. (We never hear someone report being both nervous or anxious and relaxed at the same time.)

---

[5] Other anxiety-antagonistic responses which have been used in systematic desensitization include sexual arousal, assertive behavior, anger, and humor.

Training in deep muscle relaxation (Jacobson, 1938) proceeds in a systematic fashion covering each of the various skeletal muscle groups—arms, head, face, neck, shoulders, trunk, abdomen, hips, thighs, legs, and feet. Initially, clients learn to differentiate between muscular relaxation and tension by first tensing and then relaxing each set of muscles, as the following excerpt from relaxation training instructions illustrates.

> Settle back as comfortably as you can. Let yourself relax to the best of your ability. . . . Now, as you relax like that, clench your right fist, just clench your fist tighter and tighter, and study the tension as you do so. Keep it clenched and feel the tension in your right fist, hand, forearm . . . and now relax. Let the fingers of your right hand become loose, and observe the contrast in your feelings. . . . Now, let yourself go and try to become more relaxed all over. . . . Once more, clench your right fist really tight . . . hold it, and notice the tension again. . . . Now let go, relax; your fingers straighten out, and you notice the difference once more. (Wolpe & Lazarus, 1966, p. 177)

Later in the training, clients work on creating deeper and deeper states of relaxation in their muscles(without first tensing them). Clients usually sit in a comfortable armchair, such as a recliner, close their eyes, and follow the therapist's instructions. The number of sessions needed to teach deep muscle relaxation varies from individual to individual, but on the average, less than a half-dozen sessions are required if the client practices the technique for a short time each day at home.

The construction of anxiety hierarchies

Sometimes a person will come to a therapist with a well-defined fear of a particular class of stimuli or stimulus situations, such as fear of driving or of going to the dentist. More often, however, people feel anxious at various times but are not aware of the conditions which precipitate the feeling. In such cases, it is the therapist's task to discover, by detailed questioning, the situations which cause anxiety.

When the stimuli which elicit anxiety have been enumerated, they are categorized in terms of common *themes* (e.g., fear of being alone). Within each theme, the stimuli are ordered in terms of the amount of anxiety they evoke. Examples of such *anxiety hierarchies* are presented in Table 20–1. The ranking of anxiety-evoking situations is a highly individual matter; as is apparent from the "examination" hierarchy in Table 20–1, the same scenes might be ordered differently by another person. Exploration of the nature of the person's anxiety and construction of anxiety hierarchies are usually done concurrently with relaxation training.

TABLE 20–1
Examples of anxiety hierarchies

Examination series

1. On the way to the university on the day of an examination.
2. In the process of answering an examination paper.
3. Before the unopened doors of the examination room.
4. Awaiting the distribution of examination papers.
5. The examination paper lies face down before her.
6. The night before an examination.
7. On the day before an examination.
8. Two days before an examination.
9. Three days before an examination.
10. Four days before an examination.
11. Five days before an examination.
12. A week before an examination.
13. Two weeks before an examination.
14. A month before an examination.

Discord between other people

1. Her mother shouts at a servant.
2. Her young sister whines to her mother.
3. Her sister engages in a dispute with her father.
4. Her mother shouts at her sister.
5. She sees two strangers quarrel.

Source: Wolpe, J., & Lazarus, A. A. *Behavior therapy techniques: A guide to the treatment of neurosis.* New York: Pergamon Press, 1966.

The desensitization process

Relaxation training and construction of appropriate anxiety hierarchies are the prerequisites for the actual procedure of desensitizing the stimuli associated with anxiety. In the desensitization procedure, the client is instructed to relax his or her muscles and then to visualize or imagine scenes from the anxiety hierarchy, starting with the least anxiety-provoking situation (i.e., the lowest item on each anxiety hierarchy).

Each scene is imagined for a few seconds at a time. The client is instructed to signal the therapist (usually by raising a finger) whenever any anxiety is felt, at which point the therapist immediately tells the client to stop visualizing the scene. This procedure is critical because for reciprocal inhibition to take place, the previously anxiety-producing stimulus must occur only when the client is making a response which prevents anxiety from occurring. A scene is repeated before going on to the next higher scene in the hierarchy, until the client reports experiencing virtually no disturbance while visualizing it.

To illustrate the desensitization procedure, a verbatim account of the presentation of scenes during an initial desensitization session is presented below. The client was a 24-year-old female art student who requested treatment of examination anxiety which had caused her to

fail a number of tests. When she discussed her anxiety with the therapist, it was discovered that there were also other stimulus situations
which made her anxious. Thus, four different anxiety hierarchies were
constructed, two of which appear in Table 20–1. The first scene that
she was asked to visualize was a neutral scene, one that was not
expected to elicit anxiety; this served as a "warm-up" for her imagining
anxiety-evoking scenes while remaining relaxed. The next two scenes
were the lowest items on their respective anxiety hierarchies (see Table
20–1).

I am now going to ask you to imagine a number of scenes. You will
imagine them clearly and they will generally interfere little, if at all,
with your state of relaxation. If, however, at any time you feel disturbed
or worried and want to attract my attention, you will be able to do so
by raising your left index finger. First I want you to imagine that you
are standing at a familiar street corner on a pleasant morning watching
the traffic go by. You see cars, motorcycles, trucks, bicycles, people and
traffic lights; and you can hear the sounds associated with all these things.
(Pause of about 15 sec.) Now stop imagining that scene and give all
your attention once again to relaxing. If the scene you imagined disturbed
you even in the slightest degree I want you to raise your left index finger
now. (Patient does not raise finger.) Now imagine that you are at home
studying in the evening. It is the 20th of May, exactly a month before
your examination. *(Pause of 5 sec.)* Now stop imagining the scene. Go
on relaxing. *(Pause of 10 sec.)* Now imagine the same scene again—a
month before your examination. *(Pause of 5 sec.)* Stop imagining the
scene and just think of your muscles. Let go, and enjoy your state of
calm. *(Pause of 15 sec.)* Now again imagine that you are studying at
home a month before your examination. *(Pause of 5 sec.)* Stop the scene,
and now think of nothing but your own body. *(Pause of 5 sec.)* If you
felt any disturbance whatsoever to the last scene raise your left index
finger now. *(Patient raises finger.)* If the amount of disturbance decreased
from the first presentation to the third do nothing, otherwise again raise
your finger. *(Patient does not raise finger.)* Just keep on relaxing. *(Pause
of 15 sec.)* Imagine that you are sitting on a bench at a bus stop and
across the road are two strange men whose voices are raised in argument.
(Pause of 10 sec.) Stop imagining the scene and just relax. *(Pause of 10
sec.)* Now again imagine the scene of these two men arguing across
the road. *(Pause of 10 sec.)* Stop the scene and relax. Now I am going
to count up to 5 and you will open your eyes, feeling very calm and
refreshed. (Wolpe & Lazarus, 1966, p. 81)[6]

---

[6] The reader may be interested in the outcome of this case. Wolpe and Lazarus
(1966) report that a total of 17 desensitization sessions were required for the client to
report no anxiety while visualizing the highest scene on each of her four hierarchies
(the two hierarchies presented in Table 20–1 and two additional hierarchies dealing
with being scrutinized and devalued by others). The anxiety reduction transferred from
the imagined scenes to the actual situations, and the client was able to successfully
take and pass her examinations.

Variations of systematic desensitization

Systematic desensitization has become the most frequently used behavioral therapy treatment for anxiety-related problems. Its effectiveness and efficiency have been demonstrated in hundreds of studies during the past 20 years, and the basic procedures described above have been adapted in a variety of ways, including group systematic desensitization in which a number of clients are desensitized to anxiety-evoking situations at the same time, and *in vivo* systematic desensitization in which the client is actually in the anxiety-provoking situation rather than imagining being in it.

One modification of Wolpe's (1958) basic procedures (Goldfried, 1971) is particularly worth noting because it is consistent with a growing trend within behavior therapy toward equipping clients with self-control skills (e.g., Goldfried & Merbaum, 1973; Spiegler, 1982). Systematic desensitization was originally conceived of as a passive, *counterconditioning* process for the elimination of anxiety associated with various environmental stimuli or situations (Wolpe, 1958).

An alternative conceptualization of systematic desensitization involves actively teaching the client a *skill* (deep muscle relaxation) which can be used to reduce feelings of anxiety whenever they occur. The differences between this active, self-control model and the traditional passive, counterconditioning model can be seen in a comparison of the basic procedures used in the various phases of systematic desensitization, which are summarized in Table 20–2.

TABLE 20–2
Comparison of the emphases in a counterconditioning and a self-control model of systematic desensitization

Phase	Counterconditioning	Self-control
Rationale given to clients	Replace anxiety with relaxation by reciprocal inhibition	Learn the skill of relaxation to cope with anxiety
Relaxation training	Differentiate feelings of tension and relaxation	Use tension as a cue to relax (as well as tension-relaxation differentiation)
Hierarchy construction	Common theme in each hierarchy	No common theme necessary
Dealing with tension during scene presentation	Stop visualizing scene and relax	Continue visualizing scene and use tension as a cue to relax
Practice outside therapy sessions	Practice deep muscle relaxation	Use relaxation to reduce tension that occurs in life situations (as well as relaxation practice)

Source: Adapted from Spiegler, M. D., et al. A self-control versus a counterconditioning paradigm for systematic desensitization: An experimental comparison. *Journal of Counseling Psychology,* 1976, *23,* 83–86.

The critical differences between the counterconditioning and the self-control model of systematic desensitization relate to hierarchy construction and the presentation of scenes during desensitization. Although anxiety hierarchies are constructed in both techniques, there is no need for a common theme in the hierarchy used in self-control desensitization. In the counterconditioning model, as the name implies, the relaxation response becomes associated with (conditioned to) particular *anxiety-evoking scenes* which make up the hierarchy. In the self-control model, relaxation becomes associated with *muscular tension* (i.e., with no particular external stimulus). Thus, the scenes in the self-control anxiety hierarchy need only elicit progressively greater degrees of anxiety and do not have to be related to one another.

Using the counterconditioning procedures, it is essential that the client visualize hierarchy scenes only while relaxed because this pairs relaxation (and never muscular tension) with the previously anxiety-evoking scene. The counterconditioning (substituting relaxation for muscle tension) takes place while visualizing scenes. Accordingly, clients are instructed to erase a scene from their minds as soon as they begin to experience muscular tension. In the self-control model, the purpose of imagining scenes is to evoke anxiety so that the client can practice the skill of relaxation. Thus, if the client signals the therapist that muscle tension is being experienced while visualizing a scene, the client is instructed to continue imagining the scene *and* to relax while doing so.

The self-control model of systematic desensitization has been demonstrated to be at least as effective as the counterconditioning model, and it appears that the effects of self-control procedures can generalize to situations other than the one specifically treated in therapy (Denney & Rupert, 1977; Goldfried & Goldfried, 1977; Spiegler, Cooley, Marshall, Prince, Puckett, & Skenazy, 1976; Zemore, 1975).

Aversive counterconditioning

Viewed as a counterconditioning process, systematic desensitization neutralizes threatening events by associating them with pleasant experiences (e.g., deep muscle relaxation). In other instances, just the opposite effect is called for, namely creating a negative emotional reaction to a pleasurable event. Such *aversive counterconditioning* has been used primarily in the treatment of harmful addictive behaviors (e.g., alcohol and other drug addictions, and cigarette smoking) and various sexual aberrations (e.g., exhibitionism and fetishism). These behaviors are immediately gratifying to the individual, but they have long-range negative consequences because they are socially inappropriate, culturally prohibited, or physiologically harmful.

Aversive counterconditioning involves the contiguous pairing of a UCS which normally produces an unpleasant, distasteful, revolting, or otherwise negative reaction with the conditioned stimuli associated with the behavior which is to be reduced. This counterconditioning process is continued until the CS comes to elicit a similar negative reaction. Lavin, Thorpe, Barker, Blakemore, and Conway (1961) used this strategy to treat a male transvestite, and their case will serve to illustrate the procedure.

The client, a 22-year-old married truck driver, reported that he had experienced the desire to dress as a woman since the age of eight. From age 15 and through his military service and marriage, he had derived erotic satisfaction from dressing in women's clothes and viewing himself in the mirror. At the same time, he had maintained a good sexual relationship with his wife.

In order to be able to elicit the undesirable behavior systematically (and thus pair it with a negative reaction), Lavin and his associates prepared 35-mm. slides of the client in various stages of female dress and had him make an audiotape in which he described these activities. It was then determined that the presentation of the slides and tape induced sexual excitement.

The treatment involved pairing the transvestic experience with nausea, produced pharmacologically by injection of a drug. As soon as the injection began to take effect, the slides and tape were presented, and these stimuli were terminated only after the client began vomiting. This treatment was administered every two hours for six days, a regimen which proved sufficient to completely eliminate the client's desire to don female attire. Systematic follow-up over a six-month period, including interviews with both the client and his wife, suggested that recovery was complete.

The two major unconditioned stimuli which have been used in aversive conditioning are various pharmacological agents which produce nausea, and painful (but not dangerous) electric shock (Rachman & Teasdale, 1969). An advantage of using electric shock is that its presentation and removal can be timed precisely to coincide with the CS. Another consideration for the choice of the UCS is its relevance to the CS. Thus, a mixture of smoke and hot air has been used with some success in reducing cigarette smoking (e.g., Wilde, 1964). Serber (1970, 1972b) has developed an ingenious technique called *shame aversion therapy* which involves having a person perform the deviant act (usually sexual) in the presence of other people. Obviously, for the technique to work, the person must feel ashamed, embarrassed, or humiliated by having others observe him or her perform the deviant behavior. It is also possible to symbolically induce aversion through verbal descriptions which create strong feelings of disgust, horror, and even physical reactions such as nausea. This technique is usually called *covert sensitization* (Cautela, 1967) and will be illustrated in the next section.

A major emphasis of behaviorally oriented therapists has been to teach their clients to administer their own therapy (e.g., Bandura, 1969a; Davison, 1968; Davison & Neale, 1974; Goldfried & Merbaum, 1973). One example of this approach, as it applies to counterconditioning, is a therapy procedure called *orgasmic reconditioning*. The basic technique is used to treat clients (most often males; see Marquis, 1970) who are sexually aroused by socially inappropriate stimuli. First, the client becomes sexually aroused in private by using any imaginal scene that "works," such as the client's usual deviant fantasies. The client masturbates and, just before orgasm, looks at a picture of an appropriate sexual stimulus. Then, the shift in attention to the appropriate sexual stimulus is introduced earlier and earlier in the masturbational sequence; at the same time, the appropriate stimuli are shifted from pictorial to imaginal ones. Finally, the client is instructed to apply the reoriented sexual interest to his or her personal sex life.

Orgasmic reconditioning was used to treat a young man troubled by sadistic fantasies who masturbated about five times per week, always to the imagined thought of torturing women (Davison, 1968). After a careful clinical interview and an explanation of conditioning procedures, the client was told how to proceed on his own.

> When assured of privacy in his dormitory room (primarily on the weekend), he was first to obtain an erection by whatever means possible—undoubtedly with a sadistic fantasy, as he indicated. He was then to begin to masturbate while looking at a picture of a sexy, nude woman (the "target" sexual stimulus); *Playboy* magazine was suggested to him as a good source. If he began losing the erection, he was to switch back to his sadistic fantasy until he could begin masturbating effectively again. Concentrating again on the *Playboy* picture, he was to continue masturbating, using the fantasy only to regain erection. As orgasm was approaching, he was at all costs to focus on the *Playboy* picture, even if sadistic fantasies began to intrude. It was impressed on him that gains would ensue only when sexual arousal was associated with the picture, and that he need not worry about indulging in sadistic fantasies at this point. (Davison, 1968, p. 85)

The client progressed well in the first few therapy sessions (e.g., he was able to masturbate successfully three times over the weekend to a *Playboy* picture without using sadistic fantasies). However, the client was still reluctant to ask women for dates and to give up his sadistic fantasies entirely. A form of covert sensitization was then instituted. Specifically, the client was instructed to close his eyes and

> imagine a typical sadistic scene, a pretty girl tied to stakes on the ground and struggling tearfully to extricate herself. While looking at the girl, he was told to imagine someone bringing a branding iron toward his eyes, ultimately searing his eyebrows. A second image was attempted when this proved abortive, namely, being kicked in the groin by a fero-

cious-looking karate expert. When he reported himself indifferent to this image as well, the therapist depicted to him a large bowl of "soup," composed of steaming urine with reeking fecal boli bobbing around on top. His grimaces, contortions, and groans indicated that an effective image had been found, and the following 5 min. were spent portraying his drinking from the bowl, with accompanying nausea, at all times while peering over the floating debris at the struggling girl. After opening his eyes at the end of the imaginal ordeal, he reported spontaneously that he felt quite nauseated, and some time was spent in casual conversation in order to dispel the mood. (Davison, 1968, p. 86)

Within five sessions the client had given up masturbating to sadistic fantasies entirely—he even had difficulty producing such thoughts—and was using thoughts of women and heterosexual scenes to mastur-bate. Some time after the termination of therapy, he began to date women. Even more impressive, when a relapse occurred, he was able to treat it himself, as may be seen from the following passage from a letter he wrote to the therapist describing the incident and his present state:

I bought an issue of *Playboy* and proceeded to give myself the treatment again. Once again, it worked like a charm. In two weeks, I was back in my reformed state, where I am now. . . . I have no need for sadistic fantasies. . . . I have [also] been pursuing a vigorous (well, vigorous for *me*) program of dating. In this way, I have gotten to know a lot of girls of whose existence I was previously only peripherally aware. As you probably know, I was very shy with girls before; well now I am not one-fifth as shy as I used to be. In fact, by my old standards, I have become a regular rake! (Davison, 1968, p. 89)

21 *The behavioral strategy*

The operant conditioning approach

The classical conditioning approach to personality discussed in the last chapter focuses on the conditions which antecede and elicit behavior. The operant conditioning approach deals with the effects of the *consequences* of behavior on its future performance.

Edward L. Thorndike (1874–1949), an American psychologist who is credited with initiating modern laboratory experimentation with animals, was one of the first to call attention to the importance of response consequences for human behavior. At the end of the 19th century, Thorndike was studying what he called *trial-and-error* learning. Hungry kittens were placed in a puzzle box and allowed to escape and secure food when they solved the "combination" which opened the door. The combination involved such behavior as turning wheels, pressing levers, and pulling strings. When an animal was first placed in the puzzle box, it showed much random activity, but in the course of this "aimless" behavior it eventually performed the response which opened the door. In effect, the animal arrived at the solution to the puzzle box by trial and error. Subsequently the animal made fewer responses which did not lead to the door opening (i.e., made fewer errors) and reached the solution more quickly. Eventually the animal learned to open the door without performing any erroneous responses. Thorndike took this observation as an indication that the correct response had become strongly connected to the problem.

Thorndike assumed that the mechanism which underlay this apparent "stamping in" of the correct response was a function of the *consequences* which the correct and incorrect responses produced. This idea became formalized in Thorndike's (1898) first expression of the *law of effect*, which held that the strength of the connection between a particular situation and a particular response would be increased if it were followed by a "satisfying state of affairs" (reward) and decreased if it were followed by an "annoying state of affairs" (punishment). Thorndike believed that rewards were far more powerful than punishment in trial-and-error learning.

The tradition of behaviorism, which started with the theorizing of Watson and Thorndike, is most often associated today with the name

SKINNER'S APPROACH

B. F. Skinner

*Courtesy of B. F. Skinner,
photo by Christopher S. Johnson*

of B. F. Skinner (1904–   ). Although Skinner's research contributions have emphasized the behavior of nonhuman organisms, usually rats or pigeons, he has in his writings (e.g., *Science and Human Behavior* [1953]; *Walden Two* [1948]; *About Behaviorism* [1974]) made numerous suggestions concerning the application of his findings to human behavior. In *Beyond Freedom and Dignity* (1971), Skinner developed his view of the human being as an organism whose behavior is primarily determined by *external* environmental influences, particularly the consequences of one's acts, and stated the implications of this view for designing a culture which would optimally facilitate human development and growth.[1] In essence, *Beyond Freedom and Dignity* challenges the notion that we are autonomous beings in the sense that our behavior is a function of internal influences (e.g., unconscious impulses, traits, self-actualizing tendencies), which is the model of human beings upon which the psychoanalytic, dispositional, and phenomenological strategies are based.

Psychologists who have followed in the Skinnerian tradition have made remarkable strides in recent years in developing an operant approach to the study of personality which emphasizes: (1) precise, observational personality assessment; (2) applied, yet highly controlled, research; and (3) potent personality-change techniques. In the operant approach, there is a close interrelationship among personality assessment, research, and change (which will be evident in the work described in this chapter), while personality theory plays a very minor role.

Functional analysis of behavior

Skinner has contended throughout his career (his first published book, *The Behavior of Organisms,* appeared in 1938) that psychology in general and the study of learning in particular is not yet at the stage where elaborate, formalized theorizing is justifiable. Though in principle he is not *anti*theory, Skinner asserts that psychology is not ready to establish theories of human personality. Accordingly, Skinner's own research efforts have been directed toward the complete and detailed description of behavior, which he has called the *functional analysis of behavior.* The aims of such functional analyses is to establish empirical relationships between behavior and the conditions that influence or control it. The Skinnerian approach might be summarized by the following maxim, which Skinner (1956) gleaned from Pavlov: "Control your conditions and you will see order."

While the operant approach to personality is atheoretical, it is not

---

[1] One attempt to design a culture based on Skinnerian principles, such as those depicted in Skinner's (1948) novel about a fictional society, *Walden Two,* is a community in Virginia called Twin Oaks. Its success and failures are described in a book titled *A Walden II Experiment: The First Five Years of Twin Oaks* (Kinkade, 1973).

astrategical. Operant psychologists, including Skinner, do begin with definite assumptions about the nature of behavior which, in effect, constitute a strategy for the study of personality because they provide operant psychologists with a "master plan" for studying personality which, in turn, guides their specific work. One such assumption is that the primary determinants of behavior are to be found in one's external environment. This assumption gives direction to the operant psychologists' investigations. For example, it dictates that assessment procedures should focus on measuring external, rather than internal events, that research will examine the effects of these external events on people's behavior, and that personality-change techniques will deal with modifying the environmental events which influence behavior.

In keeping with his atheoretical approach, Skinner has rejected explanations of behavior in terms of theoretical constructs, which he views as *convenient but redundant fictions.* Regarding internal influences on behavior, Skinner (1953) says:

The focus on environmental determinants of behavior

> The practice of looking inside the organism for an explanation of behavior has tended to obscure the variables which are immediately available for a scientific analysis. These variables lie outside the organism, in its immediate environment and in its environmental history. . . . The objection to inner states is not that they do not exist, but that they are not relevant in a functional analysis. (pp. 31, 35)

As an alternative, Skinner's approach is concerned with observable phenomena which fall into two main classes—*stimuli,* those observable characteristics of the environment which influence the organism, and *responses,* the overt behavior of the organism. In a sense, Skinnerian psychology deals with an "empty organism." All variables which come between, or mediate, stimulus and response, and cannot be explained in terms of stimulus or response, are considered to be outside the domain of interest of the operant approach. It should be noted, however, that this position can deal with many of the phenomena which are the basis for positing internal events in other personality approaches. Skinner (1971), for example, speaks of building "belief" by reinforcing behavior and thus increasing the probability of action. Such an explanation of belief may appear strange, at first glance, because it is construed in an unfamiliar way. But are not our strongest beliefs those which we are most likely to act upon?

Although Skinner rejects explanations of behavior in terms of theoretical constructs, he acknowledges the important role played by genetic endowment and the process of evolution in determining a person's present behavior (Skinner, 1971, 1974). Skinner views the evolution of the human species in terms of the long-range effects of contingencies of reinforcement. Contemporary *Homo sapiens* are the product of millions of years of shaping and differential reinforcement (i.e., only for adaptive- or survival-related behaviors of the species), which is Skinner's (1974) explanation of Darwin's concept of "natural selection."

The nature of operant and respondent behavior

Skinner (1938) has distinguished between two types of behavior: *operant* and *respondent*.[2] Operant behavior refers to responses which an individual *emits*, and denotes that the person is operating on the environment, changing it and being changed by it. Such behavior is controlled by the *consequences* which follow its performance.[3] Operant behavior is also called *instrumental behavior*, denoting that the behavior is instrumental in producing some effect on the environment. Examples include driving a car, dressing oneself, taking notes in class, and playing tennis. In each case, successful completion of the behavior results in some consequence, and the nature of the consequences determines whether the behavior will continue to be performed. For example, turning the steering wheel of an automobile while driving allows one to avoid the variety of obstacles which appear in the road from time to time. The behavior (e.g., turning the wheel) is under the control of its consequences in the sense that if the consequences are positive (e.g., staying in lane), the behavior is more likely to occur again, whereas if they are negative (e.g., hitting parked cars), the behavior is less likely to recur. Much of our behavior has been learned via operant, or *instrumental*, conditioning.

Respondent behavior is *elicited* by some identifiable stimulus and thus derives its name from the fact that the subject *responds* to something. The purest examples of respondent behavior are reflexes, that is, such innate responses as the pupil of the eye closing down in response to light stimulation and perspiring in response to heat. Respondents can also be learned, through classical conditioning (see Chapter 20); two common examples are blushing when someone tells you that you are attractive and feeling "nervous" (hands shaking, perspiring, stomach queasy) just before giving a speech.

Many behaviors originally learned as operants may come to function as respondents. These behaviors include acts which we colloquially call "reflexes" (since they occur almost automatically), such as stopping

---

[2] The terms *respondent* and *operant* are used both as adjectives, to refer to a type of behavior or procedure ("operant conditioning"), and as nouns, to refer to a specific response which is a member of the class of respondent or operant behavior ("writing one's name is an operant").

[3] Strictly speaking, it is logically impossible for a given response to be controlled by the consequences which accrue to it, since the consequences occur *after* the response is made. It is possible, however, for consequences which accrued to similar responses in the past to affect a given response.

when a traffic light turns red and paying close attention to teachers when they begin to talk about an upcoming examination. In each instance, some stimulus serves as a cue for the response to occur. Such a cue is called a *discriminative stimulus,* and it serves to signal the individual that the particular response is likely to be rewarded, because, in the presence of the stimulus, it has been rewarded in the past. For example, a sign in a store window saying "Sale" is a discriminative stimulus for walking into the store. The role played by discriminative stimuli in operant behavior will be discussed more fully later. For the present, it is important to remember that, although a discriminative stimulus appears to control the response, actually it only *sets the occasion* for its occurrence. Operant behavior is controlled by its consequences and not by its antecedents.

The most frequently used measure of operant behavior is its *rate of occurrence.* It is an elegantly simple measure because it involves merely counting behavior in specified time intervals; the result is expressed in terms of the number of responses per unit of time (e.g., number of words typed per minute, distractions per hour, kisses per day). Operant data are usually presented graphically, showing either the number of responses in each time period or the cumulative number of responses in each successive time period. *Cumulative records* are useful in portraying an individual's rate of responding and the change in rate. The steeper the slope (angle) of the cumulative curve, the greater is the rate of responding. Thus, a cumulative curve which comes close to being a vertical line represents a very high rate of responding, whereas a cumulative curve which approaches a horizontal line represents very little responding. *Acquisition,* or *learning, curves* rise at an angle, whereas *extinction curves* level off. Figure 21–1 is a cumulative record of one student's daily studying under three different conditions (shown in black). Compare it with the noncumulative record in Figure 21–1 (shown in color).

The measurement of operant behavior

The choice between presenting response rates cumulatively or noncumulatively depends on the purpose of the observations. For instance, if one were primarily interested in the progress or trends of a person's behavior over the course of time, then a cumulative record would be more useful. On the other hand, if one were concerned with a person's rate of responding at particular points in time, then a noncumulative record would be more helpful.

Skinner's work has stressed a thorough analysis of an individual subject's behavior. The typical experiment is not concerned with the *average* subject, for the aim of the analysis is to establish experimental

The idiographic nature of the operant approach

FIGURE 21–1
Cumulative record of daily studying (shown in black) and noncumulative record of daily studying (shown in color)

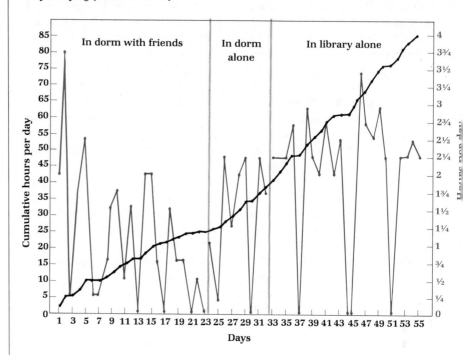

control of a particular organism's behavior. Skinner (1956) explains his concentration on the single case as follows:

> In essence, I suddenly found myself face to face with the engineering problem of the animal trainer. When you have the responsibility of making absolutely sure that a given organism will engage in a given sort of behavior at a given time, you quickly grow impatient with theories of learning. Principles, hypotheses, theorems, satisfactory proof at the .05 level of significance . . . nothing could be more irrelevant. No one goes to the circus to see the average dog jump through a hoop significantly oftener than untrained dogs raised under the same circumstances, or to see an elephant demonstrate a principle of behavior. (p. 228)

Single-subject experiments (see Chapter 2) are frequently used by operant personality psychologists to study individuals because they are at once idiographically oriented and yield results which allow conclusions about cause-and-effect relationships to be drawn, which is essential to a functional analysis.

Single-subject reversal designs

The type of single-subject experiment most frequently used to demonstrate functional relationships between environmental events and behavior is called a *reversal design* (the reason for which will become obvious in a moment). Reversal designs always involve a minimum of three phases and often have four. In the first phase, called *baseline,* the subject's behavior (the dependent variable) is merely observed and recorded to provide a "normal" level of responding before the independent variable is introduced in the second phase, the *experimental* or *conditioning* phase. If the introduction of the independent variable has influenced the dependent variable, this effect will show up as a change in the subject's behavior from the baseline to the experimental phase. However, such an observed difference might also be due to some uncontrolled-for factor other than the independent variable. This factor could have been operating during the experimental phase but not during the baseline phase.

To check on the likelihood of alternative explanations accounting for the change in the dependent variable, a third part of the experiment is instituted, the *reversal phase.* During reversal, the independent variable is withdrawn in order to see whether the dependent variable will return to the baseline level. If it does return to baseline, then it is likely that the independent variable accounted for the change observed in the dependent variable from the baseline to the experimental phase. In other words, the reversal has given us more confidence that the subject's behavior was influenced by the independent variable.

The three phases of the experiment—baseline, experimental phase, and reversal—constitute what is called an *ABA* research design. *A* stands for the absence of the independent variable (in the baseline and reversal phases), and *B* indicates the presence of the independent variable (in the experimental phase).

Frequently, a fourth phase is added to the ABA design. This is a second experimental period, or *reconditioning phase,* in which the independent variable is reinstated. With the addition of the reconditioning phase, the research design can be designated *ABAB.* The reconditioning phase will always be included when the experiment is being used to assess the effectiveness of a treatment for an actual problem behavior. (We shall see an example of this in the case of Robbie which will be described shortly.) If an effective treatment has been discovered for a particular problem, it would be unethical, to say the least, to leave the subject in the reversal phase (i.e., at baseline level). Table 21–1 summarizes the four phases of the ABAB design.

REINFORCEMENT

At the heart of the operant approach to personality is the concept of reinforcement. To reinforce is to strengthen, and reinforcement in the present context involves strengthening behavior in the sense that it will continue to be performed. *Reinforcement* occurs whenever an event that follows a behavior (i.e., a consequence) increases the likelihood that the behavior will recur. Note that this is an empirical defini-

TABLE 21–1
Phases of a single-subject reversal experiment

	$A_{(1)}$ *Baseline*	$B_{(1)}$ *Conditioning*	$A_{(2)}$ *Reversal*	$B_{(2)}$ *Reconditioning*
		Phase		
Purpose	Get "normal" comparison	Change behavior	Check whether independent variable caused change	Reinstate change in behavior
Operation	*(a)* Measure behavior	*(a)* Introduce independent variable *(b)* Measure behavior	*(a)* Remove independent variable *(b)* Measure behavior	*(a)* Reintroduce independent variable *(b)* Measure behavior
Expectation*		$B_{(1)} \neq A_{(1)}$†	$A_{(2)} = A_{(1)} \neq B_{(1)}$†	$B_{(2)} = B_{(1)} \neq A_{(1)} \neq A_{(2)}$†

* What will occur if the independent variable is affecting the dependent variable.
† The inequality can be in either direction (i.e., increase or decrease of the dependent variable in the B phases), depending on the nature of the independent and dependent variables.

tion, because we conclude that reinforcement has occurred only when an increase in the frequency of the behavior has been observed. A *reinforcer,* or *reinforcing stimulus,* is the name given the event that is a consequence of the behavior and has increased its probability of recurring. In most cases, but not always, reinforcers are pleasurable or desirable events, what we typically call rewards.

Two broad categories of reinforcement have been distinguished, positive and negative. *Positive reinforcement* refers to the case in which a stimulus is *presented* following a behavior (e.g., a father praising his son or giving him a small gift for cleaning his room), whereas *negative reinforcement* refers to the case in which a stimulus is *removed* or avoided following a behavior (e.g., a father ceasing to reprimand his son when his son cleans his room). In both cases, if the stimulus event increases the likelihood that the behavior will be repeated, reinforcement has occurred. Reinforcement always refers to increasing (or strengthening) behavior, and the designation of "positive" or "negative" merely indicates the "addition" or "subtraction" of the reinforcing stimulus. (Negative reinforcement should not be confused with "punishment" which refers to decreasing the probability of occurrence of a behavior and will be discussed later in the chapter.)

The principle of reinforcement and its role in operant conditioning will be illustrated next in the context of a single-subject reversal experiment involving an elementary school boy with studying problems.

The case of Robbie

The subject of Hall, Lund, and Jackson's (1968) single-subject reversal design experiment was Robbie, an elementary school youngster who frequently disrupted normal classroom activities and spent a minimal amount of time studying. In the first phase of the experiment, Robbie was observed unobtrusively during seven 30-minute *baseline* periods in which the students were supposed to be working in their seats. Figure 21–2 presents a record of Robbie's study behavior, which was defined as his having his pencil on paper for at least half of a 10-second observational interval. (It should be noted that such precise definition of dependent variables is typical of operant research and behavior-change procedures.) As can be seen in Figure 21–2, during the baseline observation, Robbie engaged in study behavior 25 percent of the time on the average. The remaining 75 percent of the time was taken up with such behavior as "snapping rubber bands, playing with toys from his pocket, talking and laughing with peers, slowly drinking the half-pint of milk served earlier in the morning, and subsequently playing with the empty carton" (Hall et al., 1968, p. 3). It was also observed during the baseline period that, for much of his nonstudy behavior, Robbie received the attention of his teacher, who urged him to work, put away his playthings, and so on.

Following the baseline period, the *conditioning phase* of the experiment was initiated. Now, every time Robbie engaged in one minute of continuous study behavior, the observer signaled the teacher, who then promptly reinforced Robbie for the study behavior with attention. The teacher ignored Robbie at all other times. The results of this procedure were striking, as can be seen in Figure 21–2. When Robbie received attention contingent upon his studying, the amount of studying increased markedly in the first session and continued to rise in subsequent sessions. Robbie spent an average of 71 percent of his time studying during the conditioning phase of the experiment.

It appeared, then, that the introduction of reinforcement, in the form of the teacher's attention being contingent upon study behavior, was responsible for the increased rate of studying. It is important to note that, without the baseline to which the conditioning rate could be compared, no such statement could be made. However, it is still possible that some other condition, which occurred during the conditioning phase but not in the baseline period, led to Robbie's increased studying (e.g., his parents might have begun to praise him when he reported studying at school). Thus a *reversal,* or *extinction,*[4] phase was instituted in which the teacher refrained from reinforcing Robbie with attention for his study behavior. If study behavior had been under the control of the reinforcement, then when the reinforcement was withdrawn it would be expected that the amount of study behavior would drop off. As Figure 21–2 clearly shows, Robbie's study behavior did decline during the reversal period to a mean of 50 percent.

---

[4] The term *extinction* refers to both an *experimental operation* (discontinuation of reinforcement) and a *behavioral outcome* (decreased frequency of responding).

FIGURE 21–2
A record of Robbie's study behavior

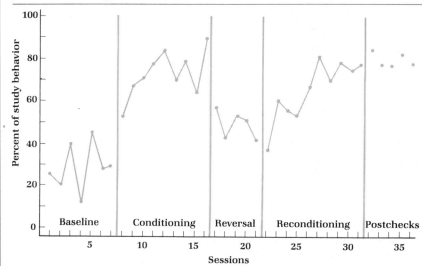

Note: Postcheck observations were made during the 4th, 6th, 7th, 12th, and 14th weeks after the completion of reinforcement conditioning.

Source: Adapted from Hall, R. V., Lund, D., & Jackson, D. Effects of teacher attention on study behavior. *Journal of Applied Behavior Analysis,* 1968, *1,* 1–12.

Since the experiment had the practical purpose of increasing Robbie's study behavior, a *reconditioning phase* was included in which the contingency relationship between study behavior and teacher attention was reintroduced. The result was an increase in Robbie's study rate, which stabilized at a level between 70 and 80 percent (see Figure 21–2). To check on the effectiveness of the operant-conditioning procedures in maintaining Robbie's study behavior, after the last reconditioning session, periodic checks were made for the remainder of the school year, the last check being made in the 14th week. These checks indicated that Robbie's studying was being maintained at an average rate of 79 percent (see Figure 21–2). Furthermore, Robbie's teacher reported that the quality of his studying had also improved; he was now completing written assignments and missing fewer words on spelling tests.

Shaping

Reinforcement is the sine qua non of operant conditioning. However, in order to reinforce behavior, it must occur. While this is certainly obvious, it is far from a trivial consideration. In the case of behavior which occurs at least occasionally, such as Robbie's studying, there is opportunity to reinforce it (although the experimenter may have to wait some time before the behavior is emitted). However, when the baseline level for a particular behavior is near zero, the standard procedures described above will not work—at least not very efficiently. This is the case with responses which have never been performed before or have not been practiced for a long period of time. It is also frequently true of complex acts, where the subject knows how to make each of the simpler component responses but has never put them together to form the complex behavior. For instance, students learning a foreign language frequently know each of the words which make up a sentence but have great difficulty in arranging them in a grammatically correct and colloquially acceptable way.

To help circumvent these problems, the desired behavior may be shaped. *Shaping,* which is also called *the method of successive approximations,* involves reinforcing progressively closer approximations of the desired behavior. A common example of shaping is the children's game of "hot and cold," in which one child has to locate a particular object in a room while a playmate directs the child toward the object by saying "hot" as the child gets closer and "cold" when the child starts to go farther away. The process of shaping is illustrated schematically in Figure 21–3 (page 470).

Complex behavior can be operantly conditioned by breaking it down into its component responses and successively reinforcing each of them. Even so-called creative behaviors, which many educators have viewed as holistic, unanalyzable, and relatively unteachable (e.g., they are "talents"), can be shaped. Examples of successful shaping include the teaching of such creative behaviors as written composition (Brigham, Graubard, & Stans, 1972) and painting (Turner, 1973).

The procedure of shaping is illustrated in the following case study of a 40-year-old male psychiatric patient who had been completely mute during 19 years of hospitalization.

> The S [subject] was brought to a group therapy session with other chronic schizophrenics (who were verbal), but he sat in the position in which he was placed and continued with withdrawal behaviors which characterized him. He remained impassive and stared ahead even when cigarettes, which other members accepted, were offered to him and were waved before his face. At one session, when E [experimenter] removed cigarettes from his pocket, a package of chewing gum accidentally fell out. The S's eyes moved toward the gum and then returned to their usual position. This response was chosen by E as one with which he would start to work, using the method of successive approximation. . . .
>
> The S met individually with E three times a week. Group sessions also continued. The following sequence of procedures was introduced in the private sessions. Although the weeks are numbered consecutively, they did not follow at regular intervals since other duties kept E from seeing S every week.
>
> *Weeks 1, 2.* A stick of gum was held before S's face, and E waited until S's eyes moved toward it. When this response occurred, E as a consequence gave him the gum. By the end of the second week, response

FIGURE 21–3
A diagram representing the principle of shaping

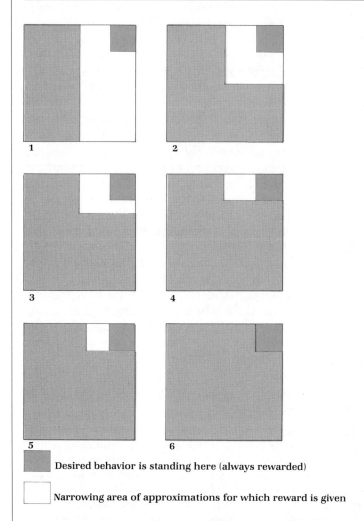

Desired behavior is standing here (always rewarded)

Narrowing area of approximations for which reward is given

probability in the presence of the gum was increased to such an extent that S's eyes moved toward the gum as soon as it was held up.

Weeks 3, 4. The E now held the gum before S, waiting until he noticed movement in S's lips before giving it to him. Toward the end of the first session of the third week, a lip movement spontaneously occurred, which E promptly reinforced. By the end of this week, both lip movement and eye movement occurred when the gum was held up. The E then withheld giving S the gum until S spontaneously made a vocalization, at which time E gave S the gum. By the end of this week, holding up the gum readily occasioned eye movement toward it, lip movement, and a vocalization resembling a croak.

Weeks 5, 6. The E held up the gum, and said, "Say gum, gum," repeating these words each time S vocalized. Giving S the gum was made contingent upon vocalizations increasingly approximating gum. At the sixth session (at the end of Week 6), when E said, "Say gum, gum," S suddenly said, "Gum, please." (Isaacs, Thomas, & Goldiamond, 1960, pp. 9–10)

A *schedule of reinforcement* is a statement of the contingency on which reinforcement is received. The most obvious schedule is to reinforce an individual every time he or she engages in the behavior to be increased. This procedure, usually referred to as a *continuous reinforcement* schedule, was used in the examples of Robbie and the mute psychiatric patient. However, continuous reinforcement often does not parallel the sort of experience which is found in actual life situations, and operant psychologists have been especially interested in the effects of reinforcement when it is not available on a continuous basis. Such schedules are referred to as *intermittent,* or *partial, schedules.*

There are four basic schedules of partial reinforcement. Each schedule is characterized by whether the reinforcement is received either after a period of time (*interval* schedule) or after a number of responses (*ratio* schedule) and whether the quantity of time or responses is either a set amount (*fixed* schedule) or a random amount (*variable* schedule). The four schedules of reinforcement which result from the combination of these four possible characteristics are depicted diagrammatically in Figure 21–4.

Schedules of reinforcement

Fixed-interval schedules

In a *fixed-interval* schedule, reinforcement is provided for the first response made after a prescribed interval of time has elapsed. Numer-

FIGURE 21–4
The four basic schedules of partial reinforcement (arrows indicate reinforcement)

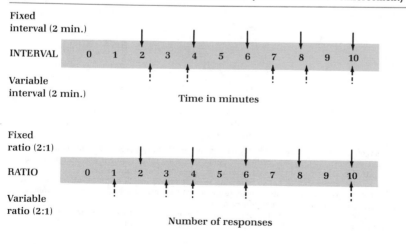

ous life situations appear to operate on fixed-interval schedules, including college examinations and salary payments. It has sometimes been recommended that infants be fed on a fixed-interval schedule (e.g., every three hours). A fixed-interval schedule produces a reliable pattern of responding that appears "scalloped" when cumulatively graphed (see Figure 21–5). The individual makes few or no responses immediately after a reinforcement but then begins to respond at an accelerated rate until the time for the next reinforcement.

> We are more willing to work harder on pay day; absenteeism is less common; the student who has dawdled along all semester suddenly accelerates his study as examination time approaches in order to secure some slight reinforcement at the end of the term; the business man makes a strong effort to "clean up his desk" in time for vacation; most people increase their efforts to make a reinforcing appointment on time. (Lundin, 1961, p. 80)

FIGURE 21–5
Stylized records of responding under basic schedules of reinforcement

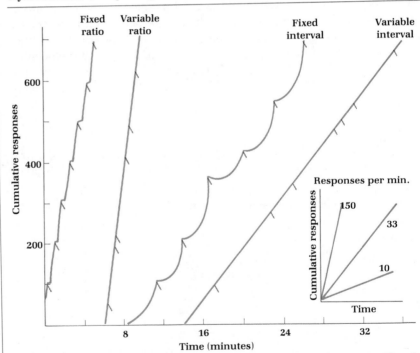

Note: Diagonal marks indicate reinforcement; the slope of various response rates is indicated at lower right. *Fixed ratio:* high rate, with brief pause following reinforcement and abrupt change to terminal rate. *Variable ratio:* high sustained rate; no pausing after reinforcement. *Fixed interval:* low overall response rate due to pause following reinforcement; length of pause increases with length of interval; gradual increase to high terminal rate as interval ends. *Variable interval:* low sustained rate; no pausing after reinforcement.

Source: Adapted from Reese, E. P. The analysis of human operant behavior. In J. A. Vernon (Ed.), *Introduction to psychology: A self-selection textbook.* Dubuque, Iowa: Brown, 1966.

Even the U.S. Congress operates on a fixed-interval schedule (Weisberg & Waldrop, 1972). Bills are passed at a very low rate for the first few months of each session, but, as adjournment draws closer, the number of bills passed increases sharply, thereby producing the "scalloped" cumulative record in Figure 21–6.

Fixed-ratio schedules

Fixed-ratio schedules are those in which reinforcement is administered only after a set number of responses has occurred. For example, a fixed ratio of 4:1 refers to a schedule in which, after every three unreinforced responses, the fourth response is reinforced. Studies with both nonhuman animals and humans suggest that fixed-ratio schedules can be made to produce considerably higher rates of responding than either continuous reinforcement or fixed-interval schedules. This can be seen in Figure 21–5, where the slope of the cumulative curve for a

FIGURE 21–6
Cumulative number of bills passed during the legislative sessions of Congress from January 1947 to August 1954

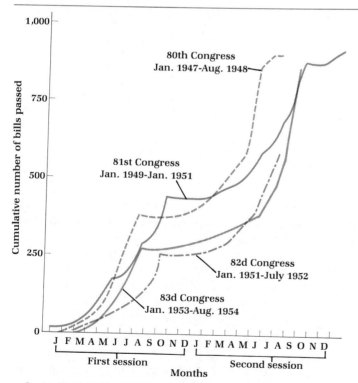

Source: Weisberg, P., & Waldrop, P. B. Fixed-interval work habits of Congress. *Journal of Applied Behavioral Analysis,* 1972, *5,* 93–97.

fixed-ratio schedule is steeper than the slope for a fixed-interval schedule.

Very high ratios of unreinforced to reinforced responses can be gradually built up. In other words, an experimenter may begin training with a 4:1 schedule and slowly increase the ratio of unreinforced to reinforced responses until the subject is rewarded as infrequently as one response in every thousand (i.e., 1,000:1). Skinner (1953) has noted both the advantages and the dangers of fixed-ratio schedules in maintaining human behavior.

> It is a common schedule in education, where the student is reinforced for completing a project or a paper or some other specific amount of work. It is essentially the basis of professional pay and of selling on commission. In industry it is known as piecework pay. It is a system of reinforcement which naturally recommends itself to employers because the cost of labor required to produce a given result can be calculated in advance. . . . A limiting factor, which makes itself felt in industry, is simple fatigue. The high rate of responding and the long hours of work generated by this schedule can be dangerous to health. This is the main reason why piecework pay is usually strenuously opposed by organized labor.
>
> Another objection to this type of schedule is based upon the possibility that as the rate rises, the reinforcing agency will move to a larger ratio. In the laboratory, after first reinforcing every tenth response and then every fiftieth, we may find it possible to reinforce only every hundredth, although we could not have used this ratio in the beginning. In industry, the employee whose productivity has increased as the result of a piecework schedule may receive so large a weekly wage that the employer feels justified in increasing the number of units of work required for a given unit of pay. (pp. 102–3)

Variable-interval schedules

In everyday life there is often variability in the schedules on which we are rewarded. A *variable-interval* schedule is one in which the interval between reinforced trials is randomly varied around a specified time value so that, *on the average,* the individual is rewarded, say, every two minutes. That is, the subject might be reinforced for responses occurring after: 1 minute, 2¼ minutes, 1½ minutes, 4½ minutes, 2½ minutes, ¼ minute; the average of these six intervals is two minutes. Lundin (1961) provides an interesting example of commonplace human behavior that is controlled by variable-interval schedules.

> Some kinds of sports activities operate on this schedule, such as hunting and fishing. A fisherman drops in his line, and then he must wait. He does not know precisely when the fish will bite (maybe not at all), nor does he know when the game will fly, even though through past conditioning history he has found certain areas to be situations in which the reinforcements occur. Although these reinforcements of catching the

fish or shooting the game are a function of his skill, the aspects of the availability of the reinforcements to him are a function of some undetermined schedule. The enthusiastic sportsman has a regularity of behavior which has had a past history of reinforcement, even though variable. (p. 88)

Variable-interval schedules produce steady (but relatively low) response rates, rather than the "scalloped" ones of fixed-interval schedules (see Figure 21–5; p. 472), and are highly resistant to extinction.

Resistance to extinction.   *Resistance to extinction* refers to the persistence of a response after reinforcement for the response has been terminated (i.e., during extinction) and thus serves as a measure of response strength. That is, the stronger a response, the longer it will be emitted without reinforcement. Behaviors which have been reinforced on partial reinforcement schedules tend to be more resistant to extinction than behaviors which have been reinforced continuously. Variable-interval schedules typically produce high resistance to extinction, as the following case illustrates.

The case involved a 21-month-old child whose bedtime temper tantrums were extinguished by his parents (Williams, 1959). By screaming and crying when they tried to leave, the child had been keeping one of his parents or an aunt, who lived with the family, in his bedroom until he fell asleep. It appeared that the child's behavior was being maintained by the adult's attention (i.e., attention was reinforcing the tantrums). To extinguish this misbehavior, reinforcement was withdrawn. The child was placed in his bed as usual, but now the adult left the room immediately despite the child's crying.

As can be seen in Figure 21–7, in the first extinction series (solid line) the child cried for 45 minutes the first time, did not cry at all the second time (it is possible that he was exhausted by the previous crying bout), cried for 10 minutes the third time, and thereafter decreased gradually to no crying. By the 10th trial, the child even smiled when the adult left. However, a week later the child cried when his aunt put him to bed, and she reinforced this behavior by remaining in the room until he went to sleep. This *single* reinforcement, which was dispensed on a *variable-interval schedule,* was sufficient to increase the rate of crying to the preextinction level and to necessitate a second series of extinction trials. As is shown in Figure 21–7 (broken line), the rate of crying reached zero by the seventh trial of the second extinction series, and no additional bedtime tantrums were reported during the following two-year period.

Variable-ratio schedules

A *variable-ratio* schedule refers to the situation in which the number of responses required for reinforcement is varied randomly around a particular ratio. For example, a "variable ratio of 20:1" might reinforce

FIGURE 21–7
Length of crying in two extinction series as a function of withdrawing reinforcement

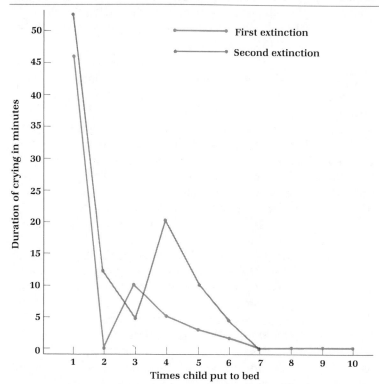

Source: Adapted from Williams, C. D. The elimination of tantrum behavior by extinction procedures: Case report. *Journal of Abnormal and Social Psychology,* 1959, *59,* 269.

a subject after every 19th, 30th, 22d, 14th, 10th, and 25th response (the average being after every 20th response). Variable-ratio schedules are among the most potent for inducing very high, steady rates of responding (see Figure 21–5; p. 472) and are very resistant to extinction.

The extremely high rates that can be generated by these schedules are illustrated in the behavior of the compulsive gambler. Even though the returns are very slim, he never gives up. Families are ruined and fortunes lost; still the high rates of behavior are maintained, often to the exclusion of all alternate forms of activity. Witness the "all night" crap games in which a single person will remain until all his funds and resources are gone. His behavior is terminated only by his inability to perform operations necessary to stay in the game. And even on these occasions, if he can muster more funds by borrowing or stealing, he will return to the game. Although gambling may involve other auxiliary reinforcements, social and personal, the basic rate of behavior is maintained by the schedule itself. The degree of control exercised by such a schedule is tremendous. In these cases almost absolute control has been achieved, so that the behavior becomes as certain as that found in respondent conditioning. The degree of control is often unfortunate and dangerous to the individual and his family, and the paradoxical thing about it is that the controlling agency (unless the gambling devices are "fixed") is the simple factor of chance. (Lundin, 1961, p. 91)

Schedules of reinforcement in daily activities

In the course of our daily activities, our behavior is influenced by a variety of schedules of reinforcement. This can be seen in the following account of the routine day of a male college student, which also serves as a review of the basic schedules of reinforcement we have discussed.[5]

Take, for example, the day-to-day activity of a college student. He eats, sleeps, takes his toilet on a variety of fixed-interval schedules, and does his assignments on ratio schedules. He takes weekly examinations in some courses (fixed interval) and is assigned only term papers in other seminar-type courses (ratio schedule). His social life operates by and large on variable-interval schedules, and much of his verbal behavior is on a . . . [continuous reinforcement] schedule, since people ordinarily speak to him when he addresses them. If he happens to work in his spare time to help pay his way through school, he can earn extra money for typing papers for his fellow students, at so much per page (fixed ratio), or he may prefer to wait on tables in the cafeteria for an hourly wage (fixed interval). He engages in sports and games on some variable-ratio schedules; the more he plays, the more likely he is to win, although the winning is not regular or absolutely predictable. (Lundin, 1961, p. 96)

OPERANT CONDITIONING OF HUMAN BEHAVIOR[6]

Demonstration 21–1

You may now wish to try your hand at operant conditioning. For this Demonstration you will need to enlist the aid of a friend who is willing to participate. Be sure that the friend has at least 45 minutes of free time. You will need a watch or clock with a sweep-second hand, and pencil and paper.

THE RESPONSE

The first step is to select the response you will teach your subject. Although the procedures to be outlined will work with complex motor or verbal responses

---

[5] Each of the four basic partial reinforcement schedules and continuous reinforcement can be combined to form *multiple schedules* (e.g., a fixed-interval followed by a fixed-ratio schedule, as occurs when a sales representative begins with a weekly salary and then switches to a commission basis) or *concurrent schedules* (e.g., fixed-interval and fixed-ratio schedules both operating at the same time, as is the case when a sales representative works for both salary and commission).

[6] The procedures used in Demonstration 21–1 are, in part, adapted from Verplanck, 1956.

TABLE 21–2
Examples of responses suitable for operant conditioning in Demonstration 21–1

Motor responses	*Verbal responses*
Opening and closing a book	Criticizing
Taking top off a pen and replacing it	Talking about the future
Standing up and sitting down	Talking about schoolwork
Nodding head	Using plural nouns

as well as simple ones, it may be best to condition a relatively simple response, at least for your first subject. Some suggested responses are listed in Table 21–2. Other than simplicity, the response you choose to condition should meet three additional requirements. First, it should **terminate fairly quickly** so that it can be reinforced. Second, the response should **end where it began.** That is, when the response is completed, the subject should be able to immediately perform the same response again without having to rearrange the situation. For example, you would not want to condition "opening a book" since this would necessitate closing the book before the subject made the response again. Such rearrangement would be a salient cue for the subject and thus would bias the operant conditioning.[7] Finally, the response should normally **occur at a speed which makes recording feasible.** Finger tapping, for example, would be a poor choice.

SHAPING

If the response you select is one your subject makes frequently, then all you have to do is wait until it occurs to reinforce it. If, however, it occurs infrequently, you may have to use shaping procedures. This will necessitate breaking down the total response into logical component parts. For example, suppose that you were going to condition "opening and closing a book." You would first reinforce (reinforcement procedures are discussed later) the first movement made, since this will start the subject moving about. **The first movement the subject makes should be the initial component of any motor response.** Next, you might reinforce (2) **movement of either hand,** (3) **movement of either hand toward the book,** then (4) **touching the book,** (5) **opening it partway,** (6) **opening it fully,** and finally, (7) **closing the book.** Similarly, the successive approximations of verbal criticism might be: (1) any verbal utterance, (2) any statement (i.e., as opposed to a question), (3) any negative statement, and finally, (4) any negative statement which is a criticism.

Keep in mind that the successive approximations for the motor and verbal responses just given are examples and will not work in all cases. For example, it may be necessary to create more steps in the sequence by breaking down some of the approximations into additional components. It is also possible that your subject will combine some of the approximations you set up, in which case the conditioning of the total response could be more rapid. Shaping is very much an art, and it is only through practice that you will "get a feel"

---

[7] If the object were to teach a particular response to someone, rather than to learn about operant conditioning, additional cues which aid the learner would certainly be used (e.g., telling the person what to do and modeling the behavior).

FIGURE 21–8
Cumulative record of "hand raising" shaped by operant conditioning

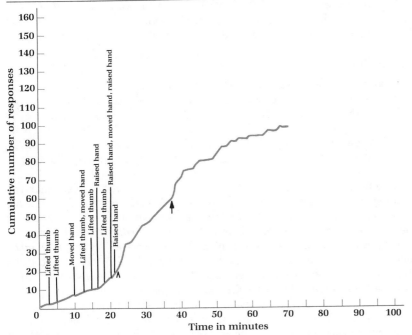

Note: Following the caret (∧) only the complete response was reinforced. Following the arrow (↑) no responses were reinforced (i.e., extinction).

Source: Verplanck, W. S. The operant conditioning of human motor behavior. *Psychological Bulletin*, 1956, *53*, 70–83.

for the procedure. Figure 21–8 illustrates a cumulative record of a response that was initially conditioned by means of shaping.

REINFORCEMENT

Each time the subject makes a correct response (or an approximation of it if shaping procedures are employed), you will say the word ***point***. (Earning points, like receiving grades, provides feedback that one is performing correctly and is an example of a *token reinforcer*, so-called because the reinforcer itself has no actual value.) The subject should be able to see a record of the points earned. This can be conveniently implemented by instructing the subject to make a tally mark on a sheet of paper each time you say "point." An alternative procedure, which is preferable only if recording points will interrupt the subject's behavior, is for you to record the points on a record sheet which is clearly visible to the subject.

The prompt and accurate administration of reinforcement is the sine qua non of operant conditioning. If reinforcement is not administered promptly, then it is likely that one or more other responses will occur between the termination of the target response (i.e., the one which you wish to increase) and the reinforcement. This will make it difficult for the subject to discriminate the response for which reinforcement is contingent. Thus, the reinforcement should be given **immediately** after the correct response (or an approximation of it) is made. Careful observation of the subject's behavior is necessary to ascertain whether the response, as you have defined it, has been made.

PROCEDURE

1. Preparation.   Before your subject arrives for your "experiment," arrange the room so that the subject will be sitting facing you. Place any equipment needed for the response (e.g., a book for the response illustrated above) in close proximity to the subject. If you are using a room with which the subject is familiar, be sure that the arrangement of the equipment necessary for the response does not look out of the ordinary lest this "give away" the correct response.

2. Instructions to the subject.   When your subject arrives, explain that you are doing an experiment or project for one of your classes. Then the following instructions should be given: *"Your job is to earn points. I will tell you each time you earn a point, and you (I) will record it immediately on this sheet of paper by making a tally mark for each point you receive. Try to get as many points as you can."* Do not give any further instructions to the subject. If the subject asks you a question, merely say: *"I'm sorry, but I'm not permitted to answer any questions. Just work for points and earn as many as you can."*

After the instructions are given, your subject may sit motionless and say nothing for several minutes. Sooner or later, however, your subject will make a response which you will be able to reinforce. Although this initial period of inactivity may be somewhat frustrating for both of you, it should not affect the success of the conditioning. Do *not* try to break the silence or awkward social situation, since this will prejudice the experiment.

OBSERVATION AND RECORDING

Once you have given your subject the instructions, your task is simply to observe the subject's behavior very carefully, record the frequency with which the correct response (or an approximation of it) is made, and reinforce correct responses. Your record sheet should be modeled after that in Figure 21–9. (Do not confuse the subject's record of the points earned with the record you keep of the subject's behavior and the procedures employed.) Your record sheet should *not* be visible to the subject. When the subject makes a correct response, you must note the 30-second time interval in which it occurred by referring to your watch with a sweep-second hand. The watch should be placed so that you do not have to move your eyes very far to see the time. Also indicate on the record sheet whether a reinforcement was given for a response by circling the check mark (see Figure 21–9), a procedure which is essential when the subject is shifted to a partial reinforcement schedule.

Finally, indicate on the record sheet all procedural changes, such as a shift in reinforcement schedule. This can easily be done by making a dark, vertical line at the point of change in procedure. As is illustrated in Figure 21–9, a small lowercase letter is placed adjacent to this line, and it is defined at the bottom of the record sheet in the space provided for comments.

FIGURE 21–9
Model record sheet for Demonstration 21–1

30-second time interval	Total For each interval	Cumu-lative	30-second time interval	Total For each interval	Cumu-lative
Response = *looking out the window and then looking back*					
√ = Response ⊘ = Reinforced response					
1.	0	0	25. √√√	3	66
2.	0	0	26. √⊘√	3	69
3. ⊘ /a	1	1	27. √√√	3	72
4.	0	1	28. ⊘√√√	4	76
5. ⊘ ⊘	2	3	29. √⊘√√	4	80
6.	0	3	30. √√⊘√	3	83
7. ⊘ ⊘	2	5	31. √√√√	4	87
8. ⊘ ⊘	2	7	32. ⊘√√	3	90
9. ⊘ ⊘ ⊘	3	10	33. d/√√√	3	93
10. ⊘ ⊘ ⊘ ⊘	4	14	34. √√√√	4	97
11. ⊘ ⊘ ⊘	3	17	35. √√√	3	100
12. ⊘ ⊘ ⊘ ⊘	4	21	36. √√	2	102
13. ⊘ ⊘ ⊘ ⊘	4	25	37. √√	2	104
14. ⊘ ⊘ ⊘ ⊘	4	29	38.	0	104
15. ⊘ ⊘ ⊘ ⊘	4	33	39. √√	2	106
16. b/ √ √√ /c	3	36	40. √√	2	108
17. √⊘	2	38	41. √	1	109
18. √√	2	40	42.	0	109
19. √√	2	42	43. √	1	110
20. ⊘√√√√	5	47	44.	0	110
21. ⊘√√√√	4	51	45.	0	110
22. √⊘√√	4	55	46.	0	110
23. √√⊘√	4	59	47.	0	110
24. √√√⊘	4	63	48.	0	110

Comments:

a = Subject asks why a point was earned
b = start of fixed-ratio 5:1
c = Subject asks why I stopped giving points
d = start of extinction

CONDITIONING

Three phases of conditioning will be used, and the procedures for each are outlined below.

1. Acquisition: Continuous reinforcement. During this phase, **every correct response** (or approximation of it) **is given a point.** Continuous reinforcement is the most efficient and effective way to initially establish a response. Continuous reinforcement should be given until the *total* response (i.e., not just a component of it) has been reinforced a minimum of 15 times. If, after a number of continuous reinforcements, the subject's rate of responding begins to decrease noticeably, you should simply say: *"Keep earning points."* This statement will usually restore the previous response rate. (Indicate on your record sheet when you gave this additional instruction to your subject.)

2. Shift to partial reinforcement.   After the response has been well established (i.e., after a minimum of 15 continuous reinforcements), you will be able to shift your subject to a partial reinforcement schedule with little difficulty. While any of the partial reinforcement schedules discussed earlier in the chapter could be used, the most convenient for the Demonstration is a *"fixed-ratio 5:1."* That is, reinforce every fifth response. This means that, although you will continue *recording* every response the subject makes, only after every five responses will you say, "Point." Note also that you will continue to record the responses in the time interval in which they occur, but the five consecutive responses required for reinforcement to be given need *not* occur in the same time interval. Under this fixed-ratio schedule, you should observe that your subject's rate of responding will increase and that there will be a brief pause after each reinforcement (see Figure 21–5; p. 472). Continue on the 5:1 fixed-ratio schedule for a minimum of 10 reinforcements (i.e., 50 responses).

When you shift to a partial reinforcement schedule, you may find that the

FIGURE 21–10
Sample cumulative record of data presented in Figure 21–9

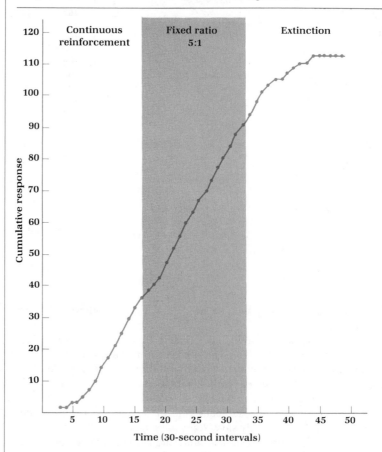

subject will begin to emit other responses and make a number of verbal comments (e.g., in the case of a fixed-ratio schedule, counting out loud and statements to the effect that points are being earned for every five responses). Do not let such behavior changes bother you; just continue with the operant procedures.

3. Extinction. The final phase of the conditioning involves extinction of the response. This is done by completely withdrawing reinforcement for the response. Continue to record the number of responses that the subject makes in each 30-second interval, but do **not** give points for any of these responses. Continue the extinction phase until the subject has failed to emit the response **during five successive 30-second recording intervals.**

PLOTTING A CUMULATIVE RECORD

Once the data for the three phases of conditioning have been collected, the frequency of responding can be plotted on a cumulative record similar to that in Figure 21–10.

To make a cumulative record, logarithmic paper is best, but any graph paper will do as long as you plan the scale of the vertical axis carefully. That is, it is necessary to make some estimate of the total (cumulative) number of responses for the entire period of recording, so that you can number the vertical axis appropriately and not have your cumulative curve run off the top of the paper.

Heavy vertical lines (i.e., parallel to the vertical axis) should be drawn on the graph to designate that a new phase of conditioning was instituted. Additionally, you may wish to note, with small vertical lines, any special changes in procedure and, in the case of shaping, the response component made. You can indicate what occurred at these points either by writing directly on the cumulative record or with a lowercase letter which refers to a statement written at the bottom of the cumulative record. Figure 21–10 is a cumulative record of the data on the record sheet in Figure 21–9 (page 481).

Learning always involves two aspects. We must learn not only *how* to perform the behavior but also to discriminate *when* and *where* it is appropriate to engage in the behavior. "Appropriateness" can be defined as those situations which are likely to lead to reinforcement (or, at least, not lead to aversive consequences). *Discriminative stimuli* are those environmental cues which tell us when it is likely that a response will be reinforced. Although operant responses are governed by their consequences, discriminative stimuli serve to set the occasion for their occurrence. Accordingly, behavior which is cued by discriminative stimuli is said to be under *stimulus control*.

Almost all operant behavior is under stimulus control. A police car up ahead is often a sufficient discriminative stimulus for decreasing the pressure of one's foot on the accelerator; the ringing telephone signals us to pick up the receiver and say hello. Other people's behavior

**DISCRIMINATION
AND STIMULUS
CONTROL**

often serves as a discriminative stimulus for one's own actions. We are more likely to smile at other people when they smile at us than when they frown at us.

The same response may be controlled by different discriminative stimuli for different people. In countries where food is scarce, people eat when their stomachs "tell" them that they are hungry, whereas in more affluent societies, such as our own, people tend to eat when the clock "tells" them that they are "hungry."

Problems arise when behavior is under too much stimulus control as well as when it is under too little. Parents of young children often must contend with the fact that their children's "good" behavior is under too much stimulus control. For example, parents discover that bedtime is likely to be observed only when they are home and not when the children are left with grandparents or babysitters. The parents are the discriminative stimuli for observing bedtime, and the children have not learned to generalize the behavior to other discriminative stimuli.

Fox (1966) points out that the study habits of college students are often under inadequate stimulus control.

> The act of studying, regardless of efficiency, is not usually under adequate stimulus control, either by time or by place. The student may study physics at random occasions and at any place he may happen to be on those occasions. Thus, he is subject to all the interfering behaviors conditioned to those occasions. No one occasion becomes uniquely related to study. Even where the student has established regular places and times for study, the immediately preceding occasion is likely to produce behavior competing with that of going to the place of study. He studies physics in the library at ten o'clock if he can resist the reinforcement involved in having coffee with his friends. (p. 86)

Fox (1966) developed a program to bring the study behavior of students under effective stimulus control, using a variety of operant procedures which have already been discussed. The program will be illustrated by the case of one of the volunteer students with whom Fox worked.

The student had a 9 a.m. physics class and was then free for an hour at 10 a.m. The student was instructed to go to the library at this time and to begin studying physics. (Students often reported an intention to do just this, but somehow never got around to it.) One of the problems involved in maintaining a schedule, as most readers doubtless know, is that a person is likely to experience some degree of discomfort or perhaps to daydream in such a situation. If this occurred, Fox instructed the student to abandon studying and go have coffee with friends or engage in any other pleasurable activity. There was, however, one small restriction—before leaving the student was either to read one page of the text carefully or to solve the easiest problem which had been assigned.

On each subsequent day the student was required to read one page more than on the previous day before leaving the study room, and, in this manner, gradually learned to spend the entire hour studying physics. After a week, a second course was similarly scheduled in a different room, and appropriate hours were set. "Eventually, every course was so scheduled, and the student was spending the whole of one hour each day on each course" (Fox, 1966, p. 87).

Each of the steps in this program was dictated by a principle of operant conditioning and therefore serves as a partial review of the preceding sections. First, social reinforcers were made contingent upon an appropriate response (some studying). Second, shaping was used by having the student work up to the full hour of study gradually. Third, a fixed-ratio schedule was employed (so many pages for the reinforcement of leaving the study situation), and the ratio was gradually increased, thereby making studying more resistant to extinction. Finally, studying was under stimulus control in that it occurred in the same room and at the same time each day.

PUNISHMENT

Punishment refers to the situation in which a response is followed by an event which *reduces* the likelihood that the response will occur again. Usually, but not always, the punishing event is aversive to the individual. Historically, punishment was thought to be much less effective than reinforcement in learning (e.g., Skinner, 1938; Thorndike, 1932, 1933), and, hence, it remained largely neglected as a topic of scientific investigation until about 20 years ago (Solomon, 1964). In recent years, applied research with humans suggests that punishment can, under some circumstances, be an effective, efficient (Rachman & Teasdale, 1969), and ethically justifiable (Baer, 1970) means of eliminating undesirable operant behavior. In one such study (Risley, 1968), the subject was a six-year-old girl who was diagnosed as having diffuse brain damage, was hyperactive, and whose only vocalizations were howls, moans, and clicking noises. Her predominant behavior was climbing in high places, although this was interspersed with sitting and rocking. Risley (1968) presents a vivid description of the potential hazards of this limited repertoire of behavior.

> Her climbing was a constant source of concern to her parents due to the threat of her life and limb (her body bore multiple scars from past falls; her front teeth were missing, having been left embedded in a two by four inch molding from which she had fallen while climbing outside the second story of her house), and the attendant destruction of furniture in the house. She had attended several schools for special children but

had been dropped from each because of these disruptive behaviors and her lack of progress. (p. 22)

Initially, Risley attempted a variety of well-established procedures for eliminating the child's potentially harmful climbing behaviors. The first of these was a procedure known as *time-out from positive reinforcement,* or *time-out* for short. When the undesired response occurs, the person is removed (for a specified time period) from circumstances in which behavior can potentially receive reinforcement. In this case, the subject's physical isolation from social interaction was made a consequence of her climbing behavior. Whenever the little girl climbed, her mother sharply said "No!," brought her back to the floor, and took her to her bedroom (with no further words and minimal physical contact) for a 10-minute time-out period. Her mother was also asked to interact with the child as much as possible when she was *not* climbing. After 17 days of employing time-out, no visible diminution of the climbing behavior occurred. Furthermore, it did not appear that the climbing was under the influence of any of the reinforcers which were supplied by either the experimenter or the mother. Thus, because of the clearly hazardous nature of the behaviors being performed, a form of punishment was applied.

The punishment was administered by a hand-held shock device. The shock was painful but it produced no lasting harmful side effects (e.g., no redness, swelling, or aching). As Risley (1968) noted, "observers of the sessions in which the shocks were applied reported that, on the basis of observable autonomic responses . . . the subject recovered from the shock episodes much faster than the experimenter" (p. 25). The contingent application of punishment effectively eliminated the hazardous climbing behavior in a very few sessions. The results are presented as a cumulative record in Figure 21–11 from which it can be seen that, after the third session in which shock was administered, the shock effectively eliminated the climbing behavior for one or more sessions (i.e., the cumulative curve leveled off indicating that the response was not being emitted).

**OPERANT
CONDITIONING
OF COVERT
BEHAVIOR**

Some personality psychologists who use a classical conditioning approach have made cognitions such as attitudes and mental imagery a part of their study (see Chapter 20). This is in keeping with the recent trend within the behavioral strategy toward studying private, covert behavior as well as public, overt behavior (see Chapter 19). Operant psychologists have been more reluctant to examine cognitive processes, but they have made some initial inroads in this regard.

The first step in this process has been to make the assumption that covert events such as thinking, ruminating, and believing follow the

FIGURE 21–11
Cumulative record of "climbing on a bookcase" showing the effects of punishment

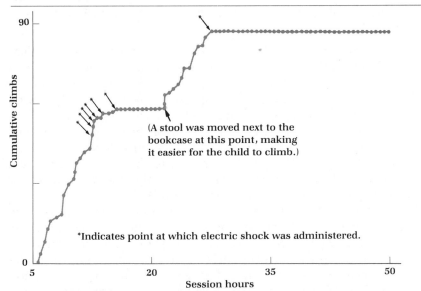

*Indicates point at which electric shock was administered.

(A stool was moved next to the bookcase at this point, making it easier for the child to climb.)

Source: Adapted from Risley, T. R. The effects and side effects of punishing the autistic behaviors of a deviant child. *Journal of Applied Behavior Analysis*, 1968, *1*, 21–34.

same principles of learning as does overt behavior (e.g., Bandura, 1969a; Homme, 1965; Mahoney, 1970, 1974; Skinner, 1953, 1963; Ullmann, 1970). More than 25 years ago, Skinner (1953) wrote: "We need not suppose that events which take place within an organism's skin have special properties for that reason. A private event may be distinguished by its limited accessibility but not, so far as we know, by any special structure or nature" (p. 257).

In 1965, Homme coined the term *coverant* as a contraction of "covert operant"—"operants of the mind"—and suggested that coverants, like their overt counterparts, are primarily influenced by the consequences which they produce. The coverants which have received the most widespread attention are *self-statements*, thoughts which are phrases or sentences that we say to ourselves. Common examples include: "I am hungry"; "I have a paper to write"; "That person is nice"; "I feel good today"; "I'm going to win this game." The simplest conceptualization of the interrelationship of "private" coverants and "public" operants is in terms of three categories:

1. *Coverants influencing operants*, as when the thought "I am tired" leads one to take a nap.
2. *Operants influencing coverants*, as when napping decreases the probability that one will think "I am tired" and increases the probability that one will think "I feel refreshed and wide awake."

3. *Coverants influencing coverants,* as when the thought "I am tired" increases the probability of making such self-statements as "I am having difficulty concentrating" or "It sure would be nice to take a nap."

Covert reinforcement (Cautela, 1970a, 1970b) refers to a procedure which involves the direct control of coverants by coverants and is primarily used therapeutically. In covert positive reinforcement the client is first trained to imagine pleasant, reinforcing scenes (e.g., swimming in a cool mountain stream on a hot summer day). Then the client is instructed to imagine doing a desired overt behavior (e.g., arriving for work on time) and then to shift attention to a reinforcing image. The therapist cues the imagery shift by saying the word *reinforcement* when the client has a clear image of performing the target behavior (which the client indicates by raising a finger).

Cautela (1970b) describes the procedures used to treat a graduate student who suffered from extreme anxiety about tests and studying. The student had failed his doctoral qualifying examination three times (despite his being an excellent student), and he was to take it for the final time in three months. First, he learned to visualize several reinforcing scenes (including skiing down a mountain feeling exhilarated, and being awarded his doctoral degree). Then, while sitting comfortably with his eyes closed, he was given the following instructions.

> Now let's work on the examination situation. It is the day of the examination and you feel confident. ("Reinforcement.") You are entering the building in which the exam is going to be given ("Reinforcement.") You remember that in all these scenes you are to try to feel confident. Now you enter the building and go into the classroom. ("Reinforcement.") You sit down and kid around with another student who is taking the exam. ("Reinforcement.") The proctor comes in with the exam. You feel good; you know you are ready. ("Reinforcement.") The proctor hands out the exam. ("Reinforcement.") You read the questions and you feel you can answer all of them. ("Reinforcement.")
>
> Now let's do that again. This time you look the questions over and you are not sure about one question, but you say, "Oh well, I can still pass the exam if I flunk this one question." ("Reinforcement.") All right, this time you look over the exam, and you can see two questions about which you are in doubt, and you say, "Well, I can still pass this exam if I take my time and relax." ("Reinforcement.") (Cautela, 1970b, p. 39)

After 10 sessions of therapist-administered covert reinforcement and self-administered covert reinforcement at home twice a day, the student reported feeling confident and relaxed about taking his qualifying examination, which he subsequently passed.

It should be noted that covert reinforcement uses coverants to directly modify other coverants which, in turn, influence operants. For example, in the case of the test-anxious graduate student, the immediate behavior which was to be increased by the covert reinforcement was a coverant—the image of performing in a relaxed and competent manner while taking an examination—but the ultimate behavior changed was an operant—actually taking an examination and doing well on it.

Attention to "inner" processes, especially cognitive processes, in the form of coverants presents some intriguing possibilities for expansion of the operant approach to studying personality. Nonetheless, it should be emphasized first of all that relatively little investigation of coverant behavior has been performed compared to the enormous amount of study of operant behavior, and second that a majority of operant personality psychologists still believe that it is most prudent to limit the scientific investigation of personality to the realm of observable behaviors (i.e., operants). The trend within the behavioral strategy toward increased attention to nonobservable events and behaviors is more prevalent in the observational learning approach to personality which is the topic of the next chapter.

22 | *The behavioral strategy*

The observational learning and cognitive-behavioral approaches

In this chapter we turn to the third major type of learning which influences personality. The study of observational learning differs in a major respect from that of classical and operant conditioning discussed in the previous two chapters. Work in both of those areas has been firmly in the tradition of radical behaviorism (see Chapter 19). On the other hand, the study of observational learning is more in keeping with methodological behaviorism because while it has been characterized by objectivity, precision, and controlled experimentation, there has been considerable theorizing and empirical research concerning the cognitive processes underlying observational learning (e.g., the question of how people come to use the information they gain from observing others). Still, these cognitive processes have generally been defined in terms of overt behavior, which is consistent with the tenets of methodological behaviorism (e.g., "acquisition" of modeled behavior, which is a covert process, is assessed by asking the observer to verbally recall or demonstrate the model's acts, which are overt behaviors).

This chapter serves a dual function. By presenting the observational learning approach to personality we are also providing a detailed example of the cognitive-behavioral approach in Chapter 19. The cognitive-behavioral approach includes cognitive factors—thoughts, expectations, beliefs, images—as well as situational and environmental factors as determinants of behavior. We shall see that it is possible to investigate covert phenomena in a reasonably objective manner, which is what makes the relatively new cognitive-behavioral approach to personality *behavioral* (methodologically but not radically). In the final major section of the chapter, we provide examples of cognitive behavior modification, personality-change procedures which are based on observational learning and/or other techniques which derive from a cognitive-behavioral perspective.

The observational learning approach to personality involves considerably more theory than do either the classical conditioning or operant approaches discussed in the previous two chapters. Furthermore, much of the theorizing concerns the underlying *cognitive* processes which

A THEORETICAL FRAMEWORK FOR OBSERVATIONAL LEARNING

Albert Bandura

Courtesy of Albert Bandura

are hypothesized to govern observational learning. Still, the approach is firmly entrenched in the behavioral strategy in that the cognitive processes are closely tied to observable behaviors and environmental events. Thus, we have the first major example of the cognitive-behavioral approach to personality, which will be discussed at length in this chapter.

We begin our examination of observational learning by briefly outlining some basic principles and a theoretical framework which stems from the social learning view of Albert Bandura (1925–   ), a psychologist at Stanford University whose name is as intimately associated with observational learning as Skinner's name is with operant conditioning. While there are other theoretical perspectives of observational learning (cf. Aronfreed, 1968; Baer & Sherman, 1964; Gewirtz & Stingle, 1968; Miller & Dollard, 1941; Mowrer, 1960; Piaget, 1952; Skinner, 1953), Bandura's (1969b, 1971, 1977b; Bandura & Walters, 1963) social learning theory is by far the most prominent.

Definition of terms

There tends to be some confusion concerning the basic terminology associated with observational learning. Thus, at the outset, we shall present some precise definitions used by psychologists who work in this area of study.

Overall, our focus of interest is on *observational learning:* the process through which the behavior of one person, an *observer,* changes as a function of merely being exposed to the behavior of another, the *model.* The phenomenon, then, always involves the behavior of at least two participants.

Modeling, as we shall use the term, refers to the behavior of the exemplar (model). Thus, models *model* and observers (sometimes) *imitate.* It would be correct to say, "Children imitate (the behavior which) adults (model)," but *incorrect* to say, "Children model (themselves after) adults." *Imitation* refers to emulating the model (though not necessarily copying or exactly reproducing the model's actions), whereas *counterimitation* refers to acting contrary to the model's behavior.

Specific components of a model's behavior are called *modeling cues.* Such cues are available almost continually in real life. Broadly, they appear in two forms: live and symbolic. *Live modeling* refers to observing models "in the flesh," so to speak—that is, models that are physically present. *Symbolic modeling* involves being exposed to models indirectly (i.e., in symbolic form) such as in movies, by reading, and through oral descriptions of a person's behaviors.

Observational learning as a three-stage process

Observational learning can be usefully conceptualized as a three-stage process: being exposed to modeling cues, acquiring (learning) them, and subsequently accepting them as a guide for one's own behav-

FIGURE 22–1
The three stages of observational learning

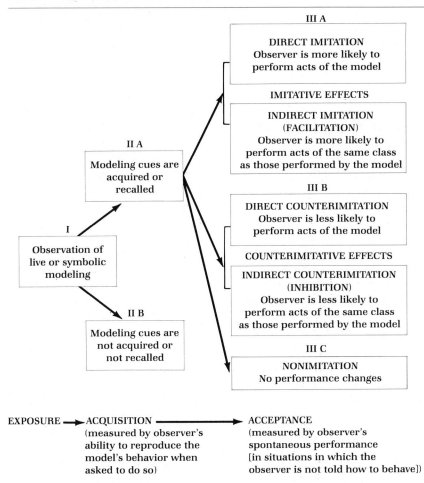

ior (Liebert, 1972, 1973). This process is depicted schematically in Figure 22–1.

Exposure to or observation of the modeling cues is the first step in the observational learning sequence. Although it is obvious that in order to learn the modeled acts people must be exposed to them in either a live or a symbolic manner, sometimes it is not readily apparent whether adequate exposure has occurred, and this becomes a critical issue.

Being exposed to modeling cues is only the first step in *potential* observational learning and implies nothing about learning from the model or subsequently imitating the model (in the third stage). *Acquisition* of modeling cues, the second stage of observational learning, does not necessarily follow from adequate exposure to them. A person can be exposed to modeling cues without acquiring new ways of behaving. This point will be obvious if you consider that we are exposed to countless models every day (e.g., noticing people cross the street, watching actors on TV) but only a handful of them have any influence on us. Acquisition requires both attention to the modeling cues and storing them in memory. Acquisition is measured by the observer's *recall* of the model's behavior—that is, the observer being able to reproduce or adequately describe it. Notice that acquisition refers to a cognitive process, a covert behavior, but that it is defined operationally in terms of an overt behavior: recall. This has the obvious advantage that acquisition is objectively and publicly verifiable. However, it also has a possible limitation because there will be times that the observer has acquired the modeling cues in the sense that they have been attended to and stored in memory, but this will not be evident in the recall measure. For instance, under some circumstances the observer may be unwilling to reproduce the model's acts, which is often the case when the model's behavior resulted in negative consequences and the observer may be reluctant to risk similar negative sanctions for performing the same behaviors. In such cases, it may be necessary to provide observers with sufficient incentives to induce them to reproduce the model's actions, as we shall see in an experiment by Bandura (1965) described later in this section.

If both exposure and acquisition have occurred, then our interest turns to the third and final step in the observational learning process: *acceptance.* Acceptance refers to the question of whether or not the observer, having been exposed to and having acquired the modeling cues, now employs or accepts them as a guide for her or his own actions. To measure acceptance, the person is observed in a situation in which he or she is free to use the model's behavior as a guide. Obviously, the observer may not choose to do this, in which case acceptance did not occur.

If the observer does choose to "accept" the model's actions to direct her or his own behavior, the acceptance will take one of four forms. We have already distinguished between two possible effects of observing a model, imitation and counterimitation (basically doing what the model did or avoiding what the model did). In each case, the influence of the model's behavior may be direct or indirect. A direct influence is said to occur when the observer engages in the same behavior as the model (i.e., matching or copying), which is called *direct imitation*, or when the observer does exactly the opposite of what the model did, which is called *direct counterimitation*. Direct counterimitation often serves an adaptive function in our lives, since it allows us to learn from the mistakes of others without having to undergo the same negative experiences ourselves. For instance, children who see a peer burned by a hot stove will typically become *less* likely to touch the dangerous appliance than they were previously; they accept the model's actions and consequences as a guide for what they should *not* do.

Modeling cues may also indirectly affect observers by suggesting acceptance of a more general class of behaviors, of which the modeling cues are perceived as an example (i.e., generalization). Consider five-year-old Doug who sees his parents regularly donate money to a variety of charities; subsequently Doug may become more willing to share his toys with his friends or to divide a piece of chocolate cake with his sister. This would be an example of *indirect imitation,* which is also called *facilitation.* In another prototypical situation, a youngster who observes a variety of models being punished regularly for handing in homework late, talking back to the teacher, and so on, may avoid school "transgressions" which the child has never seen modeled (or punished). This would be an example of *indirect counterimitation,* which is also called *inhibition.*

The three-stage scheme of observational learning makes it clear that exposure and acquisition are necessary, but not sufficient, conditions for imitation or counterimitation to occur. Simply stated, there is a distinction made between what we "see" and remember, on the one hand, and what we eventually do, on the other hand. One of the factors which influences what we do, the particular outcome in the acceptance stage, is the consequences which accrue to the model for his or her actions. The importance, indeed the necessity, of distinguishing between acquisition and acceptance,[1] as well as the role played by consequences to the model (called vicarious consequences) in determining the degree of acceptance was first demonstrated in a classic experiment by Bandura (1965), often referred to as the "Bobo doll study."

In Bandura's experiment, the observers were nursery school boys and girls, and the modeling cues were provided symbolically by a five-minute film.

> The film began with a scene in which [an adult male] model walked up to an adult-size plastic Bobo doll and ordered him to clear the way. After glaring for a moment at the noncompliant antagonist the model exhibited four novel aggressive responses each accompanied by a distinctive verbalization.
>
> First, the model laid the Bobo doll on its side, sat on it, and punched it in the nose while remarking, "Pow, right in the nose, boom, boom." The model then raised the doll and pommeled it on the head with a mallet. Each response was accompanied by the verbalization, "Sockeroo . . . stay down." Following the mallet aggression, the model kicked the doll about the room, and these responses were interspersed with the comment, "Fly away." Finally, the model threw rubber balls at the Bobo

---

[1] Bandura and Walters (1963) first made this crucial differentiation, which they called the *acquisition-performance distinction.*

> doll, each strike punctuated with "Bang." This sequence of physically and verbally aggressive behavior was repeated twice. (Bandura, 1965, pp. 590–91)

The major independent variable involved the consequences which the model in the film received as a result of his aggressive behavior. One group of children simply watched the film, as described above, and thus observed *no consequences* to the model because of his acts. A second group of children saw the same film, but with the addition of a final scene in which the model was rewarded for aggressive behavior.

> For children in the *model-rewarded* condition, a second adult appeared with an abundant supply of candies and soft drinks. He informed the model that he was a "strong champion" and that his superb aggressive performance clearly deserved a generous treat. He then poured him a large glass of 7-Up, and readily supplied additional energy-building nourishment including chocolate bars, Cracker Jack popcorn, and an assortment of candies. While the model was rapidly consuming the delectable treats, his admirer symbolically reinstated the modeled aggressive responses and engaged in considerable positive social reinforcement. (Bandura, 1965, p. 591; italics added)

A third group of children also watched the basic film, but with an added final scene in which the model was punished rather than rewarded for his acts.

> For children in the *model-punished* condition the reinforcing agent appeared on the scene shaking his finger menacingly and commenting reprovingly, "Hey there, you big bully. You quit picking on that clown. I won't tolerate it." As the model drew back he tripped and fell, the other adult sat on the model and spanked him with a rolled-up magazine while reminding him of his aggressive behavior. As the model ran off cowering, the agent forewarned him, "If I catch you doing that again, you big bully, I'll give you a hard spanking. You quit acting that way." (Bandura, 1965, p. 591; italics added)

After viewing the film, each child was brought into an experimental room which contained a plastic Bobo doll, three balls, a mallet, a pegboard, plastic farm animals, and a dollhouse which was equipped with furniture and a miniature doll family. This array of toys permitted the subject to engage either in imitative aggressive responses (i.e., the model's responses) or in alternative nonaggressive and nonimitative forms of behavior. The subject was subsequently left alone with this assortment of equipment for 10 minutes, and the subject's behavior was periodically recorded by judges who were observing from behind a one-way-vision screen. Children's aggressive behaviors in this situation constituted the *acceptance* measure.

After the acceptance test, an assessment was made of the degree to which children could demonstrate or reproduce the modeled behaviors, irrespective of whether they had performed them when alone. This constituted the *acquisition* measure. The experimenter reentered the room well supplied with sticker pictures and an attractive juice dispenser. The experimenter gave the child a small treat of fruit juice and told the child that, for each imitative response she or he could reproduce, an additional juice treat and sticker would be given. These incentives for reproducing the model's behavior were necessary to minimize possible reluctance to demonstrate the model's aggressive acts (a problem that was discussed above).

The results, shown in Figure 22–2, provide striking support for the view that acquisition and spontaneous performance (acceptance) must be distinguished. In every comparison, the children tended to perform fewer aggressive behaviors than they had acquired through observation; this was particularly true of children in the *model-punished* condition.

FIGURE 22–2
Results of Bandura's classic study of the *acquisition-acceptance* distinction in observational learning. Note that in every case acquisition is higher than acceptance.

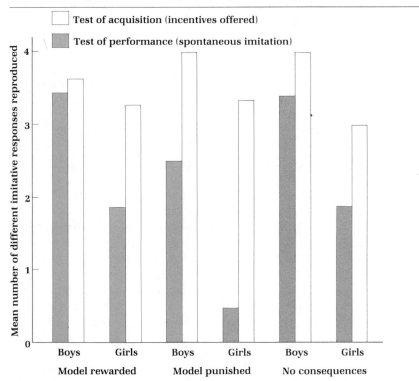

Source: Adapted from Bandura, A., & Walters, R. H. *Social learning and personality development.* New York: Holt, Rinehart & Winston, 1963.

Vicarious consequences

The reactions or consequences which modeled behavior is observed to produce furnish important information to observers, as we just saw in Bandura's (1965) experiment in which nursery school children observed a model rewarded, punished, or receive no consequences for aggressive behavior. Consequences of a model's behavior that *influence* the (acceptance) behavior of an observer are referred to as *vicarious consequences.* Two classes of vicarious consequences are usually distinguished: (1) *vicarious reward,* which applies to those outcomes which are presumably perceived by the observer as positive or desirable, and (2) *vicarious punishment,* which applies to consequences which are likely to be seen by the observer as negative or undesirable.

An informational analysis of vicarious consequences is based upon the assumption that vicarious consequences, positive or negative, convey two closely related bits of information to observers (Liebert, 1973; Liebert & Allen, 1969; Liebert & Fernandez, 1970a, 1970b). Obviously, vicarious consequences provide information as to the kind of effect an action will have—that is, whether the effect will be desirable or undesirable. In this capacity, the information provided by vicarious consequences permits observers to infer the outcomes which they will receive for similar actions. Studies have shown that vicarious reward produces direct and indirect imitation, while vicarious punishment produces direct and indirect counterimitation (e.g., Bandura, 1969b; Liebert & Fernandez, 1970a; Liebert, Sobol, & Copemann, 1972).

In addition to telling the observer the *type* of reaction which a particular behavior will elicit from others, the consequences to a model play an even more fundamental psychological role in learning. They inform the observer that certain actions are particularly likely to result in a reaction from others. This information may, in turn, signal the *importance* of what has transpired and thereby increase the likelihood that the observer will *attend* to, and try to remember, what has been observed. This attention-focusing function of vicarious consequences has been confirmed by experiments which have shown that children who see someone else *either* rewarded *or* punished for some behavior will show better acquisition of that behavior than will children who see the same behavior performed without consequences (e.g., Cheyne, 1971; Liebert & Fernandez, 1969, 1970a; Liebert et al., 1972).

The effects of vicarious consequences on both acquisition and acceptance, as predicted from the two-part informational analysis, are illustrated in an experiment which presented the modeling cues in writing (Spiegler & Weiland, 1976). College students read a brief story about a series of events involving a high school class president, the school principal, and other students. The new principal had made several changes in school policy which upset the student body (e.g., he eliminated some extracurricular activities). The class president initiated a series of actions in an attempt to bring about a change in the new policies (e.g., she wrote to the neighborhood newspaper). Depending upon the experimental condition to which the subjects were randomly assigned, the class president experienced positive, negative, or neutral consequences following each action. Within an experimental condition, only one type of vicarious consequence was presented. The only difference among the stories read by the subjects in the three conditions was the type of consequences which the model experienced. An excerpt from the modeling story is presented below, with the three types of vicarious consequences illustrated.

> Janet Halloran, the newly elected president of the senior class at Jefferson, decided that her new job was to inform both the high school administration and the local community about the attitudes and interests of her class of 428 students. She wrote an editorial for the school newspaper, *The Unicorn*, explaining the dismay of the students at the new principal's policies.
>
> [*Positive Consequences*] The principal was pleased that Ms. Halloran had chosen to go through proper channels and commended *The Unicorn* staff for allowing discussion of controversial topics.
>
> [*Negative Consequences*] The principal was so enraged that he halted publication of *The Unicorn* for the next month and severely reprimanded Ms. Halloran.
>
> [*Neutral Consequences*] The principal acknowledged Ms. Halloran's letter and told *The Unicorn* staff that he would take the editorial comments into consideration.

After reading the story, the subjects responded to written questions which asked what they would have done in a similar situation (a measure of acceptance) and which tested their recall of the modeled behaviors, vicarious consequences, and details of the story (measures of acquisition). With regard to acceptance, it was predicted that positive as well as neutral vicarious consequences would result in more imitation than would negative vicarious consequences. This would be consistent with the view that vicarious consequences provide observers with information about the acceptability and desirability of imitating modeled behaviors. Obviously, positive vicarious consequences indicate more acceptability and desirability than do negative vicarious consequences. It was predicted that the effects of neutral vicarious consequences would be similar to those of positive vicarious consequences, because, in this particular situation, the modeled behaviors—actively defying the policies of people in authority in a high school setting—typically result in negative consequences. Thus, the absence of negative sanctions inherent in neutral vicarious consequences would be expected to indicate to an observer that the modeled behaviors were acceptable. Each of these hypotheses was supported by the data.

Turning to the acquisition measure, subjects who read about a model who experienced positive or negative consequences for her actions recalled more of the total modeling cues than did subjects who read about models whose actions resulted in neutral consequences. This is consistent with the hypothesized attention-focusing function of vicarious reward and punishment. Positive and negative vicarious consequences were virtually equivalent in enhancing recall of what the model had done when compared to neutral consequences. This seems to indicate that it is the strength of the consequences, and not whether they are positive or negative, which affects subjects' acquisition of modeled responses.

If the three separate measures of recall are examined, an interesting finding emerges, as is shown in Figure 22–3. Whereas subjects who observed the model receive negative consequences had high recall of the details of the situation and the modeled behavior, they had the lowest recall of the consequences themselves. In terms of recalling vicarious consequences (but not the model's acts or the details of the situation), the valence of the consequences—whether they are positive or negative—appears to be critical.

Looking at both the acquisition and acceptance data, it can be concluded that positive vicarious consequences enhance both aspects of observational learning. In contrast, observing a model experience negative consequences decreases the likelihood that the observer will immediately imitate the model, but increases the chances that the observer will remember the model's actions and the related details. At the same time, the observer is apt to forget the negative consequences which accrued to the model's behavior. The net result appears to be that negative vicarious consequences would inhibit immediate imitation but not necessarily future imitation, because the observer would remember the model's actions and the associated details and forget that they led to negative consequences.

This finding has some possible practical implications. News reports of spectacular crimes such as skyjacking and kidnapping usually contain both positive and negative vicarious consequences. The former are more likely to appear in the initial coverage of the crime, before the criminal is apprehended and during the period when the criminal is receiving the rewards of the crime (e.g., success, money, publicity). Obviously, such reports have a potential for inspiring imitation. When the law catches up with the criminal, negative vicarious consequences predominate in the news coverage. Yet, if the results of Spiegler and Weiland's (1976) experiment can be generalized to the real-life situation, potential emulators would be more likely to remember the details of the crime, while forgetting that the criminal did not get away with the crime, and would therefore be more likely to imitate the criminal than they would if the consequences for the crime were neutral or unreported.

FIGURE 22–3
The relative amount of recall of details of the modeling story, of the modeled behavior, and of the vicarious consequences by subjects exposed to negative, positive, and neutral vicarious consequences in Spiegler and Weiland's (1976) study. Note that for the negative vicarious consequences condition, recall of story details and of the modeled behavior is high but recall of vicarious consequences is lower than that of the other two groups.

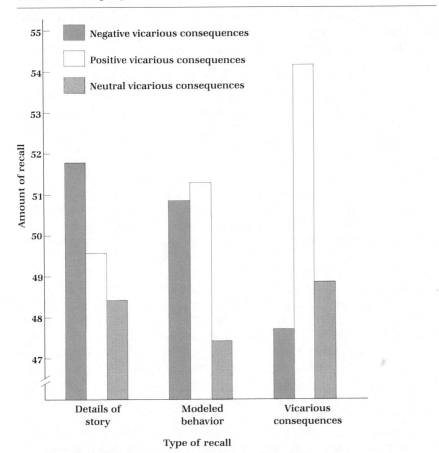

Source: Data from Spiegler, M. D., & Weiland, A. The effects of written vicarious consequences on observers' willingness to imitate and ability to recall modeling cues. *Journal of Personality*, 1976, *44*, 260–73.

Most of the research concerned with observational learning has focused either on elucidating the underlying processes of the phenomenon or on exploring the breadth of behaviors in which imitation is likely to play an important role. Examples of the former type have been discussed thus far. Now we turn our attention to the latter focus by examining the role which observational learning plays in various aspects of personality, and we shall begin by discussing the development

THE PERVASIVE ROLE OF OBSERVATIONAL LEARNING

of sex-role behavior. Our discussion will serve the dual function of exploring this important aspect of our personality and of reviewing the basic processes of observational learning which were presented in the previous sections.

Sex-role behavior

Sex roles refer to the more or less stereotyped behaviors which are deemed appropriate for males and females in a given culture or subculture. Some of our sex-role behavior is no doubt learned by direct instruction and by approval or disapproval, as is the case when parents tell their daughters that "girls don't fight" and praise their sons for being a man and not crying. However, much of our sex-role behavior is learned not through direct teaching and reinforcement from socializing agents, but by observing others (e.g., Sears, Rau, & Alpert, 1965).

Children are exposed to many people who exhibit appropriate sex-role behavior. For young children, parents are usually the most potent models. Young children usually have more exposure to their parents than to any other persons in their lives. Furthermore, parents are the most significant people in youngsters' lives in terms of the power they exert over them and the nurturance they give them. Power and nurturance are two key characteristics of models that facilitate their being imitated (for reviews, see Bandura, 1969a, 1977b; Flanders, 1968; Mischel, 1970, 1976). Other adults with whom young children come in contact, as well as siblings, also serve as models of sex-role behavior. As a child grows older, particularly upon entering elementary school, peers begin to exert an increasingly powerful influence as potential models. In addition to the host of *live* sex-role models with whom children have contact, there are also an even greater number and variety of *symbolic* sex-role models to whom children are exposed. Symbolic models are observed on television, in movies, in books and magazines, in advertising, and through the verbal description of sex-appropriate behavior by other people.

Obviously, for a child to acquire culture-appropriate sex-role behavior through observation, the models must be of the same sex as the child. Similarity between the observer and the model is another important factor that influences observational learning (Bandura, 1969a), and it appears that same sex is a particularly salient cue for both attention to (e.g., Maccoby, Wilson, & Burton, 1958) and imitation of (e.g., Hetherington & Frankie, 1967; Maccoby & Wilson, 1957) a model.

This point is illustrated in a study by Maccoby and Wilson (1957) in which seventh-grade children watched movies depicting various interpersonal behaviors between two adolescents. In one film, the lead characters were two boys, one clearly from an upper-middle-class background and the other clearly from a lower socioeconomic level. In a second film, the subjects saw the interaction between a male and a female adolescent with no apparent difference in socioeconomic level. The subjects returned a week later, and an assessment was then made of their recall of the behavior of the leading same-sexed character as compared to their recall of the leading opposite-sexed character. The subjects were also questioned about the attractiveness of each of the lead characters to obtain an "identification index." For example, they were asked which character was most like them and which they would most like to be in real life.

The results of Maccoby and Wilson's study are very enlightening. If we look first at the identification measure, we find that the subjects of both sexes indicated that they identified more with the same-sexed leading character. Of particular interest is the finding that the subjects remembered somewhat more of the actions and verbalizations of the same-sexed character. Furthermore, the specific behaviors of the model of the same sex that they remembered were linked to stereotyped sex roles: the boys remembered more aggressive content than did the girls, whereas the girls recalled more male-female interactions (involving the female lead character) than did the boys.

Interestingly, the subjects of both sexes tended to consider themselves more like the models of the socioeconomic level to which they aspired rather than the one to which they belonged. Obviously, one can change socioeconomic class more easily than gender! Mischel (1970) points out that whereas children often express a desire to be of another socioeconomic class, they report that they prefer adults of the same sex (e.g., Stevenson, Hale, Hill, & Moely, 1967) and that they do not want to change their own sex (e.g., Hartley & Hardesty, 1964; Kagan & Lemkin, 1960; Kohlberg, 1966; Minuchin, 1965).

To summarize the argument for the importance of observational learning in developing sex-role behavior, two points have been established so far. First, *exposure* to appropriate models—the initial requirement for imitation—clearly occurs in the lives of most children, since they are exposed to a variety of same-sexed adults and children. Although children come in contact with peers of both sexes, they probably have considerably more interaction with same-sexed peers than with opposite-sexed peers, as in play situations (e.g., mixed-sex groups usually do not bake pies or play football) and in segregated organized clubs and organizations (e.g., Brownies and Cub Scouts).

It is important to bear in mind that, while children tend to learn more same-sexed behavior from models, children of both sexes also acquire at least some opposite-sex behavior. For example, in the Maccoby and Wilson (1957) study discussed above, both boys and girls recalled both aggressive and interpersonal actions of the models (though boys remembered *more* aggressive behavior than did girls, and girls remembered *more* interpersonal behavior than did boys).

We are now left with two related questions. First, given that children acquire considerable same-sexed behavior through modeling, what factors account for their using this knowledge as guides for their own behavior? Second, since children also learn some opposite-sexed behavior, why do so many of them tend to exhibit predominantly same-sexed role behavior? Both of these questions concern determinants of *acceptance,* the third stage of observational learning.

Acceptance is determined by motivational factors, primarily the consequences for performing particular acts. The consequences will usually be positive (rewarding) for same-sexed behavior and negative (punishing) for opposite-sexed behavior, and they can be direct or vicarious. Examples of direct positive consequences for same-sexed behavior would be a girl receiving praise from her parents for caring for her younger cousin and a boy receiving parental approval for having aggressively fought for his rights with friends. Direct negative consequences for performing opposite-sexed role behavior would include a boy being called a "sissy" by his peers for crying when he falls off his bike and a girl being ignored by friends for wanting to play "cowboys and Indians."

Children may also observe their peers (or sometimes adults) receiving positive consequences for same-sexed behavior and negative consequences for opposite-sexed behavior. As we saw earlier in the chapter, such *vicarious consequences* can have essentially the same effect on observers' future actions as direct consequences. Vicarious punishment probably plays a more important role than does vicarious reward in the imitation of appropriate sex-role behavior. Whereas vicarious reward for same-sexed behavior is usually supplemented by direct reward, vicarious punishment for opposite-sexed behavior is less likely to be supplemented by direct punishment. Children who see same-sexed peers punished for opposite-sexed behavior will often learn from these observations and not perform the opposite-sexed behavior themselves, thereby never receiving direct negative consequences for the inappropriate sex-role acts.

The imitative and counterimitative effects we have been discussing can be either direct or indirect. Recall that direct effects refer to matching or copying the model's acts. A common example of direct imitation of sex-role behavior would be three-year-old Christopher banging wooden pegs into holes with a toy rubber hammer as his father uses a hammer and nails to make a bookcase. Direct counterimitation would be occurring in the case of seven-year-old Kathryn who watches police shows on TV because she knows that her younger and older sisters prefer family situation comedies.

Most imitative effects are indirect, involving generalization from the model's specific acts to the class of behaviors which the modeled acts exemplify. In the previous examples, Christopher's behavior might include playing with other toy tools and a range of construction or handiwork behaviors, and Kathryn may play "cops and robbers" when she is outside.

Male and female children acquire both masculine and feminine sex-role behavior through observational learning, but they usually perform only same-sexed role behavior because of the direct and vicarious consequences associated with same- and opposite-sexed acts. This points to the importance of the acquisition-acceptance distinction made earlier. It also has implications for the concept of androgyny (Kaplan & Sedney, 1980), which is a burgeoning area of study in psychology and related disciplines. *Androgyny,* in its current usage, refers to the integration of feminine and masculine sex roles in an individual (e.g., Bem, 1976; Kaplan & Bean, 1976).[2] Since we acquire both masculine and feminine sex roles through observational learning (and other learning processes), we obviously have the capacity to enact either. If our society continues to become more permissive and more rewarding of opposite-sexed role behaviors, we are likely to see an increase in androgynous behavior.

Delay of gratification

Delay of gratification refers to the self-imposed postponement of some immediate reward in favor of some potentially more valuable delayed reward. A common example is the decision not to drop out of school for a moderately good job now, but instead to persist in harsh economic circumstances in order to continue one's education (which presumably will provide a superior job after training). The ability to delay some small immediate reward for the sake of a larger outcome for which one must wait is a critical prerequisite for the achievement of success in many human endeavors.

That a willingness to delay gratification can be acquired through observational learning has been demonstrated experimentally (Mischel, 1974). For example, in a study by Bandura and Mischel (1965), fourth- and fifth-grade children were initially given a delay-of-reward test which involved confronting them with a series of 14 choices between a small immediate reward and a larger postponed reward (e.g., a small candy bar which they could have immediately or a larger one which required a week of waiting). On the basis of this assessment, the children were classified as preferring *high delay of reward* or *low delay of reward.* The purpose of the study was to demonstrate that these initial preferences could be changed (i.e., from high to low and vice versa) by exposure to an appropriate adult model who made choices between immediate and postponed rewards. The items among which

---

[2] The word *androgyny* comes from the Greek *andro,* meaning male, and *gyn,* meaning female. The Greek use of the word referred to hermaphroditism, the presence of both male and female characteristics (primarily biological) in a single organism.

the adult model chose were appropriate rewards for adults (chess sets, magazines, and so on) and were different from the items among which the subjects subsequently chose. Thus, the subjects were only able to imitate the *principle* exhibited by the model's behavior and could not merely copy the model's choices. Children whose initial preference was for high delay of reward were exposed to a model who consistently chose the immediate-reward item, whereas for those children who preferred low delay of reward, the model selected the postponed-reward item in each case. Additionally, the model briefly summarized his or her philosophy of life, which embodied the attitude toward delay of reward which was modeled, and occasionally commented on his or her choice. For instance, when the choice was between a plastic chess set obtainable immediately and a more expensive wooden set which could be obtained in two weeks, the low-delay-of-reward model commented, "Chess figures are chess figures. I can get as much use out of the plastic ones right away" (Bandura & Mischel, 1965, p. 701).

Subjects were assigned to one of three conditions. In the *live modeling* condition, the model was actually present. In the *symbolic modeling* condition, the modeling cues were presented in written form. Subjects who were just shown the series of paired objects (*no-model-present* condition) served as controls for the possible effects of mere exposure to rewards on subsequent delay-of-gratification behavior. All the children were then given a second delay-of-reward test in the model's absence. To assess the stability of changes in delay-of-reward behavior which occurred as a result of modeling, the subjects were administered a third delay-of-reward measure approximately one month later.

The results of this experiment are presented in Figure 22–4 from which it can be seen that, for both high- and low-delay-preference children, modeling produced a marked and moderately stable change in behavior. These findings have been extended to 18 to 20-year-old prison inmates who had demonstrated a low-delay-of-gratification orientation (Stumphauzer, 1972). These subjects were exposed to two older inmates with prestigious work details who modeled high-delay behavior. The subjects increased their delay behavior, and this change in delay-of-gratification orientation was still presented when it was reassessed at a four-week follow-up. Furthermore, the effect generalized to saving money.

The role of cognition in delay of gratification

Recall (from Chapter 19) that Walter Mischel (1979) has stressed the importance of studying the way in which situation and person variables interact to influence behavior. This position is evident in his work on delay of gratification. We have already seen that delay of gratification can be influenced by situational variables such as expo-

FIGURE 22–4
Mean percentage of immediate-reward choices by children who initially preferred high delay and mean percentage of delayed-reward choices by children who initially preferred low delay in Bandura and Mischel's (1965) experiment

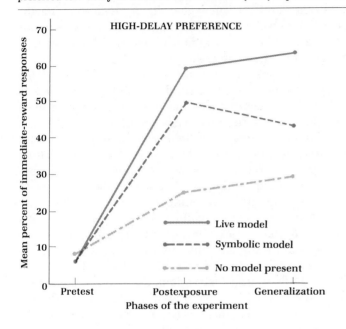

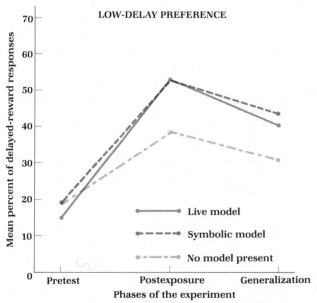

Source: Bandura, A., & Mischel W. Modification of self-imposed delay of reward through exposure to live and symbolic models. *Journal of Personality and Social Psychology*, 1965, *2*, 698–705.

sure to models who demonstrate high- or low-delay behavior (Bandura & Mischel, 1965). However, a comprehensive explanation of delay of gratification requires examination of person variables as well. For more than a decade, Mischel and his colleagues have been studying the cognitive strategies that persons use to help themselves postpone immediate rewards and wait for future rewards, and we shall briefly review some of the findings which have emerged.

Attention to rewards appears to be an important factor in delay of gratification. For example, preschool children were able to wait 10 times longer for a desired reward when the reward was not in view than when it was physically present (Mischel & Ebbesen, 1970). On the other hand, attending to *pictures of the reward* made it easier for preschool children to delay gratification (Mischel & Moore, 1973). However, the "delay of gratification story" is more complicated (and more fascinating) than these initial findings indicated. While attending to the actual reward or a symbolic representation of it during the delay can influence the degree to which a child will wait for the reward (e.g., Moore, Mischel, & Zeiss, 1976), a more important determinant of delay behavior appears to be how the child construes (cognitively represents) the reward while waiting for it. Mischel and Baker (1975) gave nursery school children brief instructions designed to encourage them to think about the reward they were waiting for in two different ways. One involved focusing on the *consummatory* qualities of the reward (e.g., how marshmallows are sweet, soft, and chewy, or pretzels salty and crunchy), and the other on *nonconsummatory* qualities of the reward (e.g., how marshmallows look like white, puffy clouds, and pretzels resemble long, thin brown logs). When children think about the reward they are waiting for in consummatory or "hot" ways, delay is difficult (Mischel & Baker, 1975). Conversely, attending to the nonconsummatory or "cool" qualities of the reward makes waiting relatively easy—in fact, easier than totally distracting themselves from the reward by not thinking about it at all would make the delay (Mischel, 1974). In sum, "hot, reward-oriented ideation decreases delay by making it more aversively frustrative and arousing. In contrast, delay is facilitated . . . by cool ideation focusing on the abstract (rather than consummatory) features of the rewards" (Mischel, 1979, p. 750).

Mischel's research on factors that account for delay of gratification clearly indicates an interaction between situation and person variables. Situational variables are important in that whether the reward or a picture of it is presented can facilitate or interfere with attempts to delay gratification; person variables are also important because people are able to enhance or impede their delay of gratification by the way they *think* about the reward for which they are waiting.

Helping behavior

Helping as a social response has been the focus of many recent studies of observational learning (e.g., Staub, 1974). It has been shown, for example, that children in a laboratory experiment are more likely to contribute some of their earnings (e.g., won in a bowling game) if they have seen an adult model do so than they are if they have not observed the adult (Liebert & Poulos, 1971; Poulos & Liebert, 1972; Rosenhan & White, 1967) and that the gift giving of adults in their place of employment is influenced by the size of the contributions made by their co-workers (Blake, Rosenbaum, & Duryea, 1955).

We shall consider two lines of research dealing with the role of observational learning in helping behavior. Unlike many other studies, the experiments of Bryan and Test (1967) and Hornstein, Fisch, and Holmes (1968) have used "street-corner" rather than laboratory settings to test their hypotheses. Such a strategy places additional demands on the ingenuity of the investigator but significantly broadens the base of evidence for hypotheses which have been supported in the laboratory.

One of Bryan and Test's (1967) naturalistic studies was designed to assess the effect of models on helping behavior. In their first experiment, titled "Lady in Distress: A Flat Tire Study," a college-age woman was stationed next to a disabled Ford Mustang; the car had a flat tire on the left rear wheel, and there was an inflated tire leaning beside it. The purpose of the experiment was to determine whether observation by passing drivers of a helping model would increase the likelihood that the drivers would stop and assist the woman. During the experimental period, an Oldsmobile was located about a quarter of a mile up the road and was clearly visible to motorists driving toward the lady and her disabled Mustang. In this "modeling scene," the Oldsmobile was jacked up, and a young woman was watching while a man changed a flat tire. During the control period, which was held at a comparable time, the modeling scene was absent. The experiment was conducted in a residential area of Los Angeles, and each treatment condition continued for the time required for 1,000 noncommercial vehicles to pass. Although the total number of vehicles which stopped to help was a small percentage of those which passed (less than 3 percent), the presence of a model significantly increased the number of drivers who stopped to offer their assistance.

Bryan and Test's data demonstrate that modeling can influence helping behavior in a naturalistic setting, but they do not elucidate the mechanisms which underlie this process. An experiment by Hornstein, Fisch, and Holmes (1968) explored this issue. The study is based on the notion that observers use a model's experiences as valid predictors of their own future experiences. This assumption leads to the expectation that, when the observer and the model are perceived as *similar,* observers will see the model's experiences as a valid predictor of what their own experiences would be if they engaged in similar behavior. Thus, in such a case, the observer should be more likely to imitate the model if the model had positive experiences than if the model had negative experiences. On the other hand, when the observer and the model are seen as very *dissimilar,* observers will not consider the model's experiences to be a valid predictor of their own. In this instance, the observer should be no more likely to imitate the model if the model had positive experiences than if the model had negative experiences.

To test these hypotheses, the investigators inconspicuously dropped addressed but unstamped envelopes containing a man's wallet and a letter on the sidewalk in a midtown Manhattan business district. The wallet's contents, for all subjects, were shrewdly designed to create the impression of an "average" owner, Michael Erwin. It contained $2 in cash, an identification card, postage stamps, membership cards for two fictitious organizations, a receipt for a rented tuxedo, the business cards of a florist and a podiatrist, and other nondescript contents that contributed to its "legitimacy."

A typewritten letter, which provided the modeling cues, gave the impression that the wallet had been *lost twice.* It appeared that when the wallet was lost initially, its finder (the model) put the wallet in an envelope to be mailed to its owner, enclosing a letter describing the model's feelings about finding and returning it. However, before

TABLE 22–1
The letters used by Hornstein et al. to vary the feelings of its original finder (model) and his similarity to the second finder (subject)

Letter condition	Model condition	
	Similar	Dissimilar
	Dear Mr. Erwin:	Dear Mr. Erwin:
Neutral*	I found your wallet which I am returning. Everything is here just as I found it.	I am visit your country finding your ways not familiar and strange. But I find your wallet which I here return. Everythings is here just as I find it.
Positive†	I must say that it has been a pleasure to be able to help somebody in the small things that make life nicer. It's really been no problem at all and I'm glad to be able to help.	It great pleasure to help sombody with tiny things which make life nicer. It is not problem at all and I glad to be able help.
Negative†	I must say that taking responsibility for the wallet and having to return it has been a great inconvenience. I was quite annoyed at having to bother with the whole problem of returning it. I hope you appreciate the efforts that I have gone through.	To take responsibility for wallet and necessity to return it is great inconvenience. Is annoyance to bother with whole problem of return and hope you appreciate effort I went to.

* The neutral letter said no more than this.
† The positive and negative letters began with the neutral statement
Source: Hornstein, H. A., Fisch, E., & Holmes, M. Influence of a model's feelings about his behavior and his relevance as a comparison other on observers' helping behavior. *Journal of Personality and Social Psychology,* 1968, *10,* 222–26.

the model could mail it, the well-intentioned finder also lost the wallet. The pedestrian who found the letter a "second" time, and who thereby became a subject in the experiment, had to decide between returning the wallet (and imitating the modeled helping behavior) and keeping the wallet and the money.

To systematically vary the similarity of observer and model, the letter was either written in familiar English (*similar model* condition) or in an ungrammatical, broken English which created the impression of a foreign writer (*dissimilar model* condition). In each of these conditions, the letter described the writer's feeling of pleasure at returning the wallet (*positive letter* condition), or expressed annoyance at being bothered (*negative letter* condition), or did not reveal any feelings (*neutral letter* condition). The letters used are shown in Table 22–1.

The percentage of wallets returned in each group is presented in Figure 22–5, from which it is clear that the researchers' predictions were supported. When the letter was apparently written by a similar model, positive and neutral experiences produced more returns than

FIGURE 22–5
Percentage of wallets returned intact in the Hornstein et al. (1968) experiment as a function of the subject's similarity to the model

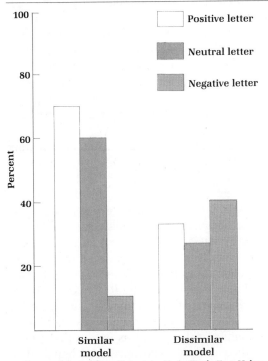

Source: Adapted from Hornstein, H. A., Fisch, E., & Holmes, M. Influence of a model's feelings about his behavior and his relevance as a comparison other on observers' helping behavior. *Journal of Personality and Social Psychology*, 1968, *10*, 222–26.

negative experiences, whereas there were no such differences for the dissimilar model condition. The study further demonstrates the role of modeling in naturalistic situations, and illustrates how two characteristics of the model—similarity to the observer and expressed feelings—may mediate such an effect.

MODELING THERAPIES AND COGNITIVE BEHAVIOR MODIFICATION

In the preceding sections of this chapter, we have seen numerous examples of how people's behavior can be changed by the observation and acceptance of models. Most of the work reviewed has been concerned with either elucidating the underlying processes of observational learning or demonstrating the role which observational learning may play in a variety of personality functions. A major offshoot of these enterprises has been a parallel effort to apply emerging principles and procedures to personality change. We will review some of the problem behaviors to which modeling procedures have been applied to illustrate the therapeutic uses of observational learning.

Two features of "modeling therapy" serve to contrast the observational learning approach to personality change with the classical and operant conditioning approaches. First, many therapeutic procedures using modeling are extremely efficient. Frequently, relatively brief exposure to appropriate models (often less than two hours and sometimes considerably less) is all that is required for significant change in the target behavior. Few other basic behavior therapy techniques work as quickly. Additionally, since modeling sequences can be presented symbolically, as in films and on audio- and videotape, many therapeutic modeling procedures can be presented to large numbers of clients at the same time and do not require professional therapists to administer treatment.

A second distinguishing feature of modeling therapies is that they are often used in conjunction with other behavior therapy techniques. In comparison to behavior therapy procedures, which have arisen primarily out of the classical or operant approaches, the designers of modeling therapies have paid more attention to developing potent therapeutic "packages" which combine observational learning procedures with techniques derived from the classical and operant paradigms. For example, modeling procedures have frequently been used in conjunction with operant conditioning techniques (see Chapter 21) in the treatment of various behavioral deficiencies. A major limitation of the operant approach in establishing behavior is that the desired response (or an approximation of it) must occur before it can be reinforced. With clients who have very limited behavioral repertoires (e.g., autistic children, psychotic adults, severely mentally retarded individuals), it is highly uneconomical to wait for responses which have a low probability of occurrence (e.g., speech in a mute child). In such instances, modeling has served a crucial role in eliciting the desired response. As Ivar Lovaas (1968), a psychologist who pioneered in teaching language and social behaviors to autistic children,[3] has commented: "In retrospect, it seems virtually impossible to have brought about certain behavioral changes . . . without an imitation approach" (p. 118).

Modeling therapies can be usefully viewed as forms of *cognitive behavior modification,* because they influence cognitive processes (e.g., knowledge of how to perform a difficult task and expectations of success in doing so) in order to change behavior. In addition to presenting examples of modeling therapies in this section, we shall also include examples of cognitive behavior modification which apply procedures other than modeling to affect therapeutic changes.

Experimental-analogue studies

In designing therapeutic techniques for the alleviation of a variety of psychological problems, it is frequently difficult and undesirable to begin by working directly with actual clients and clinical problems. The problems for which people seek professional assistance are often very complex and always unique. Ethical constraints governing the provision of efficient and effective help to the client usually do not allow sufficiently rigorous research procedures to be employed so that generalizations about the process or outcome of the therapy can be made. Thus, one tactic commonly used in developing therapeutic procedures, particularly within the behavioral strategy, is to investigate in the laboratory variables which are less complex than those that occur with clinical problems, but are *analogous* to those found in the clinical setting (Bernstein & Paul, 1971; Paul, 1969). Such investigations are called *experimental analogues.*

For example, to develop procedures for reducing fear and anxiety, many laboratory analogue studies have used subjects who were mildly afraid of, but not debilitated by, their fear of snakes. (The snake phobia of some people involves extreme reactions to snakes, such as panic behavior, and an abnormal avoidance of all situations in which snakes might possibly be encountered—for example, not going to parks or swimming in lakes.) College students who are moderately fearful of snakes are easy to obtain as research subjects, and it is possible to get relatively objective measures of their fear before, during, and after treatment by using a behavioral avoidance test (as we shall see shortly). Once potent therapeutic procedures have been developed by means of the laboratory analogue, these procedures can be more ethically attempted with actual clinical cases.

---

[3] *Childhood autism* is a very serious psychotic disorder characterized by social isolation, lack of interpersonal skills, mutism or repetitious speech, and an intolerance of change in routine.

"Coping" versus "mastery" models

One example of the experimental-analogue process in the area of modeling therapy involves the search for the optimal characteristics of the model. Basic research on observational learning, discussed earlier in the chapter, had shown that, in many circumstances, similarity between the model and the observer enhances imitation. Using undergraduate women who reported being afraid of nonpoisonous snakes as subjects, Meichenbaum (1971) compared the effectiveness of two types of models in reducing their fear: "mastery" versus "coping" models. A *mastery model* is, from the outset, competent and fearless in approaching and interacting with the feared object or situation, whereas a coping model is initially somewhat fearful, but gradually overcomes these feelings by successfully handling the situation and eventually mastering it. Because the subjects were more similar to the *coping model* than to the mastery model, the coping model was expected to be a more realistic exemplar for them to imitate and therefore to be superior to the mastery model in lowering subjects' fear. Although this hypothesis was supported in Meichenbaum's (1971) analogue study, subsequent research findings comparing the two types of models were equivocal (cf. Kazdin, 1973; Kornhaber & Schroeder, 1975). It now appears that coping models may be effective not because they are perceived as similar to the fearful observers, but because they model adaptive coping responses that mastery models never display (Kornhaber & Schroeder, 1975).

Emotional problem behaviors

In this section, we shall examine examples of modeling and cognitive-behavioral therapies which deal with alleviating excessive and maladaptive emotional reactions, such as fear, anxiety, anger, and pain.

Modeling therapies for fear and avoidance behavior

Recall from Chapter 20 that one of the procedures which Jones (1924b) used to extinguish Peter's fear of rabbits involved Peter observing two peers interact in a fearless manner with the rabbit. In the more than half a century since Jones's (1924a, 1924b) pioneering work, a large amount of evidence has been accumulated to demonstrate the efficacy of this procedure. We now know that avoidance behavior can be *vicariously extinguished* by observing appropriate models who make approach responses to feared objects or situations and do not incur any adverse consequences. Much of the evidence for this proposition also comes from experimental-analogue studies.

The initial experimental demonstrations of the efficacy of live (Bandura, Grusec, & Menlove, 1967) and filmed models (Bandura & Menlove,

1968; Hill, Liebert, & Mott, 1968) in reducing avoidance behavior involved children who were afraid of dogs. Spiegler, Liebert, McMains, and Fernandez (1969) developed a brief modeling film to reduce fear of nonpoisonous snakes in adults. Their series of studies illustrate the basic procedures used in the analogue research on vicarious extinction and also show how the treatment was subsequently validated with a clinical population.

The 14-minute modeling film used by Spiegler and his colleagues first presents the meeting of a female undergraduate (Model One) and a female herpetologist (Model Two). In successive scenes of the film, Model One gradually learns to approach and handle several snakes by following Model Two's demonstration of each behavior. As the film progresses, Model One, who was initially fearful, becomes noticeably more confident in handling the snakes and appears to be enjoying the procedure more and more. While wearing gloves, Model One learns to stroke and pick up a small snake and then repeats this procedure with a large snake. Next, Model One removes the gloves and repeats these successively more difficult tasks bare-handed. Model One is later shown confidently holding the larger snake. An accompanying narration describes what the film depicts and also includes information about snakes and their handling.

This modeling film was first tested in two analogue experiments. Women college students who reported being afraid of snakes served as subjects, and the experiments were conducted in a psychology department laboratory. These studies found that subjects who viewed the narrated film once were significantly less fearful of snakes (as measured by the behavioral avoidance test described below) than were control subjects who had not been exposed to the modeling film.

In a third experiment, adults from the local community (6 men and 15 women) were recruited via a newspaper advertisement asking for persons who were afraid of snakes and willing to participate in a study of new treatment methods. During initial screening interviews, it became apparent that these subjects were substantially more fearful than the college students who had served as subjects in the first two studies. Most of the subjects in the third experiment reported that their fear of snakes interfered with their lives in some significant way. They reported, for example, that because of this fear they had given up such enjoyable activities as gardening, waterskiing, and camping with their families.

Instead of relying on the subjects' self-descriptions of their fear of snakes as a base-rate measure to which post-treatment measures could be compared, the subjects were given a *behavioral avoidance test*. In this test, the subjects were asked to do a series of tasks which successively brought them into more contact with a snake. They were instructed to proceed only as far as they felt comfortable and able.

TABLE 22–2
Steps in the behavioral avoidance test for snakes used in Spiegler et al.'s (1969) experiments

1. Enter a room containing a caged two-foot water snake.
2. Walk to the cage, which was 15 feet away. (If the subject did not walk the entire distance, the number of feet walked was recorded.)
3. Put on a pair of gloves for handling the snake.
4. Remove the lid of the cage and look in.
5. Reach into the cage and touch the snake.
6. Pick up the snake.
7. Remove the gloves.
8. Touch the snake bare-handed.
9. Hold the snake bare-handed.
10. Walk with the snake to a chair and sit holding the snake.

The steps of the behavioral avoidance test are listed in Table 22–2.

On the basis of their performance on the initial behavioral avoidance test, subjects were matched for their level of avoidance behavior and assigned to one of three treatment conditions. In the *film* condition, subjects viewed the film described earlier. Subjects in the *film-plus-relaxation* group were taught deep muscle relaxation[4] (as used in systematic desensitization; see Chapter 20) by means of a 50-minute tape recording and then shown the modeling film. A third group was given just the *relaxation* training and, like the film-plus-relaxation group, was instructed to practice relaxation and to use it in future encounters with snakes. All subjects were treated in groups, and the treatments were administered in two sessions, one week apart.

Post-treatment behavioral avoidance tests were individually administered after the first treatment session, before and after the second session, and one week after the second session, with a new and substantially larger snake as a test for generalization. The results of these tests are presented in Figure 22–6. The addition of relaxation training to the modeling film substantially enhanced its effectiveness. Subjects in the film-plus-relaxation condition performed significantly better after the first treatment and on all subsequent tests than did participants in either of the other two conditions. As in the first two experiments, there was a significant decrease in avoidance behavior after only a single presentation of the modeling film, and a second exposure to the film served to enhance its effectiveness. Finally, it is important to note that no performance loss resulted from introducing the new and larger snake.

---

[4] Several subjects in the previous experiments had commented that, although the film seemed to help in overcoming their fear, they became somewhat "anxious" while watching *some* of the scenes. It was reasoned that if the participants were relaxed while viewing the film, its effectiveness would be enhanced. Thus, in the third experiment, relaxation training was added as a treatment component.

FIGURE 22–6
Mean number of behavioral avoidance tests passed as a function of treatment condition in Spiegler et al.'s (1969) third experiment

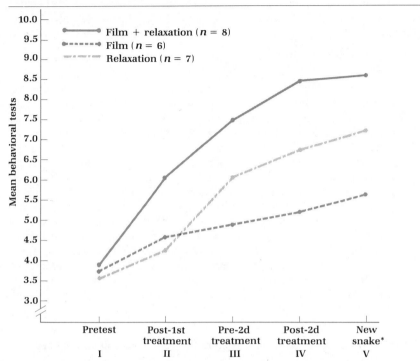

* Two subjects were unable to attend the final assessment (V), thereby reducing the number of subjects in the Film + Relaxation ($n = 7$) and Film ($n = 5$) conditions.
    Source: Spiegler, M. D., et al. Experimental development of a modeling treatment to extinguish persistent avoidance behavior. In R. D. Rubin & C. M. Franks (Eds.), *Advances in behavior therapy, 1968.* New York: Academic Press, 1969.

Participant modeling for fear and avoidance behavior

Reducing fear through exposure to symbolic modeling films is highly efficient because many clients can be treated simultaneously, and professional therapists are not needed to administer the treatment. *Participant modeling* (e.g., Bandura, Blanchard, & Ritter, 1969) is an even more potent therapy (Rachman & Wilson, 1980) although it is not as efficient as symbolic modeling. Participant modeling involves live modeling of the therapist engaging in the feared behavior and closely supervised behavioral rehearsal of feared behavior by the client. The typical sequence of procedures is as follows: first, the therapist models the anxiety-evoking behavior for the client. Then the client performs the same behavior with the therapist's verbal and physical help, if needed. Gradually, the therapist's aid is withdrawn until the client is performing the feared behavior alone. The behaviors that are modeled and practiced are arranged in a hierarchy with therapy proceeding from the least to the most anxiety-evoking behaviors. A description of the first participant-modeling session with a 49-year-old woman who had been profoundly afraid of crossing streets for the previous 10 years will illustrate these basic procedures.

> The initial . . . session was . . . held in an area adjacent to Mrs. S.'s home. A low traffic location in which a narrow street intersected with a moderately wide street was chosen. The counselor walked across the narrow street for about one minute while Mrs. S. watched. Then the counselor firmly placed her arm around Mrs. S.'s waist and walked across with her. This was repeated a number of times until Mrs. S. reported she was fairly comfortable at performing the task. . . . Street-crossing was then continued while the physical contact between counselor and Mrs. S. was gradually reduced until the counselor only lightly touched the back of Mrs. S.'s arm as she walked slightly behind her. Contact was then eliminated completely with the counselor first walking alongside Mrs. S. as the street was crossed and then slightly behind her. The counselor subsequently followed Mrs. S. approximately three fourths of the way across the street and allowed her to go the remaining distance alone. Gradually the counselor reduced the distance she accompanied Mrs. S. until eventually Mrs. S. was able to cross the street entirely alone. (Ritter, 1969, pp. 170–71)

Cognitive processes mediating fear reduction: Self-efficacy theory

There is considerable evidence that modeling, especially in conjunction with behavior rehearsal (as in participant modeling), is an effective procedure for reducing people's fears and avoidance behaviors (e.g., Bandura, 1977a; Rachman & Wilson, 1980). How do such personality changes come about? One answer to this question can be found in Bandura's (1977a, 1978) theory of *perceived self-efficacy. Self-efficacy* refers to an individual's belief or expectation that he or she can master a situation and bring about desired outcomes by personal efforts. According to self-efficacy theory, there is a common cognitive mechanism that mediates the effects of all psychological change procedures. Specifically, psychotherapeutic procedures,

> whatever their form, serve as means of creating and strengthening expectations of personal efficacy. Within this analysis, efficacy expectations are distinguished from response-outcome expectancies.
> An outcome expectancy is defined as a person's estimate that a given behavior will lead to certain outcomes. An efficacy expectation is the conviction that one can successfully execute the behavior required to produce the outcomes. Outcome and efficacy expectations are differentiated, because individuals can believe that a particular course of action will produce certain outcomes, but if they entertain serious doubts about

whether they can perform the necessary activities such information does not influence their behavior.

In this conceptual system, expectations of personal mastery affect both initiation and persistence of coping behavior. The strength of people's convictions in their own effectiveness is likely to affect whether they will even try to cope with given situations. At this initial level, perceived self-efficacy influences choice of behavioral settings. People fear and tend to avoid threatening situations they believe exceed their coping skills, whereas they get involved in activities and behave assuredly when they judge themselves capable of handling situations that would otherwise be intimidating.

Not only can perceived self-efficacy have directive influence on choice of activities and settings, but, through expectations of eventual success, it can affect coping efforts once they are initiated. Efficacy expectations determine how much effort people will expend and how long they will persist in the face of obstacles and aversive experiences. The stronger the perceived self-efficacy, the more active the efforts. Those who persist in subjectively threatening activities that are in fact relatively safe will gain corrective experiences that reinforce their sense of efficacy, thereby eventually eliminating their defensive behavior. Those who cease their coping efforts prematurely will retain their self-debilitating expectations and fears for a long time. (Bandura, 1977a, pp. 193–94)

Bandura (1977a, 1978) considers his self-efficacy theory to be a broad explanation of how diverse psychotherapeutic procedures operate, especially to reduce fearful and avoidant behaviors. Whatever the form of treatment, as a person becomes more confident that he or she can cope with a problematic situation, the person will become less fearful and more likely to engage in the previously feared and avoided behavior. These expectations of personal self-efficacy are postulated to stem from four major sources of information—performance accomplishments, vicarious experience, verbal persuasion, and emotional arousal—which various psychotherapeutic experiences provide clients.

Performance accomplishments are a powerful source of efficacy information in that they provide direct experiences of personal mastery. Through successful performance, efficacy expectations are strengthened and the threat of occasional failure is likely to be reduced. Therapeutic procedures which provide clients with direct performance accomplishments include participant modeling, behavior rehearsal, and reinforced practice. *Vicarious experience* is a second source of efficacy expectations. Observing others successfully handle a difficult situation can generate expectations in observers that they too can "do it." All live and symbolic modeling procedures provide clients with this source of self-efficacy expectations. *Verbal persuasion* is the most common source of self-efficacy expectations because of its ease and availability. By being told that they can "do it," people come to believe that they can (i.e., their efficacy expectations are increased). Traditional psychotherapies, such as psychoanalysis, rely heavily on verbal persuasion. Finally, efficacy expectations can be influenced by *emotional arousal* in threatening situations. People often rely on their state of physiological arousal (e.g., calmness, trembling) to judge their level of fear or anxiety. Feeling calm and relaxed (or even moderately aroused if some arousal is necessary for effective performance) may serve as feedback which increases competency expectations. Systematic desensitization and deep muscle relaxation training (discussed in Chapter 20) are two examples of psychotherapeutic procedures which influence efficacy expectations through regulating emotional arousal.

If perceived self-efficacy is posited to underlie the success of various therapies for reducing fearful and avoidant behavior, then it follows that the more effective a treatment is, the better it is in enhancing clients' efficacy expectations. For example, it would be predicted that "vicarious experience, relying as it does on inferences from social comparison, is a less dependable source of information about one's own capabilities than is direct evidence of personal accomplishments [e.g., as obtained in participant modeling]. Consequently, the efficacy expectations induced by modeling alone are likely to be weaker. . . ." (Bandura, Adams, & Beyer, 1977, p. 126).

This prediction was tested empirically in an experiment by Bandura, Adams, and Beyer (1977). The subjects were adults (7 males and 26 females with a mean age of 33 years) whose fear and avoidance of snakes restricted their lives in that they avoided any situation in which there was even a remote possibility that they would encounter a snake. A variety of dependent variables were employed to assess the changes in avoidance behavior and self-efficacy. The primary measure of avoidance behavior was each subject's performance on a behavioral avoidance test, similar to (but more stringent than) the one used by Spiegler et al. (1969) (see Table 22–2). To assess changes in self-efficacy, subjects rated their expectations for performing each of the steps in the behavioral avoidance test on a 100-point probability scale.

On the basis of their pretreatment behavioral avoidance test performance, subjects were matched in triads and randomly assigned to one of three conditions. Subjects in the *participant modeling* condition observed a female therapist perform a series of increasingly more threatening interactions with a snake and then practiced the same behavior with the therapist's assistance. Subjects in the *modeling* condition merely observed these modeling sequences for the same length of time. Note that, because subjects in the modeling condition did not engage in any of the modeled tasks themselves, their self-efficacy expectations could only come from vicarious experiences, whereas subjects in the participant modeling condition, who actually performed the modeled behaviors, could derive efficacy expectations from both vicarious experiences and performance accomplishments. Subjects in a control condition were jus. administered the assessment procedures at the same times as their experimental counterparts.

The results of Bandura et al.'s (1977) study are consistent with self-efficacy theory. Subjects' efficacy expectations were markedly enhanced by participant modeling (in a pre- to post-treatment comparison), moderately increased by modeling, and unaltered in the control condition. These differential changes in self-efficacy were paralleled in the subjects' overt behavior, as self-efficacy theory would predict, in that participant modeling produced slightly more approach behavior in the behavioral avoidance test than did modeling. (Both treament conditions produced significant pre- to post-treatment increases in approach behavior, whereas the control condition did not.) The close correspondence between level of perceived self-efficacy and behavior can be seen in Figure 22–7, which shows these two measures for a snake similar to the one used in treatment (similar threat) and a snake dissimilar to the one used in treatment (dissimilar threat).

Two points should be made clear about Bandura's theory of perceived self-efficacy. First, self-efficacy is considered to be situation specific—that is, to vary depending on the *particular* threatening behav-

FIGURE 22–7
Level of self-efficacy and approach behavior to a snake displayed by subjects after receiving participant modeling, modeling, or no treatment in Bandura et al.'s (1977) experiment.

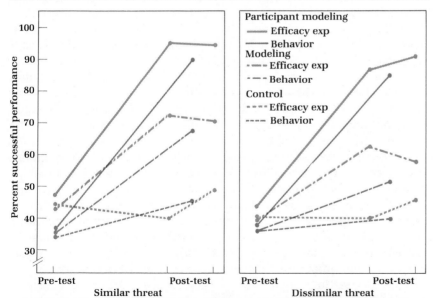

In the post-test phase, level of self-efficacy was measured prior to and after the behavioral avoidance tests with the two snakes—one similar to the snake used in treatment and one different.

Source: Adapted from Bandura, A., Adams, N. E., & Beyer, J. Cognitive processes mediating behavioral change. *Journal of Personality and Social Psychology*, 1977, *35*, 125–39.

ior called for—rather than operating as a global personality trait or motive that would influence behavior in diverse circumstances. For instance, efficacy expectations in dating would differ depending on the date's behavior, the length and intimacy of the relationship, and the specific dating activity. Second, it is acknowledged that self-efficacy is not the only factor which influences how a person will behave.

> Expectation alone will not produce desired performances if the requisite competences are lacking. Moreover, there are many things that people can do with certitude of success that they fail to perform because they have no incentives to do so. Given sufficient capabilities and incentives, however, efficacy expectations are likely to be a major determinant of people's choice of activities, how hard they strive, and how long they will persist in their attempts. These were the conditions . . . in . . . [Bandura, Adams, and Beyer's (1977)] study. All subjects had at their disposal the responses necessary for the interaction tasks and they all were motivated to overcome their phobic behavior. Under conditions in which people differ significantly in capabilities and motivation, skill and incentive factors will contribute to variance in performance. (Bandura et al., 1977, p. 138)

Bandura's theory of perceived self-efficacy represents the first major attempt to construct a unified theory of behavior change within the behavioral strategy (see Chapter 23). It has been the subject of much scrutiny and discussion among behavioral psychologists in the past few years (e.g., Borkovec, 1978; Eysenck, 1978; Kazdin, 1978; Lang, 1978; Poser, 1978; Rosenthal, 1978; Teasdale, 1978; G. T. Wilson, 1978; Wolpe, 1978b), and, not surprisingly, it has been criticized as well as lauded. To its credit, Bandura's theory has stimulated considerable research on perceived self-efficacy, which is one of the criteria upon which the merits of a theory is evaluated (e.g., Bandura & Adams, 1977; Bandura, Adams, Hardy, & Howells, 1980; Bandura & Schunk, 1981; Chambliss & Murray, 1979a, 1979b; Condiotte & Lichtenstein, 1981; DiClemente, 1981; Gauthier & Ladouceur, 1981; Gould & Weiss, 1981; Schunk, 1981; Weinberg, Yukelson, & Jackson, 1980). Furthermore, as Bandura (1978) himself acknowledges, self-efficacy theory, like any psychological theory, is speculative, and its validity needs to be tested empirically, a task in which Bandura and others are currently engaged. For example, there does appear to be a substantial correlation between efficacy expectations and behavior. However, it will be necessary to experimentally vary self-efficacy (i.e., as an independent variable) and observe the effects on behavior in order to make definitive statements that perceived self-efficacy is a causative factor in behavior. While this and other questions about self-efficacy theory wait to be answered in research studies, Bandura's efforts to generate a parsimonious, unified theory of the underlying mechanisms in diverse therapeutic methods remains impressive. Moreover, it provides a prime example of the melding of cognitive processes, situational factors, and overt behavior that is the hallmark of a rigorous cognitive-behavioral approach to personality.

Symbolic modeling treatments of fear of medical procedures

Recently, modeling approaches have been used to reduce people's fears concerning both major and minor medical procedures. The effectiveness of a modeling film in reducing the anxiety of children who were facing hospitalization and elective surgery (e.g., hernia operations, tonsillectomies) was clearly demonstrated by Melamed and Siegel (1975). The children ranged in age from 4 to 12 and had never been hospitalized before. Half of the children saw a 16-minute film titled *Ethan Has an Operation* which depicted the experiences of a seven-year-old boy who had been hospitalized for a hernia operation.

> This film . . . consists of 15 scenes showing various events that most children encounter when hospitalized for elective surgery from the time of admission to time of discharge including the child's orientation to the hospital ward and medical personnel such as the surgeon and anesthesiologist; having a blood test and exposure to standard hospital equipment; separation from the mother; and scenes in the operating and recovery rooms. In addition to explanations of the hospital procedures provided by the medical staff, various scenes are narrated by the child, who describes his feelings and concerns that he had at each stage of the hospital experience. Both the child's behavior and verbal remarks exemplify the behavior of a coping model so that while he exhibits some anxiety and apprehension, he is able to overcome his initial fears and complete each event in a successful and nonanxious manner. (Melamed & Siegel, 1975, p. 514)

The other half of the children saw a control film which presented the experiences of a preadolescent boy on a nature trip in the country. The control film had an interest value similar to that of the modeling film but was unrelated to hospitalization or surgery.

Anxiety was assessed by self-report inventories, behavioral observations, and a physiological measure the night before surgery and three to four weeks after surgery. Children who saw the modeling film exhibited a significant pre- to postoperative reduction of anxiety as compared to children who saw the control film. Furthermore, parents reported a significant posthospitalization increase in behavior problems for children who had seen the control film whereas such problems were less likely among those who saw the modeling film.

A related study has shown that a realistic modeling film depicting a child receiving an injection can reduce the apparent pain which children experience while actually receiving an injection (Vernon, 1974). Children aged four to nine who were to be hospitalized for minor surgery requiring a preoperative injection were assigned to one of three conditions. Subjects in the *no-pain-movie* condition saw an 18-minute film which showed

> eight boys and eight girls (actors) receiving injections from a nurse without apparent pain, fear, or emotional behavior. They ranged in age from 4 through 11 years. In each case the [model] was first shown playing quietly or reading in a hospital bed. The nurse then entered the room with a syringe and needle on a tray. She chatted with the [model] briefly, positioned him on his side, and then gave the injection in the [model's] lateral thigh. At the moment of injection the camera moved to a close-up of the [model's] upper torso and face, *the latter remaining expressionless throughout.* The nurse then put a bandaid on the spot of injection, said goodbye to the [model] and left the room. (Vernon, 1974, p. 795; italics added)

Subjects in the *pain-movie* condition saw the same basic movie, but at the moment of the injection the model winced, realistically exclaimed "ouch," and frowned (rather than remaining expressionless). The film was made in the pediatric ward in which the children were to be hospitalized, and the children saw it in their homes approximately 36 hours before receiving their preoperative injections. Subjects in the *control* condition saw neither movie. Children who had viewed the realistic pain movie (in which the model displayed a moderate reaction to the situation) appeared to experience the least pain when they received their injections, whereas children who had viewed the unrealistic no-pain movie seemed to experience the most pain.

There have also been a number of successful applications of therapeutic modeling (paralleling the techniques for reducing fear of surgery described above) to reduce children's fear of dentistry (e.g., Adelson, Liebert, Herskovitz, & Poulos, 1972; Johnson & Machen., 1973; Melamed, Hawes, Heiby, & Glick, 1975; Melamed, Weinstein, Hawes, & Katin-Borland, 1975; Shaw & Thoresen, 1974; White, Akers, Green, & Yates, 1974). Reducing fear of medical and dental procedures is important not only because this alleviates an uncomfortable emotional state, but also because such feelings can keep people from seeking regular checkups and obtaining necessary treatment. Modeling films have a vast potential for treating, and even preventing, the development of such fears (Melamed, 1980; Spiegler, 1980).

Modeling and cognitive behavior modification treatments for test anxiety

Considerable ingenuity has been required in designing modeling sequences to reduce anxiety about examinations. Whereas it is relatively easy to present models who are making appropriate approach responses to a feared object such as a snake, or who are demonstrating adaptive behaviors when facing surgery, coping with test anxiety involves substantially more than being able to sit down and make the motor responses required for taking an examination. Much of test anxiety involves covert, cognitive behavior—thoughts and concerns about the test, about success and failure, and about the material being tested, which interfere with the student's performance. The primary disadvantage of the test-anxious student is attentional—high-test-anxious students focus their attention on negative self-evaluative and self-depreciating thinking while taking examinations (Wine, 1971).

Most modeling treatments for test anxiety have had models verbalize their thoughts while engaging in test-related activities. Mastery models have merely verbalized adaptive thinking while taking a test (e.g., Sarason, 1973), whereas coping models have verbalized debilitating thoughts at first, then modeled the process of handling these negative thoughts by countering them with adaptive, facilitating thoughts, and finally verbalized only positive thoughts (e.g., Cooley, 1976; Cooley & Spiegler, 1980; Malec, Park, & Watkins, 1976; Sarason, 1975). Examples of scenes from modeling videotapes developed by Cooley (1976; Cooley & Spiegler, 1980) as part of a cognitive-behavioral treatment package for test anxiety appear in Table 22–3 (page 526) and illustrate the general approach using a coping model. The objective of this modeling was to train test-anxious students to use a frequently employed cognitive behavior modification technique called *cognitive restructuring* which involves (1) *recognizing* one's maladaptive self-statements (or thoughts), (2) then *challenging* their usefulness and rationality, and (3) finally *replacing* the debilitating self-statements with ones that focus the person on the task at hand and implementing adaptive behaviors.

The other approach using modeling procedures to treat test anxiety involves having test-anxious students observe other students undergoing therapy for this problem. For example, Denney (1974) found that *vicarious systematic desensitization* was as effective as direct systematic desensitization in reducing test anxiety. Horne and Matson (1977) found that listening to tapes of role-played group therapy which dealt specifically with test anxiety was more effective in reducing this target behavior than were systematic desensitization, flooding (an extinction procedure in which the client is exposed to the feared stimulus for long periods of time), and study-skills training.

Stress inoculation: A general cognitive behavior modification treatment for maladaptive emotional reactions

All of the behavior therapy procedures discussed thus far are aimed at alleviating specific problems which clients present in psychotherapy.

TABLE 22–3

Examples of scenes from modeling videotapes developed by Cooley (1976) for reducing test anxiety, illustrating the facilitating self-statements used by a coping model to counteract debilitating self-statements

Situation	Debilitating self-statement	Facilitating self-statement
Waiting for the test to be passed out.	"Oh, I'm getting nervous; I hope I don't do as badly on this test as I did on the last one."	"It's no good telling myself I'll do poorly. How I do on this test is not related to any other tests. Attend to the here and now; use your knowledge. Take your time and translate what you know into answers."
Student is not able to remember something she thinks she knows.	"I know this answer, but I can't remember it; I just studied it last night. Oh, what was it? Why can't I remember?"	"Don't let it worry me— anyone can forget something momentarily. I'll go on and answer some more. I can come back later, and I'm sure I can track the answer down."
Not knowing an answer.	"What a stupid question. How does he expect us to know that?"	"Ok, so it's a stupid question or I don't get the point. I'll do a quick job on it and invest my time somewhere else where it will pay off."
Things are going well.	—	"It's working; I'm in control; I'm thinking clearly. Now to the next question."

Source: Adapted from Cooley, E. J. Cognitive versus emotional coping skills as alternative responses for high test anxious college students. Doctoral dissertation, University of Texas at Austin, 1976.

In this section, we shall describe a cognitive-behavior therapy procedure which is broadly applicable to effectively coping with many different kinds of stressful situations.

Stress inoculation prepares clients to potentially deal with any stress-inducing event by teaching them self-control coping skills and then by having them rehearse these skills while being exposed to a variety of stressors (Meichenbaum, 1977). Stress-inoculation was developed by Donald Meichenbaum (Meichenbaum & Cameron, 1972), one of the pioneers in cognitive behavior modification.

The procedures can be divided into three phases. The first phase of stress inoculation consists of cognitive preparation of clients. Clients are provided with an adaptive way of viewing and understanding their negative reactions, such as fear or anger. Basically, the rationale offered clients is that negative emotions associated with a stressful situation are caused by the way people view the situation and the courses of action they take in relation to it, and not by the situation per se. Accordingly, clients are told that they can learn coping skills which will allow them to reconceptualize and deal with such situations without becoming emotionally upset.

In the second phase of stress inoculation, the client learns various coping skills. The coping skill most frequently employed is cognitive restructuring which is a generic term for cognitive behavior therapies that modify clients' views and ideas that are maintaining their problem behaviors. (Recall that this was one of the components of Cooley's cognitive-behavioral treatment of test anxiety discussed earlier.) Clients are taught to monitor their negative and maladaptive self-thoughts when faced with a stressful situation and to replace them with incompatible coping self-statements at each of the five stages of the coping process. Examples of possible coping self-statements applicable for different target behaviors are listed in Table 22–4.

The other specific coping skills taught depend, in part, on the target behavior being treated. For example, in the case of fear, the client might gather information about the feared situation or object, develop skills that would make the feared situation less threatening (e.g., learning to initiate and maintain conversations in the case of interpersonal anxiety), and learn deep muscle relaxation to alleviate tension.

When clients have mastered a number of coping skills, they are ready to practice applying them in the third and final phase of stress inoculation training. Clients are exposed to stressful situations and use their newly acquired coping skills to handle them. The stress-inducing circumstances might be receiving unpredictable electric shock, sub-

TABLE 22–4
Examples of coping self-statements used in stress inoculation to reduce fear or anxiety, anger, and pain

Fear or anxiety[a]	Anger[b]	Pain[c]
What is it I have to do?	What is it I have to do?	What is it I have to do?
Just think about what I can do about it. That is better than getting anxious.	This is going to upset me, but I know how to deal with it.	I have lots of different strategies I can call upon.
One step at a time. I can handle this situation.	Think of what you want to get out of this.	Don't think about the pain, just what I have to do.
This anxiety is what the therapist said I would feel. It's a reminder to use my coping skills.	I'm not going to let him get to me.	This tenseness can be an ally, a cue to cope.
I didn't handle that as well as I could have, but I'll get better.	I have a right to be annoyed, but let's keep the lid on.	When the pain mounts, I can switch to a different strategy; I'm in control.
	Can I laugh about this? It's probably not so serious.	That's better than before I used coping skills, so I'm making some progress.

Source: Adapted from (a) Meichenbaum, D. *Cognitive behavior modification.* Morristown, N.J.: General Leraning Press, 1974; (b) Novaco, R. *Anger control.* Lexington, Mass.: Heath, 1975, and (c) Turk, D., Cognitive control of pain, 1975. Masters thesis, University of Waterloo; as reproduced in Meichenbaum, D., *Cognitive behavior modification.* New York: Plenum, 1977.

merging one's arm in near-freezing water, or imagining a stressful situation.

Although such contrived stress-inducing procedures are not those encountered in real life, they do allow the client to rehearse the learned coping skills in the safe environment of the therapy session before using them to deal with actual stress-evoking situations. Furthermore, stress innoculation teaches the client *general* coping skills which are applicable in a wide range of stressful situations. Thus, it is not necessary for the stress-evoking situations used during behavior rehearsal to be the same as the particular ones clients will encounter in their natural environment (cf. the self-control model of systematic desensitization discussed in Chapter 20).

Stress inoculation has been primarily applied in the treatment of fear or anxiety (e.g., Meichenbaum, 1974), excessive anger (e.g., Novaco, 1975, 1978), and physical pain (e.g., Turk, 1975, 1978). The major differences in stress inoculation training for anxiety, anger, and pain are in the second phase where coping skills are customized to the target behavior. As seen in Table 22–4, some coping self-statements are general enough to be used with almost any type of stressful situation. In the case of controlling anger, clients are taught to view potential provocations as problems which require a solution rather than as threats which require an attack, and they rehearse alternative strategies for solving the problem at hand. One of the coping skills clients are taught for tolerating pain is to refocus their attention, such as imagining scenes unrelated to the pain-producing experience and the physical sensations of pain (cf. the cognitive strategies people use to delay gratification that Mischel and his colleagues identified in their research, discussed earlier in this chapter).

Interpersonal problem behaviors

Our discussion of therapeutic uses of modeling and cognitive behavior modification thus far has been concerned with decreasing fears, anxiety, or avoidance behavior where such responses are inappropriate, maladaptive, and/or psychologically painful. Similar procedures have also been used for the opposite purpose—increasing socially appropriate and adaptive behaviors.

Assertive behavior

Assertive behavior refers to a broad category of behavior which has as its central theme acting in a manner that assures one of not having his or her rights violated and of securing those things to which he or she is rightfully entitled. Examples of specific response classes of assertive behavior include making one's desires explicitly known (e.g., to your sexual partner), refusing unreasonable requests (e.g., when a friend asks to borrow the textbook for the course in which you are to have an exam the next day), asking for what one is entitled to (e.g., pointing out that you have received incorrect change), and not allowing oneself to be taken advantage of (e.g., when a person steps ahead of you in a line).

Modeling is one of the two procedures which are most often used to teach assertive behavior, the other being *behavior rehearsal*. The therapist or another appropriate model demonstrates assertive responses for the client (i.e., modeling), and then the client practices the responses (i.e., behavior rehearsal). (Other components of assertive training include direct instruction on how to perform an assertive response—sometimes called coaching—and feedback on the client's behavior rehearsal.)

The use of modeling and behavior rehearsal will be illustrated by an excerpt from Prince's (1975) assertion-training treatment, which was specifically designed to teach high school students to refuse unreasonable requests. The students listened to a tape-recorded description of a situation in which an unreasonable request was made, heard a role-played interaction in which a model responded to the request with an appropriate refusal, and then heard the description of the situation for a second time, after which the students practiced their own response to the situation in their minds *(covert behavior rehearsal)*. Here is an example of one situation as it was presented to students.

> You are in the middle of doing your homework when a friend phones you and says she doesn't have much to do and would like to come over for a while. Now listen to how such a situation might be handled by two people. [Friend:] "Hi, I don't have much to do. Mind if I come over for a while?" [Model:] "I'm doing my homework, and I can't take a break now. But I'd like to do it some other time." Now listen to the same situation again. This time you will be asked to respond. You are in the middle of doing your homework when a friend phones you and says, "Hi, I don't have much to do. Mind if I come over for a while?" What would you say? (15-second pause). (Prince, 1975)

In assertion training, both live models (e.g., Goldfried & Davison, 1976; Walker, Hedberg, Clement, & Wright, 1981) and symbolic models in the form of audiotapes (e.g., McFall & Twentyman, 1973; Spiegler, Marshall, Cooley, & Prince, 1978) and videotapes (e.g., Eisler, Hersen, & Miller, 1973; Rathus, 1973) have been employed.

Covert modeling is a form of symbolic modeling in which the person *imagines* rather than observes a model. This relatively new procedure will be illustrated in its application to assertion training with adults (Kazdin, 1975). Participants first practiced imagining scenes (unrelated to assertive behavior) in which a model of the same sex and similar age was present. Over the course of four therapy sessions, participants imagined a total of 35 scenes in which the model behaved assertively.

Each scene consisted of three components: (1) a description of the situation in which the assertive behavior was appropriate; (2) the model making an assertive response; and (3) the model receiving positive consequences for the assertive behavior. The following is a typical scene.

1. The person (model) is eating in a restaurant with friends. He (she) orders a steak and tells the waiter he (she) would like it rare. When the food arrives, the person begins to eat and apparently finds something wrong with the steak.
2. He (she) immediately signals the waiter. When the waiter arrives, the person says, "I ordered the steak rare, and this one is medium. Please take it back and bring me one that is rare."
3. In a few minutes the waiter brings another steak and says he is very sorry this has happened (Kazdin, 1975, p. 718).

Covert modeling has been shown to effectively increase assertive behavior (Kazdin, 1974), to be as effective as overt symbolic modeling (Rosenthal & Reese, 1976), and to be similar to overt modeling in terms of the variables which enhance imitation, such as vicarious reward and exposure to multiple models (Kazdin, 1975, 1976).

Basic social skills

Modeling therapy has proved quite potent in rapidly developing basic social skills (e.g., Goldstein, 1973; Gutride, Goldstein, & Hunter, 1973; Jaffe & Carlson, 1976; O'Connor, 1969, 1972). We shall look at several examples.

Ross, Ross, and Evans (1971) used both live and symbolic modeling to increase the social interactions of a six-year-old boy who was extremely withdrawn. The live model was a male undergraduate student who demonstrated a variety of interactions with preschool children (in the client's nursery school). At first the client would not watch the model, so that it was necessary for the therapist to verbally describe the model's behavior. Other symbolic modeling included brief presentations of stories, pictures, and films depicting the rewarding aspects of social interaction among young children. The treatment also involved role-playing and participant modeling.

> At the conclusion of seven weeks of treatment, the child had increased his social interaction to approximately the level of children who were judged socially competent. Two months after treatment, the child was given a generalization test in a playground setting that was significantly different from the protected nursery school setting. He "was able to join ongoing play groups, initiate verbal contacts, and sustain effective social interactions, all with the children who were complete strangers to him.

Furthermore . . . [he] accomplished these tasks competently, unhesitatingly, with obvious pleasure, and with no adult intervention whatsoever." (Ross et al., 1971)

In *self-modeling,* the subject serves as the exemplar in modeling sequences. Self-modeling is clearly applicable to covert modeling (described earlier), and it has also been used in symbolic overt modeling. Creer and Miklich (1970) report the successful use of the technique to modify the inappropriate social behavior of a 10-year-old boy who was a resident of a treatment center for patients with intractable bronchial asthma. Chuck spent most of his time alone, and his peers usually rebuffed his attempts to interact with them by calling him a "boob" or a "baby." He would respond by retreating to his room and throwing a temper tantrum. Chuck displayed inappropriate behavior with adults, such as giggling constantly, attempting to tickle them, and jumping into their laps during interviews. Furthermore, Chuck usually overslept, failed to make his bed or keep his room tidy, and did not show up on time for his medication.

Two self-modeling videotapes were made, one of appropriate behavior and the other of inappropriate behavior. Chuck and two other boys were asked to take part in a TV film, a request which was not considered extraordinary because the public-relations personnel who frequently visited the center sometimes made similar requests. In the *inappropriate self-modeling* scenes Chuck displayed his usual behaviors, such as asking to play with two boys and being told that he could not, and entering an office and jumping onto an adult's lap. In the *appropriate self-modeling* scenes, Chuck appropriately approached the two boys who were playing a game and asked if he could play with them, and acted appropriately with an adult in an office setting.

In the two weeks following the making of these two videotapes, no changes were observed in Chuck's behavior (change could have resulted from the role-playing involved in recording the modeling sequences). At this point, Chuck was taught to operate the videotape recorder and monitor. In the first two weeks of treatment, Chuck viewed the appropriate self-modeling tape daily, which resulted in an abrupt increase in his socially appropriate behavior that was maintained over the two-week period. In a second (reversal) phase, Chuck viewed the inappropriate self-modeling tape daily for a two-week period, which resulted in his return to inappropriate behavior in the dormitory and around others. In the final phase, Chuck again viewed the appropriate tape, which reinstated his appropriate social behavior in his daily interactions. Although the treatment terminated with this third two-week phase of viewing the appropriate tape, Chuck maintained his appropriate social behavior for the remaining six months that he was a resident at the center. Creer and Miklick (1970) note that many of the reports of Chuck's behavioral changes came from staff members who were unaware that Chuck had undergone the self-modeling treatment.

Cognitive problem behaviors

There are a number of problem behaviors that either directly involve cognitions (e.g, an inability to concentrate on a task for very long or to think of solutions to problems of daily living) or are indirectly mediated by maladaptive cognitions (e.g., telling ourselves that we can't concentrate or that there is no solution to a dilemma). We shall consider two cognitive-behavior-modification procedures that deal with a client's cognitions in conjunction with their overt behavior.

Self-instruction as applied to problems of impulsivity and inadequate creative problem solving

Self-instruction, another cognitive behavior therapy developed by Meichenbaum (Meichenbaum & Goodman, 1971), is a treatment package in which modeling and cognitive behavior rehearsal are the major components. We shall describe several applications of self-instruction to illustrate how it is used and the diversity of its applicability.

Self-instruction therapy was first used to decrease the impulsive behavior of children (Meichenbaum & Goodman, 1971). Children who act impulsively do not think before acting, which often has undesirable consequences for them as well as for other people. The general goal of self-instruction therapy for impulsive behavior is to train the children to think and plan before acting. Self-instructional training for impulsive behavior involves five steps.

1. An adult model performs a task while verbalizing an adaptive, counter-impulsive strategy (cognitive modeling). An example of what the model might say while engaging in a task involving copying line patterns is:

    > Okay, what is it I have to do? You want me to copy the picture with the different lines. I have to go slowly and carefully. Okay, draw the line down, down, good; then to the right, that's it; now down some more and to the left. Good, I'm doing fine so far. Remember, go slowly. Now back up again. No, I was supposed to go down. That's okay. Just erase the line carefully. . . . Good. Even if I make an error I can go on slowly and carefully. I have to go down now. Finished. I did it! (Meichenbaum & Goodman, 1971, p. 117)

2. The child then performs the task as the model verbalizes the instructions (cognitive participant modeling).
3. Next the child performs the task while verbalizing the instructions out loud (overt self-instruction).

4. Now the child performs the task while whispering the instructions (fading, or gradually eliminating, the overt self-instructions).
5. Finally the child performs the task while saying the instructions to her- or himself (covert self-instructions).

Using the sequence of activities just described, the child is first given practice with brief and simple perceptual motor tasks, such as coloring figures within boundaries. Gradually the length and complexity of the tasks are increased (e.g., a complex task might be solving concept-formation problems).

The use of self-instruction to teach college students creative problem solving will serve as a second illustration of the technique (Meichenbaum, 1975). The basic aim of this training is to eliminate self-talk that interferes with creative problem solving and to replace it with self-talk which enhances it. First, students are taught to be aware of the counter-creativity self-statements they make when confronted with a problem to be solved (e.g., "There is only one way to fix it and that won't work in this case"). Then students are taught to substitute creativity-enhancing self-statements for their counter-creativity self-talk (e.g., "Right now I can think of only one way to fix it, but maybe there are other ways"). The trainers model creativity-enhancing self-statements and then the students imitate and rehearse them. Below is an example of a trainer's cognitive modeling for a practice task that involved making a list of innovative ways of changing a toy monkey so that children could have more fun with it.

> I want to think of something no one else will think of, something unique. Be freewheeling, no hangups. I don't care what anyone thinks; just suspend judgment. I'm not sure what I'll come up with; it will be a surprise. The ideas can just flow through me. Okay, what is it I have to do? Think of ways to improve a toy monkey. Toy monkey. Let me close my eyes and relax. Just picture a monkey. I see a monkey; now let my mind wander; let one idea flow into another. I'll use analogies. Let me picture myself inside the monkey. . . . Now let me do the task as if I were someone else. (Meichenbaum, 1977, p. 62)

After presenting this general strategy, the trainer listed aloud possible answers to the problem and frequently modeled the use of self-reinforcement (e.g., "That's a good idea; this is fun!"). The trainer also modeled self-instructions which students could use to cope with not being able to generate any ideas and feeling frustrated (e.g., "Take it easy . . . the ideas will come, but I can't force them . . . just relax, take a break, go slowly . . ."). The self-instructional training program was individualized in that each student's notions about creativity were assessed and the self-instructions modeled for each student reflected these ideas. Self-instructional training proved successful in significantly increasing the students' originality and flexibility on tests of divergent thinking and increasing their preference for complex thinking. Additionally, it is of interest that the students reported that they were applying the self-instructional creativity training on their own to solve personal and academic problems.

Problem-solving therapy: A general cognitive-behavioral therapy

Solving problems of varying degrees of importance is a ubiquitous part of people's daily lives, and solving personal problems is the essence of psychotherapy. Thus, problem solving might be considered the most broadly applicable self-help or therapeutic skill an individual can learn. To provide clients with this useful self-coping skill, Thomas D'Zurilla and Marvin Goldfried (1971) developed an approach to problem-solving therapy that involves seven interrelated procedures or steps (Spiegler, 1982) which are briefly described below.

1. *General orientation.* The therapist explains the rationale for problem-solving therapy and stresses the importance of identifying troublesome life events as problems for which a number of alternative solutions can be generated and implemented.
2. *Problem definition and formulation.* The client is taught how to concretely and precisely define a problem and identify its maintaining conditions. Formulation of the problem involves identifying major goals and the issues or conflicts which make the situation problematic (Goldfried & Davison, 1976).
3. *Generation of alternative solutions.* Here the client is encouraged to brainstorm about possible general strategies for solving the problem; the objective in this step is to generate as many alternatives as possible without evaluating their potential effectiveness or feasibility.
4. *Deciding on a solution.* Here the client chooses the alternative generated in the previous step that has the most likelihood of successfully solving the problem.
5. *Generation of alternative tactics for implementing the solution.* Once the general solution strategy has been chosen, the client "brainstorms" to generate as many means of implementing the strategy as possible.
6. *Deciding on a tactic.* The client is helped to choose that course of action which has the highest probability of effectively and efficiently implementing the solution strategy.
7. *Action and assessment.* Finally, the client implements the chosen tactic and evaluates how well it results in a satisfactory resolution of the problem.

D'Zurilla and Goldfried's (1971) problem-solving therapy is a good example of cognitive-behavioral therapeutic approaches in that it combines direct cognitive interventions (e.g., generating alternative solutions) and direct (overt) behavioral interventions (e.g., implementing and evaluating a course of action). It is also typical of many behavior therapies in its relying on a variety of behavior therapy procedures to form a powerful treatment package. For example, the therapist may employ cognitive modeling to demonstrate how to brainstorm for solutions by verbalizing a scenario such as the following.

> How am I going to get my thesis finished by the June deadline? I could put in more hours, which would mean giving up my jogging and TV and most parties . . . even sleeping. I could hire a typist to make my rough drafts more readable so I could rewrite more quickly. Maybe I could get an English grad student to help with my grammar and spelling. Of course, I could buy a thesis from one of those companies that sells them. . . .

When alternatives are being generated, the therapist would praise the client's silly or obviously infeasible ideas as well as practical, creative ones to encourage the process of brainstorming. If the client has difficulty with brainstorming, the procedure might have to be shaped. The therapist also teaches and encourages the client to self-reinforce appropriate problem-solving behaviors. When the client is ready to implement and test a tactic for solving the problem in the final stage, it may be necessary to employ various behavior therapy procedures to facilitate the client's actions. For example, if the client felt anxious or inhibited in asking a friend for help, this difficulty would first have to be alleviated, as by systematic desensitization and assertion training.

Problem-solving behavior therapies (of which the model just described is one representative example) have been used to treat a variety of target behaviors with a wide range of clients, including helping kindergarten and grade school children learn to cooperate with peers (Spivack & Shure, 1974), reducing examination and interpersonal anxiety among college students (Mayo & Norton, 1980), and enhancing harmony among family members (e.g., Blechman, 1974). Problem-solving therapies are particularly suited for clients facing major life decisions, such as marriage, divorce, changing jobs, and even contemplating suicide. In the last example, problem-solving could help someone consider alternative solutions—besides ending one's life—to a seemingly untenable situation (Goldfried & Davison, 1976).

23 *The behavioral strategy*

Liabilities

In this chapter we shall describe six limitations of the behavioral strategy in general. They are that the behavioral strategy (1) is narrow in terms of the phenomena it studies and the theoretical explanations it advances; (2) relies on problematic situational tests in personality assessment; (3) makes unjustified extrapolations from laboratory research; (4) lacks a theory of behavioral personality change; (5) commits the logical error of affirming the consequent in relation to behavior change; and (6) is not easily accepted by many people. A seventh point is limited to the cognitive-behavioral approach, namely: (7) the cognitive-behavioral approach mistakenly casts thoughts as causes of behavior.

NARROWNESS OF THE PHENOMENA STUDIED AND OF THE THEORETICAL EXPLANATIONS

Critics have pointed out that the behavioral approach is narrow in terms of the personality phenomena examined and the variables which are posited to influence them (e.g., Pervin, 1970). For a long time, the behavioral strategy restricted its interest to overt behavior, thereby excluding private covert events from study. While this criticism is somewhat less cogent today because of the trend within the behavioral strategy to examine covert behavior, the behavioral strategy is still restrictive in the principles which it uses to explain private events. Specifically, it has made the basic assumption that covert events are governed by the same learning principles and processes that have been shown to play an important role in determining overt behavior. Though this assumption has been useful in directing behavioral psychologists toward examining the "inner" side of human beings, the assumption is still largely untested.

The narrowness of the behavioral strategy as it relates to the human experience has been eloquently stated by Sperry (1976).

> What remains of the human psyche and the mind of man in the [behaviorist] scheme of objective science seems to boil down essentially to a complex system of electrophysiochemical interactions, all causally determined and physically controlled. The resultant view of human nature and the kind of values that emerge are hardly uplifting. The color, quality, and higher meaning of life seem to be lost or destroyed; and the long-

standing separation between the material world of science on the one hand and the world of the humanities and inner experience on the other becomes increasingly wide and irreconcilable. The scientific renunciation of conscious mind and free will, flying as it does in the face of common experience and common aspiration, does little to counter the recent waning of intellectual confidence in science and opportunely feeds, instead, various sentiments of antiscience. (p. 12)

Sperry himself has championed a view of the mind in which the "phenomena of inner experience become active causal determinants in brain activity and are given a functional role and a reason for having been evolved in a physical world." Noting that his own view is confessedly speculative, he goes on to add:

It is not critical at this stage that the new interpretation lacks any firm proof. No proof is available, either, for the behaviorist-materialist position. Just the fact that a scientifically possible explanatory model [that includes private experience] is conceivable has been sufficient in itself to release the long pent-up subjectivist pressures. (1976, p. 12)

The behavioral strategy approaches personality phenomena with the fundamental postulate that *behavior is learned*. While it is certainly useful to think of *some* aspects of personality in terms of learning, it is equally clear that a complete theory of personality will have to explain some of its subject matter in other ways. We have seen, for example, that there is strong evidence for a major hereditary component in certain types of behavior even when relevant learning opportunities are held constant (see Chapter 9). The behavioral strategy makes little allowance for hereditary influences or for other biologically based individual differences that exist either before or apart from learning processes. A case in point is the suggestion made by Seligman (1971) that humans possess a "biological preparedness" to develop particular phobias which are learned rapidly (often in a single trial) and are very difficult to extinguish through various behavior therapy techniques. Thus, the development of phobias may not be explainable merely in terms of environmental effects and learning.

It is not only that a behavioral approach does not use genetic and dispositional notions; the behavioral approach tends to be *anti*dispositional and *anti*genetic and thus may be viewed as narrow and provincial. Levy (1970) has described the liability this way:

Personality theorists who have adopted a learning approach have defined their domain of interest as "the study of learned behavior." . . . Although this is a perfectly defensible position, it restricts the range of behavioral phenomena that can be studied and the kinds of explanations that can be proposed. . . . some possible qualities of behavior commonly associated with personality must be either ignored or inadequately explained as a consequence. (p. 433)

The behavioral approach can also be considered narrow in that it does not adequately take into account the role played by various psychological (as opposed to genetic and biological) dispositions. This limitation is attributable to the situation-specific perspective of the behavioral approach which holds that behavior is determined primarily by contextual variables. However, in some cases, improved prediction of an individual's behavior could be attained by attending to relevant dispositions. For example, a person's behavior in an achievement-oriented situation, such as a final course examination, might vary with the individual's achievement motivation. It is just such a possibility that has prompted cognitive-behavioral psychologists such as Mischel (1979), whose ideas were outlined in Chapter 22, to begin to investigate important person-situation interactions.

Likewise, the behavioral strategy has traditionally ignored the role played by subjective views of the external environment in determining the specific influence that the environmental factors have on behavior. This is important because people often *perceive* the same (objective) situation in different (subjective) ways. Some students may view a final course examination as anxiety evoking, whereas others may consider it a challenge. It is not even possible to make the generalization that a final examination is important for all students. Students who have extremely high or extremely low grades in a course before the final exam or who do not care what grade they receive on the exam are apt to view the test situation differently than students for whom performance on the final examination is critical in determining a course grade which is important to them. That people can view an environmental event in different ways is one explanation for individual differences in the same situation.

Again, responsive to a long-term criticism of the behavioral strategy, cognitive-behavioral psychologists such as Bandura (1977b) and Mischel (1979) have broadened the study of personality to examine the role which phenomenological influences may have on behavior as they interact with environmental conditions as well as with person variables. Bandura's (1977a, 1978) theorizing about perceived self-efficacy is a prime example of this work.

PROBLEMS WITH SITUATIONAL TESTS

Behavioral psychologists often use situational tests in their assessment of personality. An individual's personality (behavior) is assessed by observing her or him in situations which are similar to the ones which are of interest. For instance, if we were concerned with learning how individuals respond to failure, we might place subjects in several situations in which they fail at some task and observe and measure their reactions. (This tack should be contrasted with such personality assessment procedures as having the subject respond to written questions about reactions to failure, measuring the need to achieve and avoid failure by having the subject write stories in response to TAT cards, and so on.) Situational tests make sense "intuitively," inasmuch as measuring what a person does presently is an "obvious" way of determining what the person will do in the future. Partially because situational tests often have high *face validity* (i.e., they look as if they measure what is being tested for), there has been little systematic evaluation of such techniques of personality assessment.

Perhaps the most extensive development and use of situational tests occurred during World War II, when the American and British armed forces were faced with the task of selecting suitable officer candidates (Morris, 1949) and individuals for military intelligence assignments (OSS Assessment Staff, 1948). In general, the reliability of these tests was not very high (e.g., the ratings given at different "assessment stations" were not consistent). Neither was the predictive validity of the situational tests—their ability to select in advance those candidates who subsequently performed well on assignments—as high as had been hoped (Anastasi, 1976; Morris, 1949). The disappointing performance of situational tests for selecting personnel in the wartime situation is, no doubt, partially attributable to factors which were independent of the techniques themselves, such as the less than ideal circumstances of having to develop mass assessment procedures very quickly. On the other hand, some of the failure may be due to the general problems of situational tests.

One difficulty is that the act of observation by psychologists and the stresses of being "on the spot" to perform in a test situation alter the behavior of the assessee to an unknown degree. People often "flub" a demonstration of something they know how to do very well just because they are asked to perform. At the other extreme, some people may perform more competently or diligently than they are likely to in the actual situation because they know that they are being assessed or observed. Teachers who enthusiastically encourage their students while the school principal is sitting at a desk in the back of the room show that they *can* put forth an impressive effort under observation; whether they *will* be as conscientious when only the children are present cannot be judged on this basis alone.

A related problem that arises with situational tests is that the "role-playing" component which many of them have may involve somewhat different abilities than are called for in the corresponding life situations. For example, a soldier who is best able to *pretend* to be a strong leader under test conditions may not prove to be the most effective leader in the field when faced with real, rather than fictitious, enemies.

Finally, situational tests may not be "lifelike" enough to have adequate predictive validity. A person who demonstrates the ability to pick up a harmless snake in the laboratory and reports no longer being afraid of snakes may still show considerable fear when unexpectedly encountering a reptile on a solitary country lane. Indeed, such a possibility could be considered all the more likely by the behavioral strategy because of its emphasis on situational specificity.

The favored method of research in the behavioral strategy has been the controlled laboratory experiment which is most conducive to drawing conclusions regarding cause-and-effect relationships. However, to create precision in the laboratory, the problems studied are often narrow and simplified, involving the effect of one or two independent variables on several dependent variables. Experiences of people in the "real world" tend to be much more complex. Furthermore, the experimental subjects are frequently college sophomores and in some cases are nonhuman organisms. Thus, while the behavioral psychologist may conduct rigorous research, the *external validity* of the extrapolations or generalizations made from the findings is questionable.

Consider the example of classical conditioning. There is no doubt that the phenomenon Pavlov originally observed in dogs is real. It can be repeated in almost any laboratory, and, what is more, much is known about the variables that "control" such conditioning. But does this enormous body of research with nonhuman animals in specially contrived laboratory arrangements truly parallel issues in personality, such as the "conditioning" of attitudes? In fact, many patterns are not parallel. Timing, for example, which is critical in the pairings of the CS and UCS when conditioning dogs or rats (seconds, and sometimes fractions of seconds, may determine whether conditioning occurs), is less essential in humans, who are capable of symbolically "bridging the gap" between two events which are separated in time. So, too, classical conditioning of laboratory animals almost always displays a gradual acquisition curve. Is this analogous to "conditioned" emotional reactions in humans (e.g., intense fear) which are based on a single exposure to a noxious stimulus? Critics argue that classical conditioning in humans is quite different from that in lower species. There may be a variety of emotional and cognitive components which are simply ignored by referring to highly controlled and often artificial experimental situations which gloss over the complexities of real life.

Even when human subjects are studied, the artificiality of most experiments may produce simple learning responses as an artifact. The laboratory situation, in effect, "decorticates" subjects in that it restricts their behavior so as to make more complex responses impossible. That an adult *can* learn prejudicial responses because a name or a word is paired repeatedly in the laboratory with some discrete unpleasant event (e.g., an electric shock or a noxious sound or word) hardly means that most—or even any—real-life prejudices are learned this way. Simi-

UNJUSTIFIED EXTRAPOLATION FROM LABORATORY RESEARCH

larly, although there is ample direct evidence that various personality phenomena, such as delay-of-gratification, language, and sex-role behavior, can be created and modified in the laboratory setting (and sometimes in naturalistic settings), these demonstrations only serve as indirect evidence regarding the manner in which these behaviors are typically learned by people in their natural environments. Demonstrations that any particular set of learning principles accounts for complex human behavior require more than *analogies* to laboratory findings occurring under highly restricted conditions.

ABSENCE OF A THEORY OF BEHAVIORAL PERSONALITY CHANGE

Some critics have argued that no theory of learning (and certainly no single theory) underlies behavioral personality-change techniques (Spiegler, 1982); rather, behavior therapists can be said to have achieved a "nontheoretical amalgamation of pragmatic principles" (Weitzman, 1967, p. 303) from which their procedures derive strength. Weitzman suggests, for example, that the effectiveness of systematic desensitization can be explained in terms of a variety of nonbehavioral theories, such as psychoanalysis.

This liability takes on even greater force when one observes that behavioral theories of personality are not responsible for behavioral change techniques, inasmuch as the change techniques antedate contemporary behavioral approaches by many years. Breger and McGaugh (1966), two strong critics of the entire behavioral movement, write:

> It is clear that the techniques in question were in existence long before . . . learning theory. Pfaundler described an apparatus for treating enuresis in 1904 that greatly resembled Mowrer's conditioning technique, and Nye, a pediatrician, outlined a proposed method for treating enuresis in 1830 that included all of the elements of "conditioning" therapy. . . . Circus animal trainers used "operant" and "shaping" techniques for centuries. [Therefore] . . . it is not true that learning theory has been necessary or even very important in *developing* the specific techniques in question. (p. 171)

Bandura's (1977a, 1978) theory of perceived self-efficacy is an obvious exception to the liability under discussion. However, although this theory has the *potential* to provide a general theoretical explanation of diverse behavioral therapy procedures (as well as other types of personality-change techniques used in other strategies), it certainly is far too rudimentary to even approach that goal in its present form. More than likely, perceived self-efficacy will turn out, at best, to be a viable theory of a narrow range of personality-change procedures (e.g., performance-based procedures, such as participant modeling, for alleviating specific avoidance behaviors). Furthermore, the criticism that little theory of behavioral personality change exists is, in general, completely justified.

Behaviorally oriented psychologists take great pride in the success of behavior therapy techniques and often claim or imply that these successes demonstrate the validity of behavioral personality theory. The logic of this assumption can be questioned. The situation is similar to that of a person who takes aspirin for a headache; generally, the medicine will relieve the pain and thus "cure" the ailment. Still, the fact that introducing acetylsalicylic acid (aspirin) into the bloodstream eliminated the discomfort hardly means that the pain was caused by a lack of acetylsalicylic acid in the first place. Likewise, the fact that a learning and behaviorally based treatment eliminates a psychological problem does not logically imply that the problem was caused by the reverse learning process. Simply because an unrealistic fear can be eliminated by counterconditioning does not prove that it was *acquired* through conditioning. Each of these examples illustrates the logical error of "affirming the consequent"—that is, assuming that "because behavior is generated under one set of circumstances, every time this or similar behavior occurs in nature, it had developed because of the same set of controlling conditions" (Davison & Neale, 1974, p. 28).

BEHAVIOR THERAPY AND THE ERROR OF AFFIRMING THE CONSEQUENT

The final general liability of the behavioral strategy we shall discuss is more speculative than the others we have noted. People are often reluctant to view themselves, others, and human personality in general as being largely determined by the relatively simple view of behavior posited by many behavioral psychologists. (See the discussion of the parsimonious nature of behavioral personality theory in Chapter 19.) There are ways in which each of the other personality strategies has some attractive and/or compelling aspects which make it "seem" more right or palatable than the behavioral perspective.

We consider ourselves to be highly complex organisms, and the explanations of personality offered by the psychoanalytic strategy present humans as being governed by extremely complex processes. Although it may be difficult for us to accept particular psychoanalytic concepts, such as infantile sexuality, other concepts, such as the existence of an unconscious part of personality, seem helpful in providing us with reasons for many phenomena that appear to defy explanation.

The dispositional approach to personality is easy for people to accept because it presents scientific evidence for the common way in which we typically describe and view ourselves and others and "explain" behavior—that is, in terms of relatively enduring traits or needs that influence behavior in diverse settings.

The phenomenological perspective is consistent with our being predominantly self-centered beings. Although it may be less immediately obvious that our personal views of events have an important influence on our behavior, there are ample everyday examples and demon-

PROBLEMS CONCERNING THE ACCEPTANCE OF THE STRATEGY

strations of this fact which help to make the phenomenological approach to personality easily believable. Furthermore, more than any of the other strategies, the phenomenological strategy places a heavy emphasis on people's being able to determine their own behavior.

In contrast, the behavioral approach presents a more difficult "product" to sell. How can complex human beings be explained by what seem to be comparatively simple principles? Furthermore, the proposition that personality is a function of environmental factors strikes deep at the heart of the time-honored and sacred notion of free will and self-determinism. Witness the plethora of criticism launched at Skinner's (1971) book *Beyond Freedom and Dignity*. Although humans may, in fact, not possess free will, they seem to have a need to think they do, and there is good evidence that such a conceptional set can be adaptive in many circumstances (e.g., Lefcourt, 1973).

If the above arguments are correct, we can conclude that people in general resist acceptance of a behavioral approach to personality. But how does this affect the scientific study of personality through use of the behavioral strategy? Indirectly, public sentiment influences scientific investigation, particularly if that sentiment is strong and well publicized. For example, certain areas of research and practical application may be seriously hampered by state and federal laws or the loss of funding. Furthermore, personality psychologists are people (as George Kelly has pointed out) and thus may share the general public's views on human personality and the basic nature of the human species. Such biases can have definite influences on the work done by psychologists in studying personality. Thomas Kuhn, a noted philosopher of science, has very convincingly argued that changes in scientific thinking, particularly major shifts in scientific investigation, may be influenced more by nonscientific factors (e.g., the prevailing "spirit of the times" and subjective biases) than by objective scientific evidence (Kuhn, 1962).

THE COGNITIVE-BEHAVIORAL APPROACH MISTAKENLY CASTS THOUGHTS AS CAUSES OF BEHAVIOR

Many proponents of the cognitive-behavioral approach (e.g., Bandura, Mahoney) claim to be former adherents of "strict" radical behaviorism who discovered the necessity of considering cognitive processes as a result of their research or clinical work. The cognitive-behavioral approach has thus been called the new wave in behaviorism. However, radical behaviorists have expressed a number of serious reservations about the cognitive-behavioral approach (Skinner, 1974; Rachlin, 1977; Wolpe, 1978).

Radical behaviorists do not deny that thoughts occur, or that they are "real," but they do not consider thoughts to operate as independent causes of behavior. Rather, according to radical behaviorism, our thoughts are the *effect* of our reinforcement histories and biological condition, and not a *cause* of behavior. Thus, the radical behaviorists would reply to Bandura that favorable experiences (e.g., exposure to appropriate models and teachers) lead us both to perform better and to feel that we have personal efficacy. The feeling of efficacy is thus an effect of experience and not a mental way station between experience and performance.

What are the implications of this dispute between the two groups? In the practice of behavior therapy, it may be that very much the same principles of treatment apply in behavior therapy regardless of whether or not the therapist has a cognitive orientation. Thus Rachlin, after reading Mahoney's (1974) book, *Cognition and Behavior Modification,* commented:

> [Cognitive] therapy does not stop after the irrational idea is uncovered and the rational idea presented. If ideas themselves could control behavior [as cognitive behaviorists assert] then one would expect the change of ideas to result simply in a change of behavior, as when a general orders his army to advance or retreat. But far from ending after the client's ideas are changed, therapy barely begins at that point. The therapy consists of homework assignments that to all intents and purposes are identical with the sorts of things noncognitive behavior therapists do as a matter of course. (1977, pp. 372–73)

References

Abraham, K. The Influence of oral eroticism on character formation. In K. Abraham, *Selected papers on psychoanalysis*. London: Hogarth, 1927.

Adelson, R., Liebert, R. M., Herskovitz, A., & Poulos, R. W. A modeling film to reduce children's fear of dental treatment. *International Association for Dental Research Abstracts*, March 1972, 114.

Adler, A. *Social interest: A challenge to mankind*. New York: Putnam (Capricorn Books), 1964.

Adler, A. *Superiority and social interest: A collection of later writings*. (H. L. Ansbacher & R. R. Ansbacher, Eds.) New York: Viking Press, 1973.

Allen, E., Sociobiology: A new biological determinism. In Sociobiology Study Group of Boston (Eds.), *Biology as a social weapon*. Minneapolis: Burgess, 1977.

Allport, G. W. *Pattern and growth in personality*. New York: Holt, Rinehart & Winston, 1961.

Allport, G. W. *Letters from Jenny*. New York: Harcourt, Brace, & World, 1965.

Allport, G. W. Traits revisited. *American Psychologist*, 1966, *21*, 1–10.

Allport, G. W., & Allport, F. H. *The A-S reaction study*. Boston: Houghton Mifflin, 1928.

American Psychological Association. Testing and public policy. *American Psychologist*, 1965, *20*, 857–993.

Anastasi, A. *Psychological testing* (3d ed.). New York: Macmillan, 1968.

Anastasi, A. *Psychological testing* (4th ed.). New York: Macmillan, 1976.

Ansbacher, H. L., & Ansbacher, R. R. *The individual psychology of Alfred Adler: A systematic presentation in selections from his writings*. New York: Harper & Row, 1956.

Aronfreed, J. *Conduct and conscience*. New York: Academic Press, 1968.

Aronson, E. *The social animal*. San Francisco: Freeman, 1972.

Aserinsky, E., & Kleitman, N. Regularly occurring periods of eye motility, and concomitant phenomena, during sleep. *Science*, 1953, *118*, 273–74.

Aspy, D. *Toward a technology for humanizing education*. Champaign, Ill.: Research Press, 1972.

Aspy, D., & Roebuck, F. From humane ideas to humane technology and back again, many times. *Education*, 1974, *95*, 163–71.

Atkinson, J. W. (Ed.) *Motives in fantasy, action, and society*. Princeton, N.J.: Van Nostrand, 1958.

Atkinson, J. W. Studying personality in the context of an advanced motivational psychology. *American Psychologist*, 1981, *36*, 107–12.

Atkinson, J. W., & Litwin, G. H. Achievement motive and test anxiety conceived as motive to approach success and motive to avoid failure. *Journal of Abnormal and Social Psychology*, 1960, *60*, 52–63.

Atkinson, J. W., & McClelland, D. C. The projective expression of needs, II. The effect of different intensities of the hunger drive on thematic apperception. *Journal of Experimental Psychology*, 1948, *38*, 643–58.

Ayllon, T. Some behavioral problems associated with eating in chronic schizophrenic patients. In L. P. Ullmann & L. Krasner (Eds.), *Case studies in behavior modification*. New York: Holt, Rinehart & Winston, 1965.

Bach, G. R. The marathon group: Intensive practice of intimate interactions. *Psychological Reports*, 1966, *181*, 995–1002.

Baer, D. M. A case for the selective reinforcement of punishment. In C. Neuringer & J. L. Michael (Eds.), *Behavior modification in clinical psychology*. New York: Appleton-Century-Crofts, 1970.

Baer, D. M., & Sherman, J. A. Reinforcement control of generalized imitation in young children. *Journal of Experimental Child Psychology*, 1964, *1*, 37–49.

Bandura, A. Psychotherapists anxiety level, self-insight and psychotherapeutic competence. *Journal of Abnormal and Social Psychology*, 1956, *52*, 333–37.

Bandura, A. Influence of models' reinforcement contingencies on the acquisition of imitative responses. *Journal of Personality and Social Psychology*, 1965, *1*, 589–95.

Bandura, A. *Principles of behavior modification*. New York: Holt, Rinehart & Winston, 1969. (a)

Bandura, A. Social learning theory of identificatory processes. In D. A. Goslin (Ed.), *Handbook of socialization theory and research*. Chicago: Rand McNally, 1969. (b)

Bandura, A. (Ed.). *Psychological modeling: Conflicting theories*. Chicago: Aldine-Atherton, 1971.

Bandura, A. Self-efficacy: Toward a unifying theory of behavioral change. *Psychological Review*, 1977, *84*, 191–215. (a)

Bandura, A. *Social learning theory*. Englewood Cliffs, N.J.: Prentice-Hall, 1977. (b)

Bandura, A. Reflections on self-efficacy. In S. Rachman (Ed.), *Advances in behaviour research and therapy* (Vol. 1). Oxford: Pergamon Press, 1978.

Bandura, A., & Adams, N. E. Analysis of self-efficacy theory of behavioral change. *Cognitive Therapy and Research*, 1977, *1*, 287–308.

Bandura, A., Adams, N. E., & Beyer, J. Cognitive processes mediating behavioral change. *Journal of Personality and Social Psychology*, 1977, *35*, 125–39.

Bandura, A., Adams, N. E., Hardy, A. B., & Howells, G. N. Tests of the generality of self-efficacy theory. *Cognitive Therapy and Research*, 1980, *4*, 39–66.

Bandura, A., Blanchard, E. B., & Ritter, B. The relative efficacy of desensitization and modeling approaches for inducing behavioral, affective, and attitudinal changes. *Journal of Personality and Social Psychology,* 1969, *13,* 173–99.

Bandura, A., Grusec, J. E., & Menlove, F. L. Vicarious extinction of avoidance behavior through symbolic modeling. *Journal of Personality and Social Psychology,* 1967, *5,* 16–22.

Bandura, A., & Menlove, F. L. Factors determining vicarious extinction of avoidance behavior through symbolic modeling. *Journal of Personality and Social Psychology,* 1968, *8,* 99–108.

Bandura, A., & Mischel, W. Modification of self-imposed delay of reward through exposure to live and symbolic models. *Journal of Personality and Social Psychology,* 1965, *2,* 698–705.

Bandura, A., & Schunk, D. H. Cultivating competence, self-efficacy, and intrinsic interest through proximal self-motivation. *Journal of Personality and Social Psychology,* 1981, *41,* 586–98.

Bandura, A., & Walters, R. H. *Social learning and personality development.* New York: Holt, Rinehart & Winston, 1963.

Barash, D. P. *Sociobiology and behavior.* New York: Elsevier, 1977.

Barash, D. P. Evolution as a paradigm for behavior. In M. S. Gregory, A. Silvers, & D. Sutch (Eds.), *Sociobiology and human nature.* San Francisco: Jossey-Bass, 1978.

Barrett-Lennard, G. T. Dimensions of therapist response as causal factors in therapeutic change. *Psychological Monographs,* 1962, *76* (43, Whole No. 562).

Bem, S. L. Probing the promise of androgyny. In A. G. Kaplan & J. P. Bean (Eds.), *Beyond sex-role stereotypes: Readings toward a psychology of androgyny.* Boston: Little, Brown, 1976.

Benedek, T. Climacterium: A developmental phase. *Psychoanalytic Quarterly,* 1950, *19,* 1–27.

Benfari, R. C. Relationship between early dependence training and patient-therapist dyad. *Psychological Reports,* 1969, *25,* 552–54.

Berger, R. J., & Oswald, I. Eye movements during active and passive dreams. *Science,* 1962, *137,* 601.

Bergin, A. E. The evaluation of therapeutic outcomes. In A. E. Bergin & S. L. Garfield (Eds.), *Handbook of psychotherapy and behavior change.* New York: John Wiley & Sons, 1971.

Bergin, A. E., & Jasper, L. G. Correlates of empathy in psychotherapy: A replication. *Journal of Abnormal Psychology,* 1969, *74,* 477–81.

Bergin, A. E., & Solomon, S. Personality and performance correlates of empathic understanding in psychotherapy. In J. T. Hart & T. M. Tomlinson (Eds.), *New directions in client-centered therapy.* Boston: Houghton Mifflin, 1970.

Bergin, A. E., & Strupp, H. H. *Changing frontiers in the science of psychotherapy.* Chicago: Aldine-Atherton, 1972.

Berkowitz, L., & Knurek, D. A. Label-mediated hostility in generalization. *Journal of Personality and Social Psychology,* 1969, *13,* 200–206.

Berne, E. *Transactional analysis in psychotherapy.* New York: Grove Press, 1961.

Berne, E. *Games people play.* New York: Grove Press, 1964.

Bernstein, A. Some relations between techniques of feeding and training during infancy and certain behavior in childhood. *Genetic Psychology Monographs,* 1955, *51,* 3–44.

Bernstein, D. A., & Paul, G. L. Some comments on therapy analogue research with small animal "phobias." *Journal of Behavior Therapy and Experimental Psychiatry,* 1971, *2,* 225–37.

Bertrand, S., & Masling, J. M. Oral imagery and alcoholism. *Journal of Abnormal Psychology,* 1969, *74,* 50–53.

Bettelheim, B. *The uses of enchantment.* New York: Alfred A. Knopf, 1976.

Bieri, J. Changes in interpersonal perceptions following social interaction. *Journal of Abnormal and Social Psychology,* 1953, *48,* 61–66.

Bindrim, P. A report on a nude marathon: The effect of physical nudity upon the practice interaction in the marathon group. *Psychotherapy: Theory, Research, and Practice,* 1968, *5,* 180–88.

Birney, R. C. Research on the achievement motive. In E. F. Borgatta & W. W. Lambert (Eds.), *Handbook of personality theory and research.* Chicago: Rand McNally, 1968.

Birns, B. Individual differences in human neonates' responses to stimulation. *Child Development,* 1965, *36,* 249–56.

Blake, R., Rosenbaum, M., & Duryea, R. A. Gift-giving as a function of group standards. *Human Relations,* 1955, *8,* 61–73.

Blechman, E. A. The family contract game: A tool to teach interpersonal problem solving. *Family Coordinator,* 1974, *23,* 269–81.

Block, J. *The challenge of response sets.* New York: Appleton-Century-Crofts, 1965.

Block, J. Advancing the psychology of personality: Paradigmatic shift or improving the quality of research? In D. Magnusson & N. S. Endler (Eds.), *Personality at the crossroads.* Hillsdale, N.J.: Lawrence Erlbaum Associates, 1977.

Bolles, R. C. Whatever happened to motivation? *Educational Psychologist,* 1978, *13,* 1–13.

Bootzin, R. R., & Nicassio, P. M. Behavioral treatments for insomnia. In M. Hersen, R. Eisler, & P. Miller (Eds.), *Progress in behavior modification* (Vol. 6). New York: Academic Press, 1978.

Borkovec, T. D. Self-efficacy: Cause or reflection of behavioral change? In S. Rachman (Ed.), *Advances in behaviour research and therapy* (Vol. 1). Oxford: Pergamon Press, 1978.

Bottome, P. *Alfred Adler: A portrait from life.* New York: Vanguard, 1957.

Bowers, K. S. Situationism in psychology: An analysis and a critique. *Psychological Review,* 1973, *80,* 307–36.

Breger, L., & McGaugh, J. L. Learning theory and behavior therapy: A reply to Rachman and Eysenck. *Psychological Bulletin,* 1966, *65,* 170–73.

Bregman, E. An attempt to modify the emotional attitude of infants by the conditioned response technique. *Journal of Genetic Psychology,* 1934, *45,* 169–98.

Brenneis, C. B. Male and female ego modalities in manifest dream content. *Journal of Abnormal Psychology*, 1970, *76*, 434–42.

Brenner, C. *An elementary textbook of psychoanalysis*. Garden City, N.Y.: Doubleday Anchor Books, 1957.

Brigham, T. A., Graubard, P. S., & Stans, A. Analysis of the effects of sequential reinforcement contingencies on aspects of composition. *Journal of Applied Behavior Analysis*, 1972, *5*, 421–29.

Brooks, P. The crypto-biologist. *The New York Times Book Review*. February 10, 1980, pp. 9 and 26.

Brown, J. L. Alternate routes to sociality in jays—with a theory for the evolution of altruism and communal breeding. *American Zoologist*, 1975, *14*, 63–80.

Brown, N. O. *Life against death*. New York: Random House, 1959.

Brown, R. *Social psychology*. New York: Free Press, 1965.

Bruhn, J. G., McCrady, K. E., & du Pleissis, A. Psychological predictors of sudden death in myocardial infarction. *Journal of Psychosomatic Research*, 1974, *18*, 187–93.

Bruner, J. S. A cognitive theory of personality. *Contemporary Psychology*, 1956, *1*, 355–56.

Bryan, J. H., & Test, M. A. Models and helping: Naturalistic studies in aiding behavior. *Journal of Personality and Social Psychology*, 1967, *6*, 400–7.

Burian, R. More than a marriage of convenience: On the inextricability of history and philosophy of science. *Philosophy of Science*, 1977, *44*, 1–42.

Burnham, J. C. Historical background for the study of personality. In E. F. Borgatta & W. W. Lambert (Eds.), *Handbook of personality theory and research*. Chicago: Rand McNally, 1968.

Buros, O. K. (Ed.). *The sixth mental measurements yearbook*. Highland Park, N.J.: Gryphon Press, 1965.

Buros, O. K. (Ed.). *The seventh mental measurements yearbook*. Highland Park, N.J.: Gryphon Press, 1972.

Buss, A., & Plomin, R. *A temperament theory of personality*. New York: Wiley-Interscience, 1975.

Buss, A. H., Plomin, R., & Willerman, L. The inheritance of temperaments. *Journal of Personality*, 1973, *41*, 513–24.

Butcher, J. N. Use of the MMPI in personnel selection. In J. N. Butcher (Ed.), *New developments in the use of the MMPI*. Minneapolis: University of Minnesota Press, 1979.

Campbell, D. T. Recommendations for APA test standards regarding construct, trait, or discriminant validity. *American Psychologist*, 1960, *15*, 546–53.

Campbell, D. T., & Fiske, D. W. Convergent and discriminant validation by the multitrait-multimethod matrix. *Psychological Bulletin*, 1959, *56*, 81–105.

Cantwell, D. P. Psychiatric illness in the families of hyperactive children. *Archives of General Psychiatry*, 1972, *27*, 414–17.

Cartwright, R. D., & Ratzel, R. Effects of dream loss on waking behaviors. *Archives of General Psychiatry*, 1972, *27*, 277–80.

Cattell, R. B. *Personality and motivation structure and measurement.* Yonkers, N.Y.: New World Book, 1957.

Cattell, R. B. *The scientific analysis of personality.* Baltimore: Penguin Books, 1965.

Cattell, R. B. *Personality and learning theory* (Vol. 1). New York: Springer, 1979.

Cattell, R. B., & Kline, P. *The scientific analysis of personality and motivation.* New York: Academic Press, 1977.

Cattell, R. B., & Warburton, F. W. *Objective personality and motivation tests: A theoretical introduction and practical compendium.* Urbana, Ill.: University of Illinois Press, 1967.

Cautela, J. R. Covert sensitization. *Psychological Reports,* 1967, *20,* 459–68.

Cautela, J. R. Covert negative reinforcement. *Behavior Therapy and Experimental Psychiatry,* 1970, *1,* 273–78. (a)

Cautela, J. R. Covert reinforcement. *Behavior Therapy,* 1970, *1,* 33–50. (b)

Chambliss, C. A., & Murray, E. J. Cognitive procedures for smoking reduction: Symptom attribution versus efficacy attribution. *Cognitive Therapy and Research,* 1979, *3,* 91–96. (a)

Chambliss, C. A., & Murray, E. J. Efficacy attribution, locus of control, and weight loss. *Cognitive Therapy and Research,* 1979, *3,* 349–54. (b)

Cheyne, J. A. Effects of imitation of different reinforcement combinations to a model. *Journal of Experimental Child Psychology,* 1971, *12,* 258–69.

Chiang, H., & Maslow, A. H. (Eds.). *The healthy personality: Readings* (2nd ed.). New York: Van Nostrand, 1977.

Chodorkoff, B. Self-perception, perceptual defense, and adjustment. *Journal of Abnormal and Social Psychology,* 1954, *49,* 508–12.

Clark, K. *Civilisation: A personal view.* New York: Harper & Row, 1970.

Coates, T. J., & Thoresen, C. E. *How to sleep better: A drug-free program for overcoming insomnia.* Englewood Cliffs, N.J.: Prentice-Hall, 1977.

Cohen, J. B., Matthews, K. A., & Waldron, I. Coronary-prone behavior: Developmental and cultural considerations. In T. M. Dembroski, S. M. Weiss, J. L. Shields, S. G. Haynes, & M. Feinleib (Eds.), *Coronary-prone behavior.* New York: Springer-Verlag, 1978.

Colarusso, C. A., & Nemiroff, R. A. Some observations and hypotheses about the psychoanalytic theory of adult development. *International Journal of Psycho-Analysis,* 1979, *60,* 59–71.

Comrey, A. L. *A first course in factor analysis.* New York: Academic Press, 1973.

Condiotte, M. M., & Lichtenstein, E. Self-efficacy and relapse in smoking cessation programs. *Journal of Consulting and Clinical Psychology,* 1981, *49,* 648–58.

Cooley, E. J. Cognitive versus emotional coping skills as alternative responses for the high test anxious college student. Doctoral dissertation, University of Texas at Austin, 1976.

Cooley, E. J., & Spiegler, M. D. Cognitive versus emotional coping responses as alternatives to test anxiety. *Cognitive Therapy and Research*, 1980, *4*, 159–66.

Cooperman, M., & Child, I. L. Differential effects of positive and negative reinforcement on two psychoanalytic character types. *Journal of Consulting and Clinical Psychology*. 1971, *37*, 57–59.

Crain, W. C. *Theories of development*. Englewood Cliffs, N.J.: Prentice-Hall, 1980.

Crandall, V. J. Achievement behavior in young children. In *The young child: Reviews of research*. Washington, D.C.: National Association for the Education of Young Children, 1967.

Crandall, V. J., Dewey, R., Katkovsky, W., & Preston, A. Parents' attitudes and behaviors and grade-school children's academic achievement. *Journal of Genetic Psychology*, 1964, *104*, 53–66.

Crandall, V. J., Katkovsky, W., & Preston, A. Motivational and ability determinants of young children's intellectual achievement behaviors. *Child Development*, 1962, *33*, 643–61.

Creer, T. L., & Miklich, D. R. The application of a self-modeling procedure to modify inappropriate behavior: A preliminary report. *Behaviour Research and Therapy*, 1970, *8*, 91–92.

Cronbach, L. J. Statistical methods applied to Rorschach scores: A review. *Psychological Bulletin*, 1949, *46*, 393–429.

Cronbach, L. J. Review of the California Psychological Inventory. In O. K. Buros (Ed.), *Fifth mental measurements yearbook*. Highland Park, N.J.: Gryphon Press, 1959.

Cutter, H. S. G., Boyatzis, R. E., & Clancy, D. D. The effectiveness of power motivation training in rehabilitating alcoholics. *Journal of Studies on Alcohol*, 1977, *38*, 131–41.

Dahlstrom, W. G. Screening for emotional fitness: The Jersey City case. In W. G. Dahlstrom & L. Dahlstrom (Eds.), *Basic readings on the MMPI: A new selection on personality measurement*. Minneapolis: University of Minnestoa Press, 1980.

Damon, A. Physique and success in military flying. *American Journal of Physical Anthropology*, 1955, *13*, 217–52.

Darley, J. M., & Aronson, E. Self-evaluation vs. direct anxiety reduction as determinants of the fear-affiliation relationship. *Journal of Experimental Social Psychology*, 1966, (Suppl.), *1*, 66–79.

Darley, J. M., & Latané, B. Bystander intervention in emergencies: Diffusion of responsibility. *Journal of Personality and Social Psychology*, 1968, *8*, 377–83.

Darwin, C. *On the origin of the species* (6th ed.). New York: MacMillan, 1859/1927.

Davidson, M. A., McInnes, R. G., & Parnell, R. W. The distribution of personality traits in seven-year-old children: A combined psychological, psychiatric, and somatotype study. *British Journal of Educational Psychology*, 1957, *27*, 48–61.

Davis, W. N. Drinking: A search for power or for nurturance? Doctoral dissertation, Harvard University, 1969.

Davison, G. C. Case report: Elimination of a sadistic fantasy by a client-controlled counter-conditioning technique. *Journal of Abnormal Psychology*, 1968, *73*, 84–90.

Davison, G. C., & Neale, J. M. *Abnormal psychology: An experimental-clinical approach.* New York: John Wiley & Sons, 1974.

Davison, G. C., & Neale, J. M. *Abnormal psychology* (2nd ed.). New York: John Wiley & Sons, 1978.

DeCharms, R. *Enhancing motivation in the classroom.* New York: Irvington, Halsted-Wiley, 1976.

DeFries, J. C. Genetics of animal and human behavior. In G. W. Barlow & J. Silverberg (Eds.), *Sociobiology: Beyond nature/nurture?* Boulder, Col.: Westview Press, 1980.

Dekker, E., & Groen, J. Reproducible psychogenic attacks of asthma: A laboratory study. *Journal of Psychosomatic Research*, 1956, *1*, 58–67.

Dekker, E., Pelser, H. E., & Groen, J. Conditioning as a cause of asthmatic attacks. *Journal of Psychosomatic Research*, 1957, *2*, 97–108.

Dement, W. C. An essay on dreams: The role of physiology in understanding their nature. In *New directions in psychology* (Vol. 2). New York: Holt, Rinehart & Winston, 1965.

Dement, W. C., & Kleitman, N. The relation of the eye movements during sleep to dream activity: An objective method for the study of dreaming. *Journal of Experimental Psychology*, 1957, *53*, 339–46.

Dement, W. C., & Wolpert, E. The relation of eye movements, body motility, and external stimuli to dream content. *Journal of Experimental Psychology*, 1958, *55*, 543–53.

Denney, D. R. Active, passive, and vicarious desensitization. *Journal of Counseling Psychology*, 1974, *21*, 369–75.

Denney, D. R., & Rupert, P. A. Desensitization and self-control in the treatment of test anxiety. *Journal of Counseling Psychology*, 1977, *24*, 272–80.

Diamond, S. *Personality and temperament.* New York: Harper & Row, 1957.

DiClemente, C. C. Self-efficacy and smoking cessation maintenance. *Cognitive Therapy and Research*, 1981, *5*, 175–87.

Dixon, N. F. *Subliminal perception: The nature of a controversy.* London: McGraw-Hill, 1971.

D'Zurilla, T. Recall efficiency and mediating cognitive events in "experimental repression." *Journal of Personality and Social Psychology*, 1965, *37*, 253–56.

D'Zurilla, T., & Goldfried, M. Problem solving and behavior modification. *Journal of Abnormal Psychology*, 1971, *78*, 107–26.

Eckert, R. E., & Stecklein, J. E. Academic woman. *Liberal Education*, 1959, *45*, 391–97.

Edwards, A. L. *Manual for Edwards Personal Preference Schedule.* New York: Psychological Corporation, 1953.

Edwards, A. L. *The social desirability variable in personality research.* New York: Dryden, 1957.

Edwards, A. L., & Abbott, R. D. Measurement of personality traits: Theory and technique. In *Annual Review of Psychology,* 1973, *24,*

Eiseley, L. *Darwin's century.* New York: Doubleday, 1958

Eisler, R. M., Hersen, M., & Miller, P. M. Effects of modeling on components of assertive behavior. *Journal of Behavior Therapy and Experimental Psychiatry,* 1973, *4,* 1–6.

Ellenberger, H. F. *The discovery of the unconscious: The history and evolution of dynamic psychiatry.* New York: Basic Books, 1970.

Epstein, S. Some theoretical considerations on the nature of ambiguity and the use of stimulus dimensions in projective techniques. *Journal of Consulting Psychology,* 1966, *30,* 183–92.

Epstein, S. The self-concept revisited: Or a theory of a theory. *American Psychologist,* 1973, *28,* 404–16.

Epstein, S. Explorations in personality today and tomorrow: A tribute to Henry A. Murray. *American Psychologist,* 1979, *34,* 649–53.

Erdelyi, M. H. A new look at the new look: Perceptual defense and vigilance. *Psychological Review,* 1974, *81,* 1–25.

Erikson, E. H. The dream specimen of psychoanalysis. *Journal of the American Psychoanalytic Association,* 1954, *2,* 5–56.

Erikson, E. H. *Childhood and society.* New York: W. W. Norton, 1963.

Erikson, E. H. *Identity, youth, and crisis.* New York: W. W. Norton, 1968.

Eysenck, H. J. *The scientific study of personality.* London: Routledge & Kegan Paul, 1952.

Eysenck, H. J. The effects of psychotherapy. In H. J. Eysenck (Ed.), *Handbook of abnormal psychology.* New York: Basic Books, 1961.

Eysenck, H. J. *Crime and personality.* Boston: Houghton Mifflin, 1964.

Eysenck, H. J. *The structure of human personality* (3d ed.). London: Methuen, 1970.

Eysenck, H. J. *The inequality of man.* San Diego: Edits Publishers, 1975.

Eysenck, H. J. *Crime and personality.* London: Routledge & Kegan Paul, 1977.

Eysenck, H. J. Expectations as causal elements in behavioural change. In S. Rachman (Ed.), *Advances in behaviour research and therapy* (Vol. 1). Oxford: Pergamon Press, 1978.

Fadiman, J. Motivation in children: An exploratory study. Honors essay, Stanford University, 1960.

Feldman, F. Results of psychoanalysis in clinic case assignments. *Journal of the American Psychoanalytic Association,* 1968, *16,* 274–300.

Fiedler, F. E. A comparison of therapeutic relationships in psychoanalytic, nondirective, and Adlerian therapy. *Journal of Consulting Psychology,* 1950, *14,* 436–45. (a)

Fiedler, F. E. The concept of the ideal therapeutic relationship. *Journal of Consulting Psychology,* 1950, *14,* 239–45. (b)

Field, W. F. The effects of thematic apperception upon certain experimentally aroused needs. Doctoral dissertation, University of Maryland, 1951.

Fischer, M. Genetic and environmental factors in schizophrenia. *Acta Psychiatrica Scandinavica,* 1973, Suppl. 238.

Fisher, S., & Greenberg, R. P. *The scientific credibility of Freud's theories and therapy.* New York: Basic Books, 1977.

Fiske, D. W. The subject reacts to tests. *American Psychologist,* 1967, *22,* 287–96.

Fiske, D. W. *Measuring the concepts of personality.* Chicago: Aldine, 1971.

Fiske, D. W., & Pearson, P. H. Theory and techniques of personality measurement. *Annual Review of Psychology,* 1970, *21,* Palo Alto, Calif.: Annual Reviews.

Fjeld, S. P., & Landfield, A. W. Personal construct consistency. *Psychological Reports,* 1961, *8,* 127–29.

Flanders, J. P. A review of research on imitative behavior. *Psychological Bulletin,* 1968, *69,* 316–37.

Fox, L. Effecting the use of efficient study habits. In R. Ulrich, T. Stachnik, & J. Mabry (Eds.), *Control of human behavior.* Glenview, Ill.: Scott, Foresman, 1966.

Frank, J. D. Nature and functions of belief systems: Humanism and transcendental religion. *American Psychologist,* 1977, *32,* 555–59.

Freedman, D. G. *Human sociobiology: A holistic approach.* New York: The Free Press, 1979.

Freedman, D. G., & Keller, B. Inheritance of behavior in infants. *Science,* 1963, *140,* 196–98.

French, E. G., & Lesser, G. S. Some characteristics of the achievement motive in women. *Journal of Abnormal and Social Psychology,* 1964, *68,* 119–28.

French, T. M. Interrelations between psychoanalysis and the experimental work of Pavlov. In *Psychoanalytic interpretations: The selected papers of Thomas M. French.* Chicago: Quadrangle Books, 1970. (Originally published in the American Journal of Psychiatry, 1933.)

French, T., & Fromm, E. *Dream interpretation.* New York: Basic Books, 1964.

Freud, A. Adolescence. *Psychoanalytic Study of the Child,* 1958, *13,* 255–78.

Freud, A. *The ego and the mechanisms of defense* (Ref. ed). New York: International Universities Press, 1966.

Freud, S. On the history of the psycho-analytic movement. In J. Strachey (Ed.), *The standard edition of the complete psychological works of Sigmund Freud* (Vol. 14). London: Hogarth, 1957. (Originally published, 1914.)

Freud, S. Character and anal eroticism. In J. Strachey (Ed.), *The standard edition of the complete psychological works of Sigmund Freud* (Vol. 9). London: Hogarth, 1959. (Originally published, 1908.)

Freud, S. *The interpretation of dreams* (J. Strachey trans. and Ed.). New York: Science Editions, 1961. (a)

Freud, S. Two encyclopedia articles. In J. Strachey (Ed.), *The standard edition* of the complete psychological works of Sigmund Freud (Vol. 18). London: Hogarth, 1961. (Originally published, 1923.) (b)

Freud, S. Introductory lectures on psycho-analysis (Vol. 15). In *The standard edition of the complete psychological works of Sigmund Freud* (J. Strachey trans. and Ed.). London: Hogarth Press, 1963.

Freud, S. New introductory lectures on psychoanalysis. In J. Strachey (Ed.), *The standard edition of the complete psychological works of Sigmund Freud* (Vol. 22). London: Hogarth, 1964. (Originally published, 1933.)

Freud, S. *New introductory lectures on psychoanalysis.* New York: W. W. Norton, 1965.

Freud, S., & Jung, C. G. *The Freud/Jung letters* (W. McGuire, Ed.). Princeton, N.J.: Princeton University Press, 1974.

Friedman, M., & Rosenman, R. H. *Type A behavior and your heart.* London: Wildwood House, 1974.

Fromm, E. *Man for himself: An inquiry into the psychology of ethics.* New York: Rinehart, 1947.

Fromm, E. *The anatomy of human destructiveness.* New York: Holt, Rinehart and Winston, 1973.

Fromm, E. *The art of loving.* New York: Bantam Books, 1963.

Gallagher, J. J. The problem of escaping clients in non-directive counseling. In W. U. Snyder (Ed.), *Group report of a program of research in psychotherapy.* Psychotherapy Research Group, Pennsylvania State University, 1953.

Galton, F. Measurement of character. *Fortnightly Review,* 1884, *42,* 179–85.

Garfield, S. L., & Bergin, A. E. Personal therapy, outcome and some therapist variables. *Psychotherapy: Theory, Research and Practice,* 1971, *8,* 251–53.

Garn, S. M., & Gertler, M. M. An association between type of work and physique in an industrial group. *American Journal of Physical Anthropology,* 1950, *8,* 387–97.

Gauthier, J., & Ladouceur, R. The influence of self-efficacy reports on performance. *Behavior Therapy,* 1981, *12,* 436–39.

Gedo, J. E. *Beyond interpretation.* New York: International Universities Press, 1979.

Geer, J. H. A test of the classical conditioning model of emotion: The use of nonpainful aversive stimuli as unconditioned stimuli in a conditioning procedure. *Journal of Personality and Social Psychology,* 1968, *10,* 148–56.

Geer, J. H., Davison, G. C., & Gatchel, R. I. Reduction of stress in humans through nonveridical perceived control of aversive stimulation. *Journal of Personality and Social Psychology,* 1970, *16,* 731–38.

Gewirtz, J. L., & Stingle, K. C. The learning of generalized imitation as the basis for identification. *Psychological Review,* 1968, *75,* 374–97.

Gill, L. J., & Spilka, B. Some nonintellectual correlates of academic achievement among Mexican-American secondary school students. *Journal of Educational Psychology,* 1962, *53,* 144–49.

Glass, D. C. *Behavior patterns, stress, and coronary disease*. Hillsdale, N.J.: Lawrence Erlbaum Associates, 1977. (a)

Glass, D. C. Stress, behavior patterns and coronary disease. *American Scientist*, 1977, *65*, 177–87. (b)

Glueck, S., & Glueck, E. *Unraveling juvenile delinquency*. New York: Commonwealth Fund, 1950.

Glueck, S., & Glueck, E. *Physique and delinquency*. New York: Harper & Row, 1956.

Goffman, E. *The presentation of self in everyday life*. Garden City, N.Y.: Doubleday, 1959.

Goldfried, M. R. Systematic desensitization as training in self-control. *Journal of Consulting and Clinical Psychology*, 1971, *37*, 228–34.

Goldfried, M. R., & Davison, G. C. *Clinical behavior therapy*. New York: Holt, Rinehart & Winston, 1976.

Goldfried, M. R., & Goldfried, A. P. Importance of hierarchy content in the self-control of anxiety. *Journal of Consulting and Clinical Psychology*, 1977, *45*, 124–34.

Goldfried, M. R., & Merbaum, M. (Eds.). *Behavior change through self-control*. New York: Holt, Rinehart & Winston, 1973.

Goldstein, A. P. *Structured learning therapy: Toward a psychotherapy for the poor*. New York: Academic Press, 1973.

Gottesman, I. I. Heritability of personality. *Psychological Monographs*, 1963, *77* (9, Whole No. 572).

Gottesman, I. I., & Shields, J. Schizophrenia in twins: Sixteen years' consecutive admissions to a psychiatric clinic. *British Journal of Psychiatry*, 1966, *112*, 809–18.

Gough, H. G. What determines the academic achievement of high school students? *Journal of Educational Research*, 1953, *46*, 809–18.

Gough, H. G. *California Psychological Inventory*. Palo Alto, Calif.: Consulting Psychologists Press, 1956.

Gough, H. G. Theory and measurement of socialization. *Journal of Consulting Psychology*, 1960, *24*, 23–30.

Gough, H. G. Academic achievement in high school as predicted from the California Psychological Inventory. *Journal of Educational Psychology*, 1964, *55*, 174–80.

Gough, H. G., & Sandhu, H. S. Validation of the CPI socialization scale in India. *Journal of Abnormal and Social Psychology*, 1964, *68*, 544–47.

Gould, D., & Weiss, M. Effect of model similarity and model self-talk on self-efficacy in muscular endurance. *Journal of Sport Psychology*, 1981, *3*, 17–29.

Graham, W., & Balloun, J. An empirical test of Maslow's need hierarchy theory. *Journal of Humanistic Psychology*, 1973, *13*, 97–108.

Grasha, A. F. *Practical applications of psychology*. Cambridge, Mass.: Winthrop, 1978.

Greene, D. L., & Winter, D. G. Motives, involvements, and leadership among Black college students. *Journal of Personality*, 1971, *39*, 319–32.

Gregory, M. S., Silvers, A., & Sutch, D. (Eds.), *Sociobiology and human nature.* San Francisco: Jossey-Bass, 1978.

Grieser, C., Greenberg, R., & Harrison, R. H. The adaptive function of sleep: The differential effects of sleep and dreaming on recall. *Journal of Abnormal Psychology,* 1972, *80,* 280–86.

Guerney, B. G. Jr., Andronico, M. P., & Guerney, L. F. Filial therapy. In J. T. Hart & T. M. Tomlinson (Eds.). *New directions in client-centered therapy.* Boston: Houghton Mifflin, 1970.

Guilford, J. P. *Personality.* New York: McGraw-Hill, 1959.

Guinan, J. F., & Foulds, M. L. Marathon group: Facilitator of personal growth? *Journal of Counseling Psychology,* 1970, *17,* 145–49.

Gutride, M. E., Goldstein, A. P., & Hunter, G. F. The use of modeling and role playing to increase social interaction among asocial psychiatric patients. *Journal of Consulting and Clinical Psychology,* 1973, *40,* 408–15.

Hall, C. S. *A primer of Freudian psychology.* New York: New American Library, 1955.

Hall, C. *The meaning of dreams.* New York: McGraw-Hill, 1966.

Hall, C. S., & Van de Castle, R. L. An empirical investigation of the castration complex in dreams. *Journal of Personality,* 1963, *33,* 20–29.

Hall, R. A., & Closson, W. G. An experimental study of the couch. *Journal of Nervous and Mental Disease,* 1964, *138,* 474–80.

Hall, R. V., Lund, D., & Jackson, D. Effects of teacher attention on study behavior. *Journal of Applied Behavior Analysis,* 1968, *1,* 1–12.

Halpern, J. Projection: A test of the psychoanalytic hypothesis. *Journal of Abnormal Psychology,* 1977, *86,* 536–42.

Hanley, C. Social desirability and responses to items from three MMPI scales: D, Sc, and K. *Journal of Applied Psychology,* 1956, *40,* 324–28.

Harrell, T. W. High earning MBAs. *Personnel Psychology,* 1972, *25,* 523–30.

Harris, B. Whatever happened to little Albert? *American Psychologist,* 1979, *34,* 151–60.

Harris, J. G., Jr. Nomovalidation and idiovalidation: A quest for the true personality profile. *American Psychologist,* 1980, *35,* 729–44.

Hartley, R. E., & Hardesty, F. P. Children's perception of sex roles in childhood. *Journal of Genetic Psychology,* 1964, *105,* 43–51.

Hartmann, H. Ego psychology and the problem of adaptation. In D. Rapaport (Ed. and trans.), *Organization and pathology of thought: Selected sources.* New York: Columbia University Press, 1951.

Hathaway, S. R., & Monachesi, E. D. The Minnesota Multiphasic Personality Inventory in the study of juvenile delinquents. *American Sociological Review,* 1952, *17,* 704–10.

Hersen, M., & Barlow, D. H. *Single case experimental designs: Strategies for studying behavior change.* New York: Pergamon Press, 1976.

Hetherington, E. M., & Frankie, G. Effects of parental dominance, warmth, and conflict on imitation in children. *Journal of Personality and Social Psychology,* 1967, *6,* 119–25.

Hill, J. H., Liebert, R. M., & Mott, D. E. Vicarious extinction of avoidance behavior through films: An initial test. *Psychological Reports,* 1968, *22,* 192.

Hjelle, L. A., & Ziegler, D. J. *Personality theories: Basic assumptions, research, and applications* (2nd ed.). New York: McGraw-Hill, 1981.

Hobson, J. A., & McCarley, R. W. The brain as a dream state generator: An activation-synthesis hypothesis of the dream process. *American Journal of Psychiatry,* 1977, *134,* 1335–1438.

Hoffer, A., & Pollin, W. Schizophrenia in the NAS–NPC panel of 15, 909 veteran twin pairs. *Archives of General Psychiatry,* 1970, *23,* 469–77.

Hoffman, L. W. Fear of success in males and females: 1965 and 1971. *Journal of Consulting and Clinical Psychology,* 1974, *42,* 353–58.

Hogan, R., DeSoto, C. B., & Solano, C. Traits, tests, and personality research. *American Psychologist,* 1977, *32,* 255–64.

Hollander, E. P. *Leaders, groups, and influence.* New York: Oxford University Press, 1964.

Holmes, D. S. Repression or interference? A further investigation. *Journal of Personality and Social Psychology,* 1972, *22,* 163–70.

Holmes, D. S. Projection as a defense mechanism. *Psychological Bulletin,* 1978, *85,* 677–88.

Holmes, D. S., & Schallow, J. Reduced recall after ego threat: Repression or response competition? *Journal of Personality and Social Psychology,* 1969, *13,* 145–52.

Holmes, D. S., & Tyler, J. D. Direct versus projective measurement of achievement motivation. *Journal of Consulting and Clinical Psychology,* 1968, *32,* 712–17.

Holtzman, W. H., Thorpe, J. S., Swartz, J. D., & Herron, E. W. *Inkblot perception and personality: Holtzman Inkblot Technique.* Austin: University of Texas Press, 1961.

Homme, L. E. Perspectives in psychology, 24. Control of coverants, the operants of the mind. *Psychological Record,* 1965, *15,* 501–11.

Horne, A. M., & Matson, J. L. A comparison of modeling, desensitization, flooding, study skills, and control groups for reducing test anxiety. *Behavior Therapy,* 1977, *8,* 1–8.

Horner, M. S. A psychological barrier to achievement in women: The motive to avoid success. In D. C. McClelland & R. S. Steele (Eds.), *Human motivation: A book of readings.* Morristown, N.J.: General Learning Press, 1973.

Horney, K. *New ways in psychoanalysis.* New York: W. W. Norton, 1939.

Hornstein, H. A., Fisch, E., & Holmes, M. Influence of a model's feeling about his behavior and his relevance as a comparison other on observers' helping behavior. *Journal of Personality and Social Psychology,* 1968, *10,* 222–26.

Houts, A. C. *Initial clinical judgement in psychotherapy: The role of theoretical orientation.* Doctoral dissertation, State University of New York at Stony Brook, 1981.

Hull, D. L. Sociobiology: Scientific bandwagon or traveling medicine show? *Transaction Society,* 1978, *15,* 50–59.

Hyman, R. *The nature of psychological inquiry*. Englewood Cliffs, N.J.: Prentice-Hall, 1964.

Inkeles, A., & Levinson, D. J. National character: The study of modal personality and sociocultural systems. In G. Lindzey & E. Aronson (Eds.), *The handbook of social psychology* (Vol. 4, 2nd ed.). Reading, Mass.: Addison-Wesley, 1969.

Isaacs, W., Thomas, J., & Goldiamond, I. Application of operant conditioning to reinstate verbal behavior in psychotics. *Journal of Speech and Hearing Disorders*, 1960, *25*, 8–12.

Jaccard, J. J. Predicting social behavior from personality traits. *Journal of Research in Personality*, 1974, *7*, 358–67.

Jackson, D. D. (Ed.). *The etiology of schizophrenia*. New York: Basic Books, 1960.

Jackson, D. N. A sequential system for personality scale development. In C. D. Spielberger (Ed.), *Current topics in clinical and community psychology* (Vol. 2). New York: Academic Press, 1970.

Jackson, D. N. The dynamics of structured personality tests: 1971. *Psychological Review*, 1971, *78*, 229–48.

Jackson, D. N. *Jackson Personality Inventory manual*. Port Huron, Mich.: Research Psychologists Press, 1976.

Jackson, D. N. Interpreter's guide to the Jackson Personality Inventory. In P. McReynolds (Ed.), *Advances in psychological assessment* (Vol. 4). San Francisco: Jossey-Bass, 1978.

Jackson, D. N., & Messick, S. Content and style in personality assessment. *Psychological Bulletin*, 1958, *55*, 243–52.

Jacobson, E. *Progressive relaxation*. Chicago: University of Chicago Press, 1938.

Jaffe, P. G., & Carlson, P. M. Relative efficacy of modeling and instructions in eliciting social behavior from chronic psychiatric patients. *Journal of Consulting and Clinical Psychology*, 1976, *44*, 200–7.

James, W. *Principles of psychology* (Vols. 1 and 2). New York: H. Holt, 1890.

Jenkins, C. D. Rosenman, R. H., & Zyanski, S. J. Prediction of clinical coronary heart disease by a test for the coronary-prone behavior pattern. *New England Journal of Medicine*, 1974, *290*, 1271–75.

Johnson, G. B. Penis envy or pencil needing? *Psychological Reports*, 1966, *19*, 758.

Johnson, R., & Machen, J. B. Behavior modification techniques and maternal anxiety. *Journal of Dentistry for Children*, 1973, *40*, 272–76.

Jones, E. *The life and works of Sigmund Freud* (Vol. 1). New York: Basic Books, 1953.

Jones, M. C. The elimination of children's fear. *Journal of Experimental Psychology*, 1924, *7*, 382–90. (a)

Jones, M. C. A laboratory study of fear: The case of Peter. *Pedagogical Seminar*, 1924, *31*, 308–15. (b)

Jones, R. *The new psychology of dreaming*. New York: Viking Press, 1970.

Jourard, S. M. *Healthy personality: An approach from the viewpoint of humanistic psychology.* New York: Macmillian, 1974.

Jung, C. G. *Modern man in search of a soul* (W. S. Dell & C. F. Baynes, trans.). New York: Harcourt Brace Jovanovich, 1933.

Jung, C. G. General aspects of dream psychology. In *The collected works of C. G. Jung* (Vol. 8). Princeton, N.J.: Princeton University Press, 1969. (a)

Kagan, J., & Lemkin, J. The child's differential perception of parental attributes. *Journal of Abnormal and Social Psychology,* 1960, *61,* 440–47.

Kagan, J., & Moss, H. A. *Birth to maturity.* New York: John Wiley & Sons, 1962.

Kaplan, A. Ethics, evolution, and the milk of human kindness. *Hastings Center Report,* 1976, *6,* 20–25.

Kaplan, A. G., & Bean, J. P. *Beyond sex-role stereotypes: Readings toward a psychology of androgyny.* Boston: Little, Brown, 1976.

Kaplan, A. G., & Sedney, M. A. *Psychology and sex roles: An androgynous perspective.* Boston: Little, Brown, 1980.

Katahn, M., & Koplin, J. H. Paradigm clash: Comment on "some recent criticisms of behaviorism and learning theory with special reference to Breger and McGaugh and to Chomsky." *Psychological Bulletin,* 1968, *69,* 147–48.

Kazdin, A. E. Covert modeling and the reduction of avoidance behavior. *Journal of Abnormal Psychology,* 1973, *81,* 87–95.

Kazdin, A. E. Effects of covert modeling and reinforcement on assertive behavior. *Journal of Abnormal Psychology,* 1974, *83,* 240–52.

Kazdin, A. E. Covert modeling, imagery assessment, and assertive behavior. *Journal of Consulting and Clinical Psychology,* 1975, *43,* 716–24.

Kazdin, A. E. Conceptual and assessment issues raised by self-efficacy theory. In S. Rachman (Ed.), *Advances in behaviour research and therapy* (Vol. 1). Oxford: Pergamon Press, 1978.

Kelly, G. A. *The psychology of personal constructs* (Vols. 1 and 2). New York: W. W. Norton, 1955.

Kelly, G. A. The autobiography of a theory. In B. Maher (Ed.), *Clinical psychology and personality: Selected papers of George Kelly.* New York: John Wiley & Sons, 1969.

Kelly, G. A. A brief introduction to personal construct theory. In D. Bannister (Ed.), *Perspectives in personal construct theory.* New York: Academic Press, 1970.

Kern, S. Freud and the discovery of child sexuality. *History of Childhood Quarterly,* 1973, *1,* 117–41.

Kettlewell, H. B. D. Further selection experiments on industrial melanism in the Lepidoptera. *Heredity,* 1956, *10,* 287–301.

Kimble, G. A. *Hilgard and Marquis' conditioning and learning* (2d ed.). New York: Appleton-Century-Crofts, 1961.

Kinkade, K. *A Walden II experiment: The first five years of Twin Oaks.* New York: William Morrow, 1973.

Kipnis, D. *Character structure and impulsiveness.* New York: Academic Press, 1971.

Kleinmuntz, B. *Personality measurement: An introduction.* Homewood, Ill.: Dorsey Press, 1967.

Kline, P. *Fact and fantasy in Freudian theory.* London: Methuen, 1972.

Klinger, E. Fantasy need achievement as a motivational construct. *Psychological Bulletin,* 1966, *66,* 291–308.

Klopfer, B., & Davidson, H. H. *The Rorschach technique: An introductory manual.* New York: Harcourt, Brace & World, 1962.

Kluckhohn, F., & Strodtbeck, F. *Variations in value orientation.* Evanston, Ill.: Row, Peterson, 1961.

Knapp, P. H., Levin, S., McCarter, R. H., Wermer, H., & Zetzel, E. Suitability for psychoanalysis: A review of 100 supervised analytic cases. *Psychoanalytic Quarterly,* 1960, *29,* 459–77.

Knapp, R. R. *Handbook for the Personal Orientation Inventory.* San Diego: Edits Publishers, 1976.

Kohlberg, L. A cognitive-developmental analysis of children's sex-role concepts and attitudes. In E. E. Maccoby (Ed.), *The development of sex differences.* Stanford, Calif.: Stanford University Press, 1966.

Kopp, S. *This side of tragedy.* Palo Alto, Calif.: Science and Behavior, 1977.

Kornhaber, R. C., & Schroeder, H. E. Importance of model similarity on extinction of avoidance behavior in children. *Journal of Consulting and Clinical Psychology,* 1975, *43,* 601–7.

Kosinski, J. N. *Being there.* New York: Harcourt Brace Jovanovich, 1970.

Krasner, L., & Ullmann, L. P. *Behavior influence and personality: The social matrix of human action.* New York: Holt, Rinehart & Winston, 1973.

Krantz, D. S. The social context of obesity research: Another perspective on its place in the field of social psychology. *Personality and Social Psychology Bulletin,* 1978, *4,* 177–84.

Kretschmer, E. *Physique and character: An investigation of the nature of constitution and of the theory of temperament* (W. J. H. Sprott trans.). New York: Harcourt, 1926.

Kris, E. On preconscious mental processes. *Psychoanalytic Quarterly,* 1950, *19,* 540–60.

Kuhn, T. S. *The structure of scientific revolutions.* Chicago: University of Chicago Press, 1962.

Kuhn, T. S. *The structure of scientific revolutions* (2d ed.). Chicago: University of Chicago Press, 1970.

Kurtz, R. R., & Grummon, D. L. Different approaches to the measurement of therapist empathy and their relationship to therapy outcomes. *Journal of Consulting and Clinical Psychology,* 1972, *39,* 106–15.

Lang, P. J. Self-efficacy theory: Thoughts on cognition and unification. In S. Rachman (Ed.), *Advances in behaviour research and therapy* (Vol. 1). Oxford: Pergamon Press, 1978.

Langer, E. J., & Abelson, R. P. A patient by any other name. . . "Clinician group difference in labeling bias." *Journal of Consulting and Clinical Psychology,* 1974, *42,* 4–9.

LaPiere, R. T. Attitudes vs. actions. *Social Forces,* 1934, *13,* 230–37.

Lavin, N. I., Thorpe, J. G., Barker, J. C., Blakemore, C. B., & Conway, C. G. Behavior therapy in a case of transvestism. *Journal of Nervous and Mental Disease,* 1961, *133,* 346–53.

Lazarus, R. S. *Adjustment and personality.* New York: McGraw-Hill, 1961.

Lefcourt, H. M. The function of the illusions of control and freedom. *American Psychologist,* 1973, *28,* 417–25.

Leon, G. R., & Roth, L. Obesity: Psychological causes, correlations, and speculations. *Psychological Bulletin,* 1977, *84,* 117–39.

Lesser, G. S. Achievement motivation in woman. In D. C. McClelland & R. S. Steele (Eds.), *Human motivation: A book of readings.* Morristown, N.J.: General Learning Press, 1973.

Lesser, G. S., Krawitz, R., & Packard, R. Experimental arousal of achievement motivation in adolescent girls. *Journal of Abnormal and Social Psychology,* 1963, *66,* 59–66.

Lessler, K. Cultural and Freudian dimensions of sexual symbols. *Journal of Consulting Psychology,* 1964, *28,* 46–53.

Levinson, D. The mid-life transition. *Psychiatry,* 1977, *40,* 99–112.

Levy, L. H. *Conceptions of personality: Theories and research.* New York: Random House, 1970.

Lewis, M. The meaning of a response, or why researchers in infant behavior should be Oriental metaphysicians. *Merrill-Palmer Quarterly,* 1967, *13,* 7–18.

Lewis, O. *The children of Sanchez: Autobiography of a Mexican family.* New York: Random House, 1961.

Liebert, R. M. Television and social learning: Some relationships between viewing violence and behaving aggressively. In J. P. Murray, E. A. Rubinstein, & G. A. Comstock (Eds.), *Television and social behavior* (Vol. 2). *Television and social learning.* Washington, D.C.: U.S. Government Printing Office, 1972.

Liebert, R. M. Observational learning: Some social applications. In P. J. Elich (Ed.), *The Fourth Western Symposium on Learning.* Bellingham, Wash.: Western Washington State College, 1973.

Liebert, R. M., & Allen, M. K. Effects of a model's experience on children's imitation. *Psychonomic Science,* 1969, *14,* 198.

Liebert, R. M., & Baron, R. A. Some immediate effects of televised violence on children's behavior. *Developmental Psychology,* 1972, *6,* 469–75.

Liebert, R. M., & Fernandez, L. E. Vicarious reward and task complexity as determinants of imitative learning. *Psychological Reports,* 1969, *25,* 531–34.

Liebert, R. M., & Fernandez, L. E. Effects of vicarious consequences on imitative performance. *Child Development,* 1970, *41,* 847–52. (a)

Liebert, R. M., & Fernandez, L. E. Imitation as a function of vicarious and direct reward. *Developmental Psychology, 1970, 2,* 230–32. (b)

Liebert, R. M., Neale, J. M., & Davidson, E. S. *The early window: Effects of television on children and youth.* New York: Pergamon Press, 1973.

Liebert, R. M., & Poulos, R. W. Eliciting the norm of giving: Effects of modeling and the presence of a witness on children's sharing behavior. *Proceedings of the 79th Annual Convention of the American Psychological Association,* 1971, *6,* 345–46.

Liebert, R. M., Sobol, M. P., & Copemann, C. D. Effects of vicarious consequences and race of model upon imitative performance. *Developmental Psychology,* 1972, *6,* 453–56.

Liebert, R. M., & Spiegler, M. D. *Personality: Introduction to theory and research.* Homewood, Ill.: Dorsey Press, 1970.

Liebert, R. M., & Spiegler, M. D. *Personality: Strategies for the study of man* (Rev. ed.). Homewood, Ill.: Dorsey Press, 1974.

Lindsley, O. R. An experiment with parents handling behavior at home. *Johnstone Bulletin* (Johnstone Training Center, Bordentown, N.J.), 1966, *9,* 27–36.

Lindzey, G., & Herman, P. S. Thematic Apperception Test: A note on reliability and situational validity. *Journal of Projective Techniques,* 1955, *19,* 36–42.

Loehlin, J. C., & Nichols, R. C. *Heredity, environment, and personality.* Austin: University of Texas Press, 1976.

Lorand, S. *Technique of psychoanalytic therapy.* New York: International Universities Press, 1946.

Lovaas, O. I. Some studies on the treatment of childhood schizophrenia. In J. Schlein (Ed.), *Research in psychotherapy.* Washington, D.C.: American Psychological Association, 1968.

Lubin, B., Wallis, R. R., & Paine, C. Patterns of psychological test usage in the United States: 1935–1969. *Professional Psychology,* 1971, *2,* 70–74.

Lundin, R. W. *Personality.* New York: Macmillan, 1961.

Lundy, R. M. *Changes in interpersonal perception associated with group-therapy.* Master's thesis, Ohio State University, 1952.

Lykken, D. T. A study of anxiety in the sociopathic personality. *Journal of Abnormal and Social Psychology,* 1957, *55,* 6–10.

Maccoby, E. E., & Wilson, W. C. Identification and observational learning from films. *Journal of Abnormal and Social Psychology,* 1957, *55,* 76–87.

Maccoby, E. E., Wilson, W. C., & Burton, R. V. Differential movie-viewing behavior of male and female viewers. *Journal of Personality,* 1958, *26,* 259–67.

Maddi, S. R. *Personality theories: A comparative analysis* (3d ed.). Homewood, Ill.: Dorsey Press, 1976.

Mahoney, M. J. Toward an experimental analysis of covert control. *Behavior Therapy,* 1970, *1,* 510–21.

Mahoney, M. J. *Cognition and behavior modification.* Cambridge, Mass.: Ballinger, 1974.

Malec, J., Park, T., & Watkins, J. T. Modeling with role playing as a treatment for test anxiety. *Journal of Consulting and Clinical Psychology*, 1976, *44*, 679.

Malinowski, B. *Sex and repression in savage society*. London: Routledge & Kegan Paul, 1927.

Marks, P. A., & Seeman, W. *An atlas for use with the MMPI: Actuarial description of abnormal personality*. Baltimore: Williams & Wilkins, 1963.

Marquis, D. A study of frustration in newborn infants. *Journal of Experimental Psychology*, 1943, *32*, 123–38.

Marquis, J. N. Orgasmic reconditioning: Changing sexual object choice through controlling masturbation fantasies. *Journal of Behavior Therapy and Experimental Psychiatry*, 1970, *1*, 263–71.

Masling, J. M. The influence of situational and interpersonal variables in projective testing. *Psychological Bulletin*, 1960, *56*, 65–85.

Masling, J. M., Johnson, C., & Saturansky, C. Oral imagery, accuracy of perceiving others, and performance in Peace Corps training. *Journal of Personality and Social Psychology*, 1974, *30*, 414–19.

Masling, J. M., Rabie, L., & Blondheim, S. H. Obesity, level of aspiration, and Rorschach and TAT measures of oral dependence. *Journal of Consulting Psychology*, 1967, *31*, 233–39.

Masling, J. M., Weiss, L., & Rothschild, B. Relationships of oral imagery to yielding behavior and birth order. *Journal of Consulting and Clinical Psychology*, 1968, *32*, 89–91.

Maslow, A. H. Deficiency motivation and growth motivation. In M. R. Jones (Ed.), *Nebraska symposium on motivation: 1955*. Lincoln, Neb.: University of Nebraska Press, 1955.

Maslow, A. H. Self-actualizing people. In G. B. Levitas (Ed.), *The world of psychology* (Vol. 2). New York: Braziller, 1963.

Maslow, A. H. *Toward a psychology of being*. Princeton, N.J.: Van Nostrand, 1962.

Maslow, A. H. *Toward a psychology of being* (2nd ed.). Princeton, N.J.: Van Nostrand, 1968.

Maslow, A. H. *Motivation and personality* (Rev. ed.). New York: Harper & Row, 1970.

Maslow, A. H. *The farther reaches of human nature*. New York: Viking Press, 1972. (a)

Maslow, A. H. Self-actualizing and beyond. In A. H. Maslow, *The farther reaches of human nature*. New York: Viking Press, 1972. (b)

May, R. Existential psychology. In T. Millon (Ed.), *Theories of psychopathology*. Philadelphia: Saunders, 1967.

Mayo, L. L., & Norton, G. R. The use of problem solving to reduce examination and interpersonal anxiety. *Journal of Behavior Therapy and Experimental Psychiatry*, 1980, *11*, 287–89.

McArthur, C., Waldron, E., & Dickinson, J. The psychology of smoking. *Journal of Abnormal and Social Psychology*, 1958, *56*, 267–75.

McArthur, L. Z., & Eisen, S. V. Achievements of male and female storybook characters as determinants of achievement behavior by boys and girls. *Journal of Personality and Social Psychology*, 1976, *33*, 467–73.

McCarley, R. W., & Hobson, J. A. The neurobiological origins of psychoanalytic dream theory. *American Journal of Psychiatry*, 1977, *134*, 1211–21.

McClelland, D. C. *The achieving society*. Princeton, N.J.: Van Nostrand, 1961.

McClelland, D. C. Toward a theory of motive acquisition. *American Psychologist*, 1965, *20*, 321–33.

McClelland, D. C. *The achieving society*. New York: Free Press, 1967.

McClelland, D. C. The impact of power motivation training on alcoholics. *Journal of Studies on Alcohol*, 1977, *38*, 142–44.

McClelland, D. C. Managing motivation to expand human freedom. *American Psychologist*, 1978, *33*, 201–10.

McClelland, D. C. Inhibited power motivation and high blood pressure in men. *Journal of Abnormal Psychology*, 1979, *88*, 182–90.

McClelland, D. C., Atkinson, J. W., Clark, R. A., & Lowell, E. I. *The achievement motive*. New York: Appleton-Century-Crofts, 1953. (Reprinted 1976 by Irvington Publishers.)

McClelland, D. C., & Burnham, D. H. Power is the great motivator. *Harvard Business Review*, 1976, *54*, 100–10.

McClelland, D. C., Davis, W. N., Kalin, R., & Wanner, E. *The drinking man*. New York: The Free Press, 1972.

McClelland, D. C., & Winter, D. G. *Motivating economic achievement*. New York: Free Press, 1969.

McFall, R., & Twentyman, C. T. Four experiments of relative contributions of rehearsal, modeling, and coaching to assertion training. *Journal of Abnormal Psychology*, 1973, *81*, 199–218.

McFarland, R. A. *Human factors in air transportation*. New York: McGraw-Hill, 1953.

McGaw, W. H., Rice, C. P., & Rogers, C. R. *The steel shutter*. La Jolla, Calif.: Film Center for Studies of the Person, 1973.

McIntyre, J. J., & Teevan, J. J., Jr. Television violence and deviant behavior. In G. A. Comstock & E. A. Rubinstein (Eds.), *Television and social behavior* (Vol. 3). *Television and adolescent aggressiveness*. Washington, D.C.: U.S. Government Printing Office, 1972.

McKeachie, W. J. Motivation, teaching methods, and college learning. In M. R. Jones (Ed.), *Nebraska Symposium on Motivation, 1961*. Lincoln, Neb.: University of Nebraska Press, 1961.

McKenna v. *Fargo*, 451 F. Supp. 1355 (1978).

Mead, M. *Male and female*. New York: William Morrow, 1949.

Meichenbaum, D. Examination of model characteristics in reducing avoidance behavior. *Journal of Personality and Social Psychology*, 1971, *17*, 298–307.

Meichenbaum, D. *Cognitive behavior modification.* Morristown, N.J.: General Learning Press, 1974.

Meichenbaum, D. Enhancing creativity by modifying what subjects say to themselves. *American Educational Research Journal,* 1975, *12,* 129–45.

Meichenbaum, D. *Cognitive-behavior modification: An integrative approach.* New York: Plenum, 1977.

Meichenbaum, D., & Cameron, R. Stress inoculation: A skills training approach to anxiety management. Unpublished manuscript, University of Waterloo, 1972.

Menchenbaum, D., & Goodman, J. Training impulsive children to talk to themselves: A means of developing self-control. *Journal of Abnormal Psychology,* 1971, *77,* 115–26.

Melamed, B. Prevention of medical and dental anxiety. In M. D. Spiegler (Chair), *Behavioral primary prevention: A challenge for the 1980s.* Symposium presented at the meeting of the Association for Advancement of Behavior Therapy, New York, 1980.

Melamed, B. G., Hawes, R. R., Heiby, E., & Glick, J. The use of filmed modeling to reduce uncooperative behavior of children during dental treatment. *Journal of Dental Research,* 1975, *54,* 797–801.

Melamed, B. G., & Siegel, L. J. Reduction of anxiety in children facing hospitalization and surgery by use of filmed modeling. *Journal of Consulting and Clinical Psychology,* 1975, *43,* 511–21.

Melamed, B. G., Weinstein, D., Hawes, R., & Katin-Borland, M. Reduction of fear-related dental management problems using filmed modeling. *Journal of the American Dental Association,* 1975, *90,* 822–26.

Meltzoff, J., & Kornreich, M. *Research in psychotherapy.* New York: Atherton, 1970.

Merrill, R. M., & Heathers, L. B. The relation of the MMPI to the Edwards Personal Preference Schedule on a college counseling center sample. *Journal of Consulting Psychology,* 1956, *20,* 310–14.

Meyers, A. W., Stunkard, A. J., & Coll, M. Food accessibility and food choice: A test of Schachter's externality hypothesis. *Archives of General Psychiatry,* 1980, *37,* 1133–35.

Miller, N. E., & Dollard, J. *Social learning and imitation.* New Haven: Yale University Press, 1941.

Millon, T. (Ed.). *Theories of psychopathology.* Philadelphia: Saunders, 1967.

Mintz, E. Time-extended marathon groups. *Psychotherapy,* 1967, *4,* 65–70.

Minuchin, P. Sex-role concepts and sex typing in childhood as a function of school and home environments. *Child Development,* 1965, *36,* 1033–48.

Mischel, W. *Personality and assessment.* New York: John Wiley & Sons, 1968.

Mischel, W. Continuity and change in personality. *American Psychologist,* 1969, *24,* 1012–18.

Mischel, W. Sex-typing and socialization. In P. H. Mussen (Ed.), *Carmichael's manual of child psychology* (Vol. 2). New York: John Wiley & Sons, 1970.

Mischel, W. *Introduction to personality.* New York: Holt, Rinehart & Winston, 1971.

Mischel, W. On the empirical dilemmas of psychodynamic approaches: Issues and alternatives. *Journal of Abnormal Psychology,* 1973, *82,* 335–44. (a)

Mischel, W. Toward a cognitive social learning reconceptualization of personality. *Psychological Review,* 1973, *80,* 252–83. (b)

Mischel, W. Processes in delay of gratification. In L. Berkowitz (Ed.), *Advances in experimental social psychology* (Vol. 7). New York: Academic Press, 1974.

Mischel, W. *Introduction to personality* (2d ed.). New York: Holt, Rinehart & Winston, 1976.

Mischel, W. On the interface of cognition and personality: Beyond the person-situation debate. *American Psychologist,* 1979, *34,* 740–54.

Mischel, W., & Baker, N. Cognitive appraisals and transformations in delay behavior. *Journal of Personality and Social Psychology,* 1975, *31,* 254–61.

Mischel, W., & Ebbesen, E. Attention in delay of gratification. *Journal of Personality and Social Psychology,* 1970, *16,* 329–37.

Mischel, W., & Moore, B. Effects of attention to symbolically presented rewards upon self-control. *Journal of Personality and Social Psychology,* 1973, *28,* 172–79.

Moll, A. *The sexual life of the child.* New York: Macmillan, 1912. (German edition, 1909).

Montague, E. K. The role of anxiety in serial rote learning. *Journal of Experimental Psychology,* 1953, *45,* 91–96.

Moore, B., Mischel, W., & Zeiss, A. Comparative effects of the reward stimulus and its cognitive representation in voluntary delay. *Journal of Personality and Social Psychology,* 1976, *34,* 419–24.

Morris, B. S. Officer selection in the British Army, 1942–1945. *Occupational Psychology,* 1949, *23,* 219–34.

Morrison, J. R., & Stewart, A. M. A family study of the hyperactive child syndrome. *Biological Psychiatry,* 1971, *3,* 189–95.

Motley, M. T., & Baars, B. J. Laboratory verification of "Freudian" slips of the tongue as evidence of prearticulatory semantic editing. In B. Ruken (Ed.), *Communication yearbook 2.* New Brunswick, N.J.: Transaction, 1978.

Mowrer, O. H., & Mowrer, W. M. Enuresis—A method for its study and treatment. *American Journal of Orthopsychiatry,* 1938, *8,* 436–59.

Mullen, J., & Abeles, N. Relationship of liking, empathy, and therapist's experience to outcome of therapy. In *Psychotherapy, 1971, an Aldine annual.* Chicago: Aldine-Atherton, 1972.

Müller, F. M. *Biographies of words.* New York: Longmans, Green, 1888.

Murray, H. A. *Explorations in personality.* New York: Science Editions, 1962.

Murstein, B. I. *Theory and research in projective techniques (emphasizing the TAT).* New York: John Wiley & Sons, 1963.

Myerson, A. The attitude of neurologists, psychiatrists, and psychologists towards psychoanalysis. *American Journal of Psychiatry,* 1939, *96,* 623–41.

Neale, J. M. Personal communication, 1968.

Neale, J. M., & Liebert, R. M. *Science and behavior: An introduction to methods of research.* Englewood Cliffs, N.J.: Prentice-Hall, 1973.

Neale, J. M., & Liebert, R. M. *Science and behavior* (2nd ed.). Englewood Cliffs, N.J.: Prentice-Hall, 1980.

Neale, J. M., & Weintraub, S. Personal communication, 1977.

Neisser, U. *Cognition and reality.* San Francisco: Freeman, 1976.

Nisbett, R. E. Determinants of food intake in human obesity. *Science,* 1968, *159,* 1254–55.

Nisbett, R. E., & Storms, M. D. Cognitive, social, psychological determinants of food intake. In H. London & R. E. Nisbett (Eds.), *Cognitive modification of emotional behavior.* Chicago: Aldine, 1975.

Nisbett, R. E., & Temoshok, L. Is there an external cognitive style? *Journal of Personality and Social Psychology,* 1976, *33,* 36–47.

Nisbett, R. E., & Wilson, T. Telling more than we can know: Verbal reports on mental processes. *Psychological Review,* 1977, *84,* 231–59.

Nisenson, S., & DeWitt, W. A. *Illustrated minute biographies.* New York: Grosset & Dunlap, 1949.

Noll, V. H. Simulation by college students of a prescribed pattern on a personality scale. *Educational and Psychological Measurement,* 1951, *11,* 478–88.

Norman, W. T. Development of self-report tests to measure personality factors identified from peer nominations. *USAF ASK Technical Note,* 1961, No. 61–44.

Norman, W. T. Toward an adequate taxonomy of personality attributes: Replicated factor structure in peer nomination personality ratings. *Journal of Abnormal and Social Psychology,* 1963, *66,* 574–83.

Novaco, R. *Anger control: The development and evaluation of an experimental treatment.* Lexington, Mass.: Heath, 1975.

Novaco, R. W. Anger and coping with stress: Cognitive behavioral interventions. In J. P. Foreyt & D. P. Rathjen (Eds.), *Cognitive behavior therapy: Research and application.* New York: Plenum, 1978.

Nunnally, J. C., Duchnowski, A. J., & Parker, R. K. Association of neutral objects with rewards: Effect on verbal evaluation, reward expectancy, and selective attention. *Journal of Personality and Social Psychology,* 1965, *1,* 270–74.

Nuttall, R. L. Some correlates of high need for achievement among urban Northern Negroes. *Journal of Abnormal and Social Psychology,* 1964, *68,* 593–600.

O'Connor, R. D. Modification of social withdrawal through symbolic modeling. *Journal of Applied Behavior Analysis,* 1969, *2,* 15–22.

O'Connor, R. D. Relative efficacy of modeling, shaping, and the combined procedures for modification of social withdrawal. *Journal of Abnormal Psychology,* 1972, *79,* 327–34.

Oppenheimer, R. Analogy in science. *American Psychologist,* 1956, *11,* 127–35.

Orgler, H. *Alfred Adler: The man and his work.* New York: Putnam (Capricorn Books), 1963.

OSS Assessment Staff. *Assessment of men.* New York: Holt, Rinehart & Winston, 1948.

Overall, J. E. Note on the scientific status of factors. *Psychological Bulletin,* 1964, *61,* 270–76.

Palombo, S. R. *Dreaming and memory.* New York: Basic Books, 1978.

Parker, R. K., & Nunnally, J. C. Association of neutral objects with rewards: Effects of reward schedules on reward expectancy, verbal evaluation, and selective attention. *Journal of Experimental Child Psychology,* 1966, *3,* 324–32.

Parnell, R. W. Physique and choice of faculty. *British Medical Journal,* 1953, *2,* 472–75.

Parnell, R. W. Physique and mental breakdown in young adults. *British Medical Journal,* 1957, *1,* 1485–90.

Passini, F. T., & Norman, W. T. A universal conception of personality structure? *Journal of Personality and Social Psychology,* 1966, *4,* 44–49.

Paul, G. L. Behavior modification research: Design and tactics. In C. M. Franks (Ed.), *Behavior therapy: Appraisal and status.* New York: McGraw-Hill, 1969.

Paul, I. H., Gill, M. M., Simon, J., Fink, G., & Endicott, N. A. *The differential effect of different interventions.* In preparation, 1969. Cited in Luborsky, L., & Spence, D. P. Quantitative research on psychoanalytic therapy. In A. E. Bergin & S. L. Garfield (Eds.), *Handbook of psychotherapy and behavior change: An empirical analysis.* New York: John Wiley & Sons, 1971.

Pavlov, I. P. *Conditioned reflexes.* New York: Liveright, 1927.

Pawlik, K., & Cattell, R. B. Third-order factors in objective personality tests. *British Journal of Psychology,* 1964, *55,* 1–18.

Payne, D. E. Role constructs versus part constructs and interpersonal understanding. Doctoral dissertation, Ohio State University, 1956.

Pekarik, E. G., Prinz, R. J., Liebert, D. E., Weintraub, S., & Neale, J. M. The Pupil Evaluation Inventory: A sociometric technique for assessing children's social behavior. *Journal of Abnormal Child Psychology,* 1976, *4,* 83–97.

Perls, F. S. *Gestalt therapy verbatim.* Lafayette, Calif.: Real People Press, 1969.

Pervin, L. A. *Personality: Theory, assessment, and research.* New York: John Wiley & Sons, 1970.

Pierce, J. V. Personality and achievement among able high school boys. *Journal of Individual Psychology,* 1961, *17,* 102–7. (a)

Pierce, J. V. *Sex differences in achievement motivation.* Quincy, Ill.: Quincy Youth Development Project, 1961. (b)

Piliavin, I. M., Rodin, J., & Piliavin, J. A. Good samaritan: An underground phenomenon? *Journal of Personality and Social Psychology,* 1969, *13,* 289–99.

Plomin, R. Behavior genetics and personality. In R. M. Liebert & R. Wicks-Nelson, *Developmental psychology* (3rd ed.). Englewood Cliffs, N.J.: Prentice-Hall, 1981.

Plomin, R., & Foch, T. T. A twin study of objectively assessed personality in childhood. *Journal of Personality and Social Psychology,* 1980, *39,* 680–88.

Plomin, R., & Rowe, D. C. Genetic and environmental etiology of social behavior in infancy. *Developmental Psychology,* 1979, *15,* 62–72.

Poser, E. G. The self-efficacy concept: Some theoretical, procedural and clinical implications. In S. Rachman (Ed.), *Advances in behaviour research and therapy* (Vol. 1). Oxford: Pergamon Press, 1978.

Posner, M. Coordination of internal codes. In W. Chase (Ed.), *Visual information processing.* New York: Academic Press, 1973.

Poulos, R. W., & Liebert, R. M. Influence of modeling, exhortative verbalization and surveillance on children's sharing. *Developmental Psychology,* 1972, *6,* 402–8.

Price, J. M., & Grinker, J. Effects of degree of obesity, food deprivation, and palatability on eating behavior of humans. *Journal of Comparative and Physiological Psychology,* 1973, *85,* 265–71.

Price, J. S. The genetics of depressive disorder. In A. Coppen & A. Walk (Eds.), *Recent developments in affective disorders. British Journal of Psychiatry,* Special Publication 2, 1968.

Prince, H. T. The effects of covert behavioral rehearsal, modeling, and vicarious consequences in assertive training. Doctoral dissertation, University of Texas at Austin, 1975.

Psychiatry on the couch. *Time,* April 2, 1979, p. 74 ff.

Quarti, C., & Renaud, J. A new treatment of constipation by conditioning: A preliminary report. In C. M. Franks (Ed.), *Conditioning techniques in clinical practice and research.* New York: Springer, 1964.

Rachlin, H. Review of M. J. Mahoney's *Cognition and behavior modification. Journal of Applied Behavior Analysis,* 1977, *10,* 369–74.

Rachman, S., & Teasdale, J. *Aversion therapy and behaviour disorders: An analysis.* Coral Gables, Fla.: University of Miami Press, 1969.

Rachman, S. J., & Wilson, G. T. *The effects of psychological therapy* (2nd ed.). Oxford: Pergamon Press, 1980.

Ramond, C. K. Anxiety and task as determiners of verbal performance. *Journal of Experimental Psychology,* 1953, *46,* 120–24.

The Random House dictionary of the English language. New York: Random House, 1969.

Rangell, L. The role of the parent in the Oedipus complex. *Bulletin of the Menninger Clinic,* 1953, *19,* 9–15.

Rank, O. *The trauma of birth.* New York: Harcourt, Brace, 1929.

Raskin, N. Studies on psychotherapeutic orientation: Ideology in practice. *AAP Psychotherapy Research Monographs,* Orlando, Fl.: American Academy of Psychotherapists, 1974.

Rathus, S. A. Instigation of assertive behavior through videotape-mediated assertive models and direct practice. *Behaviour Research and Therapy,* 1973, *11,* 57–66.

Razran, G. S. Conditioning away social bias by the luncheon technique. *Psychological Bulletin,* 1938, *35,* 693.

Razran, G. S. Conditioned response changes in rating and appraising sociopolitical slogans. *Psychological Bulletin,* 1940, *37,* 481.

Read, P. P. *Alive: The story of the Andes survivors.* Philadelphia: J. B. Lippincott, 1974.

Rees, L. Constitutional factors and abnormal behavior. In H. J. Eysenck (Ed.), *Handbook of abnormal psychology.* New York: Basic Books, 1961.

Reisman, D., Glazer, N., & Denney, R. *The lonely crowd.* New York: Doubleday, 1950.

Risley, T. R. The effects and side effects of punishing the autistic behaviors of a deviant child. *Journal of Applied Behavior Analysis,* 1968, *1,* 21–34.

Ritter, B. Eliminating excessive fears of the environment through contact desensitization. In J. D. Krumboltz & C. E. Thoresen (Eds.), *Behavioral counseling: Cases and techniques.* New York: Holt, Rinehart & Winston, 1969.

Roazen, P. *Freud and his followers.* New York: Alfred A. Knopf, 1975.

Robins, L. N. *Deviant children grown up: A sociological and psychiatric study of sociopathic personality.* Baltimore: Williams & Wilkins, 1966.

Rodin, J. Effects of obesity and set point on taste responsiveness and ingestion in humans. *Journal of Comparative and Physiological Psychology,* 1975, *89,* 1003–9.

Rodin, J. The externality theory today. In A. J. Stunkard (Ed.), *Obesity.* Philadelphia: Saunders, 1980.

Rodin, J. Current status of the internal-external hypothesis for obesity: What went wrong? *American Psychologist,* 1981, *36,* 361–72.

Rogers, C. R. A theory of therapy, personality, and interpersonal relationships, as developed in the client-centered framework. In S. Koch (Ed.), *Psychology: A study of a science* (Vol. 3). New York: McGraw-Hill, 1959.

Rogers, C. R. *On becoming a person.* Boston: Houghton Mifflin, 1961.

Rogers, C. R. Toward a science of the person. In T. W. Wann (Ed.), *Behaviorism and phenomenology.* Chicago: University of Chicago Press, 1964.

Rogers, C. R. *Client-centered therapy.* Boston: Houghton Mifflin, 1965.

Rogers, C. R. The process of the basic encounter group. In J. F. T. Brugental (Ed.), *The challenges of humanistic psychology.* New York: McGraw-Hill, 1967.

Rogers, C. R. *Freedom to learn: A view of what education might become.* Columbus, O.: Charles E. Merrill, 1969.

Rogers, C. R. *Carl Rogers on encounter groups.* New York: Harper & Row, 1970.

Rogers, C. R. Some new challenges. *American Psychologist,* 1973, *28,* 379–87.

Rogers, C. R. In retrospect: Forty-six years. *American Psychologist,* 1974, *29,* 115–23.

Rogers, C. R. Empathic: An unappreciated way of being. *The Counseling Psychologist,* 1975, *5,* 2–10.

Rogers, C. R. *A way of being.* Boston: Houghton Mifflin, 1980.

Rogers, C. R., & Dymond, R. F. (Eds.). *Psychotherapy and personality change.* Chicago: University of Chicago Press, 1954.

Rokeach, M., & Kliejunas, P. Behavior as a function of attitude-toward-object and attitude-toward-situation. *Journal of Personality and Social Psychology*, 1972, *22*, 194–201.

Rorer, L. G. The great response-style myth. *Psychological Bulletin*, 1965, *63*, 129–56.

Rosen, B. C., & D'Andrade, R. G. The psychosocial origins of achievement motivation. *Sociometry*, 1959, *22*, 185–218.

Rosenhan, D., & White, G. M. Observation and rehearsal as determinants of pro-social behavior. *Journal of Personality and Social Psychology*, 1967, *5*, 424–31.

Rosenman, R. H. Introduction. In T. M. Dembroski, S. M. Weiss, J. L. Shields, S. G. Haynes, & M. Feinleib (Eds.), *Coronary-prone behavior*. New York: Springer-Verlag, 1978.

Rosenman, R. H., Brand, R. J., Jenkins, C. D., Friedman, M., Straus, R., & Wurm, M. Coronary heart disease in the Western Collaborative Group Study: Final follow-up experience of 8½ years. *Journal of the American Medical Association*, 1975, *233*, 872–77.

Rosenman, R. H., Friedman, M., Straus, R., Wurm, M., Kositchek, R., Haan, W., & Werthessen, N. T. A predictive study of coronary heart disease: The Western Collaborative Group Study. *Journal of the American Medical Association*, 1964, *189*, 15–22.

Rosenman, R. H., Friedman, M., Straus, R., Wurm, M., Kositchek, R., Haan, W., & Werthessen, N. T. Coronary heart disease in the Western Collaborative Group Study: A follow-up experience of 4½ years. *Journal of Chronic Disease*, 1970, *23*, 173–90.

Rosenthal, D. *Genetic theory and abnormal behavior*. New York: McGraw-Hill, 1970.

Rosenthal, T. L. Bandura's self-efficacy theory: Thought *is* father to the deed. In S. Rachman (Ed.), *Advances in behaviour research and therapy* (Vol. 1). Oxford: Pergamon Press, 1978.

Rosenthal, T. L., & Reese, S. L. The effects of covert and overt modeling on assertive behavior. *Behaviour Research and Therapy*, 1976, *14*, 463–69.

Rosenwald, G. C. Effectiveness of defenses against anal impulse arousal. *Journal of Consulting and Clinical Psychology*, 1972, *39*, 292–98.

Ross, A. O. Deviant case analysis: A neglected approach to behavior research. *Perceptual and Motor Skills*, 1963, *16*, 337–40.

Ross, D. M. Relationship between dependency, intentional learning, and incidental learning in preschool children. *Journal of Personality and Social Psychology*, 1966, *4*, 374–81.

Ross, D. M., Ross, S. A., & Evans, T. A. The modification of extreme social withdrawal by modeling with guided participation. *Journal of Behavior Therapy and Experimental Psychiatry*, 1971, *2*, 273–79.

Rotter, J. B. *Social learning and clinical psychology*. Englewood Cliffs, N.J.: Prentice-Hall, 1954.

Ruse, M. *Sociobiology: Sense or nonsense?* Dordrecht, Holland: D. Reidel, 1979.

Rychlak, J. The psychology of personal constructs: George A. Kelly. In J. Rychlak (Ed.), *Introduction to personality and psychotherapy*. Boston: Houghton Mifflin, 1973.

Rychlak, J. F., & Brams, J. M. Personality dimensions in recalled dream content. *Journal of Projective Techniques*, 1963, *27*, 226–34.

Sahlins, M. D., *The use and abuse of biology*. Ann Arbor, Mich.: University of Michigan Press, 1976.

Sanford, R. N., Adkins, M. M., Miller, R. B., & Cobb, E. A. Physique, personality, and scholarship. *Monographs of the Society for Research in Child Development*, 1943, *7*, No. 34.

Sarason, I. G. Test anxiety and cognitive modeling. *Journal of Personality and Social Psychology*, 1973, *28*, 58–61.

Sarason, I. G. Test anxiety and the self-disclosing coping model. *Journal of Consulting and Clinical Psychology*, 1975, *43*, 148–53.

Sarbin, T. R., Taft, R., & Bailey, D. E. *Clinical inference and cognitive theory*. New York: Holt, Rinehart & Winston, 1960.

Sarnoff, I., & Corwin, S. M. Castration anxiety and the fear of death. *Journal of Personality*, 1959, *27*, 374–85.

Scarr, S. Genetic factors in activity motivation. *Child Development*, 1966, *37*, 663–73.

Scarr, S. Social introversion-extroversion as a heritable response. *Child Development*, 1969, *40*, 823–32.

Schachter, S. *The psychology of affiliation*. Stanford, Calif.: Stanford University Press, 1959.

Schachter, S., Goldman, R., & Gordon, A. Effects of fear, food deprivation, and obesity on eating. *Journal of Personality and Social Psychology*, 1968, *10*, 91–97.

Schachter, S., & Latané, B. Crime, cognition, and the autonomic nervous system. In D. Levine (Ed.), *Nebraska symposium on motivation, 1964*. Lincoln, Neb.: University of Nebraska Press, 1964.

Schachter, S., & Rodin, J. *Obese humans and rats*. Washington, D.C.: Erlbaum/Halsted, 1974.

Schaefer, W. S., & Bayley, N. Maternal behavior, child behavior, and their intercorrelations from infancy through adolescence. *Monographs of the Society for Research in Child Development*, 1963, *28*, 1–27.

Schafer, R. Review of *Introduction to the Szondi Test: Theory and practice* by S. Deri. *Journal of Abnormal and Social Psychology*, 1950, *45*, 184–88.

Schaffer, H. R., & Emerson, P. E. Patterns of response to physical contact in early human development. *Journal of Child Psychology and Psychiatry*, 1964, *5*, 1–13.

Schill, T. Sex differences in identification of the castrating agent on the Blacky Test. *Journal of Clinical Psychology*, 1966, *22*, 324–25.

Schloss, G. A., Siroka, R. W., & Siroka, E. K. Some contemporary origins of the personal growth group. In R. W. Siroka, E. K. Siroka, & G. A. Schloss

(Eds.), *Sensitivity training and group encounter: An introduction.* New York: Grosset & Dunlap, 1971.

Schramm, W., Lyle, J., & Parker, E. *Television in the lives of our children.* Stanford, Calif.: Stanford University Press, 1961.

Schunk, D. H. Modeling and attributional effects on children's achievement: A self-efficacy analysis. *Journal of Educational Psychology,* 1981, *73,* 93–105.

Schutz, W. C. *Joy: Expanding human awareness.* New York: Grove Press, 1967.

Sears, P. S. Correlates of need achievement and need affiliation and classroom management, self-concept, achievement, and creativity. Unpublished manuscript, Stanford University, 1962.

Sears, R. R. *Survey of objective studies of psychoanalytic concepts.* New York: Social Science Research Council, Bulletin 51, 1943.

Sears, R. R., Rau, L., & Alpert, R. *Identification and child rearing.* Stanford, Calif.: Stanford University Press, 1965.

Sechrest, L. The psychology of personal constructs: George Kelly. In J. M. Wepman & R. W. Heine (Eds.), *Concepts of personality.* Chicago: Aldine, 1963.

Sechrest, L. Personal constructs theory. In R. J. Corsini (Ed.), *Current personality theories.* Itasca, Ill.: Peacock, 1977.

Seligman, M. E. P. Phobias and preparedness. *Behavior Therapy,* 1971, *2,* 307–20.

Serber, M. Shame aversion therapy. *Journal of Behavior Therapy and Experimental Psychiatry,* 1970, *1,* 219–21.

Serber, M. The experiential groups as entertainment. In P. S. Houts & M. Serber (Eds.), *After the turn-on, what? Learning perspectives on humanistic groups.* Champaign, Ill.: Research Press, 1972. (a)

Serber, M. Shame aversion therapy with and without heterosexual retraining. In R. D. Rubin, H. Fensterheim, J. D. Henderson, & L. P. Ullmann (Eds.), *Advances in behavior therapy.* New York: Academic Press, 1972. (b)

Seward, G. H. The relation between the psychoanalytic school and the value problems in therapy. *American Journal of Psychoanalysis,* 1962–63, *22–23,* 138–52.

Shane, M. A rationale for teaching analytic technique based on a developmental orientation and approach. *International Journal of Psycho-Analysis,* 1977, *58,* 95–108.

Shaw, D. W., & Thoresen, C. E. Effects of modeling and desensitization in reducing dentist phobia. *Journal of Counseling Psychology,* 1974, *21,* 415–20.

Sheldon, W. H. *The varieties of temperament: A psychology of constitutional differences.* New York: Harper & Row, 1942.

Sherwood, G. G. Classical and attributive projection: Some new evidence. *Journal of Abnormal Psychology,* 1979, *88,* 635–40.

Sherwood, M. *The logic of explanation in psychoanalysis.* New York: Academic Press, 1969.

Shostrom, E. L. *Personal Orientation Inventory.* San Diego: EdITS/Educational & Industrial Testing Service, 1963.

Shostrom, E. L. An inventory for the measurement of self-actualization. *Educational and Psychological Measurement,* 1964, *24,* 207–18.

Shostrom, E. L. *Manual for the Personal Orientation Inventory.* San Diego: Edits/Educational & Industrial Testing Service, 1974.

Shostrom, E. L., Knapp, L. F., & Knapp, R. R. *Actualizing therapy: Foundations for a scientific ethic.* San Diego: EdITS/Educational & Industrial Testing Service, 1976.

Silverman, L. H. Psychoanalytic theory: "The reports of my death are greatly exaggerated." *American Psychologist,* 1976, *31,* 621–37.

Simonton, O. C. *Getting well again.* New York: Bantam, 1980.

Skinner, B. F. *The behavior of organisms.* New York: Appleton-Century-Crofts, 1938.

Skinner, B. F. *Walden two.* New York: Macmillan, 1948.

Skinner, B. F. *Science and human behavior.* New York: Macmillan, 1953.

Skinner, B. F. A case history in scientific method. *American Psychologist,* 1956, *11,* 221–33.

Skinner, B. F. Behaviorism at fifty. *Science,* 1963, *140,* 951–58.

Skinner, B. F. Behaviorism at fifty. In T. W. Wann (Ed.), *Behaviorism and phenomenology.* Chicago: University of Chicago Press, 1964.

Skinner, B. F. *Beyond freedom and dignity.* New York: Alfred A. Knopf, 1971.

Skinner, B. F. *About behaviorism.* New York: Alfred A. Knopf, 1974.

Skinner, H. A., Jackson, D. N., & Rampton, G. M. The personality research form in a Canadian context: Does language make a difference? *Canadian Journal of Behavioural Science,* 1976, *8,* 156–68.

Smith, G. Usefulness of peer ratings of personality in educational research. *Educational and Psychological Measurement,* 1967, *24,* 967–84.

Smith, M. B. The phenomenological approach to personality theory: Some critical remarks. *Journal of Abnormal and Social Psychology,* 1950, *45,* 516–22.

Smith, R. T. A comparison of socioenvironmental factors in monozygotic and dizygotic twins: Testing an assumption. In S. G. Vandenberg (Ed.), *Methods and goals in human behavior genetics.* New York: Academic Press, 1965.

Snyder, C. R. Acceptance of personality interpretations as a function of assessment procedures. *Journal of Consulting and Clinical Psychology,* 1974, *42,* 150. (a)

Snyder, C. R. Why horoscopes are true: The effects of specificity on acceptance of astrological interpretations. *Journal of Clinical Psychology,* 1974, *30,* 577–80. (b)

Snyder, C. R., & Larson, G. R. A further look at student acceptance of general personality interpretations. *Journal of Consulting and Clinical Psychology,* 1972, *38,* 384–88.

Snyder, F. The organismic state associated with dreaming. In N. W. Greenfield

(Ed.), *Psychoanalysis and current biological thought.* Madison: University of Wisconsin Press, 1965.

Solomon, R. L. Punishment. *American Psychologist,* 1964, *19,* 239–53.

Spence, J. T., & Spence, K. W. The motivational components of manifest anxiety: Drive and drive stimuli. In C. D. Spielberger (Ed.), *Anxiety and behavior.* New York: Academic Press, 1966.

Sperry, R. W. Changing concepts of consciousness and free will. *Perspectives in Biology and Medicine,* 1976, *20,* 9–19.

Spiegler, M. D. A classroom demonstration of the classical conditioning of attitudes. Unpublished manuscript, University of Texas at Austin, 1970.

Spiegler, M. D. Behavioral primary prevention: Introduction and overview. In M. D. Spiegler (Chair), *Behavioral primary prevention: A challenge for the 1980s.* Symposium presented at the meeting of the Association for Advancement of Behavior Therapy, New York, 1980.

Spiegler, M. D. *Contemporary behavioral therapy.* Palo Alto, Calif.: Mayfield, 1982.

Spiegler, M. D., Cooley, E. J., Marshall, G. J., Prince, H. T., II, Puckett, S. P., & Skenazy, J. A. A self-control versus a counterconditioning paradigm for systematic desensitization: An experimental comparison. *Journal of Counseling Psychology,* 1976, *23,* 83–86.

Spiegler, M. D., & Liebert, R. M. Some correlates of self-reported fear. *Psychological Reports,* 1970, *26,* 691–95.

Spiegler, M. D., Liebert, R. M., McMains, M. J., & Fernandez, L. E. Experimental development of a modeling treatment to extinguish persistent avoidance behavior. In R. D. Rubin & C. M. Franks (Eds.), *Advances in behavior therapy, 1968.* New York: Academic Press, 1969.

Spiegler, M. D., Marshall, G. J., Cooley, E. J., & Prince, H. T. *The role of observational learning in assertive training.* Unpublished manuscript, Providence College, 1978.

Spiegler, M. D., & Weiland, A. The effects of written vicarious consequences on observers' willingness to imitate and ability to recall modeling cues. *Journal of Personality,* 1976, *44,* 260–73.

Spielberger, C. D. Theory and research on anxiety. In C. D. Spielberger (Ed.), *Anxiety and behavior.* New York: Academic Press, 1966.

Spielberger, C. D., & Gorsuch, R. L. *Mediating processes in verbal conditioning: Report of United States Public Health Service Grants MH-7229, MH-7446, and HD-947.* Unpublished manuscript, Vanderbilt University, September, 1966.

Spivack, G., & Shure, M. B. *Social adjustment of young children.* San Francisco: Jossey-Bass, 1974.

Staats, A. W., & Staats, C. K. Attitudes established by classical conditioning. *Journal of Abnormal and Social Psychology,* 1958, *57,* 37–40.

Stagner, R. Traits are relevant: Theoretical analysis and empirical evidence. In N. S. Endler & D. Magnusson (Eds.), *Interactional psychology and personality.* Washington, D.C.: Hemisphere, 1976.

Staub, E. Helping a distressed person: Social, personality, and stimulus determinants. In L. Berkowitz (Ed.), *Advances in experimental social psychology* (Vol. 7). New York: Academic Press, 1974.

Sternberg, S. Memory scanning: New findings and current controversies. *Quarterly Journal of Experimental Psychology*, 1975, *27*, 1–32.

Stevenson, H. W., Hale, G. A., Hill, K. T., & Moely, B. E. Determinants of children's preferences for adults. *Child Development*, 1967, *38*, 1–14.

Stroller, F. H. Accelerated interaction: A time-limited approach based on the brief intensive group. *International Journal of Group Psychotherapy*, 1968, *18*, 220–35.

Strasburger, E. L., & Jackson, D. N. Improving accuracy in a clinical judgmental task. *Journal of Consulting and Clinical Psychology*, 1977, *45*, 303–9.

Strupp, H. H. The performance of psychoanalytic and client-centered therapists in an initial interview. *Journal of Clinical Psychology*, 1958, *22*, 265–74.

Strupp, H. H. *An introduction to Freud and modern psychoanalysis.* Woodbury, N.Y.: Barron's Educational Series, 1967.

Stumphauzer, J. S., Increased delay of gratification in young prison inmates through imitation of high-delay peer-models. *Journal of Personality and Social Psychology*, 1972, *21*, 10–17.

Stunkard, A., & Koch, C. The interpretation of gastric motility, I. Apparent bias in the reports of hunger by obese persons. *Archives of General Psychiatry*, 1964, *11*, 74–82.

Sullivan, H. S. *The interpersonal theory of psychiatry.* New York: W. W. Norton, 1953.

Sulloway, F. J. *Freud, biologist of the mind.* New York: Basic Books, 1979.

Szasz, T. S. The myth of mental illness. *American Psychologist*, 1960, *15*, 113–18.

Tanner, J. M. *Growth at adolescence.* Springfield, Ill.: Charles C Thomas, 1955.

Tart, C. T. Toward the experimental control of dreaming: A review of the literature. *Psychological Bulletin*, 1965, *64*, 81–91.

Tausch, R. Personal communication, 1973. Cited in C. R. Rogers, *A way of being.* Boston: Houghton Mifflin, 1980.

Tausch, R., Bastine, R., Friese, H., & Sander, K. Variablen und Ergebnisse bei Psychotherapie mit alternierenden Psychotherapeuten. *Verlag für Psychologie*, 1970, XXI/I, Göttingen. Cited in C. R. Rogers, *A way of being.* Boston: Houghton Mifflin, 1980.

Taylor, J. A. A personality scale of manifest anxiety. *Journal of Abnormal and Social Psychology*, 1953, *48*, 285–90.

Taylor, J. A., & Spence, K. W. The relationship of anxiety level to performance in serial learning. *Journal of Experimental Psychology*, 1952, *44*, 61–64.

Teasdale, J. D. Self-efficacy: Toward a unifying theory of behaviour change? In S. Rachman (Ed.), *Advances in behaviour research and therapy* (Vol. 1). Oxford: Pergamon Press, 1978.

Thigpen, C. H., & Cleckley, H. A case of multiple personality. *Journal of Abnormal and Social Psychology*, 1954, *49*, 135–51.

Thomas, A., & Chess, S. *Temperament and development.* New York: Brunner/Mazel, 1977.

Thomas, A., Chess, S., & Birch, H. G. The origin of personality. *Scientific American,* 1970, *223,* 102–9.

Thompson, C. Cultural pressures in the psychology of women. In P. Mullahy (Ed.), *A study of interpersonal relations.* New York: Hermitage Press, 1950.

Thompson, C. *Psychoanalysis: Evolution and development.* New York: Grove Press, 1957.

Thorndike, E. L. Animal intelligence: An experimental study of the associative processes in animals. *Psychological Review,* 1898, *2* (Monogr. Suppl. 8).

Thorndike, E. L. *The fundamentals of learning.* New York: Columbia University Teachers College, 1932.

Thorndike, E. L. *An experimental study of rewards.* New York: Columbia University Teachers College, 1933.

Tippett, J. S. A study of change process during psychotherapy. Doctoral dissertation, Ohio State University, 1959.

Trivers, R. L. The evolution of reciprocal altruism. *Quarterly Review of Biology,* 1971, *46,* 35–57.

Tryon, W. W. The test-trait fallacy. *American Psychologist,* 1979, *34,* 402–6.

Tupes, E. C., & Christal, R. E. Stability of personality trait rating factors obtained under diverse conditions. *USAF WADC Technical Note,* 1958, no. 58–61.

Tupes, E. C., & Christal, R. E. Recurrent personality factors based on tract ratings. *USAF ASD Technical Report,* 1961, no. 61–67.

Turk, D. Cognitive control of pain: A skills training approach for the treatment of pain. Masters thesis, University of Waterloo, 1975.

Turk, D. C. Cognitive behavioral techniques in the management of pain. In J. P. Foreyt & D. P. Rathjen (Eds.), *Cognitive behavior therapy: Research and application.* New York: Plenum, 1978.

Turner, A. J. Personal communication, 1973.

Turner, J. H. *The structure of sociological theory.* Homewood, Ill.: Dorsey Press, 1974.

Ullmann, L. P. On cognitions and behavior therapy. *Behavior Therapy,* 1970, *1,* 201–4.

Ullmann, L. P., & Krasner, L. *A psychological approach to abnormal behavior.* (2d ed.). Englewood Cliffs, N.J.: Prentice-Hall, 1975.

Ulrich, R. E., Stachnik, T. J., & Stainton, N. R. Student acceptance of generalized personality interpretations. *Psychological Reports,* 1963, *13,* 831–34.

Valentine, C. W. The innate bases of fear. *Journal of Genetic Psychology,* 1930, *37,* 394–420.

Van de Castle, R. L. *The psychology of dreaming.* Morristown, N.J.: General Learning Press, 1971.

Vandenberg, S. G. Contributions to twin research in psychology. *Psychological Bulletin,* 1966, *66,* 327–52.

Vandenberg, S. G. Hereditary factors in normal personality traits (as measured by inventories). In J. Wortis (Ed.), *Recent advances in biological psychiatry* (Vol. 9). New York: Plenum, 1967.

van der Veen, F. Client perception of therapist conditions as a factor in psychotherapy. In J. T. Hart & T. M. Tomlinson (Eds.), *New directions in client-centered therapy.* Boston: Houghton Mifflin, 1970.

Vernon, D. T. A. Modeling and birth order in responses to painful stimuli. *Journal of Personality and Social Psychology,* 1974, *29,* 794–99.

Veroff, J. Development and validation of a projective measure of power motivation. Doctoral dissertation, University of Michigan, 1955.

Veroff, J. Development and validation of a projective measure of power motivation. *Journal of Abnormal and Social Psychology,* 1957, *54,* 1–8.

Veroff, J., Atkinson, J. W., Feld, S. C., & Gurin, G. The use of thematic apperception to assess motivation in a nationwide interview study. *Psychological Monographs,* 1960, *74* (12, Whole No. 499).

Verplanck, W. S. The operant conditioning of human motor behavior. *Psychological Bulletin,* 1956, *53,* 70–83.

Viederman, M. Adaptive and maladaptive regression in hemodialysis. *Psychiatry,* 1974, *37,* 68–77.

von Bracken, H. Mutual intimacy in twins. *Character and Personality,* 1934, *2,* 293–309.

von Euen, E. [The psychology of diet behavior: Examinations of patients with kidney failure.] *Zeitschrift für Psychotherapie und medizinische Psychologie,* 1974, *24,* 31–35. (Abstracted in *Psychological Abstracts,* 1975, *53,* No. 10307.)

Walker, C. E., Hedberg, A., Clement, P. W., & Wright, L. *Clinical procedures for behavior therapy.* Englewood Cliffs, N.J.: Prentice-Hall, 1981.

Watson, J. B. *Behavior: An introduction to comparative psychology.* New York: H. Holt, 1914.

Watson, J. B. *Psychology from the standpoint of a behaviorist.* Philadelphia: J. B. Lippincott, 1919.

Watson, J. B., & Rayner, R. Conditioned emotional reactions. *Journal of Experimental Psychology,* 1920, *3,* 1–14.

Webb, W. B. *Sleep: The gentle tyrant.* Englewood Cliffs, N.J.: Prentice-Hall, 1975.

Weinberg, R. S., Yukelson, D., & Jackson, A. Effect of public and private efficacy expectations on competitive performance. *Journal of Sport Psychology,* 1980, *2,* 940–49.

Weisberg, P., & Waldrop, P. B. Fixed-interval work habits of Congress. *Journal of Applied Behavior Analysis,* 1972, *5,* 93–97.

Weiss, S. L. Perceived effectiveness of psychotherapy: A function of suggestion? *Journal of Consulting and Clinical Psychology,* 1972, *39,* 156–59.

Weitzman, B. Behavior therapy and psychotherapy. *Psychological Review,* 1967, *74,* 300–17.

Weitzmann, E. A note on the EEG and eye movements during behavioral sleep in monkeys. *EEG Clinical Neurophysiology,* 1961, *13,* 790–94.

Wesman, A. G. Faking personality test scores in a simulated employment situation. *Journal of Applied Psychology,* 1952, *36,* 112–13.

White, R. W. *The enterprise of living: A view of personal growth* (2nd ed.). New York: Holt, Rinehart & Winston, 1976.

White, W., Akers, J., Green, J., & Yates, D. Use of imitation in the treatment of dental phobias in early childhood: A preliminary report. *Journal of Dentistry for Children*, 1974, *26*, 106.

Whyte, L. *The unconscious before Freud*. New York: Basic Books, 1960.

Wicker, A. W. An examination of the "other variables" explanation of attitude-behavior inconsistency. *Journal of Personality and Social Psychology*, 1971, *19*, 18–30.

Wiggins, J. S. *Personality and prediction: Principles of personality assessment*. Reading, Mass.: Addison-Wesley, 1973.

Wilde, G. J. S. Behavior therapy for addicted cigarette smokers: A preliminary investigation. *Behaviour Research and Therapy*, 1964, *2*, 107–9.

Willerman, L. Activity level and hyperactivity in twins. *Child Development*, 1973, *44*, 288–93.

Willerman, L. *Individual and group differences*. New York: Harper's College Press, 1975.

Willerman, L., & Plomin, R. Activity level in children and their parents. *Child Development*, 1973, *44*, 854–58.

Willerman, L., Turner, R. G., & Peterson, M. A. A comparison of the predictive validity of typical and maximal personality measures. *Journal of Research in Personality*, 1976, *10*, 482–92.

Williams, C. D. The elimination of tantrum behavior by extinction procedures: Case report. *Journal of Abnormal and Social Psychology*, 1959, *59*, 269.

Williams, R. B., Jr., Friedman, M., Glass, D. C., Herd, J. A., & Schneiderman, N. Mechanisms linking behavioral and pathophysiological processes. In T. M. Dembroski, S. M. Weiss, J. L. Shields, S. G. Haynes, & M. Feinleib (Eds.), *Coronary-prone behavior*. New York: Springer-Verlag, 1978.

Williams, R. J. The biological approach to the study of personality. In T. Million (Ed.), *Theories of psychopathology*. Philadelphia: Saunders, 1967.

Wilson, E. O. *Sociobiology: The new synthesis*. Cambridge, Mass.: Harvard University Press, 1975.

Wilson, E. O. Introduction: What is sociobiology? In M. S. Gregory, A. Silvers, & D. Sutch (Eds.), *Sociobiology and human nature*. San Francisco: Jossey-Bass, 1978. (a)

Wilson, E. O. *On human nature*. Cambridge, Mass.: Harvard University Press, 1978. (b)

Wilson, G. T. The importance of being theoretical: A commentary on Bandura's "Self-efficacy: Towards a unifying theory of behavioral change." In S. Rachman (Ed.), *Advances in behaviour research and therapy* (Vol. 1). Oxford: Pergamon Press, 1978.

Wilson, W. H., & Nunnally, J. C. A naturalistic investigation of acquired meaning in children. *Psychonomic Science*, 1971, *23*, 149–50.

Wine, J. Test anxiety and direction of attention. *Psychological Bulletin*, 1971, *76*, 92–104.

Winter, D. G. Power motivation in thought and action. Doctoral dissertation, Harvard University, 1967.

Winter, D. G. Need for power in thought and action. In *Proceedings of the 76th Annual Convention of the American Psychological Association,* 1968, *3,* 429–30.

Winter, D. G. The need for power in college men: Action correlates and relationship to drinking. In D. C. McClelland, W. N. Davis, R. Kalin, & E. Wanner (Eds.), *The drinking man.* New York: Free Press, 1972.

Winter, D. G. *The power motive.* New York: Free Press, 1973.

Wolman, B. B. *The unconscious mind: The meaning of Freudian psychology.* Englewood Cliffs, N.J.: Prentice-Hall, 1968.

Wolpe, J. *Psychotherapy by reciprocal inhibition.* Stanford, Calif.: Stanford University Press, 1958.

Wolpe, J. Cognition and causation in human behavior and its therapy. *American Psychologist,* 1978, *33,* 437–46. (a)

Wolpe, J. Self-efficacy theory and psychotherapeutic change: A square peg in a round hole. In S. Rachman (Ed.), *Advances in behaviour research and therapy* (Vol. 1). Oxford: Pergamon Press, 1978. (b)

Wolpe, J., & Lazarus, A. A. *Behavior therapy techniques: A guide to the treatment of neurosis.* New York: Pergamon Press, 1966.

Woodworth, R. S. *Personal data sheet.* Chicago: Stoelting, 1920.

Worchel, P. Anxiety and repression. *Journal of Abnormal and Social Psychology,* 1955, *51,* 201–5.

Wrightsman, L. S. Wallace supporters and adherence to "law and order." *Journal of Personality and Social Psychology,* 1969, *13,* 17–22.

Wylie, R. C. The present status of self theory. In E. F. Borgatta & W. W. Lambert (Eds.), *Handbook of personality theory and research.* Chicago: Rand McNally, 1968.

Yalom, I. D., & Lieberman, M. A. A study of encounter group casualities. *Archives of General Psychiatry,* 1971, *25,* 16–30.

Yates, A. J. *Behavior therapy.* New York: John Wiley & Sons, 1970.

Zeller, A. An experimental analogue of repression, II. The effect of individual failure and success on memory measured by relearning. *Journal of Experimental Psychology,* 1950, *40,* 411–22.

Zeller, A. An experimental analogue of repression, III. The effect of induced failure and success on memory measured by recall. *Journal of Experimental Psychology,* 1951, *42,* 32–38.

Zemore, R. Systematic desensitization as a method of teaching a general anxiety-reducing skill. *Journal of Counsulting and Clinical Psychology,* 1975, *43,* 157–61.

Zerbin-Rüdin, E. Endogene Psychosen. In B. Becker (Ed.), *Humangenetik: Ein Kurzes handbuch in fünf banden* (Vol. 2). Stuttgart: Verlag, 1968.

Zucker, R. A., Manosevitz, M., & Lanyon, R. I. Birth order, anxiety, and affiliation during a crisis. *Journal of Personality and Social Psychology,* 1968, *8,* 354–59.

Author index

Subject index

A

Ability tests, and personality tests, 237–39
Abreaction, 133
Acceptance, in observational learning, 494, 504
Achievement motive; *see* Need for achievement
Acquisition curves, 463
Acquisition-performance distinction, 495 n
Activity level
  defined, 192
  as influenced by genetic factors, 190, 192
Actone, distinguished from need, 252
Actualizing tendency, 314–15; *see also* Self-actualization
Adjustment emphasis in personality, defined, 10
Aggression
  defined (G. A. Kelly), 386
  sociobiological view, 196–97
Altruism and kin selection theory, 196
  and sociobiology, 195–96
  defined, 195–96
  hard-core, 196
  soft-core, 196
Anaclitic identification, 100; *see also* Defensive identification
Anal compulsive character, 78
Anal expulsive character, 77
Anal stage, 78–79; *see also* Psychosexual development
Androgyny, defined, 505, 505 n
Antecedent conditions; *see* Maintaining conditions
Anxiety, 324, 381; *see also* Moral anxiety; Neurotic anxiety; Primary anxiety; *and* Signal anxiety
  as classically conditioned response, 445–46
  and defense, 324–26
Anxiety hierarchies, 448–50
Approach tendencies, and motivation, 251

B

B-love, 355
B-motives; *see* Being motives
Baseline, 467
Bedwetting; *see* Enuresis, treatment of
Behavior modification, 429; *see also* Cognitive behavior modification
Behavior rehearsal, 529
Behavior therapy, 429
Behavioral avoidance tests, 514
Behaviorism, 419; *see also* Methodological behaviorism; Radical behaviorism
Being motives (B-motives), 354
Bell-and-pad apparatus, 447
Birth trauma, 75
Bisexuality, 96
Body types, 175–77
  asthenic, 175–76
  athletic, 175–76
  dysplastic, 175–76
  ectomorphic, 175–77
  endomorphic, 175–77
  mesomorphic, 175–77
  pyknic, 175–76
Breakdown and disorganization, process of (Rogers), 327–28

C

California Psychological Inventory (CPI), 230–31

Archetypes, 95–97
  anima, 96
  animus, 96
  defined, 95
  persona, 96
  shadow, 96
Assertive behavior and modeling, 528–30
Asthma, and classical conditioning, 444–45
Attributive projection, 108
Aversive counterconditioning; *see* Counterconditioning, aversive
Avoidance tendencies, and motivation, 251

Cardinal dispositions (traits), 204
Case study method, 23–24, 43–48
  evaluation of, 46–47
Castration anxiety, 80; *see also* Anxiety
Catharsis, 133 n
Cathartic method, 133
Cathexis, 70–71
Central dispositions (traits), 204
Cerebrotonia, 175
Character disorders, 140, 140 n
Character structure, Freud's view, 61, 73–74
Childhood autism, 513 n
Choice corollary, G. A. Kelly's, 383–86
Classical conditioning, 419, 436
  of attitudes, 440–43
  aversive, 444
  of emotional reactions, 443–44
  of fear, 438–40
  and personality change, 446–56
Classical projection, 108
Client-centered therapy, 331–35
  defined, 331
Cognitive behavior modification, 431, 512–35
Cognitive-behavioral approach, 419
Cognitive restructuring, 525
Collective unconscious (Jung), 95–97
Common traits, 204–6
Commonality Corollary, G. A. Kelly's, 388–89
Composite profile approach to assessment, 236–37
Condensation (in dream work), 117
Conditioned response (CR), 437
Conditioned stimulus (CS), 436–37
Conditions of worth, 322
Conflict in psychoanalytic therapy, 59–60, 101–2, 116
Conscious, 68, 93; *see also* Consciousness, levels of
Conscious ego (Jung), described, 94
Consciousness, levels of, 68, 93–97; *see also* Conscious; Preconscious; Subconscious; *and* Unconscious

This book has been set CAP, 10 and 9 point Vermilion, leaded 2 points. Section numbers and titles and chapter numbers and titles are Zapf demibold. The overall type area is 37 by 47½ picas.